Xurt'an

Native Literatures of the Americas and
Indigenous World Literatures Series

Xurt'an

*The End of the World and
Other Myths, Songs, Charms,
and Chants by the Northern
Lacandones of Naha'*

SUZANNE COOK

UNIVERSITY OF NEBRASKA PRESS | LINCOLN

This book is published as part of the Recovering
Languages and Literacies of the Americas initiative.
Recovering Languages and Literacies is generously
supported by the Andrew W. Mellon Foundation.

Library of Congress Cataloging-in-Publication Data
Names: Cook, Suzanne, 1956– author.
Title: Xurt'an: the end of the world and other myths,
songs, charms, and chants by the Northern Lacandones
of Naha' / Suzanne Cook.
Description: Lincoln: University of Nebraska Press,
[2019] | Includes bibliographical references.
Identifiers: LCCN 2019007033 | ISBN 9780803271555
(cloth: alk. paper) | ISBN 9781496222244 (paperback) |
ISBN 9781496216373 (epub) | ISBN 9781496216380 (mobi) |
ISBN 9781496216397 (pdf)
Subjects: LCSH: Lacandon Indians—Folklore. | Lacandon
Indians—Religion. | Lacandon mythology. | Lacandon
incantations. | Lacandon cosmology. | Maya literature—
Translations into English.
Classification: LCC F1221.L2 C67 2019 |
DDC 398.20897/427—dc23 LC record available
at https://lccn.loc.gov/2019007033

Set in Merope by Tseng Information Systems, Inc.

CONTENTS

PART ONE. THE HACH WINIK 'TRUE PEOPLE'

PART TWO. MYTHS

PART THREE. POPULAR STORIES

PART FOUR. SONGS

PART FIVE. RITUAL SPEECH: INVOCATIONS, CHANTS, AND CHARMS

PART SIX. DESCRIPTIONS OF METEOROLOGICAL AND ASTRAL PHENOMENA

ILLUSTRATIONS

TABLES

PREFACE

This book took me twenty-five years to write, even though I only began to compose it five years ago. My motivation was Chan K'in Viejo, the last civic and religious leader of the northern Lacandones. He was ninety years old when he had expressed to me his deep concern that the old traditions, particularly the religion, was being abandoned by the younger generation. He believed that recording the Lacandon stories, songs, and rituals would help to preserve Lacandon tradition for the next generation and for the outside world to appreciate what would soon be forgotten.

That conversation occurred in 1991. At the time, I had just completed my documentary *Solitary Journey* and was looking for another subject to film. Chan K'in's lament over the loss of his culture articulated my own concern about the negative impact of Western culture on traditional cultures. The focus of *Solitary Journey* was on the effects of the first conquest of Mount Everest on the Sherpas.

Five years after my meeting with Chan K'in, filming in his community of Naha', and numerous failed attempts at raising interest from broadcasters to fund the completion of the film, I shelved the documentary. I went back to university, obtained degrees in linguistics, and then returned to Naha' with a new focus. By then Chan K'in Viejo had died and the community had transformed into cement-block houses with red laminate roofs. Evangelical temples had sprouted up on the front lawns of several homes. Most of the men had cut their hair, and many wore Western clothes. The seemingly abrupt changes had, in fact, not been abrupt at all; the Lacandones had been undergoing a process of transformation decades prior to my initial contact with them (see McGee 2002, 20). But the dramatic change that met me was all the incentive I needed to work harder, faster, and longer at documenting what was left of their cultural heritage. I intensified my fieldwork, returning to the village every year and staying longer each time. I took up permanent residence in Chan K'in's household and worked every day with Chan K'in's wives and their sons, their families and in-laws. The focus of my documentation shifted to collecting all the Lacandon narratives, songs, chants, magic charms, and any other forms of speech that expressed their culture. Lacking the recordings of previously translated texts, I had to re-record them all and then transcribe and translate them with the help of Lacandon assistants.

Although many of the texts in this book appear in earlier publications,[1] they differ from the others in a number of ways. The book represents the most recent collection of Lacandon oral literature, the last anthology having been published over thirty years ago. Some of these publications synthesize versions of a single narrative, thereby draining the narrative of valuable information for a comparative analysis of the individual narratives. A great deal of the Lacandon oral literature is unavailable to English readers, as most of the anthologies are published in Spanish, German, and French translation. Moreover, a number of these lack the Lacandon transcription, rendering them unusable for linguistic studies of the language. Finally, many of the extant texts were provided by the same few Lacandon contributors, all of whom were men.

This book broadens the scope of the existing repository of Lacandon oral literature by including the voices of some of these previous contributors in addition to newer, younger voices, both male and female. It supplements texts published in translation only by providing Lacandon transcriptions for each recorded performance. In this way, the book offers a practical resource for synchronic and diachronic analyses of Lacandon literature, performance, and style. Finally, each text is introduced by relevant historical and ethnographic information, to provide context for the narratives, songs, and ritual speech.

ACKNOWLEDGMENTS

I am indebted to those who welcomed me into their homes, fed me, and put up with me: the work was difficult, tedious, and long. Despite this, my hosts were generous and accommodating, their patience and good humor never wavering. Over ten Lacandones contributed to this book. I appreciate them all for helping me achieve my goal. The following five individuals, without whom the book would never have gotten off the ground, warrant special mention:

Antonio Martinez is the last of the three main patriarchs of Naha'. The others were Chan K'in Viejo and Mateo Viejo. Like the others were, Antonio is a dedicated practitioner of the traditional religion. He was born in Sa'am (Monte Líbano) around 1925 and raised by his mother and grandparents. He moved to Naha' during the resettlement of the Lacandon communities and has lived there ever since. Now in his nineties, he still rises early to tend his three *milpas* 'cornfields'. During the heat of the day he is often found in his god house. He is now the most respected elder, a font of traditional knowledge and skilled in ceremonial procedures.

Bor Ma'ax is one of the eldest sons of Chan K'in Viejo and Koh Maria, and Antonio's son-in-law. Now in his fifties, he has minimal formal education but is fluent in Spanish and Lacandon. As a youngster, he learned many of the stories and the ceremonial protocol from Chan K'in Viejo, imbibing his traditional wisdom on a daily basis. He was born in Naha', married Antonio's daughter, and lives next door to him with his wife, Chan Nuk, and his married son and his wife and child. In addition to narrating many of stories in this volume, he helped with the transcription and translation of numerous other narratives, songs, and chants performed by other contributors.

Juana Koh is the half-sister of Koh Maria, Chan K'in Viejo's elder wife. She is in her eighties and a monolingual speaker of Lacandon. A widow for many years, she lives with her brother in a small, traditional hut a short distance from the community. She, along with most women in the community, now observes the Christian faith. She was the only woman in the community willing to sing the "women's work songs." She also enjoyed narrating traditional stories and reciting charms.

K'ayum Ma'ax is the older brother of Bor Ma'ax. Close to sixty years old and with little formal education, he is nonetheless educated in the traditions of his people. He is also fluent in Spanish. He is well known in parts of Mexico and Europe for his painting, having traveled extensively to Mexico City, the United States, and Europe to exhibit his work. Most of his work depicts scenes from Lacandon traditional stories. Although well traveled, he prefers to remain in Naha', where he continues to cultivate his milpas and work in the community.

Chan K'in Quinto "Säk Ho'or" ("white head") is the fifth Chan K'in born to Chan K'in Viejo. His nickname distinguishes him from the others, as well as identifying him as an albino. He is also the third youngest child of Chan K'in's third wife, Koh Paniagua. Although one of the youngest of her ten children, he still recalls as much of his father's stories and sacred songs as his older siblings and excels in elucidating obscure sections in the ritual performances and texts. He contributed many of the songs and "secrets" and numerous narratives, in addition to assisting with their transcription and translation.

I am also grateful for the financial assistance I have received over the years from foundations. They include the Volkswagen Foundation, the Firebird Foundation, the Endangered Language Fund, the Foundation for Endangered Languages, and the California Indian Language Center. Their funds helped to get me into the field, survive in the field, and pay my Lacandon hosts and consultants. The effort would have been wasted if it hadn't been for Barry Carlson. His support and encouragement helped buoy my resolve to carry on and carry through in spite of innumerable frustrations and setbacks.

INTRODUCTION

On December 21, 2012, throngs of tourists stood at the foot of classic Mayan monuments waiting for the end of the world. The last day of the 5,200-year Maya Long Count calendar was about to expire, marking the end of time. Despite the apocalyptic alarm bells, the *xurt'an* came and went without incident, and the next day dawned just like any other. In dignified silence Mayan shamans packed up their paraphernalia, and somewhat disappointed, the crowds dispersed.

But for the shamans, as it is for all Mayas, the xurt'an signifies both the end of the world and its rebirth. The apocalyptic connotation of the term derives from its twofold meaning. The literal translation is 'the end of speech' and in this context alludes to worship. The sweet words of the mortals sustain the gods, who in turn maintain the momentum and order of the universe. Self-preservation motivated the gods in the past to destroy the world and its neglectful mortals and replace it with a new creation with better mortals who would nourish and adore them.

This belief traces its origin to the Creation story, in which the gods spoke the world into existence. They tried several times to create sentient beings who would acknowledge their work and venerate them. When their creations failed to do so, they destroyed the world and started over. After three failed attempts they finally succeeded in creating respectful, sentient beings out of maize. Their venerations sustained the world in a reciprocal agreement between themselves and their creators.

Xurt'an is also on the minds of the Lacandones. Numbering fewer than four hundred men, women, and children, they were the last Mayas to have practiced the religion of the ancient Mayas. They survived the Conquest intact, while all other Mayas were exterminated or forced into Catholic mission towns. The Lacandones call themselves *hach winik* 'True People', but to the Spanish they were the Lacandones, an exonym that derives from the Mayan phrase meaning 'those who set up (and worship) stone'. The conquistadors applied the label to all indomitable heathens who had fled into the frontier of southeastern Chiapas and the Guatemalan Petén. Concealed under the canopy of the forest, the fugitives dispersed their homesteads and continued to propitiate their gods well into the twentieth century. By 1970 the hach winik had all but dissolved into legend.

The demise of the hach winik was prophesied by their last religious leader, Chan K'in Viejo. Burgeoning colonization in the forest had forced the semi-nomadic Lacandones into settlements; deforestation, a shrinking arable land base, and a lack of privacy to conduct their rituals hampered their ability to continue their traditional way of life. The religious contexts for transmitting the traditions disappeared, and, one by one, families shelved their incensories, portals of communication to the gods.

Shortly after his death in 1996, Chan K'in's prophesy was borne out when his wives dismantled his temple and replaced it with a church. His eldest son declined to succeed him, leaving Antonio Martinez, now in his nineties, as the only one left to propitiate the gods on behalf of the world. The day that he dies will be the day that the world comes to an end.

Lacandon is an oral culture, which means that knowledge, ideology, and values are passed on through speech, and hence it requires the cultural contexts in which to communicate the traditions. Having lost the religious and attendant social contexts, Lacandon myths, chants, songs, women's work songs, and medical incantations have lost their relevance to the community. But they are not yet forgotten.

Xurt'an is a collection of oral literature from the northern Lacandones of Naha'. Texts were recorded and transcribed in the community between 2000 and 2015 with help from fluent Lacandon speakers who possessed extensive knowledge of their traditional myths, rituals, songs, and magical charms.

The book is organized into six parts. The first chapter in part 1 introduces the Lacandones, their language, and the historical context within which they emerged as an identifiable ethnic group. This is followed by an ethnographic sketch of their traditional culture and *cosmovision*. This sketch is meant to establish a context for the Lacandon texts, and the reader will find a wealth of information on Lacandon society, culture, religion, and history. There are numerous references to technical articles, books, research papers, and documentary efforts.[1]

The second chapter describes Lacandon oral literature and compares it with the literary conventions and rhetoric of the ancient Maya. Oral literature is a form of creative language, sharing with written forms the distinctive literary techniques and devices that exploit language at every linguistic level. It differs from written literature in that it only emerges during performance and constitutes an event.[2] In this section, Lacandon literary style—word choice, sentence structure, figurative language, and sentence arrangement—is revealed and compared to ancient Mayan literary style. Lacandon genres are explored as well.

Parts 2 through 6 present the Lacandon texts, organized into genres: parts 2 and 3 divide traditional narratives into myths (part 2) and "popular stories" (part 3), so called because the term "folk tale" still carries negative connotations. Part 4 presents songs, part 5 ritual speech. Part 6 includes three Lacandon descriptions of meteorological and astral phenomena.

The division into myths and "popular stories" is based on the content of the narratives. Myths deal with stories of creation and the origin and development of humanity. They take place in mythic time and involve the gods and ancestors from the distant past. In most cases they are believed to be true. "Popular stories" are fictive, involving animals and supernatural, usually malevolent beings, and are typically cautionary tales.

These narratives were collected as individual texts over a period of fifteen years, and it is unclear whether the Lacandones would impose a chronological order on them. The sequence presented here was determined by the author.

Xurt'an

1

The Hach Winik 'True People'

The Lacandones

ORIGIN

The Lacandones constitute one of the smallest linguistic communities in the world, with fewer than eight hundred speakers.[1] They call their language *hach t'an* 'true language' and themselves *hach winik* 'true people'. They live in the Lacandon forest, also called La Selva Lacandona, in Chiapas, Mexico. They speak a Yucatecan language closely related to Itza, Yucatec, and Mopan. These four languages were once a single language that was spoken throughout the Yucatan peninsula. Around AD 950 the language began to diverge into the four Yucatecan languages spoken today. Mopan split off first in AD 950, followed by Itza in 1250, northern Lacandon in 1500, and finally southern Lacandon and modern Yucatec in 1700 (Hofling 2014, 1).

The diversification occurred at pivotal points in Maya history. Mopan separated at the close of the Classic period, when the focus of cultural development moved from the southern (or central) lowlands north to the Yucatan Peninsula with the ascendency of Mexicanized Maya merchant-warriors and the invasion of the Toltecs. The region experienced a cultural transformation that combined Mexican and Mayan ideologies and aesthetic expression, and increased trade and economic prosperity that spurred a widespread movement of people (Coe 1993, 130–31).

LANGUAGE

Lacandon shares morphology (word structure), syntax (word order and grammar), and phonology (sound system) with (modern) Yucatec, Itza, and Mopan. Apart from a few phonetic features and some vocabulary items, they are essentially the same language from a linguist's perspective.

The language is mildly agglutinative, with person, number, transitivity (based on whether a verb takes one or more arguments[2]), causation, reflexivity, and other word-building elements affixed to the root, or the core meaning of the word. Most of the inflectional and derivational affixes are suffixes, but tense, aspect, and mood also occur as preverbal elements.

Some roots belong to more than one word class—for example, verb, noun, adjective. Compounding is an active process in the language, which involves the blending of two or more free morphemes (or words)—for example, *ya'axk'in* 'year' < *ya'ax* 'green/blue' + *k'in* 'day/time'. The basic word order is vos, where V stands for verb, O stands for object, and S stands for subject. Other word orders (vso and svo) are also possible, reflecting pragmatic considerations, such as focus-comment, or to achieve rhetorical effect, such as narrative highlighting.

Lacandon is divided into two variants (or dialects). The northern Lacandon spoken in Naha'[3] is closer to the Itza Maya language in its retention of the (Proto-Yucatec[4]) /l/ phoneme and lack of (Proto-Yucatec) tone.[5] Southern Lacandon is closer to Yucatec Maya in its retention of lexical tone and markedly pronounced intervocalic glottal stops.[6] All the Yucatecan languages, except Yucatec Maya, have a sixth vowel /ä/. Table 1 presents the orthographic conventions used by various scholars of the Mayan languages. The right-hand column provides characters from the International Phonetic Alphabet (IPA), which is used to transcribe the sounds of all languages. The orthographic conventions used in this book follow Bruce.

PRONUNCIATION GUIDE

Consonants

' glottal stop—achieved by a brief closure of the vocal cords restricting the flow of air

b **b**aby

ch **ch**eck

ch' glottalized alveolar affricate, cat**ch'** it /kætʃ'ɪt/

h **h**ouse

k **k**iss

k' glottalized voiceless velar stop, take it /teɪk'ɪt/

l **l**ate

m **m**other

n **n**ice

p **p**uppy

p' glottalized voiceless bilabial stop, sto**p** it /stɑp'ɪt/

Table 1. Lacandon orthographic conventions and pronunciation guide

Lacandon (Bruce)	Lacandon (Baer)	Yucatec (Bricker)	Yucatec (Tozzer)	Itzaj (Hofling)	Colonial Maya	IPA
'	'	ʔ		'		ʔ
b*	b	b'	b	b'	b	ɓ
ch	č	č	tš	ch	ch	ʧ
ch'	č'	č'	tš'	ch'	cħ	ʧ'
h	j	h	h	j	h	h
k	c, qu	k	k	k	c	k
k'	c', q'u	k'	q	k'	k	k'
l, r**	r	l	l	l(r)	l	l, ɾ
m	m	m	m	m	m	m
n	n	n	n	n	n	n
p	p	p	p	p	p	p
p'	p'	p'	p'	p'	₽, pp	p'
s	s	s	s	s	ç, z	s
t	t	t	t	t	t	t
t'	t'	t'	t'	t'	tħ, th	t'
ts	ts	ȼ	c	tz	tz	ts
ts'	ts'	ȼ'	c'	tz'	dz	ts'
w	w	w	w	w	u, v	w
x	x	š	š	x	x	ʃ
y	y	y	y	y	i, y	j
a	a	a	a	a	a	a
ä	ʌ			ä	ə	ə
e	e	e	e	e	e	e
i	i	i	i	i	i	i
o	o	o	o	o	o	o
u	u	u	u	u	u	u

* Consensus holds that this is a bilabial implosive [ɓ], but the implosion is difficult to detect in the speech of the northern Lacandones.

** In northern Lacandon (spoken in Naha'), the /l/ and /r/ are in complementary distribution: the /l/ always and only occurs word-initially, despite the addition of prefixes on the root/stem of the word. The /r/ occurs word-medially and word-finally, never word-initially. In word-medial position, /r/ is pronounced as flap [D]. In word-final position, /r/ is often pronounced as [h] or omitted altogether.

s   sun
t   tool
t' glottalized voiceless alveolar stop, kitten /kɪt'ən/
ts bits
ts' glottalized alveolar affricate, itsy-bitsy /ɪt͡s'ibɪt͡s'i/
w   wow
x   shine
y   yellow

Vowels

a   father /fɑːðər/
ä   about /əbaʊt/
e   tell
i   peep
o   open
u   shoot

Long vowels (v:) are pronounced the same as their short counterparts, except that the sound is sustained for a longer period.

HISTORY

As the most conservative of all other Mayas, the Lacandones are regarded by many to be survivors of the ancient Mayas. According to Bruce (Perera and Bruce 1982), they represent the last lords of Palenque, the Classic Maya dynasty that flourished in the seventh century. But given the linguistic diversification of the Yucatec language family, the Lacandones emerged eight centuries later, in the Postclassic period.

Around AD 950 Palenque and the other Classic Maya dynasties in the southern Lowlands collapsed when political power and economic control shifted to the Yucatan in the northern Lowlands.[7] This shift marked the beginning of the Postclassic period, inaugurated by Toltec invaders from Mexico. At the vanguard of this change were the Pútun merchant-warriors, who later became known as the Itza.

Mayan civilization transformed under the new military regime, which jettisoned the dynastic rule characteristic of the Classic Maya period and introduced a political hierarchy rooted in militarist ideology.

The Toltecs introduced a pantheon of gods, at the center of which was Quetzalcoatl 'The Feathered Serpent'.[8] He symbolized the divinity of the state (Schele and Freidel 1990, 394–95). The cult of Quetzalcoatl swept throughout the Maya lands, through the network of trade routes (Sharer and Traxler 2006, 582–83, 619). This melding of the divine and militaristic ideology was also reflected in the multilevel political hierarchy (Coe 1993, 146), the pantheon of gods increasing with the deification of ruler-warriors. These gods assumed their positions alongside Mayan and Mexican gods in a hierarchy that mirrored the political hierarchy of the state.

The Toltecs were succeeded by the Itza (Coe 1993; J. Thompson 1970, 1977), who not only emulated the Toltec ideology but intensified it. They established the cults of the Sacred Cenote and Ixchel Goddess of Medicine, introduced a form of joint-rule government between the formerly independent Mayan lords and Itza rulers, and founded the League Mayapan, which became the capital of the Yucatan.

The Postclassic period maintained its economic and sociopolitical momentum until the mid-fifteenth century, when hostilities between the Xiu (formerly a Mexican lineage) and the Cocom (an Itza lineage) erupted, culminating in the expulsion of the Itza at Chichén Itza. They returned to the Petén, where they established Tayasal on the shore of Lake Petén Itza. Around the same time, the Xiu leader and his allies, the Couoh,[9] migrated into the northern Petén as well.

The enmity between the Itzas and the Xiu and Couoh resumed in the Petén. Joining the fray were other Mayan groups who had been pushed to the margins by Itza expansionism.[10] Among them were the Cehach,[11] Chinamitla,[12] Mopan, and Itza subgroups, one of which was the Chak'an Itza.

By now they had become known as "the Lacandones," an exonym the Spanish applied to Mayan infidels and rebels. Between AD 1646 and 1648 a group of them was discovered at Nohha 'Great Water' in a region the Spanish dubbed El Próspero located between Palenque and Tenosique. The missionaries who came across them noted their wild appearance, their naked, black-painted bodies, long hair adorned with feathers, earrings, and nasal septa pierced through with reeds.[13] Most spoke Yucatec Maya, except for a Ch'ol-speaking group called the Locenes, who lived apart from the others in seven or eight settlements (Scholes and Roys 1948, 46). But Spanish soldiers left them alone, having shifted their focus to the Itza and quelling their rivals in the Petén. The Itza ruler at Tayasal had expressed an interest in collaborating with the Spanish, if for no other reason than to maintain control over Tayasal. But his enemies discovered the plan and escalated their attacks.

Beleaguered by incessant interethnic conflicts, fatal diseases introduced by an invigorated Spanish offensive, and concomitant population losses, the Itza ruler capitulated to the Spanish in AD 1697. As for his recalcitrant adversaries, they fled into the forest and disappeared into the folds of the mountains. There in the jungle fastness they continued their clandestine habits—venerating their gods and assailing the Spanish and their Christian converts.

Immediately preceding the conquest of the Itza, a coordinated Spanish offensive had effectively expunged a group of aggressive Ch'ol rebels that had retreated to the southern Lacandon forest. One of their strongholds was called Lacam Tun, a name that is believed to be the source of the Spanish exonym "Lacandon" (Nations 2006, 158–160).[14] Trusting that they had now cleared the forest of infidels, the Spanish withdrew. But in the eighteenth century a new influx of Maya fugitives streamed into the Lacandon forest from various points along the upper Usumacinta River. Many of them were apostates fleeing captivity in *reducciones* 'Spanish settlements' and Itza reactionaries. Others crossed the Lacantún River from Guatemala.

That they constituted the ancestors of the present-day Lacandones is corroborated by historical and linguistic evidence. Colonial and government registers include the patronyms B'alam, Chan, Couoh,[15] Hau,[16] Kalsiya,[17] Keho', Kob', Koho', Mis, Naguate (Nawat), Nistisyaho', Puc, Taxo', Tut, Uuko', and Yaxuno'—all of which survive as Lacandon "ceremonial" names.[18] Reminiscent of a taboo against speaking or writing the given names of exalted persons, these "ceremonial" names are only uttered in sacred contexts and myths. Each ceremonial name embraces a set of Lacandon *onen*, akin to clans. Details on the Lacandon onen and corresponding ceremonial names are supplied in appendix 1.

Late in the eighteenth century a small contingent of Lacandones ventured into Palenque to trade. They said they had come from *yucum* 'the river',[19] where their ancestors had fled to escape Spanish soldiers. The Franciscan priest of the mission at Palenque, Fray Manuel Joseph Calderón, welcomed them, giving them gifts in exchange for their bundles of cacao and various artifacts. These Lacandones continued the transactions, settling in San José Gracia de Real, a mission outpost that Calderon had founded for them. The priest's primary aim, of course, was to convert the Lacandones, but his attempts to teach them the Christian doctrine only resulted in a few marriages between Lacandon men and indigenous women in Palenque, and a few baptisms that ailing Lacandones eagerly accepted, thinking they were a kind of curing ritual (Boremanse 1998, 5). For the most part the Lacandones were interested in doing business. After Calderon died, they abandoned the mission and drifted back into forest. The Lacandones continued sporadic contact with other outsiders throughout the nineteenth and early twentieth centuries.

In 1878 the timber industry expanded operations in Mexico, developing tracts throughout the Lacandon forest, using its network of rivers to float booms of precious hardwoods to Tenosique for shipment to the west. Logging camps sprang up along riverbanks, and their stores of metal tools, salt, shotguns, sugar, and other foreign novelties lured the Lacandones into contact with the lumbermen.

Consummate traders by now, the Lacandones not only embraced foreign goods but also, as trading continued, depended on them. Steel tools alleviated the drudgery of carving out cornfields with stone axes; shotguns were more effective and accurate than bamboo spears in taking down large game; bolts of cotton cloth reduced the time it took to spin cotton and weave garments on a backstrap loom. Lacandon settlements moved closer to the stores, thus reducing the time and distance of having to search for food and materials in the forest.

But along with these blessings, the lumbermen exposed the Lacandones to foreign diseases—measles, small pox, influenza—which spread like wildfire through the trading network, wiping out enclaves of Lacandones in their path. Two yellow fever outbreaks occurred, reducing the population to all-time lows. After one epidemic, the Southern Lacandon population plunged to just one hundred men, women, and children (Baer and Merrifield 1971).

The Lacandones were given a slight reprieve when the Mexican Revolution broke out. A band of revolutionaries mounted a series of raids on the logging camps, managing to destroy half a dozen of them and freeing the indentured Maya laborers. Although they failed to halt the industry altogether, they had reduced its capacity. More importantly, they had impeded the spread of contagions (De Vos 1988, 228). Several years later, in 1925, the Mexican government prohibited foreign title to Mexico's timber along its international borders. Since the Lacandon forest straddled a contested zone between Mexico and Guatemala, one of the major logging operations in Chiapas went out of business (Nations 2006, 123).[20]

After the industry collapsed, the forest fell silent, and the cycle of life returned to normal. The Lacandon population rebounded, and families resumed their quotidian lives in peace. Ensconced in this refuge, they were far removed from problems developing in the rest of Mexico, yet they would soon feel the impact. Although numerous *ejidos* (collective Indian villages) were formed and began to prosper, it took forty more years for the Mexican government's agrarian reforms to take effect and return appropriated lands to their indigenous owners. But over a third of the arable land remained in the hands of less than 0.5 percent of the population.[21] Landlessness and poverty continued, and discontent escalated. To mitigate the problem and avert another revolt, the government opened tracts of wilderness for colonization. Following overgrown logging tracks, the disenfranchised peasants slashed and burned their way through the Lacandon forest, establishing settlements as they went. A decade later, the Lacandones were surrounded by colonies of Tzeltal, Tzotzil, Ch'ol, and Tojolabal Mayas.

At this time, there were a total of two hundred Lacandones, aggregated into four main groups. The Tzendales group[22] lived near the river by the same name and along the Lacantún River; the Cedro-Lacanha' group were settled near Lake Lacanha' and along the Lacanha' River downstream from Bonampak; and the Jatate (or San Quintín) group occupied an area near the confluence of the Jatate and Perlas rivers (Baer and Merrifield 1971; Blom and Blom 1969). The fourth and largest group, the northern Lacandones, comprised several small subgroups. The Petha'[23] group occupied the region around the lakes of Mensäbäk and Itsanohk'uh and near the Santo Domingo River (Bruce 1968, 16). The others were located along the Chocolha' River, Chancala, Tenosique, and Piedras Negras. Portraits of some of the Lacandon groups taken by the first explorers are presented in the illustration gallery.

Colonization accelerated, and so did deforestation. By the 1970s the effects of burgeoning population and concomitant environmental degradation compelled the government to intervene by dedicating the Lacandon forest as a national park. Numerous settlers were displaced and moved outside the park's boundary, while three Lacandon settlements, Mensäbäk, Naha', and Lacanha' Chan Sayab, remained inside.

ETHNOGRAPHY

Before this onslaught, Lacandones had the forest to themselves. It offered them a cornucopia of fruits, seeds, and nuts. The rivers and myriad lakes provided quality protein from many species of fish, turtles, crabs, and snails. They were also a magnet for a diversity of birds and game, particularly peccary, monkey (spider and howler), deer, armadillo, agouti, and coatimundi. Of the various birds, the great curassow and quail were hunted for food, while parrots and macaws were coveted for their feathers. The Lacandones hunted with bow and arrow and perhaps the *atlatl* (spear thrower).[24] They also fished with bow and arrow in addition to hand lines tied at the end with hooks of palm spines. They stripped the fiber from various trees for cords and ropes and selected specific trees and palms from which to construct their houses.[25]

While the forest provided all their essential needs, the Lacandones were basically farmers. They practiced a system of swidden agriculture that preserved the integrity and vitality of the forest. Swidden agriculture entails slashing and burning vegetation to clear land for cultivation. The method incorporates the rotation of a several milpas, as soil fertility is quickly depleted after a few years of cultivation. In earlier times each Lacandon family had up to five milpas in various stages of regeneration distributed throughout a large territory. Sometimes this required families to move their households closer to the active milpas. The old milpas, however, were never abandoned, as they supplied a store of fruits, tubers, and edible "weeds" throughout the year. Above all, they provided quality protein from small animals that foraged in the undergrowth.

The foremost subsistence crop is maize, which the women process with slacked lime or snail shells to release the niacin. The dough is patted out into tortillas, folded into tamales, and sieved and boiled into various kinds of beverages.

Second and third in importance are beans and tubers. Beans accompany almost every meal, forming a complete protein when eaten with corn. Although beans and corn are enough to sustain life, the Lacandones prefer a little more variety. Tubers, especially the yucca (cassava) and sweet potatoes, are enjoyed roasted and boiled. The cassava is mixed with corn dough to add a chewy texture and sweetness to tortillas. A second-choice tuber comes from the 'elephant ears' plant (*Xanothsoma mafaffa* Schott).

In addition to these staples, the Lacandones cultivate *chayote* 'vegetable pear' (*Sechium edulea* Jacq. Sw.), varieties of hot chilies, cherry tomatoes, avocados, sugar apples, and an assortment of squashes. Wild plants are also cultivated for food. The primary ones are the *balche'* tree, whose bark is used to make the ceremonial liquor; the 'Mayan breadnut', for its nutritious nuts; and two varieties of Chamaedorea palms, for their edible inflorescences. A comprehensive description of cultural uses and preparation of plants among the Lacandones can be found in Cook (2016).

In the first half of the nineteenth century timber and chicle industries expanded operations into the Lacandon forest, bringing with them foreign food plants, among them bananas and plantains, citrus fruits, and sugarcane.

Before the Colonial period, honey was the only sweetener available. Lacandones obtained it from the hives of wild, stingless honey bees. Very few Lacandones raised their own bees, unlike the Mayas in the Yucatan. Honey was primarily used to ferment the balche'. When sugar was introduced, Lacandones began to cultivate sugarcane. They also raised tobacco—for everyone, including the children, smoked cigars—and cotton for weaving their traditional tunics.

The Lacandon population was never very large, mainly due to living in a difficult environment, fatal foreign diseases, and a dearth of marriageable women. The cycle of swidden farming also affected the size, composition, and distribution of the Lacandon population. Family members would split up in search of fertile land, where they might join other groups. Disputes within the families or between *caribales* occasioned the hiving off of caribales (G. Soustelle 1959, 144).

The family, or *caribal*, was (and still is) the main unit of social organization. Caribales were united through onen affiliation. An onen is an animal name that functions like a surname and is passed down through the father's line (McGee 2002, 10). Each onen pairs with another to form a (once) larger social unit, identified by a "ceremonial" name (e.g., *ma'ax* 'spider monkey' and *ba'ats'* 'howler monkey' are pairs of onen under the Karsiya name). As discussed above, ceremonial names correspond to the patronyms of the Mayas who entered the Lacandon forest in the seventeenth and eighteenth centuries.

At the turn of the twentieth century, there were twenty-four Lacandon onen. Today, only three survive: *ma'ax*, *k'ek'en*, and *yuk*. The ma'ax is the predominate onen among the northern Lacandones, and the k'ek'en predominates in the south.[26] Although they share a similar lifestyle, customs, beliefs, and history, and they speak mutually intelligible dialects,[27] the two groups differ with respect to kinship terms, postmarital settlement patterns, and religious mythologies. Each regards the other as different, attested by the names they call each other: the northerners call the southerners the "long tunics," and the southerners call the northerners "far away people." Unsurprisingly, each has its own origin story.

The name *hach winik* is a relatively recent endonym, a name that a group calls itself to assert its ethnic identity. Hach winik appears to have formed in the 1940s, when Phil Baer, an Evangelist missionary from the Summer Institute of Linguistics, began converting the southern Lacandones. Descriptions of the Lacandones published before this time make no mention of the name hach winik.

The name derives from a *halach winik* 'true person', a title bestowed on pre-Columbian governors in the Yucatan. The Lacandon definition of *hach winik* was one who could "see the gods." Today, it means a Lacandon who has never been Christianized. Chan K'in Viejo was considered hach winik, although he always denied it. Antonio Martinez, his son-in-law and last of three old patriarchs of Naha', says that no one is hach winik anymore. Today, the hach winik are an ethnic identity in name only. All the "true people" have passed away, leaving a legacy that the business savvy new generation of Lacandones exploit to draw tourists.

LACANDON RELIGION

The Lacandones preserved many ritual practices of the ancient Maya, and their mythology includes common themes and motifs that express a core system of Mesoamerican beliefs. Lacandon rituals are indeed ancient survivals, yet their religion and their mythology are products of a millennia of social and political change.

Maya religion underwent revisions between the Classic, Postclassic, and Colonial periods. The Classic period religion was a theocracy: rulers embodied the gods on earth and became the gods after death. When the monarchy collapsed, the religion became secularized under a Toltec regime. Maya and Toltec religions intermingled, blending their mythologies, gods, and religious practices and producing an increase in the number of household oratories. The same process occurred again in the Colonial period; after the Spanish established their base in northern Yucatan in AD 1546, they began to impose Christianity upon the Maya. This was a time of great disruption, and the events and their consequences—deaths from European diseases, conscription of native labor, and violent struggles between ethnic groups and between them and the Spanish—were incorporated into a syncretic blend of Mayan and Catholic religion and mythologies.

Northern Lacandon Religion

The religion that the Lacandones inherited was in all probability that of the Mayan fugitives who had escaped the Spanish. When noted anthropologist Alfred Tozzer encountered the northern Lacandones in the early twentieth century, he found them living in isolated family homesteads. There were no priests and diviners, astronomers and mathematicians, or physicians among them. Religion was under the purview of the family head of the household. His ceremonial regalia was made of bark cloth, and his temple was a simple shelter of pole and thatch. The focus of his rituals revolved around matters of the home, his fields, and the forest. In many ways his practices were like those of the sixteenth-century Yucatec Mayas described by Bishop Diego de Landa.[28]

The Lacandon ritual of the greatest importance was the changing of the god pots, clay incensories that represent the gods. Reminiscent of the ancient ceremonies commemorating the inauguration of a new ruler at the conclusion of the Calendar Round, the renewal ceremony involved symbolically killing and reinstating the gods. A similar ritual was enacted during the New Year renovation rituals performed by the Mayas described by Landa, in which the people destroyed all their ritual paraphernalia, including the incensories (Landa 1864, chap. 40:242, 276, cited in Tozzer [1907] 1978, 106n2).

For this ceremony to have endured in the simple homes of the Lacandon Maya is remarkable. They also performed ritual blood-letting and continued to burn copal in the Mayan ruins, and they retained other traditions that evoke the practices of the Mayan aristocracy. But it does not prove that they were survivors of ancient Maya nobility, as Perera and Bruce (1982) claim. More likely they were from common stock.

What follows is a description of northern Lacandon religion and cosmology. It begins with an overview of the core features of ancient Mayan religion and ideology, much of which the Lacandones preserved, and some of which they changed or abandoned.

Mayan Religion

Mayan religion incorporated a polytheistic pantheon of deities that embodied the natural forces of the universe. The forces, at once animistic and solar, were the manifestations of an amorphous intelligence named *k'uh*. At the center of this pantheon was the sun, constantly and reliably rising every day from the cosmic hearth. As the sun mapped the limits of the world, its endless rising and setting rhythm brought order to the universe. The word for sun is *k'in*, and its journey across the sky was therefore called *k'in*, meaning day. K'in was the smallest unit of time in the Mayan calendars and formed the first digit in the Maya vigesimal or base 20 numeral system. Twenty k'ins were called *uinic* 'man'. Thus, time was an animate being, and his twenty trips across the sky established the standard by which Mayas, and Mesoamericans in general, reckoned time and envisioned the structure of the world. Four limbs with five digits on each represented the four corners and sides of the universe. The heart, hearth, fire, and force of the divine formed the fifth direction. Although a wellspring of life, it was also a place of return and death.

The Mayan universe carved space into pairs of opposing sides. The eastern and western sides aligned with the equinoxes, indicating the transitions between the wet and dry seasons. When the sun arrived at these two stations, it told farmers when to plant and when to harvest. Rituals were performed to commemorate the beginning of spring and the beginning of fall, the time of renewal and the time of fruition. The solstices represent a similar idea, as they are twice-a-year occurrences, and on those days the sun reaches its highest or lowest altitude in the sky above the horizon at solar noon. The winter solstice marked the sun's awakening from its winter slumber in the underworld. The summer solstice marked the time of the peak rainy season in the year, a stage in the development of maize, and, symbolically, the rising of the Maize God.

TIME AND THE STRUCTURE OF THE UNIVERSE

Mayan astronomers observed and noted the points along the horizon where the sun rose and set on its diurnal and annual passages. They also noted the points where it paused and then reversed direction, the points at which the days and nights were equal in length, and the points where the sun stood directly overhead twice a year. They plotted these stations of the sun on a cosmogram, which divided the world into quadrants that represented the cardinal and intercardinal directions and the seasons. Where the quadrants converged marked the upper and lower limits of the universe and the center of the universe where life began (Villa Rojas 1988, 127–29). In Maya cosmology it is represented as a giant green ceiba tree, the Maya Tree of Life.

The cosmogram portrayed the creators and rulers of space and time as pairs of deities located at each station of the sun. Two more deities were in the center, sitting back-to-back on either side of the ceiba tree. Each pair represented opposing forces, up–down, youthful–aged (mature), life–

death; at zenith sit celestial gods, perhaps representing the sun's physical maturity and its imminent transition into old age; at nadir sit two other gods, perhaps representing the end of the sun's journey to death and the beginning of the journey to life. Other pairs of deities facing each other across the horizon mark the portals into the underworld: those deities on the east side represent the ascent of the sun from the underworld, and those on the west, the descent of the sun into the underworld. Deities were positioned at the corners, marking the rest stops of the sun on its journey; the motion of the sun was indicated by footsteps radiating out from the center to these rest stops; the footsteps continue to trace the periphery of the cosmogram, indicating the direction of the sun around the celestial sphere.

The sun's metronomic lift, glide, drop, glide rhythm established a regularity for the people's existence. Its endless rising and setting and rising again formed and reaffirmed for them that time was cyclical. People saw in the sun's journey the cycle of their lives. Like the sun, they rose from the east at birth, ascended the sky as they grew, stopped at zenith at middle age, and descended to the west as they continued to age. They continued through the sun's portal in the earth and followed the path of the sun through the underworld to the east where they ascended again. The cycle of their lives was duplicated in the seasonal growth of maize: from the gestation of the seed in the earth to its emergence in the spring, to the development of its future generations in the rows of kernels, and to their return to the earth. Maize thus represented both their substance and their sustenance.

As Mayan society became more complex, so too did the structure of the universe and the pantheon of gods that controlled it. The monarchy, having established itself at the center of the world, asserted its control by appropriating the sun: during their reign, rulers were the sun incarnate; after their deaths they rose to the sky as the sun itself. Through lineal descent, rulers continued the cycle through their heirs, thus preserving the order of the cosmos and their central position within it.

To justify the monarchy's position in the theocratic hierarchy, Mayan astronomers and mathematicians expanded the basic three-realm universe into thirteen levels of heaven rising above the earth and nine levels of underworld descending beneath.[29] In Classic Maya cosmology the thirteen celestial gods were embodied by Oxlahun ti' K'uh 'Thirteen Gods'.[30] While they ruled the celestial realm, nine gods ruled the underworld. They were called B'olon ti' K'uh 'Nine Gods'.[31] Though temporally and spatially opposed, Oxlahun ti' K'uh and Bolon ti' K'uh were unified in the diurnal cycle, their characters and elements interpenetrating the middle realm of the mortals. Calamity and chaos in the natural world imputed the recurring struggle between the Oxlahun ti' K'uh and the B'olon ti' K'uh for supremacy.

Cycle endings were met with dread, the people unsure whether the Oxlahun ti' K'uh would rise victorious. Ceremonies were held at the New Year, reenacting the destruction of the world through private rituals that entailed the destruction of all household and ritual items, and, in preparation for a new beginning, the gods were nourished with offerings of copal and blood. Longer cycles coincided with shifts in political offices or governors. The longest cycle of fifty-two years was solemnized in a stately ceremony that inaugurated a new ruler, the sun god's proxy on earth. His ascendance to the throne was accompanied by human sacrifices to induce the sun to rise again.

Before the Spanish had made landfall on the shores of the Yucatan, the Mayas were venerating a large, dynamic pantheon of gods that functioned in numerous roles. After colonization many of the gods disappeared into the folds of Christian saints. Those who endured were disguised in their clothes or sheltered inside the saintly effigies. Several gods continued to be venerated openly in areas beyond the sphere of Spanish influence.

LACANDON GODS

Largely because of their geographic isolation in the forest, the Lacandones preserved the religion that was practiced during the Postclassic period. Tozzer noted that some of the thirty-six gods and goddesses still venerated by the Mayas of the Yucatan in the sixteenth century had been preserved in the pantheon of the northern Lacandon community of Petha'. Although most of these gods had preserved their names, their original functions and attributes had been changed (Tozzer [1907] 1978, 80). These changes likely reflected the ethnic Mayan diversity in the forest, each group having maintained their special patron gods. Recall that the Mayas were free to venerate whatever gods that they wanted; thus the gods in one household may not have been venerated in another household.

The northern Lacandon community of Naha' comprises descendants of some, but not all, of the people from Petha'. Bruce (1968) counted nine principal gods and twenty-two assistant deities, goddesses, and minor deities. Davis (1978) reported a total of seventeen gods among the same group. Clearly the pantheon had shrunk from its former, Postclassic size and continued to shrink during the latter part of the twentieth century.

The decline in the number of Lacandon deities may account for the relatively small Lacandon universe compared to that of the ancient Mayas. It embraces five to seven levels supported by pillars anchored in the underworld. Through the center rises the ceiba tree, joining the levels together. This axis mundi is the birthplace of the Lacandon gods.

The levels are organized into a hierarchy of realms, each occupied by one god or several gods ranked in ascending order according to the degree of power they exert. At the top of the hierarchy is Kak'och, creator of the northern Lacandones' major gods, the primordial sea, the first sun, and maize. He corresponds to the creator god(s) or grandparents in all the various Mesoamerican cosmogonic myths. Although Kak'och is the god of the gods, being so far away from the earth, he exerts little influence over the lives of the Lacandones.

Directly below him resides Hachäkyum, creator of the Lacandones, the earth, the underworld, sky, stars, moon, and the second sun. He is accompanied by his wife, Äkna'il Hachäkyum, who corresponds to the (aged) moon goddess and is called Xk'änle'ox in ceremonial contexts. She created the female Lacandones, introduced weaving, oversees childbirth and protects pregnant women and newborns, and is petitioned during parturition. Their youngest son, T'uup, resides in Hachäkyum's sky, where he guards the (second) sun and carries it across the sky of the earth. He is responsible for covering the sun during a solar eclipse.

Two additional main celestial gods are the elder brothers of Hachäkyum. They live on lower levels of the universe. Their position indicates their rank relative to Hachäkyum, as well as their physical location in the universe. Sukunkyum 'Lord of the Underworld', eldest of the triumvirate, is caretaker of the sun at night, custodian of Kisin 'Lord of Death', and the god who decides the fate of souls. Mourners petition him during funerals to show leniency toward the souls of their loved ones, and he is supplicated in ceremonies commemorating the beginning of planting season to deliver a fruitful harvest. He corresponds to various aspects of the B'olon ti' K'uh in the Mayan pantheon but does not function as the Lord of Death. That role is filled by Kisin, the epitome of decay and death who occupies a part of the underworld, called Metlan. He works together with Sukunkyum by meting out the requisite punishments on every soul. He is associated with earthquakes, which he causes by kicking the pillars supporting the earth to collapse the world. He corresponds to the ancient deities Cizin (God A) and Ah Puch, in the Mayan pantheon.

Akyant'o' 'Our Middle Lord',[32] is the god of Christians. He took his mortals to the "other side of the sea," where he then created Western goods, money, foreign diseases, and medicine to cure them. He lives in a cliff near Tenosique.[33] He may correspond to the Postclassic god Ek Chuah, the patron god of the Mayan merchant-warriors (Bruce 1968, 125).

As the middle brother of the Lacandon triumvirate, Akyant'o' is portrayed in Lacandon myth as the embodiment of an advanced stage in sociocultural evolution, which implies a linear path of social progress from simplicity to complexity. When Akyant'o' left the forest, he literally left the Lacandones behind. He was supplanted by Ak'inchob 'Lord of the Milpa', who became protector of the cornfields and the go-between for the Lacandones and Hachäkyum. In terms of sociocultural evolution, he embodies the agricultural stage of development. As the central deity in Lacandon culture, he essentially represents the middle realm of the Lacandon universe.[34]

Above the realm of Kak'och is the realm of the *chembehk'uho'*, who are souls of all the people annihilated in the previous world destructions. Also called the "wandering gods," they drift in dark, cold intergalactic space beyond the walls of the "cosmic house." Lacandones say that this is where the souls of all the people and creatures will go after the next destruction of the world.

Directly below Hachäkyum's realm is a layer of clouds, called the "the Vultures' Sky," occupied by the "king" vulture and his family. The role and significance of this king are unclear; but during an eclipse Hachäkyum lowers the Vultures' Sky, causing the earth to heat up and burn the crops (Rätsch and Ma'ax 1984, 183–84).[35]

Directly below the Vultures' Sky stretches the plane of the earth. It is occupied by numerous gods who control the forces of nature. The main god is Mensäbäk 'Maker of Soot', the Lord of Rain and superior commander of the *ha'ha'nahk'uh* 'rain gods', who seed the clouds with soot, produce the thunder and lightning, and whip up the winds with their enormous fans. Mensäbäk corresponds to the Mayan god Chac and the Mexican god Tlaloc. Mensäbäk and Tlaloc guard the souls of the dead in their aquatic abodes.

Mensäbäk lives near his two brothers, Ts'ibanah 'Painter of Houses', who is renown in the creation myth for painting the gods' houses with the blood of mortals sacrificed during the second destruction of the world, and Itsanohk'uh 'God of Hail', who makes hail and regulates the population of crocodiles. All three brothers live in the caves or cliff faces surrounding three interconnected lakes in the northern Lacandon territory. The home of Ts'ibanah is a large ceremonial site; its monumental architecture and habitation platforms, large deposits of human remains, and ritual artifacts suggest it was always an important pilgrimage site (Palka 2014, 168). According to my Lacandon consultant, Bor Ma'ax, this is the gateway to Mensäbäk's realm where good souls spend the afterlife.

K'ak' 'Lord of Fire' is located on another lake that connects with the other three. He epitomizes the protector god, introduced the bow and arrow, and bequeathed his archery skill and courage to the Lacandones. In one myth he slays the two-headed jaguar and becomes the jaguar when he paints his tunic with spots of blood (see "Ka'wäts'äk uho'or Barum yeter K'ak'" 'The Two-Headed Jaguar and the Lord of Fire', this volume). K'ak' is associated with the Lacandon onen *yuk* 'deer', the emblem of Mayan warriors. In Mesoamerican mythology, the jaguar represents the gods of the underworld, symbols of darkness and the night sun, and rules over the celestial forces of day and night. He is the embodiment of leadership, control, and confidence.[36]

The last of the notable terrestrial gods is Kanank'aax 'Guardian of the Forest'. He lives in the small ruins throughout the forest. His main role is to protect the animals and their habitats.

Most of the gods have their sets of assistants (Hachäkyum and Kak'och have identical sets), who carry out the work of the gods. Tozzer ([1907] 1978, 158) notes that "the gods themselves never do any real work." Their assistants are comparable to the ritual and civic functionaries in Postclassic Mayan society. Bor 'Lord of the Balche' and K'ayum 'Lord of Song' resemble officers within the ancient Mayan *holpop* 'council' that oversaw public feasts and ceremonies (Bruce 1968, 130); Itsanah,[37] first assistant to Hachäkyum, corresponds to *batab* 'municipal president' in the Postclassic political hierarchy (130); Säkäpuk, second assistant, corresponds to *ahkuchkab* 'city councillors' under the batab (130); Ahk'in 'The Sun' corresponds to the Ah K'in, a Maya priest who conducted public and private rituals, divined and interpreted portents, and determined the appropriate ritual actions; and K'urer,[38] third assistants who carry out basic civic tasks under the authority of first and second assistants (130),[39] including the inspection of the mortals' cornfields. In this capacity they are reminiscent of the agents who collected tribute from the rulers' subjects (Davis 1978, 250). A full list of the gods and their functions, together with their ancient Maya analogues, is provided in appendix 2.

In the creation story the gods emerged from the birth flower of their creator, Kak'och. They were followed by the goddesses, who became their wives. By this time the gods had founded their positions and established their roles, but they did not execute their duties until their wives had emerged.[40]

All the goddesses are called Äkna' 'Our Mother'. Äkna' also means 'moon'. Äkna' is the quintessential mother who represents the womb of the universe and the phases of fetal development. In Classic Maya mythology, she had a multiplicity of personas and names. In the Lacandon pantheon she represents the wives of all the gods and thus takes on, or reflects, their various characteristics: she is Äkna'il Hachäkyum, Goddess of the Creator; Äkna'il Sukunkyum, Goddess of the Underworld; and Äkna'il Akyant'o', Goddess of Foreigners and of Western Medicine. The preeminent goddess, Äkna'il Hachäkyum 'Lady of Our True Lord', resembles the aged aspect of the Mayan moon goddess (Goddess O). In rituals the Lacandones call her Xk'änle'ox 'Lady Yellow Ramon Leaf', which associates her with the south, nadir, harvest, and abundance.[41] She worked in concert with her husband

Hachäkyum (God D) to create Lacandon mortals; she made the women, taught them distaff tasks, including weaving, and represents childbirth and midwifery.

Her youthful aspect is reflected in her daughter Äkna'ir Ak'inchob 'Goddess of the Maize God'. As the symbol of fruitfulness and procreation, she corresponds to Goddess I, in the Classic Mayan pantheon.

Äkna' (Xk'änle'ox), Hachäkyum, Sukunkyum, and Ak'inchob constitute the essential deities venerated in every (northern) Lacandon household, because they embodied life and death, fecundity and proliferation, and sustenance.

RELATIONSHIP BETWEEN GODS AND MORTALS

The gods set the moral, social, and spiritual values they expected from their mortals. They were born on earth, where they lived, procreated, and died. They tended their cornfields, formed alliances, intermarried, engaged in battle, and venerated their creator, Kak'och, with sacrifices and offerings in return for their existence.

In addition to following the gods' example, the mortals adopted the divine-inspired onen system. Like the gods, the mortals divided into the *ma'ax* 'monkey', the oneñ of the celestial gods, and *k'ek'en* 'peccary', the onen of the terrestrial gods. The ma'ax and k'ek'en people intermarried, and by this means they united the sky and the earth. The gods and the mortals were also bound together by an agreement that entailed reciprocity: the mortals were to nourish the gods with sweet words and offerings, and the gods would deliver what they needed to survive.

Though the gods and the mortals coexisted on parallel universes and lived similar lives, they were not equal. Generally benevolent toward the mortals, the gods were also irascible and vengeful, especially if the mortals defaulted on the agreement. The gods demonstrated their displeasure by sending illnesses, causing injuries, covering up the sun, whipping up storms, and delaying rains. As one Lacandon said, "We are really only toys in the gods' hands."

The standards of correct behavior and the concept of indebtedness to the gods were established at the beginning of time and form the foundation of the Maya ideology. This ideology is expressed in the Lacandon creation myth.

THE MAYAN CREATION MYTH

"Perhaps the most basic and profound premise of Maya cosmology is the recurrence of eras of the world, each with its creation, its people, their failure to worship their gods correctly, their condemnation, and their destruction" (Bruce 1975, 340). These eras are more clearly defined in the myths of some Mayan groups than in the myths of others.

The Quiché Maya Book of Counsel, the *Popol Vuh,* is the classic source of the Mayan creation story against which all other Maya myths have been compared by scholars. It clearly defines each era on a narrative time line that follows a forward trajectory: In the beginning, the gods created beings that only squawked, and so they condemned them to be the creatures of the forest and to give their flesh to future mortals. Next the gods made beings from mud, but they could not keep their shape and were incapable of active thought, and so they were left out in the rain to dissolve into the earth. Next, the gods made mortals from wood, but they had no heart and were belligerent, so they were destroyed in a flood. Some of them managed to escape but turned into monkeys. Finally the gods made mortals from maize; they were sentient, intelligent, dutiful, and, above all, pious. Unfortunately, they were too perfect: they were as powerful and omniscient as the gods themselves. So, the gods "clouded their eyes" and stripped them of their immortality. Like the maize plant, they would live, procreate, and die in an endless cycle.

THE LACANDON CREATION MYTH

Unlike the *Popol Vuh,* the Lacandon creation myth provides no obvious cycles that represent the various eras. The mortals in each era do not go through the evolutionary stages implied in the *Popol Vuh.* They remain physically the same. Instead, their progress from one stage to the next is expressed in terms of social, moral, biological, and spiritual development and eventual loss of immortality. But the sequence of episodes in which these developments take place is quite fluid. Despite the efforts of some scholars (Bruce 1968, 1975; Bruce, Robles, and Ramos Chao 1971; Marion 1999) to connect the events (and characters) in the Lacandon creation myth with those in the *Popol Vuh*, the connections remain tenuous. The (northern) Lacandon creation story adheres well enough to the first few chapters in the *Popol Vuh*, but after that the Lacandon myth reads as a collection of disparate episodes that may or may not evoke episodes in the *Popol Vuh*. McGee (1993, 1997a) also comments that the Lacandon creation story lacks cohesion, finding that the order of events fails to adhere to a "logical" narrative time line. While Boremanse (1986) and Marion (1999) present the episodes in an order that reflects a sequential progression, they also refer to other stories to give each episode they present some context. The context is usually another story that could precede or follow the episode under discussion. Below I present a simple structure that seems to be universally accepted among the Lacandon researchers.

In the beginning Kak'och was the only being in the universe. He was alone, in a dark, aqueous void. He planted a tuberose in the sea which brought forth the first three principal gods.[42] They were brothers and they emerged in the following order: Sukunkyum, Akyant'o', and Hachäkyum. Although the youngest, Hachäkyum stepped down from the blossom first and began to firm the land. His brothers followed him and together they established their home in Palenque.[43]

Kak'och then departed for the penultimate layer of the universe, but before he left, he gave maize to Hachäkyum, who gave it to his wife, Akna'ir Hachäkyum, and together they developed ways to prepare it.

Hachäkyum set out to finish the task of making the universe inhabitable for his mortals. He sowed the sky with the seeds of trees, thereby establishing his level in the sky. As they grew, their roots perforated the roof of the second layer below, creating pinholes of light in the dark dome over the earth.

By now the terrestrial gods had begun to emerge from the tuberose. The first of these was K'ak' 'Lord of Fire, Courage, and the Hunt'. He was followed by Mensäbäk 'Lord of Rain' and his brothers Ts'ibanah 'Painter of Houses' and Itsanohk'uh 'Lord of Hail'. K'ak', Mensäbäk, Ts'ibanah, and Itsanohk'uh established their houses around the lakes. Mensäbäk's cave would become the place for souls in the hereafter. The houses of Ts'ibanah and Itsanohk'uh would become the gateway through which the souls would pass.

Hachäkyum's in-law 'Hachir Hachäkyum' emerged next and moved to the ruins of Bonampak. He was followed by Kanank'aax 'Guardian of the Forest'.

After the gods had emerged, their wives followed. The primary goddess was Äkna'ir Hachäkyum, the wife of Hachäkyum. She was followed by Äkna'ir Sukunkyum and Äkna'ir Akyant'o'. They, along with all other goddesses, joined their respective husbands and settled down in their assigned abodes.

After some time a second generation of gods was born. They were retrieved from among the roots of a ceiba tree. Akna'ir and Hachäkyum had a daughter, Äkna', who would become Äkna'ir Ak'inchob, and three sons — K'ak'bäk'äkyum Chäk Xib, Upaläkyum Chäk Xib,[44] and T'uup. The Chäk Xib brothers would eventually be stranded on earth, and T'uup would eventually ascend to the sky and become the guardian of the sun.[45]

Ak'inchob 'Lord of Maize', son of Hachil Hachäkyum and his wife, was born on the earth. He was the only celestial god that did not emerge from the tuberose. The blood from his birth was covered up by Hachäkyum, who wanted to hide "the indecency" (Bruce 1974, 43). Ak'inchob would marry Hachäkyum's daughter, the (youthful) Moon Goddess, and become Hachäkyum's dutiful son-in-law.[46]

Five days after all the gods had emerged, Hachäkyum created Kisin 'Lord of Death' in the blossom of the 'aak'älyoom 'night foam' (*Cestrum nocturnum L.*). Hachäkyum gave Kisin a wife. They settled at Palenque in a house behind Hachäkyum, after which they bore two sons and a daughter. Kisin had a neighborly relationship with Hachäkyum until the day Hachäkyum turned his clay human prototypes into animals.[47]

By now Hachäkyum had ordered the world. The land had forests and mountains and rivers and was ready for the mortals. Hachäkyum, Akyant'o', and Mensäbäk collected the clay and sand, mixed up the paints, and set to work on making their mortals: Hachäkyum made the male Lacandones, and his wife made the females; Akyant'o' made the foreigners; and Mensäbäk made the Tzeltales.[48]

Kisin saw the gods working and desired his own mortals, so he produced his set of clay mortals. Before he could bring them to life, as the other gods had done to their figurines, Hachäkyum turned them into animals and decreed that they would be game for his own mortals and provide them with the names of their lineages (onen). Kisin retaliated by defacing the (still inert) mortals of the other gods. From that day on, Kisin pursued Hachäkyum, attempting to kill him (and his mortals) at every opportunity (see "Hachäkyum and Akyant'o' Create Their People and Kisin Creates Their Onen," this volume).

At this point the world was still in darkness. The only light was a faint glimmer coming from Kak'och's sun far up in the sky. This was the sun that brought light and warmth to Hachäkyum's realm, but it was too weak for Hachäkyum's mortals. The light from Kak'och's sun was not only faint and weak but also intermittent, because Kak'och kept covering it up. Because of this, the mortals were cold and starving, so Hachäkyum made a second sun and set it in his own sky. But it just hung in the sky and never moved, and the mortals complained they could not sleep.[49] So, Hachäkyum told T'uup he would have to carry it across the sky each day and hand it over to Sukunkyum to carry through the underworld each night.

At the same time, Hachäkyum created the moon to keep the sun company. He gave her a loom that radiated a cold light. She used it to defend herself against his pet jaguars (Rätsch and Ma'ax 1984).

During this period Hachäkyum was constantly beleaguered by Kisin. So, he made a palm leaf replica of himself as a ruse to make Kisin believe he was beating up the real Hachäkyum. While his proxy was being tormented by Kisin, the real Hachäkyum devoted his time in the underworld to secure a place for Kisin.

Together with his brothers and his son-law, Ak'inchob, Hachäkyum set to work building the underworld. When he emerged, Kisin was standing at the edge of a pretend tomb, where Hachäkyum's son T'uup had "buried" him after his proxy was "killed" by Kisin. When the ground opened up, Kisin and his family tumbled in, and the earth snapped shut behind them.

At the same time, T'uup was receiving the same treatment from his elder brothers, the Chäk Xib, as his father was receiving from Kisin. Like his father, T'uup made an effigy of himself to feign his existence and his death at the hands of his brothers. He departed with his father to his celestial realm. Hachäkyum subsequently cut off the route to his sky, stranding the Chäk Xib brothers on earth. Now the world was complete.

Following the first creation, Hachäkyum destroyed the world three times because the mortals failed to appropriately venerate him. He destroyed the first mortals because they failed to honor him adequately. He sent his sons, the Chäk Xib, to stir up the Chäk Ik'al 'Hurricane', which flattened the world and then rained down a torrent of fire (resin) that burned up the land.

After the land had been cleared and renewed, the souls of those dead returned to earth and repopulated the earth.[50] But they too disappointed Hachäkyum, and he initiated the end of the world with an eclipse. In the darkness the celestial and terrestrial jaguars came up on all sides of the mortals and devoured them. Those whom Hachäkyum set aside, survivors, were taken to Yaxchilan, and their throats were cut. Hachäkyum reserved the blood from each onen, and Ts'ibanah used the rest to paint the houses of the gods (see "Xurt'an, Hachäkyum Uxatik Uche'ir Ukaar" 'Hachäkyum Cuts the Mortals' Throats', this volume). (It is in this era that human sacrifice was performed and that the Lacandones realized they had to nourish the gods to survive.)

Then Hachäkyum created the world for the third time. He reseeded the earth with the blood of the mortals he had reserved, and they multiplied. During the eras, the mortals lost their divine omniscience and immortality, developed reproductive and sexual anatomies, gave birth instead of retrieving their babies from under the ceiba tree, and developed other characteristics and experienced other situations that constitute human existence (see "Äkich'e'ex" 'Our Eyes', "Nacimiento" 'Birth', and "Uyählehir Bah" 'The Mole Trapper', this volume).

And they learned to respect the gods and supplicate them. The gods now departed from their terrestrial home in Yaxchilan. They had given the Lacandones god pots with which to communicate with them and send their offerings, reminding the mortals of their obligation to the covenant set down in Yaxchilan a long time ago.

But as time passed, the mortals' fighting and their continued irreverence toward the gods compelled Hachäkyum to end the world yet again, this time with a flood. He secured the species of each plant and crea-ture, selected two pairs of mortals from each onen, and shut them up in a large canoe in advance of the flood. The rest of humanity was left to drown and be devoured by crocodiles. After the rains had stopped and the waters receded, the creatures and the mortals disembarked the canoe, and Ak'inchob reseeded the earth; the fourth and current era, in which we are living now, began.

But the mortals failed Hachäkyum yet again, so he prepared to end the world for good. He gave the sun to T'uup, and as he was about to cover it up, Akyant'o' came rushing in, intercepted it, and placed it back in the sky. He and Hachäkyum's wife defended the mortals, and together they persuaded Hachäkyum to reconsider.

LACANDON RELIGIOUS BELIEFS AND RITUALS

The Lacandon creation myth expresses the core religious beliefs, practices of worship, and ethics of the pre-Columbian Mayas. The focus of religion is to maintain order and balance in the universe, which can only be achieved by nourishing the gods.

In historical times the Mayan ruler was the sun god's surrogate on earth. He also functioned as the channel through which the beneficence of the sun god flowed down to the people, and their tributes flowed up to him. As the intermediary between the god and the people, the ruler sustained his semidivine position, so long as he honored this covenant.

FORMS OF TRIBUTE

Blood, preferably human blood, was the ideal tribute. A beating heart was better still, pumping its vital fluid through the arteries to the four extremi-ties of the human being, akin to the life force issuing from the hearth in the center of the universe and flowing through the Tree of Life out to the four corners of the cosmos.

Mayas also performed self-sacrifice, which entailed bloodletting from various parts of the body. Because blood symbolized fertility, it was often drawn from the penis. Bloodletting continued to be performed by the northern Lacandones in the twentieth century. The *chak hu'un* headbands, worn by both celebrants and the god pots during the important *k'ämkih* renewal ceremony, attest to the ancient practice. *Chak hu'un* means 'red paper' and represents the blood-soaked paper that was burned in censors by Lacandon ancestors and their ancient Mayan predecessors.[51]

Just as blood was the life force that coursed through the body, it also coursed through the trees. The Lacandon word for blood and tree resin is the same, *k'ik'*. Just as blood is vital for survival, so too were trees. In a forest environment they are the primary resource for the Lacandones' material existence. Species of pine and the copal tree were tapped for their aromatic resins, which the Lacandones say smell like blood to the gods.

Copal is one of the principal foods of the gods (maize is the other). Copal and maize share a network of associations, given their similar appearance. Copal is the maize of the gods. It was mashed into a thick, gooey paste and then offered in various forms, representing tortillas, tamales, and human beings. As lumps, it was simply (divine) corn dough. When rolled into balls and lined up in rows on an offering board, it represented rows of males and females, who, when burned, would drift up to the heavens and become the servants of the gods. At other times these male and female servants were arranged as cones and flattened discs stacked in layers (Tozzer [1907] 1978, 125).

Rubber. The latex of certain rubber trees, also called k'ik', was formed into rubber figurines with humanoid features. They too represented human servants (Tozzer [1907] 1978, 127). The males and females were called *kohoh* and *cher*, respectively, evoking the names of ancient Mayan characters.[52]

The Lacandones call the copal and rubber figurines *gente* 'people'. According to Tozzer ([1907] 1978, 127), the word *gente* is also used for the small censors in which the offerings are burned. Lacandones refer to specific servants as *uk'anir* (see "Kak'och yeter Uk'anir Hach Winik" 'Kak'och and His Human Assistant', this volume).[53] They may correspond to the souls of dead warriors and sacrificed personages among the ancient Maya who ascended to the highest heaven reserved for the brave and the innocent.[54]

Balche', another indispensable edible offering, is the ceremonial liquor first introduced by the gods. Balche' is included in practically every ritual, and celebrants drink it for the express purpose of getting intoxicated. Lacandones believe that being in this altered state of mind enables them to visit the gods. Still another sacred food is honey. Before sugar was introduced, honey was used to ferment the balche', which accounts, in part, for its sacred association. Lacandon myths describe honey as being the food of the gods and unsuitable for human nourishment (see "Mensäbäk yeter Hach Winik Tukinsah" 'Mensäbäk and the Ancestor He Killed', this volume). It is also the symbol of femininity, fertility, and procreation (see "Uk'aay Box" 'The Gourd Song', this volume).

Maize is the most important form of sustenance for the Lacandones. Like other Mesoamericans, the Lacandones consider it sacred. Unlike other Mesoamericans, they do not regard it as a deity, but as a sentient being with a soul. One Lacandon man compared it to a young child, who needs protection and loving care. To abuse or misuse it is a grave offense. Corn also has the power to obstruct evil forces; they say its rows of kernels are like an army of soldiers that repel Kisin and ghosts. Lacandones place ears of corn next to sacred objects and babies that will be left unattended for long periods, and insert them in the corners of the god house and in the doorways of empty houses.

Ceremonial tamales called *nahwah* 'great bread' are offered. Some are small, consisting of one layer of dough and one layer of beans; others are large, with five layers of dough alternating with beans.[55] The tamales are stacked into groups of five. Tucked inside every fifth tamale is a supplicant's request. These are reserved for the gods (Davis 1978, 205).

When offerings are made, an interesting thing happens. They reverse their attributes. Mortals and gods live parallel lives in parallel realms. Their realms are mirror images of each other. In ritual contexts supplicants need to reverse the meaning of their words and the attributes of the offerings so that they are received by the gods as intended: if the gods require a large portion of an offering, the supplicant will offer a small portion, and vice versa. Likewise, the supplicant describes the opposite of what he is offering (Boremanse 1998a; Bruce 1975; Davis 1978; McGee 2002).

Associated items, such as copal and corn dough, also reverse their attributes. Mashed copal resembles corn dough and is regarded as corn dough by the gods. Lacandones say that copal is food for the gods just as corn is food for themselves. So, when they offer copal to the gods, it transforms into corn for the gods. The focus of the opposition is on whoever owns the object, or who it is fit for, rather than on the object itself: the polarity shifts between the gods and mortals.

Rubber may transform into blood, but since the word for both is k'ik', it is unclear whether rubber would necessarily convert into human blood. Some researchers (Bruce 1975; Davis 1978; McGee 1983) maintain that the offering of the rubber figurines represents human sacrifice. It is possible that the transformation represents the ascendance of the souls of the rubber figurines in the afterlife in Lacandon (and pan-Mesoamerican) eschatological beliefs. The Lacandones believe that the soul and the body are separated at death, and that the soul embarks on its journey through the underworld following the path of the night sun.

RELIGIOUS CEREMONIES AND RITUALS

Lacandon religious ceremonies are organized sequences of rituals (Davis 1978). Rituals are performed to placate the gods for a *si'ipir* 'fault' that has been committed. There are three types of faults (Boremanse 1998a): those that are committed against the social order (such as murder, suicide, stealing, lying, the killing of dogs, incest, and despoiling the dwellings of deities); those that are committed against nature (such as hunting techniques that cause suffering and wasting food, especially corn and game); and those that involve ritual oversights (such as neglecting the god pots or the careless handling of sacred objects) (Boremanse 1998a, 71).

Gods mete out punishments commensurate with the fault. Most take the form of injury, illness, and death. Lacandones attribute mishaps, snake bites, crop failures, and epidemics to their having broken one or more of these moral or social injunctions. Reparations must be made immediately to repair the situation with supplication.

Lacandon rituals are requests and entreaties to the gods, not expressions of selfless adoration, although they may contain a thread of sincere thanksgiving when prayers are answered. The main purpose of rituals is to compensate the gods with an offering or a promise of atonement and to restore the harmony between the offender and the gods. If offenders die without making amends, they will receive their comeuppance in the underworld.

Therefore, rituals invariably focus on renewal. Serious situations call for ceremonies that integrate several rituals (see Davis 1978). The largest and most prolonged is the *k'ämkih* ceremony, which is dedicated to renewing the god pots (discussed below). Therapeutic ceremonies range in size and complexity, depending on the condition of the patient (see Davis 1978, 252, 278). Preventative rituals tend to be smaller and performed more often. They include requests to prevent tree limbs from falling on one's head or apologies for small mistakes and other peccadillos. Another simple rite performed daily involves burning copal to grant the supplicant and his family good health (McGee 2002, 145).

Ensuring the benevolence of the gods requires honoring the covenant of reciprocity. The first fruits ceremony is an important form of repayment to the gods for allowing the crops to grow and flourish. Aptly called *uts'ahik ho'or* 'give the head',[56] this simple ritual entails offering the gods the first pick of each crop as it matures (McGee 2002, 146). A similar ceremony, *uhanlikol* 'the food of the milpa', was performed by the Mayas of the Yucatan during the early part of the twentieth century (Tozzer [1907] 1978, 160). Another agricultural ceremony is the *uho'ol ubäker*,[57] which is conducted at the beginning of the corn-planting season (McGee 2002, 145). It is a ritual that returns the seeds reserved from the previous year's crop to the soil and thereby commemorates the end of the cycle.

In all types of ceremonies, supplicants are working to placate the gods. But before supplication can proceed, the cause and requirements of the gods must be determined. Without knowing what kind of crime has been committed or which god has been offended, remedial action is impossible. Therefore, a *k'inyah* 'divination' must be performed. Davis (1978) provides a description of the various forms a divination takes. People who are unable to divine for themselves need to request help from someone who can.

RITUAL PLACES

There are three main sacred places where Lacandones communicate with the gods and ancestors. The first is the *yatoch k'uh* 'house of the gods', where all the ceremonial artifacts are stored and where most rituals take place. Another is Yaxchilan, a great city on the Usumacinta River built in the Classic period. Lacandones believe this was the second terrestrial home of their main gods. In the past they made pilgrimages to venerate the gods and obtain sacred stone relics from the houses of the gods who were will-ing to be represented in the pilgrim's god house. Still other sacred sites include caves, especially those around the northern lakes of Mensäbäk, Itsanohk'uh, and Ts'ibanah, named after the gods who live there. North-ern Lacandones believe that these caves are the place where souls spend the afterlife. Caches of bones and skulls, some recent and others ancient, suggest to archeologists that these caves were used as sacred burial sites; the Lacandones say the bones belong to Mensäbäk and his brothers, who once lived on earth but died from an epidemic. Their spirits have pene-trated deep into the cave and the cliff face. Stools, offering bowls, and other artifacts in the caves suggest that people in the area, including the Lacan-dones, went there to communicate with the gods and their dead ancestors (Palka 2014, 167).

RITUAL EQUIPMENT

By far the most important piece of equipment is the god pot. God pots are living replicas of the gods and the vital means for communicating with the gods. The gods had initially lived on earth, before they died from an epi-demic that swept through the forest. But their spirits departed into the sky, the underworld, and the caves and cliff faces. Lacandones believed that the gods' life force permeated their terrestrial homes in the ruins of Yaxchilan. Lacandones made pilgrimages to Yaxchilan to retrieve small stones from the gods' houses. The major gods originally inhabited the Maya ruins of Palenque, but later, for reasons that are still unclear, they moved to Yax-chilan.[58] Although Palenque remained important to the northern Lacan-dones, Yaxchilan became the center of the world and the destination for ritual pilgrimages (Bruce 1968, 12; McGee 2002, 130). Many of the offering bowls archeologists have found in these ruins date back to the eighteenth century (Palka 2014, 178) and probably earlier. Explorers and clergymen in the seventeenth and eighteenth centuries reported that many Mayas were still conducting rituals in Yaxchilan and other ruins (Cogolludo 1688, bk. 4, chap. 7: 198; Landa 1864, chap. 227: 158; Sapper 1891, 891; Sapper 1897, 265; Stephens 1841, 2:196; Villagutierre 1701, bk. 4, chap. 14: 264; all are cited in Tozzer [1907] 1978, 82–83).

The god pot represents the god's body, or the "house of his soul," in the same way the physical body may be conceived of as the house of a person's soul (Boremanse 1998a, 91). It contains his entrails in the form of cacao beans. The exterior of the pot is its head, presenting a stylized face with a lower projecting lip on which offerings of food and drink are placed. A stone inside is its life force, which receives and responds to the supplicants' petitions.[59]

This sacred stone was obtained from the terrestrial houses of the gods who had, through divination, agreed to be represented in the Lacandon god houses. This relic was deposited in a special incensory, a god pot, which was the means by which the supplicant communicated with the god. The stone inside symbolized the god's life force and his seat, which he uses when he descends from the sky to partake of the gifts offered by supplicants when they request his aid and beneficence.

Like a physical body, a god pot grows old and moves on to the underworld. In the k'ämkih ceremony, reminiscent of the Calendar Round ceremonies, celebrants "kill" the old god pots (or the gods themselves) and then resurrect them. The old god pots have their cacao beans and the sacred stone removed and placed in the new god pots, and then their painted clothing is burned off (McGee 2002, 136). The "dead gods" are moved to the west side of the temple, following Lacandon mortuary custom of laying out the body of the deceased with its head pointed toward the west (Boremanse 1998a, 94). They are given their last food offerings, as are the deceased, who are buried with food supplies for the journey through the underworld, and then their heads are covered with a cacao pod.[60] After this they are laid to rest under the ledge of a sacred cave.

The new god pots are brought into the temple, placed on the east side, and then awakened.[61] A song that accompanies the awakening describes the destruction of the world. The singer tells the gods sleeping inside to wake up and observe the end of the world. He implores them to wake up and partake of all the offerings in front of them. Bruce (1974) and Davis (1978) supply similar versions of the song sung by the late Chan K'in Viejo, who was likely the last officiant to perform the ceremony.

The Lacandon ceremony used to be performed every year, presumably to commemorate the New Year (Tozzer [1907] 1978, 106). After Tozzer, subsequent researchers noted that Lacandones changed the god pots less and less frequently until, in the end, they abandoned the practice altogether (Perera and Bruce 1982; McGee 2002).

CHANGES

The Lacandon religion was on the wane when linguist Robert Bruce arrived in Naha' in 1953 (Perera and Bruce 1982). During that period they were lamenting that their sons had abandoned the gods. Yet later McGee (1983) discovered that the young Lacandon men were nevertheless just as conversant in the religion as their fathers, though they did not practice it as vigorously. The reason for this, McGee surmises, is that after the communities had aggregated into settlements, the main patriarchs conducted the ceremonies on behalf of the entire community, since they were the senior heads of the families in the community. While their sons said they were prepared to take over the religious obligations when their fathers died, they never did (McGee 1983, 73–77). Lacandon young men have begun to forget the religion, saying that they need to write down the words of ceremonies, ritual songs, and chants to remember them. But most never learned to write.

Much that has been lost can never be recovered, but many Lacandon sacred myths, songs, chants, and rituals have been transcribed, and although versions vary from one contributor to the next, the structure and rhetorical expression of their present-day performances preserve the literary style reminiscent of ancient Mayan oratory.

Northern Lacandon Oral Literature

The ancient Mayas were an oral society that transmitted knowledge, ideas, and cultural material in oral and dramatic performances. Nobles delivered their messages to the nonliterate masses in recurring patterns of sounds, words, meanings, and sentence structure. Mayan scribes transcribed the sounds, syllables, and concepts into blocks (glyphs) of hieroglyphic script and arranged them into two columns. Read from left to right, a glyph in the left column paired with the adjacent glyph in the right column forms a unit of meaning reminiscent of a couplet. A couplet is a literary device that merges two successive lines of text that have the same meter and share a single theme. The second line expands on the first to produce a complete thought. Figure 1 presents an example of couplets and triplets in a hieroglyphic text on the east side of Quirigua, Stela C, Copan (from Josserand and Hopkins 2011, 20).

Lines A(1)A(2) form a couplet by establishing the time frame of the event. B(1)B(2) form a couplet by identifying the number of Stones that were set. C(1)C(2)C(3) form a triplet by naming the individual gods, the name of the Stone (or their dominion), and the location where they set the Stone.

Parallelism is a formal rule of design used to achieve balance, proportion, rhythm, and cohesion. The ancient Mayas exploited it in every sphere of their lives, not only in their literature. But when Mayan scribes were forced to abandon hieroglyphic writing and adopt the Latin orthography, the poetry of Mayan oratory was obscured in the blocks of printed text.

LACANDON LITERARY STYLE

The same principles of design are preserved in Lacandon oral performances. The sounds and rhythms of speech contribute to the structure of a text, usually, but not always, coinciding with structural divisions forged by semantic and syntactic parallelism. An excerpt from a Lacandon women's

13.0.0.0.0 4 Ahau 8 Cumku, the creation Event took place.	**A1**	
Three stones were set.	**B1**	
The Paddler Gods erected a stone, in the First Five Sky place; the Jaguar Throne Stone.	**C1**	
The Black Deity erected a stone, in the Large Town place; the Snake Throne Stone.	**C2**	
And then it came to pass that Itzamna set a stone, the Water Throne Stone, in the Sky place.	**C3**	
This was the First Three Stones (the First Hearth).	**B2**	
13 b'ak'tuns were completed, under the supervision of the Six Sky Lord.	**A2**	

Fig. 1. Poetic structure of Quirigua stela C. Adapted from Josserand and Hopkins 2011.

work song "Uk'aay ti' K'uuch" 'Song for Spinning Thread' is organized into four verses that are established by syntactic and semantic parallelism, and reinforced by prosody. The first verse consists of a couplet (BB) played against line (1.i) that precedes it. The second verse also contains a couplet (DD), introduced by line 2.iv. Verse three consists of a single line interposed between verses 2 and 4. Verse four is a triplet (FFF), preceded by line 3.vii.

Poetic and prosodic structure of Juana Koh's spinning song

1.	i	Yan atar at'a(h)sik ten	You must come heap it on for me
	ii	ti' u'a(r)ar inpits'	so that my thread stretches out
	iii	ti' ut'a(h)ar.	so that it increases.
2.	iv	Yan (a)tar ti' awaantiken inpits'eh tu' way yane'ex	You must come help me spin where you are here
	v	Kabar, lah boona.	below, how many (you) all are.
	vi	Kab(ar) awaant(iken).	Below you help me.
3.	vii	Ku(r)e(n) but' (eh) awaar te(n) way.	Sit down and stuff in your brood for me here.
4.	viii	Yan atar abut'ik.	You must come stuff it in.
	ix	Yan atar ats'äpik ten inpits' a' way.	You must come and pile it on my thread right here.
	x	Yan atar ats'äpik ten a' way.	You must come and pile it up for me here.

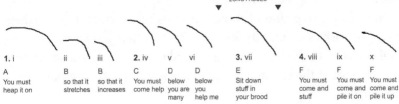

LONG PAUSES

1. i	ii	iii	2. iv	v	vi	3. vii	4. viii	ix	x
A	B	B	C	D	D	E	F	F	F
You must heap it on	so that it stretches	so that it increases	You must come help	below you are many	below you help me	Sit down stuff in your brood	You must come and stuff	You must come and pile it on	You must come and pile it up

The text is a charm to help ease the spinner's labor. She summons the help of spiders, ordering them to add their silk to the thread on her spindle. The first verse focuses on increasing the thread. The couplet is introduced by a demand marked by the obligatory mode (line i) telling the spiders they must put their silk on the spindle.

The second verse focuses on helping the singer spin; lines v and vi constitute a couplet in that each begins with the word "below."

The third verse interrupts the rhythm established by preceding couplets with a spike in the pitch contour. It also shifts from the usual obligatory mood to imperative mood—Sit down! Stuff in! The disruption of the rhythm and shift in mood are reinforced by two long pauses on either side of the verse.

In the fourth verse (lines viii, ix, x) the rhythmic pattern and use of the obligatory mood resume.

Since prosody is the key contributor to the organization of oral performances, it is the first device that a transcriber normally uses to help segment the stream of speech into prosodic units. As demonstrated in the example, pauses and intonation often operate in lockstep with syntactic and semantic parallelism. Falling pitch over a line or a group of lines is graphically represented by indentation. Text that rises in pitch is set flush left, marking the beginning of a new prosodic unit (or verse). Pauses are represented as empty lines on the page. Like syntactic and semantic parallelism, pauses and pitch contours recur in patterns, which establish cohesive units of text.

While parallelism is one of the key literary devices Lacandon performers exploit, other forms of repetition they use include alliteration (the repetition of the initial consonants of adjacent words, e.g., "mash," "mince," "mulch"); anaphora (the repetition of the word at the beginning of successive lines and verses); and epistrophe (the repetition of a word or words at the end of successive clauses).

In addition to repetition, Lacandones press into service features of their language, such as lexical substitution, which involves juxtaposing semantically related words (e.g., *muxik* 'grind' and *mäxik* 'mash'). The sound correspondence of the pair enhances the rhetorical effect and establishes a firm rhythm.

Lacandones commonly employ periphrasis (many words are used to describe a thing or situation where fewer words would suffice). This strategy is used to embellish texts for lyrical effect. An example, from one of Antonio Martinez's chants, is *muxur matan* 'ground gift'. It refers to *pom* 'copal'. When he chants "he' inmuxur matan" 'here is my ground gift', he is not just offering copal, but describing a gift that he has specially prepared into a fragrant paste. It implies a request for help, since *matan* means not only 'gift' but also 'beg for'. Whether intentional or not, the alliteration lends a poetic resonance to the phrase.

Lacandones make extensive use of metaphors, many of which are unusual and imaginative. In the "Song to the Gourd," also entitled "Song to a Woman," a cup of balche' (traditional liquor) is a young woman, inebriation is her embrace, and her embrace is communion with the gods (McGee 1987).

They also exploit homophony, which entails the pairing of words that sound similar but differ in meaning. An example from the same song pairs *läk* 'drinking gourd' and *laak'* 'spouse, wife', and *chan* 'little' and *ch'en* 'cure'. The singer deliberately reverses the usual word order of *chan laak'* 'little woman' to *laak' chan* to evoke *läk ch'en* 'curing bowl' (Bruce 1974, 291).

LACANDON LITERARY GENRES

Repetition, metaphorical language, lexical substitution, periphrasis, and other literary devices discussed above are employed to greater or lesser degree in all forms of Lacandon oral literature and discourse. But there are discernable formal and stylistic characteristics and subject matter that define certain Lacandon genres.

Tsikbal refers to discourse, any kind of talk, whether a myth or factual event, that happened in the recent distant past, a personal history, a description, and a report. Generally, the term is applied to ordinary conversation. The Lacandones with whom I worked distinguish narratives that are "traditional" and those that are not.[1] They further divide traditional stories into myths and fiction. Lacandones sometimes refer to myths as *historia* 'history' and nonmythic stories as *cuento* 'story'. Historias are set in a timeless past. The themes and characters are cosmological. Protagonists are typically deities but sometimes include the ancestors (e.g., see "Nacimiento" 'Birth', this volume). Themes center on the origin of the universe and the birth of humanity, the acquisition of religion, morality, marriage, and the evolution of lineages. In short, historias reflect the realities to which the Lacandon society had to adjust and the various stages of its cultural evolution.[2]

The opposite can be said of cuentos: their main purpose is to entertain, though they often include didactic subtext. They feature monsters, ogres, and animal-gods (or transformers), talking animals who often interact with the ancestors and sometimes enter into reciprocal exchanges.

Characters and motifs in Lacandon cuentos are also found in the narratives of other Mayan groups, including the Tzotzils, Tzeltales, Chujes, Yucatecans (Bierhorst 1986), Ch'oles (Josserand 2003), and Mopanes and Yucatecans living in southern and central Belize (J. Thompson 1930). The similarities suggest cultural contact, undoubtedly facilitated by the reducciones established by Catholic missionaries. The story of the rabbit, a trickster, and his dupe, a jaguar (this volume), is popular throughout the Mayan lowlands; the innumerable versions retain the motif of holding up the cave or a boulder to prevent the world from crashing down, a motif that recurs in many deception tales featuring tricksters and dupes other than the rabbit and the jaguar.[3]

Still other narratives fall somewhere between myth and legend—a story that has some basis in historical fact and whose protagonist was a real person, but that contains elements that are fantastical.

Narratives that are apparently Mayan incorporate motifs that are European. For example, there is an event in the story of Hachäkyum and Kisin (see "Hachäkyum yeter T'uup yeter Kisin" 'Hachäkyum, T'uup, and the Devil', this volume) in which the maize field of a dishonest farmer turns into stones. A similar event occurs in a Zinancantec (Tzotzil Maya) narrative (Laughlin 1977) and other narratives throughout Mesoamerica. Although deceptively Mayan, the scene traces back to a thirteenth-century Latin manuscript (Dähnhardt 1912, 2:95–107) that was brought to Europe from the Near East by the crusaders (Laughlin 1977, 8).[4] Whether the Lacandones received this story from the Tzotziles or another group is uncertain. Tracing the sources is time-consuming and, in many cases, impossible.

NARRATIVE STRUCTURE

Traditional narratives are formally structured. They employ formulaic openings and closings, which include an acknowledgment to the originators of the narratives, typically *aknukire'ex* 'our ancestors'. In so doing, narrators are authenticating the stories and linking them to a meaningful past (Bauman 1991, 126).

Narratives are structured into units of organization, from the phrase, clause, sentence, paragraph, and larger sections, such as scene and episode. The segmentation of these units is achieved by changes in intonation patterns and pauses, syntactic and semantic parallelism, and other forms of repetition that include back tracking. Higher levels of organization, such as episodes, are typically marked by the discourse particles *bay* 'okay' and *ele* 'well, and so'. *Bay* marks changes in time and setting and frequently signals shifts in dialogue. *Ele* functions similarly and introduces a scene or the narrator's commentary. Another particle, *pachir* 'then', operates at lower levels of organization, typically introducing shifts in action or speaker turns in conversation that are embedded in the narrative. Practically every narrative includes dialogue and, if it is a retelling of someone else's story, embeds that dialogue within a dialogue.

Narratives contain a great deal of conversation and are, in themselves, conversational. In oral societies telling stories is a collective process; the audience actively participates in developing the narrative by interpolating the narrative with anecdotes or adding comments and corrections, which often veer the story into other directions.

Narratives may also contain songs and chants, thus marking narrative as an all-inclusive or default genre. Ordinary speech is often punctuated with narratives, anecdotes, and embedded conversation.

More than any other genre, songs and incantations display a versified structure that fully exploits syntactic and semantic parallelism, sound symbolism or word play, metaphorical language, and lexical substitution. The following describes each of these genres with examples.

K'aay 'song'. The Lacandones distinguish two kinds of songs: *hach k'aay* 'real song', and *baxal k'aay* 'play song'.[5] Most hach k'aay are sung in the context of rituals (secular and sacred), ceremonies, or activities associated with ceremonies. Since ritual practice is the purview of men, hach k'aay are only sung by men. Other hach k'aay relate to hunting, fishing, and trapping and are sung to lure game. For example, "Uk'aay Käy" 'Fish Song' calls upon the help of aquatic creatures to round up the fish, and "Uk'aayir Ma'ax" 'Song of the Monkeys' helps the hunter locate and lure monkeys to the offering plates (Antonio Martinez pers. comm.). Still other hach k'aay are sung to protect oneself against insect bites and animal attacks (see "Uk'aayir Xux" 'Song of the Yellow Jacket Wasps', and "Uk'aay Barum" 'The Jaguar Song', this volume). Because of their protective and preventative function, these types of songs are also referred to as *sekretos* 'secrets' (see Ritual Language, below).

Whereas hach k'aay follow a culturally established pattern and were given to the mortals by the lord, Ak'inchob, singers are also free to make up their own songs. These types of songs are called *baxar k'aay* 'play songs'.

Ritual Language. Sacred texts and magic charms are the most difficult to translate because of their pervasive figurative language, abstract references, and unusual sentence structure.[6] The complexity of ritual speech varies according to the occasion and its purpose. The list below describes the kinds of ritual speech performed in different contexts.

***Sekreto* 'secret'.** A *sekreto* is a charm recited to produce a positive effect, such as to increase the amount of yarn, hasten the grinding of maize, or produce immaculate arrowheads. Others are aimed at prevention, such as disempowering wasps to prevent them from stinging. Many sekretos solicit the assistance of specific creatures or invoke plants with specific qualities. Since sekretos are often sung, they are also referred to as k'aay. Examples of sekretos include "Uk'ayir Tok'" 'Song of the Flint', which invokes a variety of birds and palms with strong, straight bones and ribs to help flake durable, straight flint blades; "Uk'aay Xux" 'Song of the Yellow Jacket Wasps', which induces impotence; "Uk'aay ti' Huuch'" 'Song for Grinding', which calls upon the birds to help grind the maize; and "Uk'aay ti' K'uuch" 'Song for Spinning Thread', which invokes the spiders and bees to help with the task. Apart from their magical purpose, most sekretos are instructive and of considerable taxonomic value.

Ut'anir, literally 'its words', is slightly different from a sekreto. The difference lies in the addressee and the location in which it is performed.

While sekretos are addressed to things in the natural world or invoke their inherent essences, *ut'anir* are directed to the gods or sacred elements. Sekretos may be conducted in any environment, usually in the context of some relevant activity, whereas ut'anir are performed in ritual contexts and usually in sacred spaces, such as the god house, Mayan ruins, and caves.

K'asar k'uh 'praying (to sacred images)'[7] <k'a'ah-s-ar 'cause to remember'[8] is a monotonic chant punctuated by short bursts of rapid, high-pitched speech. The particle *ber* is often uttered at the end of lines, along with a fall in pitch and a decrease in amplitude.[9]

K'inyah 'divination' <k'in-'prophesy'-yah 'pain' is a short ritual performed by one person to determine the cause of a misfortune, the god or gods willing to intervene, and the kinds and amounts of offerings they desire.[10]

Kunyah 'curing ritual' <kun-'relieve'-yah 'pain' is a curing ritual, usually addressed to the gods, but it may include invoking certain creatures, plants, or their essences. The ritual is sometimes accompanied by smudging the patient with the smoke of copal.

Pokikbäh 'worship, pray'[11] is like k'asar k'uh but involves the burning of incense. It may include all the forms of ritual speech described above.

TRANSCRIPTION CONVENTIONS AND PROCEDURES

Most of the texts were prompted by me to provide the audio complements to the published Lacandon texts that lack recordings or are otherwise unavailable. The performers contributed additional narratives and descriptions during recording sessions and informal interviews.

Performances were transcribed and translated with the help of Lacandon consultants, who were familiar with the texts and had experience in transcription and translation.[12] The procedure entailed playing a short stretch of speech on the computer and having the consultant repeat what he heard. It was a slow process, taking on average one hour to transcribe and translate one minute of speech. The texts were then checked with the same consultant or another one to verify their accuracy.

Texts are mostly presented in broad phonetic transcription, which means that the abstract form of the words are given, rather than idiosyncratic forms in pronunciation. An English example of an idiosyncratic form of 'going to' is 'gonna'. Hyphenation between morphemes (e.g., *t-in-lah-han-t-ah* 'I ate it all up') is avoided, because it is an artefact of linguistic analysis. The sentence in the example would be written as *tinlah(h)antah*. Elided sounds are restored in parentheses, as in the previous example. Parentheses also enclose material in the English translations, to clarify otherwise obscure concepts or render the translation more grammatical and semantically precise.

Stress marks on syllables (e.g., Nahá', Lacandón, and Lacanhá') are omitted, because they reflect Spanish pronunciation, namely accent. In Maya transcriptions, stress marks indicate tone, which carries grammatical meaning. Northern Lacandon does not, as far as can be determined, have tone, therefore stress marks are omitted. In keeping with the Lacandon phonemic inventory (a set of distinct speech sounds), the phoneme /h/ is transcribed as *h*, rather than *j*, which is also prevalent in the extant Lacandon literature. Moreover, instead of Lakantun, I use the conventional spelling Lacandon because this is how it is spelled in most publications (see table 1).

Pauses and pitch contours are the primary guides for transposing the oral performance to the printed page. A line of text is indicated by an initial high or rising pitch and a final low or falling pitch and a pause. A period is placed at the end of the line that immediately precedes a line marked by a return to high pitch. Several of these pitch contours often embed within an overarching intonation phrase, creating a gradual downward trend over more than one line of speech. Ideally, these embedded contours are presented as indented lines of text, but in this work they are simply marked by commas. Intonation and pauses also inform higher levels of organization beyond the line, such as stanzas and verses, scenes and episodes, or acts. These divisions are displayed on the page as empty lines (white spaces). Emotions, intensity, and volume are represented by literary devices, such as italics, capitalization, and punctuation, including dashes and exclamation marks. Commas are used to mark a short breath or hiatus in a stream of speech, and periods are used to demarcate complete sentences.

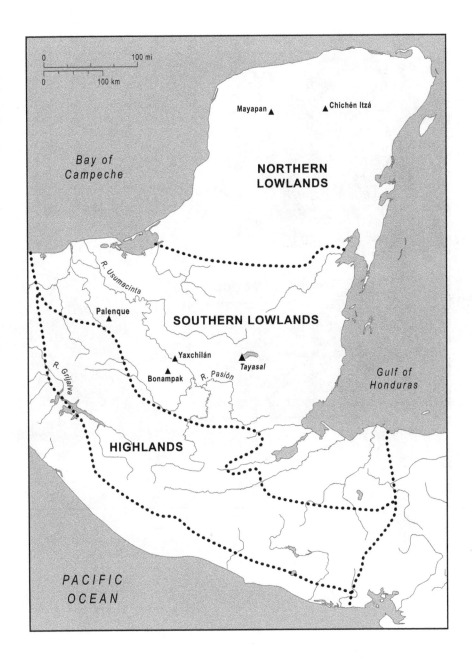

Fig. 2. Geocultural areas. Map created by Erin Greb.

Fig. 3. Maya Lowlands and ethnic territories during the Postclassic and Colonial periods. Map created by Erin Greb.

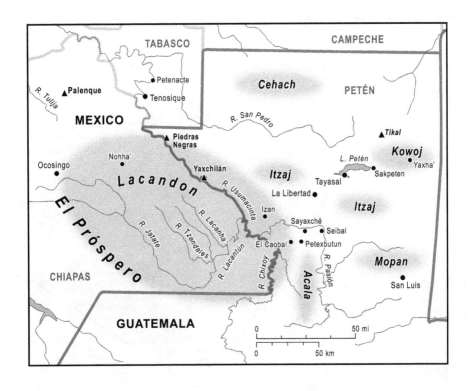

Fig. 4. Close-up of El Próspero. Map created by Erin Greb.

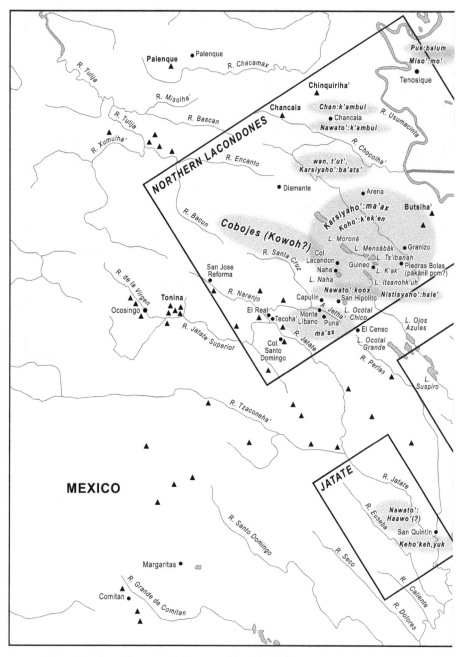

Fig. 5. Four Lacandon areas. Map created by Erin Greb.

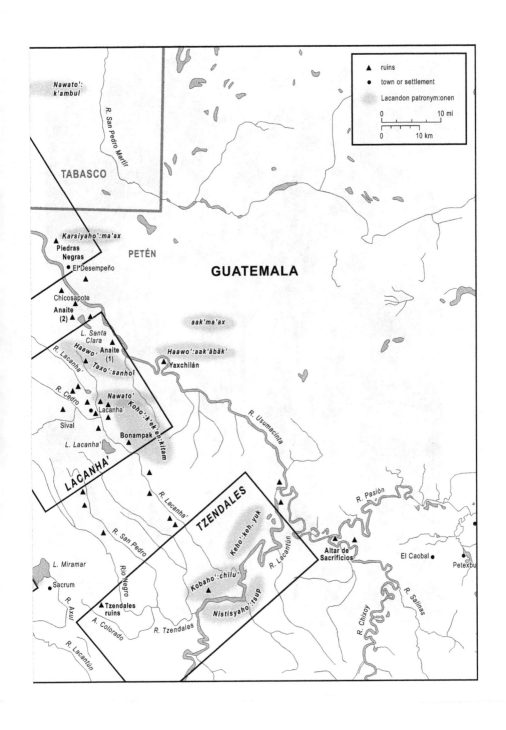

ruins
town or settlement
Lacandon patronym:onen

0   10 mi
0   10 km

Nawato':
k'ambul

R. San Pedro Martir

TABASCO

▲ *Karsiyaho':ma'ax*
Piedras
Negras
● El'Desempeño
▲

PETÉN

GUATEMALA

Chicosapote
Anaite
(2) ▲

L. Santa
Clara
Haawo': Anaite
R. Lacanha' (1)
Taxo':sanhol

aak'ma'ax

Haawo':aak'äbäk'
▲ Yaxchilán

R. Cedro

Nawato'
▲ ▲
Lacanha'
Sival ▲ ▲ *Koho':k'ek'eh:kitam*

L. Lacanha'

Bonampak

R. Usumacinta

LACANHA'

R. Lacanha'

TZENDALES

Keho':xeh.yuk

R. Pasión

R. San Pedro

R. Lacantún

L. Miramar

Río Negro

Altar de
Sacrificios

El Caobal ●

Petexbu

Sacrum

Kobaho':chilu'

R. Axul

▲ Tzendales
ruins

A. Colorado

Nistisyaho':tsup

R. Tzendales

R. Chixoy

R. Salinas

R. Lacantún

Fig. 6. Menche Bol (center), indomitable Lacandon leader of Yaxchilan.
Photo by Desiree Charnay, c. 1880. Courtesy of Société de Géographie.

Fig. 7. Lacandon men, Petha'. Photo by Teobert Maler. Courtesy
of the Peabody Museum of Archaeology and Ethnology, Harvard
University, PM#2004.24.1939 (digital file #130710010).

Fig. 8. Lacandon women and children, Petha'. Photo by Teobert Maler
1898. Courtesy of the Peabody Museum of Archaeology and Ethnology,
Harvard University, PM#2004.24.1935 (digital file #130710006).

Fig. 9. Northern and southern Lacandon
settlements today. Map created by Erin Greb.

2

Myths

Birth of the Gods

Bor Ma'ax

In the beginning the world was nothing but still waters in the darkness.[1] There was only one god, Kak'och.[2] He created a single tuberose[3] from which three gods emerged: Sukunkyum was born first,[4] then Akyant'o', and finally Hachäkyum. Kak'och left it to these gods to complete the earth, but all he gave them was a little mound of earth and the seeds of the trees.[5]

The brothers grew very quickly. Hachäkyum, although he was the youngest, climbed out of the tuberose first.[6] While his older brothers still huddled in the blossoms, Hachäkyum walked about the earth testing the ground. He tried to tamp it down as he walked, but the ground was too soft. So he went looking for something to firm it up. He walked a ways before he spotted a mound that Kak'och had left. As he approached it he called out to his brothers, telling them that he had found the perfect material to make the ground solid. Taking handfuls of sand, he turned this way and that, distributing it all around. As he did, the ground began to solidify. After this, he sowed the seeds that Kak'och had given him to replenish the earth.

When Hachäkyum had finished all this, his brothers descended from the tuberose, and they went off to found their home in Palenque.[7]

Voy intsikbartik utsikbar ka'(ah) toop'ih k'uh ti' Parenke.
I'm going to tell the story about when the gods were born in Palenque.

Be'ik utsikbartah ka'ah toop'ih yok'or baknikte', hunkuri' ahbaknikte' la 'oxheek' uk'ä' ahbaknikte'. Uyanchuni(n), ka'ah wak(ih) utoop' ahbaknikte', lahih usuku'un kyum hook'ih. Pachir, wakih uher uhump'er uk'äb, utoop', ele tarih uk'aba', Akyant'o'. Ele ti' yan uher hump'er uk'äb; ele ka'ah wak(ih) utoop', ele ubähi(r) Hachäkyum hook'ih tun.

They say that when they were born in the tuberose flower—(each one emerged from) one of three (flower) branches—when the first (flower) opened, the eldest brother of our Lord came out. Then, another flower opened on another branch, and out came Akyant'o'. And then, there is another branch; when the flower opened, Hachäkyum came out.

[Be'ik tutsikbartah uchik unuki(r) (winik) aknukire'ex. Uya'arik, la' suku'un akyum, ma' tupees(ah) ubäh. Toh ka'(ah) toop'ih yok'or ahbaknikte', ma' ximnah; ma' peeknah. La' ket yeter Akyant'o', ma' ximnahih.]

[This is how our ancestors recounted it. They say, the eldest brother of our Lord didn't move. As soon as he was born in the tuberose, he didn't walk (on the earth); he didn't move. The same for Akyant'o', he didn't walk (on the earth).]

Ele, ubähi(r) ahHachäkyum, ka'ah wakih la' toop' ahbaknikte', tupurah uyok seeb yok'o(r) lu'um. Seeb uxim(b)asik yok'o(r) lu'um. Tupurah uyok ahHachäkyum, uyirik. "Ma' tsoy," kih. "Ne huup." Kupurik uyok—*hup*.[8] Ne huup.

And so, when the flower of the tuberose opened, Hachäkyum quickly jumped down onto the earth. Quickly he walks back and forth on the earth, tamping it down. Hachäkyum (had) step(ped) down and look(ed) at it. "The earth is not good," he says. "It's soft." He puts his foot down— *sloosh*. It's very soft.

"Ehhh," (u)hook'or ut'an ubähi(r) ahHachäkyum. "Eh maaa' tsoooy lu'um. Eh ma' tsoy lu'um. Tint'an yan inwutskintik."

"Ehhh," Hachäkyum calls out. "Ehhh, the earth is nooo good. The earth is no good. I think I have to fix it."

Tan uman uwich ubähi(r) ahHachäkyum. Eh kupu(ri)k uwich yan kura'an chan pukwits. Ne tikin a' lu'um. Eh, kupu(ri)k ut'aan bin ubähi(r) ahHachäkyum ti' usuku'uno', "Eh ma wa ne tsoy a' kura'an wits. He' inbin inwirik. Wa ne tsoy (inbin) intasik (ti') inka'lahwutskintik a' lu'um, ti' uchichtar, t(i') upak' ubah."

Hachäkyum is scanning the area. Then he spots a small knoll standing there. The soil (appears to be) very dry. So, Hachäkyum calls out to his older brothers, "Eh, the knoll (might be) good. I'll go see if it's good. If it's good, I'm (going to) spread it out, to fix the earth again, so it hardens, so it settles."

Binih uyaaka' bin ahHachäkyum. Chik chik bin utäreh la' kura'an chan wits'. Kutärik ne tikin.

Hachäkyum went quickly (toward it). He walks and walks to investigate the knoll there. He tests it to (see if) it is very dry.

"Eh," kuhook'or ut'an ahHachäkyum, "Ehhh, tinwirah, bäkan. Ne tsoy, bä-kän, a' he'."

"Ehhh," Hachäkyum announces, "Ehhh, I see this here is very good."

Tan upäyoktik t(i') uk'äb ahHachäkyum bin. Kutärik ne chich. Ele, kutekch'a'tik—*wiii*. Kupäyoktik ti' uk'äb, kupurik—*wiii*. Eh, kuka'sutik ubah tupach, kupurik tupach—*wiii*—kuka'sutik ubah te' tahan.

Hachäkyum is scooping up handful(s). He tests it and (finds) it is very firm. And so, he grabs more (and throws it)—*whizzz*. He takes another hand-ful and throws it—*whizzz*. He turns back and forth (throwing the soil)—*whizzz*.

Ele, ne seeb uka'bin uxim(b)aseh. Ne seeb kubin uka'tunt(ik) uximbartik. Seeb t(an) uts'a(hi)k ubah a' lu'um; ma' ne yäka'(an) yok'or ahHachäkyum uxim(b)ar te'.

And then, he quickly walks (back and forth) again. Very quickly he is trying out the land; it's not that swampy there (where) Hachäkyum walks.

"Ehhh, ne tsoy. Eh, tint'an, bähe' binet k'in ti' kunahbin kuta(r) ti' lu'um(o'). Ne tsoy ti' umeyah, ne tsoy. Bähe' chich, ma' huup." Le' ne tsoy uyor ahHachäkyum.

"Ehhh, it's very good. So I think that now the earth is going to stay like this forever for the mortals. It's very good for doing things, very good. Now it's hard, not soft." Hachäkyum is elated.

Kuk'atik ti' ubäho', Sukunkyum, "Eh tech, tu' kabin tech?"

He asks his eldest brother, Sukunkyum, "So now, where are you going to go?"

Sukun akyum tuya'arah, "Ten, tint'an ma' ten kinbin inkänäntik way. Tint'an, tech."

Sukunkyum said, "I don't think I'm going to take care of (things) here. I think you should."

"Eh bay."

"All right," (says Hachäkyum).

Ele, ubähi(r) usukun akyum tuya'arah, "Tint'an ten kinbin inkänäntik (u)yaram lu'um."

And then Sukunkyum said, "I think I'm going to take care of the Underworld."

Eh, ubähi(r) ahAkyant'o' tunuukah ti', "Ten, tint'an ten mäna' inkurta(r) way ten inmeyah way. Ma' inp'aata(r) ten. Ten ti' kin bin ch'ik t(i') upach k'ak'na'⁹ (ti') uher lu'um. Ti' kinbin ten."

And his brother Akyant'o' said, "As for me, I don't think there is any work for me here. I'm not staying. I'm going way over to the other side of the sea to another land. I'm going there."

And so, the brothers separated. Hachäkyum continued his work in the forest, Sukunkyum departed for the underworld, and Akyant'o' set out for the "other side of sea," where he created many different races of people, foreign diseases and the medicine to cure them, technology and metal tools, domestic animals, and money.

Five days later all the rest of the gods came out of the tuberose. They came in the following order: Itsanal, Säkäpuk, K'ulel, Bol 'Lord of Wine', K'ayum 'Lord of Song', AhK'in 'Lord Sun', AkK'ak' 'Lord of Fire', Mensäbäk 'Lord of Rain', Ts'ibanah 'Painter of Houses', Itsanohk'uh, Uhachil Hachäkyum 'Hachäkyum's co-parent in-law',[10] AhK'ak' Mensäbäk, and all the *chembel k'uho'* 'minor gods' (Chan K'in Viejo, in Bruce 1974). Ten days later the lords' wives were born.

Hachäkyum and Akyant'o' Create Their People and Kisin Creates Their Onen

Bor Ma'ax

After Hachäkyum fixed the earth, he set about to create mortals with his brother Akyant'o'.[1] Hachäkyum made his *hach winik*, the 'true people', and Akyant'o' made his *ts'ul*, the 'foreign people'. When Kisin, the Devil, tried to make his own people, Hachäkyum turned them into forest animals that became food for his mortals and the *onen* 'animal-named lineages' of the hach winik.[2]

Hachäkyum created many onen and assigned each its own territory. First, he created the *ma'ax* 'spider monkey'; then the *k'ek'en* 'white-lipped peccary', which he placed about thirty centimeters away from the ma'ax; then the *k'ambul* 'curassow', which he placed about eighty centimeters from the other two; then the *keh* 'brocket (mule) deer', which he placed about two and a half meters away from the k'ambul; and, finally, the *mo'* 'macaw', which he placed about three meters away from the rest (Boremanse 1986, 31, translated by Cook).

This story differs from the southern Lacandon version, which has onen emerging from a hole in the ground. Four are mentioned: the k'ek'en, *kitam* 'collared peccary', *yuk* 'white-tailed deer', and keh. They emerged simultaneously, but some had more difficulty than others getting out. The yuk and the keh sprang out and landed far from the hole, because they had long, strong legs. But the short and stout k'ek'en and kitam heaved themselves up and out and collapsed at the edge of the entrance (Boremanse 1986, 273).

The order and placement of the onen implies a series of migrations by different Mayan groups, each group arriving at different times and settling in different areas. Distances between the groups also suggest the existence of alliances and animosities: according to the northern Lacandones, there are two groups of k'ek'en; the one in the north intermarries with the ma'ax, whereas the one in the south does not. By the northern Lacandon account, the mo' are furthest away from the ma'ax, conceivably because the ma'ax feared them and kept their distance (Boremanse 1986, 31). There were many more Lacandon onen than the ones mentioned here. A full list of the onen and their associated Mayan patronyms (or "ceremonial" names), along with their locations and affiliations, can be found in appendix 2.

The northern Lacandon origin myth also differs from the Classic Mayan version, which describes the gods' failed attempts at making mortals from mud and then wood before succeeding with maize. The birth of humanity is depicted in Mayan iconography as a stalk of maize, symbolizing both humanity's substance and sustenance. The ancient Mayas believed that human beings, and life itself, emerged from the waters of the underworld. That the northern Lacandones believe humans were created on earth could explain why the mortals were made of clay and not, save for their teeth, from maize.

PART 1. HACHÄKYUM AND AKYANT'O' CREATE THEIR MORTALS

Ele ne tsoy uyor. Lahih tukatar uyoro'. Tan uya'arik bin ubähi(r) ahHachäk-yum, "Le ten way kinbin inwutskintik tuworor ba'ink'i(r), ten."

And so, Hachäkyum was very happy. He and his brothers had come to an understanding.[3] Hachäkyum is saying to his brothers, "I am going to fix everything here."

Ele, kura'an utukrik ubäh, "*Ba'inkin kakbin akme(n)tik way?*"

And so, Hachäkyum is seated there thinking to himself, "*What are we going to do here?*"

Bay.

Okay.

[Lahih usukun akyum, ma' täy[4] ume(n)teh la' (yaram)lu'um. Ma' xik (ti' u)yaram lu'um, ma' täy. Ti' yan bähe' ich Parenke.]

[The eldest brother of our lord hasn't made the underworld yet. He hasn't gone to the underworld yet. He is still in Palenque.]

Ubähi(r) ahHachäkyum, tutukrah ubäh yete(r) Akyant'o'. Ele ubähi(r) Hachäkyum tuya'arah, "Tint'an bin ink(ah) inkäxtik k'ät. Bin ink(ah) inkäxtik sa'am."

Hachäkyum and Akyant'o' thought to themselves. And then Hachäkyum said, "I think I'm going to go look for clay. I'm going to go look for sand."

Eh ubähi(r) ahAkyant'o' ku nuukik ti', "P'isi(r) ten. Ne pochen ti'."

And Akyant'o' replies, "So am I. I really want to."

"Wa bin inme(n)tik (winik), bin inkäxtik k'ät."

"If I'm going to make (people), I'm going to look for clay," (says Hachäkyum).

"P'isi(r) ten. Bin inkah inkäxtik ten ti' inme(n)tik inwinik ten."

"Me too. I'm going to look for it to make my own people," (says Akyant'o').

"Eh bay!" kih Hachäkyum. "Eh, ko'ox akkäxtik uk'äti(r). Ko'ox!"

"All right!" says Hachäkyum. "So, let's go look for their clay. Let's go!"

Uhook'or ubino' ket kubino'.

They set out together.

Kuk'uchu(r) kubin uho'ots'eh k'ät. Tuyirah k'ät, tuho'ots'ah. Lahih tuyanu'rsah la' k'ät. Pachi(r) ka'ah binih ukäxt(ik) usa'am.

They arrive and go scoop out the clay. They saw the clay and they scooped it out. They brought all the clay back first. Then they went in search of the sand.

Ele, tulahu'rsah sa'am, ele kuya'ach'tik.

So, they brought back all the sand, and then they kneaded it (with the clay).

"Ele bähe', kakpäteh tun. Kakpäteh," uya'arik ti' Akyant'o' ahHachäkyum.

"So now, let's form them. Let's form them," Hachäkyum says to Akyant'o'.

Ele tuya'arah ubähi(r) Hachäkyum, "Ten inme(n)tik hach winik. Ma' ne pim."

Then Hachäkyum said, "I am making the 'real people'.[5] There won't be many."

Eh, Akyant'o' kunuukik ti', "Eh ten bin ink(ah) inme(n)tik inmeyahkaheh. Bin ink(ah) inme(n)tik inwinik ten."

And Akyant'o' replies, "I'm going to make my own creations. I'm going to make my own people."

"Eh bay." Ne tsoy uyor.

"All right," (says Hachäkyum). He is very happy.

Tan upätik; tan uya'ach'tik k'ät. Ne tsoy uyor. Tan ume(n)tik.

He is forming them; he is kneading the clay. He is in good spirits. He is making them.

Bay.

Okay.

Hachäkyum, tan ume(n)tik. Kisin, ma' usamtar utar. (Toh ti' yan ahKisin ti' Parenke.) Kutich'ir la' Kisin uya'arik, "Eh, ba'inkin ame(n)tik tech yumeh?"

Hachäkyum is making them. By and by Kisin comes along. [Kisin is still in Palenque.]⁶ When Kisin approaches he says, "Eh, what are you doing, Lord?"

"Eh, mäna'. Tan inme(n)tik ink'ät. Tan inme(n)tik inwinik ten."

"Nothing much. I'm working my clay. I'm making my own people."

"Eh hah!" Kisin.

"Ah, indeed!" (says) Kisin.

Ne su' utar uch'eene'etik, ahHachäkyum bin. Mäna' kuxantar—kutichir uch'eene'etik tu' kumeyah Hachäkyum, tan ume(n)tiko'one'ex. Tan uya'ach'tik k'ät.

He is always visiting Hachäkyum. He doesn't waste any time—he comes to visit Hachäkyum where he is making us. He is kneading clay.

Hach ma' ne san, kuka'tichir ahKisin. "Tan ameyah yum."

A little while later, Kisin comes again. "You are working, Lord."

"Tan."

"I am."

"Eh ba'inki(r) kubin ume(n)tik ti' tech?"

"So, what is your work going to do for you?"

Ele ubähi(r) Hachäkyum kunukik, "Eh, la' he' kinme(n)tik ti' uts'ahik ma'ats', ti' uts'ahik ten, wa k'ik', hu'un, nahwah, tum(b)en lek.⁷ Ele lahih kuts'ahik ten."

And Hachäkyum replies, "These that I'm making are for giving me *posol* or rubber, bark cloth, tamales, (and) incensories. They are going to give these to me."

"Eh hah," kih Kisin.

"Ah, indeed," says Kisin.

Uhook'or ubin Kisin, ti' ukäxtik uk'ätir ti' ume(n)tik uwinik ti' Kisin. Bin ukäxteh sa'am. Kura'an uya'ach'teh uk'ät. Bekir ti' ahHachäkyum, la' bix tume(n)tah Hachäkyum, bekir ti' Kisin ti' naka'an ume(n)tik, tan uya'ach'tik uk'ät.

Kisin leaves and goes to look for clay to make people for himself. He goes to look for sand. He is seated kneading his clay. In the same way Hachäkyum did it, Kisin is crouched as he works. He is kneading his clay.

Ele, tarih ahKisin, upäyeh ahHachäkyum. "Yumeh," kih, "he' wa (a)tar awireh inmeyah ten?"

Then, Kisin came and wav(ed) Hachäkyum over. "Lord," he says, "will you come and see my work?"

"Eh he'ere'," kih Hachäkyum.

"Certainly," says Hachäkyum.

"Ko'oten awireh inmeyah. He' wa uts'ahik ma'ats' ti' ten! Ne pochen bik a' bix tech. He' wa uts'ahik ma'ats'. He' wa uts'ahik hu(')un. He' wa ts'ahik ba' ten. Yan uts'ahik ten usiihi(r) tum(b)en lek. He' ut'äniken."

"Come see my work. They will give me posol! I really want it to be the way it is for you. They will give me posol. They will give me bark cloth. They will give me things. They will have to give me incensories. They will pray to me."

"Ele he'," Hachäkyum kunuukik. "Ele he're'."

"Yes indeed," Hachäkyum replies. "Yes indeed."

Bay.

Okay.

Ti' yan ti' yan ubin uyirik ahKisin.

Kisin has to go again to see (Hachäkyum).

Uch'eene'etik ahHachäkyum. Upäyik, "Ko'ox!"

He visits Hachäkyum. He waves him over, "Let's go!"

Hachäkyum, ma' hach uk'at. Tan umeyah, t(an) ume(n)tik uwinik ti', tan ume(n)tik. Ket kuriko' yete(r) Akyant'o' tan ume(n)tik. [Be'ik utsikbartah, ka'ka'tuu(r) ka'ka'tuu(r) ume(n)tiko' ubähi(r) Hachäkyum. Tume(n)tah huntuur xira(r) huntuur ch'upra(r). Beki(r) Akyant'o'; tan ume(n)tik ti' huntuur xira(r) huntuur ch'upra(r). Tan ulahme(n)tik ka'ka'tuu(r) ka'ka'tuu(r). Ele, ts'o'okih ulahme(n)tik, täsa'an tumentah ti' utihi(r).]

Hachäkyum doesn't really want to. He is working, he is making his own people, he is making them. He is sitting with Akyant'o' making them. [It's like they say: Hachäkyum makes them in pairs. He made one man and one woman, and so does Akyant'o'; he is making one man and one woman. He is making them in pairs. And then, when they finished making them all, they spread them out to dry.]

Ele, Kisin kutar, "Ah he're' wa uts'ahik ma'ats' ten. Ko'ox ti' awirik yumeh," kih.

So, Kisin comes along, "They will give me posol. Come see them, Lord," he says.

Ele, lik'ih ahHachäkyum, "Eh ko'ox." Upäyik ubäho' Akyant'o', "Ko'ox akireh umeyah Kisin."

So, Hachäkyum got up (and says), "Okay. Let's go." He waves over his brother Akyant'o', "Let's go see Kisin's work."

"Ko'ox."

"Let's go," (Akyant'o' says).

Uk'uchur ubin uyireh.

They come over to see.

"Hah, bik uyirah inmeyah. He' wa uts'ahik ma'ats' ten."

"So, how does my work look? Perhaps they will give me posol," (says Kisin).

"Eh," tunukah ahHachäkyum. "Ele, he're' tint'an le tech uts'ahik ma'ats'. He' uts'ahik. He' ut'änikech."

"Eh," replied Hachäkyum. "Indeed, I believe they will give you posol. They will give it to you. They will pray to you."

"Eh, bay!" kih. Ne tsoy uyor.

"Oh good!" says (Kisin). He is delighted.

Ele, ba'axtar, ahHachäkyum ma' boon ulahts'o'okor ulahme(n)tik uk'ät. Ulahme(n)tiko' yete(r) Akyant'o'. Uti'ri(') ti' Hachäkyum; uti'ri(') ti' Akyant'o' umeyah ti'. La la'eh ti' hu(n)p'eri' xok'or, lahih mäna' uxaaktik. Ti'ri(') ti' Hachäkyum uti'ri(') ti' Akyant'o'.

And so, Hachäkyum has almost finished making all his clay (people). He and Akyant'o' (made) them all. Hachäkyum's work is set apart from Akyant'o''s work; Hachäkyum's work is separate from Akyant'o''s work. They are close, (but) he doesn't mix them together. Those of Hachäkyum are separate from those of Akyant'o'.

Ele, Hachäkyum yete(r) Akyant'o' bin(ih) ti' uhe'eseh ubah; bin(ih) ti' uhana(n). Ti' yan umeyah Hachäkyum u'eek'. Ti' yan umenman u'eek' ti' ubanik umaaktun akiche'ex. Hachäkyum yan ti' ubanik aktso'otser akho'or 'eek'.

And then, Hachäkyum and Akyant'o' went to rest; they went to eat. Black paint is there for Hachäkyum's work. He has made black (paint) to paint our eyebrows. Hachäkyum has to paint our hair black.[8]

Bek ahKisin tarih. Ma' ti' yan Hachäkyum. Ok(ih) a' tu' kumeyah Hachäkyum. Ele, tukäräxmentah umeyah ahHachäkyum. Beki(r) umeyah Akyant'o'. Tulahkäräxme(n)tah ahKisin: tuch'a'ah la' 'eek' tulahba'axtah la' k'ät yete(r) 'eek'. (T)ulahban(ah) ume'ex. Tulahbanah tuworo(r), tuworo(r) tulahbanah.

So, as usual, Kisin came around. Hachäkyum wasn't there. He went into to where Hachäkyum was working. And then, he ruined all Hachäkyum's work. He did the same to Akyant'o''s work. Kisin ruined them all: he grabbed the black paint and painted them all over. He painted on moustaches. He painted everywhere.

Uk'uchur uyireh ume̒yah Hachäkyum yete(r) Akyant'o'. "Ehhh mäna'. Ma' tsoy. Tukäräxme(n)tah Kisin akmeyah."

Hachäkyum and Akyant'o' arrive (and) see their work. "Ohhh no. This is terrible. Kisin ruined our work."

Eh, ma' hach tsoy uyor Hachäkyum yete(r) Akyant'o'. Ts'iik ti' Kisin, porque Kisin tar(ih) tukäräxme(n)tah umeyah.

Hachäkyum and Akyant'o' aren't very happy. They are annoyed with Kisin because Kisin came and ruined their work.

K'eex uyor Kisin, ne k'eex uyor.

Kisin was jealous, very jealous.

Bay.

Okay.

Tulahp'o'ah, Hachäyum, tulahp'o'ah. Chen ma' ki'luk'ih; ti' yan ne 'eek' tulahbanah ahKisin.

Hachäkyum washed them; he washed them, but they really didn't come
clean; there was black (where) Kisin painted them.[9]

[La' be'in kawirik yan winik. Naachi(r) ts'ur umeyah Akyant'o'; yan ts'ur säk
uyo'ote(r) yan ts'ur 'eek'; lati' Kisin tukäräxme(n)tah. Bex tutsikbartah. Bex
tuyiraho'. Bex utsikbar uchik unuki(r) winik.]

[That's why you see people (like this). The foreigners are the work of
Akyant'o'; there are foreigners with white skin and foreigners with black
skin, which are the ones that Kisin ruined. That's what they said. That's how
they saw it. That's what the ancestors said.]

PART 2. HACHÄKYUM MAKES THE ONEN FOR HIS MORTALS

Ele, pachi(r) ka'(ah) tuyirah bin, tuya(h)sah umeyah Hachäkyum yete(r)
Akyant'o' la' ket tuya(h)sah (u)winik. Kutar bin uyireh ahKisin bin,
kura'an bin tuyahs(ah)o'on. AhHachäkyum tuyahsaho'on. La' ket umeyah
Akyant'o'. La' lik'ih winik, tun; ya ma' k'ät. La' lik'i(h) uwinik. Kurenkur
kura'an huntuur, kura'an huntuu(r), lah yete(r) ulaak'i(r).

So then, when they saw it, they awakened their creations. Together, Hachäkyum and Akyant'o' awakened their people.[10] (When) Kisin comes around
to visit, (the mortals) are seated there. He (had) awakened us; Hachäkyum
had awakened us. It was the same for Akyant'o''s creations. They got up
as people; they were not clay anymore. They got up as people. Some were
seated here and others, there, still others were with their spouses.

Ele, Kisin kutich(ir), "Eh, tawahsah tech awinik!"

And then, Kisin approaches, "Eh, you awakened your people!"

"Tinwasah," kih Hachäkyum.

"I awakened them," says Hachäkyum.

"Le' hah. TSK!" Ne tsoy uyor Kisin. "Ko'ox awireh ten yumeh!" kih. "Ko'ox!
He' awirik bik uyaha(r) ten inwinik."

"Ah, yes. TSK!" Kisin is very excited. "Come see them, Lord!" he says. "Come on! You're going see how my people wake up for me."

AhHachäkyum kura'an utukreh yete(r) Akyant'o', *"Bähe', umeyah Kisin wa. Ma' akyant'an; ma' akyansä(')sä('a)k't'an. Ti' kirik ubin umeyah Kisin."*
Hachäkyum is seated there with Akyant'o' ruminating, *"Now, it's Kisin's work. We (won't) speak at first; we won't make small talk at first. We (will) just see how Kisin's work is going."*

Ele, Kisin, *"K'o'ox, yumeh!"*
And so, Kisin (says), "Let's go, my Lords!"

Ele, baayla' Hachäkyum yete(r) Akyant'o' tutohtukrah, *"Bähe' tint'an ume-yah Kisin bin a(k)ka(h) kpurik uyonen inmeyah."*
But, Hachäkyum and Akyant'o' had already thought it through. (Hachäk-yum says,) "Now, I think we are going to convert Kisin's work into lineages for my creations."

"Eh, ne tsoy. Bay," kih Akyant'o' kunuukik. *"Ele ne tsoy yumeh,"* kih. *"Tint'an, tuha(h)i(r), p'isi(r) ten. Yan uwaaya(r). He' akpurik uyone(n) akwinik. He' akharik uyone(n). Ko'ox akirik umeyah Kisin. Ko'ox!"*
"Ah, very good. Okay," Akyant'o' says. "That's very good, my Lord," he says. "I think it'll be the same for me. (Kisin's work) must transform. We will con-vert (them into) the lineages of our people. We will pull out their lineages. Let's go see Kisin's work! Let's go!"

[Kisin mäna' ts'aabar ti': mäna' ubin winik. Bäk' ubin waaya(r) ti' umeyah Kisin.]
[Nothing is going to be given to Kisin: his (work) won't turn into people. Kisin's work is going to turn into animals.]

Hach tuha(h)i(r).

Sure enough, it (came) true.

Ma' boon utar uk'uchur, ma'. Ne xok'o(r) kuk'uchu(r) tu' nika'an umeyah Kisin—AHEEEYI,[11] kulik'i(r) kuku(r)k'ä'teh ubäh umeyah Kisin. Woro(r) bäk' ulik'i(r) ukuku(r)k'ä'teh ubah, xäka'an huntu(u)r kitam kubin; huntu(u)r k'ek'en kubin; ma'ax kulik'i(r) umeyah Kisin ch'äxk'äräk ubin.

It doesn't take (them) long to get there. They get close to where Kisin's work is strewn about—AHEEEYI, Kisin's work gets up on all fours. All around the animals get up, they sit with their hands on the floor; a peccary goes on all fours, a white-lipped peccary goes; the spider monkeys get up from Kisin's work and go about with their arms swinging.

"Ehhh määäna' ten inwinik." Ti' uman ne ts'iik. "Bik yani(r) yumeh, bik yani(r) lik'ih bäk' inmeyah ten? Ma' ubin uts'ahik ma'ats' ten!"

"Ohhh noooo, my people." (Kisin) angrily paces back and forth. "Why, oh Lord, why did my work rise up as animals on me? They're not going to give me posol!"

Hachäkyum mäna' ume(n)tik t'an. Ne tsoy uyor. Hachäkyum. Ket yete(r) Akyant'o' ne tsoy uyor. Tutohtukrah bin Hachäkyum yete(r) Akyant'o'.

Hachäkyum doesn't say a word. He is delighted. Both he and Akyant'o' are delighted. Hachäkyum and Akyant'o' had already (planned) this.

Hachäkyum, "Ele, bähe' bäk' lik'ih ti' umeyah Kisin, ti' upurik uyone(n) akwinik ton."

Hachäkyum (says), "So, now the animals (have) emerged from Kisin's work to (provide) the lineages for our people."

"Hah," kih Akyant'o'. "Tarak akwu'yik uts'iiki(r) Kisin, hoy ti'. Mäna'. He' utubur."

"Indeed," says Akyant'o'. "Even though we feel Kisin's rage (now), it doesn't matter. It's unimportant. He'll forget about it."

Ele, be'ik ka'(ah) lik'ih, uya'arah, "Mäna'!" Kisin ne ts'iik. "Mäna', ma' ubin uts'ahik ma'ats' ti' ten, mäna'. Binih ti' ubäk'i(r)!"

And so, when the animals got up like this, (Kisin says,) "There aren't any!" Kisin is furious. "None of them are going to give me posol. They turned into animals!"

"Ehhh," tuya'arah Hachäkyum. "Hoy ti'. Xa'ateh tawor, Kisin. Lahbinih t(i') ubäk'ir ameyah tech. Tint'an lahih kubin uchi'ik inmeyah ten; inlu'umo' lahih kubin uchi'ik. Tint'an bähe' bek ubin ku(r)tar binet k'in. Le' kubin yan bäk' ti' uchi'iko' inmeyah."

"Ehhh," said Hachäkyum. "Forget it. Calm down, Kisin. Your creations all turned into animals. I think my creations will eat them; my mortals will eat them. I think, now it will be this way forever. They are going to be game for my creations to eat."

"Ah bay."

"Very well," (says Kisin).

Eh, ma' het la'eh. Lehih ka'(ah) nahkura'an Kisin. Hoy ti'. Ts'o'ok.

And so, they were unable to stay with Kisin. The issue was closed. That was it (he would never have mortals to venerate him).

Hachäkyum Makes the Ants and Snakes

Antonio Martinez

After creating his mortals, Hachäkyum rolls off the clay that remains on his hands, inadvertently creating ants and snakes.[1]

(Ts'o'ok umentik winik,) Akyumeh tume(n)tah tuhäxah uk'ä' ti'.
(When he finished making people,) our Lord made them (when) he rubbed his hands together.

Upuustik uk'ä',
He dusts off his hands,

wäwäkeh[2]
twisting out (little) threads

—*wah, wah*.[3]
—*wah, wah*.

Ele sinik! Bini(h) sinik! Lehi(h) bin yok'o(r) lu'um,
And then ants! They turned into ants! They go on the ground,

—*p'ätäch, p'ätäch*[4]—kubin yok'or (lu'um).
—*plop, plop*—they go on (the ground).

Woror k'ät uk'äb p'ätäch, p'ätäch, eh lehi(h) ulahbin te' lahbin(ih) ahsinik.
Woror sinik kubin—*purrr*—kubin ahsinik.

All the clay (he rubs from) his hands turns into ants. All the ants go—
purrr—(along the ground).

Ele, tak bähe' kura'an to'one'ex way.
And so, up to now they (have) (remained) with us here.

La'eh p'isir ahkan. Ahkan! Hook'i(h) ahkan.
The same thing (happens with) the snakes. Snakes! The snakes came out.

Eh, kuhäxärk'ä'tik
Eh, Hachäkyum rubs his palms together

—*wah, wah.*
—*wah, wah.*

Hachäkyum, kuts'o'okor ume(n)tik, Hachäkyum a' chukuch chukuch (u)ber a' waan a' k'ät.
When Hachäkyum finishes, he makes a long length of clay.

Eh! *Pih.*
Eh! *Plop.*

"Eh! Kan!"
"Eh! A snake!"

"Ehhh, eh yan waar inmeyah kubin."
"Ehhh, it is the coil(?) of my work that is going."

Eh! Kubin huntuur. Kubin huntuur te'.
Eh! Another one goes. Another one goes after that.

Ne pim! Tuts'ä('n) tuts'ä('n) kubin.[5]
There are a lot of them! They go stretched out in all directions.[6]

Ele ts'o'okih.
And so it was.

Bähe', lahp'aat.
Today, they all remain.

Uhaax[7] uk'ä' bin,
His hands rub together,

kuhäx(i)k uk'ä' way.
he rubs his hands together here.

K(u) (h)äx(i)k uk'ä'.
He rubs his hands together.

Tuharah a' pat
He removed the clay

—*wah, wah*—uk'ä'.
—*wah, wah*—went his hands.

"Ehhh yärär[8] inpat. Kinbin inpurik."
"Ehhh, the remains of my clay. I'm going to fling them down."

—HUM—
—HUM—

(U)tak'a(r), P'AAAH, yok'o(r) näk' che'.
It sticks, SPLAT, against a tree.

Eh, *ter-ter-ter*, kubin. A' lah pat kuna'akar.

Then, *ter-ter-ter*, they go. All the (pieces of) the clay climb up.⁹

"Eh! T(an) uyärär inpat."

"Eh! My clay is separating."

Eh, tuya'arah Hachäkyum, "Eh, binet k'in, lehi(h) kubin p'atar yok'or k'aax."

Then Hachäkyum said, "Eh, these are going to stay in the forest forever."

Bek tutsikbartah uchik.

This is how they recounted it long ago.

Hachäkyum Makes the Sky

Bor Ma'ax

After Hachäkyum created his people, the land was still in darkness.[1] The only sun belonged to Kak'och, Hachäkyum's creator.[2] It shone high up in the ether, where Kak'och had retreated after he had left the earth. His sun illuminated and warmed Hachäkyum's realm immediately below, but it was too far away from the earth to benefit the mortals; they were always cold, and their crops did not grow well. Moreover, every year Kak'och covered up his sun. This worried Hachäkyum, for it threatened the survival of his mortals. All his attempts to stop Kak'och from doing this failed, so he decided to create another sun and another sky in which to place it for his mortals.[3]

First he stretched out the sky and then sowed the stars. But the stars did not produce enough light. Then he made the sun and placed it in the middle of the sky. But it shone all the time, keeping the poor mortals awake. So he drew a path across the sky for the sun to follow from east to west. He put his brother Sukunkyum in charge of retrieving the sun after it set and depositing it on the horizon in the morning. During the journey through the underworld Sukunkyum fed the sun to keep up its strength.[4]

It is said that Hachäkyum created the moon to provide a little light during the night and as a means for his mortals to schedule their sowing and harvesting according to its phases.[5]

Ele, kura'an (tan) utukr(ik) ubähir ahHachäkyum, *"Ele bähe', yan uher inmeyah. Tint'an, bin ink(ah) inmentik inka'an ten."*

And so, Hachäkyum is seated there thinking to himself, *"So now, I have another job to do. I think I'm going to make my own sky."*

[Ka'ah yantop'ih ahHachäkyum mäna' uka'anir. Yan uka'anir, Kak'och. Le kuk'änik ahHachäkyum uyähtich'k'ä'ir leh(ih) umeyah Kak'och, la' k'in

kuk'änik ahHachäkyum. Xuri' bähe' bek tutsikbartah uchik intet. Tutsikbar bin la' Kak'och, lehih uk'uur ahHachäkyum. Hachäkyum kut'änik k'uh.
Hachäkyum kupokik. Kut'änik uk'uur. Lehih uk'uur ahKak'och. Be'ik tutsikbartah.]

[When Hachäkyum was born, there wasn't any sky. There was Kak'och's
sky, which Hachäkyum uses. The sun he uses is Kak'och's creation. It is still
like this, like my father said a long time ago. He talks about how Kak'och
is Hachäkyum's god. Hachäkyum prays to (his) god. Hachäkyum burns
offerings. He prays to (his) god. Kak'och is his god. That's how (my father)
told it.]

Bay.

Okay.

Ele kura'an utukr ubähir Hachäkyum. Kura'an utukur abäh, *"Bähe' tint'an
yan inmentik ten ka'an. Yan insinik ka'an."* Ele, kura'an utukr ubähir Hachäkyum, *"Bähe' bin ink(ah) insinik ten inka'an."*

So, Hachäkyum is seated there thinking to himself. He is seated there
thinking, *"Now I think I have to make my own sky. I have to stretch out a sky."*
He is thinking to himself, *"Now I'm going to stretch out my sky."*

…Toh yan umeyah winik ahHachäkyum. Ka'(ah) tuyirah bin utich'ir la' p'is
muuyar utich'ir bin. Kutich'ir bix a' muuyar ka' tich'ir bin säkware'en, ka'
tich'ir bin. Ka'(ah) tuyirah la(h)nup', ele uka'anir Hachäkyum. Ele ts'o'ok
ulahsinik a' ka'an ahHachäkyum.

… Hachäkyum already had his people. When they (see) it (happen), it
(comes across) the way clouds (come across). It (comes across) like clouds
do, like a sheet of whiteness,[6] when it (comes across). Then they saw it close
(over), and that was Hachäkyum's sky. And so Hachäkyum finished stretching the sky.

Ele uhook'or utukr ubähir Hachäkyum, *"Le bähe' tint'an bin ink(ah) inmentik ten k'in. Bin ink(ah) inme(n)tik akna'."* Kura'an utukrik ubäh bin ahHachäkyum, *"Bin ink(ah) inme(n)ntik ten ink'in."*

And then Hachäkyum goes out and thinks to himself, *"Now, I think I'm going to make the sun. I'm going to make the moon."* Hachäkyum is seated there thinking to himself, *"I'm going to make my sun."*

Tuyanmentah bin. Kura'an umenteh ubähir ahHachäkyum. Bähe' k'in. Binih utäk'unteh chun a' ka'an bin.

He made it first. Hachäkyum is seated there making it himself. Now (there is) the sun. He went to stick it at the base of the sky.

Ne tsoy kutich'ir.

It rises very well.

Ele, uhook'or ume(n)tik akna' p'isir, akna'. Tume(n)tah ti', bin utäk'kunteh.

And then he goes out and makes the moon the same way. He made the moon and went to stick it in.

La' k'in, kuyantich'ir bin. Che(n) ubichka' a' k'in, ele kutich'ir akna'. Ele ne tsoy.

The sun arrives first. And (when) the sun goes down, the moon arrives. And so this was very good.

Ele bähe' kura'an utukr ubäh ahHachäkyum, *"Bähe' ne tsoy. Yan ti' binet k'in bähe' te' ti' lu'umo'. Yan uyähtich'k'a'ir. Yan k'in ti'."*

So now Hachäkyum is seated there thinking, *"Now it's good. It must be like this forever for the people. They have their light. There is a sun for them."*

Ele, Hachäkyum kura'an utukur abäh, *"Ele bähe' ha'ri' way, kuren way. Yan inwatoch yan."*

And so, Hachäkyum is seated there thinking to himself, *"So now I (will) just stay here. I have my house."*

Yan, bin ume(n)tik Yaxchilan uher hump'er yatoch. Bin ume(n)tik.
He goes to make another house in Yaxchilan. He goes to make it.[7]

Ele, ya'arah ubähir Hachäkyum tun, le ts'o'ok ulahme(n)tik uyatoch to'an Yaxchilan, bin ume(n)tik uyatoch ich ka'an. Ele ti' kubi(n) ku(r)ta(r). Ba'lah Hachäkyum mäna' ukahar way. Ts'o'ok. Tu' yankurahih, tu' yantoop'ih ich Parenke, mäna' ukurtar. Tume(n)t(ah) uka'an, uka'anir, ti' binih ich uka'anir Hachäkyum. Lati' tulahbisah uti'a'ar, tuworor ulaak', yet tubisah. Ti' binih. Bex utsikba(r)tah.

It is said that after Hachäkyum finished making his house in Yaxchilan, he went to make a house in the sky. And there he goes to settle. Thus, Hachäkyum does not live here anymore. That is over. At first he was in Palenque, where he was born. But he didn't stay. Hachäkyum made his sky, and he went to his sky. He took everyone, his son, his wife, he took them all with him. They went there. That's what they say.

Ulu'ubir Ba'arka'an Umentik Petha'
'A Star Falls and Creates the Lagoon'

Antonio Martinez

Once a star fell into the forest.[1] An ancestor went to investigate and discovered that it was decorated with precious stones of various sizes.[2] He collected them and went back to his village to show the others. When they saw these jewels, they wanted some too. Later another star fell in the forest, and two ancestors rushed to collect its precious stones. But one of them tarried too long. While he was greedily plucking off as many stones as he could, the star began to melt, and the stones began turning into fish, turtles, and crocodiles. His companion urged him to retreat, but he ignored his companion and continued collecting the stones. But he took one step too far, fell into the water, and was immediately swallowed by a crocodile.

This story echoes the belief of the pre-Columbian Mexicans and Mayas that the crocodile and the stars are intertwined. From an astronomical perspective, when the Milky Way arches from the southwest to northeast quadrants of the sky, it resembles the shape of a crocodile.

In addition, Mayas believe that the world rests on the back of a crocodile floating in a vast lagoon (Freidel, Schele, and Parker 1993; J. Thompson 1970, 200). How the crocodile ended up on the earth is recounted in the *Chilam Balam of Maní*, a myth about Bolon ti' K'uh, the Nine Lords of the Night, who turned the sky and the earth upside down and then slayed the (starry) crocodile. As this happened, a great cataclysm occurred, and the blood of the crocodile inundated the earth. Bolon ti' K'uh then spread the corpse of the crocodile over the sea of blood; thereupon it formed the land of Petén (Craine and Reindorp 1979, 117–18). This event is preceded by an eclipse (Velasquez 2006, 6).[3]

Correspondingly, the Lacandon story has the star-crocodile crashing into the earth and flooding the land. The myth does not specify any particular lagoon, so it could be any huge body of water, not just Lake Naha'. The image of aquatic creatures that emerge from the "stars" on the back of the crocodile evokes the association between the crocodile, fertility, and, by extension, accession, depicted in Mayan iconography (see Schele and Miller 1986, 45).

Additionally, in Lacandon mythology aquatic creatures, especially turtles, are relatives of the crocodile, and thus their emergence from the back of the crocodile alludes to the connection between fertility and descent. See "Chäk Xok" 'The Sirens' (this volume).

NARRATOR'S SUMMARY

[Aknukire'ex tuyirah upitk'ab uba'arka'an. Lubih. Tuyu'yah peeknah lu'um. *Pi-i-i-i-ih*. Ne nunka'an cherih. Ele, binih. Bin t(i') uximba(r). Kubin na'ak(ar) uyaaka'. Ti' yan up'u'uyeh ti' upach. Lehih kuläkik t(i') upach up'u'uy yanir. La' huntu(u)r ubäho' ahnukuch winik ma' seeb k'uchih uläkeh up'u'uyeh. La' huntuur nukuch winik seeb tuch'a'ah—a' hum(b)u(h)-k'ä'ir tuch'a'ah. Tan uk'ana(r) yok—sahak ti'. La' huntu(u)r mäna' uluk'ur.]

[Our ancestors saw a star suddenly come loose. It fell. They felt the earth move. *B-o-o-o-m*. There was a great rumble. And so, they went. They went walking. They go scampering up (the star). There are lumps on its back. These they pull off its back. One of the ancestors wasn't as fast getting there to remove those lumps. The ancestor who got there first grabbed them quickly—he grabbed five of them. (Then) he (runs) away very fast—he is afraid. The other one doesn't leave.]

"Ko'ox!" kih.

"Let's go!" says (the first one).

"Mäna' ma' intar," kih. "Ch'ukteh. T(an) inya(n)läkik te'."

"No, I'm not coming," he says. "Wait. I'm removing (some lumps) first."

La' kupur(i)k ubäh ha'. TUM.

He jumps (and into) the water. SPLOOSH.

Ma' het la'eh tu' bin. Ti' chi'b t(i') 'ayim. Ti' ts'o'ok ti'.

There is no way he can get out. He was eaten by a crocodile. He was finished.

Ba'(ale') a' hunt(uur)eh t(an) uhachp'e(nk')ächk'ana(r) yok. Puts'ih. Bi-i-i-n(ih) t(i') uyatoch. Ele, 'u'ri(h) tuya'arah, "Mäna'. Ele bähe' mäna'. Ta(ra)k int'äni(k) ta(ra)k int'äni(k), ma' uk'uchur inmuuk'. Tan inpäyik 'Ko'ox!' Mäna'. La'eh chi'(i)b ti' 'ayim. Bäh(e') mäna'. Ti' ts'o'ok ti' upetha'(il) tun."

But the other one ran away at full tilt. O-o-o-ff he went to his house. Well, he returned and said, "He's no more. He's no more now. Although I told him, although I told him (to come), (because) I wasn't strong enough (to save him), I was calling (to him), 'Let's go!,' but he didn't (want to). He was eaten by a crocodile right there. Now he's no more. He was finished there in the lagoon."

Hook'(ih) uch'eene'etah. Ubin petha'. Woro(r) 'ayim lähan. Toh käy t(an) umeyah bähe' — chäkrah. Ba'axtäk käytäk. Tuworo(r) ne yaab.

They went out to see. It (had converted) into a lagoon. There are crocodiles lined up everywhere. Mojarras are already reproducing now. There are all kinds of fish. They are everywhere.

"Ele hah. Ma' mäna' a' winik," kih. "'U-u-u-tsereh. Tuko(h)kintah ubah winik. Ma' het la'eh. Hach ma' ba'inki(r) akme(n)tik ti'."

"Well it's clear the man isn't (here) anymore," they said. "O-o-o-h boy. The man was careless. It's impossible now. There is really nothing we can do for him."

"Ele hah. Ma' het la'eh. Ma' tuyu'(y)ah t'an. La' huntuur lahputs'i(h). He' toh mäna' tuyu'yah t'an, ti' ts'o'ok ti'."

"That's true. There is no way. He didn't listen. The other one ran away. This one here didn't listen and he was finished there."

"Ele bay. Eh ma' het la'eh," kih. "Ele bähe' wa bik kabin alutskäy, yan amen-tik a' chem. He're' awok(or) alutseh käy. Bähe' mäna' abäho'. Ti' chi'(i)b yok'or ha'."

"Well, okay. Now it's impossible," they say. "From now on you have to make a canoe to go in to fish. Now you don't have your companion. He was eaten in the water."

Ti' bini(h) bek tutsikba(r)tah aknukire'ex. "Ele tuko'okintah," kih. "Ele ma' het la'eh."

This is how the story went, as told by our ancestors. "He was careless," they say. "It was impossible (to save him)."

'Ayim ... uba'arka'an; p'iis 'ayim, ... ka'(ah) t(u)(y)i(r)aho'. Hach awa'arik toh 'ayim upach, ma la'eh ... Ten ti' ha' ti' upuk'u(r). Lahpuuk' tuworo(r) ele lah petha' äka'an. Lahbin(ih) t(i') upetha'.

The star was a crocodile; it was the same as a crocodile, ... when they saw it. You could really say (the star) was a crocodile's back, (but) it wasn't that ... It dissolved to water. Everything completely dissolved and the lagoon was laid out. It all turned into a vast lagoon.

Hachäkyum yeter T'uup yeter Kisin
'Hachäkyum, T'uup, and the Devil'

Bor Ma'ax

Ever since Hachäkyum turned Kisin's mortals into animals, Kisin has pursued Hachäkyum, beating him up at every opportunity. In this story Kisin is at it again. Unbeknownst to him, it is Hachäkyum's body double that Hachäkyum has left as a ruse. The real Hachäkyum is busy creating the underworld.[1] Believing that Hachäkyum had died and his son T'uup had buried him, Kisin and his family stood poised at his tomb waiting for Hachäkyum's soul to emerge, as souls are wont to do. On the day of emergence, the earth shuddered, and the ground opened. Instead of capturing Hachäkyum's soul, Kisin and his family tumbled into the crevasse. Hachäkyum passed them on his way out, and after he climbed out, the ground closed up behind him.

Imprisoned in the underworld, Kisin assumes the role of the 'Lord of Death'. He represents the opposite of Hachäkyum: whereas Hachäkyum is life and light, Kisin is death and darkness. On a practical level, life would be impossible without death. For this reason Hachäkyum prohibits T'uup from killing Kisin.

This story evokes the struggle for power between Venus (the lord of the underworld) and the celestial gods in pre-Columbian Mayan creation narratives (see Vail and Hernandez 2013, xxiii).

PART 1. KISIN PURSUES HACHÄKYUM

Bay.

Okay.

Hachäkyum ne ch'ihanchahih, ne 'uchben. Lah hutur ukoh. Hachäkyum mäna' ukoh. Ne ch'ihir. Kisin ne p'eek uyirik Hachäkyum.

Hachäkyum had become old. He's very old. All his teeth have fallen out. Hachäkyum doesn't have any teeth. He's very old. Kisin hates the sight of Hachäkyum.

Bay.
Okay.

[Kisin, ka'tu(ur)o' Kisin, bin uhäts'ik Hachäkyum ich uyatoch.]
[There are two Kisins who (regularly) go and beat up Hachäkyum in his house.][2]

K'uchur häts'ik como 'aak'bi(r). K'uchur uhäts'ik.
They arrive at night to hit him. They arrive and hit him.

—BUH—

—BUH—

"UGH!" uyawat Hachäkyum.
"UGH!" cries Hachäkyum.

—BUH—

—BUH—

"UGH!"
"UGH!"

Tar uKisin. Tan uhäts'ik,
The Kisins came. They are hitting him,

—BUH—

—BUH—

"UGH!"
"UGH!"

"Ta'aken T'uup! Ko'oten! Ta'aken!"
"Protect me, T'uup! Come here! Protect me!"

Mix T'uup. Ne ki' uwenen. Ma'.
T'uup doesn't (hear) anything. He is fast asleep.

Ne ki' uwenen, mix uyoher wa tan uhäts'ah utet.
He is fast asleep. He does not know (that) they are hitting his father.

— K'ÄP PIN —
— THWACK —

"UGH."
"UGH."

— BUH —
— BOOF —

"UGH," tan uyawat Hachäkyum
"UGH," Hachäkyum cries.

Maaa, k'oopi(h) uxikin ahT'uup,
Then finally (his cries) jolt T'uup awake,

"Ele! Intet kuhäts'a'."
"Oh! My father is being beaten."

Kuk'uchur uyireh utet. Tan uhäts'ah ti' naka'an Kisin; tan uhachts'ahik.

He arrives to see his father. The Kisins are bent over him; they are really giving it to him.

—BUH, BUH—

—BUMF, BUMF—

Ti' chara'an Hachäkyum.

Hachäkyum is lying there.

Uhook'or ulisik uyok ahT'uup tulaxah Kisin.

T'uup lifted his foot and kicked (one of) the Kisins.

—BUH—

—BUMF—

Naach binih bich'tar Kisin. Tuka'tärah huntuur naach bin naktar. Ele, toh hach p'enk'äch uk'anar uyok ahKisin.

Kisin went sprawling. T'uup hit the other one and sent him sprawling. Then, the Kisins dash off.

Ele, k'uchih ut'äneh utet ahT'uup,

Then, T'uup went over to talk to his father.

"Tet," kih, "tubäräxhäts'tah tech ahKisin."

"Father," he says, "the Kisins beat you up."

"Ele, T'uupken, tan uhäts'iken Kisin."

"Oh, my dear T'uup, the Kisins are (always) beating me up."

"Hah bähe' binih. Tinlaxah. Bini(h)."

"Yes, well now they're gone. I beat them up. They left."

Bay.
Okay.

Le lahi(h) tu' bini(h), maaa tumaasah boon k'in, hu(n)buhk'äb k'in, uher kuka'tar uhäts'e(h) k'äb.
Wherever they went, so many days (later), perhaps five days, they come back again to slap him around.

—BUH—
—BUMF—

"UGH!" utet.
"UGH!" (cries) his father.

Bay.
Okay.

Ele, uhook'or uku(r)tar tan utuk(r)ah ahT'uup, *"Bähe' bin inkah inme(n)teh aht'eer, inwäht'eer."*
So then, T'uup goes out and sits down. He is thinking, *"Now I'm going to make a rooster, my very own rooster."*

Tukäxtah k'ät. Tupätah. Ele, tuki'me(n)tah ut'eer. Tupätah yeter k'ät, tu-purah—HUM PAH.
He looked for the clay. He formed it. He made the rooster well. He formed it with clay, and then he threw it down—THUD.

Ulik'i(r) ch'iktar aht'eer, uhook'or ulik'i(r) ch'iktar, HOF-HOF-HOF-HOF.

The rooster stands up, it comes out, it stands up (and ruffles its feathers loudly), HOF-HOF-HOF-HOF.

"Eeehhh," kuhook'or t'an ahT'uup. "Bähe' yan inwäht'eer tun. Ele, tint'an, lahih kubin uyahsiken."
"Eeehhh," T'uup exclaims. "Now, I have my pet rooster. Now, I think, he'll wake me up."

Toh ahT'uup ne yan utukur a' la'eh tume(n)tah aht'eer ti' uyahsah (tuk'in) utar ahKisin t(i') uhäts'ik.
This was a really good idea that T'uup (had), to make a rooster to wake him up (when) the Kisins come to beat up (Hachäkyum).

"Eh lech k'aynahen, t'eer!"
"Now sing, rooster!"

Tan ut'änik (ti') uyäht'eer.
He is talking to his pet rooster.

"Eh lech t'eer, k'aynahen!"
"Now rooster, sing!"

Ele, lech tan upeeksik, *pi-pi-pi-pi-pi* uxik' aht'eer.
And now the rooster is flapping his wings, *pi-pi-pi-pi-pi*.

Uhäts'ik uxik' aht'eer, *pi-pi-pi-pi-pi*.
The rooster flaps his wings, *pi-pi-pi-pi-pi*.

Ele, "TÄÄÄÄSÄÄÄH," aht'eer uyawat.
And then, "COCK-A'DOODLE-DOO," the rooster crows.

"TÄÄÄÄSÄÄÄH. TÄÄÄÄSÄÄÄH."

"COCK-A'DOODLE-DOO. COCK-A'DOODLE-DOO."

Ele, ne tsoy t'eereh. Ne tsoy uyor ahT'uup.

And so, this rooster is very good. T'uup is very pleased.

"Bähe' yan inwäht'eer ti' uyähsiken."

"Now, I have my very own rooster that is going to wake me up."

Le' tumakah uyok ut'eer, upu(r)ik tu' kuwene(n) utet ahHachäkyum.

Then he tied the rooster's legs together. He put it where his father, Hachäk-yum, sleeps.

Ele, tutoht'anah uxikin ut'eer,

And then, he whispered right into the rooster's ear,

"Le t'eeren wa tawu'yik uk'uchur ahKisin uhäts'ik intet, k'aayen! Le' kak'aay wa! Ma' axu(r)ik ak'aay ma' wa."

"Now, my rooster, if you hear the Kisins coming and they beat my father, sing! You will sing, then! Don't stop singing."

Tan uk'uchur tup'is tuk'inir ahKisin ti' uhats'ik Hachäkyum.

The Kisins (arrive) at the usual time to beat (Hachäkyum).

"TÄÄÄÄSÄÄÄH!"

"Cock-a'doodle-DOO!"

K'uchi(h) la' Kisin.

The Kisins arrived.

"TÄÄÄÄÄÄÄSÄH! TÄÄÄÄÄÄÄSÄH!!!"
"Cock-a'doodle-DOO! Cock-a'DOODLE-DOO!!!"

Ma (ah)T'uup, ne ki' uwenen. Ele, lik'ih yaaka' T'uup.
But T'uup is fast asleep. But then (he heard it), (and) T'uup got up and ran.

"UGH! He'eh ton, T'uupeh. Tan ukinsiken Kisin. Tan ulaxiken Kisin."
"UGH! Over here, T'uup. The Kisins are killing me. The Kisins are punching me!"

K'uchi(h) yaaka'.
(T'uup) came rushing in.

"Kuxan hah Kisin."
"So it's true. It's the Kisins," (thinks T'uup).

T'uup yeter umaska'. Tuhiitah umaska' ahT'uup, y
T'uup (came with) his machete. T'uup pulled out his machete, and

—CHAAASH—CHAAASH.
—SLASH—SLASH.

Tuki'lakch'äktah uche'ir ukaar ahKisin. Kulik'i(r) huntuur, tulakch'äktah.
Ba'axta(r) tulahkinsah tuka't(uu)ri' ahKisin ton.
He chopped off the head of (one) Kisin. When the other (Kisin) gets up, he chopped off his head (too). He killed both Kisins.[3]

Ele, bin(ih) ahT'uup ti' uyatoch.
And then, T'uup went (back) to his house.

Kusaastar kubin uyireh utet ahT'uup.

In the morning, T'uup goes to visit his father.

"Eh hah, bik yanech tet?" kih.

"Eh, how are you father?" he says.

"Eh mäna'. Tsetseri' 'asyah inbäk'e(r)."

"Eh, not bad. My body aches a little bit."

Bay.

Okay.

Kisin täsän ka't(uu)ro'. Ubähi(r) ahHachäkyum kut'an, "Eh, T'uup ku(r)kin-teh uho'oro' ahKisin. 'Otsir Kisin."

The two Kisins are sprawled out. Hachäkyum says, "Eh, T'uup, set the Kisins' heads back on. Poor Kisins."

"Ele, mäna' tet," kih. "Ma', che(n) ti' ulaxikech. Mäna', chen ti' ukinsik-ech. Lati' mäna' ma' intäkik, hoy ti', Kisin ma' tsoy inwirik ten. Chen t(an) uhäts'ikech."

"Oh no, father," he says. "No, for they will only punch you. No, for they will kill you. I won't stick their heads back on. Forget it. I see that the Kisins are evil. They just beat you."

"Ehhh ma', T'uupeh," kih. "'Otsi(r) Kisin. Täkeh uho'(or)."

"Ohhh no, T'uup," he says. "Poor Kisins. Stick their heads back on."

'Oy uyor ut'an utet ahT'uup. Tuch'a'ah Kisin uho'(or). Tuku(r)kintah t(i') uch'a(r)a'ati(r). Kubin ahKisin, *chik, chik.*

T'uup is tired of listening to his father. He grabbed (one of) the Kisins' heads. He set it on his ribs. Kisin goes along, *chik, chik.*

Huntuur tuku(r)kintah t(i) upach. Kubin, *chik, chik.* CHI-I-I-K, kubin. Maan t(i') upach kumaan Kisin.

He set (the head) of the other one on (backward). He goes along, *chik, chik,* CHI-I-I-K. Kisin walks along with his head on backward.

"Eh," ubähi(r) Hachäkyum tuka'pu(r)ah ut'an ti' T'uup,

"Eh," Hachäkyum called out to T'uup again,

"Ma' tar ubin Kisin. T(i') upach uch'ara'ati(r) kubin."

"Kisin doesn't walk straight. He goes with his head on his ribs.

"Mäna' tet," kih. "Mäna'. Hoy ti'. Xi'ki bin. Ma' tsoy Kisin."

"No, father," he says. "No. Forget it. Let it go. Kisin is evil."

Ubähir ahHachäkyum tuka'päyah ahKisin. Tuka'päyah, "Ko'oten Kisin way."

Hachäkyum called the Kisin(s) over. He called them over, "Come here, Kisin."

(U)hook'or uki'k'uchur ahKisin, uki'takkuntik t(i') uho'or. Ele, beki(r) huntuur. Tulahtahkuntah. Lah ne 'uts uxim(b)a(r) tun.

The Kisins come over. (Hachäkyum) adjusts the head (of one) and then the other. He adjusted (their heads) completely. They walk well now.

Ele, "Xen Kisin!"

And then (he says), "Now go, Kisin!"

Eh bih.

And they took off.

Ele, tumaasah ka'buhk'ä' k'in, ma' yantari(h) ti' uhäts'ik Hachäkyum. Ma' yantari(h) porque (t)usähta(r)—tula(k)ch'eeptah uche'ir kaar.

Well, ten days passed. They didn't come at first to beat Hachäkyum, they didn't come at first because they were afraid—he chopped off their heads.

Ele, ba'aleh Hachäkyum, tun, maaa ti' uhaats'a(r) (ah)Kisin ele chunk'in tun.

However, the Kisins then beat Hachäkyum at midday.

Ele, yah chunk'in, tan ulik'(ir), tan uputs'ur Hachäkyum.

So now, at midday Hachäkyum gets up and flees.

Ba'a(leh) Kisin lik'(ih) tukäxtah Hachäkyum tun, ti' ukinsik, ti' häts'ik, ti' uhixtik.

However, the Kisins got up and looked for Hachäkyum, to kill him, to beat him, to whip him (at midday).

Maaa, lahi(h) k'ini(r) tan upäk'när ahhach winik äknukire'ex. Tan upäk'ik när. Tan uputs'ur ahHachäkyum maaa ti' k'o'opir yok'or a' la'eh (koor) tu' kupäk'ik unär äknukire'ex.

Welll, that day (one of) our ancestor(s) is sowing his maize. He is sowing maize. Hachäkyum is fleeing toward the hollow (of the cornfield) where our ancestor is sowing his maize.

Ele, tichi(h) Hachäkyum—*chik, chik, chik*—ich ukool.

And Hachäkyum approached—*click, click, click*—into the cornfield.

"Ehhh pare(r), tan apaak'(ar) anär."

"Ehhh son, you are sowing your maize," (he says to the ancestor).

"Tan inpäk'ik chen birin tunich inpäk'ik a' ten."

"I am sowing it but they're stones that I sow."

"Eh, hah, paareh," kih. "Mäna' wa k'äs awo'och ma'ats' wa ats'ahik ten tinwuk'ik? Ne 'uk'ahen."

"Ah, uh-huh, son," he says. "You wouldn't have a little posol that you could give me to drink? I'm very thirsty."

"Ele tu' kutar ma'ats'eh? Toh mäna', birim tunich kinpäk'ik. Tan inkimi(r) yete(r) inwi'ihi(r)."

"Well where would the posol come from? There isn't any yet (because) I'm sowing stones. I'm starving," (says the man).

[Lahi(h) hach ubähi(r) Hachäkyum a' la'eh.]

[This is the real Hachäkyum (he's talking to).]⁴

"Eh, bay," kih Hachäkyum. "Mäna' awo'och ma'ats'."

"Okay, fine," says Hachäkyum. "You don't have any posol."

"Ele, mäna'."

"Unfortunately, there isn't any."

"Bay. Puts' inkah. Bin inkah tumen tan ukäxtiken Kisin, ton ti' ukinsiken."

"Okay. I'm on the run. I'm going now because the Kisins are looking for me to kill me."

"Eh hah," kih.

"Ah, uh-huh," says (the ancestor).

[Mäna' äknukire'ex, mäna' utukrik ahHachäkyum.]

[Our ancestor doesn't think that this is Hachäkyum.]

Bay.
Okay.

Ch'ikanch'ikan Hachäkyum,
Hachäkyum stands around for a moment.

"Bay. Bin inkah."
"Okay. I'm going," (he says).

"Xen."
"Goodbye," (says the ancestor).

Binih.
He left.

[La'eh ma' ts'aabi(r) ma'ats' ti' Hachäkyum. Ma' ts'a(a)bi(r) ti'.]
[Posol wasn't given to Hachäkyum. It wasn't given to him.]

Bay.
Okay.

Kutichir ahKisin pachi(r) ti' a(h)Hachäkyum.
Kisin arrives after Hachäkyum passed through.

Toh ka't(uu)ro' ahKisin. Tich'iknäk uni' bin utar —*sniff, sniff*—
There are still two Kisins. They come with their noses raised —*sniff, sniff*—

"Way ubok."

"His scent is here," (says one).

"Tu' bini(h)?"
"Where did he go?" (says the other).

"Way tari(h)."
"He came here," (says the first one).

"Wa maanih way äkyum?"
"Did our Lord pass through here?" (they ask the ancestor).

"Eh, way maanih. Te' binih."
"Eh, he passed through here. He went that way."

"Ah bay," kih. Ne tsoy uyor ahKisin.
"Ah good," they say. The Kisins are jubilant.

Ele, uk'atik ma'ats' ahKisin ti' äknukire'ex, "Yan wa ma'ats'?"
Then, the Kisins ask our ancestor, "Is there any posol?"

"Yan ma'ats'. Kuren 'uk'eh.
"There is posol. Sit down and drink."

[Uyirik Hachäkyum ma' tuts'ahah ti'. Ha'ri' Kisin tuts'ahah.]
[He (saw) Hachäkyum (but) he didn't give it to him. He only gave it to the Kisins.]

Bay.
Okay.

Ba'aleh, ka'bini(h) Hachäkyum; binih ti' uher koor to'an äknukire'ex tan upäk'när. Ele, ti' utichi(r). Ba'aleh Hachäkyum ne 'uk'a'.

Then Hachäkyum went again; he went to a second cornfield where our ancestor is sowing maize. And so, he approaches. By then Hachäkyum is very thirsty.

"Ehhh bay," kih. "Tan apaak'(ar) anär."

"Ehhh splendid," (Hachäkyum) says. "You're sowing your maize."

"Tan yumeh."

"I am, Lord."

"Eh. Kawirik bik inmaan, ne 'uk'ahen. Mäna' ma' wa k'äs awo'och ma'ats' ats'ats'ah ten?"

"Eh. You see how I'm passing through like this, I'm very thirsty. There wouldn't be any posol of which you could give me a little?"

"Eh yan, yumeh! Kura'an ma'ats' yok'o(r) chuh. Le' ch'a'eh."

"Eh, there is, my Lord! Posol is there in the jug. Take it."

Hach tan unich'k'ä'(ik?) t(i') ubäh —*ha-s-o-o*. Tulahbich'kuntah uchuhir ele tuku(r)kintah uchuri(r).

He clutches the jug in both hands —*glug, glug, glug*. He knocked back the entire jug and then he set the jug back down.[5]

Bay.

Okay.

Äknukire'ex as maani(h) utukur, "*Ele, mäna', inwo'och ma'ats'. He' insut, tarak wa ma' tints'o'oksah. Saaman he' inka'tar inpäk'eh.*"

A thought crossed our ancestor's mind, "*Well, now, I have no more posol. I will have to go back (to the house), even though I haven't finished. I'll come back again tomorrow to sow.*"

Bik utukrik ubäh äknukire'ex.

This is what our ancestor is thinking to himself.[6]

Bay.

Okay.

Hachäkyum ne tsoy uyor. Tan uya'arik ti' äknukire'ex, "Eh paareh. Bay. Tats'aah ten awo'och ma'ats', paareh. Tan inhach kimi(r) yete(r) inwuk'u(r). Tan ukinsiken Kisin. Ele, he're' uts'o'okor apäk'ik paareh?"

Hachäkyum is very content. He is chatting to our ancestor, "Eh, son. Thank you. You gave me your posol, son. I (was) dying of thirst. The Kisins are out to kill me. So now, have you've finished your sowing, son?"

"Eh ma', tak ma' ts'o'oki(h). Saama(n)."

"Oh no, it's not finished yet. Tomorrow."

"Eh, takeh he' uts'o'okor. He' ats'o'oksik, paareh. He' ats'o'oksik apäk'ik. Bay. Bähe', intoha'ari(k) tech, wa ts'o'ok apäk'ik, le' ma' ayantar awireh ka'buhk'ä' humbuhok k'in katar awireh wa, chen ahook'(or) ach'eene'teh. Eh, katar ach'a'eh ats'ahik uho'(or) ti' kyum."

"Eh, not yet, but it will (be finished) tomorrow. You will finish it, son. You will finish sowing it. Okay. Now, I'm telling you straight, when you finish sowing, you are not to come and (check) it at first. You (may) come back in fifteen days to see it, but just go out and look at it. (Later) when you come to collect the (ears), offer (the first fruits) to our Lord."

"Eh bay."

"Okay," (says the ancestor).

"Wa tawi(r)ik utar ahKisin, tan ukäxtiken, ma' awa'arik wa maanen way, ma'. Ma' awa'arik ti' Kisin."

"If you see the Kisins come by, they are looking for me, don't say that I passed through here. Don't tell the Kisins."

"Bay, yumeh," kih. "Mäna' inwa'arik wa ti' maanech."

"Okay, my Lord," he says. "I won't say you passed through."

Bay.
Okay.

Äknukire'ex tan useebseeb umaan ubabahpäk'tik unär (ti')ulahsätik ubok ahHachäkyum. Tarak uta(r) ahKisin, tarak umaan ukäxtik, mäna' ubok ahHachäkyum (tumen) turahsätah äknukire'ex. Ti' tuluk'sah.

Our ancestor quickly goes around sowing his maize all over the place, to diffuse Hachäkyum's scent.[7] Although the Kisins come, although they walk around looking for him, there (will be) no scent of Hachäkyum (because) the ancestor completely made it vanish. He erased it.

Ele, kutichi(r) Kisin, "Yan wah maani(h) äkyum way?"

And then, the Kisins approach, "Has our Lord passed through here?"

"Mäna', ma' maanih way Hachäkyum. Way ma' maani(h)."

"No, Hachäkyum didn't pass through here. He didn't pass through here."

"Bik tari(h) ubok way."

"It seems like his scent came here."

Ti' kumaan tich'i(r) kumaan uni', ti' kumaan uyu'yik ubok. Mäna' uyu'yik ubok maani(h).

With their noses raised the Kisins go around sniffing for his scent. They don't smell any scent.

"Bik way tari(h) uboke(r)."
"It seems his scent came here," (say the Kisins).

"Mäna'."
"There isn't any," (says the ancestor).

"Way ma' maani(h) äkyum way."
"Our Lord didn't pass through here."

[Ma' lati' äknukire'ex ma' tuye'esah uber tu' maani(h) ti' Kisin.]
[That ancestor of ours didn't show the Kisins which way he went.]

"Way maani(h) äkyum. Mäna'."
"Our Lord didn't pass through here. There isn't any (scent)."

Ele, b-i-i-i-h äkyum.
And so, (by now) our Lord is long gone.

PART 2. HACHÄKYUM "DIES" AND KISIN IS INTERRED IN THE UNDERWORLD

Ele, mäna' uts'o'oko(r), Hachäkyum. Wo(r)o(r) tan ulaxik lati' ahKisin. Ele, kuk'uchur tuka'ten tup'is(ir k'inir?) uk'aay aht'eer. Leh(ih?) kuyu'yik uk'aay aht'eer, "TEESEH, TEESEH."

Well, it's not over for Hachäkyum (yet). The Kisins are still beating him. And so, the time comes for the rooster to crow again. (T'uup) hears the rooster's crowing, "COCK-A'DOODLE-DOO, COCK-A'DOODLE-DOO."

Ele T'uup kulik'i(r).

So T'uup gets up.

"Lahi(h) in tet! Kuhäts'ik!"

"It's my father! They're beating him!" (he says to himself).

Lik'ih yaaka' seeb. K'uchi(h) yaaka'.

He got up and rushed out. He came running in.

"Kuxa'an lahih intet."

"My father is alive," (he says to himself).

Le' beki(r) tulahkinsah Kisin.

Well, he killed Kisin the same way (as before).

"Mäna'. Ele, ne ma' tsoy," tan uya'arik ti'. *"Le' mäna', ma' tsoy, tet. Kisin ma' tsoy."*

"They are no more. They're evil," he is saying to (his father). "They're finished. They're evil, father. The Kisins are evil."

"Le' ma' T'uupeh," kih. *"Hoy ti'. Ka'liseh Kisin."*

"No, T'uup," (Hachäkyum) says. "Never mind. Pick the Kisins up again."

"Le' mäna'. Chen t(an) ukinsikech tet. Le' mäna'."

"I won't do that. They will only kill you, father. I won't do that."

Ele, tunekukuxhäts'ah tun, ahHachäkyum. Tunebä(r)äxhäts'ah tun.

Well, they (had beaten) Hachäkyum half to death, by then. They (had beaten) him all over, by then.

Ele, hoopi(h) uchäkwir. Le' ma' tupi(h) uchäkwir tun.

And then he came down with a fever. But the fever didn't break.

Ele, ma' nahtupih. Ele, kimi(h).

Well, it didn't break. And so, he died.[8]

Eh ba'aleh, T'uupeh ok'or ukah, "Mäna' intet. Kimih."

So then, T'uup begins to cry, "I don't have my father. He died."

Ele ts'o'ok. Kimih utet tun. Tumukah. Ts'o'oki(h) umukik utet tun.

And so, it's over. His father died. (T'uup) buried him. He buried his father.

Ele, ba'aleh Kisin seebseeb tulahma(r)a(h) uba'a(r) ubäh. (U)laak' ahKisin tulahma(lah) . . . tuworo(r) ba'axtäk uba'a(r) ubäh . . . Tulahmuuch'ah uti'a'ar, leti' bini(h) ukananteh upixan Hachäkyum.

Well then, the Kisin(s) hastily picked up all of their belongings. Kisin's wife picked up . . . all their things . . . She gathered her children together (and) they went (to Hachäkyum's tomb) to guard Hachäkyum's soul.[9]

Tu(k'in) (u)k'uchu(r) t(i') unah k'in ahHachäkyum. Nah k'ini(r) ti' ubin upixan ahHachäkyum t(i') uyaram lu'umeh. Le toh ti' nika'(a)n kura'an t(i') umuk(r)an ahHachäkyum. Ma' uhook'or upixan Hachäkyum. Ele, hach t(i') unah k'ini(r) le tuyu'yah t(an) uhe'(ik) ubäh umuk(r)an ti' Hachäkyum— BIZ-Z-Z-Z-Z-Z.

Hachäkyum [had been] dead for five days. On the fifth day, Hachäkyum's soul [was still in] the underworld. (The Kisins) are still gathered there at Hachäkyum's grave. Hachäkyum's soul [hadn't yet] come out. But on that fifth day they heard Hachäkyum's tomb opening—BIZ-Z-Z-Z-Z-Z.

Ele, Kisin bini(h) kuru-kuru-kuru(r) ti' uyaram lu'um. Ele, lahi(h) ka'(ah) tuka'nup'ah umuk(r)an Hachäkyum.

And so all the Kisins went toppling into the underworld. Then Hachäkyum's tomb closed over again.

Ele, taki(r) bähe' tun, lahbini(h) Kisin tun. Mäna', mäna' way yok'o(r) k'aax tun. Ti' bini(h) yok'o(r) yaram lu'um. Le lahi(h) ka'ah ts'o'ok.

And so, up to now, the Kisins are all gone. They're not here in the forest anymore. They went into the underworld. That is when (the fight between Hachäkyum and Kisin) ended.

Hachäkyum yeter T'uup yeter Chäk Xib
'Hachäkyum, T'uup, and Chäk Xib'

Bor Ma'ax

When the story begins, Hachäkyum is already very old and is being cared for by his dutiful, youngest son, T'uup.[1] His eldest son,[2] Chäk Xib, despises them both and tries to kill T'uup. But T'uup outsmarts him by feigning his own death before joining his father in the sky. He makes a straw replica of himself, which his brother thinks is real and proceeds to slash to pieces. When Chäk Xib discovers that it is not his little brother, T'uup has already ascended to Hachäkyum's sky. Hachäkyum disconnects the route to the sky, stranding Chäk Xib[3] on earth. According to the narrator, the moral of the story is to respect your parents, especially when they are old.

Rivalry between younger and elder brothers and fratricide is a common theme in Mayan mythology. T'uup corresponds to the young twins in the *Popol Vuh*, Hunahpu and Xbalanque, who were mistreated by their jealous half-brothers, Hun Batz and Hun Chouen. The young twins got even when they lured their evil brothers up a tree to retrieve birds that the twins had allegedly shot. While they are up there, the tree grows so high that the brothers cannot get down. The twins tell them to take off their loincloths and tie them round their waist like tails, to help lower themselves down. When they do this the elder brothers turn into monkeys and, later, become the patrons of artists and scribes in Mayan mythology.

Later on, the twins are summoned to the underworld to play ball with the Lords of the Underworld. While there they endure many harrowing trials, before defeating the lords. After this they ascend to the sky where they become the sun and moon (or Venus). In Mayan mythology twins symbolize the dualism of life and death, sky and earth, day and night, and the sun and moon.

Like the twins, T'uup fools his brothers and ascends to the sky where he becomes the guardian of the sun. Meanwhile, his brothers are relegated to the margins of the earth.

Bay. Bin inkah intsikbartik utsikbar yete(r) Hachäkyum, Chäk Xib yete(r) T'uup. Chäk Xib, lehih uyanchuni(n) upaara(r) äkyum. AhT'uup, uk'aba' T'uup porke ha'ri' ut'uupi(r).

Okay. I'm going to tell the story about Hachäkyum, Chäk Xib, and T'uup. Chäk Xib is Hachäkyum's first son. T'uup is called T'uup only because he is the youngest.

Bay.

Okay.

T'uup ne 'otsir uyirik utet. Woro(r) ahT'uup ne 'otsir uyirik utet. Wa tu' kubin utet uyet bin. Tu' kubin tu' kumeyah, uyet bin ahT'uup. Ha'ri' T'uup ma' up'ätik utet. Ma' up'ätik utet ahT'uup. Ne 'otsir uyirik utet.

T'uup dotes on his father. T'uup has always doted on his father. Wherever his father goes T'uup goes with him. Wherever he goes to work, T'uup goes with him. Only T'uup doesn't abandon his father. T'uup doesn't abandon his father; he dotes on his father.

Eh, upaara(r) äkyum, Chäk Xib, mäna', ma' hach 'otsir uyirik utet. Ma' 'otsir uyirik. Kuch'eene'(e)tik chen bay ma' ne 'otsir uyirik utet. Eh upaara(r) äkyum Chäk Xib ha'ri' uch'eene'etik utet como ne nuxi' utet. Ba'ar uk'a't uya'areh ti' utet: "Ne ch'iha'an intet, yahah nuxibi(r). Ya hupuk chi' intet. Mäna'. Ne ch'ihi(r)."

Hachäkyum's son Chäk Xib doesn't care about his father at all. He doesn't care about him. He'll go and visit him, but he doesn't really care about him much. Chäk Xib just visits his father (because) his father is old. He says whatever he wants to his father: "My father is ancient, he's become a really old man. My father's mouth is already sunken in. He's had it. He's ancient."

Le lahih upaara(r) äkyum Chäk Xib. Ne ma' k'a't uyirik utet. Ha'ri' T'uup, huntuuri' yet(er) tu' kuxbin utet yet bin. Ba'inkin kubin ume(n)tik, kiri' kubin ahT'uup. Kubin te' ka'an, uyetbin ti' ka'ani(r) ahT'uup. Ha'ri' upaara(r) äkyum Chäk Xib ti' yan ich Parenque, bex utsikbartah äknukire'ex.

That's what the son of Hachäkyum, Chäk Xib, thinks. He doesn't want to even look at his father. Only T'uup, the other one, goes with his father wherever he goes. Whatever he goes to do, T'uup goes too. When he goes to the sky, T'uup goes to the sky with him. Only Hachäkyum's son Chäk Xib lives in Palenque, our ancestors say.

Bex utsikbartah kimih ahHachäkyum tun ya tumukah utet ahT'uup. Ba'axta(n) mäna'. Bayla', ahHachäkyum, bex utsikbartah äknuki(r) winik, ma' (kimih): tutohlahk'äxah ahxa'an, p'is ubähi(r) ahHachäkyum tuk'äxah la' xa'an. La la'eh kimih. Toh ma' ubähi(r) ahHachäkyum. Xa'an. Lahih tutusah ukimi(n). Ubähi(r) ahHachäkyum ma' kimih. Kuxa'an.

They say Hachäkyum died and that T'uup buried his father. Thus, his father is no more. However, our ancestors say that Hachäkyum didn't die: he (had) made a dummy of himself out of palm leaves, and this is what (had) really died. It wasn't the real Hachäkyum. It was his palm leaf dummy. He faked his death. The real Hachäkyum didn't die. He was (still) alive.

Entonces, "kimih" ahHachäkyum, y tumukah ahT'uup

And so, Hachäkyum "died," and T'uup buried him.

Yan 'oxkuru' uka'ani(r) uyatoch ahT'uup, 'oxkuru' uka'ani(r) yatoch.

T'uup's house is on the third level in the sky.

Tix kura'an tanux ok'or. T'uup ok'or ukah, "Mäna' intet. 'Otsir intet. Bähe' ma' het usut intet. Kimin intet.

He sits there and sits there, crying and crying. T'uup is crying, "I don't have my father anymore. My poor father. My father can't come back now. My father is dead."[4]

Eh ba'la' usukun ahT'uup, upaara(r) Chäk Xib, ti' yan ne tsoy uyor ti'. "Ele, kimi(n) intet—luk'ih," tuya'arah. "'Oy inwor ti'. Ne ch'iha'an, yahah hupuk uchi'."

But T'uup's older brother, Chäk Xib, is elated. "My father is dead—eliminated," he said. "I was so tired of him. He was so old with his old mouth sunken in."

Mäna', ahT'uup. Tix kura'an tanux (tan-ux-?) ok'or ti' uxur uchi' uyatoch t(i') uka'ani(r). Tix (ti' x-?) kura'an. Tan yok'or.

T'uup doesn't feel the same way. He sits there and sits there, crying and crying at the far end of his house in the sky. He sits there and sits there crying.

Eh, upaara(r) äkyum Chäk Xib yan uch'upra(r) uti'a'ar. Tutuchi'tah uch'upra(r) uti'a'ar.

Hachäkyum's son Chäk Xib has a daughter. He sent his daughter (to T'uup).

"Eh xen, xen pureh ma'ats' ti' inwits'in T'uup," kih. "Xen, uk'useh. Xen pureh wah ti'."

"Go and put down some posol for my little brother, T'uup," he says. "Go and give him a drink. Go put down tortillas for him."[5]

Tan ut'ana(r) uyixkit ti' T'uup,

T'uup's niece is saying to him,

"Eh wa ahantik wo'och ma'ats'?"

"Hey, why don't you eat some posol?"

"Mäna', ma' ink'a't," kih T'uup. "Mäna' ma' inwuk'ik."

"No, I don't want any," says T'uup. "I don't want to drink any."

Utukur ne yah. Tan yak'tik ti' utet. Kura'an tanux ok'or, "Mäna', ma' wi'ihen. Mäna' inhanan. Ne yaab intukur mäna' intet."

He is inconsolable. He is crying for his father. He is seated and keeps crying, "I'm not hungry. I don't (want) to eat any. I am so sad that my father is no more."

Tix kura'an ahT'uup, tanux ok'or.

T'uup just sits there crying and crying.

"Ba'wih tech kawak'tik (ak)tet? Yahah nuxi(b). Yahah ch'iha'an. Yahah hupuk chi'. Luk'. Hoy ti'."

(Chäk Xib says to T'uup), "Why do you cry for (our) father? He's old. He's ancient. His mouth is sunken in. Drop it. Forget about him."

Maa, 'oy uyor—mäna' ma' utu'pur, woror ok'or ukah, kurik woror ok'or ukah ahT'uup.

He is tired of it—it never ends, he is crying all the time. All T'uup does is sit there and cry.

Bek tutsikba(r)tah uchik äknukire'ex, la'eh ahT'uup, mäna' ma' kura'an tan uyok'or, pero ma' ubähi(r), ahT'uup xa'an tuk'äxah. Xa'an. Ubähi(r) ahT'uup yet bin(ih) utet ti' uka'an. Yet bin(ih) utet. A' la'eh tup'ätah kurtar la'eh uxa'an. Ti' kura'an tan uyok'or uk'äx xa'an ahT'uup.

Like our ancestors said, that's not T'uup seated there crying, but a dummy of himself that he made from palm leaves.[6] The real T'uup left with his father for the sky. He went with his father. He left the palm leaves behind. It is the dummy of T'uup sitting there crying.

Ba'lah upaara(r) äkyum Chäk Xib, ne p'eek ti' utet. "Mäna'. Luk' intet. Hoy ti'."

So now Hachäkyum's son, Chäk Xib, really detests his father. "He's gone. My father has been erased. Forget about him."

"Ba'wih inwits'in T'uup up'isik ubäh uyak'tik (ak)tet?" kih. *"Yahah nuuuxibi(r)."*

(He thinks to himself,) *"Why does my little brother T'uup cry so much over our father? He'd gotten so ooold."*

Uhook'or usukun ahT'uup, upaara(r) äkyum Chäk Xib, tuch'a'ah uharar. Bin uhureh uyits'in T'uup tu' kura'an ti' uyatoch. Bin uhureh. HUP. Tak lu'um binih uyits'in T'uup.

T'uup's older brother, Chäk Xib, grabbed his bow and arrows. He went to shoot his little brother, T'uup, where he's sitting by his house. He went to shoot him. TWANG. His little brother T'uup fell to the ground.

"Luk' inwits'in tun. Hoy ti'! 'Oy inwor ti' woror uyak'tik ti' intet. Ba'wih ti' intet kuyak'tik? Luk'i(h)."

(He says to himself,) *"Now my little brother is gone. Forget him! I was tired of his constant crying over my father. Why (did) he cry so for him? He's gone."*

La'eh ma' bin(ih) uyireh a' la'eh ahpaara(r) äkyum Chäk Xib. Ma' k'uchih uyireh uyits'in T'uup, porque T'uup lubih. Uch'upra(r) uti'a'ar hook'ih uch'eene'eteh. Eh, kuyirik kura'an, tu' kuuchi(r), ok'or ukah ti' utet, *"'Utsere(r). Ma' het la'eh intet. Kimi(n)."*

Chäk Xib didn't go see him. He didn't arrive to see his little brother T'uup, because T'uup (had fallen). His daughter went out to have a look. And, she sees him sitting there, in that place, crying over his father, "Dear me. It's no use. My father is dead."

Ahch'upra(r) uti'a'ar Chäk Xib 'u'rih tuya'arah ti' utet, "Kuxa'an awits'in T'uup. Ti' kura'an t(an) uyok'or."

Chäk Xib's daughter returned and told her father, "Your little brother, T'uup, is alive. He is sitting there, crying."

"TSK! Ehhh. Bähe' ma' tu' bin xi'ik inwits'in T'uup. Bähe' ten bin inkah in-hureh."

"TSK! Ehhh. Now there is nowhere for my little brother T'uup to go. Now I'm going to shoot him."

Okor ukah bin uhureh. Uhurik. Lubur uyits'in T'uup. Kuk'uchu(r), kuhach-ki'lahp'e'p'e'ch'äkt(ik) uyits'in T'uup—ch-a-a-ah, ch-a-a-ah.

He goes in (T'uup's house) to shoot him. He shoots him. His little brother, T'uup, falls. He goes over and hacks his little brother T'uup to pieces—ch-a-a-ah, ch-a-a-ah.

Tuki'lahp'ip'i(k)ch'äktah. Tulahp'eext'ah ubäk'er.

He chopped him all up. He whittled his body down.

"Ele bähe' mäna' uyaaha(r) inwits'in T'uup. Bähe' luk'. Hoy ti'. 'Oy inwor ti' woro(r) yak'tik ti' intet."

(He thinks to himself,) *"So now my little brother T'uup will never wake up. Now he's erased. Forget it. I was so tired of his constant crying over my father."*

Bähe' mäna' uyits'in T'uup. Tukinsah. Hook'or ukah; bin uyireh ubähi(r) ahpaarar äkyum Chäk Xib. K'uch(ih) uyaaka' uyireh. Chen xa'an, yahah pätan tuhachlahp'ep'e'ch'äk. Woro(r) xa'an puka'an—sä(k)kete(r).

Now his little brother, T'uup, is no more. He killed him. Chäk Xib goes out to check his brother. He ran over to check him. But they are palm leaves, large banana (leaves) (that) he chopped all up. They're just palm leaves (that) are destroyed—T'uup's dummy.

"Eh hah! Mäna'!" kutubur ut'an upaara(r) äkyum Chäk Xib. "Ma' bäk'er inwits'in T'uup bäkan. Ma' tinkinsah bäkan, chen uk'ax xa'an(ir) inwits'in T'uup. Ubähir inwits'in T'uup, mäna' bäkan. Toh yet bin(ih) intet ka'ah binih."

"Aha! There isn't any (body)!" Chäk Xib snorts. "This isn't the body of my little brother, T'uup. I didn't kill him after all, only the palm leaves of my little brother, T'uup. My real brother, T'uup, isn't here after all. He left with my father when he went (to the sky)."

Ele, ti' ts'o'ok ti' la' la'eh ahT'uup.
And so, that's the end of T'uup.

Ele, ti' kuru(r) yahah a' pa(a)k'a(r) (ah)k'uche' tupäk'ah ahChäk Xib. Leti' upaara(r) kyum Chäk Xib (t)upäk'ah ahk'uche', yahah kura'(an) ne ha(ch)ch'ik yum. Tupäk'ah ahk'uche' chi' uyatoch.
Well then, there is a large cedar tree that Chäk Xib (had) planted. This cedar tree Chäk Xib planted is enormous. He planted it at the side of his house.

Tix tar(ih) ahtunse(r). "BOOOX," kih, ahtunse(r).
This woodpecker came along. "BRRRAP" goes the woodpecker.

—Boh-boh-boh-boh. Boh-boh-boh—
—Boh-boh-boh-boh. Boh-boh-boh—[7]

Mix uyo(h)e(r) upaara(r) äkyum Chäk Xib wa lahih yits'in T'uup kubin uch'äka(r) ahk'uche'. Bix ta(r) bin—"boh, boh"—bey ahtunse(r).
Chäk Xib doesn't know (that) it is T'uup who is going to chop down the cedar tree. He is going like this—"boh, boh"—like a woodpecker.

Ba'axta(n),[8] ka'ah tuyu'yah bin tun, tan uläkchah a' la'eh yahah pak'a(r) k'uche'. Tan chumuk kutar ich uyatoch a' la'eh tu' kura'(an) uyatoch upaara(r) kyum Chäk Xib. Ma ten k'uy ukah chik utich, ehh utichi(r). Chich umuuk' k'uchi(h)—PUHHH—ti' bin utser uyatoch ti' lub. b-i-i-i-IX.[9]

But then he heard it; the great big cedar was coming loose. It was heading toward the middle of Chäk Xib's house. And then it starts to tilt, coming closer and closer. It comes down with great force—PUHHH—toward the side of the house, where it fell—k-a-a-a-BOOM.

Eh, hook'o(r) bi(n) yir(eh) upak'ar k'uche' yah puk'a'anta(r) ch'aak.

He goes out to see that the cedar tree (had been) chopped.

"Ehhh hah," tuya'arah upaara(r) äkyum Chäk Xib. "Eh toh inwits'in T'uup tuch'äk(ah) inpak'a(r) k'uche'. Ne tak uts'ahik ten. Ne tak ukinsiken."

"Ehhh, aha," said Chäk Xib. "It's my little brother T'uup who chopped down my cedar tree. It just about took me out; it nearly killed me."

Ele, ba'ale' ti' tuyirah upaara(r) äkyum Chäk Xib, *"Ele inwits'in T'uup p'oka'an. Mäna', ma' ints'ahik ti'. Hoy ti'. Yetbinih intet. Ubähi(r) inwits'in, T'uup, yetbinih intet."*

But then, Chäk Xib saw him there, *"Eh, my little brother, T'uup, is perched there. I didn't take him out. Never mind. He left with my father. My real little brother, T'uup, left with my father."*

Ele, bex utsikbartah.

So, this is like they tell it.

Bähe' upaara(r) äkyum Chäk Xib ti' p'aatih ti' Parenke. Ma' tubisah ahHachäkyum, porque ma' 'otsir uyirik utet ahChäk Xib.

Today Chäk Xib stayed behind in Palenque. Hachäkyum didn't take him (to his sky), because Chäk Xib didn't care about his father.

Hachäkyum Uxatik Uche'ir Ukaar
'Hachäkyum Cuts the Mortals' Throats'

Bor Ma'ax

The following text is an account of the second end of the world.[1] Hachäk-yum is still displeased with his mortals' behavior and wants to rid the land of the miscreants. He orders T'uup to cover the sun. T'uup obeys and pro-duces an eclipse. After this Hachäkyum orders all the mortals to gather at Yaxchilan, where he cuts their throats and tests their blood for purity.[2] He collects the pure blood in a special cauldron, boils it up, and then gives it to Ts'ibanah to paint the houses of the gods. It is said that the gods relish the scent of fresh blood. Hachäkyum saves some of the pure blood[3] to repopu-late the world in the next creation and then casts the bodies and heads to his ravenous pet jaguars.

This event is reminiscent of the blood sacrifice prevalent among the Maya as described in the Mayan chronicles and codices. Archeological ex-cavations and forensic examinations of pre-Columbian human remains confirm human sacrifice was commonplace in Mayan society (Marcus 1978; Tiesler and Cucina 2006). Although there is little consensus on why human sacrifice occupied a central place in Maya ritual, Diego de Landa Calderón, Spanish bishop of the Roman Catholic Archdiocese of Yucatán, noted that "plagues, rebellions, droughts, or like ills" were some reasons (Landa [1937] 1978, 91). Children, who represented life and purity incar-nate, were sacrificed as part of dedication ceremonies for laying the foun-dations of new temples and during the accession of a new king or to cele-brate a new year. Their beating hearts were removed, and their blood was used to anoint the idols.

Bay.

Okay.

Hachäkyum tuxurah a' t'an. Uyanchuni(n) tuye'esah uxurt'an. Hachäkyum woro(r) ya'axk'in, boon uk'uchur ya'axk'in tan uk'uchur ya'axk'in uxurik t'an. Uk'uchur ya'axk'in, poch uxurik t'an.

Hachäkyum ended the world. (He had already) demonstrated the end of the world (once before). When the (new) year arrives, Hachäkyum wants to end the world.

Yan äknukire'ex unuki(r) winik upokik. Upokik ti' Hachäkyum. Uts'ahik ba'che', k'ik', hu'un, nahwah, ch'ur(h)a'—tuworo(r) ubo'otik ti' kyum tema' uxurik t'an.

Our ancestors pray to him. They pay Hachäkyum. They give him balche', rubber, bark cloth, tamales, posol—they offer everything to our Lord so that he doesn't end the world.

AhHachäkyum ne poch uxurik t'an. Tan uk'uchur ya'axk'in, poch uxurik t'an; tan uk'uchur ya'ak'in, poch uxurik t'an. Aknuki(r) winik ubo'otik ti' Hachäkyum.

But Hachäkyum really wants to end the world. A new year arrives, and he wants to end the world; then another new year arrives, and he wants to end the world. Our ancestors (continue to) give offerings to Hachäkyum.

Bay.

Okay.

Hachäkyum uch'a'ik ma'ats', ch'a'ik k'ik', uch'a'ik tuworo(r), tum(b)en lek y ma' uxurik t'an. Tsoy uyor chichin, chen ma' hach tsoy uyor. Hachäkyum poch uxurtik yete(r) T'uup.

Hachäkyum takes the posol, he takes the rubber, his new god pots, he takes it all, and he doesn't end the world. He's satisfied but not very happy. Hachäkyum (still) wants to end the world with (his son) T'uup.

Bay.

Okay.

Äknukire'ex ne sahak, ne sahak ti' uxurt'an. Uya'arik ti' ubäho', "Bähe' tint'an tech apokik ti' kyum, tema' uxurt'an, tema' uxurik t'an to'on."

Our ancestors are very afraid, very afraid of the end of the world. One says to his companions, "Now I think you (had better) pray to our Lord, to prevent the end of the world, to prevent him ending the world for us."

Uya'arik unuki(r) winik, "Ten tinpokah, ten int'anik k'uh, int'anik Hachäkyum; int'anik ulekil T'uup; tuworo(r) ints'a'ik ti' inbo'otik tema' uxurik t'an. Ne yah inwu'yik utar uxurt'an. Ne yah inwu'yik utar inkimi(n)."

(Another) ancestor says, "I pray, I speak to the gods, I speak to Hachäkyum; I speak to T'uup's god pot; I give them everything so that they (won't) end the world. I (will) suffer when the end of the world comes. I (will) suffer a lot (when) my death comes."

[Utsikbar uchik: Tu' kakbine'ex, mäna' ma' saasir tu' kubin äkpixane'ex. Ma' saasir tu' kubin äkpixane'ex. Be'ik utsikbartah: Tu' kubin äkpixane'ex, mäna' uher ka'an, mäna' k'in, ma' saasir, ha'ri' 'aak'bi(r) tu' kakbine'ex. Bex tutsikba(r)tah unuki(r) winik.]

[They said before: Where we go, there isn't any light where our souls go. There is no light where our souls go. That's what they say: Where our souls go, there isn't another sky, there isn't a sun, there is no light, just darkness where we go. That's how the ancestors put it.]

Bay.

Okay.

Hachäkyum turaka(r) tutuntah uxurik t'an. Hachäkyum turaka(r) tutuntah uxurik t'an ti' lu'umo'. Woro(r) ne poch uxurik t'an. AhHachäkyum yeter uti'a'ar, T'uup, ne poch, ne poch, ne p'enk'äch poch.

Hachäkyum always tried to end the world. Hachäkyum always tried to end the world for the people. He yearned to end the world. Hachäkyum and his son, T'uup, really, really yearned to do it, they yearned so much to do it.

Bay.

Okay.

K'uchih tuk'in ahHachäkyum tuläkah a' k'in yete(r) T'uup. Tan uyaak'ä'-chah; 'aak'ä'chahih; mäna' k'in. Barum kuhum—tan uyu'yik siis. Lahih ku-yanhum uyawat way yok'or k'aax. Lahih kuyanhum uyaakan yok'or k'aax. Uhach barumi(r) k'aax kuyaakan; kuyawat. Tuworo(r) bäk' ulahto'ochta(r); tuworo(r) barum ulahto'ochta(r); tan uyawat.

The time came, (and) Hachäkyum and T'uup unfastened the sun. It's getting dark; darkness fell; there isn't any sun. The jaguars make noise—they are cold. First, they make a noise, they cry out in the forest, here. They first make noise; they roar in the forest. The true jaguars of the forest are roaring; they are crying out.

Pachir tan utar siisir, ne siis. Nukuch winik tan upokik; tan upokik yok'or uleki(r) k'uh ti' Hachäkyum. Ma' k'uchu(r) umuuk', ne siis. Ma' bik upok-or lahto'ochir yete(r) siisi(r). P'isi(r) barum. Lahto'ochir. Lahkimih. Lah-to'ochir yete(r) siisi(r).

Then it is getting cold, very cold. The ancestors are burning offerings; they are burning offerings in Hachäkyum's incensory. They don't have any strength, (because) it is cold. They're unable to pray (because) they're frozen stiff. The same goes for the jaguars. They're completely frozen. They all died. They're frozen stiff.

Ti' yan uhaan Hachäkyum. Uk'aba' Ak'inchob. Lahih kuman'aaka' uyireh lu'umo' yok'or k'aax, tema' uchi'bi(r) ahbarum. Ne yan utukur. Ak'inchob seeb tan umaan ukänänteh.

Hachäkyum's son-in-law is there. His name is Ak'inchob. He is running through, keeping an eye on his mortals in the forest, so that they don't get eaten by jaguars. He is worried. Ak'inchob rushes around to protect them.[4]

Akna'i(r) Hachäkyum ne tukur ukah, "'Otsir inwaar — bähe' mäna'. Bin ukah chi'bi(r) ten ahbarum."

Hachäkyum's wife is very worried, "My poor children — now it's hopeless. They're going to be eaten by the jaguars."

Lahkimin yok'o(r) lu'um. Uhaan ahHachäkyum, Ak'inchob, tan umanaaka' ti' uyirik a' winiko' tema' uchi'bi(r) ten barum, tema' utäreh ten barum. Ti' kumanaaka' ukananteh.

They're dead on the ground. Hachäkyum's son-in-law, Ak'inchob, is rushing around to make sure that they are not eaten by the jaguars, so that they are not touched by the jaguars. He is rushing around (trying) to protect them.

Bay.

Okay.

Pachir, Ak'inchob ubin ulahahsik ti' uheebe(r) uyor. Mix uyu'yik uximba(r). Tuworo(r) yete(r) uchan mehen ti'a'ar ulaak', tuworo(r) mix t(an) uximba(r). Seebseeb ka'(ah) tuyu'yah ich Yaxchilan äknukire'ex saasi(r)chah. Ha'ri'; chen tuworo(r) k'aax, aak'bi(r).

Later, Ak'inchob goes to wake them all up, to revive them. None of them sense that they are walking. All of them, including the children and the wives, don't walk (at all). Instantly, when they sensed (they were) in Yaxchilan,[5] our ancestors (noticed) it was getting light. But it was only (here); the rest of the forest was dark.

Ti' yan Yaxchilan. Uchik unuki(r) winik uk'aba' ka'anan xokra'. Tuworo(r) lah ti' yan ka'anan xokra', Yaxchilan. Uyirik yan k'in ne saasi(r). Uyirik ne pim k'uho' kurukbar — ahk'uh'o', chem(b)ehk'uho', tuworo(r); Yahanah, tuworo(r); Ts'ibanah, tuworo(r); Mensäbäk, tuworo(r). Lah ti' yan uyirik bik uxurik t'an ahHachäkyum. Ne tsoy uyirik. To'one'ex äknukire'ex, ne tsoy uyor tambien. Uyirik ubin umentik ti' to'one'ex Hachäkyum.

They were in Yaxchilan. The ancestors used to call it *Ka'anan Xokra'*.[6] All of them were in ka'anan xokra', or Yaxchilan. They see that it is very bright and sunny. They see many gods sitting around; the gods, the little gods that walk around the mountains, all of them; Yahanah, all of them; Ts'ibanah, all of them; Mensäbäk, all of them.[7] All of them are there to see how Hachäkyum ends the world. They are eager to see it. Our ancestors are also eager to see what Hachäkyum is going to do.

"Ba'inkin kubin umentik to'one'ex?"

(And the ancestors are thinking,) *"What is he going to do to us?"*

Ele, äknukire'ex upäktik uyireh yan nukuch kan, yan nukuch barum, yan unukuch 'ayim. Ba'la' Hachäkyum ti' kura'an. AhHachäkyum tan ucha'antik (u)nukuch winik; uyirik bik uxurik äknukire'ex.

Then, our ancestors look around and see enormous snakes, enormous jaguars, (and) enormous crocodiles all around. But Hachäkyum is sitting there. Hachäkyum is watching the ancestors; he sees how he is going to finish off our ancestors.

Tuworo(r) lahk'uchih, tuworo(r) lahkahankah yok'or k'aax. Tuworo(r) lati' tulahmuuch'ah ubah ti' Yaxchilan. Lati' lahk'uchih.

All of them arrived (from) all the surrounding settlements. All of them gathered together at Yaxchilan. They all arrived.

La' boon äknukire'ex toh uyoher bin ukah uxurik a' t'an ahHachäkyum yete(r) T'uup. Äknukire'ex tutohp'u'uktah tok'. Ma' uyoher Hachäkyum; manih uwich ma' tuyirah wa yan (u)tok' ti' up'u'uk.

(Some) of our ancestors already know that Hachäkyum and T'uup are about to end the world, (so) (they) (had) already filled their cheeks with arrowheads. Hachäkyum does not know this; he scanned (the people), but he did not see if they had arrowheads in their cheeks.

Hachäkyum uyantehtik; le ba'axtar lah ti' yan tuworo(r) nukuch winik. Boon ahk'uho' lah ti' kurenkur ucha'anteh.

Hachäkyum begins to select them; that is why all the ancestors are there. How many gods there are sitting here and there to watch.

Ele, kut'ana(r) ahHachäkyum ubähi(r), *"Bähe' tuneh, bin inkah inteh-teh inwaaro' to'an ne tsoy uk'ik'er. La' he' inwaaro' ne tsoy uk'ik'er, eh la' he'ra' inwaaro' ma' tsoy. Te' kubin lähtar y la' he'ra' inwaaro' te' kubin lähtar."* ... Ha-chäkyum uya'arik, "La' he'ra' ne tsoy; la' he'ra' ma' tsoy," uhätsik uti'ri(').

And then, Hachäkyum says to himself, *"Now then, I'm going to select my chil-dren that have pure blood. My children here have pure blood and my children there have impure blood. The ones right here will line up here, and the ones there will line up over there."* ... Hachäkyum says, "These here are good; those there are not good." And he separates them.

Ti' yan äknukire'ex umeek'man upom; ch'a'aban upom ti' uts'ahik ti' kyum.

There are (some) of our ancestors who have been clutching copal; they had brought copal to give to Hachäkyum.

Eh huntuur äknukire'ex tan utukrik, *"Ne tsoy inwor. Ten bin inkah p'aata(r). Bin ukah up'atiken. Bin ukah tutiisahen. Ma' inbin kimi(r) ten, porke tuya'arah Hachäkyum ten, 'A' he'ra' ne tsoy inwaaro'; a' he'ra' ma' ne tsoy.'"* Äknukire'ex ne tsoy uyor, *"Bähe' ten ma' inbin kimi(r) ten."* Eh, ahuntuur äknukire'ex tan utukrik ubah, *"Tuya'arah Hachäkyum ten, 'Ma' tsoy inwaaro.' 'Utsereh chen ten bin inkah kimi(n)."*

Another one of our ancestors is thinking, *"I'm very happy. I'm going to be spared. He is going to spare me. He is going to put me aside. I'm not going to die, because Hachäkyum said to me, 'These of my children are good; those are not good.'"* Our ancestor is very happy, "Now I'm not going to die." And, there is another of our ancestors who is thinking to himself, *"Hachäkyum said to me, 'My children (here) are not good.' Oh dear, I'm going to die."*

Ba'la' Hachäkyum ne tsoy uyor. Kurukbar yete(r) ahT'uup. (U)haan ahHachäkyum, Ak'inchob, ti' yan tukur ukah, *"Otsi(r) lu'umo'. Mäna', ma' pim.
Ma' inwoher bik yani(r) Hachäkyum ne seeb uxurik t'an. 'Otsi(r)."*

But, Hachäkyum is very happy. He is sitting with T'uup. Hachäkyum's son-
in-law, Ak'inchob, is worried, *"The poor mortals. There (won't be) any left.
They are so few. I don't know why Hachäkyum is ending the world so quickly.
Poor things."*

Ba'aleh, ahbarum charenchar. Mäna' upeek. Nukuch barum, nukuch kan,
nukuch 'ayim.

Then, the jaguars are lounging here and there. None of them move. They
are large jaguars, large snakes, and large crocodiles.

"Ele'," tuya'arah Hachäkyum, "la' he'ra' inwaaro', ts'aah ti' inwäräko'. A'
he'ra', ts'aah ti'."

"And so," said Hachäkyum, "my children there, give them to my pets. Those
there, give them to them."

Y uk'ani(r) Hachäkyum utench'intik äknukire'ex ti' barum. Kubin ti' barum. Kutar. HÄP. Tuluk'ah äknukire'ex. Y kuch'a'ik huntuur. Utench'intik
huntuur ti' yan ahnukuch kan. Tuluk'ah. Kutar huntuur ti' yan 'ayim.
Tuluk'ah äknukire'ex.

And Hachäkyum's assistants shove our ancestors at the jaguars. They go to
the jaguars. They come. GULP. They swallowed our ancestors. And they grab
another one. They shove another one at a large snake. It swallowed him.
Another one comes to a crocodile. It swallowed our ancestor.

Ti' yan huntuur äknukire'ex up'u'ukman tok'. Ka'(ah) tuyirah ahHachäkyum, hä'käräk uman nukuch barum. Mäna'. Tan ukimi(n). Ahkan kubin
hä'käräk; tan up'irisbah; hä'käräk; tan ukimi(n).

There are other ancestors who had arrowheads (tucked) inside their
cheeks. When Hachäkyum looked at it, the large jaguar is rolling around.

There isn't any of him left. He's dying. A snake is floundering; it is twitching; it is wallowing; it is dying.

"Eh ba'inki(r) tumentah inwäräk' barum?" kut'an Hachäkyum, ka'(ah) tuyirah hook'(ih) ch'ika'an (äknukire'ex). Tup'eesah uchooche(r) ahbarum, hook'(ih) ch'iktar.

"Eh, what did he do to my pet jaguar?" says Hachäkyum, when he saw that (the ancestor) had gotten out and was standing there. He (had) split open the jaguar's belly, gotten out, and stood up.[8]

"Eh! Ma' tsoy. Tukinsah inwäräk' barum. Ma' inwoher wa ti' yan p'u'ukman tok'. Eh bähe' tint'an xatbin uche'ir ukaar ... tumen ma' bin ukah ulahkinsik inwäräk'o'. Tukinsah inwäräk' kan. Mäna'. San tukinsah."

"Eh! This is not good. He killed my pet jaguar. I (didn't) know (that) he had an arrowhead inside his cheek. So now I think their necks (will) be chopped. Their necks will be chopped ... because they are going to kill all my pets. He killed my pet snake. It's gone. He just killed it."

Bay.

Okay.

Hachäkyum tuya'arah ti', "Ne tsoy." La'eh (tu)lahxatah uche'i(r) ukaar.

Hachäkyum said to them, "Very well." (And) they cut their throats.

Hachäkyum kuya'arik, "Ne ma' tsoy uk'ik'e(r), eh la' ne tsoy."

Hachäkyum (inspects the blood and) says, "(Their blood) is bad, but theirs (over there) is very good."

Bin ukah ulahxatik uche'i(r) ukaar ulahts'ahik ti' uyäräk' barum.

He is going to cut off their heads and give them to his pet jaguars.

Yaxchilan toh ti' yan 'aktun umena('an) ti' yan (u)hoor ti' kutäkik uyok äknukire'ex ti' uchurux uk'ik'er yok'or kum. Ti' yan ukuminir a(k)k'ik'e'ex.

A cave is already prepared in Yaxchilan that has a hole (where) they stick the feet of our ancestors to drain their blood into a pot. There is a special pot for our blood.[9]

Kuts'o'okor ulahch'a'ik, ulahturur ukumir ak'ik'ere'ex. Ele, lahih kuch'a'ik ahHachäkyum a' to'on ne tsoy uk'ik'er, mäna' ba' mee(n)mah ma' ukinsmah winik k'as ba' umeenman. Ele, lahih kuch'a'ik uk'ik'er ahHachäkyum ti' ubanik uyatoch, ti' ubanik 'aaktun, bixyan ts'ibanah. Tuworo(r) ulahbanik tum(b)en.

When he (had) finished taking them all, he fills up the cauldron with our blood. And then, Hachäkyum takes the blood from those of us that have the purest blood, (those who) haven't done anything bad. Then, Hachäkyum takes this blood to paint his house, to paint the stone houses like the one Ts'ibanah has. All (the gods) paint their houses anew.

[Be'ik tutsikbatah, ne tsoy uyirik uchäkir a(k)'ik'ere'ex, ubanik uyatoch. Eh, ne ki' uyu'yik ubok. Ne p'enk'äch ki' uyu'yik ubok. Le' bex tutsikba(r)tah äknukire'ex.]

[(Our ancestors) told it like this: (The gods) liked the color of our blood to paint their houses. And it smelled good to them. They savored its aroma. This is how our ancestors told it.]

"Eh hah!" äknukire'ex. "Hachäkyum ka'ah tuxurah t'an, ne yaah."

"It's true!" our ancestors (said). "When Hachäkyum ended the world, there was great suffering."

[Maa, lati' ma' tuhachxurah. Tusa(')asah. Hachäkyum tusa(')asah.]
[But, he didn't really end it. He forgave (us). Hachäkyum forgave (us).]

Bähe', chen uk'ik'er tuch'a'ah tut'isah uyiihma(n). Tut'isah uyiihman, ha'ri' tut'isah, "La' ne tsoy uk'ik'er. Ma' ukinsman. Mäna' ba'(ar) umeenman. Ne tsoy. Tuworo(r) la' ut'änik k'uh. Woro(r) la' utukur ut'änik k'uh."[10]

And now, the blood that he took he put it aside as "seed stock."[11] He put the "seed stock" aside. He just put it aside (saying), "This is very good blood. (These people) haven't killed anyone. They haven't committed any crimes. They are very good. They always pray. They all think about the gods."

Ele, lati' tut'isah ahHachäkyum. Tut'isah uyonen. La' uyonen tut'isah k'ek'en, huntuur ch'upra(r) huntuur xira(r). Wa ma'ax uyonen—huntuur ch'upra(r), huntuur xira(r); wa barum, tut'isah. Tuworo(r) tulaht'isah ahHachäkyum. Tut'isah tuworo(r) uyiihman. Ka'ka'tuu(r), ka'ka'tuu(r) tulaht'isah barum, tulaht'isah bäk', k'ek'en, yuk, k'ambur—tuworo(r) tulaht'isah. Ele bex tumentah ahHachäkyum.

And so, Hachäkyum put them aside. He separated them into lineages. He reserved one woman and one man of the white-lipped peccary lineage. If the spider monkey was their lineage—one woman and one man. If it was the jaguar, he separated them. Two by two, two by two he separated them (into lineages) of the jaguar, the white-lipped peccary, the deer, the curassow, all of them—he separated them all. And so, this is how Hachäkyum did it.

Ba'lah upixane'ex lahkimi(h), (tu)xatah uche'i(r) ukaar, upixano' bin ch'ik ti' uts'o'oki(r) ka'an. Mäna' k'in, mäna' ba'a(r)ka'an, mäna' mix k'äs ba'. Leti' bin upixano'. Ti' yan akpixane'ex aknuki(r). Hasta bähe' yan, ti' yan. Ti' p'aatih t(i') uts'o'oki(r) ka'an.

But the souls (of) all those who died, (the ones whose) heads he cut off, their souls went to the outer limits of the sky. There isn't any sun, there aren't any stars, there isn't anything at all. This is where the souls went. To this day, they are (still) there. There they remained at the outer limits of the sky.

Äkiche'ex 'Our Eyes'

Bor Ma'ax

After Hachäkyum had made his mortals he discovered that they saw too much.[1] He was not pleased that they could see his activities, especially with his wife, and so he shortened their sight. He left the dog's sight intact, because the dog denied seeing Hachäkyum and his wife together. This story is reminiscent of other Mayan myths in which the first humans were omniscient.[2]

Utsikbar nukuch winik yete(r) akiche'ex yete(r) Hachäkyum yete(r) aknukire'ex yete(r) pek'.

It is a story about the ancestors and our eyes, Hachäkyum, the ancestors, and the dog.

Bay.

Okay.

Hachäkyum tume(n)tah akiche'ex. Lahi(h) tulame(n)tah akiche'ex ti' kirik.

Hachäkyum made our eyes. He made our eyes so we could see.

Bay.

Okay.

To'one'ex nukuch winik ne saasir uwich. Ubin uwich ne naach. Wa upurik uwich ulah'irik. Ne naach tuworo(r) ne chäkan. Ne saasir uwich nukuch winik.

Our ancestors had very clear vision. Their vision (went) very far. When they cast their gaze they (could) see everything. They (could) see everything that is far away. The ancestor's vision was very clear.

Bay.

Okay.

Lah ket yete(r) pek'. Pek' p'isi(r). Saasir uwich. Ulah'irik. Lah ket yet(er) nu-kuch winik yete(r) pek', ne saasir uwich.

It was the same for the dog. The dog's vision was the same. His vision was clear. He (could) see everything. The ancestors' vision was as keen as the dog's.

Bay.

Okay.

Pachir, Hachäkyum tutukrah,"*Bay, tint'an bin intuntik inwaaro' wa yiriken. Yan inbin yet(er) akna'. Inbin ich kor intuntik inwireh wa uyirik ba'inkin inmen-tik ich kor.*"

Then, Hachäkyum thought, *"All right, I think I'm going to test my children to see if they can see me. I have to go with Our Mother. I'm going into the cornfield to see if they can see the things I do in the cornfield."*

Bay.

Okay.

Hachäkyum bini(h) yete(r) akna'e'ex. K'uchih ich kor, unaachi(r) hunp'e(r) he're(r).

Hachäkyum left with Our Mother. Hachäkyum arrived in the cornfield, which was about one rest stop away.[3]

Umeek'ik akna'e'ex.
He embraces Our Mother.

Uki' meek'ik.
He fully embraces her.

Uts'uuts'(ik) uchi'.
He kisses her mouth.

Uki'utsmentik.
He makes her swoon.

"Ah bay."
"Okay," (he says).

Ele, kusut yet(er) akna'e'ex tun. Kuyu'(r), kuk'atik ti' aknukire'ex, "Eh paa-reh," kih. "Tawirah ba'inki(n) tinme(n)tah yet(er) ana'e'ex?"
Then, he returns with Our Mother. When he returns, he asks our ances-tors, "Well, children," he says. "Did you see what I did with your Mother?"

"Le tinwirah! Tinwirah! Tinwirah aki'meek'ik akna'e'ex. Tinwirah aki'ts'uuts'ik. Tinwirah ats'uuts'ik uchi'."
"Yes, I saw it! I saw it! I saw you embrace Our Mother. I saw you really kiss her. I saw you kiss her mouth."

"Eh tawirah?"
"So you saw it?"

"Tinu'irah(?)."
"I often see that."

"Ah bay."

"Okay," (says Hachäkyum).

Uk'atik ti' pek', "Eh, tech pek', tawirah ba'inki(n) tinme(n)tah yet(er) ana'?"

He asks the dog, "And you, dog, did you see what I did with your Mother?"

"Le' ten ma' tinwirah. Mix tink'äs'irah. Miiix. Tarak tinpurah inwich, ma' tinwirah."

"I didn't see it. I didn't see anything at all. Nooothing. Although I looked, I didn't see it."

"Eh bay."

"Good," (says Hachäkyum).

Ele, tuya'arah Hachäkyum, "Eh bay. Tint'an bin inkink'eerik uwich."

And then, Hachäkyum said, "All right. I think I'm going to toast their eyes."

Tuch'a'ah (u)xämäch. Tut'achkuntah yok'or k'ak'. Ele, "Ts'ahten awich, paa-reh," kih.

He took out his griddle. He placed it on the fire. And then (he said), "Give me your eyes, sons," he says.

Tulahk'ooyah—k'ooyoch, k'ooyoch—tuka'p'e(r). Ele, tumaasah yok'o(r) (u)xämäch—*wah, wah*. Ts'ets'eri(r) tuasmaasah yok'o(r) (u)xämäch—*wah, wah*.[4] Ele tuka'but'ah akiche'ex.

They scooped both of them out—pop, pop. And then he moved them around in the griddle—*swish, swish*. He moved them little by little on the griddle—*swish, swish*. And then he put our eyes back in.

Ts'o'ok uka'lahbut'ik, ele kuka'bin tuka'ten yet(er) akna'e'ex.

He finished putting them all back in, and then he leaves again with Our Mother.

"Ele, bin inkah tuka'ten. Bin inkah yet(er) akna'e'ex wa. Päkteh awireh ba'(in)ki(n) inme(n)tik yet(er) ana'e'ex wa."

"So, I'm going again. I'm going with your Mother. Look to see what I do with your Mother."

"Bay," kih nukuch winik.

"Okay," said the ancestors.

Uk'uchul ti' ukuuchi(r) tu' bini(h) uchik, hunp'e(r) he're(r) unaachi(r). Ts'o'ok uki'meek'ik akna'e'ex. Ts'o'ok uki'ts'uuts'ik uchi', uki'utsmentik. Ele kuka'sut.

They get to the place where they went to before. He finished embracing Our Mother. He finished kissing her, making her swoon. Then he comes back.

Kuyu'(r), ele kuk'atik ti' aknukire'ex, "Hah tawirah, paareh? Tawirah ba' tin-me(n)tah yet(er) ana'e'ex?"

He returns, and then asks our ancestors, "So, did you see it, children? Did you see the things I did with your Mother?"

"Le bähe' mäna'. Ma' tinwirah. Miiix. Tarak inpäktik ma' ubin inwich. Ma' chäkan. Ma' tinwirah."

"Now I didn't see anything. I didn't see it. Nooothing. Although I looked I didn't see anything. It wasn't clear. I didn't see it."

Pek', uka'k'atik ti', "Tech tawirah?"

He asks the dog again, "Did you see it?"

"Mäna', ten mäna'. Miiix ink'äs'irik, ma'. Tarak inpäktik, ma' chäkan inwi-rik. Ma' inbin inwich. Ma' saasi(r)."

"Nothing, I (didn't see) anything. I saw nooothing much at all, no. Although I looked, I (couldn't) see clearly. My eyesight is short. It isn't clear."

"Ehhh, ne tsoy." Ele, ne tsoy uyor Hachäkyum.

"Ahhh, very good." Now Hachäkyum is satisfied.

"Bähe'," uya'arik ti' akna'e'ex, "tint'an bähe' bin ukah ku(r)ta(r) ti' lu'umo' binetk'in. Mäna' ne bin uwich ne naach. Tarak wa ba'i(n)k(in) ume(n)tik uboho' ma' uyirik. Wa umak, wa utet, kubin ich k'aax, ba'i(n)k(in) ume(n)tiko', mix kuyirik. Ma' bin uwich. Mäna'. Tarak upäktik, ma' ubin. Ha'ri' inwaaro' mäna' ubin uwich naach."

"Now," he says to Our Mother, "I think now it's going to stay this way forever for the humans. Their sight won't go too far. Even if their companions do things, they won't be able to see it. If it's another person, perhaps their father(s), when they go into the forest and do whatever, they won't see anything. Their sight won't go (that far). (They won't see) anything. Although they look, their sight won't go (far). (But) only my children's sight won't go far."

[Pek' ne ta'ah. Ma' tutoha'arah. Ma' tuya'arah wa saasir uwich. Ne yo(h)e(r) pek', ma' tutoha'arah. Xuri(') bähe' ne saasir uwich, ubin uwich. Pek', tarak ne naach, yan uwiniki(r) be'ik bix Palenkeh, hasta kuk'uchur uyirik uyoocher uwiniki(r). Ne saasir uwich. Tuworo(r) ba'i(n)ki(n) uyirik. Kulah'irik utar tuworo(r). Kuyaak'ächah saasir uwich uyirik pek'.]

[The dog is intelligent. He kept quiet. He didn't say if his vision was clear. The dog (knew) but he kept quiet. The dog's vision is still clear; it goes (far). Even if the dog's master is far away, like in Palenque,[5] (the dog) sees the image of his master (before) he arrives. His vision is very clear. He sees everything. He sees everything coming. The dog can see very clearly at night.][6]

Be'ik tutsikbartah uchik, uchik aknukire'ex winik.

This is how our ancestors told the story long ago.

Nacimiento 'Birth'

Bor Ma'ax

In the beginning, the ancestors were immortal and genderless. Like the goddesses Akna'ir Hachäkyum and Akna'il Ak'inchob, mortal women felt no pain in childbirth: they just felt a little twinge, at which point they knew it was time to collect their babies from under a papaya tree.[1]

This all changed the day a woman and her husband disobeyed Ak'inchob and ate a watermelon before he could offer it to Hachäkyum.[2] Although the woman swore that it was Ak'inchob himself who had told her that it was all right to eat the watermelon, it was actually Kisin disguised as Ak'inchob who told her.[3] Nevertheless, Ak'inchob deemed that from then on all women would have to endure the pain of childbirth.[4] She began to argue with Ak'inchob, which made him angrier. Fearful of Ak'inchob's wrath, the woman's husband inadvertently swallowed a melon seed, which lodged in his throat. When he tried to speak, his voice had changed to a deep, croaking sound. Ak'inchob told them that neither they nor any other mortal would see him again (Ak'inchob was still living on earth then). Before he left, he gave the husband an incense burner and told him to petition the gods to protect his wife and child during parturition. He decreed that all men would have to petition the gods when their wives went into labor.[5]

This story evokes the Fall, suggesting a Christian influence.

Bay.

Okay.

Inbin intsikbartik utsikbar unuki(r) winik uchik, lati' ka'(a)h toop'i(h) äknukire'ex yok'or uchun put. Lahi(h) ka'(ah) tuyirah Ak'inchob, lahi(h) tume(n)tah yeter una'i(r) Ak'inchob bex tume(n)tah uchik äknukire'ex.

Ma' tuyu'yah yahir bik utoop'or mehen paara(r), ti' kubin ukäxtik uti'a'ar yok'o(r) chun put.

I'm going to tell the story about when the ancestors were born at the base of the papaya (tree), when they saw Ak'inchob and his wife do it in the past. They didn't feel the pain of childbirth; they (simply) went to look for their babies at the base of a papaya tree.

Bay.

Okay.

Una'i(r) Ak'inchob uyänchuni(r) ti' kukuchik uti'a'ar t(i') uchoocher. Boon uk'uchur—ka'buhk'ä akna'—yah kuyu'yik ma' boon tutoop'or [kuyu'yik yah uhämnen ulaak' ahch'uprar] kukäxtik yok'or uchun put.

Ak'inchob's wife was the first to carry her children in the (womb). Some (time) goes by—ten months or so—she feels pain at the point of giving birth [just like wives feel pain in their belly] (and) she goes to look for her baby at the base of a papaya (tree).

Bay.

Okay.

Äknukire'ex toh ti' kubin ukäxtik t(i') uchun ahput Toh uyo(h)e(r): "Ten inchanti'a'ar kubin toop'or." Toh kuyu'yik uyok'or uchun a(h)put. Äknukire'ex toh uyoher ti' kubin ukäxtik uch'a'ik looch'ik.

Our ancestors already know about going to look for the baby at the base of the papaya (tree). They already know: "My baby is going to be born (there)." They already hear it crying at the base of the papaya (tree). Our ancestors already know to go look for them, pick them up, and cradle them.

[Le' bek utsikbartah äknukire'ex uchik.]

[That's how our ancestors recount it.]

Bex tume(n)tah Ak'inchob y akna'i(r) Ak'inchob. Bex tutukrah tuk'atah uyor yete(r) uhaan yeter uchuprar uti'a'ar Hachäkyum.

Ak'inchob and his wife did it the same way. Thought about it and they agreed, (along) with Hachäkyum's son-in-law and daughter, that it (would) be like this.

Chen ma' biki(r), tutukrah ubäh Hachäkyum yet(er) una'i(r) Hachäkyum yeter ubähi(r) una'i(r) Ak'inchob tuk'axah utukur para ti' ukäxtik bik ume(n)tik t(an) uyuutsta(r).

But Hachäkyum and his wife and the companions of Hachäkyum's wife change(d) their minds on how (the mortals) give birth.

Tuya'arah ti' Ak'inchob, "Eh bay, bähe' bin akah apak'arsanyah."

(Hachäkyum) said to Ak'inchob, "Okay, now you are going to sow watermelons."

Tupak'ah sanyah ...

He sowed watermelons ...

Ch'uuyur uwich ahsanya, tari(h) Kisin. Tume(n)tah ubäh p'is Ak'inchob; p'isir uwich.

(When) the watermelons were hanging down, the Devil came. He made himself look like Ak'inchob; his face was the same.

Tutoh'a'arah ti' (äknukire'ex): "He'ra' a(h)sanya. Ma' (a)t'akik ma', ma' at'akik ma' ahantik ma' wa. Chäka'an ten wa kintare(r) kints'ahik uho'or ti' äkyum."

Ak'inchob (had) already told (our ancestors): "These here are the watermelons. Don't cut them, no. You don't cut them down, don't eat them, all right? Let's see, when I come I am going to offer it to our Lord."

Bik'in tar(ih) ahKisin, tut'akah la' sanyah. Ma' ti' yan Ak'inchob; ma' ha-kan(?) tuxim(b)a(r)

When the Devil came, he snapped off a watermelon. Ak'inchob isn't there; he had already gone for a walk.

. . .

. . .

Bik'in äknukire'ex ahch'uprar ne poch ti' la' sanyah, bini(h) umuk'ur (ti' u)t'aka' ahsanyah tuki'hantah y lah ket yet(er) ahxira(r) äknukire'ex kura'an uhanteh la' sanya.

When our female ancestor craved the watermelon, she went and hid, (then) cut the watermelon (and) ate it up. Together she and the male ancestor (her husband) (ate) the watermelon.

Eh kupäktik utichi(r), la' hach ubähi(r) Ak'inchob yeter una'i(r) Ak'inchob.

Then, they spot Ak'inchob, the real Ak'inchob, approaching with his wife.

"Eh, eh mäna'. Eh, eh ma'. Ch'ik san tahantah ahsanyah. Tinwa'arah ma' (a)t'ak(eh) ahsanyah."

"Eh, oh it can't be. Oh, oh no. You just ate the watermelon. I told you not to cut the watermelon," (says Ak'inchob).

Tunuukah, "Eh mäna'. Lahi(h) tats'aah ten a' la'eh."

The woman replied, "It's nothing. You gave this to me to eat."

"Ehhh, mäna'."

"Oooh no," (says Ak'inchob).

La' ch'upra(r) ne chich uyor. Tan uya'arik, "Mäna'," kih. "Mix, mäna'. Ne tsoy. He' inhantik. Mäna' ut'an sanyah."

The woman is very bold. She is saying, "No. It's nothing. It's quite all right. I will eat it. The watermelon (won't) object."

Ba'aleh ahxira(r) äknukire'ex, ti' k'ari(h) t(i') uk'o'och tun. La' sanyah ma' bini(h) uluk'ik ti' (u)xur t(i') uk'o'och.

And now it is stuck in our ancestor's throat. The watermelon didn't go (down) (and) is stuck (at the bottom) of his throat.

"Eh! Ma' het la'eh'."

"Eh! I can't (swallow)."

Ba'aleh ahch'upra(r) tan uts'ahik uk'eyah, "Mäna'," kih. "Yo ma' inwuut-sta(r)," kih. "He' inbin inch'a'eh (ti') (u)chun (ah)put. Mäna', mäna' ink'äs-wu'yik yahi(r). Ne seeb he' inbin inch'a'eh (ti') (u)chun ahput."

Now the woman is shouting, "No!" she says. "I (will not) give birth to my baby," she says. "I will go get it (from) the base of the papaya (tree). I (won't) feel much pain. I will go quickly to collect it at the base of the papaya (tree)."

Eh bähe' tan uki'p'aktik a' bähe' uhaan Hachäkyum. "Eh mäna'. Ma' het la'eh. Ne sam tukäräxme(n)tah ubäh tun, Kisin."

Well, now she is really annoying Hachäkyum's son-in-law. "Oh, no. That is not possible. Kisin himself just spoiled it."

Bay.

Okay.

Äknukire'ex ah xira(r) bin tun, ma' bin uluk' ahsanyah. Lati' k'a'a(r) t(i') uk'o'och, "EHHH." A' ba'aleh ahxira(r) tun, ka'(a)h bini(h) tun, tunuukah, "EHHH," ba'axta(r) ne 'aar ut'an. Ya nahkuur uk'o'och tun; ne 'aar ut'an ahxi-ra(r). Ya k'aaxbah.

Our male ancestor can't swallow the watermelon (seed). It was stuck in his throat, "EHHH." Now when the man went (to speak), he replied, "EHHH," his voice is very low. It stuck in his throat now; the man's voice is very low. It had changed.

Ba'alah ahAk'inchob tan uya'arik tun, "Bähe' ma' het la'eh paare'ex," kih. "Bähe' ma' het la'eh. Bin akah abäh(eh) pom. Bähe' bin akah käxteh pom ti' apokik alaak'. Yan ti' at'änik k'uh."

And then, Ak'inchob is speaking now, "Now it is impossible, son," he says. "Now it's impossible (to change the situation). You are going to tap copal resin. Now you are going to search for copal to offer it on behalf of your wife. You have to pray to the gods."

"Eh, eh hah," äknukire'ex.

"Ah, ah yes, certainly," (says) our ancestor.

Ba'alah ulaak' äknukire'ex tan uts'ikir. "Mäna'," kih. "Yo'omir. Inwutstar seeb; mäna' inkimi(n). Mäna' inkimi(n). Seeb, inbin inch'a'eh inwäräk' ne seeb."

And now the wife of our ancestor is angry. "No!" she says. "I am pregnant. I (want) to give birth quickly; I don't (want to) die. I don't (want to) die. I'm going to go quickly and get my newborn. It will be very quick."

Ba'alah ahAk'inchob tan uya'arik, "Mäna', bähe' ts'o'ok. Kisin tukäräx-me(n)tahe'ex tun ts'o'ok. Bähe', tint'an bähe' tuworo(r) lu'umo', tuworo(r) k'aax tu' ch'ikin bin k'aax, tuworo(r) tu' kahenkah woror bek kubin utstar, yan t(i')upokik. Yan t(i') upok(ik) ulaak'; yan t(i') ut'änik k'uh. Ele, he' uyuutsta(r)."

And now Ak'inchob is speaking, "No. That's over now. The Devil spoiled you all now. Now, I think that now all of humanity, no matter how far they go in the forest, everyone living in towns here and there, all of them are going to give birth this way, (and) (the husbands) have to burn offerings. They have to burn offerings for their wives; they have to pray to the gods. After this, they will give birth."

Le' bek tutsikbartah uchik äknukire'ex. Wa mäna' ahKisin kachik ukäräx-me(n)tik, ti' uts'ahik ahsanya uhantik äknukire'ex kachik, eh ma' xuri(h), yok'o(r) chun (ah)put uch'a'ik uti'a'ar.

So, this is how our ancestors explained it. Had Kisin not spoiled the ancestors before, by giving the watermelon to the ancestors to eat, then fetching their babies from the base of the papaya (tree) would not have ended.

AhKisin tari(h) ne seeb. Tuhantah la' sanyah y tulahkäräxme(n)tah. Ma' het uyuutsta(r) tun t(i') uchun (ah)put, ts'o'ok, (u)chun (ah)put.

Kisin came quickly. He gave the watermelon and he ruined the ancestors. Birth at the base of the papaya tree is impossible, now. Giving birth under the papaya (tree) is over.

"Ele bähe' tun," Ak'inchob, "bähe' tun," kih, "bähe' yan ti' abähike'ex apome'ex, paare'ex. Yan ti' abo'otik yan ti' apokik. Ma' boon utar uyuutsta(r) tan uyu'yik yah uhämnen alaak' tun. Ka('ah) bin at'anik k'uh, yan una'i(r) Ak'inchob kat'änik. Lehi(h) kubin uyaantik ukunyah ti' alaak' ti' uyuutsta(r).

"So now," Ak'inchob (says), "now you will have to tap your copal resin, sons. You have to pay (the gods). You have to pray. Just before giving birth your wives are going to feel pain in their belly. When you go pray to the gods, you will pray to the wife of Ak'inchob. This (prayer) is to request her help for your wives during childbirth.

Le' binet k'in tuworo(r) k'aax tuworo(r) ch'ikin bini(h). Yan ti' uyuutsta(r) ba'ik, yan ti' ut'änik k'uh, yan ti' upokik, yan ti' uts'ahik ma'ats', yan ti' uts'ahik ch'ur(h)a', ba'che'; yan ti' uts'ahik tuworo(r), k'ik', ba'inkin, hu'un. Ele bek kubin ku(r)tar."

This will be forever, throughout the entire forest however far the people have gone. They (will) have to give birth in this manner, they (will) have to pray to the gods, they (will) have to give offerings of posol, *ch'urha'*, balche'; they have to offer everything, rubber and whatever else, bark cloth. And so, this is the way it's going to be."

Ele bex ka'(ah) ts'o'oki(h) uyuutstar yok'o(r) chun put.

And so, this giving birth like this at the base of the papaya (tree) was finished.

Uyählehir Bah 'The Mole Trapper'

Bor Ma'ax

This is the story about the Mole Trapper's journey through the underworld where he witnesses what happens to the souls of the dead.[1]

Lured into the underworld by Kisin's daughter, the Mole Trapper travels through a landscape like the one on earth. The only difference is that time is turned upside down: when the Mole Trapper left the earth, the sun was setting, but when he went underground, the sun was rising.

He arrives at the house of Sukunkyum, the Lord of the Underworld. Because he arrives alive, Sukunkyum and his wife hide him from Kisin 'the Devil' and his sons, who can smell humans.[2] Sukunkyum's wife hides the Mole Trapper in a pot with a burning chili, to deter Kisin. When Sukunkyum returns after setting the sun on the eastern horizon, he learns that the Mole Trapper has arrived in human form. So, to mask his human scent, he gives the Mole Trapper one of his old tunics to put on.[3] He instructs the Mole Trapper on the ways of the underworld and orders him to spend time with Kisin to observe how he lives and works in Metlan 'Hell'.[4] Sukunkyum tells him that he must report all that he learns to his companions when he returns to the earth.

Shortly after his arrival in Metlan, the Mole Trapper transforms into a hummingbird. Kisin and his sons shoot him down, but Kisin's daughter snatches him up and hides him in her bed.

That night Kisin and his wife begin to sneeze (undoubtedly because the Mole Trapper still had chili residue on him).[5] They get up and discover a man in their daughter's bed. They are delighted to learn that they now have a son-in-law.[6]

The Mole Trapper begins his residence with his father-in-law, where he observes the ways of Kisin: his food is rotten, his tortillas are tree fungus, and his firewood is the bones of the dead. He learns that Kisin shoots the souls of humans while they sleep. These souls appear as monkeys swinging through the trees. The Mole Trapper also witnesses Kisin's methods of torturing the souls, which involve alternately burning them in his fires and freezing them in water, putting firebrands on their mouths and anuses, and turning the worst of them into his domestic animals.

The time to depart for the earth draws near and the Mole Trapper readies himself to exit. As the earth yawns open, the Mole Trapper jumps out. He thinks his wife is behind him, but she is still sweeping the house[7] when the earth snaps shut, stranding her in the underworld.[8] Saddened but undeterred, the Mole Trapper finds his people and reports all that he has witnessed in the underworld.

The story of the Mole Trapper is similar and yet different from the journey of the Hero Twins in the *Popol Vuh*, who descend into the underworld, slay the lords of the underworld, resuscitate their father, and then return to the earth. Both narratives include descriptions of the subterranean topography and the relationships between the underworld gods. Their experiences elucidate the limits and options of human beings and their interactions with the underworld gods. Both stories allude to Mayan eschatological beliefs in death and rebirth.

The two stories differ in the objectives the heroes fulfill. The Hero Twins set out to avenge the death of their father (and uncle), defeat the lords of the underworld, and resurrect their father. The Hero Twins are gods who participate in the creation of the world, such that the resuscitation of their father results in the emergence of the Maize God, the sustenance of humanity. In the end they ascend to the sky where they become the sun and the moon (or Venus).

By contrast, the Mole Trapper was lured into the underworld by the daughter of the Kisin and is compelled, rather than elects, to experience what happens to souls after they die, underscoring the importance of leading a moral life. As such, the story of the Mole Trapper is also a cautionary tale. Rather than a god, the Mole Trapper is a simple mortal who dies in the end.

PART 1. INTRODUCTION

Bay.

Okay.

Bähe' intsikba(r)tik utsikbar unukuch winik. Lati' be'ik utsikbar nukuch winik. Tuya'arah uyählehi(r) bah. Lati' woro(r) ukäxtik woro(r) bah. Ukäx-tik ti' ubin ulehik. Woro(r) k'in ubin ukäxtik ulehik uyo'och bah. Tanux maan ukäxtik uyo'och bah. Woro(r) la' kuchi'ik. Woro(r) la' kuhantik. Lahi(h) uki'ir uyo'och.

Now I'm going to tell the story about the ancestor. It is the same story the ancestors (tell). They called him the Mole Trapper. He is the one who searches for all the moles. He looks for them to trap. Every day he goes looking for and trapping his moles. He goes around looking for his moles. This is all he eats. He only eats this. This is his favorite food.

Bay.

Okay.

Pachi(r), tanux maan ukäxtik uyo'och bah. Ume(n)tik uleh. Uya(h)chuni(r) tulehah uyo'och bah. Yan (ti') ne kubin uyirik uleh, kubi(n) yan ti' yan. Ne tsoy uyor. "Bähe' yan inwo'och bah. Ne ki' inhanan. Ne tsoy inwor."

Then, he is looking for his moles daily. He sets his traps. In the beginning, he set his traps. Now he must go check his traps. When he goes, (the moles) are there. He is delighted. "Today I have my moles. My food is very tasty. I am very happy."

Bay. Woro(r) k'in, woro(r) k'in, sastar ukah bin ulehik uyo'och bah.

Okay. So every morning he goes to trap his moles.

Chen bikir k'uchi(h) tuk'in lahxupi(h) ubah. Tulahhantah tulahkinsah. Ubin uyirik uleh. Mäna'. Lahxupi(h) ahbah. Chen uleh yan, chen mixba'(ar), mix ahbah.

But then the day came when all his moles were finished. He (had eaten) them all. He (had) killed them all. He goes to check his traps. There aren't any. All the moles are finished. His traps are there but there aren't any moles.

"*Eh,*" nukuch winik, uyählehi(r) bah tutukrah ubäh.
"*Eh,*" the ancestor, the Mole Trapper, thought to himself.

"*Eh bik yani(r) mäna' inwo'och bah? Bähe' ba'i(n)ki(r) bin inhantik? Män(a') uki'ir inwo'och. 'Otsiren.*"
"*Why don't I have my moles? Now what am I going to eat? There isn't any (more) of my favorite food. Poor me.*"

Tuhuunar tan utukrik ubäh,
He is thinking to himself,

"*Aaah 'otsiren. Bähe' mäna' mix ba'(ar) inhantik. Mäna' inwo'och bah. 'Otsiren.*"
"*Aaah, poor me. Now there isn't anything for me to eat. I don't have my moles. Poor me.*"

Tutukrik ubäh,
He is thinking to himself,

"*Bik yani(r) mäna' inwo'och bah? Lahxupi(h). 'Otsiren.*"
"*Why don't I have any moles? They're all finished. Poor me.*"

Bay.
Okay.

Pachir, tuyirah ti' kura('an) ahchi'. Ti' kura('an) uche'i(r) ahchi'. Ne täk'än uwich. Tuyirah ne täk'än uwich. Na'ak ut'akik uwich umäk'ik. Ukäxtik uyirik uyan ne täk'än. Pachi(r) ut'akik umäk'ik.

Then, he saw a nance tree standing there. The fruit was very ripe. He saw that the fruit was very ripe. (So) he climbed up to pick the fruit and eat it. He searches for the ripest ones. Then he snaps them off (and) eats them.

"Bay. Ne ch'uhuk. Ne ki'."
"Okay. These are very sweet. They're very tasty."

Bay.
Okay.

Pachi(r), tuyeensik uwich nukuch winik t(i') uyaram. Tan utukrik ubäh,
Then, the ancestor looks down at the ground. He is thinking to himself,

"*Otsiren. Bähe' mäna' inwo'och bah. Bik yani(r) mäna'? 'Otsiren.*"
"Poor me. Now I don't have any food. Why don't I have any? Poor me."

Pachi(r), tuyirah häbäch uhoor a' lu'um. Tuhe'ah ubah a' lu'um uhoor. Pachir uhook'or (u)winik, ch'iktar. Nukuch winik uyählehi(r) bah kura('an). Tubi(h) ti' uyo'och bah. Tubi(h).
Then, he noticed a crack in the ground. The ground opened a little. Then a person comes out and stands up. The ancestor, the Mole Trapper, is sitting there. He forgot about his moles. He forgot.

Ch'ikikbar uwinik utichi(r). Ma' una'aksik uwich ka'(a)nan. Chen ch'ikikbar, uximba(r) chichin. Ha'ri' upäktik ti' lu'um.
The person stands up and approaches. She doesn't look up. She just stands there, (then) walks around a little. She only looks at the ground.

Pachi(r), uyirik uläkik uho'(or). Utsiktik uho'(or) yete(r) uxaache'. Uki'tsiktik uho'(or). Uki'tsiktik uho'(or). Pachi(r), uka'na(k)ku(n)tik uho'(or). Yan uho('o)r. Uyirik ch'uprar. Ne tsoy uwich.

Then, he sees her unfasten her head. She combs her hair. She combs her hair well. She combs her hair well. Then, she puts her head back on. She has her head (back on). She looks like a girl. She is very pretty.

"Oooh, ahch'uprar tinwirah! Ne tsoy uwich."
"Oooh, it's a girl I saw! She is so pretty."

Tan umäk'ik ahchi'. Tupurah uneek' ahchi' t(i') uho'(or). Tuch'inah. Utsa'ay-pah t(i') uho'(or) — BAP.

He is eating the nance fruit. He hurled a seed of the fruit at her head. He threw it. It hit her head — BAP.[9]

Mix tuna'asah uwich. Mix.

She never looked up. Never.

Uka'mäk'ik hump'e(r), uch'inik. Mix tuna'asah uwich.

He eats another (and) throws (the seed). She never looked up.

Unukuch winik uyählehi(r) bah tutukrah, *"Chen bik yani(r) ma' una'asik uwich? Ne tsoy uho'(or). Ki' tsiktik uho'(or) (ah)ch'uprar."*

The ancestor, the Mole Trapper, thought, *"But why doesn't she look up? Her hair is pretty. The girl combs her hair nicely."*

Pachi(r), uyirik uka'bin tuka'ten ti' kura('an) chan suuk. Tulakah. Tu-lakp(a)ytah ahsuuk. Ti' ka'(ah)bini(h) tuyirah yan uhoor. Ti' bini(h), en-tonse tuka'mäkah ubäh a' lu'um. Tuka'mäkah ubäh.

Then he sees her go (back) to where there is a tuft of grass. She loosened it (and) yanked the grass up. He noticed there was a door where she went. She went in, then the ground closed. It closed.

Bay.

Okay.

PART 2. THE MOLE TRAPPER'S JOURNEY THROUGH THE UNDERWORLD (PART 1)

Nukuch tutukrah ubäh, *"Eh, tinwirah ubin. Bay. Bähe' bin inkah 'eemer inkäx-tik inwirik. Poch inbin inwirik tu' bini(h)."*

The ancestor thought to himself, *"Eh, I saw her go. Now I'm going to go down (and) look for her. I want to go see where she went."*

Nukuch winik ts'o'ok umäk'ik ahchi'. Tub ti' uyo'och bah tuworo(r). Eemi(h) uyirik. Ubi(n) ukäxtik uyirik to'an tu bini(h). Lati' la' ch'uprar tuyirah ne tsoy uwich. Bin ukäxtik. Uyirik. Mäna'. Sa'atih. Ma' uyoher to'an.

The ancestor finished eating the nance. He forgot all about his moles. He went down to see (where she went). He goes to look where she went. The girl he saw was so beautiful. He goes to look for (the spot where she entered). He looks for it. It's not there. He (has) lost it. He doesn't know where it is.

"Mäna'. To'an? Ma' inyoher to'an."

"There isn't anything. Where is it? I don't know where it is."

Pachir, na'aki(h) tuka'ten t(i') uyirah. Bay. Bähe' ne ki' (u)yirah to'an suuk. Xok'or.

Then, he climbed up again to see. Okay. Now he sees clearly where the grass is. It is near.

"Bay. Bähe' bin inläkik. Bin inläkik inwireh wa to'an tu' bini(h)."

"Okay. Now I'm going to pull it out. I'm going to pull it out to see where she went."

Bay.

Okay.

Eemi(h) tuka'ten. Maan ukäxtik. Uka'maan ukäxtik. Uch'uyik chichin la' suuk tu' kura('an).

He (climbed) down again. He walks around looking for it. He walks through again and finds it.

(U)lahkäch; ulakar ahsuuk.

He lifts the grass a little bit; the grass all separates.

Bay.

Okay.

(U)yahlehi(r) bah nukuch winik ne tsoy uyor. "Inwirik bähe' ber. Yan inbin. Bähe' yan inbin inwirik tu' bini(h) a' la'e', la' winik tinwirah ch'uprar. Bähe' ti' kinbin inwirik tu' bini(h). Yan (u)ber." Ubin, nukuch winik uyählehi(r) bah ubin seeb.

The Mole Trapper is elated. "Now I see the path. I must go. Now I must go see where that person went, the female person that I saw. Now I will go there to see where she went. There is a path." The Mole Trapper goes quickly.

Pachi(r) uxim(b)a(r) ma' ne nach, uyirik seeb ukaxik ubäh yah uhe(r) lu'um. Uhe(r) lu'um; (u)k'in kutichir; ne hats'ka'.

After he (has walked) a short way, he quickly sees the land change. It is another land; the sun is (rising); it's early morning.

[Uyanchuni(r), uyählehi(r) bah mäna' k'in ka'(ah) tuyirah—ti' yan k'in ni'che'.]

[In the beginning, the Mole Trapper didn't see the sun; there wasn't any sun—the sun was at the tree tops (before he went underground).[10]]

Bay.

Okay.

Uxim(b)a(r) ma' ne naach. Pachir uyirik tan ukaxbar. Uyirik p'is be' chäkan. Ne äka('a)n. Yan k'in kutichir; ne hats'ka'.

He doesn't walk very far. Then he sees (the landscape) changing. He sees something like an old milpa; it's very flat. The sun is rising; it is early morning.

Bay.

Okay.

Tan uximba(r) nukuch winik. Tan ukäxtik tu' bini(h) a' ber. Tan uxim(b)a(r). Uxim(b)a(r) mas uyirik ti' yan nah. Mas bin(ih). Ne tsoy uyor.

The ancestor is walking along. He is looking for where the path went. He is walking along. He walks further (and) sees a house there. He walked on. He is very happy.

"Bähe' inbin inwirik mak," kih.

"Now I'm going to see people," he says.

Uk'uchur (ah)nukuch winik. Uk'uchur xok'or to'an nah. Ti' yan ulaak' usuku'un kyum. Uk'uchur uyählehi(r)bah xok'or to'an uhoor uyatoch. Ulaak' usuku'un kyum tan uhuuch'. Tan uhuch'ik uyo'och wah. Eh kupur(ik) uwich ulaak' usuku'un kyum.

The ancestor arrives. He gets close to the house. The wife of Sukunkyum is there. The Mole Trapper gets close to the door of the house. The wife of

Sukunkyum is grinding corn. She is grinding (corn for) tortillas. And the wife of Sukunkyum spots him.

"Ehhh. Tutichir inwaaro'. Eh, tukuxta(r)kih. Ma' kimen. Ma' sooreban (u)bäh,[11] ma'. T(an) ukuxta(r)kih kutichir."

"Ehhh. Our son approaches. Eh, he's alive. He's not dead. He hasn't shed his skin, no. He's alive when he comes."

Umasxok'or unuki(r) winik. Upur(ik) ut'an, "Taren."

The ancestor gets nearer. He calls out, "I have come."

"Eh, ko'ten paareh," ut'an una'ir usuku'un kyum.

"Eh, come here son," says the wife of Sukunkyum.

Bay.

Okay.

Uki'irik una'ir Sukunkyum,

Sukunkyum's wife looks at him closely,

"Ehhh. *Bähe' inwaaro' bäkän ma' tusoorentah ubäh; tukuxta(r)kih, bäkän. Bik kinbin inmee(n) ti'? Takeh ma' ti' yan äkyum. Ma' kura('an). Eh bay.*"

"Ehhh. *Our son hasn't shed his skin; he's still alive. What am I going to do with him? Our Lord is not here. Our Lord isn't here yet. He's not (at home). Very well then.*"

Tutukrah una'i(r) usuku'un kyum, "*Bähe' bik kinbin inmeen ti'? Porque Kisin ti' yan ne xok'or, ne xok'or, uyu'yik ubok nukuch winik. Ne seeb bin uyu'yik ubok. Ne xok'or.*"

Sukunkyum's wife thought, "*Now what am I going to do with him? Because Kisin is very near, very near, he can smell the ancestor's scent. Very soon they're going to smell his scent. They are very near.*"

[Yan ka'tuur mehen kisin.]

[There are two of Kisin's children.]

Una'i(r) usuku'un kyum ne yan utukur, *"Bähe', bik kinbin inme(n)tik ti(')*
inwaaro' bähe'? K'uchi(h), tukukuxta(r)ki(h) k'uchi(h)."

Sukunkyum's wife is clever, *"Now, how am I going to do it for our son? He ar-*
rived, he arrived alive."

Bähe' ti' kura('an) unukuch kum, ne nuk, tu' kuk'intik uyo'och ma'ats'. Tutukrah ubäh, *"Bähe' bin ink(ah) inkäxtik. Bik inme(n)tik, bik inta'akik inwaaro'?*
'Otsir."

A large pot is sitting there, a very big (one) in which she warms up posol.
She thought to herself, *"Now I'm going to look for it. How am I going to do it?*
How do I protect our child? The poor thing."

Äkna'i(r) usuku'un kyum ubin ukäxtik ukum. Tut'oh(ah) uyit ukum, ti'
ukänäntik nukuch winik.

Sukunkyum's wife goes to look for the pot. She struck (a hole in) the bottom of the pot, to guard the ancestor.

"Tarak kutar Kisin, ma' uyu'yik ubok."

"Even if the Kisins comes, they won't smell his scent."

Bay.

Okay.

Tumäka(h). Ne yan utukur äkna'i(r) usuku'un kyum. Tumäkah nukuch
winik yok'or kum. Chen Kisin ne xok'or kutar ka'tu(u)r. Äkna'i(r) usuku'un
kyum yan upak'ar ik t(i') upach uyatoch. T(i') useeb bin ut'akik upak'ar ik.

Tuk'eerah yok'or xämäch. Seebseeb tuk'eerah. Seebseeb tuk'eerah. Ubin uyähk'intik t(i') upach ukum tu' mäkan ahnukuch winik.

She shut him up (inside the pot). Sukunkyum's wife is smart. She shut up the ancestor in the pot. But Kisin is very close. The two of them are coming. Sukunkyum's wife has chili plants in the back of her house. Quickly she went and cut the chili plants. She toasted them on the griddle. Rapidly she toasted them. Rapidly she toasted them. She (was) going to warm them up first near the back of the pot, where the ancestor is sealed in.[12]

Hach ma' ne sahin, umehen Kisin kutichir,

In no time, (one of) the little Kisins approaches,

"Ba'inki(r) a' kubok, Chaxnuk? Ba'inki(r) a' kubok ich awatoch?"

"What smells, Chaxnuk?[13] What smells inside your house?"

Äkna'i(r) usuku'un kyum kunuukik, "Mäna' ba'(ar) kubok way. Tub(ah) in-harik ba'(ar) way, mäna' ba'(ar) way ich inwatoch."

Sukunkyum's wife replies, "There isn't anything that smells here. There is nothing here in my house."

"Ma' Chaxnuk. K'äs cha'eh inmaan. Ba'inki(r) a' kubok ich awatoch?"

"No, Chaxnuk. Please, let me come in. What smells in your house?"

"Ten mixba'(ar) a' way. Maanen käxtah awireh wa yan."

"I don't have anything here. Come in and search to see if there is anything."

Umaan Kisin. Yah ok. Ukäxtik tan umaan. Uk'uchur to'an (u)kum, *sniff-sniff-sniff*.

Kisin passes through. He (has) already entered. He searches the house. He is going around. He gets to the pot, *sniff-sniff-sniff*.

"Ba'inki(n) kubok ne xok'or, Chaxnuk? Eh, maane(n) u'ye(h) awu'ye(h) kuuchi(r) to'an kum."

"What smells near here, Chaxnuk? Come over and smell around where the pot is."

Ti' äka'an ik.

The chili is lying there.

Sniff-sniff-sniff.

(Kisin sniffs again) *sniff-sniff-sniff.*

AYYYCH! AYYYCH! AYYYCH! AYYYCH!

ACHOOO! ACHOOO! ACHOOO! ACHOOO!

"Chaxnuk! Ik! Ne ma' tsoyech. Takäräxme(n)ti(k)en!"

"Chaxnuk! Chilies! You're wicked. You hurt me!"

"Toh tech apochi(r) maan akäxtik. Tawa'a rah, 'Ti' yan way.'"

"You're the one who really wanted to come through to look for it. You said, 'It is here.'"

"Ma', Chaxnuk!"

"No, Chaxnuk!"

Bini(h) tuk'anah yok mehen Kisin. Bini(h).

The young Kisin sped away. He left.

Pachir, ma' ne sanih, huntuur utichir.

Then, a little later, the other one approaches.

"Ba'inki(r) kubok way Chaxnuk?" *Sniff-sniff-sniff.*
"What smells here, Chaxnuk?" *Sniff-sniff-sniff.*

"Mäna'. Mixba'(ar) way."
"There isn't anything. There's nothing here."

"Ma', Chaxnuk." *Sniff.*
"No, Chaxnuk." *Sniff.*

"Ti' yan way. Ne ki' ubok."
"It is here. It smells delicious."

"Mäna'."
"There isn't anything."

"K'as cha'eh inmaan inkäxtik."
"Please let me come through and look for it."

"Maanen."
"Come in."

Äkna'i(r) usuku'un kyum ne yan utukur,
Sukunkyum's wife is thinking hard,

"Bähe', uyu'yik ubok ik."
"Now, he (will) smell the scent of the chilies."

Maani(h) Kisin ich uyatoch. K'uchur to'an (u)kum.
Kisin passed through the house. He gets to the pot.

"Bik way unehook'or ubok? Ne ki'."

"How come a delicious aroma is coming from here?"

Kumasxak'ik uni' Kisin.

Kisin's nose comes nearer.

Sniff.

Sniff.

Beki(r).

The same thing happened.

AYYY! AYYY! AYYY!

ACHOOO! ACHOOO! ACHOOO!

"Chaxnuk! Ik!"

"Chaxnuk! Chilies!"

"Eh, tintoh'a'arah tech akäxt(eh) abah. Ten mana' ba'(ar) ich inwatoch."

"Well, I just told you to look for yourself. I don't have anything in my house."

Lati' bini(h) mehen Kisin ka'tu(u)r. Bini(h). Tuk'ana(r) (u)yok. Ne ma' ki' ubok ik.

That second little Kisin left. He left. He sped away. The smell of chilies was terrible.

Nukuch winik tan uch'e'extik uyu'yik. Ti' kura'(a)n ichir (u)kum. Mäkan ich (u)kum.

The ancestor is listening intently. He is sitting inside the pot. He is shut in the pot.

Bay.

Okay.

Ma' ne sahin Sukunkyum kuyu'(r). Kutichir Sukunkyum. Ka'ni(h) chichin.
Ti' tari(h) upurik a' k'in t(i') uchun ka'an. Tan uyu'(r).

A short time later Sukunkyum returns. Sukunkyum approaches. He was a
little bit tired. He has come back (from) putting the sun at the base of the
sky.[14] He is returning.

Äkna'i(r) usuku'un kyum tan uyuk'u(r)sik. Seeb upuk'ik ma'ats'. Tuyuk'u(r)sah äkna'i(r) usuku'un kyum. Tan uyuk'u(r)sik, seeb.

Sukunkyum's wife is (making) Sukunkyum a drink. Sukunkyum's wife
rapidly mixes the posol. Sukunkyum's wife gave it to him to drink. She
quickly gives him a drink.

Bay.

Okay.

Äkna'ir Sukunkyum tuya'arah ti',

Sukunkyum's wife said to him,

"Eh, bähe' k'uchi(h) inwaaro'. Tukuxta(r)ki(h) k'uchih. Ma' usoorenmah
ubäh, ma'. Tunahwinkiri(r)."

"Well, today our child arrived. He arrived alive. He hasn't shed his skin.
He's still a person."

Usuku'un kyum tunuukah,

Sukunkyum replied,

"Eh. Eh 'otsir. Tukuxta(r)ki(h). Tukuxta(r)ki(h). Ma' kimen. Ma' kimen—
tukuxtiki(h). Ma' usoorenmah ubäh, ma'. Tukuxta(r)ki(h). Eh bay. Tsoy. Eh
to'an?"

"Eh. The poor thing. He is alive. He is alive. He's not dead. He's not dead—he's alive. He hasn't shed his skin. He is alive. Okay. Where is he?"

"Ti' yan. Inmäkmah ich kum. Ti' yan. Inkänä(n)mah. Awoher yan Kisin, ne ma' tsoy mehen Kisin. T(an) ukäräxme(n)tik inwaaro'."

"He is here. I have closed him in the pot. He is there. I have protected him. You know that Kisin's children are around. They are wicked. They are bothering our child."

Sukunkyum, "Ne tah."

Sukunkyum replied, "That's the right thing to do."

Tunuukah,

He replied,

"Eh bay. Ne tsoy. Ne tsoy takänä(n)tah."

"Okay. That's very good. It's very good that you protected him."

PART 2. THE MOLE TRAPPER'S JOURNEY THROUGH THE UNDERWORLD (PART 2)

Bay.

Okay.

Sukunkyum uya'arik ti' ulaak',

Sukunkyum says to his wife,

"Bähe' ne ti' yan inwor. Bähe' inwaaro' uk'uchur way. Upuur ubäh tukux-ta(r)ki(h). Bähe' bin inkah inwe'esik ti' way. Bin ukah ukänik tuworo(r) ba' way yok'or yaram lu'um to'an Kisin, bik umeyah Kisin, bik umeyah way ten."

"Today I am pleased. Today our son (has) arrive(d) here. He jump(ed) in alive. Now I'm going to show it to him here. He is going to learn about everything (that happens) here in the underworld—where Kisin is, how he works, how he works here for me."

Äkna'i(r) Sukunkyum tuya'arah,
The wife of Sukunkyum said,

"Ne tsoy. Tech awoher."
"Very good. You know."

"Bay. Yan a(k)känä(n)tik."
"Okay. We have to protect him," (says Sukunkyum).

Unuki(r) winik uyählehi(r) bah tan uyu'yik utsikbar.
The Mole Trapper is listening to the conversation.

Una'i(r) usuku'un kyum tuya'arah,
Sukunkyum's wife said,

"Bik inme(n)tik? Yan ka'tu(u)ro' mehen Kisin ukäräxme(n)tik inwaaro'. Bik inme(n)tik? Ne yan ne ki' ubok. Ne yan ubok. Kisin ne ni' ukäxtik."
"How do I do it? There are two Kisin boys (that) bother our son. How do I do it? He really smells good (to them). He really smells. Kisin has a good nose for finding him."[15]

Sukunkyum tutukrah ubäh,
Sukunkyum thought,

"*Bähe' yan inlä'xikur ints'ahik ti'.*"
"*I have my old tunic that I can give him for a while.*"

Unook' unukuch winik yan ti' upitik ti' up'o'ah ti' yete(r) k'urta'an yete(r) ik, tumen ti' uluk'ur ubok. Ulä'nook' usuku'un kyum, lahi(h) tumahantah (ti') uyählehi(r) bah. Tumahantah tumen ten ma' uyu'yah ubok.

As for the clothes of the ancestor, he should take them off so that they can be washed with quick lime and chilies, because this will remove his scent. The old tunic of Sukunkyum, this he loaned to the Mole Trapper, because it didn't have any scent.

Nukuch winik tan ulahu'yik utsikbar usuku'un kyum äkna'i(r) usuku'un kyum. Tan ulahu'yik. Känänta('a)n ti' yan ich kum, uyählehi(r) bah tan ulahu'yik tuworo(r) utsikba(r) usuku'un kyum (yeter?) (u)äkna'i(r) usuku'un kyum.

The ancestor is listening to Sukunkyum and his wife. He is listening to everything. Protected in the pot, the Mole Trapper is listening to everything Sukunkyum and his wife say.

Bay.
Okay.

Sukunkyum tan ukäxtik unook' ti' umahantik ti' unuki(r) winik ti' ubukintik. Tuts'aah.
Sukunkyum is looking for his tunic to lend to the ancestor for him to put on. He gave it (to him).

Bay.
Okay.

Äkna'i(r) usuku'un kyum bin up'o'ik unook' nukuch winik yete(r) k'urta'an.
Sukunkyum's wife goes to wash the ancestor's clothes in quick lime.

Bay.

Okay.

Okih k'in, tubukintah unook' usuku'un kyum unuki(r) winik. Oki(h) k'in.
Hach mäna' a' k'in; tan ubin ni'che' k'in.

At sunset, (the ancestor) dressed in Sukunkyum's tunic. It is sunset. There
is hardly any sun; the sun is (down) at the tree tops.

"Usuku'un kyum tint'an lati' unook'."

"I think this is Sukunkyum's tunic."

Tubukintah. Nukuch winik oki(h) t(i') uts'unu'.

He put it on (and) the ancestor turned into a hummingbird.

Bin t(i') uts'unu'ni(r). Ne ya'ax.

He turned into a hummingbird. He is very blue.

Bini(h) t(i') uyuk'ik utop'che'.

He went to drink (from) the flower(s).

Tan umaan uyuk'ik utop'che'. Ti' kumaan. Uk'aba' ahya'ax pos.

He is going around drinking the flowers. He is going around. He is called
ya'ax pos.[16]

Ma taak'ih uwich uyirik tan umaan a' ya'ax pos.

(The two kisins) spot the ya'ax pos passing by.

"Ne tsoy."

"How pretty."

Tan umaan uyuk'ik utop'che'. Uhook'or ut'an uti'a'ar Kisin,
He is going around drinking the flowers. The sons of Kisin shout,

"Inwähya'ax pos!"
"It's my ya'ax pos!"

"To'an?" kunuukik huntuur.
"Where is it?" the other replies.

"La' kumaan," kih.
"He's passing by," (the first one) says.

"Ah!" kih. "To'an?"
"Oh!" says (the other). "Where?"

"La' kumaan. Inwähya'ax pos."
"He is passing by. It's my ya'ax pos."

"Bik awähya'ax pos? Ma'," kih. "Inbin inchi'ik! Ne ki'. Inbin inki'sasa(r)chi'tik."
"How is he your ya'ax pos? No (he's not)," he says. "I'm going to eat him! He's very tasty. I'm going to eat him bones and all."

"Eh hah," kih. "To'an? Taaseh ten inharar. Taasheh inharar."
"Uh-huh," (the other) says. "Where is he? Bring me my bow and arrows. Bring my bow and arrows."

Uteto' Kisin kunuukik, "To'an? Ba'(in)k(ir) awirik?"
The kisins' father (says), "Where is he? What do you see?"

"Inwähya'ax pos," kih.
"It's my ya'ax pos," he says.

"To'an?"

"Where?"

Uteto' Kisin ti' chara'an ti' uxuur uchi' uk'ak'. Ne ch'iha('a)n. N-e-e-e nu-xi(b). Ne ch'iha'(a)n. Ti' chara'(a)n (ti' u)xuur uchi' uk'ak'. Tan ulik'ir uteto' Kisin.

The kisins' father is lying down at the edge of the fire. He's very old. He's v-e-e-e-ry old. He's ancient. He is lying down at the edge of the fire. The kisins' father is getting up.

"To'an?" kih. "Hah! Eens(eh) ten inharar. Taaseh inharar."

"Where is it?" he says. "Aha! Bring me down my bow and arrows. Bring my bow and arrows."

Uch'uprar uti'a'ar Kisin la' mak tutaasah. Lati' ti' yan ne xok'or to'an tu' kumaan ahts'unu' ya'ax pos. Ne xok'or ti'. Ne poch uchukik. Lahlik'i(h) ka'tu(u)r mehen Kisin. Lati' yan poch uchukik.

Kisin's daughter is the one who brought them. She is very close to where the ya'ax pos is moving about. She is very close to him. She really wants to catch him. Both the kisin (boys) got up. They really want(ed) to catch it.

Bay.

Okay.

Uyahahteto' Kisin tan upur(i)k ut'an ti' uti'a'ar uch'uprar,

Their ancient father, Kisin, is calling out to his daughter,

"Xen! Taas(eh) inharar t(i') inhurik, t(i') insäsärchi'tik. He' inhanan!"

"Go! Bring my bow and arrows so I can shoot it, so I can eat it bones and all. Here is my food!"

Uk'anik (u)yok to'an uharar Kisin. Tutaasah ti' seeb. Tuhurah. Maanih uk'orhurtik. Cheeri(h)—p'ih.

She runs off to where Kisin's bow and arrows are. She quickly brought them to him. He shot an arrow. It grazed (the hummingbird). He fell—plunk.

Ne seeb uch'uprar uti'a'ar Kisin, ne seeb tuchukah uyählehi(h) bah. Seeb tuchukah.

Quickly, Kisin's daughter grabbed the Mole Trapper. She grabbed it quickly.

Utar huntuur ka'tu(u)r uxirar (u)ti'a'ar Kisin,

One of the two kisin boys comes over,

"Ten! Ts'ah(eh) ten!"

"It's mine! Give it to me!"

"Ma'. Bik ints'ah(i)k tech?"

"No. Why should I give it to you?"

Uputs'ur uti'a'ar Kisin. Uputs'ur seeb.

Kisin's daughter runs away. She runs away quickly.

"K'as ts'ah(eh) ten," uteto' kunuukik. "Ts'ah(eh) ten t(i') inchi'ik."

"Please, give it to me," their father (says). "Give it to me to eat."

"Ma'! Ma' ints'a(h)ik."

"No! I won't give it."

Uputs'ur uch'uprar (u)ti'a'ar. (U)känäntik. Puts'(ih) tuk(')anah (u)yok.

His daughter runs away. She protects it. She ran away.

(U)yahahteto' Kisin, ma' ha(ch) tsoy yor. Ma', ma' ts'aabir ti'. Uch'uprar uti'a'ar, lahi(h) ne seeb lap'(ih) uk'äb uchukik a' ts'unu'. Ya'ax pos ne tsoy uyirik, ne tsoy. Eh uti'a'ar uch'uprar Kisin ne tsoy uyor.

Their ancient father, Kisin, isn't very happy (that) it wasn't given to him. As for his daughter, she snatched up the hummingbird in her hands. She loves the ya'ax pos very much. Kisin's daughter is very happy.

"Yan inwähts'unu'."

"I have my pet hummingbird."

Ok(ih) k'in, ti' kumaan uch'uprar (u)ti'a'ar Kisin. Tan uyuk'u(r)sik käxtik utop'che'. Tan ukänäntik.

It is late afternoon (and) Kisin's daughter is walking around. She is giving it a drink from the flowers she finds.[17] She is taking care of him.

Bay.

Okay.

Kisin, uyahahteto', tub ti'. Tucha'ah uch'uprar uti'a'ar t(i') ukänänt(ik). P'isi(r) uxirar ubäho'. Lahtub ti' uyo'och ahts'unu'. Binih.

Kisin, their ancient father, forgot about him. He let his daughter take care of it. Same for her brothers. They forgot all about their hummingbird. They left.

Bay.

Okay.

Oki(h) k'in, mäna' 'aak'ä'chahi(r), uch'uprar uti'a'ar Kisin tuchukah la' chan ts'unu'. Tukänäntah. Tukäxtah ubooxir. Tu but'ah yok'or ubooxi(r).

Tuki'chantapah. Tuch'a'ah ti' uwenen yeter. Ket charakbar tuxaax. Ne 'otsi(r) yirik.

At sunset, it's not dark (yet), Kisin's daughter took the little hummingbird. She cared for him. She looked for a gourd bowl. She put him in the bowl. She wrapped him up well. She took it to sleep with her there. They lie down together. He is dear to her.

. . . Chen k'uchi(h) ma' ne sah(i)n uyaak'ä'chah(ar). A' sah(i)n uyaak'ä'-chah(ar). Uteto' Kisin ti' chara'(a)n t(i') uwenen (ti' u)xuur uchi' uk'ak'. Ulaak' ahKisin, ne ch'iha'(a)n. Lähcharanchar. P'isi(r) ubäho' ahKisin— uka't(uu)ro' la' mak kutookik akpixan. Lah ti' yan.

. . . And soon night fell. Soon night fell. Their father, Kisin, is lying down to sleep at the edge of the fire. Kisin's wife is very old. They're lying side by side. The same goes for Kisin's companions[18]—the two who burn our souls. They're all there.

Bay.

Okay.

(U)yahahteto' ti' chara'(a)n lehi(h), yan lik'(ih) uyahahteto',

Their ancient father gets up sneezing,

"AAYCH! AAYCH! AAYCH! AAYCH!" hook'or uyahaht'an uteto'.

"ACHOOO! ACHOOO! ACHOOO! ACHOOO!" booms their father.

"Ehhh."

"Ehhh."

Eh, kulik'i(r) ulaak' ahKisin, kulik'i(r),

Then, Kisin's wife gets up,

AACH! AACH!

ACHOOO! AACHOO!

"Eh ne tak inxeeh, ne tak."
"Eh, I'm about to vomit."

Eh, kutubu(r) ut'an uyahahteto' Kisin,
Their father Kisin exclaims,

"Eh! Inhaan! Eh, inhaan!"
"Eh! It's my son-in-law! Eh, it's my son-in-law!"

Eh uyixkit (ku)tubur ut'an,
And his mother-in-law (Kisin's wife) exclaims,

"Ehhh! Akhaan. Bik (u)yirah uwich akhaan."
"Ehhh! He is our son-in-law. It looks like he's our son-in-law."

Seebseeb ulik'ir yaaka' uyireh tu' chara'(a)n tu' kuwenen uch'uprar uti'a'ar Kisin. Kulik'i(r) yireh ti' chara'(a)n.
They scramble up and run over to look at him where Kisin's daughter lies sleeping. They get up to see him lying there.

Tuya'arah,
They said,

"Ma', ma' ts'unu'. Ok(ih) t(i') uwiniki(r)."
"He's not a hummingbird anymore. He (has) turned into a person."

Winik chara'(a)n t(i') uxaax uti'a'ar Kisin.

It's a person lying next to Kisin's daughter.

"Eh hah. Inhaan. Tinwirah inhaan."

"It's true. He's my son-in-law. I (see) my son-in-law."

Ne tsoy uyor uyahahteto' Kisin. Ne ne tsoy uyor,

Their ancient father, Kisin, is elated. He's elated,

"Yan inhaan bähe'."

"I have a son-in-law now."

"Eh hah," upurik ut'an ti' ulaak'. "Yan akhaan. Eh hah. Yan akhaan."

"Ah yes," his wife says. "We have a son-in-law. That's true. We have a son-in-law."

"Eh, eh bay." Ne tsoy uyor.

"Eh, very well, " (they say). They're very happy.

Bay.

Okay.

Nukuch winik, mäna' ubok. Yah lahluk'i(h) ubok tuworo(r). Mäna', mix umehen Kisin, mäna' ma' uk'äräxme(n)tik.

The ancestor doesn't have any scent. All his scent (had) already (been) removed. There wasn't any trace of it. None of them, not even the little kisins, bother him anymore.

Ka't(uu)ro' mehen kisin, lati' kutookiko'on akpixan, ma' uk'äräxme(n)tik k'axpah(ih) ubok—mäna' ubok; lahluk'i(h).Tuwaaysah ubäh t(i') uts'unu'ir.

The two little kisins, the ones who burn our souls, they don't harm him (because) his scent was changed—he had no scent; it was erased. He (had) turned himself into a hummingbird.

Bay.

Okay.

Saasi(r), nukuch winik tutoha'arah ti' usuku'un kyum:

In the morning, the ancestor (recalled) Sukunkyum's warning:

"Ma' ahantik uyo'och Kisin, ma'. Tarak kawirik uts'a(h)ik tech, wa wah, wa bu'ur, ma' (a)hantik. Wa ma'ats', ma' hantik ma' awuk'ik."

"Don't eat the food of Kisin, don't. Although you see him give it to you, be they tortillas or beans, you don't eat it. If it is posol, you don't eat it, you don't drink it."

Unuki(r) winik uyählehi(r) bah tutohtukrah tuworo(r). Ma' tuhantah uyo'och Kisin. Eh . . . ti' kubin t(i') uhana(n) to'an usuku'un kyum. Ti' kubin t(i') uhana(n).

The ancestor, the Mole Trapper, had already thought about all this. He didn't eat Kisin's food. So . . . he goes to eat at Sukunkyum's (house). He goes there to eat.

Kuhantik hach o'ochi(r). Ne ki'. Ne ki' mena'(an). Uyo'och Kisin, ma' ki'. Woro(r) bu'ur kuhantik uye'(er) ya'axkech. Wa wah lati' ukuxumche'. Woro(r) ma'ats' lati' aktu'i(r)e'ex. Leh(ih) uhana(n). Lehi(h) uyuk'ur: tu'i(r) winik.

He eats proper food. It's very tasty. It's very well prepared. Kisin's food is terrible. All the beans he eats are maggots. If they're tortillas, they are tree fungus. All the posol is our rotten (flesh). This is his food. That's his drink: rotting people.

[Bahik utsikba(r)tah (ah)nuki(r) winik. Bahik utsikba(r)tah.]
[That's what the ancestors say. That's what they say.]

Bay. Uyählehi(r) bah, tulahu'yah utsikbar usuku'un kyum. Ma' tuhantah yo'och wah Kisin mix tuhantah uyo'och Kisin. Xurbah (bexir) a'arah ti':

Okay. The Mole Trapper listened to Sukunkyum's advice. He didn't eat the Kisin's tortillas. He didn't eat any of Kisin's food. He obeyed what was said to him:

"(U)yo'och Kisin, ma' ahantik. Ä(k)kunteh awireh. Kusaastar, kabin awirik ba'inki(r) uyo'och Kisin."

"Don't eat Kisin's food. Set it down and look at it. In the morning, you're going to see what Kisin's food is."

Eh, nukuch winik, tuyä(k)kuntah uyo'och Kisin.

So, the ancestor set down Kisin's food.

Saasi(r), kuyirik eh tuhahir. Usuku'un kyum ne tah tuya'arah, "Ma' ahantik. Woro(r) kuxumche'. Woro(r) bu'ur ahya'axkech, uye'e(r) ya'axkech, nok'or. Eh woro(r) ma'ats' aktu'i(r)e'ex'."

In the morning, he sees that it is true. Sukunkyum was right (when) he said, "Don't you eat it. It's nothing but tree fungus. All the beans are maggots. All the posol is our rotting flesh."

Saasi(r), tuhahir, tuyirah. Tutukrah ubäh (u)yählehi(r) bah, *"Lati' tuhahir. Ne tah tuya'arah ten ma' tinhantah uyo'och Kisin. Hach tuhahir. Ne tah."*

In the morning, he saw that it was true. The Mole Trapper thought to himself, *"It's really true. He was right when he told me not to eat the food of Kisin. It's true. He was right."*

Bay

Okay.

Uyählehi(r) bah bini(h) to'an usuku'un kyum. Ti' kubin tuhana(n), ti' kuyuk'ur ti'. Usuku'un kyum ma' uhantik tu'i(r) winik. Ma' uhantik ukuxumche'. Ma' uhantik. Tuworo(r) hach ne ki' o'ochi(r) kuhantik.

The Mole Trapper goes to (the house of) Sukunkyum. He goes there to eat
(and) drink there. Sukunkyum doesn't eat rotting people. He doesn't eat
tree fungus. He doesn't eat it. All the food he eats is very tasty.

Bay.

Okay.

Sukunkyum yan utsikbar yete(r) nuki(r) winik (u)yählehi(r) bah. Yan utsikbar yete(r),

Sukunkyum must speak to the Mole Trapper. He must speak to him,

"Eh, paareh bähe' tawirah, bik umeyah Kisin. Tawirah ba'inki(r) uhana(n)
Kisin. Tawirah. Bin awirik paareh ma' ts'o('o)kok. Bin awirik. Ma' ts'o('o)kok
awirik. Ba'i(n)k(ir) kabin awirik way umeyah Kisin. Bin awirik ba'i(n)ki(r)
(k)uki'xit'ik: bin awirik ahKisin, mehen Kisin ka'(ah) bin ukäxtik uyo'och
bäk'. Abin alahkänik tuworo(r). He' abin awirik tuworo(r) ba'inki(r) umeyah Kisin way yok'o(r) (u)yaram lu'um. Bin awirik bik yirah. Bin alahkänik
tuworo(r). Yan alahirik."

"So son, now you saw it, what the work of Kisin is. You saw what Kisin
eats. You saw it. You are going to see that it's not over yet. You are going to
see it. You haven't seen it all. What you are going to see here is the work
of Kisin. You are going to see what unfolds: you are going to see it when
the little kisins look for their meat. You are going to learn all about it. You
will go and see everything that Kisin does here in the underworld. You are

going to see what it looks like. You are going to learn all about it. You have to observe everything."

Uyählehi(r) bah tutukrah ubäh,
The Mole Trapper is thinking to himself,

"Ne tsoy. Ne tsoy inlahkänik."
"Very good. Very good, I (will) learn it all."

Bay.
Okay.

Päytan, unuki(r) winik bini(h) t(i') upach Sukunkyum tu' ubin upurik k'in.
First, the ancestor followed Sukunkyum to where he goes to throw down the sun.

Bahik utsikba(r)tah uchik: Usuku'un kyum lati' ukuchik a' k'in ubisik to'an uchun ka'(a)n. Lehi(h) kukänäntik k'in; lehi(h) kubisik chun a' ka'(a)n. Kubin hats'ka', upurik k'in (u)chun ka'(a)n. Kubin k'in kubin ukäxtik usuku'un kyum. Lehi(h) umeyah usuku'un kyum.

This is how they (the ancestors) recounted the story before: Sukunkyum is the one who carries the sun on his back and takes it to the base of the sky. He takes care of the sun; he carries it to the base of the sky. At daybreak, he throws down the sun at the base of the sky. When the sun goes down, Sukunkyum goes to find it. This is Sukunkyum's job.[19]

Bay.
Okay.

Unuki(l) winik tuyirah bini(h) t(i') upach. Bini(h) t(i') upach usuku'un kyum. (U)känik (u)yirik bik umeyah, bik upurik k'in, bik ubin uch'a'ik.

The ancestor saw him; he followed Sukunkyum. He learns about it. He sees how he works, how he throws down the sun, how he goes and takes it (through the underworld).

[Be'ik tutsikba(r)tah la' k'in, winik. K'in winik p'is to'one'ex, chen ha'ri' ma' uxim(b)a(r). Usuku'un kyum kubin uk'ochik. Utaaseh. Bek tutsikbar(r)tah unuki(r) winik.]

[They said that the sun is a person. The sun is a person, like us, only it doesn't walk. Sukunkyum carries the sun on his shoulder. He brings it (across). This is what the ancestors said.]

Bay.

Okay.

(U)yählehi(r) bah tuyirah bik umeyah usuku'un kyum. Lahi(h) umeyah.

The Mole Trapper saw how Sukunkyum works. This was his work.

Bay.

Okay.

Usuku'un kyum tuya'arah,

Sukunkyum said,

"Tint'an sama(r), paar'eh, kabin awirik. Abin ti' upach uti'a'ar Kisin. Bin awirik ba'inki(r) kubin uhurik. Sama(r) ba'inki(r) kubin ukinsik uyo'och Kisin. T(an) awirik. T(an) akänik."

"I think that tomorrow, son, you're going to see it. You (will) follow the sons of Kisin. You are going to see what they shoot at, what the food of Kisin (will be) (that) they kill tomorrow. You (will) see it. You (will) learn about it."

Uyählehi(h) bah tutukrah ubah,

The Mole Trapper is thinking to himself,

"*Bay. Yan inbin inwirik ba'inkin kubin ukäxtik, Kisin uyo'och bäk', ba'inki(r) uhurik saman.*"

"*Okay. I have to go and find out what game the kisins are going to find and shoot tomorrow.*"

PART 2. THE MOLE TRAPPER'S JOURNEY THROUGH THE UNDERWORLD (PART 3)

Saasi(r) bini(h) yete(r), bini(h) t(i') uxim(b)a(r). Yan ka'tu(u)ro' mehen Kisin. Bin ukäxtik. Nukuch winik uyählehi(r)bah ubin t(i') upach. Ubin t(i') upach (u)ti'a'ar Kisin.

In the morning, he went with them. They went for a walk. There are the two small kisin boys. He goes to look for them. The ancestor, the Mole Trapper, follows, he follows Kisin's sons.

Ma' unenaachtar, ma' ne naach ubin uyirik utichir ma'ax, tichir k'ä' che'. Ch'uyirak kutar. Ne pim. Umehen Kisin tan uyirik, tan ukäxtik to'an mas kaba(r) kutar, ti' uhurik. Ma' chen uyirik, ne ka'ana(r) ma' uk'uchur uhär-är.[20]

He does not go very far, he does not go very far (when) he sees monkeys coming, coming (through) the tree branches. They come swinging. There are a lot. The little kisins are looking at them, they are looking for (those that) come lower, to shoot them. But they don't see them (because) they are too high (and) the arrows don't reach them.[21]

[Lati' be'ik tutsikba(r)tah nukuch winik: Wa to'one'ex ka'(ah) kmakik a(k)k'ane'ex ne ka'ana(n), wa akwene(n) akpixan kuyirik ahKisin. Ne kaba(r) a' wa ne kaba(r) a(k)k'an akch'ukintik ke wen(e)ko'one'ex akpixan, umaan yaram lu'um uyiriko'on ne ka'ana(n) ahKisin. Ma' uk'uchur uhurik ne ka'ana(n) kumaan. Ne ka'ana(n) tach'ukintah kan, lah ma'ax ne kaba(r) kutichir. Ne kaba(r) ne seeb uhurik.]

[It's like the ancestors said: If we tie our hammocks very high (when) we are sleeping, Kisin sees our souls. If we hang our hammocks very low, when we are sleeping our souls pass through the underworld, Kisin sees us (as being) very high. His arrows do not hit them (because) our souls are passing by very high. You hang your hammock very high, all the monkeys appear very low and Kisin quickly shoots them.]

[Lah mix mäk bähe'. Wa yan k'an, aki'ch'u(y)kintik ma' ne ka'(a)na(n) tumen wa akwene(r), ka('ah) kwene(r), akpixan yaram lu'um kuyirik Kisin ne ka'(a)na(n), ma' uhurik. Ti' yan huntu(u)r, huntu(u)r tutsikbar ne ka'(a)na(n) uk'an tuch'ukintah, tuhurah Kisin. Tuhurah, lubi(h). Tuchi'ah.]

[Nobody today (sleeps in a hammock). If there is a hammock, we don't hang it very high because, when we sleep, Kisin sees our souls in the underworld (as being) very high (and) he can't shoot them. There was a (person), one they said (who) hung his hammock high (and) Kisin shot him. He shot him (and) he fell. Then he ate him.][22]

Bay.

Okay.

Uyählehi(r) bah, (u)yirik, bik uyirik a'arah ti', tukänah.

The Mole Trapper, he sees it, he sees it just like it was told to him (and) he learned it.

"Bähe' awirik," Sukunkyum tuya'arah. "Bähe' yan akänik. Awirik tukinsah ma'ax Kisin huntu(u)ri' Tukinsah. Bay. Huntu(u)ri' tukinsah, huntu(u)ri'.

Bay. Bähe' … awirik … bik uk'uchur akpixane'ex. 'Oxp'e(r) k'in kuk'uchur. La' tawirah Kisin, tuhurah ma'ax, tuhurah akpixane'ex. 'Ooxp'e(r) k'in mäna' umaan uk'uch(ur) akpixane'ex way. Yan ti' ach'uktik hats'ka'."

"Now you (have) see(n) it," Sukunkyum said. "Now you have to learn it. You (have) see(n) (that) Kisin killed a monkey. He killed it. Okay. He killed one of them. Okay. Now … you (will) see how … how our soul arrives. It (will) arrive in three days. You saw that (when) Kisin shot the monkey he shot our soul. In three days, without fail, our soul (will) pass through and arrive here. You must wait for it at dawn."

Uyählehi(r) bah tuch'uktah. Ti' bini(h) uch'ukteh to'an uyatoch usuku'un kyum. Hach tuhahir, ne hats'ka' kura('a)an uch'uktik uyählehir bah ti' uyirik wa'an be(r) tan utich(ir). Hach tuhahir, 'ooxp'e(r) k'in, ma' maani(h), kutichir a(k)pixane'ex. Yan uba'ay. Yan tuworo(r) pooxa(r).[23] Ch'a'ban tuworo(r) ba'(ar) (ku)tichir. Tah kutar to'an uyatoch usuku'un kyum. K'uchur ch'iktar to'an ho(o)r uyatoch.

The Mole Trapper waited for it. He went to wait at Sukunkyum's house. True enough, at dawn he sits and waits (at) Sukunkyum's and he sees it approaching on the road. True enough, (in) three days, without fail, our soul approaches. It has its net bag. It has all its shoulder bags. All its things are carried with it (when) it approaches. It comes directly to Sukunkyum's house. It arrives (and) stands at the door of his house.

"Ehhh," Äkna'e'ex t(i') usuku'un kyum tan uki'irik.

"Ehhh," Our Lady of Sukunkyum is looking at our soul very carefully.

"Ehhh, kutichir, apixane'ex. Ehhh usooremah ubäh. Ma' kuxta(r)k(ih)."

"Ehhh, our soul approaches. Ehhh, it has shed its skin. It's not alive."

Uyählehi(r) bah tan uyirik tuworo(r).

The Mole Trapper is watching it all.

Äkna'i(r) usuku'un kyum,

Sukunkyum's wife (says),

"Eh, bähe' inwaaro', usooremah (u)bäho', usooremah (u)bäho'. Ma' t(an) ukuxta(r)ki(h). Kimen."

"Eh, as for our child, now he has shed his skin. He's not alive. He's dead."

Uki'irik.

She peers at it.

"Mäna' ma' yaab uk'ak'ir. Mäna' usi'ipir. He' uhook'or ti' kubin ti' uyits'(i)no', wa ti' Mensäbäk, wa ti' Itsana(r), ti' kubin."

"There aren't many sins. There aren't any crimes. It will leave (the underworld) to go (live with) its brothers and sisters, or it will go to Mensäbäk or to Itsanal."

Tuworo(r) ulahirik.

She looks it all over over.

[Usuku'un kyum, ma' ti' yan. Bin upurik (a') k'in.]

[Sukunkyum isn't there. He went to put down the sun.]

Äkna'e'ex tan uki'yirik ne 'uts, mäna' uk'ak'ir yaab.

Our Lady is inspecting it (to see if the soul is) good, that it has not committed many sins.

Eh, uyaksik uts'ahik uk'anche' ti'.

Then, she invites it in (and) gives it a seat.

"Oken ku(r)ta(r) yok'or ink'anche'."

"Come in and sit down on my bench," (she says).

"Eh bay."

"Thank you," (it says).

Akpixane'ex uyokor ku(r)ta(r) yok'o(r) k'anche'. Uyokor, uku(r)ta(r). Äk-na'i(r) (u)Sukunkyum upuk'ik ma'ats'. Uts'ahik ti'.

Our soul goes in (and) sits down on the bench. It enters (and) sits down. Sukunkyum's wife mixes posol. She gives it to it.

"Uk'eh."

"Drink it."

"Bay."

"Thank you."

Bay.

Okay.

Ma' ne santa(r), Kisin kutichir. Yan uni'. Ne seeb uyu'yik. (U)tichir Kisin. Ne seeb utar.

Soon the (two) kisin(s) approach. They have good nose(s). They smell it instantly. The kisin(s) approach. They come quickly.

"Ba'i(nkir) ubok way?" *Sniff-sniff.*

"What smells here?" *Sniff-sniff.*

"Eh mäna'."

"It's nothing," (says Sukunkyum's wife).

Ti' yan. (U)k'uchur kura('a)n akpixane'ex; kura('a)an tan uyuk'ur ma'ats'.
It is there. Our soul is sitting there; it is sitting there drinking posol.

"Ts'aaah(eh) ten!" tuk'atah ti' äkna'i(r) usuku'un kyum. "Ts'aaah(eh) ten!"
"Giiive it to me!" they (say) to Sukunkyum's wife. "Giiive it to me!"

Unuuki(k) una'i(r) usuku'un kyum,
The wife of Sukunkyum replies,

"Mäna'. Mäna' ints'ahik tech. Ma' ti' (yan) äkyum."
"No. I won't give it to you. Our Lord (Sukunkyum) isn't here."

"Eh ma'. K'as ts'ah(eh) ten. K'as ts'ah(eh) ten. Seeb k'as ts'ah(eh) ten."
"Eh, no. Please give it to me. Please give it to me. Please give it to me quickly."

Poch uhi(i)tik. Poch uhi(i)tik t(i') ukura('a)an.
They want to drag it out. They want to drag it from where it is seated.

Äkna'i(r) Sukunkyum ma' uk'a(')t.
Sukunkyum's wife doesn't want to.

"Ma'. Ma' ti' yan äkyum."
"No. Our Lord isn't here."

"Ts'ah(eh) ten."
"Give it to me!"

"Ma'."
"No."

Ma' ubin uti'a'ar Kisin. Ka'tu(u)ro' ti'a'ar Kisin ne poch uch'a'ik ubisik ti' utookik ich k'ak'.

Kisin's children don't leave. The two kisins want very much to grab (the soul) and bring it back to burn it in the fire.

Bay. Uyoher ka'nan una'i(r) usuku'un kyum.

Okay. They realize that Sukunkyum's wife is tired.

"Bay. Ch'a'eh pero awoher ma' tech yani(r). (U)yits'ino' yani(r)."

"Okay," (she says). "Take it but you know it's not yours. It belongs to (Sukunkyum's) brothers."[24]

Kisin seeb uch'a'ik ubisik. Seebseeb ubisik uhiitik. Seebseeb. Ne tsoy (u)yor, "Ko'ox!"

The kisins grab it swiftly and take it away. Rapidly they grab it and drag it out. They are elated, "Let's go!"

Uk'uchu(r) to'an k'ak' Metlan.

They get to the fires at Metlan.

(U)purik yok'o(r) k'ak' — PFFF.

They throw it into the fire — PFFF.

"Ahhh, ne yah. Inweere(r)!"

"Ahhh, it hurts. I'm burning!"

— PFFF —

— PFFF —

"Ne yah aweere(r)?"

"Does the burning really hurt you?"

Toh ti' kura('a)an ukuumi(r) sisiis ha' — PFFF —
Right there is a pot of freezing cold water — PFFF — (they dunk it in)

"Ahhh, ne siis, ne siis!"
"Ahhh, it's cold, it's cold!"

Tuka'ten, ich k'ak'.
Again, into the fire.

"Ayyy, ne chakar!"
"Ayyy, it's hot!"

"Ne chakar te', siis ha' (te')."
"It's very hot there; it's cold (here)," (the kisins say).

"Ahhh, ne siis!"
"Ahhh, it's very cold!" (screams the soul).

Lati' umeyah Kisin. Uyählehi(r) bah tuyirik.
That is the work of Kisin. The Mole Trapper sees it.

Bay.
Okay.

Seebseeb uyeere(r). Tulahma(n)sah.
Very quickly they burn it. They passed it back and forth (from the fire to the water).

Seeb, akpixane'ex uyawat. Uyawat, "Ayyy, ne yah inweere(r)!"
Instantly, our soul screams. It screams, "Ayyy, it hurts. I'm burning!"

"Ne yah aweere(r)?" Kisin uya('ar)ik. "Ne yah aweere(r)? Tame(n)tah tu' maanech tu' yok'o(r)bir lu'um."

"Does your burning really hurt?" says Kisin. "Does your burning really hurt? You did (bad things) while you were on earth."

"Hah! Bähe' ma' su'en," unuuki(h) äkpixane'ex. "Bähe' ma' su'en. Sa'aseh ten."

"Yes! Now I won't do it again," replies our soul. "Now, I won't do it again. Forgive me."

Kisin ne mix uyu'yik. Bay, (u)ka'ch'ukik (u)purik ich k'ak'
Kisin doesn't listen at all. Well, he grabs him again (and) throws him into the fire

—PFFF—
—PFFF—

"Ahhh, ne yah inweere(r)!"
"Ahhh, it really hurts. I'm burning!"

"Bay. Ne yah aweere(r) te'yan siis ha'."
"Okay. Does your burning hurt a lot? Over there it's cold."

—PFFF—
—PFFF—

"Ahhh ne siis!"
"Ahhh, it's really cold!"

Bay.
Okay.

[Tumuuts'ichtah una' yan chakar maska' upäk'ik.]

[When one scowls at his mother there is a piece of hot iron he plants (on our eyes).]

—sh-sh-sh-sh—

—s-i-z-z-l-e—

"Ahhh ne yah yeere(r) box inwich!"

"Ahhh, it hurts a lot. My eyelids are burning!"

"Ne yah uyeere(r) ubox awich? Tamuuts'ichtah ana'."

"Does the burning of your eyelids really hurt? This is because you scowled at your mother."

Bay.

Okay.

[Hump'er umaska t(i') uchi' tuts'ikintah t(i') una' o tet. Wa tutsutsukt'äntah una' o tet päk'ik chakar maska'.]

[Another iron is for the mouth for getting angry with one's mother or father. Or if one insults (their) mother or father under their breath, (Kisin) plants a hot iron (on your lips).]

—psh-sh-sh-sh—

—s-i-z-z-l-e—

"Ahhh, ne yah inchi'. Uyeere(r)!"

"Ahhh, it really hurts. My mouth is burning!"

"Ne yah uneyah achi'? Tatsutsukt'äntah ana'. Tats'ikintah; tawa'arah ba'(ar) t(i') ana' ma' tah!"

"Does your mouth really hurt? You insulted your mother. You got angry; you said things to your mother that weren't true!"

"Bähe' ma' su'en. Sa'aseh ten!"
"Now, I won't do it again. I'm sorry!"

Kisin mix uxurik. Poch utookik.
Kisin doesn't stop. He wants to burn him.

Bay.
Okay.

Tulahirah uyählehi(r) bah. Lati' unukuch winik uyählehi(r) bah tulahirah, lati' akpixane'ex tan utookik Kisin, lati' män(a') uk'ak'i(r).
The Mole Trapper saw it all. That ancestor, the one that the Mole Trapper saw, that soul of ours that Kisin is burning, that one doesn't have any sins.

Bay.
Okay.

Tuya'arah Sukunkyum,
Sukunkyum said,

"Tawirah? Ma' ne yaab. Utookik. Lati' ma' yaab usi'ipir; mä'a(n) uk'eban yaab; ma' tukinsah winik. Mix usi'ipi(r) lati', lati' pixan lati' tawirah utookik."
"You saw it? It's not much of a (punishment). He burns it. That one didn't commit many crimes; it doesn't have many sins; it didn't kill people. That one has no faults, that soul, that one you saw burn."

[AhKisin ne poch ulahtookike'ex. Chen usuku'un kyum toh uyoher ma' yaab a(k)k'ak'i(r). Seeb kutakikech kupurikech ti' uyits'(i)no'.]

[Kisin really wants to burn us. But Sukunkyum knows if we don't have many faults. He quickly snaps you up and sends you to his brothers.]

"Ah bay," uyählehi(r) bah tuya'arah.

"Ah, okay," said the Mole Trapper.

[Bik yani(r) ne seeb? Ma' ulahbisik yok'or k'ak', ma'?

[Why so quickly? (Why) doesn't he (put) it completely on the fire?[25]

Bay, utar usuku'un kyum utakik, "Eh. P'ehas! Ts'o('o)k bähe'. P'ehas! Ma' tech yani(r). Inwits'no' yani(r)."

(It's because) Sukunkyum comes and snaps it up (and says to Kisin), "Eh. That's enough! It's over now. That's enough! He's not yours. He belongs to my brothers."

Kisin kuyarik, "Bik yani(r) ma' (a)ts'ahik ten?"

Kisin says, "Why don't you give him to me?"

"Ma'. Tech ma'. Ts'o'ok."]

"No," (says Sukunkyum). "It's not yours. It's over."][26]

Bay.

Okay.

Sukunkyum ulahpustik k'ak' tuworo(r) tu' eri(h) chichin yok'or k'ak'.

Sukunkyum shakes all the embers off where (the soul) burned a bit in the fire. (Then he says to the soul,)

"Bay. Ko'ox. Ko'ox paareh. Bähe' ts'o('o)k. Ko'ox."

"Okay. Let's go. Let's go, son. It's all over now. Let's go."

Umaan akpixane'ex to'an uyatoch usuku'un kyum. (U)kuchik uba'(ar).

Our soul passes through (again) Sukunkyum's house. It carries its belongings.

Bay.

Okay.

Uye'esik (u)be(r). Uya'arik, "Bay. Tech abin te' he' ti' Mensäbäk. Inwits'(i)n ti' kabin. Lati' ma' ne nuk be(r). Chichin."

(Sukunkyum) shows it the way. He says, "Okay. You go over there to Mensäbäk. You will go to my younger brother. That road isn't very large. It's small."

Bay. Ti' kubin akpixane'ex to'an Mensäbäk, wa to'an Itsanar. Ti' kupuriko'on.

Okay. Our soul goes to Mensäbäk or Itsanal. He sends us there.[27]

Le tulahirah uyählehi(r)bah.

The Mole Trapper saw all of it.

Bay.

Okay.

Tuya'arah ti',

(Sukunkyum) said to (the Mole Trapper),

"Bähe' abin awirik wa. Bähe' kubin (u)tichir ne yaab uk'ak'ir abähe'ex wa. Lati' ukinsmah ubäho'. Ma' tutukrah ubäh. Tula(a)k'intah ubäho' uyits'ino', una', tuworo(r). Tukinsah bäho'. Bähe', beki(r) kabin awireh wa. Way kubi(n) (u)k'uchur akpixane'ex way. Bay. Mäna' uhook'or a' la'eh abähe'ex, turah ulah'ere(r), turah ulah'ere(r) yok'or k'ak'. Hach tuhahir."

"Now maybe you will see it. Now (another soul) who has a lot of sins is going to arrive. That one killed his brother. He didn't think. He slept with his brothers' wives, his sisters, his mother, all of them.[28] He killed his brother. Now, you're going to see the same thing happen (to him). Your soul is going to arrive here and he isn't leaving until he burns up, until he burns up in the fire. That's the truth."

[Bähe' boona kukinsik ahma'ax ahKisin lah boona kukinsik ahma'ax, 'ooxp'e(r) k'in, mäna' umaan kuk'uchu(r) akpixane'ex.]

[Now, as many monkeys that Kisin kills, however many monkeys he kills, three days (later), without fail our souls arrive.][29]

Kura'(a)n uyireh bähe'. Ukura'(a)n uch'ukteh uyireh. Yählehi(r) bah kura'(a)n. Hach tuhahir, ne hats'ka', kutich(ir).

He is there to see it, now. He is sitting there waiting to see it. The Mole Trapper is sitting there. Sure enough, at dawn, it comes.

"Eh," una'i(r) usuku'un kyum kunuukik. "Eh, kutichir akpixane'ex. Le' tawa'arah."

"Eh," Sukunkyum's wife replies. "Eh, our soul is arriving. Like you said," (she says to Sukunkyum).

"Hah," kunuukik uyählehi(r) bah. "Hah."

"It is true," replies the Mole Trapper. "It is true."

(U)k'uchur. Äkna'i(r) usuku'un kyum (u)ki'irik.

It arrives. Sukunkyum's wife peers at it.

"Ehhh, määäna'. Ne yan uk'ak'ir. Bähe' ma' teni(r). Ma' (in)wits'(i)no' yan-i(r). Kisini(r) yani(r). Kisin yani(r)."

"Ehhh, noooo. He has a lot of faults. He's not mine, now. He doesn't belong to my younger brothers. He belongs to Kisin."

Äkna'e'ex ne saasi(r) uwich uyirik; toh uyoher ma' ti' kubin ti' Mensäbäk, ma' ti' kubin ti' Itsana(r).

Our Lady sees very clearly; she already knows that he is not going to Men-säbäk, he is not going to Itsanal.

Bay.

Okay.

Ma' ne samtar[30] (u)k'uch(ur) akpixane'ex.

Our soul doesn't take long to arrive.

Mix ma'ats' kuyuk'ik, ne seeb utar Kisin, uch'a'ik, ubisik.

He doesn't drink any posol, (because) Kisin comes very quickly, grabs him, and carries him off.

Uk'aatik 'oxwäts uk'atik Kisin. "He' wa ts'ahik ten?"

Kisin asks for it three times. "Will you give it to me?"

"Ma'."

"No," (says Sukunkyum's wife).

"He' wa ts'ahik ten?"

"Will you give it to me?"

"Ma'. Ma' ints'ahik tech."

"No. I won't give it to you."

Ki' (u)lahi(ri)k,

(Then) she peers at it,

"Ah mäna'. Ne yaab usi'ipi(r). Mäna'."
"Ah, no. He has a lot of faults. No good."

"Bay," Sukunkyum uya'arik ti'. "Ch'a'(eh). Tech yani(r)."
"Okay," Sukunkyum says to (Kisin). "Take him. He's yours."

"Ah bay." Kisin ne tsoy uyor. "Yan inmeyah tuworo(r) k'in. Yan inmeyah ten.
Yan ints'imin, inwäht'eer. Lahi(h) intukrik inharik.
"Ah good." Kisin is elated. "I have work to do every day. I have my work.
I have my horse (and) my pet rooster. I think these are what I (will) pull
out."[31]

[Lati' be'ik tutsikbar(r)tah 'uchik (u)nukuch winik, lati' ne yaab usi'ipi(r).
Ne yaab usi'ipi(r). Tukinsah winik.]
[This is the one ancestor that (Sunkunkyum) talked about before, the
one that committed many crimes. He committed many crimes. He killed
people.]

[Lati' Kisin umeyah wolol ya'axk'in. Hach turah ulaheere(r) ne chichin.
Pachir, Kisin kuharik wa ts'imin wa kax. Lahi(h) kubin uharik.]
[Kisin works all year round.[32] The soul burns up into nothing. Then, Kisin
pulls it out as either a horse or a chicken. This is what he's going to pull out.]

Bay.
Okay.

"Lati' ne yaab usi'ipi(r) tuworo(r)."
"This one has (committed) many crimes of every kind."

Ulahtookik.

(Kisin) burns it up.

Be'ik tutsikba(r)tah, bek tuyirah uyählehi(r) bah.

This is just like what he reported, it is just like what the Mole Trapper saw.

Bay.

Okay.

Pachi(r) a'arah ti' uyählehi(r) bah [utsikbar yete(r) usuku'un kyum yete(r) uyählehi(r) bah],

Then the Mole Trapper is told [Sukunkyum is talking to the Mole Trapper],

"Bähe' paareh tawirah ba'inki(r) (u)meyah Kisin."

"Now son, you (have seen) Kisin's work."

"Tinwirah."

"I saw it," (says the Mole Trapper).

"A' tawirah."

"You saw it," (says Sukunkyum).

"Tinwirah."

"I saw it."

"Le' ma' ts'o'(o)kok awi(ri)k. Yanta(r) ... Kabin awirik ulahmeyah Kisin tuworo(r). Kabin awirik ba'inki(r) uk'ichintik."

"You haven't finished seeing it. There's more ... You're going to see all Kisin's work. You're going see what he warms (himself) with."

"Bay."

"Okay," (says the Mole Trapper).

"Bin awirik ba'inki(r) uche' Kisin."

"You're going to see what Kisin's wood is made of."

Uyählehi(r) bah tutukrah, *"Bähe' poch inbin inwirik ba'inki(r) uche' Kisin."*
The Mole Trapper thought, *"Now I want to go and see what Kisin's (fire)wood is."*

Bin uyirik. Lahi(h) uche' ubaker winik. Lahi(h) uche' uk'ak'. Woro(r) akba-kere'ex uk'ichintik. Ma' uk'ichintik hach che'. Woro(r) baak, woro(r) akba-kere'ex. Lehi(h) uche'. Lehi(h) uche' Kisin.

He goes to see it. Kisin's wood is the bones of people. This is his firewood. He warms (himself) with all our bones. He doesn't warm (himself) (with) real wood. It's all bones, all our bones, the bones of people. This is his (fire) wood. This is Kisin's (fire)wood.

[Ne chi'ha('an)n Kisin. Woro(r) ti' kuwene(n) (u)chi' (u)k'ak'.]
[Kisin is very old. He's always sleeping at the edge of the fire.]

Uyählehi(r) bah bini(h) (u)yirik to'an che' tu' kutaasik; bin uyirik; bin uxa-tik. Lati' uyählehi(r) bah sahak; sahak uyirik lati' akbakere'ex. Tulahirah lati' uyählehi(r) bah. Lati' tulahirah ba'(in)ki(r) uche' Kisin.

The Mole Trapper went to see where he gathers his wood; he goes to see it; he goes to chop it. The Mole Trapper is afraid; he is afraid to look at it (be-cause) these are our bones. The Mole Trapper saw it all. He saw what Kisin's (fire)wood was made of.

Bay.

Okay.

Pachir (tu)ye'esah ti' bik tuyirah uyokman lu'um. Tulahirah uyokman lu'um.

Then (Sukunkyum) showed him what the pillars of the earth looked like. He studied the pillars of the earth. The pillars are planted in the ground.

Ne nuk uyokman lu'um. Yan utaan a' lu'um. La' yan upäk'man tah xämän. Te' kubin nohor, kir ubin k'in, kir uta(r) k'in—lahket sina('an) uyokman lu'um.

The pillars are very big. They have girders supporting the earth. They are planted directly north. From here they go south, west, east—the pillars of the earth are all stretched out together in rows.

Ulahki'irik uyählehi(r) bah. Uki'rah cha'(a)ntik tuworo(r) bik (u)irah uyokman lu'um yete(r) ubähi(r) usukun akyum. Tuye'esah ti' uyählehi(r) bah, aknukire'ex.

The Mole Trapper studies all of this. He studies how the pillars of the earth are with Sukunkyum. He showed them to the Mole Trapper, our ancestor.

'A'arah ti', "Ireh, awireh, paareh. A' he' kawirik uyokman lu'um. La' Kisin lahi(h) kutench'intik yete(r) uyok. Be'in kawirik upeek a' lu'um."

He is told, "Look, look at it son. Here you see the pillars of the earth. Kisin kicks (the pillars). Because of this you see the earth move."[33]

"Eh eh hah, be'ik bäkan."

"Uh-huh, so it's like that then," (says the Mole Trapper).

"He' kawirikeh paareh ke lahi(h) uyokman lu'um."

"You will see, son, that these are the pillars of the entire earth," (Sukunkyum says).

. . .

. . .

Tan uki'lahcha'a(a)ntik tuworo(r) uyählehi(r) bah. Tan uki'lahirik.

The Mole Trapper is observing everything. He is studying it all.

"Leti' up'atar teche'ex, ti' abähe'ex, tumen ti' atsikba(r)tik ti' abähe'ex, ti' alaht'axik ti' abähe'ex. Bähe' ma' aputs'(s)ik, ma'."

"This (knowledge) will remain for all of you, for your companions, because you (will) talk about it to your companions, share (the word) with all your companions. Now, don't forget it, don't."

"Bay," kih uyählehi(r) bah.

"Okay," says the Mole Trapper.

Bay. Tuworo(r) utsikbar usukun kyum tuworo(r) tulahkänah tulahu'yah. Bähe' yan ti' ulahts'ahik ti' ubäho'. Yan ti' utaxik. Ma' utup'u(r) ti' . . .

Okay. He learned everything he heard from Sukunkyum. Now he must pass it on to his companions. He must spread (the word). He doesn't forget it . . .

Bay.

Okay.

Uyählehi(r) bah suti(h). Suti(h) t(i') uhanan. Ket kuhanan yete(r) Sukunkyum. Ket kuhe're(r) ket yete(r). Tan utsikba(r) yaab yete(r). Tsoy uyor. Ti' yan uyor.

The Mole Trapper returned. He returned to eat (his meal). He eats with Sukunkyum. They rest together (afterward). They are chatting a lot. They are very happy. They are relaxed.

"Bähe'," uya('ar)ik ti' uyählehi(r) bah, "bähe', paareh," kih, "bähe' talahkänah bik umeyah way Kisin. Tawirah yok'or yaram lu'um bik umeyah."

"Now," (Sukunkyum) says to the Mole Trapper, "now, son," he says, "now you (have) learned how Kisin works here. You saw how he works in the underworld."

"Tinwirah," unuuki(k) winik uyählehi(r) bah. "Tinwirah."
"I saw it," the ancestor, the Mole Trapper, replies. "I saw it."

"Bay, ne tsoy. Bähe' ma' utubur tech. Ma.' Ma' utubur. Turah alahtsik-ba(r)t(ik) abähe'ex. Turah alahirik ba'(in)ki(r) umeyah Kisin, bik aweere'ex. Ba'inki(r) tawirah way, bik uk'uchur apixane'ex ba'inki(r) umeyah Kisin. Tawirah. Ma' utubur tech. Ma'."
"Okay, very good. Now don't forget. Don't. Don't forget. You must tell all your companions everything. You must see everything that Kisin does, how you all burn. (Tell them) what you saw here, how your souls arrive (and) what Kisin does. You saw it. Don't forget. Don't."

"Bay," uyählehi(r) bah unuukik. "Bay. Bähe' mäna' ma' tubu(r) ten."
"Okay," the Mole Trapper replies. "Okay. Now I won't forget anything."

PART 3. THE MOLE TRAPPER LEAVES THE UNDERWORLD

Bay.
Okay.

Ya ne xok'or usut uyählehi(r) bah t(i') upach tuka'ten tu' yok'o(r)bir lu'um.
The Mole Trapper is getting ready to go back to the earth.

Bay.
Okay.

Uch'uprar uti'a'ar Kisin, lati' ulaak' uyählehi(r) bah, lehi(h) ulaak'.[34] Ne tsoy (u)yor uyählehi(r) bah. Yan ulaak.'

The daughter of Kisin is the Mole Trapper's wife. The Mole Trapper is very happy. He has his wife.

Bay. Ba'axta(r) ne xok'or utar usut tuka'ten. Chen biki(r) uch'uprar uti'a'ar Kisin ma' seeb t(an) uts'o'okir (u)maarik ulu'um ti' uyatoch. Ma' seeb tumaar(ah) ulu'um. Ti' p'aati(h). Ti' p'aati(h) uch'uprar Kisin.

Okay. He is close to returning. But the daughter of Kisin isn't very quick about sweeping her house. She didn't pick up the sweepings quickly enough. She stayed behind. Kisin's daughter stayed behind.

Bay.

Okay.

Ne seeb, hook'i(h) lati' nukuch winik uyählehi(r) bah. Ne seeb uhook'or upurik (u)yokyok'o(r) lu'um. Uch'uprar (u)ti'a'ar Kisin ma' seeb hook'ih. Ne seeb tumak(ah) ubäh uhoor a' lu'um. Ba'axta(r) tan uhook'or uyaaka' uyählehi(h) bah, ulu'um kubin ne seeb (u)nup'ik. Ya p'aatih uti'a'ar Kisin. Ha'ri' uyählehi(h) bah hook'ih.

Hurridly, that ancestor, the Mole Trapper, departed. Hurridly, he exits and steps out onto the earth. Kisin's daughter didn't get out quickly enough. The door of earth instantly shut. As the Mole Trapper is running out, the ground is quickly closing. Kisin's daughter was left behind. Only the Mole Trapper got out.

Bay.

Okay.

[Bek tutsikba(r)tah unuki(r) winik. Bek tutsikba(r)tah intet. Bek tutsik-
ba(r)tah.]

[This is how the ancestors told it. This is how my father told it. That is how
they told it.]

Bay.

Okay.

Uyählehi(h) bah tan utukur, *"Bähe' ti' p'aati(h) mäna' inlaak'. Ma' het la'eh,
ma' het inka'sut. Ma' het la'eh. Ma' het la'eh, ma' het la'eh t(i') uhook'or. Ma' het.
Tumäk(ah) ubäh a' lu'um."*

The Mole Trapper is thinking, *"Now she stayed there, I don't have my wife. It's
impossible, I can't go back (for her). It's impossible. It's impossible, it's impossible
for her to go out. It's impossible. The earth (has) covered over."*[35]

Bay.

Okay.

Suti(h) uyählehi(r) bah ich uyatoch. Yan utukur tuworo(r) ulahtuyirah
ba'inki(r) umeyah ti' uyaram a' lu'um Kisin, ba'inki(r) a'alah ti' Sukunkyum.

The Mole Trapper returned to his house. He must think about all of Kisin's
work he saw in the underworld, (about) what he (had) been told by Sukunkyum.

Bay.

Okay.

K'uchih saasi(r) bini(h) uyählehi(h) bah bin(ih) uya'arik ti' ubäho'. Ubin
uya'arik utsikbar ba'inki(r) tuyirah yok'o(r) uyaram lu'um to'an Kisin. Ubin
utsikbar tuworo(r) ti' ubäho'.

In the morning, the Mole Trapper went to talk to his companions. He goes to tell the story of what he saw in the underworld where Kisin is. He went to pass it on to all his companions.

"Bähe' ten ti' taren to'an uyaram lu'um. Tinwirah ba'inki(r) umeyah usuku'un kyum. Tinwirah ba'inki(r) umeyah Kisin. Tinwirah bik akeere'ex. Tinwirah tuworo(r) ba'(ar) ti' uyaram a' lu'um, bik uyirah uyaram lu'um, bik uyirah uyokman a' lu'um. Tuworo(r) tinlahirah. Tinwirah be'ik(ir) umeyah Kisin.

"Now, it is I who have come from the underworld. I saw the work of Sukunkyum. I saw the work of Kisin. I saw how (our souls) burn. I saw all these things in the underworld, how the underworld looks, how the pillars of the earth look. I saw it all. I saw the work of Kisin.

"Bähe' inwa'arik teche'ex: Känänt(eh)e'ex abähe'ex. Tukr(eh) abah. Wa yan ati'a'ar, akansik, tema' ume(n)tik k'as ba'(ar), tema' ukinsik abäho', tema' ume(n)tik k'as ba'(ar) ti' uyits'(i)no' ti' uch'uprar yits'(i)no'. Tuworo(r) yan 'eerer ti' Kisin. Ten tinwirah. Hach tuhahir. Ten ti' taren ti' uyaram a' lu'um. Ti' meyahnahen to'an Kisin.

"Now I'm telling you all: Take care. Think about it. If you have children, teach them not to do bad things, not to kill their brothers, not to do bad things to their younger brothers and sisters. All (those who do these things) (will) be burned by Kisin. I saw it. It's true. I came from the underworld. There I had worked where Kisin is.

"Bähe' tukrehe'ex abähe'ex. Tints'ahah intsikba(r) ti' teche'ex. Bähe' yan ti' atukrike'ex abähe'ex. Yan ti' akansik. Yan ti' awa'arik ti' abähe'ex. Wa tech ma' akänik la' tintsikbartah tech, utookikech ahKisin."

"Now think about it. I (have given) you my account. Now you must think about it. You must teach it. You must tell it to your companions. If you don't (heed) what I (have) told you, Kisin (will) burn you."

Le' lati' umeyah uyählehi(r) bah. Uyählehi(r) bah tu' kura('an) yok'or uyaram a' lu'um (ti') hump'e(r) ya'axk'in chumuk uka'sut t(i') uyok'o(r)bir lu'um.
Pachi(r), ma' ne xanahi(h), kimi(h). Ka'ts'it äkna' kimi(h). Chen ts'o('o)k
ulaht'axik utsikba(r) tuworo(r), kimi(h).

So, that was the work of the Mole Trapper. The Mole Trapper was there in
the underworld (for) one and a half years (before) he return(ed) to earth.
Then, not long after that, he died. He died two months later. But he (had)
shared the whole story with everyone (before) he died.[36]

DISCUSSION

This story is about not only a hero's journey and his message to humanity,
but also the journey of death as a journey that everyone takes, a common
theme in most Mayan eschatology. Souls follow a path through the underworld, cross a wide river, and confront a myriad of obstacles along the way
before arriving at their final resting place. In preparation for this journey,
Lacandon burial rites include providing the deceased with food for the
journey and a few articles to protect it along the way. These articles include
(four) dogs made of palm leaves, who will guide the soul across the river of
tears; a bone, to give the jaguars in Metlan (wild dogs, according to McGee
1983, 157); a bowl of corn to feed the chickens that block the path; and a
lock of hair, to deter the lice (McGee 1983, 152; Perera and Bruce 1982, 107).

The Mole Trapper's reemergence from the underworld symbolizes
his immortality (Marion 1999, 254); his delivery of information from the
underworld events to the mortals symbolizes his role as intermediary between humankind and the supernatural (Bruce, Robles, and Ramos Chao
1971, 113). The Mole Trapper could also be regarded as a demigod, the blue
feathers of the hummingbird representing his deification (blue being the
color of the divine). In other versions of this story, the Mole Trapper is
given a "lotus flower" wand called *äsäb*, which was used to resurrect the
dead (McGee 1983, 148). The Mole Trapper's wife found it, unwrapped it,
and showed her companions its magic, whereupon the instrument lost its
power, and the Mole Trapper could no longer bring the dead back to life.
Davis (1978, 77) mentions *äsäh in wäsäbeh*, which she describes as colored

beads of clay believed to have been part of the gods' necklaces. These are used by the officiant of the *k'ämkih* ceremony, who strikes the new god pots with these beads to awaken them.

Bruce, Robles, and Ramos Chao (1971, 116) equate the Mole Trapper with the hero twins of the *Popol Vuh*, who vanquish the Vucub-Caquix, and equate the Vucub-Caquix with the survivors of the "men of mud" of the first creation. Most were destroyed in the flood; the few survivors transformed into the Vucub-Caquiz, a demon-bird of pre-Columbian mythology who pretended to be the sun and moon in the era before the sun had emerged.

Xurt'an Uburur 'The World Ends with the Flood'

Bor Ma'ax

Hachäkyum is growing tired of the mortals' behavior and wants to end the world. He had ended the world twice before, each time decapitating the mortals and reserving the blood of the virtuous for reseeding the earth. This time he ends the world in a deluge.

The flood story is ubiquitous not only in Mesoamerica mythology. A comparison of their flood myths reveals parallels with the biblical account, albeit with some modifications: the ark is replaced by a canoe in stories from cultures that rely on canoes for travel; after the flood recedes, fish emerge; survivors who anger the gods are turned into monkeys. Some myths recount saving male and female pairs of humans and animals. The theme of cleansing the world of corruption and sin is present in a small percentage of Mesoamerican myths.[1]

The Lacandon flood myth has also been attributed to Christian influences. For example, the canoe may be a substitute for the biblical ark. Yet the flood myth appears in both the *Popol Vuh*, considered a truly indigenous text (Horcasitas 1988, 189), and the books of the *Chilam Balam*, which preserves many ancient myths and miscellany from the Yucatec Mayas. Both sources are believed to be based on ancient Mayan accounts of the first creation, in which the blood of the cosmic caiman inundated the world after his head was severed by the supreme God. For details on this story and other accounts of the deluge from the Postclassic and Colonial Maya manuscripts, see Velásquez-García (2006).[2] Moreover, the canoe may symbolize the Milky Way, which was ferried across the sky by the Paddler Gods to deposit the hearth fires and then the embryo, or maize seed, of the Maize God into the center of the universe (see Freidel, Schele, and Parker 1993). Nevertheless, many maritime cultures that use the canoe as the main mode of transportation and that have been influenced by Christianity supplant the biblical ark with a canoe. So, we cannot be certain that the flood myth is entirely Mayan. If viewed from the cultural perspective of the Lacandones, however, the flood story is "not merely one version of a pan-Maya flood myth [but] a chronicle of the catastrophic consequences of a hurricane" (McGee 1989, 68). In this respect history, mythology, and the environmental conditions the Lacandon experience coalesce into a unique rendition of the flood that, according to McGee, is by all accounts traditionally Lacandon.

There are two aspects of the Lacandon myth that are definitely Mayan: first, the flood was caused by the mortals' failure to venerate their gods; second, the Lacandones say that the world grows old and therefore needs to be renewed. Both ideas form the core of Mayan religious cosmology. The gods proclaim their intent to end the world with a solar eclipse. Wind, fire, and torrential rains are their methods of destruction, but the order in which they occur varies among the Mayan groups (Horcasitas 1988, 188) and among Lacandon narrators.

The version here is close to those collected by Boremanse (1986) and Bruce (1974); it differs from them in that it omits an episode that takes place after the flood in which the gods make incensories for each other and leave them with the mortals to communicate with them after they have ascended to their home in the sky.

Bay.

Okay.

AhHachäkyum tuya'arah ti' (T'uup), Ak'inchob, "Bin aka(h) akme(n)tik chem. Bin akah akmentik."

Hachäkyum said to (T'uup) and Ak'inchob, "We are going to make a large canoe. We are going to make it."

Yan unukuch k'uche'. Tuch'akah a' k'uche' tumentah a' chem. Toh uyo(h) e(r) ahHachäkyum bin ukah nuk uburu(r), bin ukah uxureh tun.

There is an enormous cedar tree. They chopped down an enormous cedar tree (and) made a canoe. Hachäkyum already knows that there is going to be a great deluge that is going to end the world.

Ele tume(n)tah, tume(n)tah nukuch chem. Tuch'akah la' k'uche', ne nuk, tume(n)tah a' chem, nukuch chem.

This they made, they made a large canoe. They cut down the cedar, an enormous one, (and) made a canoe, an enormous canoe.

Eh bay.

Okay.

Ele, Hachäkyum tutoh'a'arah, "Bähe' bin ink(ah) inxureh, tun. Bururbi(r) kubin."

And then, Hachäkyum simply said, "Now I'm going to end it. It's going to be flooded."

Tan ume(n)tiko'. Seebseeb ume(n)tiko'. Tuch'akah, tulahbuhah.

They are making (the canoe). Quickly they make it. They chopped down (the tree) and they split it.

Toh uyo(h)e(r) Hachäkyum.

Hachäkyum already knew (what he was going to do).

Tuya'arah, "Ele bähe', T'uupeh, bin a(k)kah akläkeh uyähtich'k'a'i(r). Bururbi(r) kubin a' lu'umo'. Ha' kubin tuursik. Ch'ik hasta ti' una'ka'an kubin na'aka(r)."

He said, "So now, my T'uup, we're going to detach the sun. The humans are going to be flooded. The rains will fill up the earth. All the way up to the belly of the sky the (water) will rise."

"Eh bay, tet."

"Okay, father."

Täk'a'an uwich bin, aknukire'ex. Ka'(ah) tuyu'yah bin la' aknukire'ex bin, ka'(ah) tuyu'yah tuhachtärar ha'

The ancestors stared. Then the ancestors heard the rain hit hard

—*TEEEEX.*

—*TEEEESH.*

Umaanan la' k'in. Umaanan la' 'aak'ä'. Ha', mäna'. Ne k'a'am.

The days pass. The nights pass. And there is only rain. It (comes down) very hard.

Täk'a'an uwich ka'(ah) tuyirah tan una'aka(r) (ha'). Tan uturu(r)—be'ik tutsikbartah Haawo', be'ik tuyiraho'.

The (people) stared when they saw (the water) rising. (The land) is filling up—just like the Haawo' talked about, like they had seen it.[3]

Boon a' chem yok'o(r) petha' lah(h)ook'(ih) (ti' u)'ayim! Bix a' baab lahhook'(ih) (ti' u)käy. Bini(h) t(i') ukäy, lahwaayih t(i') ukäy. A' hach chem waayi(h) yok'or a' petha', lahbinih 'ayim. Yan k'än 'aak. Lahbinih.

How many canoes in the lagoon turned into crocodiles! The oars all turned into fish. They turned into fish. They all turned into fish. The canoes in the water turned into crocodiles. There were yellow turtles. They all turned into (these creatures).

Ele, ahHachäkyum tutohtukrah. Tut'iisah; tume(n)tah a' chem ti' ut'iisik, ti' ubut'ik aki'ime'ex, ti' ut'iisik uyi'iman ahbäk', tuworo(r) a' bix la' bäk', barum, ka'ka'tuu(r); ka'ka'tuu(r) k'ambur; tuworo(r)—yuk, ha're', hach k'ek'en, kitan, ma'ax, ba'ats', tuworo(r). Tuhachlahmarah sinik, kan. Tulahmuuch'ah—tuworo(r)—ka'ka'tuu(r), ka'ka'tuu(r) yete(r) uch'upi(r).[4]

And so, Hachäkyum had already thought about it. He set them apart; he made the canoe to save us, to save the seeds of every kind of creature, like the jaguar, (they came) two by two; two by two curassow; (pairs of) all of them—the deer, the spotted cavy, the white-lipped peccary, the collared peccary, the spider monkey, the howler monkey—all of them. He gathered up all the ants (and) the snakes, (and) piled them together—all of them, two by two, two by two with their females.

Ele, "La'he'," tuya'arah Hachäkyum, "la'he' le kubin; int'iisah ti' uyaarän-ka(r), ti' uka'pimtar tuka'ten."

"These," said Hachäkyum, "these here are going to carry on; I save them so they will make babies, so they will multiply again."

Ele, tulahmuuch'ah la' uhaan ahHachäkyum. Tulahmuuch'ah tuworo(r) la' bäk', ti' tulahbut'ah yok'o(r) la' chem.

And so, Hachäkyum's son-in-law gathered together (pairs) of all the animals. He gathered all the animals together (and) put them all in the canoe.

Ele, uts'o'okor ulahbut'ik yok'o(r) chem, tuworo(r) a' la'eh a' bäk'.

And then, he finishes putting all these animals into the canoe.

Ele, Hachäkyum tuya'arah, "P'isi(r) lu'umo'; bin ink(ah) int'iisah uyi'iman."

And then Hachäkyum said, "The same goes for the humans; I'm going to separate (the best) seeds."

Wa uyoone(n) k'ek'en, wa uyoone(n) ma'ax, wa ba'inkin uyoone(n), tuworo(r), wa yuk wa keh, tuworo(r) turah kulahbut'ik. Ka'ka'tuu(r), ka'ka'tuu(r), tulahbut'ah ti'ri(') tu' bähan a' bäk'. Ti'ri(') tulahbut'ah.

If their lineage is the white-lipped peccary or the spider monkey, whatever their lineage, the brocket deer or the mule deer, he had to put them all in (the canoe). He put them in the canoe, two by two, two by two where the animals were stowed. He put them in together.

Le ka'(ah) tuyu'yah bin aknukire'ex—*t-e-e-e-e-x*. Tan una'aka(r), tan una'aka(r), tan una'aka(r) uburu(r). Täk'an uwich uyirik. Mäna'. Na'ak(ih) yok'o(r) ka'an. [Bex tutsikbartah Haawo'.]

Then our ancestors heard it—*t-e-e-e-e-sh*. The (water) was rising, rising, rising. They looked around (but saw) nothing. They rose into the sky. [This is just like the Haawo' recounted it.]

Hump'eri' ya'axk'in, äka('a)n. Tuuri(h) ka'an. Hump'eri' ya'axk'in, ka'(ah) eemi(h), ka'ah ka'saahi(h). Ele, neki'tsaabi(r) saahi(h). Ele ki'ki'tsaabi(r) usaahar.

After one year, the (water) leveled off. It (had) reached the sky. A year (later) then it went down again, it started to dry up again. Very slowly it dried up. Little by little it dried up.

Ba'areh ahma'ax, ahba'ats'mana' upeek. Ti'ri'ti'ri' kurenkuu(r) ti' uchi' chem. La ti' yan tuworo(r) o'ochir ich uchem. Hachäkyum tutohmuuch'ah a' o'ochi(r) ti' tuworo(r). Tulahmuuch'ah uwich, uwich a' che'o' ba'axtäk—puuna', puk'te', k'uche', ya', tuworo(r). Tulahmuuch'ah uwich. Toh Hachäkyum tulahmuuch'ah uwich a' che'o' tuworo(r), ti' uka'päk'ik tuka'ten. [Le' bex tutsikbartah Haawo'. Tuyirah bik xur(i)ki(r) t'an, be'ik tume(n)tah Hachäkyum.]

But the spider monkeys and the howler monkeys didn't move. They sat here and there on the side of the canoe. All their food is in the canoe. Hachäkyum (had) already gathered the food for all of them. He (had) gathered the seeds from all kinds of trees—mahogany, *kanchan*, cedar, chicle, all of them. He gathered all the seeds. Hachäkyum (had) already gathered all the seeds from all the (different kinds of) trees to sow again. [This is just like the Haawo' recounted it. The Haawo' saw the ending of the world, (and) how Hachäkyum did it.]

Bay.

Okay.

Ele, saahih a' petha'. Mäna' a' che'o'. Ulahkimi(n); lahtihih; lahkimi(n). Ele, tuyirah, pachi(r) Hachäkyum tulahtookah. Tutookah tuworo(r) ch'ik bini(h) tuworo(r) k'aax. Lah'eerih, lah'eerih. Tumen ti' utumenchah a' lu'um tuka'ten. [Le' be'ik tutsikbartah—ti' uka'tumenchah a' lu'um.]

Then, the lagoon dried up. There weren't any trees. All of them were dead; they had dried up; they were all dead. And when he saw this, Hachäkyum burned up (the land). He burned everything as far as the forest went. It burned and it burned. (He did this) to make (the land) new again. [That's how they recounted it—to make the land new again.]

Ele, ts'o'ok ulah'eerer.

And then, the burning stopped.

Ele ubähir Hachäkyum utukrik ubin upäk'ik uher a' che'o'. Ulahokik uwichtäk ahpuuna', uwichtäk ahek'ba'che', uwichtäk a' ba'axtäk che'o' tuworo(r). Uhook'or ubähir ahHachäkyum ulahustik ulahte'täk ulahsutik ubah tuworo(r) te' tupach. Tan ulahsutik uk'äb te' kir uta(r) k'in, te' nohor, te' kubin k'in, te' tu' kutar xämän. Ele, tulahpurah uneek' a' wich a' che' ti' useebta(r). Tulahpurah tuworo(r) ti' k'aax, ti' useebta(r).

And then Hachäkyum thinks about sow(ing) new trees. He takes a handful of mahogany seeds, seeds of the black cork tree, seeds of all the various trees. Hachäkyum goes out and blows them (from his palms) while he turns around. He turns his hands to the east, to the south, to the west, to the north. And then, he flung all the seeds of the fruit of the trees. He flung them throughout the forest, so that they (would grow) quickly.

[Be'ik tutsikbartah Haawo', äknukire'ex. Be'ik utsikbar bin.]

[This is how the Haawo', our ancestors, recounted it. This is how the story goes.]

Ma' xanahi(r), hunts'it na' seeb. Seeb ch'ihih a' che'. Seebseeb unukta(r). Ma' uxantar uch'ihi(r).

In no time, (perhaps) one month, the trees grew very quickly. They grew up very fast. They didn't take long to grow.

[Bex tutsikbartah Haawo'. Tuya'arah, "K'uh tupäk'ah, Hachäkyum tupäk'ah la' che'. Ma' uxanta(r), seeb kunukta(r) tuworo(r) seebseeb. Ka'ts'it na', yan uwich, tuworo(r) ba'axtäk che'."]

[This is like the Haawo' recounted it. They said, "The Lord Hachäkyum sowed the trees. In no time, all of them (grew). In two months, all the trees (had) fruit."]

Boon a' che'o'! Seeb uwichanka(r) che' tumen ti' uhantik a' bäk'o', ma'ax, ba'ats', k'ambur. Seeb ch'ihi(h) puuna', tuworo(r) pahok. Yan kun, xa'an. La' seebseeb ch'ihiho'.

How many trees there were! Quickly the trees fruited for the animals, the spider monkeys, howler monkeys, curassows, to eat. The mahogany grew quickly, all the *pahok* palms.[5] There were give-and-take palms (and) sabal palms. They grew very quickly.

[Bex tuyirah aknukire'ex Haawo'. Bex tuyirah ka'(ah) tuyirah uxurik a' t'an Hachäkyum yeter ahT'uup.]

[This is how the Haawo', our ancestors, saw it. They saw it like this when they saw Hachäkyum and T'uup end the world.]

Hachäkyum ne tsoy uyirik.

Hachäkyum likes what he sees.

"Bähe' inwaaro', ti'ri('), le ne tsoy uk'ik'e(r). Ulah ne tsoy. Mäna', mäna' kin-sah ti' uk'äb. Bähe' bin ukah ka'pimtar inwaaro' tuka'ten. Bin ukah pim-ta(r). Kuka'pimta(r), he' inka'xurik ti'. Inka'xurik t'an."

"Now my children are separated, their blood is pure. It's all very good. There isn't (going to be) any more killing. Now my children are going to multiply again. They are going to multiply. When they multiply, I will end it again for them. I (will) end the world again."

Akyant'o' No Permite Uxurt'an
'Akyant'o' Prevents the End of the World'

Bor Ma'ax

In this story, Akyant'o' 'God of Foreigners' learns of Hachäkyum's intention to end the world.[1] Alarmed that this would destroy his own people, in addition to wiping out the small population of Lacandones, he persuades Hachäkyum and his son, T'uup, to reconsider. In the end, they agree to decide together when the time will come to end the world.[2]

El ultimo xurt'an bek tutsikbartah uchik: uxurt'an yeter Hachäkyum yeter T'uup y Akyant'o'.

They recounted the final end of the world like this: the end of the world with Hachäkyum, T'uup, and Akyant'o'.

Bek tutsikbartah Haawo'. Haawo' tuyirah uxurt'an. Lati' aknukire'ex Haawo'.

This is how the Haawo' recounted it. The Haawo' saw the end of the world (coming). The Haawo' are our ancestors.[3]

Bay.

Okay.

Päytan Hachäkyum ne tsoy uyirik uxuri(r) t'an. Ne uk'a't ba'i(n)k(in) ume(n)tik lu'umo'. Wa yan kinsah, uyan ukinsik ubäho', Hachäkyum ne p'eek uyirik. Yan uhurik ubäho'. Ne p'eek uyirik. Poch utoh uxurik t'an ne seeb.

In the beginning Hachäkyum enjoyed seeing the end of the world.[4] He really wants it (because of) the things that the mortals do. If there is war, they kill their brothers; Hachäkyum really hates it. They shoot their brothers with arrows. He really hates it. He still wants so much to end the world quickly.

Bay.

Okay.

Pachir, Hachäkyum yeter T'uup, uyarik ti' T'uup, "Tint'an bähe' bin inkah inxurtik t'an, tun. Ne 'oy inwor ti' lu'umo'."

Later, Hachäkyum is with T'uup, and he says to T'uup, "So now I think I'm going to end the world. I'm fed up with the mortals."

[Ne baaxä(r) yan t(i') uk'äb.]

[They are really toys in his hands.]

"Mäna'. Ne p'eek inwirik. Ma' tsoy. Bähe' bin inkinxurtik t'an, tun. Tech T'uup tech yeter ten kakbineh tap'ik a' k'in."

"There isn't anything (to save them now). I hate them. They are bad. So now I'm going to end the world. You, T'uup, you and I are going to cover up the sun."[5]

"Bay," kih ahT'uup. Ne tsoy uyor.

"Okay," says T'uup. He is elated.

Bay.

Okay.

Akyant'o' ma' uyohe(r). Ne naach yan ch'ik pach k'ak'na'. Ha'ri' uhaan Ha-chäkyum, Ak'inchob, lehi(h) kuyaantik lu'umo'. Kupokik (ti') ma' uxurt'an. Kume(n)tik ti' usiiri(r) yeter tum(b)en lek. Ele, lati' kubo'(o)tik, äknukire'ex uchik; kubo'otik ti' Hachäkyum, tema' (u)xurik t'an ti' to('o)ne'ex.

Akyant'o' doesn't know (the plan). He is far away on the other side of the sea. Only Hachäkyum's son-in-law, Ak'inchob, helps the mortals. They pray (to him) so the world doesn't end. They give offerings and a new god pot to him. And then our ancestors pay Hachäkyum so that he doesn't end the world on us.[6]

Pero Hachäkyum ma' k'a't utä(r)ik ba'che', ma' k'a't utä(r)ik nahwah. Ma' k'at utärik siiri(r). Tum(b)en lek, ma' uk'a't Hachäkyum mäna', mix nahwah, mix ch'ur(h)a'—mix. Eh, kutä(r)ik, mäna' utä(r)ik. Mix T'uup. Mäna' utä(r)ik. Lah ket yet(er) utet.

But Hachäkyum doesn't want to touch their balche', he doesn't want to try their tamales. He doesn't want to touch their braziers. The new god pots,[7] Hachäkyum doesn't want them, or the tamales or the posol—nothing. Well, he touches it (but) he doesn't accept it. Neither does T'uup. He doesn't touch anything. He sides with his father.

Bay.

Okay.

Nukuch winik tan uts'o'oksik ba'che' yete(r) huun, tuworo(r), "Ma' uxurik t'an Hachäkyum. Ma' axurik t'an yete(r) T'uup. Ma' axurik t'an. Ne yah inwu'yik."

The ancestors are finishing their (offerings) (of) balche' and bark cloth, everything. "Don't end the world, Hachäkyum. Don't end the world with T'uup. Don't end the world. We will suffer a lot."

Tarak uxurt'an.

But the end of the world had already (begun).

Bay.

Okay.

K'uchi(h) tuk'in. Lehi(h) k'uch(ih). T(i') up'iis uk'ini(r) ti' uxurik t'an ti' utap'ik ahk'in. "Ele, bay," T'uup yete(r) Hachäkyum. "Ele lehi(h) bähe' ka'(ah) bin axureh, T'uup." Bähe' kubin (u)tap'ik la' k'in, tun. Ts'o'ok'i(h) ti' lu'umo' tun. Ts'o'ok.

The time came. It came. At the same time he ends the world (T'uup) covers up the sun. "All right," Hachäkyum (says to) T'uup. "So, it is now that you will end it, T'uup." Now he will go and cover up the sun. It's over for the mortals now. It's over.

Uhaan ahHachäkyum, Ak'inchob, ne tukur ukah, "'Utsereh, bik inbin in-me(n)tik? Bähe' kuhachbin a' xurt'an tun. Mäna' kubin ti'ri(') lu'umo'."

Hachäkyum's son-in-law, Ak'inchob, is getting very worried. "Dear me, what am I going to do? He's really going to end the world now. None of the mortals are going to be saved."

"Boon?" akna'e'ex ti' Hachäkyum tukur ukah. "'Utse(re)h bähe' inwaa(r)o' ma' bin uti'ri('). Bin ukah lahkimi(n)."

"How many (will die)?" Hachäkyum's wife is getting worried. "Dear me, now none of my children are going to be saved. They're all going to die."

Haawo' ti' kura'(a)n ti' uka'ani(r) Hachäkyum. Tan uche'extik uyu'yeh ba'i(n)ki(n) kutsikbartik Hachäkyum yete(r) T'uup. Tan ulahu'yik Haawo'.

The Haawo' are there in Hachäkyum's sky. They are listening to what Hachäkyum is saying to T'uup. The Haawo' hear everything.

Uhaan Hachäkyum lehi(h) kumanaaka' utaasik. Kukusik pom, hu'un, k'ik'. Tuworo(r) ba'(ar) kulahkusik ti' Hachäkyum, ti' uyäkan.

Hachäkyum's son-in-law races to deliver (the people's offerings to Hachäk-yum). He brings copal resin, bark cloth, rubber. He brings everything to Hachäkyum, his father-in-law.

Hachäkyum mäna' utä(r)ik t(i') uhaan. Mäna' utä(r)ik ti'. Mäna'. (Tu)cha'ah ukusik nika'(a)n. Ma' uhantik. Yan nahwah—tuworo(r) ba'(ar); ma'ats', tuworo(r). Boon ahpom kuts'ahba(n) ti', woro(r) pom. Mäna' utä(r)ik Hachäkyum.

Hachäkyum doesn't touch anything from his son-in-law. He doesn't touch anything from him, nothing. He lets him bring them and pile them up. He doesn't eat them. There are tamales—everything; posol, everything. So much copal is given to him, all of it (pure) copal. Hachäkyum doesn't touch any of it.

Bay.

Okay.

Akyant'o' ma' uyohe(r). Ne naach, yan ne ch'ik pach k'ak'na' yani(n).

Akyant'o' doesn't know. He is far away, way off on the other side of the sea.

Ele, tuch'ahah ahk'in tun. Tuyaak'ächa(r). Yah tutap'ah ahk'in t(i') uku(r) urmeek'mah ahT'uup. Umeek'mah yok'or uk'äb. Hunxet' uk'äb umeek'mah akna'.

And then, (T'uup) seized the sun, now. It is getting dark. T'uup has just covered up the sun and is sitting with it in his arms. He hugs it in his arms. Under one arm he has cradled the moon.

Ele, uhaan ahHachäkyum bin uk'ana(r)yok. Bin ukäxtik up'äyik ahAkyant'o' ch'ik pach k'ak'na' bin(ih). T(i') uhachk'ana(r) yok ka'(ah) bini(h.). Uhaan Hachäkyum, Ak'inchob, tak ch'ik pach k'ak'na' bini(h).

And then, Hachäkyum's son-in-law rushes off. He goes off to look for him, to alert Akyant'o' way over on the other side of the sea. He is running hard. Hachäkyum's son-in-law, Ak'inchob, went to the other side of the sea.

K'uchi(h) to'an pach k'ak'na' t(i') ukaha(r) ahAkyant'o'. Ma' uyohe(r) ti' Akyant'o'. Uher k'aax ti'. Uher k'ine(r). Ma' ma' la' kahtich'k'ä'i(r) ma' a' la'eh ti' Akyant'o' kuk'anik. Ti'ri(') ti'.

He got to Akyant'o''s town on the other side of the sea. He doesn't know (this place of) Akyant'o'. The forest is different there. It has another sun. The light is not ours. Akyant'o' uses a separate one.

K'uchih. Bin uyaaka' Ak'inchob. Ne ka'ni(h), tumen ti' yaaka' ka'(ah) bin(ih). Ne ka'ni(h) ka'(ah) k'uch(ih).

Ak'inchob arrived. He is very tired, because he (had been) running. He is very tired when he arrived.

"Ti' yan way, yum?" kih. "Ti' yan? Mäna'. Ti' yan? Mäna'."

"Are you here, Lord?" says (Ak'inchob). (He mutters to himself,) *"Is he there? No, he's not. Is he there? No, he's not."*

AhAkyant'o' hak'a' t(i') uxim(b)a(r), ma' ku(r)a'(a)n ich uyatoch. Ma' ti' yan ich uyatoch.

Akyant'o' had left for a walk a moment ago. He's not sitting in his house. He's not in his house.

Se(e)b bin t'anah t(i') uyani(n). Se(e)b bini(h) payah. Se(e)b suti(h), Akyant'o'. Se(e)b tari(h).

Quickly (Ak'inchob) went where he is to talk to him. He quickly went to call him. Akyant'o' spun around and hurried back.

"Eh ba'i(n)k(in) kume(n)tik?"

"Eh, what's going on?" (asks Akyant'o').

"(U)lu'umo'," kih. "Tar(en) . . . inwireh a tech, yumeh," kih. "Wa h(e') atar awireh t(i') uka'ani(r) Hachäkyum. 'Otsi(r) lu'umo'. Mäna'. Bin ukah xurt'an ti'."

"It's the mortals," he says. "I came to see . . . you, my Lord," he says. "Will you come to Hachäkyum's sky? The poor mortals. There is no (hope for them). The end of the world has begun for them."

Eh kunuukik Akyant'o', "Hach hah wa tan uxurik t'an ti' lu'umo'?"
And Akyant'o' replies, "Is that true he is ending the world for the mortals?"

"Akyum bin uxurik ti' lu'umo'. He' wa (a)tar awireh?"
"Our Lord is going to end it for the mortals. Will you come see (him)?"

"He'e'!" kih. "He' intar."
"Of course," (Akyant'o') says. "I'm coming."

Lik'ih Akyant'o'. "Ko'ox!"
Akyant'o' got up. "Let's go!" (he says).

Tuhachk'ana(r) yok.
They rush off.

Akyant'o' t(i') useebta(r) uk'uchur t(i') uka'ani(r) Hachäkyum, tu' kura'(a)n Hachäkyum tu' ka'ana(n). Se(e)bse(e)b t(an) uhachk'ana(r) yok.
Akyant'o' has to hurry to get to Hachäkyum's sky, where Hachäkyum is seated above. He is really running hard.

K'uch(ih) uyaaka' Akyant'o'. Tuya'arah ti', "Ehhh." [Toh naach ka'(ah) tuyirah.]
Akyant'o' came running. (Hachäkyum) said to (T'uup), "Ehhh." [Akyant'o' is still in the distance when Hachäkyum saw him.][8]

"Tan utichi(r) Akyant'o'," tuya'arah, Hachäkyum yete(r) T'uup. "T'uupeh," kih tuya'arah Hachäkyum, "bähe' ma' ame(n)tik t'an ti' kyum, tarak wa kuch'a'ik a' k'in, mäna' ma' to'on yani(r), akyum kubin uya'areh wa."

"Akyant'o' is approaching," Hachäkyum said (to) T'uup. "T'uup," says Hachäkyum, "now don't say a word to our Lord, even if he grabs the sun and says it isn't ours."

"Bay," tuya'arah T'uup. "Bay."

"Okay," said T'uup. "Okay."

Ele, k'uchi(h) Akyant'o' tu' kura'an Hachäkyum.

And then, Akyant'o' arrived where Hachäkyum is seated.

(U)pur(ik) ut'an, "Akyant'o'eh!"

(Hachäkyum) calls out, "Hey, Akyant'o'!"

"Kux ba'i(n)ki(n) kame(n)tike'ex? Lu'umo' bin yumeh," kih.

"What are you doing? It's about the mortals, Lord," (Akyant'o') says.

Eh tunuukah Hachäkyum, "Ele tan inxurik ti' lu'umo'. 'Oy inwirik woro(r) maska' yan t(i') uk'äb. Ne 'oy inwor ti' be'in kinxurik tanah."

And Hachäkyum replied, "Well, I'm ending it for the mortals. I'm tired of seeing (them) with machetes in their hands all the time. I'm so tired of it, so now I'm going to end it."

Eh tunuukah Akyant'o', "E-h-h-h, 'otsi(r) lu'umo'. Ma' pim. Ma' 'as pim ame(n)tikech ameyah. Awinik tech, yum," kih.

Akyant'o' replied, "E-h-h-h, the mortals are piteous. They aren't many; you (didn't) make very many. They're your (only) people, Lord.'"

Eh unuukik Hachäkyum, "Pero ne 'oy inwor ti', woro(r) kinsah yan t(i')
uk'äb. Woro(r) (u)kinsik ubäho'; ne woro(r) huur yan ti'. Mäna'. Ne 'oy inwor ten. Ma' ink'a't inwireh bek."

And Hachäkyum replies, "But I'm so sick of it, all the wars, the killing all
around. They kill their brothers; they all have arrows. It's no use. I'm sick
of it. I don't want to see it like this."

Tunuukah Akyant'o', "'Otsi(r) lu'umo', yumeh," kih. "Ma' pim awaar tech.
Ten inmeenkahi(r) ne pim. Bay. Tan uturik (u)k'aax. Tu(r)ur hach turik
k'aax. Yan kinsah. Yan chäkpipit tu' yan tuworo(r) maska' t(u)me(n)tah ti'.
Baayla' kumaan lu'um. Eh baayla' kumaan ka'ana(n)."

Akyant'o' replied, "Poor mortals, my Lord," he says. "Your children are few.
My creations are many. Okay, they're filling up the forest; they have really
fill(ed) up the forest. There is killing. (The land) is bare where they (have)
used their machetes. Thus, the earth will pass on. Thus, the sky will pass
on."[10]

AhHachäkyum (u)kurur (u)ch'e'ext(ik) uyu'yah, mäna' nuukik. Mix T'uup,
mix unuukik. Kura'(a)n.

Hachäkyum sits and listens closely (but) he doesn't respond. Neither does
T'uup respond. He (just) sits there.

Ele, tuya'arah Akyant'o', "Wa he're', yumeh," kih, "tech kabin akänäntik in-
meenkahi(r) ch'ik pach k'ak'na'."

And then, Akyant'o' says, "Will you, my Lord, protect my creations way
over on the other side of the sea?"

Eh tunuukah Hachäkyum, "Ele ma', yumeh."

And Hachäkyum replied, "Alas, no, my Lord."

Akyant'o', "Ten kinsuut inkänä(n)tik way yok'o(r) k'aax ti' lu'umo'. Ne
'otsi(r) inwi(r)ik, lu'umo'. Ne ki' umeyah, ne ki' tuworo(r) a' nika'(a)n. He'

pom, nahwah, ba'che'. Ne ki' meen(a'an) awo'och, yumeh," kih. "Bik yani(n) ma' tach'a'ah ti' lu'umo'. Ne 'otsi(r) lu'umo'. Ma' k'äs pim ameyah tech, yumeh."

Akyant'o' (said), "I will return to take care of it here in the forest of the mortals. I feel so sorry for the mortals. Their work is very good, all of it piled up here is very good. Here there is copal, tamales, ba'che'. Your food is well made, my Lord," he says. "Why don't you take it from the mortals? The poor mortals. There are hardly any of your creations, my Lord."

Hachäkyum kura'(a)n. T'uup kura'an. Mix ut'an. Ele, "Bay, yumeh," kih. "Bin ukah siistar lu'umo' tun," kih. "Ts'a(eh?) ten la' k'in, tun."

Hachäkyum sits there. T'uup sits there. Neither speaks. And then, (Hachäkyum) says, "All right, my Lord. The mortals are going to freeze, now. Give me the sun, now," (Hachäkyum says to T'uup).

K'uch(ih) uyaaka' Akyant'o' tu' kura'(a)n ahT'uup. Tumeek'ah la' k'in Akyant'o' bin upu(r)eh ch'ik chun ka'an seeb. Hach ma' sahih ubin, k'uchih chun ka'an Akyant'o' ut'äkik a' k'in.

Akyant'o' runs over to where T'uup is sitting. Akyant'o' clutched the sun and left quickly to put it way up in the center of the sky. Soon after he goes, Akyant'o' arrived at the center of the sky (and) sticks in the sun.

Ha(ch) ma' sahin (u)bin—POHPOHPOH aht'er. Ele, "TERESEHHH."

Shortly after that a rooster goes (ruffling its feathers)—POHPOHPOH. And then (it goes), "COCK-A'DOODLE-DOO."[11]

Ba'axta(r) ahbarum, ch'een kuhum ahbarum. Boon ahbarum a' k'aax lahch'een uhum. Ubarum a' ka'an lahch'eeni(h). Mäna.'

Just then, the jaguars stop making noise. There is no (noise). All the jaguars of the forest stop making noise. The jaguars of the heavens all stopped. There isn't any (noise).[12]

Ba'axta(r) nukuch winik täsa(n) ton; ma' chich umuuk'. Lahto'ochi(h) yete(r) siisi(r). 'Otsir, mäna'. Uhaan ahHachäkyum, lehi(h) kukänä(n)tik ulu'umo' tema' chi'bir ten barum. Lehi(h) ka'lah'eemi(h) uyä(h)seh se(e)b. Uhaan ahHachäkyum, lehi(h) umaan uyä(h)seh tuworo(r) ti' uka'lik'ir äknukire'ex uchik. T(an) uhätsä' ten sisi(r), porque mäna' k'ak'. Mäna'. Lah tu'p(b)i(r). Boona tan upok(ik) ubäh yok'or ich uk'ur lahto'och. Ti' ween(ih) ti' ch'eeri(h) ti'.[13] Lah to'och yete(r) si(i)si(r).

Now the ancestors are lying spread-eagle; they don't have any strength. They are frozen stiff. Poor things, they don't have any strength. The son-in-law of Hachäkyum guards the mortals so that they don't get eaten by the jaguars. He descended again to shake them awake. The son-in-law of Hachäkyum goes around waking them all, so that our ancestors get up again. They are succumbing to the cold, because there isn't any fire. There isn't any; it went out. All (the men) that (were) praying in the god house are stiff. They went to sleep there (and then) fell over. They are frozen stiff.

Tuya'arah Akyant'o', "Bähe' tint'an, yumeh, ten kinbin, ten kinlisik ut'ani(r). Tech yete(r) ten yete(r) T'uup ka(k)k'atik akoor (h)asta kintar inwa'areh ne tur inmeenkahi(r) wa kurenturu(r) k'aax, kurenturu(r) wa, ele inbähi(r) ten kintar way inwarik ele turi(h) tun k'aax. Ele kintar way, yumeh."

Akyant'o' said, "Now I think, my Lord, I'm going to go and lift (Hachäkyum's) order. You (Hachäkyum) and I and T'uup will agree, together (when to end the world). I will say when my creations are complete, when the (world) is overflowing with them. Then I'll come here, in person, to say that the forest full. I will come here, my Lord."

Hachäkyum kura'(a)n.

Hachäkyum just sits there.

T'uup kura'(a)n. Mix unuukik.

T'uup just sits there. Neither answers.

"Ele, bähe', yumeh," kih. Kupurik uwich Akyant'o' bin nika'(a)n a' ba'che', tuworo(r) le'. "Ne ne ki' meena('an)." Bin yaaka' Akyant'o', bin t(i') unika'an ba'che' tutekch'a'atah. "He' tech yumeh," kih. "'Uk'eh! Umeyah alu'umo'."

"So, now, my Lord," Akyant'o' looks at all the balche' and everything else laid out there. "It is very well made." Akyant'o' ran over to the balche' and grabbed it. "This here is for you, my Lord," he says. "Drink it! It is the work of your mortals."

Kutar kuch'a'ik Hachäkyum. Kumaasik ti' T'uup. Kutar kuch'a'ik T'uup.

Hachäkyum comes over (and) takes it. He passes it to T'uup. T'uup comes over and takes it.

Ele kupurik ut'an Akyant'o', "Pur(eh) uho'or tech, yumeh," kih. "Tech! T'uup, pur(eh) uho'o(r)."

And then Akyant'o' announces, "You, send the first drop, my Lord," he says. "You, T'uup, send the first (drop)."[14]

"Bay." Ele upur(ik) uho'(or) bin. T(an) ulahpur(ik) (u)ho'(or), "(U)tar uho'(or) tech yum, ba'che'. (U)tar uho'(or)."

"Okay," (says T'uup). And so he offers the first (drop). He is offering the first (drop) (while he chants), "The first offering of balche' comes to you, Lord. It comes to the (god pot)."

Le' tuyuk'ah Akyant'o' ba'che'.

Then he drank Akyant'o''s balche'.

Hachäkyum tuyuk'ah ti'. Y T'uup lah tulah'uk'ah.

Hachäkyum drank it. And T'uup drank it all up.

Ba'axta(r), tan utsikbar Akyant'o'. Ne tsoy uyor. Tuyarah, "Bähe', yan ti' kak'atik akoor ma' ha'ri' tech, yumeh, yete(r) T'uup ka'(ah) (a)bin axurik t'an ti' lu'umo'; mäna' (h)asta kintar ten ket kak'atik akoor. Ele, kurentuu(r) (in)meenkahi(r) ten, kulahxupik k'aax, mäna' tuworo(r) lu'um, ele ten kintar. Wa tawirah mäna' intar, ma' täy[15] xuruk t'an. Lu'umo' tan uts'ahik ba'che'; tan uts'ahik tum(b)en lek; tan uts'ahik siir; tan uts'ahik chäk hu'un; k'ik'; tuworo(r). Ch'a'eh! 'Otsir, ka'n!"

And now Akyant'o' is talking. He is in good spirits. He said, "Now we must agree that it is not only you, my Lord, and T'uup (that) will end the world for the mortals; not until I come will we agree. When my creations have filled (the earth), when they (have) destroy(ed) the forest, (when) there is nothing (left) of the land, then I will come. If you don't see me come, (then) the world will not end. The mortals are offering balche'; they are offering new god pots; they are offering small braziers (of copal); they are offering red bark cloth;[16] rubber; everything. Take it! Poor things, they are tired!"

"Ak'inchob, ka'n uyok. Kukusik tech, cha'eh, yumeh! Ne ki' umeyah lu'umo'."

"Ak'inchob's feet are tired. When he brings (their offerings) to you, take them, my Lord! The work of the mortals is very good."

Ele Kyantho'[17] tuya'arah, "Cha'eh!"

Akyant'o' said, "Take it!"

"Ne ki'. Ten inmeenkahi(r). Ten mäna' inp'aktik inmeyah ten, inmeenkahi(r). Mäna' inp'aktik. Tan uts'ahik ten. Tan inch'a'ik."

(Hachäkyum says,) "It's delicious. They are my creations. I don't detest my work, my creations. I don't detest them. They are giving (their offering) to me (and) I am taking it."

Ele, Kyanto' tuya'arah, "Mäna' nen pim, inmeenkahi(r). Ne yan kinsah, ne yan tuworo(r). Mäna' inwa'(ar)ik kinxurik (u)t'an. Tech, yumeh, ki' tukreh awoher; ma' pim awaarech tech. Mäna' pim. Mäna'. 'Otsir. Ne ki' umeyah. Ch'a'eh! Hanteh! Bähe', ts'o'ok."

And then, Akyant'o' said, "There aren't many of them, but my people are many. There is so much fighting everywhere. I couldn't say when I (would) destroy the world. (But) you, my Lord, think about it carefully: your children are few; there aren't many, no. Poor things. Their work is good. Take it! Eat it! Now (the threat of ending the world) is over."

Ele, bex tutsikbartah äknukire'ex, Haawo'. Lati' tuyu'yah; Haawo' tuyu'yah utsikbar be'ik tume(n)tah Hachäkyum yete(r) T'uup yete(r) Kyantho'.

Well, that is how our ancestors, the Haawo', told the story. They heard it. The Haawo' heard the discussion among Hachäkyum, T'uup, and Akyant'o'.

'Ähah

Antonio Martinez

The 'Ähah[1] were orphans who were not quite human and not quite super-natural but were of a race of men who were endowed with an unusually long penis.[2] It was so long that it served as a loincloth.[3] This put the boys at a grave disadvantage: they could not marry because they managed to kill every woman that they slept with. Unable to keep a wife and fulfill the role as husband and provider, the boys became despondent.[4] In the end, one hanged himself, and the other was annihilated by a bolt of lightning hurled at him by one of the ha'ha'nahk'uh rain deities.[5]

The reason for their creation is unclear, but Hachäkyum saw the neces-sity of eliminating them after the second 'Ähah had seized the great fan of the ha'ha'nahk'uh, which they use to stir up storms and set in motion the beginning of the Deluge.

Little rain deities are ubiquitous in the indigenous stories from the Americas. Like the ha'ha'nahk'uh, they live under rocks and in caves throughout the landscape. A common sequence in many Mayan stories entails an errant boy getting into trouble with the rain deities and unleash-ing a thunderstorm (e.g., "The Rainmaker's Apprentice" [Bierhorst 1998] and "Chac" [Bierhorst 1986]).

'Ähah, bik tuyarah äknukire'ex, kutoop'o(r) 'Ähah bin, chan 'Ähah ne tsoy. Ma' k'äs ts'iik; ne kukäxan kab. 'Ähah ne kuch'a'(ik) kab. Ne tsoy uyor äkna'e'ex ti'. Äkna' way. 'Ähah kutseentik. Te' huntuur 'Ähah, te' huntuur 'Ähah. Eh ne tsoy uyirik 'Ähah.

The 'Ähah, as our ancestors said, when the 'Ähah are born, the little 'Ähah were very good. They are docile; they just look for honey. The 'Ähah collect honey all the time. Our ancestor mothers are very happy with them. Our mother(s) here[6] raise the 'Ähah as their own. One 'Ähah belongs to one and the other 'Ähah belongs to another. They love the 'Ähah very much.

Ma' k'äs ts'iik; ne kukäxan kab, woro(r) ch'ach'a'(ik) kab. Mäna' bin ubu(h)hartik kab. Na'ak(ih) k'ä' che', bix uk'ä' unukuch che' kuna'akar uyeens(ik) 'Ähah.

They are well behaved; they look for honey all the time, they just collect honey. They don't do anything else but split open (hives) and remove the honey. The 'Ähah climb up the branches of large tree(s) and bring down the honey.

Ele, ka'ah 'oy uyor bin tun. Ele tan utsikbartik, tun, äknukire'ex bin, "Eh, bähe', na'eh," kih. "Na'exeh, bin aka(h) (a)wir(eh) ints'o'ok inch'äkik kab bähe' ten. Bin inkins(ik) inbah. Ts'o'ok(ih) inmeyah. Ts'o'okih way ten inna'eh," kih.

And then, one becomes bored. So then, our ancestor is talking about it (with his mother), "So now, mother," he says. "Mother dear, you are about to see me stop collecting honey. I'm going to kill myself. My work is finished. It's finished for me here, mother," he says.

"Ma' 'Ähah," kih. "Ma' (a)kins(i)k abah."

"No, 'Ähah," she says. "Don't kill yourself."

"Ma'. Bin inkins(ik) inbah, na'exeh," kih. "Ne 'oy inwor ti'. Ts'o'ok(ih) inmeyah way yok'o(r) k'aax. Ts'o'ok inhanan. Ts'o'ok."

"No. I'm going to kill myself, mother," he says. "I'm so bored with it. My work here in the forest is finished. My food is finished. It's finished."

Ts'o'ok ulaht'ot'o(h)ch'äktik. Bin (u)na'aka(r) (u)k'äb la' nukuch che', bix a' nuk kura'(an) nukuch säk pukte'. (T)ulahharah (u)yaak'i(r). Tulahxatah bin. (T)ulahxatah k'äbche'—CHA!

He finished hacking away all the vines. He's going to climb up the branch of a large tree, like the large *säk pukte'* [7] standing there. He pulled off all the vines. He cut them all with his machete. He chopped all the branches off—CHA!

Toh ulahhari(k), eeeh lech kuhook'or ut'an, "Bähe', na'exeh," kih ...
As soon as he removes them all, he suddenly announces, "Now, mother dear ..."

Hach chen yu'yah utar bin—*wwwoooosh*—
She only heard him coming—*wwwoooosh*—

"aaAH!"—PIIIN.
"aaAH!"—THUD.

Tupurah uk'äb ti' bix to'one'ex äkbäk'ere'ex to'an tu' kuch'ur[8]—HANECH—(tu)hu(r)che'et(ah) ich uhoor ukaar.
He put this hand on his penis—YANK—and thrust it down his throat.

Le' x-i-i-i-b, bin 'Ähah, mäna'.
Th-i-i-i-s 'Ähah is gone, he is finished.

Le' ts'o'ok 'Ähah.
This 'Ähah is finished.

[Baayi huntu(ur) kukimi(n). Baayi(h) huntu(ur) kukimi(n). Tuworo(r) yok'o(r) k'aax ah'Ähaheh bin.]
[The other one is going to die, too. The other one is going to die, too. The 'Ähah went everywhere in the forest.][9]

Ele, binih huntuu(r). Tarih huntuur ah'Ähahi(r). [Woro(r) bex tukins(ah) ubäho' yok'o(r) (u)k'äb che', tukinsah ubah.]
So the other one went. The other 'Ähah came. [Just like his brother (who) killed himself on the branches, he killed himself (too).]

Ele, tarih huntuu(r). Tuyirah tuyaaka'tah ahhuh. La' bix ahnukuch winik
una' bin(ih) tun, "K'äs ts'ah(eh) awo'och 'Ähah ten ahuh," kih, "porque ne
ti(n) ts'i'o(r)t(ik)."

So, the other one came along. He saw an iguana and chased it. Just like the
(other) ancestor's mother, she went (to him) now, "Please 'Ähah, give me
your iguana," she says, "because I really crave it."

"Ma' na'exeh. Ma' ints'ahik tech inwo'och huh. Ma' ints'ahik tech. Ne ki'
uchi'ah chuhuchuh uyoot'e(r)."

"No, mother dear. I won't give you my iguana. I won't give it to you. The
charred skin is good to chew on."[10]

"K'äs ts'aah ten a' he'ra'; ne ch'ik yum."

"Please give me that very big one."

"Ma' la'eh." Uki'teet(ik) bin ti'. Suum(ir) uyo'och uyahahkuchk'äxman
uyok. Ulahk'äxman uk'äb, ulahk'äxman uyok. Woro(r) huh. A' bix ahtorok.

"Not that one." He carefully selects (another one) for her. His food on the
rope hangs heavily by their feet. All their hands and all their feet are tied
together. They are all iguanas. (They're) like the basilisk lizards.[11]

Ele uteetik bin ti' una'. Kuts'ahik, "He'eh."

And so he goes to select (one) for his mother. He gives it to her, "Here."

T-o-o-o(h)kächkih. Bähe' hitich niiki(r). To(k)k'ah, t'äkchäh tu' ch'uya'(an)
bin hayniki(r). "UyyyAAAiyee."[12]

(The rope) is splitting. Now it's loose and (the iguanas) are piled up (on the
ground). They fell suddenly, they snap off from where they were hanging
and scatter. "UyyyAAAiyee."

"Eh! Taputs'ah inwo'och huh na'exeh!" kih.

"Eh! You let my iguanas escape, mother!" he says.

Ye-e-e-t bin(ih) kansutu(r) umaan …

He went after them, propelling (himself) from side to side …

"Mäna'. Taputs'ah inwo'och huh. He' awu'yik bin ayaah t(i') ink'äb na'e'exeh. He' awirik ten wa. Tech taputs'ah inwo'och huh."

"They're gone. You let my iguanas escape. You're going to feel the (sting) of my hand, mother. You're going to get it. You let my iguanas escape."

Upäktik ubin huntu(ur). Ti' ok(ih) yok'o(r) muuri(r) tunich bin, *k-o-r-r-r-um*.

He spots another one go. It entered a pile of rocks, *k-o-r-r-um*.

Yet ok(ih) tu' ok(ih)! Ti' utar *k'ooro(r)*, kupaani('i)h.

He went in after it! There comes a *bump-clunk*, as the (rocks) collapse there.

"Hook'en 'Ähah! Hoy ti'," kih. "Binih."

"Get out of there, 'Ähah! Forget about it," says (the mother.) "It's gone."

"Ma' na'exeh. Ch'ukteh. Ka'(ah) hook'en pur inwok, he' awu'yik bin aya'h t(i') ink'äb."

"No, mother. Wait for me. When I jump out of here, you're going to feel the (sting) of my hand."

"Mäna'," kih. Ch'en kut'ana(r). Ele, t(an) utar *ch'e'* E-E-E-H.

"No," she says. She stops speaking. And then, a *rrrruU-U-U-MBLE* comes.

…

…

"K'äs! Hook'en 'Ähah!"

"Please! Get out, 'Ähah!" (says the mother).

"Mäna' ma' inhook'o(r)," kih. "Le bähe' turah inharik inwo'och huh. Ch'ukteh. Ka'(ah) hook' inpur inwo'ocheh h(e') inyaatikech ink'äb."

"No, I'm not coming out," he says. "Now I have to pull out my iguana. Wait (here). When I come out and throw down my food, I'm going to slap you."

"Ma', 'Ähah ..."

"No, 'Ähah ..."

Eh, ma' uyant'ant'antik. Ts'o'ok.

And then, she isn't chattering anymore. (Her chattering) stopped.

Täka'an uxikin.

He listens intently.

"*Ch-i-i-i-n,*" kih.[13]

"*R-a-t-t-l-e.*"

Bin(ih) taami(r) tun. Binih. Tulahmäk ube(r) tu' hook'ih. Lahtsärah a' tunich tu' hook'(ih) tu' ube(r).

He went deep(er) now. He went. The path covered over (with boulders) behind him. All the rocks tremble on the path behind him.

Ele, hach ma' xanahih, bin tuneh, hook'(ih) yaaka' haräkniki(r). Ha'-ha'nahk'uh bin ka'(ah) hook'ih tun. Ha'ha'nahk'uh.

And then, in no time, the ha'ha'nahk'uh ran out now. The ha'ha'nahk'uh (came) when he went out then. The ha'ha'nahk'uh.

Lahi(h) binih 'Ähah a' la'eh. Ele iik' kutichi(r) bin. Hach ho(ch)charakche' hach läk. Tahantahan kutsarik uyiik'ar bin a' ha'ha'nahk'uh. A(h)'Äha la(hih) ch'ikrah.

The 'Ähah went in there. And then the wind comes up. The trees are yanked up. Back and forth he churns up the wind (with the paddle) of the ha'ha'nahk'uh. The 'Ähah stands there.

Ch'ika('a)n bin, t(an) upeeksik ch'ikrik, tan usutik uwaar ahk'uh. Tan uhachki'sutik uyiik'al. Bix a' che' ho(ch)chal ubin. Mix pak'al, mäna' pätan, mäna' ts'in, mäna' ba'(al).[14]

He is standing there, fixed on the spot, he is moving it, he is spinning the fan of the gods. He is really churning the wind. Consequently the trees are getting pulled out of the earth. There aren't any plants, there aren't bananas, there aren't manioc bushes, there isn't anything (left).

. . .

. . .

Eknukire'ex bin t'anih ti' ha'ha'nahk'uh, "Xen at'aneh. Le' 'Ähah uwiniki(r)."

Our ancestors went and called upon the ha'ha'nahk'uh, "Go call him. The 'Ähah has taken over (the fan)."

Bin yaaka' ti' ha'ha'nahk'uh. Tuts'aah ahha'ha'nahk'uh bin. tekts'o'ok te', ma' k'uchih.[15] Pur(ih) turah uxuur unäk'i(r). Teench'intah ten uyiik'ar.

The ha'ha'nahk'uh sped (toward) him. The ha'ha'nahk'uh gave it their all, they went head on (into the wind), but they didn't get there. They skirted to the side. They were pushed aside by the wind.

. . .

. . .

Ele, t(an) uts'aaba(r) ti' Hachäkyumeh, "Eh 'eeme(n) 'ireh," kih. "Le' tan uxurt'an tun. Ma' tsoy ba' tume(n)tik 'Ähah."

And then, (the order) is being given by Hachäkyum, "Eh, go down and see," he says (to other ha'ha'nahk'uh). "He's bringing about the end of the world. What the 'Ähah is doing is very bad."

Tan ubin uyaaka'.[16]

They go running off.

'Eemih uyaaka' ubähi(r) ha'ha'nahk'uh. K'uch(ih) tu' ch'ika'(a)n . . . Tan upee(k)sik uwaar . . .

(One of them) came down running. He got to where he is standing . . . (The 'Ähah) is moving the fan . . .

"Ma' bik inme(n)tik," kih. "Bik inme(n)tik ti'? Bin ink(ah) inch'akeh wa."

"I don't know how to do it," (the ha'ha'nahk'uh) says. "What shall I do with him? I'm going to cut him down."

Tupurah uk'äb tekchuktah a' waar bähe', "T-A-A-H-H-H."

He threw out his hand and snatched the fan, "T-A-A-H-H-H" [lightning strikes].

Bex 'a'arabi(h) lahpeknah lu'um. CHUX-UX-UX-UH. Lahpeknah ka'. Le' nahch'ikrik 'Ähah; chäkhare'n ch'ikrikeh.

It was said that the entire land quaked. CHUX-UX-UX-UH. The entire earth quaked. The 'Ähah was still standing; he stood there glowing red.

Ele, chen uta'ani(r) ah'Ähah. Lah'eeri(h) bin. Kah lahpuk'i(h) uta'ani(r), mäna'. Le' bähe ts'o'okih 'Ähah.

But then the 'Ähah (turns to) ashes. He burned up. When his ashes dissolved, there was nothing left of him. So now the 'Ähah is finished.

Bähe' mäna' 'Ähah,

Now the 'Ähah is no more.

Iik' bin hum. Lah ts'o'ok iik'. Mäna'.

The wind died down. The wind completely stopped. There was nothing left of him.

Tarak bähe', ts'o'oki(h) (u)ya'axk'in utar iik' ti' 'Ähah.

Up to now, that was to be the last year the 'Ähah's wind would come.

"Le' ma' yan toop'ih 'Ähah," tuya'ara(h) Hachäkyum. Ma' uk'a't. "Ts'o'ok."

"The 'Ähah must not be born," declared Hachäkyum. He didn't want them. "It's over."

Ba'wih 'Ähah kuhook'o(r) yok'o(r) k'aax? 'Ähah ma' k'uchur umuuk' (ti') ha'ha'nahk'uh. Poch ukatik umuuk' yete(r) ha'ha'nahkuh, pero ma'. Ts'o'ok. Tuch'akah. Ts'o'ok. Ele, ts'o'okih 'Ähah. Takih bähe' mäna' akhook'ore'ex 'Ähah.

Why (did) the 'Ähah go out in the forest? The 'Ähah was no match for ha'ha'nahk'uh. He wanted to copy the power of the ha'ha'nahk'uh, but no. It was over. (The ha'ha'nahk'uh) cut him down. And so, the 'Ähah are finished. Up to now, there are none of us who come out like 'Ähah.

Bek tutsikbartah uhistoria ahnukuch winik.

This is how the ancestors recounted the story.

Ka'wäts'äk uho'or Barum yeter K'ak'
'The Two-Headed Jaguar and the Lord of Fire'

Säk Ho'or

In this story K'ak' 'Lord Fire, Courage' confronts and then kills the two-headed jaguar, Ka'wäts'äk uho'(or) Barum.[1] During this period, the ancestors had not yet been created. The land was populated by terrestrial deities, some of whom were the *chemberk'uho'* 'pedestrian gods'.[2]

In this story the chemberk'uho' are wondering what to do about the two-headed jaguar. Their attempts to kill it fail because he splits into two fearsome jaguars when shot with an arrow. K'ak' hears about the problem and steps in to help. It takes him three tries before he is able to defeat the two-headed jaguar. His quick thinking and good aim kill both of them with one arrow. He plunges his hand into the jaguar's chest, yanks out his heart, and eats it. Then he daubs the blood all over his tunic. In his blood-stained grandeur he returns to the chemberk'uho' to announce his victory.

Lacandones regard K'ak' as the embodiment of courage, the lord of the hunt, and the maker of arrows.[3] He is associated with the jaguar in the mythology of all Mesoamerican cultures. As one of the most efficient and aggressive of all predators, the jaguar was integrated into Mayan religious and secular spheres as the symbol of courage and power. Warriors and hunters appropriated the jaguar as their emblem. They donned jaguar pelts to infuse themselves with his essence.[4] Like K'ak', Mayan warriors would paint spots on their bodies with the blood of their victims, in imitation of the jaguar.

Bay.
Okay.

A' ka'wäts'äk uho'(ol) ti' xäkan. Uk'aba', Nah Ts'u(l)u'. Nah Ts'u(l)u' uk'aba' ka'wäts'äk uho'(ol).

The two-headed jaguar is standing there. His name is Nah Ts'ulu'. Nah Ts'ulu' is the name of the two-headed jaguar.[5]

Bay.

Okay.

Chem(b)e(r)k'uho' ne pim ubäho', lah ket.

The "little gods that walk around" have many companions.

Uya'arik ti' ubäho', "Bay. Barum ka'wäts'äk uho'(or), ma' inkinsik. Awirik ne nuk. Ne nuk barum ka'wäts'äk uho'(or). Ma' ukuch inmuuk'."

(One) says to his companions, "Okay, the two-headed jaguar, I (can't) kill it. You see he is very big. The two-headed jaguar is very big. I'm not strong enough."

Bay.

Okay.

Pachi(r) bini(h) K'ak', bini(h) ti' uyireh la'eh barum. Bini(h) uyireh ka'wäts'äk uho'(or) barum. K'uch(ih) uyireh tuha(h)i(r).

Then K'ak' went there to see that jaguar. He went to see the two-headed jaguar. He got there to see if it were true.

Ti' yan ka'wäts'äk uho'(or). Kuhu(r)ik mix kuchukik kuhu(r)ik. Kuhu(r)ik mix kukimi(n).

The two-headed jaguar is there (indeed). He shoots him (but) none of (the arrows) he shoots grabs hold. He shoots him but he never dies.

Ne nuk, ne ch'ik yum ka'wäts'äk uho'(or) barum. Wa kukimi(n), kuxatik ubäh ubäk'er; kuwaaya(r) ka't(uu)ro' akinsik kuwaaya(r) ka't(uu)ro'.

The two-headed jaguar is enormous. When he dies, his body splits and turns into two (jaguars). When you kill him, he becomes two.

Bay.

Okay.

Pachi(r), ka'ah u'ri(h) K'ak' tuya'arah t(i') ubäho', "Tuha(h)i(r), tinwirah nu-kuch barum ka'wäts'äk uho'(or). Ma' ukuch(ur) (in)muk' inkinsik. Ne nuk. Ne ch'ik yum ka'wäts'äk uho'(or). Ne tak ukinsiken. Ne tak uts'ahik ti' ten."

Later, when K'ak' returned, he said to his companions, "It's true, I saw the huge two-headed jaguar. I didn't have the strength to kill him. He's big. The two-headed jaguar is enormous. He very nearly kill(ed) me. He very nearly did me in."

"Eh hah," kih. "Tuha(h)i(r). Ma'ah. Tawirah ten; ka'(ah) tari(h) ne taki(r) ukinsiken. Ne tak uchi'iken. Ne nuk ka'wäts'äk uho'(or) barum."

"Ah, yes," (one of them) says. "It's true. You saw (what happened) to me; when he came he almost kill(ed) me. He almost (ate) me. The two-headed jaguar is enormous."

"Bay," tuya'arah ti' ubäho'. "Tint'an inbin inwirik," tuya'arah K'ak'. Ten kin-bin inwireh wa (u)kuch(ur) inmuuk' inkinseh. Ma' inwoher wa inkinsik inbin inwireh."

"Okay," he said to his companion(s). "I think I'm going to visit him (again)," said K'ak'. "I'm going to see if I'm strong enough to kill him. I don't know if I can kill him (but) I'm going to see."

Bay.

Okay.

K'ak' bini(h). Bini(h) K'ak'. Tuka'irah barum. Tuya'arah ti' K'ak', "Bay. K'ät abäh. K'ät abäh barum. Barum (u)k'ät abäh," kih.

K'ak' left. He visited the jaguar a second time. K'ak' said to him, "Okay. Turn sideways. Turn sideways, jaguar. Jaguar, turn sideways," he said.[6]

Bay. Barum ka'wäts'äk uho'(or) tuk'ätah ubäh. Tusut(ah?) ubäh; tuk'ät(ah) ubäh.

Okay. The two-headed jaguar turned sideways. He spun around; he turned sideways.

Pachi(r), tulamah. [Yan ulom ti' ulamik ba'(ar).] Tulamah. Tuhu(r)ah. [Ka'ts'it uhuu(r) tuch'a'ah ka'(ah) bini(h)—ka'ts'it uhuur.] Tuch'a'ah, tu-hu(r)ah.

Then, (K'ak') speared him. [He has a spear to spear animals.] He speared him. (Then) he shot him with an arrow. [He (had taken) two arrows when he left—two arrows.] He took them and shot them.

Bay. Ma' kimi(h). Tu(ka')lamah. Eh, kimih.

Okay. (The jaguar) didn't die. He speared him (again). And then, he died.

Bay.

Okay.

Pachi(r) tuhaarah upixan. Tulahhaarah upixan, tuworo(r) tulahbaaxtah tu-woro(r) unook'. Tulahmentah (u)nook'. [Yan uyek'e(r) unook' p'iis barum.] Tuharah upixan tulahbaaxtah[7] yete(r) uk'ik'er. Tuworo(r) (u)nook' tulah-baaxtah.

Then, he took out the heart. He removed the heart entirely (and) stained his entire tunic (with the blood). He did this all over his tunic. [His tunic has spots like a jaguar.] He removed the entire heart and stained his (tunic) all over with the blood. He stained his tunic all over with blood.

Ka'(a)h 'u'ri(h), ka'(a)h 'u'rih lati' tuya'arah, "Eh ba'(ar)inki(n) kume(n)tik ahK'ak'?" tuya'arah ubäho'. "Ba'(ar)inki(n) kume(n)tik ahK'ak'? Ba'(ar)in-ki(n) kume(n)tik ka'ah (a)tichir K'ak'?"

When he returned, his companions said, "Eh, what (did) K'ak' do? What (did) K'ak' do? What (did) K'ak' do that he arrives (like this)?"

Chäkape'(e)n[8] unook', lah yan ubaaxban unook'.

His tunic is splotched red all over. His clothes are stained (with blood).

K'ak' tuya'arah, "Tinkinsah ka'wäts'äk uho'(or) barum. Tinkinsah. Ten tin-kinsah."

K'ak' said, "I killed the two-headed jaguar. I killed him. I am the one who killed him."

Bay.

Okay.

Lati' K'ak' tukinsah. Tuya'arah, "Awirik ten, hach tuha(h)i(r). Ten chich in-wo(r). Ten tinkinsah."

K'ak' is the one who killed him. He said, "You see me, it is true. I am brave. I killed him."

Bay.

Okay.

Taki(r) bähe', p'aati(h) bähe' utsikbar lati' ti' K'ak'. Ka'wäts'äk uho'(or) uchik hach tuha(h)i(r) yan.

Up to now, the legend of K'ak' has remained. It is true that the two-headed-jaguar existed.

Hach tuha(h)i(r) yan ka'wäts'äk uho'(or) barum. Lati' p'aati(h) ti' uchik nu-kuch winik.

It is true that there was the two-headed jaguar. (The story) remained for the ancestors (as a model of courage).

Yan nukuch winik chich uyor ma' sahak ti' ba'(ar). Lati' uya'arik ti', "Ten wa inwirik barum inkinsik. Ma' insahtik ten."

There were valiant ancestors that weren't afraid of anything. They say to (others), "If I see a jaguar, I will kill it. I don't fear it."

Yan huhuntu(u)r chich uyor, ma' tuworo(r).

There were some who were valiant, but not everyone.

Lati' K'ak' tukinsah porque K'ak' ma' hach winik, K'ak' lati' k'uh. Lati' uk'an-i(r) k'uh. Lati' uk'aba' ahK'ak'. Lati' tukinsah ka'wäts'äk uho'(or) barum.

It is K'ak' who killed him, because K'ak' is not a man, K'ak' is a god. He is an assistant god. His name is K'ak'. He is the one who killed the two-headed jaguar.

Mensäbäk yeter Hach Winik Tukinsah
'Mensäbäk and the Ancestor He Killed'

K'ayum Ma'ax

Mensäbäk 'Lord of Rain' was jealous of Hachäkyum because he had human assistants that served him.[1] So, one day he stole one of them. But as Mensäbäk only had responsibility over the souls of mortals, he could only take its soul. He captured the assistant by placing his loincloth on the path that the assistant usually took, and when he passed by it, the loincloth turned into a snake and bit him. Mensäbäk absconded with the wounded assistant to his cave on the lake by the same name.[2] He tried desperately to care for it, feeding it lots of honey, but the soul got progressively worse and eventually died.[3]

Meanwhile Hachäkyum was wondering where his assistant got to. He sent Ak'inchob to look for him. Ak'inchob found him in a severely decomposed state in Mensäbäk's house.

When Hachäkyum learned about this, he invited Mensäbäk to drink balche' with him. But Mensäbäk regarded the invitation as a ruse to castigate him, so he declined. He received several more invitations, but he ignored them all. Time went by, and he forgot about the incident. But one day it hit him, literally, when a huge star came careening toward his house.[4] Mensäbäk decided it was time to pay Hachäkyum a visit. When he arrived, Hachäkyum greeted him cordially, offering him balche'. They sat down and proceeded to get very drunk. However, Hachäkyum had not forgotten Mensäbäk's crime, and his anger began to peak. To calm him down, Mensäbäk sang him a song. Although this relaxed Hachäkyum somewhat, it was only after Mensäbäk vomited great torrents of balche' that Hachäkyum forgave him.

He instructed Mensäbäk to take better care of the souls and not to go around killing mortals to acquire their souls. Rather, he must wait for them to be sent to him after they ascended from the underworld. His job would be to protect the souls in the hereafter.

Hachäkyum's invitation to Mensäbäk to partake in a social drink is reminiscent of the forced drinking ritual the Lacandones hold to castigate a suspected liar. In the ritual event an alleged liar is forced to drink copious amounts of balche' to the point of vomiting. If he vomits, he purges himself of his crime, cleansing himself both body and soul. If he does not vomit, it proves he was innocent all along.[5] The act of purging not only restores the body and the soul but also serves a social function by restoring harmony to the group.

Hachäkyum's purpose for subjecting Mensäbäk to the same ritual is the same.

Mensäbäk tuch'a'ah a' la'eh uwinik Hachäkyum. Tupurah ahkan, chi'bih ten kan.

Mensäbäk took (one of) Hachäkyum's mortals. He threw down a snake, and the mortal was bitten by the snake.

Hachäkyum tuyirah, mäna' uwinik. Tutuchitah uhaan, Ak'inchob.

Hachäkyum noticed that his mortal was missing. He sent his son-in-law Ak'inchob (to look for him).

"Mäna'," kih. "Eh mäna', yumeh," kih. "Ma ma' kuxa'an. Ti' yan t(i') ahMensäbäk."

"He is no more," (Ak'inchob) says. "Eh, he is no more, Lord," he says. "He isn't alive. He is with Mensäbäk."

Ento(nces,) *"Hah. Tuha(h)i(r), porke bik yani(r) k'eex uyor ten Mensäbäk tuch'a'ah inwinik."*

Then Hachäkyum (thinks to himself), *"Yes, of course. Mensäbäk took my mortal because he is jealous."*

Ma' la'eh ahhach winik. He' uwinik. Leh(ih) uyähts'aah uyo'och ba'che', ma'ats' ahHachäkyum. Lehih uyähbärir uk'uuts (ah)Hachäkyum. Lehih uyäht'äbir uk'uuts ahHachäkyum. Ne suuk ti' ahHachäkyum.

He is no ordinary ancestor. He is a man who serves balche' and posol to Hachäkyum. He is the roller of Hachäkyum's cigars. He is the lighter of Hachäkyum's cigars. He is devoted to Hachäkyum.

Chen biki(r) Mensäbäk tupurah ahkan. Chi'bi(h). Kimih. Mensäbäk tuts'aah kab yaab ti' upixan nukuch winik. Yaab kab tuts'ahah uyuk'eh. Ne huy ch'uhuk. Entonces tseemen ahhach winik yete(r)yete(r) kab. 'Otsir, ne tse'eme(n).

But then Mensäbäk threw down a snake. (The assistant) is bitten. He died. Mensäbäk gave the ancestor's soul lots of honey. He gave him lots of honey to drink. It was too sweet. So the ancestor (grew) very thin on the honey. The poor thing was very thin.[6]

Chen bikir, (u)k'uch(ur) hunts'it na' tu(k'in) kim(ih) ahhach winik, k'uch(ih) ahAk'inchob, "Ti' yanech yumeh?"

One month after the man (had) died, Ak'inchob arrived, "Are you there, my Lord?" (he calls out).

"Eh, ti' yanen," kih.

"Yes, I'm here," (Mensäbäk) says.

"Eh, taren inwa'ar(eh) tech he' wah atar (a)ch'eene'et(eh) äkyum. Bek tuya'arah ten, inmaa(n)sik t'an tech."

"Well, I've come to tell you to come and visit our Lord. This is what he told me to pass on to you."

"Eh bay," kih. "He' intar inch'eene'eteh," kih.

"Well, all right!" he says. "I'll come and visit him," he says.

Eh, che(n) bikir toh uyoher Mensäbäk ba'inkir usi'ipir. Yan usi('i)pir tumen tukinsah a' la'eh hach winik. Mäna' ba'ar tub ti'. Ma' tar(ih) uch'een(e'e) t(eh). Ma maanih hunts'it na' tuka'ten, tara(k) tupäyah, mäna' ma' tar(ih). Ma' bin(ih) ahMensäbäk. Ma' bin(ih) uch'eene'et(eh) (ah)Hachäkyum. Tub ti'. Ma, mixba'(ar) ahMensäbäk, tub ti' ba'i(n)ki(r) usi'ipir.

Well, Mensäbäk already knows what his crime is. He (committed) a crime by killing the ancestor. (But) Mensäbäk (had) forgotten about it. He didn't go visit. A second month passed, and although they summoned him (again), he didn't go. Mensäbäk didn't go visit Hachäkyum. He forgot. Mensäbäk forgot he did anything wrong.

Kuyu'yik utar bin, a' bix huysuus ahk'uh. Uyu'y(ik) utar bin tun. "Eh kutich(ir). Utar uba'a(r)ka'an," kih. Hook'(ih) (u)yaaka' ahMensäbäk. Tut'ank'a'tah (ah)Ts'ibanah, ahK'ak'. Hook'(ih) utekla(a)t'ik bin a' ba'arka'an, che(n) k'uchih (t)uyatoch. Hach tuya(to)ch ahMensäbäk bin(ih). Uyaareh orak uhe(e)nse(h). Eh kuhook'(or) uka'tekrat'(t)ik. Tuchukah tubisah yok'or ka'an tuka'ten. Eh, ma' sanhir ka'u'rih.

(Then) he hears it coming; it's something like the whirring sound that the ha'ha'nahk'uh stir up.[7] He hears it coming now. "Eh, it is approaching. A star is coming," he says. Mensäbäk went running out. He called on Ts'ibanah and K'ak'. They went out to buoy the star up, but it continued into his house. It went right into Mensäbäk's house. The weight of it almost collapses it. They go out and immediately buoy it up again. They grabbed it and took it into the sky again. A little while later (Mensäbäk) went back (to his house).

"Eh, ne tak uts'a(hi)k ten yumeh," kih. "Eh, ne tak uts'ah(i)k ten."

"Well, it almost got me, my Lords," he says. "It almost got me."[8]

Ele ma k'uchu(r) boon k'in, "Ahhh lahih yan insi'ipir ti' (in)yum bäkan ti'. Eh lat(i') tutinkinsah (u)winikir. Che(n) ma' bik insutik ma' het la'eh." Kimen. Ma' bik usutik upixan. Wa ma' kimi(h) kachik, he' usutik upixan.

Well, some time passes (and then Mensäbäk remembers), "Aahh, so that's my crime against my Lord. I killed his servant. But I don't know how to return him." He's dead. He can't return his soul. If it (hadn't) died, he (could have) returned the soul.

Ma k'uchi(h) boon (k'in) bin, eh (u)hook'(or) ubin Mensäbäk yok'or uka'anir ti' ahHachäkyum.

So many days went by and then Mensäbäk leaves to go to Hachäkyum's sky.

Ma Hachäkyum yan uyo'och ba'che'. Ma lahih k'inir k'uchih uyo'och ba'che'
ahHachäkyum. Ne yäk uyo'och ba'che'.

Hachäkyum has balche'. That day Hachäkyum's balche' (had) arrived. His
balche' is very strong.⁹

"Eh! Oke(n), yumeh."

"Eh! Come in, my Lord," (Hachäkyum says to Mensäbäk).

"Eh tar(en) inwi(ri)kech."

"I've come to see you," (says Mensäbäk).

"Ko'oten, yumeh. Oke(n)."

"Come here, my Lord. Come in," (says Hachäkyum).

La' hook' uyuk'u(r) bin.

They go out and drink.

Chen bikir, ma tuyuk'ah a' bache' mas yaa(b). Ele, ma k'a'ah ti' ahHachäkyum.

But then, (as) they drank more and more balche', it occurred to Hachäkyum (why he had summoned Mensäbäk).

"Ah, yumeh. K'a'ah tech tech takins(ah) inwinikir. Y tinpäyah ma' tarech."

"Ah, my Lord. You remembered you killed my servant. And I called, (but)
you didn't come."

"Eh hah, yumeh, tuhahir. Eh hah tuhahir."

"Eh, yes, my Lord, that's true. Eh, yes that's true."

Ti' yan akna'ireex ti' Hachäkyum, utar ... ti' uk'aasik uyik', "Ma'ech," kih.
"Ma'ech," kih.

Hachäkyum's wife is there and she comes over . . . (and) reminds Hachäkyum, "Don't," she says.

Tuts'iiktar Hachäkyum tun. Ya poch uhaats'ik tun. Kuts'iikta(r).

Hachäkyum is getting angry now. He already wants to strike him now. He's getting angry.

"Mäna'," kih. "He're' k'aaheh tech takins(ah) inwinik!" kih.

He says, "No!" he says. "You remember you killed my servant!"

"Eh, tuhahir, yumeh!" kih. "Sa'aseh ten yumeh!" kih. "Ele, mäna'," kih.

"Yes, it's true, my Lord!" he says. "Forgive me, my Lord!" he says. "Unfortunately, he is no more," he says.

Eh, umuurur t'anah bin. Wo(r)or (u)ka'mu(urur) t'an. Eh, ts'o'ok.

(The people) huddle around advising (Hachäkyum) to calm down. All of them huddle around to calm him down again. Then, his anger subsided.

"Ch'ukt(eh) ink'äyik, yumeh," kih. Yan uk'aay (ah)Mensäbäk.

"Hold on, my Lord, I'll sing something," says (Mensäbäk).

T(an) uch'i(k)k'at(ik) ubäh t(i') uk'aay. Ne p'enk'äch tsoy uk'aay ahMensäbäk. La' bix la' ch'anex ahts'ikren uk'aay bex tsoy.

He has a song. He is standing with his (arms) crossed in front of himself to sing. The song Mensäbäk sings is exceptionally lovely. His song is as lovely as the (song of) cicadas, of the *ts'iklen* cicadas.[10]

Ele, tub t(i') ahHachäkyum porque tuk'äyah bin ahMensäbäk bin ne p'enkäch tso(y) uk'a(ay). Ele, eh tub t(i') ahHachäkyum, ele ma' sanhir bin ele ts'o'ok.

And then, Hachäkyum forgot (why he was angry), because Mensäbäk sang such a beautiful song. And so Hachäkyum forgot about it, and soon after (his anger) subsided.

Eh, tuyuk'ah ba'che' ba'axtah, Mensäbäk bin, maa, ne na'a(h)char bin yete(r) uba'che', tuxehah. Ne yaab tuxehah bin—xixxx—kih. Eh mäna'. (U)bäk'ä(r) ubin käch'arak ubin yete(r) ha' tu' kuxeeh.

Then Mensäbäk drank balche', well then [narrator chuckles] he got very full with balche' and threw up. He vomit(ed) a great deal—SHISHHH—he couldn't help it. The corncobs went tumbling end over end where he vomited.

Tuya'arah, "Sa(')aseh ten yumeh," kih.

He said, "Forgive me, my Lord."

Tub ti' (ti') tuk'aaynah(eh) ... a' ti' tuk'aaynah a' la'eh ahMensäbäk bin. Tub ti'. Ya ma' het uyank'a'aha(r) ti'. Ya tub ti' Hachäkyum.

Hachäkyum (had already) forgot(ten) about (his crime), because Mensäbäk sang. He had forgotten about it. Now, he couldn't remember. Hachäkyum had already forgotten about it.

Lahih utsikbar a' la'eh Mensäbäk yete(r) hach winik yete(r) hach winik tukinsah.

That's the story about Mensäbäk and the ancestor he killed.

Kak'och yeter Uk'ani(r) Hach Winik
'Kak'och and His Human Assistant'

Bor Ma'ax

The gods have assistants who live with them and perform a variety of jobs. Most are mortals with exceptional strength and abilities. They are not to be confused with the minor deities that emerged from the sacred tuberose.[1] The mortal assistants travel the paths of the gods that connect the earth and sky,[2] but rarely do they interact with their earth-bound counterparts.

In this story the assistants of Hachäkyum and Kak'och compete to see who can ascend the fastest up their individual roads. Kak'och is the god of Hachäkyum; his realm as the First Creator is higher than Hachäkyum's. No mortal has ever seen Kak'och. Hachäkyum's assistant extended the challenge because he really wanted his companion to reveal the route to Kak'och's sky. His companion agrees, and they set off. But Hachäkyum's assistant quickly loses sight of his companion and his route. To this day Kak'och remains as a remote and inaccessible god.

Kak'och yan uk'ani(r)[3] ti' hach winik.

Kak'och has a human assistant.

Y Hachäkyum yan uk'ani(r) ti' hach winik.

And Hachäkyum has a human assistant.

Huhuntu(u)r yan uk'ani(r).

Each one has an assistant.[4]

Bay.

Okay.

Nukuch winik tan uyuk'ik. Tume(n)tah ba'che', tan uyuk'ik ich uyatoch k'uh. Ne tsoy uyor. Utsikbar nukuch winik yeter bäho',

The ancestors are drinking. They (had) made balche' (and) they're drinking balche' in the god house. They're in good spirits. One ancestor is talking to his companion,

"Ah ne tsoy. Tan usa'atar inwor. Ne ki' ba'che'."

"Ah, this is very good. I'm (getting) drunk. The balche' is very good."

"Eh bay," tu nukah uk'ani(r) Kak'och. "Ne tsoy akor, tan akuk'ik ba'ché. Ne ki'."

"Ah, yes," replied Kak'och's assistant. "We're in high spirits. We're drinking balche'. It's very good."

Bay.

Okay.

Nukuch winik tan uyuk'ik uyo'och ba'che'. Ne ki'. Tan uyuk'ik. Tan usa'atar uyor. P'isir uk'ani(r) Hachäkyum. Tan usa'atar uyor, lah ket. Ne tsoy uyor.

(Kak'och's assistant) is drinking his balche'. It is delicious. He is drinking it. He is getting drunk. So is Hachäkyum's assistant. They are both getting drunk together. They are very happy.

Tan utsikbar. Uya'arik ti' ubäho',

They're talking. (Hachäkyum's assistant) says to his companion,

"Eh, tech aw(oh)e(r) wa to'an ube(r) äkyum Kak'och?"

"Eh, do you know where the road of our Lord Kak'och is?"

Tunuukah uk'ani(r) ahKak'och, "Eh, tuts'aah (u)be(r) ten, chen ma' hach inw(oh)e(r)."

Kak'och's assistant replied, "Eh, he gave me the road, but I don't know it very well."

Eh, unuukik uk'ani(r) Hachäkyum, "Ele! Ten ne yan tuts'aah (äh)kyum ten. Yan ube(r) ten. Ne seeb inbin ten. Poch inbin tsikbar yeter kyum Hachäkyum—tsk—seeb. Bähe' ka'(ah) hook'en ha(r)aknikir, seeb kinbin ti' ka'an. Tuts'aah ube(r) ten, Hachäkyum."

And Hachäkyum's assistant replies, "Well! There is one Hachäkyum gave to me. There is a road for me. I (can) travel very rapidly. (Whenever) I want to go talk to our Lord Hachäkyum—tsk—it's quick. Now, when I go outside I go rapidly into the sky. Hachäkyum gave his road to me."

Uk'ani(r) Kak'och unuukik, "Eh ne tsoy. Wa hach tuha(h)i(r) tuts'aah tech (u)be(r) akyum, ne tsoy. Ha'ri' tech yan (u)be(r) tech."

Kak'och's assistant replies, "Eh, that's great. If it's true that our Lord gave you his road, that's great. His road is only for you."

Bay. T(an) uma(s)sa'at(ar) uyor. T(an) umasuk'ik ba'che', mas yaab. Eh uka'nuukik uk'ani(r) Hachäkyum, "Bay. Tuk'in aktuntik ku'yeh ti' (ak)katik akaaka' boon uchichir ana'akar tech?"

Okay. He is getting drunker. He is drinking more balche', a lot more. Hachäkyum's assistant replies again, "Okay. When do we race (to see) how quickly you can climb?"

Ma' hach tak unuukik uk'ani(r) ahKak'och.

Kak'och's assistant is hesitant to answer.

"Bay. Tech kawa'arik wa tuk'in a(k)katik akbin boon mak mas chich ubin mak chich ubin."

"Fine. You say when we race (to see) who goes the fastest."

Uk'ani(r) Hachäkyum ma' uxurik. Ne poch ubin ukatik uyaaka', ti' ubin ka'an.

Hachäkyum's assistant doesn't stop (pestering him). He really wants to race to the sky.

Ah tan umas saatar uyor, tan umassaatar uyor. Uya'arik ti',

He is getting drunker and drunker. He says to him,

"Ten, bay. Ma' tuhachts'aah (u)be(r) ten Kak'och. Ma' ti' ki' kuts'ah(ik) ten uber ten—uts'aabar ten, chen ma' ohernah ba'inki(r) uk'aba' ts'aab(ir) ti' (u)xikur, ke lehi(h) umuk' ti' ubin ka'ana(n)."

"As for me, well. Kak'och didn't really give me his road. It (was) given to me, but it is unknown what the (word) is that is given to his tunic, wherein lies the power to go high."

Bay.

Okay.

Ele tuya'arah uk'ani(r) ahKak'och, "Hach tuha(h)i(r) poch a(k)katik akbin ka'ana(n)?"

And then Kak'och's assistant said, "Do you really want to race to the sky?"

Unuukik uk'ani(r) Hachäkyum, "Ne poch! Ko'ox bähe'! Ko'ox!"

Hachäkyum's assistant replies, "I want to go! Let's go now! Let's go!"

"Yan ti' atuntik; yan ti' ame(n)tik, 'ᴛᴜᴜᴜɪ, ᴛᴜᴜᴜɪ.' Yan ti' ame(n)tik. A' p'is ch'ich' bi(n) (u)yawat, 'ᴛᴜᴜᴜɪ, ᴛᴜᴜᴜɪ.'"

(Kak'och's assistant said), "You have to try it; you have to make (the sound), 'ᴛᴜᴜᴜɪ, ᴛᴜᴜᴜɪ.' You have to make (that sound). It's like a bird calling, 'ᴛᴜᴜᴜɪ, ᴛᴜᴜᴜɪ.'"

Lah ket hook'ih ha(r)akniki(r) ch'iktar. Tuhunar saatih. P'iis saatih, tuhuunar bini(h).

Together they went outside and stopped. They disappeared, one and then the other. It's like they disappeared, they left one and then the other.

Bay.

Okay.

Mas seeb bini(h) uk'ani(r) Kak'och. Lehi(h) mas chich bini(h), mas seeb bini(h).

Kak'och's assistant went faster. He went stronger and faster.

Eh uk'ani(r) Hachäkyum ume(n)tik ti', "TUUUI, TUUUI."

Hachäkyum's assistant (goes), "TUUUI, TUUUI."

Ti' yan chumuk che'. Mix ubin, ma' n(e) chich ubin.

He is half-way up the trees. He neither goes (fast) nor steadily.

Eh uka'nuukik tuka'ten uk'ani(r) Kak'och, "TUUUI, TUUUI." Mas neka'ana(n), ti' yan t(i') uni'yor nukuch che'.

Kak'och's assistant answers again, "TUUUI, TUUUI." He is much higher up, at the top of a tall tree.

Eh kuka'nuukik uk'ani(r) Hachäkyum, "TUUUI, TUUUI."

Hachäkyum's assistant replies again, "TUUUI, TUUUI."

Ch'ik ti' yan uni'yor ek' bahche'. *"Eh mana' be(r)."*

He gets as far as the top of the black cork trees.[5] *"There isn't any road,"* (he says to himself).

Tarak ukäxtik ubäho', mix tuyirah be(r) ti'.

Although he searches for his companion, he (doesn't) see any road there.

Tusätah tu' bini(h). Tarak uche'extik uka'me(n)tik, "TUUUI, TUUUI," ya(n) ne naach utar. Mäna' ma' k'uch uyu'yik ume(n)tik uk'aay.

He lost (sight of) where he went. Although he listens to the "TUUUI, TUUUI," it comes from very far off. His song is faint.

Ele, bärak'i(h) y ch'ik bini(h) na'akih ka'ana(n). Tusätah (u)bäho' uk'ani(r) Kak'och.

So, he turned around and climbed higher into the sky. He lost (sight of) his companion, Kak'och's assistant.

Ele, bini(h) tun (u)k'anir Kak'och. Kuman toh lahi(h) uk'ani(r) Kak'och tak t(i') uka'anir Kak'och bin ti', eh uk'ani(r) Hachäkyum, p'aat kabar.

So, Kak'och's assistant is gone now. Kak'och's assistant has almost (reached) Kak'och's sky, and Hachäkyum's assistant is left below.

'Oxp'er k'in uka'irik ubäho',

Three days (later), he sees his (other) companion again,

"Hah tawirah tu' bineh? Hah tawirah tu' bineh?"

"Did you see where (Kak'och's assistant) went? Did you see where he went?" (asks his friend).

"Ele hah. Ma' tinwireh," uya'arik ti'.

"Well, no. I didn't see," he says to him.

"Ah hah, tech tint'an ne tsoy. Tuts'aah (u)be(r) Kak'och tech."

"Indeed, I think (you must be) very pleased. He offered you Kak'och's road."

"Ten mäna'. Ma' hach chich inbin yeter. Mäna' ma' chich inbin. Ube(r) Kak'och, leti' mas ne chich ubin. Tir[6] ube(r) Kak'ocheh tir ube(r) Hachäk-yum."

"Not to me. I (didn't) go that far with him. I didn't go strong enough. Kak'och's road, that is much harder to travel. Kak'och's road is different from Hachäkyum's road."

Ak'inchob Takes a Human Wife

Antonio Martinez

Ak'inchob[1] is the Lacandones' emissary to Hachäkyum, delivering the Lacandones' prayers and offerings to help their crops and to cure or avert illnesses. Because he spends a good deal of time on earth, he marries a human wife. But after giving her only honey to eat, she gets pregnant and then dies.[2] Bereft, Ak'inchob gives the Lacandones a curing prayer to help prevent death during pregnancy and childbirth.[3]

Ak'inchob ukäxtik ulaak' ti' nukuch winik. Uk'aatik uch'upra(r) uti'a'ar ti' nukuch winik. Uxatik uche'i(r) k'ak', uxatik utaasik. Uxukik ti' uyäkan.

Ak'inchob looks for a wife from the ancestor. He asks the ancestor for his daughter. He chops firewood, he chops it and brings it (to him). He arranges the wood in a circle in the hearth for his father-in-law.[4]

Nukuch winik ma' uts'ahik uch'upra(r) uti'a'ar. Tarak uk'atik, mäna' uts'ahik ti'. Kulahharik uche'i(r) uk'ak' uwehch'intik ti' haräkniki(r). Ma' utärik uche' tarak uk'aatik.

The ancestor doesn't give him his daughter. Even though (Ak'inchob) asks for her, (the ancestor) doesn't give her to him. (The father) removes all the firewood and pitches it outside. He doesn't accept the wood, even though (Ak'inchob) asked for her.[5]

Uya'arik nukuch winik, "Ma' ak'aatik inti'a'ar!"
The ancestor says, "Don't ask for my daughter!"

Tuyirah tan utar uxira(r) uti'a'ar ti' nukuch winik. "Ma' tats'aheh inwits'ineh? Ma' tats'aah? La' la'eh ma' winik, tet. Ak'inchob. K'uh."

He saw his son coming, (who says), "Why didn't you give him my sister? Why didn't you give her (to him)? He is no ordinary man, father. He is Ak'inchob. He is a god."

"Bay. He' ints'ahik ti'. He' ints'ahik ti'!"
"Okay. I will give her to him. I will give her to him!"

"Bähe' bin ukah sata(r) inwits'in tech."
"Now my sister is going to lose (him) because of you."

"Le ma' usata(r). He' ints'ahik."
"She won't lose (him). I will give her (to him)."

"Eh bay. Ne tsoy."
"Okay. Good."

Le' okih k'in uka'taasik uxukeh che'. He' tuts'aah ti'. Eh, tuts'aah ti'; tuhitah uk'äb tuts'aah ti'. Ne seeb; ma' ne xanta(r).

That evening he brings wood again to set up in the hearth. And, the (ancestor) gave her to him; he released her hand and gave her to him. It was quick; it didn't take long.[6]

Eh, tuts'aah ch'uhuk. Tuts'aah ti' ulaak' ti' uyuk'ik. Wo-o-o-ro(r) ch'uhuk kuts'ahik ti', okor ukah k'in. Ne yan kab; kuch'a(ak)ab. Woro(r) kab kuts'ahik.

And then, (Ak'inchob) gave her honey. He gave it to his wife to drink. He just gives her honey every afternoon. There is a lot of honey; he is always collecting honey. It's only honey he gives her to drink.

Eh, ma' utsir. Yan uchan ti'a'ar. Ma' utsir. Kimih.

Well, she is unwell. She is with child. She is pregnant. (And) she died.

"Eh mäna'," Ak'inchob tan uyok'or, uyak'tik ulaak'. "Ma' het la'eh."

"Oh, she is no more," Ak'inchob is crying, crying for his wife. "There is nothing (that can be done)."

Eh, uch'upra(r) uti'a'ar Hachäkyum, uka'tuur ulaak' Ak'inchob, ti' yan ich uyatoch. Ele tuyirah kimih ulaak' tun. Ele tuye'ens(ah) ubah ti' (uka'tuur ulaak' Ak'inchob). Sut(ih) tsikbarnahih yet(er) ulaak'.

And then, Hachäkyum's daughter, Ak'inchob's second wife, is in her house (in the sky).[7] She saw that his wife died, now. And then she went down (to see). She went back (to the sky) and talked to her husband.

"Le' mäna' inwits'in. Kimih. Ts'o'ok. Tech awoher to'an."

"My little sister is no more.[8] She died. She is finished. You know (why)."

"Ten, yan kunyah ten."

Ak'inchob (says), "I have a curing prayer."

Ak'inchob tupurah ukunyah way, yok'o(r) lu'um.

Ak'inchob sent down his curing prayer here, to earth.

3

Popular Stories

Maya Kimin 'The Mayan Death'

Säk Ho'or

This myth recounts a time when yellow fever spread through the forest and decimated most of the Lacandon population (Baer and Merrifield 1971, 39).[1] The Lacandones blamed this plague on the Maya Kimin, which they describe as small monkey-like beings that whizz through air. The story goes that anyone who came near them or ate their meat came down with a terrible fever, began vomiting, and later died (Bruce 1976, 45).

Yellow fever spread through the Mayan lowlands in the mid-seventeenth century (Roys 1933, 120). In part, it was responsible for the annihilation of the Putún Maya of Campeche (J. Thompson 1970, 59). A large population of monkeys also contracted it (Bruce 1976, 132, in Boremanse 1986, 181n2). Monkey meat was a delicacy and a valued food offering to the gods.

Those who died from yellow fever were thought to have contracted the disease from eating the meat. Yellow fever is now known to be caused by the Flavivirus, a virus that is transmitted to humans and primates by an infected *Aedes aegypti* mosquito. Among other systems and organs in the body, the virus prevents the body's blood-clotting mechanism, causing hemorrhaging.[2]

Bay. Bähe' kinbin intsikbarteh.
Okay. Now I'm going to tell the story.

A' 'uchik tuya'arah 'uchik unuki(r) winik, wa tuha(h)i(r) wa ma' tuha(h)i(r),
Long ago the ancestors said, whether this is true or not,

bex tuya'arah umaya kimin.
this is what they said about the Mayan Death.

Bay. Maya Kimin.
Okay. The Mayan Death.

'Uchik unuki(r) winik ma' uyohe(r) ba'(in)ki(n) a' la'eh kuyu'yik umaan.
Long ago an ancestor didn't know what he was hearing passing by.

Bay. Tutukrik ba'ats';
Okay. He thinks it's a howler monkey;

o tukrik ma'ax kubin ka'ana(n).
or he thinks it's a spider monkey going along above (in the trees).

Bay, ti' tuch'a'ah uhuur. Bin uhure(h).
So, he took his arrows. He went off to hunt (it).

Bay. Pachi(r) tuya'arah t(i') ulaak', "Kakme(n)tik äkchi'e(h) ti' äkhantik.
Okay. Then he said to his wife, "Let's prepare it to eat.

Ne ki', äkhantik."
It's delicious, let's eat it."

Bay.
Okay.

Ti' cha'(an)nika'(an) tuworo(r) uti'a'ar uboho'bi(r). Ne xoko(r) nikrik.
Sitting there are all the children of his companions. They are sitting very close together.

"Bay," tuya'arah.

"Okay," he said.

"Kakchi'eh. Bähe' bin akchi'eh."

"Let's eat it. Now we're going to eat it."

[Tumen 'uchik, ma' uyoher ba('in)ki(r) a' la'eh maya kimin. Utukrik mäna' yahi(r).]

[Because before, they didn't know about the Mayan Death. They didn't know anything about illness.[3]]

Bay.

Okay.

Kuts'o'ok(or) uhantik, tulahhantah,

When they finished eating it, (after) they ate it all up,

pachi(r) tuyu'yah ma' 'uts.

they didn't feel well.

Tuworo(r) tan ulahkimi(n).

All of them were dying.

Tuworo(r) tan ulahkimin, tuworo(r) yete(r) yahi(r).

All of them were dying from an illness.

Lati' ubäyn[4] kuya'arah umaya kimin,

That is why they call it the Mayan Death,

tumen lati' maya kimin
because the Mayan Death

p'is kisin.
is like a demon.

Yan uyahi(r). Ne yaab yahi(r) uch'a'aban.
There (was) sickness. A great deal of sickness was caught.

Bay.
Okay.

Unuki(r) winik,
The ancestor,

lehi(h) 'uchik hunt(uu)ri' p'aati(h) uyirnah,
he was the only one left to bear witness,

hunt(uu)ri' p'aati(h), uhunt(uu)ri' up'aati(h). Ma' kimi(h).
the only one left, the only one left. He didn't die.

P'aati(h). Ma' kimi(h).
He remained. He didn't die.

Bay. Ti' tuya'arah,
Okay. He said,

"Bähe' yan inbin inwa'arik ti', 'Awirik ba(')inki(r) ahmaya kimin,
"Now I must go tell them,⁵ '(If) you see the Mayan Death,

ma' akinsik,
don't kill it,

tumen, awirik, 'uchik ten inboho' lah kimi(h).
because, you see, all my companions died before.

Lah kimi(h) tuworo(r).
All of them died.

Mix p'a(a)ti(h). Ha'ri' hunt(u)ri' p'a(a)ti(h).
No one was left. Only one remained.

Lah kimi(h).
All the others died.

Ba('in)k(in) inwa'arik ma' (a)kinsike'ex.
What I'm saying to you is, do not kill it.

Ma' (a)chi'ike'ex. Ne yaab yahi(r) ti'.
Do not eat it. It contains a great deal of sickness.

Wa kuchere(r),
If it falls,

yan xeh.
there will be vomiting.

Yan chäkwi(r).
There will be fever.

Yan yah uho'ori(r).
There will be headache.

Yan tuworo(r) uhupnäk'i(r).
All will have bloody diarrhea.

Tuworo(r) ne yaab yahi(r) yan ti' uk'uchpah.'"
All will catch a great deal of sickness that arrives.'"

Lehi(h) bähe' tuya'arah ahmaya kimin.
This, now, is what they say about the Mayan Death.

Yan uneeh.
It has a tail.

Mäna' uxik'. Mäna'.
It doesn't have wings. It doesn't have any.

Che(n)bay ubin.
Nevertheless, it (flies).

Ha'ri' a' la'eh utsikba(r) 'uchik unuki(r) winik.
That is all there is to the story from the ancestors.

Chäk Xok 'The Sirens'

Bor Ma'ax

The *chäk xok* are sirens that snatch unsuspecting bathers and carry them off to their watery abode beneath the lagoon.[1] In this story, there are two chäk xok, a male and a female, who are looking for human spouses. The "merman" approaches a poor fisherman and his wife and strikes a deal: the fisherman will hand over his daughter in return for all the fish he could ever eat. The fisherman agrees. The merman hauls the daughter to the depths of the lagoon and leaves the fish on the shore. The "mermaid" arrives and asks the fisherman for his son. She too makes the same deal with the man and is thus granted the fisherman's son, in return for fish. But the son overhears them plotting his capture and flees. He embarks on a fantastic quest to find his sister. Helped along the way by deities and the white falcon, he travels to the "other side of the sea," where he marries the daughter of a king and starts a new life.[2]

The chäk xok are reminiscent of the half-reptilian and half-human rain gods in Mayan mythology. In this respect, they are the equivalent to the *chicchan* in Ch'orti' mythology and the *chaacs* in Yucatec Maya mythology. The chicchan are gigantic beings that live in underwater caves. When they swim they create powerful currents, their sudden movements often causing earthquakes (Marion 1999, 351). Similarly the Lacandones believe that the chäk xok are responsible for rough waters, and hence they are summoned to churn the balche' beverage to aid fermentation (see "Ut'anir Ba'che'" 'The Secret of the Balche'', this volume).

Among the Yucatec Maya there exists a similar mythical fish, called Ah Chac Uayab Xok 'Great Demon Shark' (J. Thompson 1970, 321). The chäk xok in Lacandon lore are related to fish in that fish are produced through the copulation between the chäk xok and turtles. That turtles are their relatives is borne out by another reference to the chäk xok: *umiim 'aak* 'grandchildren of the turtle' (Boremanse 1986, 240n1). The chäk xok are also related to the crocodile, as demonstrated by the narrator's uncertainty over whether to identify the grandmother of the male chäk xok as a turtle or a crocodile.

Whereas the chaacs and the chicchan are also deities that reside at the four corners of the world (Marion 1999, 351), the chäk xok are a pair of malicious beings that appear to be unassociated with any cardinal direction.

PART 1. THE ANCESTOR GIVES AWAY
HIS DAUGHTER TO THE MERMAN

Bähe', intsikbar yete(r) nukuch winik yete(r) chäk xok. Bek tutsikbartah uchik chäk xok yete(r) nukuch winik.

Now, my story is about the ancestor and the sirens. It is like the story they told long ago (about) the sirens and the ancestor.

Päytan, nukuch winik, tuworo(r) bin lutskäy yok'or petha'. Woro(r) okor ukah k'in ubin yet(er) ulaak' lutsi(k) uyo'och käy.

In the beginning, the ancestor went fishing every day in the lagoon. Every afternoon he goes with his wife to catch their fish.

Woro(r) käy kuchi'ik. Ne ki' uyu'(y)ik. Lehi(h) uyo'och.

They only eat fish. They really like the taste. This is their food.

Lahi(h) kuchi'ik woro(r) käy.

They eat only fish.

Okol ukah k'in, (u)bin yet(er) ulaak' lutsik uyo'och käy. Yaab ne su' kubin.

In the late afternoon, he (goes) with his wife to catch their fish. He goes regularly.

Bay.

Okay.

Tanux bin ulutsik uyo'och käy. Kulutsik, chen ma' ne nuk. Chan mihin. Woro(r) chan mihin käy. Mäna' nuk.

He is always fishing. He fishes, but the fish aren't very big. They're tiny. All of them are tiny fish. None of them are big.

Bay.

Okay.

Ubin tanux (u)bin o(k)k'in. Kulutsik ma' nuk. Woro(r) chan mehen, mehen käy.

He always goes in the late afternoon. He catches fish, none of them are big. They're all small, baby fish.

Chen bikir, wa nukuch winik yet(er) ulaak' tutukrah mäna'. Ma woro(r) chan mihin käy kulutsik. Ma' ulutsik unuki(r). Woro(r) chan mehen. Woro(r) mehen chäklah. Yan bik utar ahsäktan, eh lehi(h) kuyu'(r)sik uchäk(eh) uchi'eh.

Perhaps the ancestor and his wife thought there (weren't) any (big fish). All the fish they catch are tiny. They don't catch the big ones. All of them are little babies. All of them are little *mojarras*.[3] At times sardines come along, so he brings them home to cook and eat.

Chen bikir wa, woror o(k)k'in ubin. Mäna' kuman. Woror o(k)k'in ubin.

Nevertheless, every afternoon he goes. He doesn't let a day go by. He goes every afternoon.

K'uch(ih) tuk'in ti' yan ahchäk xok. Kuyu'(y)ik utubur ut'an, "Eh, ba'inki(r) kalutsik tech?"

The time came when a siren (appeared). He hears a voice blurt out, "Hey, what are you fishing for?"

"Eh," tunukah nukuch winik, "eh mäna'. Inlutsik inwo'och käy."
"Oh," the ancestor replied, "nothing much. I'm fishing for my fish."

"Eh bay. Wa yan uch'uprar ati'a'ar ats'ahik ten?" ...
"Very well. Do you have a daughter to give me?" ...

Tunuukah ahnuki(r) winik, "Eh, yan uch'uprar inti'a'ar."
The ancestor replied, "I have a daughter."

[La' la'eh tut'anah lati' xirar. Lati' chäk xok xirar.]
[The siren that spoke is a man. That is a male siren.]⁴

Bay.
Okay.

Tan ukäxtik ulaak'. Ahchäk xok tuya'arah, "Wa ats'ahik ten ati'a'ar, inwäk-antikech. Inwäkanech."
He is looking for a wife. The merman said, "If you give me your daughter, I will make you my father-in-law. You (will be) my father-in-law."

Nukuch winik tan utukrik.
The ancestor is thinking.

"Bay. Ch'ukt(eh). Inyantukrik inwohe(r). Ch'ukt(eh). Inyantsikbar yete(r) una'. Yan (in)tukrik inwohe(r) wa he' ints'ahik inti'a'ar ti' tech."
"Okay. Wait. I have to think about it first. Wait. I must talk to her mother first. I have to think about whether I will give my daughter to you."

Chäk xok ne tsoy uyor. Seeb poch uyu'(y)ik wa he' uts'ahik uti'a'ar nukuch winik.

The merman is very happy. He's anxious to hear if the ancestor will give away his daughter.

Nukuch winik uk'atik ti' ulaak',

The ancestor asks his wife,

"Kon he're' akts'ahik akti'a'al?"

"Should we hand over our daughter?"

Tuya'arah ulaak' unukuch winik, "Ma' ten inwoher. Wa tech, wa kutukrik, he're' p'isi(r) ten. He're'."

The ancestor's wife said, "I don't know. If you think so, then so do I. Yes."

"Ah, bay."

"Ah, good," (he says).

Chäk xok toh ti' yan chi' chem tan uyu'(y)ik utsikbar nukuch winik.

The merman is right there by the edge of the canoe listening to the ancestors' conversation.

"Eh," uka'k'aatik ti' nukuch winik. "Ha(h) bik awa'arik? Ha(h) he're' ats'ahik ten uch'uprar (a)ti'a'ar?"

"Eh," he asks the ancestor again. "What do you say? Are you really going to give me your daughter?"

"He're', pero wa h(e') ats'ahik ten woro(r) nukuch käy. Kabin ataasik ten."

"Yes, but only if you give me nothing but big fish. You are going to bring them to me."

Chäk xok tuya'arah, "He're', ints'ahik tech käy—woro(r) ne nuk, mäna' umeheni(r), Woro(r) ne nukuch käy. Kintaasik tech. Ink'uhsik. Ink'uhsik. O(k)k'in katar ach'a'eh way, kuuchi(r). Way tinwirahech, way katar ach'a'eh, saman. Kintaasik tech käy ne yaab."

The merman said, "Certainly, I (will) give you fish—all very big ones, no small ones, all very big fish. I will bring them to you. I (will) bring them. I (will) bring them. When you come in the afternoon, you (will) take them (from) here, at this place. Here, (where) I saw you, you will come here and take them tomorrow. I will bring you a lot of fish."

Bay.

Okay.

Suti(h) nukuch winik. Yan. Tulutsah. Tuch'a'ah uyo'och käy. Ma ka'saasi(r) ka'bini(h) (tu)ch'a'ah (u)yo'och käy nukuch winik yet(er) ulaak'. [Mäna' up'ata(r). Uyetbin ulaak'. Uyetluts käy. Ulaak'i(r) uyetbin ich petha'.] K'uch(ih) t(i') ukuuchi(r) tu' tsikbarnah(ih) yete(r) chäk xok.

The ancestor returned. They are there. He (the merman) (had) caught them. The next day the ancestor and his wife went and took the fish. [She never stays behind. She goes with her husband. They go fishing together. His wife goes with him to the lagoon.] They arrived at the place where (the ancestor) (had) chatted with the merman.

(U)k'aatik ti' nukuch winik, "Hah, h(e') ats'ahik ati'a'ar wäkan?"

The merman asks the ancestor, "So, will you hand over your daughter, father-in-law?"

"Eh, he' ints'ahik," tuya'arah nukuch winik. "He're', he' ints'ahik tech. Toh awohe(r) käy kats'ahik ten. Woro(r) käy kabin ats'ahik ten."

"I'll hand her over," the ancestor said. "Certainly, I'll give her to you. You know you're still going to give me fish. You are going to give me nothing but fish."

"He're'," tuya'arah ahchäk xok. "Ne tsoy inwor. He' ints'ahik tech!"

"Of course," said the merman. "I am very happy. Yes, I will give them to you!"

Bay.

Okay.

"Bik ints'ahik inti'a'ar?"

"How am I to give my daughter?"

"Eh, ak'uch(ur) apäyik ten. Apäyik (ti') (u)chi' chem. Päyeh up'ees ahkäy. Kin toh awirik ubin, pureh ich ha'."

"Eh, you arrive and call her over to me. You call her over to the side of the canoe. Call her over to gut fish. (As soon as?) you see her go (in), throw her into the water."

"Ma' atukrik wa 'ayim uchi'ik?"

"Don't you think a crocodile will eat her?"

"Ma' 'ayim. Toh ten tinch'a'ah."

"There aren't any crocodiles. I already caught them."

"Eh, bay," tuya'arah nukuch winik. "Eh, bay. Bähe' intaasik ti'a'ar.

"Very good," said the ancestor. "Very good. I (will) bring my daughter today."

Seeb suti(h). Nukuch winik yan uyo'och käy. Woro(r) ne nuk. Mäna' mehen-i(r). Ne nuk. Woro(r) ne nuk.

He returned quickly. The ancestor has his fish. All of them are big. None are babies. They're very big. All of them are very big.

Bay.

Okay.

K'uchih (ti' u)chi' upetha'i(r).

He got to the edge of the lagoon.

[Ti' yan ne xok'or uyatoch, xok'o(r) (u)chi' petha'.]

[His house is very close to the edge of the lagoon.]

Tut'än(ah) uch'upra(r) (u)ti'a'ar, "Katar way awaant(ik) inp'eeseh käy."

He called to his daughter, "You're going to come over here (and) help me gut fish."

Ma' uyohe(r) uch'upra(r) uti'a'ar, ne seeb tarih uyaantik up'eesik käy yet(er) una' yet(er) utet nukuch winik. Ne seeb uk'uchur purik uyok (ti' u)chi' chem. Mas okor tu' mas tam, seeb uch'a'ik—HEEEY—bihin.

The daughter doesn't know (the plan), so she came quickly to help gut the fish with her mother and her father. She arrives quickly and steps (at the) side of the canoe. (When) she goes in where it is a bit deeper, he snatches her (and)—HEEEY—she plunges in.

Nukuch winik toh uyohe(r) (ah)chäk xok (u)ch'a'ik. Ne tsoy uyor. Uyohe(r) lahi(h) yan uhaan chäk xok.

The ancestor already (knew) the merman (would) grab her. He's very happy. He knows that the merman is (now) his son-in-law.

Bay.

Okay.

Mix, mix utukrik. Ne tsoy uyor. Nukuch winik yet(er) ulaak' ne tsoy uyor.
Ne ki' uhanan. Woro(r) käy kabin uch'a'ik. Okor ukah k'in woro(r) käy,
woro(r) mäna'. Woro(r) lah uhana(n). Ne ki'. Woro(r) käy kutaasik ne nuk.
Chäk xok woro(r) lah uluts käy.

He doesn't worry about anything. He is very happy. The ancestor and his
wife are very content. Their food is good. They just go and take their fish.
Every afternoon they (get) all their fish, nothing else. This is all they eat.
It's delicious. All the fish they take away are very big. The merman does all
the fishing.

Bay.

Okay.

Lati' uch'uprar uti'a'ar nukuch winik bini(h) t(i') uyit ha' yete(r) chäk xok.
Bini(h). Tsoy uyor chäk xok. Tuch'a'ah ulaak'. Yan ulaak'. Tubisah t(i') uyit
ha'.

The ancestor's daughter went to the bottom of the lagoon with the merman.
She went. The merman is very content. He took his woman. He has his
wife. He took her to bottom of the (lagoon).

PART 2. THE ANCESTOR GIVES AWAY HIS SON TO THE MERMAID

Chen biki(r), yanta(r) huntuu(r) chäk xok. Lati' uch'upra(r). Lati' tan ukäxtik ulaak'. P'isi(r) lati' ch'upra(r) chäk xok tan ukäxtik xira(r). Mäna' xira(r)
ti'.

However, there is another siren. She is a woman. She is looking for a
spouse. Just like the (merman), the mermaid is looking for a man. There
aren't any men for her.

Nukuch winik (u)k'aata(r) ti', "Ehhh, wäkaneh, yan uxira(r) ati'a'ar ats'ahik
ten?"

She asks (the ancestor), "Ohhh, father-in-law, do you have a son to give me?"

Nukuch winik kunuukik," Eh, mänä'."
The ancestor replies, "Eh, there aren't any."

"Yan! Ti' yan. He' ats'ahik ten uxira(r) ati'a'ar. Mänä' inlaak'. 'Otsiren; ten mänä' xira(r) ten."
"There is! There is one. You will give me your son. I don't have a husband. Pity me; there aren't any men for me."

"Eh, mänä'. Mänä' uxira(r) inti'a'ar."
"There aren't any. I don't have any sons."

"He' ats'ahik ten, wäkän! He' ats'ahik ten, wäkän. Inwäkänech. H(e') ats'ahik ten. Mänä', mänä' xira(r) ti'a'ar ten. 'Otsiren."
"You will give him to me, father-in-law! You will give him to me, father-in-law. You are my father-in-law. You will give him to me. There aren't any men for me. Poor me."

"Eh bay."
"All right."

Nukuch winik uk'aati(k) ti' ulaak' tuka'ten, "Bik akme(n)tik? Tan uk'aat(ik) äkti'a'ar huntuur, lati' äkti'a'ar huntuur xira(r). 'Otsir chäk xok. Män(a') ulaak'. 'Otsi(r). Mänä', mänä' xira(r) ti'."
The ancestor asks his wife a second time, "What are we going to do? She is asking for our other child, our son. The poor thing. She doesn't have a husband. The poor thing. There aren't any men for her."

Eh bay.
Okay.

Chäk xok mäna' uxurik. Ne su' uk'aat ti('). "Inwäkanech. He' ats'ahik ten ati'a'ar. Intaasik käy. H(e') ints'ahik tech he'. Woro(r) käy kabin achi'ik mäna' umeheni(r); woro(r) ne nuk intaasik tech."

The mermaid doesn't stop it. She asks him constantly. "You are my father-in-law. You will give me your son. I (will) bring fish here. I will give them to you here. All the fish you are going to eat won't be little ones; I'll bring you all big ones."

Nukuch winik ne tsoy uyor. "Yan inhaan. Yan ka't(uu)ro'. Bähe' yan inwo'och käy," uya'arik ti' ulaak'. "Bähe'. O(k)k'in kaka'kbine(r) akirik ak'o'och käy. Yan äkhaan lehi(h) kulutsik to'on."

The ancestor is very happy. "I have my son-in-law. There are two (sirens). Now I have my fish," he says to his wife. "This afternoon we are going to go again to see our fish. We have our son-in-law (who) catches fish for us."

. . .

. . .

Bay.

Okay.

Uch'uprari(r) chäk xok ne män(a') uxurik uk'aatik. Ne su' uk'aatik ulaak' ti' nukuch winik, "Hah he' ats'ahik ten uxirar ati'a'ar, wäkan?"

The mermaid doesn't stop asking for him. She constantly asks the ancestor for her husband, "So will you give me your son, father-in-law?"

"Eh ma yan ti' inyank'aatik inwu'yeh ti' una'."

"Well, I have to ask his mother first to hear (what she says)."

"K'aateh awu'yah bik uya'arik."

"Ask her to hear what she says."

Nukuch winik uk'aat ti' ulaak', "Kohe(?) äkts'ahik ti' äkti'a'ar huntuur ahxira(r)?"

The ancestor asks his wife, "Should we hand over our other child, the boy?"

"Ma' ten inwohe(r)," tuya'arah ulaak' nukuch winik. "Ma' ten inwohe(r). Tech awohe(r) utetech. Ba'inki(r) kuts'ek tech, wa käy?"

"I don't know," said the ancestor's wife. "I don't know. You know. You are his father. What's she going to give you, fish?"

"Tuworor käy ubo'ori(r) ati'a'ar."

"All fish is her payment for your son," (he says).

Le' ne tsoy uyor nukuch winik. Ne tsoy. Ne ki' uhanan yete(r) tuworor käy.

This (thought) (makes) the ancestor very happy. It's going to be great. He (will) eat very well with all this fish.

Tuya'arah ti' ch'uprari(r) chäk xok,

He said to the mermaid,

"Eh bay. Wa hach tuhahi(r) ahachlutsik käy, ma' atusiken, he' intaasik."

"Okay. If it's really true that you are going to catch fish (and) you're not lying to me, I will bring him."

"Way katare(r) ach'a'eh akäy wayi', tu' tsikba(r)nah(o'on) wayi'. Wayi' kak'uch(ur) ach'a(')a(eh?) akäy."

"You come here and fetch your fish here, where (we) chatted here. Here you will come and get your fish."

"Bay!" nukuch winik.

"Okay!" (says) the ancestor.

Ne tsoy uyor nukuch winik yete(r) ulaak'. Ok ukah k'in woro(r) bin uch'a('i)k (uy)o'och käy. Ok ukah k'in woro(r) käy kubin uch'a'ik ... Woro(r) ne nuk. Mäna' umeheni(r).

The ancestor and his wife are very happy. Every afternoon they go collect their fish. Every afternoon they just go collect fish ... They are all very big. None are babies.

Bay.

Okay.

Ti' yan uxirar uti'a'ar nukuch winik. Lati' ch'upra(r) chäk xok, toh xok'or. Ti' yan t(i') uchi' ha', (ti' u)chi' (u)chem. Eh tan uch'e'extik uyu'yik bik ut'änik (ti'?) uti'a'ar nukuch winik. T(an) upäyik (ti') (u)chi' a' chem.

The ancestor's son is there. The mermaid is already nearby. She is there on the shore, at the side of the canoe. She is listening to what the ancestor is saying (to) his son. He is calling him to the side of the canoe.

Upäyik, "K'ayum! K'ayum, katar ap'eese(h) la' käy!"

He calls to his son, "K'ayum! K'ayum, you come gut the fish!"

Nukuch winik ne yan uxikin. Tutohu'yah ut'an chäk xok; ti' yan (ti' u)chi' (a') chem. Ele tuyu'yah ut'an chäk xok,

The ancestor has good ears. He already heard what the mermaid said; she is there (at) (the) edge of the canoe. And he heard the mermaid (whisper),

"Päyeh ati'a'ar ka' ta(r)ak way xok'or, päyeh (a)k'a' mas xok'or ten t(i') inch'a'ik."

"Call your son so that he comes closer, call him closer to me so I can grab him."

"Bay."

"Okay," (says the ancestor).

Upurik ut'an, "Ma' ne yahah. Buuy ukah. Man(en) ti'. Ma' ne yahah. Ko'oten 'aante(h) inp'eeseh käy, K'ayum!"

He calls out, "It's not that difficult. (The shore) is beginning to harden. Pass over there. It's not that difficult. Come here and help me gut fish, K'ayum!"

"Intet tan uk'ub(i)ken ti' chäk xok bähe'. Inkik, bini(h) t(i') uyit ha' yete(r) chäk xok. P'isi(r) ten. Tan uk'ubiken ti' chäk xok."

"My father is handing me over to the mermaid now. My older sister went to the bottom of the lagoon with the merman. He's doing the same with me. He is handing me over to the mermaid."

Tuyu'yah ut'an lati' uch'upra(r) chäk xok, "Taaseh ati'a'ar. Seeb! Päyeh ka' ta(ra)k."

He heard that mermaid say, "Bring your son. Hurry up! Call him to come."

Nukuch winik seeb seeb upäyik uti'a'ar uk'uchur up'eesik käy.

The ancestor frantically calls his son over to come and gut fish.

Unukuch winik chich upäyik uti'a'ar, "Ko'oten! Seeb!"

The ancestor calls out sharply to his son, "Come here! Hurry up!"

Chen biki(r) nukuch winik ne yan utukur. Ma' xok'i(h) t(i') uchi' chem. Ne seeb bini(h). Uxira(r) uti'a'ar nukuch winik tutukrah ubäh,

However, the (ancestor's son) is smart. He did not go near the edge of the canoe. He darted away. The ancestor's son thought to himself,

"Bin inkah puts'u(r) ten. Bähe' bin inkah ten. Intet bäkan tan uk'ub(i)ken ti' chäk xok, bäkan. Intet tan uk'ubiken. Ne ma' tsoy intet. Tuworo(r) käy uhanan.

Woro(r) käy uhanan intet mäna' uki' uyo'och. T'ära(r) intet. Tuk'ubah inkik. Ti' bini(h) t(i') uyit ha'. Lehi(h) ten bähe' kuk'ub(i)ken intet. Bähe' ten mäna' inku(r)tar t(i') inwatoch. Bin inkah ten."

"I'm going to run away. I'm going right now. Despite what he says, my father is going to hand me over to the mermaid. My father is handing me over. My father is very wicked. All he does is eat fish. My father only eats fish. There isn't any (other) food as good. My father is getting in the habit of it. He gave away my older sister. She went to the bottom of the lagoon. This is what (he intends to do) to me. Now my father (plans) to give me away. Now I'm not going to hang around in my house. I'm leaving."

Bek utukul nukuch winik.

This is what the ancestor is thinking.

"Bähe' ten bin inkah. Bin inp'ätik intet. He' uyirik ten intet. He' uyirik ten inna' Mäna' inku(r)tar bähe'. Bin inkah inputs'u(r)."

"Now I'm going. I'm going to leave my father. Surely my father will see me. Surely my mother will see me. I'm not going to hang around now. I'm going to run away."

. . .

. . .

Nähch'ika'(an) (u)mächm(an) kuchiyo ti' up'ees(i)k ukäy. Lahih ka'ah tuyirah utet ahnukuch winik yet(er) una', tusutk'ah ubäh. Maani(h) t(i') uyatoch, okih ich uyatoch ukäxtik ubaay. Yan uhärär. Tuch'aah uhärär, b-i-i-i-h ich k'aax. Puts'ih.

He is still standing there holding the knife for gutting the fish. When he saw his father and his mother he spun around. He went (to) his house. He entered his house and looks for his bag.[5] He has arrows. He took his arrows (and) took off into the forest. He ran away.

Tan uyok'or tan ubin nukuch winik,

The ancestor is crying as he goes,

"'Utse(r)eh. Intet ne ma' baay intet. Uk'ubiken ti' chäk xok. Ne ma' bay. Ne ma' tsoy intet. Woro(r) käy uhanan, mäna', mäna' ba' kuchi'ik intet—woro(r) käy. Tuk'ubah inkik. Ten tanah bähe'. Kuk'ubiken tanah. Mäna' ma' tutukur ubah intet. Woro(r) käy uhanan. 'Otsi(r)en. Ma' tuba' inbin. Tuk'ubahen ti' chäk xok."

"Woe is me. My father is a phony. He's handing me over to the mermaid. He's a fraud. My father is wicked. All he does is eat fish, nothing else—just fish. He handed over my older sister. Now it's me. Now he's handing me over. There isn't anything (else) my father thinks about. He only eats fish. Poor me. There is nowhere for me to go. He handed me over to the mermaid."

Bay.

Okay.

Tan ubin nukuch winik, tuhunin ich aak'bir. Tan uyok'or tan ubin ti'. Tan uyok'or tan ubin. Tan uyok'or tan ubin,

The ancestor is going along, alone in the darkness. He is crying (as) he is going. He is crying (as) he is going. He is crying (as) he is going,

"Ne ma' tsoy intet. Be'in intet ma' inwohe(r) bik yani(r), ma' utukur intet. Uk'ubiken ti' chäk xok. Inkik binih (ti') (u)yitha'. Bähe' inkik ti'yan ti'. Bähe' tan uk'ubiken intet ti' chäk xok."

"My father is wicked. I don't know why my father is like this. He doesn't think. He hands me over to the mermaid. My older sister went to the bottom of the lagoon. Now my older sister is there. Now my father is handing me over to the mermaid."

PART 3. THE BOY'S JOURNEY

Tan ubin, tan ubin, tan ubin nukuch winik ich k'aax. Tan uyok'or tan ubin. Yan uyo'och wah, yan uyo'och k'ayem. (Chan kuchmach chichin.) Leh(ih) tu' kubin yet(er) yan uhärä(r) yan.

He is going and going, the ancestor is going (through) the forest. He is crying, (as) he is going. He has his tortillas; he has his posol. (He's got a little [in a small bag] he carries in his hand.) This and his bow and arrows go with him where(ever) he goes.

(U)k'uchur boon ubin nukuch winik tunup'ah chem(b)e(r)k'uho'.[6] Uyirik woro(r) barum. Kulik'ir uk'anik (u)yok, "HAAYII! Barum!" Ne pim. Chäk barum.

The ancestor gets so far (when) he encounters the little gods of the forest. He sees only jaguars. He gets up and runs, "YIKES! Jaguars!" There were a lot. They are red jaguars.[7]

Ele, uhook'or ut'an lati' chäk barum, "Ma' asähtiken paareh," kih. "Tu' kabin tech?"

Then, (a) red jaguar speaks out, "Don't be afraid of me, son," he said. "Where are you going?"

"Eh, mäna'," kih. "Puts'ur inkah. Intet tan uk'ubiken ti' chäk xok."

"Nowhere," he says. "I am running away. My father is handing me over to the mermaid."

"E-h-h-h. Ne ma' tsoy atet."

"E-h-h-h. Your father is wicked."

"Ha'ri' chäk xok, lati' intet tuk'ubah inkik. Tuk'ubah inkik. Toh ch'a'ahbi(h) inkik ten chäk xok". A' bähe', ten ti' uch'upra(r) chäk xok. Tuk'ubahen intet."

"My father already handed my sister over to the merman. My sister is already taken by the merman. And now it is I who belongs to the mermaid. My father gave me away."

Y chem(b)e(r)k'uho' tuya'arah,

And the little gods of the forest said,

"Eh, 'otsirech, paareh. Bähe' ne ma' tsoy atet uk'ubikech. Eh 'otsirech."

"Eh, poor you, son. Your father is very wicked to give you away. Poor you."

La' la'eh chem(b)e(r)k'uho' yan uyo'och yuk. Ti' chara'(a)n uyo'och yuk. Tukinsah uyo'och yuk. Ne pim ahbarum la'eh chem(b)e(r)k'uho'. Ma' ba-rumi(r), chem(ber) k'uho', xim(b)a(r) k'uho' yok'o(r) k'aax. [Leti' tsik-bar(r)nah yete(r) nukuch winik uchik. Ba'ik utsikbartah.]

Those little gods of the forest have deer meat. Their deer is lying there. They (had) killed a deer. There are a lot of those little gods of the forest. But they aren't (really) jaguars. They are little gods of the forest, the gods that walk in the forest. [They used to talk with the ancestors long ago. They used to talk with them like this.]

Ahchem(b)er k'uho' xim(b)a(r) k'uho' tuya'arah, "'Otsirech, paareh. Eh, tu' kabin?"

The little gods of the forest, the gods that walk said, "Poor you, son. So where are you going?"

"Mäna' ti'. Way kinbin wene(n) ti' inhuni(n) yanen."

"There isn't any(where). I'm going to sleep here because I'm all alone."

"Eh, eh hah. 'Otsirech paareh. Ne ma' tsoy atet. Ma' (t)utukrah atet. Tuk'ubahech ti' chäk xok. Eh, bay."

"Ah, yes indeed. Poor you, son. Your father is wicked. Your father didn't think. He gave you away to the mermaid. Ah, well."

Tuya'arah lati' xim(b)a(r) k'uho', chem(ber) k'uho', "Eh, wi'hech paareh?"

That little god that walks, the little god of the forest, said, "Eh, are you hungry, son?"

"Wi'hen," kih. "Chen ma' inchi'ik che'che' yuk. Ten ma' inchi'ik yuk che'che', chen täk'an. Täk'an inhanan, k'ak'bir."

"I am hungry," he said. "But I don't eat raw deer meat. I don't eat deer meat raw, only cooked. My food is roasted."

"Eh hah. Ne poch inwu'yik. Paareh, bik yu'yah? Uki' awo'ocheh? Ne pochen."

"Eh yes. I want to try it. So, son, how does it taste? Is your food good? I really want (to try it)."

"Eh bay," la' nukuch winik tuya'arah.

"All right," the ancestor said.

Chem(b)e(r) k'uho', xim(b)a(r) k'uho' k'aaxo' lati' ne poch utuntik bäk' k'ak'bir, täk'an. Tuya'arah ti' nukuch winik,

The little gods of the forest, the gods that walk around the forests, they really want to try the meat roasted, cooked. They said to the ancestor,

"Wa awohe(r) uk'ak'ta(r), he' wa ak'ak'tik, ne poch intuntik awo'och."

"If you know how to roast it, if you will roast it, (then) (we) really want to try your food."

Tuya'arah lati' nukuch winik, "He're'! He' ink'ak'tik. Xen käxtik uk'ak'i(r). He' ink'ak'tik atuntik awu'yeh."

The ancestor said, "Of course! I will roast it. Go look for fire. I will roast it and (then) you try it and see what you think."

"Eh bay."

"That's fine," (say the little gods).

Lati' chem(b)e(r)k'uho' binih huntuuri' yok'o(r) ka'an bin utaasik k'ak'. Ma'
ne sahin ubin, ka'u'rih. Eh, tutaasah k'ak'.

One of the little gods of the forest went to the sky. He went to fetch fire. Not
long after he left he came back. So, he brought back fire.[8]

Seeb tukäxtik uche' ti' umut ti' uk'ak'tik a' bäk'. Ubin umehenk'upik a'
bäk'. Boon upimen ahbarum! Le a'la'eh chem(b)e(h)k'uho'. Le ma' barum.
Xim(b)a(r) k'uho'. Le ne poch utuntik, ne seeb, ne poch utunti(k).

Quickly (the ancestor) looked for wood to build a fire to roast the meat. He
proceeds to cut up little pieces of meat. How many jaguars there are! They
are little gods of the forest. They aren't jaguars. They're the little gods that
walk. They really want to try it. They are eager to try it.

Ele, nukuch winik tan uk'ak'tik ubäk'er ahyuk. Tan uk'ak'tik. Seebseeb ulah
wä(r)k(')äsik. Upeesik. Ne t'ab(bir) uk'ak'. Ne chäkhar(e'en) uk'ak'. Ele,
tähi(r) tumentah ubäk'er ahyuk.

And so, the ancestor is roasting the meat of the deer. He is roasting it.
Quickly, quickly he turns it over and over. He moves it around. The fire is already lit. The fire is blazing. And then, he cooked the flesh of the deer well.

Ele, ubin sinta(r). La'eh ahbarum la'eh ahchem(b)e(r)k'uho' a' la'eh. Uya'arik, "Ma', ma', ma' (a)ts'ahik ten t(i') uk'äb ma'. Yan ti' ach'inik, paareh,
ubäk'e(r) t(i') intuntik inwu'yeh awo'ochech tech, bik (u)yu'y(e)h täk'an."

Then, they line up. The little gods of the forest are jaguars. (One) says, "No,
no, don't give it to me by hand. You have to throw the meat, son, so I (can)
try your food and see how it tastes cooked."

"Bay," kih nukuch winik. "Bay."

"Okay," said the ancestor. "Okay."

La'eh uchem(b)e(r)k'uho' bini(h) usiinta(r). Ket ku(r)ta(r) ket siinah. Ele, nukuch winik tuch'a'ah a' bäk' ne täk'an—tuch'inah—HUMMM. Kutar, "häp," kih t(i) uho'or ukaar, ne tah uho'or ukaar. Kutar, "HÄP," seeb (kutar) ne tah uchi'. Ma' uch'a'ik t(i') uk'äb.

The little gods of the forest went and formed a line. They sit down in a straight line. So then, the ancestor took the well-cooked meat and threw it—HUMMM. It comes, "gulp," into their throats, straight into their throats. It comes, "GULP," (it goes) straight (into) their mouths. They don't take it from his hand.

"Ehhh, ne p'enk'äch ki' awo'ochech, paareh," ut'an lati' chem(b)e(r)k'uho', xim(b)a(r) k'uho'. "Ne ki' awo'ochech, paareh. 'Otsirech atet uk'ubikech ti' chäk xok. P'ateh. Inbin inwu'yeh ti' kyum, wa bik uya'alik akyumeh, he' inwaantikech."

"Ehhh, your food is incomparably delicious, son," says one little god of the forest. "Your food is delicious, son. It's a pity for you that your father is handing you over to the mermaid. Wait here. I'm going to hear (what) our lord (says). If our lord says so, I will help you."

Bini(h) lati' chem(b)e(r)k'uho' t(i') uka'ani(r) to('a)n äkyum. K'uch uk'aatik,

That one little god of the forest went to the sky where our lord is. He arrived and asks him,

"Ko'n 'otsi(r) luumo'. 'Otsi(r) mehen. K'uba'abih ten utet ti' chäk xok."

"Our poor mortal. The poor child. He was handed over by his father to the mermaid."

"Ehhh, mäna'. Wa k'uba'abih ti' (u)chäk xok, hoy ti'. Chäk xok yani(r). Ut'ani(r) utet. Ut'ani(r) una'."

"Ehhh, there isn't anything (that can be done). If he was handed over to the mermaid, then forget it. He belongs to the mermaid. It is his father's order. It is his mother's order."

"Eh, eh hah."
"Yes, that's true." (says the little god).

"Le mäna'."
"There isn't anything (that can be done now)."

"Mäna'."
"There is no way," (says the little god).

"'Otsi(r). Xiiki(h) bin. Chäk xok yani(r)."
"Poor thing. He has to go. He belongs to the mermaid," (says Hachäkyum).

"Bay."
"Very well," (says the little god).

U'lih chem(b)e(r)k'uho' uka'tsikbartik ti' nukuch winik.
The little god of the forest came back and talks to the ancestor again.

"Hah bik uya'arik?"
"So, what does he say?" (asks the ancestor).

"Mäna' bin. 'Otsirech. Atet usi'pi(r). Ana' usi'pi(r). Woro(r) käy kuchi'ik.
Lahi(h) uk'ubikech, ma' het la'eh. Yan ti' abin."
"He says there's nothing. Poor you. It's your father's fault. It's your mother's
fault. All they (care about) is eating fish. This is (why) they gave you away,
so it is impossible (to do anything). You have to go."

"Bay."
"All right," (says the ancestor).

Lati' chem(b)e(r)k'uho' tutuntah umeyah nukuch winik. Ne ki' umeyah tuyu'yah; tuch'i'ah yuk täk'an, k'ak'bi(r). Ne p'e(n)k'äch ki' tuyu'yah.

That little god of the forest tasted the work of the ancestor. His work was very delicious; he ate the cooked, roasted deer. He tasted its incomparably delicious flavor.

Lati' chem(b)e(r)k'uho' yan ulä'p'ook. Tuts'aah ti' nukuch winik, tusihah ti'.

That little god of the forest has an old hat. He gave it to the ancestor, he gave it as a gift to him.

"Ele, he're', paareh. Yan inlä'p'ook. Insihik tech te' akuchik te' abin. Ma' ap'ätik inlä'p'ook.

"Here, son. I have an old hat. I'm giving it to you to carry where you go. Don't leave my old hat behind.

Yan tu' kabin awetbin. Ma' ap'ätik inlä'p'ook."

You must take it with you where you go. Don't leave my old hat behind."

"Bay."

"Okay."

Nukuch winik tukuchah lati' up'ook (ti') chem(b)e(r)k'uho'. Bin yete(r).

The ancestor carried that hat (of) the little god of the forest. He left with it.

"Bay. Bin inkah ten."

"Okay. I'm going now."

"Xen, paareh! 'Otsi(r), ma' ba' inme(n)tah tech. Tuk'ubahech atet. Usi'ipi(r). Ne 'otsirech. Ma' ba' inme(n)tik. Ma' bik inwaantikech, ma'. Taren inwu'yik ti' äkyum. 'Mäna',' tuya'arah. 'Mäna'. Hoy ti'.'"

"Go on, son! Poor thing, there is nothing I can do for you. Your father gave you away. It is his fault. Poor, poor you. There is nothing I can do. I don't know how to help you. I came back, I heard from our Lord, 'There is no way,' he said. 'There is nothing (that can be done). Forget it.'"

"Bay."
"Okay," (says the ancestor).

Kuka(')bin. Tan uxim(b)a(r).
He sets off once more. He is walking.

Xuba(h) a'arah ti' ten xim(b)a(r) k'uho',
The little god that walks around called after him,

"T(e') awirah paareh, te' awirah kurik a' wits. Ne ka'ana(n) ti' ahook'or ku(r)tar. Ti' kahook'or ku(r)tar. Ti' kahook'or ku(r)tar yok'o(r) uho('o)r a' wits. Ma' p'ätik inlä'p'ook. Ma'."
"You (will) see a hill standing over there. You go out there, way up high, and sit down. You go out there and sit down. You go out there and sit down on top of the hill. Don't leave my old hat behind. Don't."

"Bay."
"Okay."

Nukuch winik tan ubin. Tuyirah wits ne ka'ana(n). Ti' na'ak(ih) ku(r)tar. Xuba(r) la' lä' p'ook ts'a'(a)b ti' ukuchban. Tan ubin.
The ancestor is going along. He saw the very steep hill. He climbed up it and (sat) down. He still carries the old hat that was given to him to carry. He is going along.

Tan uyok'or nukuch winik,
The ancestor is crying,

"'Utse(r)eh. Ne ma' baay intet. Tuk'ubahen ti' chäk xok. Ma' het la'eh, ma'
bik insut ma'."

"Woe is me. My father is a phony. He gave me away to the mermaid. It's impossible, there is no way I can return."

Tan uyok'or nukuch winik.

The ancestor is crying.

Hook'ih ho'or wits ku(r)tar. Tan uyok'or. Tan utukrik ubäh,

He came out on the top of the hill and sat down. He is crying. He is thinking to himself,

*"Uts(er)eh, ne ma' tsoy intet. Tuk'ubahen ti' chäk xok. Inkik ti' yan t(i') uyit ha'
bähe'."*

*"Oooh my father is wicked. He gave me away to the mermaid. My older sister is at
the bottom of the lagoon now."*

Ma' ne sanih utukrik ubäh nukuch winik lati' kutar säk ch'iich'. Kaba(r) kumaan. Usutik ubäh säk ch'iich'. Sut kumaan, usutik ubäh. Tan utan yawat
ahsäk ch'iich',

The ancestor was not thinking very long before a white falcon comes. He
passes by low. The white falcon turns around. He passes by again and turns
around. The white falcon is screeching,

"IIIYYYOO. IIIYYYOO."

"IIIYYYOO. IIIYYYOO."

Nukuch winik tan utukrik ubäh,

The ancestor is thinking to himself,

"Wa ba'ik inten ahsäk ch'iich'en, wa ba'ik inme(n)tik inbah, yan inxik' bix ahsäk ch'iich', . . . he' inbin inwir(ik?) inkik. Turah inbin inwireh inmam, chäk xok. He' inbin inch'eene'etik inkik to'an tukura'(a)n t(i') uyit ha'."

"If I were like the white falcon, if I (could) make myself like him, with wings like the white falcon that passes by, . . . I would go see my older sister. I (would) have to go see my brother-in-law, the merman. I would go visit my older sister where she is at the bottom of the lagoon."

Eh, säk ch'iich' kukuru(m) — KURUM.

The white falcon lands — KURUM.

Tan uki'paak'tik nukuch winik tukura'(a)n. Eh, kuyu'yik ut'an ahsäk ch'iich',

The ancestor is (anxiously) waiting where he is seated. Then, he hears the white falcon speak,

"Eh, ba'i(n)ki(r) kawirik tech kurikech way?"

"Eh, what are you looking at seated here?"

Tan uteknuktik nukuch winik,

The ancestor answers immediately,

"Ele mäna' aten. Puts'ur inkah. Intet tuk'ubahen ti' chäk xok. Ma' tubah inbin, ma'."

"Eh, nothing. I'm running away. My father gave me away to the mermaid. There is nowhere for me to go."

"Eh, eh hah. Puts'ur akah."

"Eh, uh-huh. You're running away."

"Puts'ur inkah. Ma' tubah inbin. Mäna'. Inkik tutohk'ubah intet ti' chäk xok. Toh ti' yan yitha' bähe'. A' la'eh intech wa be'ik a' bix tech(ir) yan axik'e(h), h(e') inbin inwir(ik) inkik. Tur(ah) inbin inwireh t(i') uyit ha' tu' yan inkik. 'Otsir inkik. Intet tuk'ubah ti' chäk xok, inten tan uk'ubiken ti' chäk xok. Tutohk'ubahen intet."

"I'm running away. There is nowhere for me to go. Nowhere. My sister, well, my father has already handed her over to the merman. She's at the bottom of the lagoon now. If I had wings like you, I would go see my older sister. I must go see my older sister at the bottom of the lagoon. My poor sister. My father gave her away to the merman, and now it is me that my father is giving away to the mermaid. My father (has) already given me away."

"Ehhh, eh hah," kunuuk ahsäk ch'iich'. "Eh hah, ne ma' tsoy atet. Bay ne woro(r) käy uhana(n) ateti(h) wa?"

"Ehhh, I see," replies the white flacon. "Indeed, your father is wicked. So, is it true your father only eats fish?"

"Eh, woro(r) käy uhana(n) intet."

"Yes, my father only eats fish."

"Eh, ne ma' tsoy. 'Otsirech, paaleh."

"Well, that's very bad. Poor you, son."

[Lati' säkch'iich' ma' hach säkch'iich'. Int'än lati' k'uh, wa chem(b)e(r)k'uho'.]

[That white falcon is not really a white falcon. I think he is a god, or one of those little gods that walk around.]

"Eh bay. Eh, hach tuha(h)i(r) poch abin awirik akik tu' yanih yit petha'?"

"Very well. Do you really want to go see your older sister at the bottom of the lagoon?"

"Lehih ne poch inbin inwirik inkik," (u)ya'(ar)ik (ah)nukuch winik. Ne tsoy uyor.

"I really want to go see her," says the ancestor. He is elated.

"Eh hah. Yan akuchmah alä'p'ook?"
"Very well. Have you brought your old hat?"

"Ti' yan ten. Tuts'aah ten."
"It's with me. He gave it to me. "

"Eh ne tsoy. Kuch(eh). Ma' p'äti(k)."
"Very good. Carry it. Don't leave it behind."

"Bay."
"Okay."

"Hach poch akänik?" uya'arik ti' nukuch winik. "Hach poch akänik uk'aayi(r) uxik'. Yan uk'aay."
"Do you really want to learn it?" he says to the ancestor. "Do you really want to learn the song of the wings? There is a song."

Tunukah nukuch winik,
The ancestor replied,

"Ten ne pochen.
"I really want to.

Wa h(e') akana(n)siken inkänik."
If you will teach me I (will) learn it."

"Eh bay. Le, ach'e'extik awu'yik ink'aay wa. Ma' aputs'ik, ma'."
"Okay. Pay attention to my song, then. Don't forget it."

"Bay," nukuch winik tunuukah. "Bay. Ma' inputs'ik. He' inch'e'extik inwu'y-eh. Bay."

"Okay," the ancestor replied. "Okay. I won't forget it. I will pay attention. Okay."

Tan uk'aay säk ch'iich' ti' ukaansah nukuch winik.

The white falcon is singing, to teach the ancestor.

Bay. Ts'o'ok uk'aay ahsäk ch'iich'. Le' kuk'atik,

Okay. The white falcon finished singing. He asks him,

"Tawu'yah? Tawu'yah ink'aay?"

"Did you hear it? Did you hear my song?"

"Tinwu'yah."

"I heard it."

"Le ma' p'ätik ma' wa. Ma' aputs'ik ut'ani(r) ink'aay."

"Don't leave it, don't. Don't lose the words of my song."

"Bay," kih, nukuch winik tunuukah.

"Okay," the ancestor replied.

"Eh, bay. Chäkan wa takänah ink'aay, wa poch abin awirik akik. Tawarah ne poch abin ch'ik yitha' kabin akäxtik akik."

"Good. Let's see if you learned my song, if you want to go see your sister. You said you really wanted to go far to the bottom of the lagoon to look for your sister."

"Le' he're' bek! He' inbin inwirik inkik. Ne poch intsikbar yete(r) mam. Ne poch inwirik inkik. Intet tuk'ubah ti' chäk xok."

"This is so! I will go see my sister. I really want to talk to my brother-in-law. I really want to see my sister. My father handed her over to the merman."

"Eh, hah. Bay." Tuya'arah säk ch'iich', "Ten kinyanbin päytan wa. Tech paachi(r) wa. La' ink'aay tinka(')ans(ah)ech ma' (a)tubsik ma' wa."

"Of course. Okay." The white falcon said, "I'm going to go first. You next. This song of mine that I taught you, you won't forget it, will you."

"Bay!" kih nukuch winik tuya'arah. "Bay, ma' intubsik."

"Okay!" the ancestor said. "Okay, I won't forget it."

Ulik'(ir) ya(a)ka' (ah)säk ch'iich'—wooosh. Eh (U)lik'(ir) yok'or uxik', poh-poh-poh-pokeh. (U)hook'(or) uyawat ahsäk ch'iich',

The white falcon lifts-off—wooosh. And he lifts off on his wings, flap-flap-flap-flap. The white falcon screeches,

"IIIYOOO."

"IIIYOOO."

Nukuch winik kulik'i(r) ya(a)ka' ti' tupaach. (U)hook'(or) uxik' ti' p'is la' ket säk ch'iich'. Tan ubin. Nukuch winik kuhook'or (u)k'aay ti' lati' le ket uk'aay säk ch'iich'.

The ancestor lifts off behind (him). His wings come out the same as the white falcon's. He is going. The ancestor's song goes out like the falcon's song.

La' ket uk'aay yete(r). Lati' tuyu'yah ahsäk ch'iich' ut'an. Be'iki(r) ti' nukuch winik (u)hook'o(r) uk'aay,

It's the same song as his. He listened to the words of the white falcon. The ancestor's song goes out like his,

"IIIYOOO."

"IIIYOOO."

Nukuch winik tukanah uk'aayi(r) uxik' yete(r) säk ch'iich'. (U)nech'ik-na'aka(r). Lati' nukuch winik unech'ikna'aka(r). Ch'ik bini(h) tu' ya'axi(h) ka'an.

The ancestor learned the song of the wings with the white falcon. He climbs way up high. That ancestor climbs way up high. He went way up to where the sky is bluest.

Eh, lati' hach säk ch'iich' 'eemi(h) kaba(r), mas kaba(r) yan. Nukuch winik mas ne na'aki(h) tu' yaaxi(r) ka'aneh. Chäkan uyirik ukik t(i') uyit ya'rir, t(i') uyit a' petha' tu' kura'(an) umam.

Then, the real white falcon went down much lower. The ancestor climbed higher to where the sky is bluest. He looks to see where his sister is at the bottom of the water, at the bottom of the lagoon where his brother-in-law is.

Chäkan uyirik umam.

He looks to see (if) his brother-in-law (is there).

Ti' yan (u)mam. Ti' yan ukik.

His brother-in-law is there. His sister is there.

PART 4. THE BOY FINDS HIS SISTER

Lati' nukuch winik ubin chumuk petha'. Uyirik ukik. (U)purik u(bah?) yet(er) uxik' ubin ch'ik yit ha'. Ok(ih) uyir(ik) ukik. Ti' yan. K'uch. Uk'uchur to'an ukik. Uyirik. Ti' yan ukik', tan uhuch'. Ma' 'utsk'in ti'. Poch uharik, lati' nukuch winik, poch uharik ukik, ti' uharik ti' ukansik ut'ani(r) uxik'. Chen bikir, ma' utsk'in ti'. Yan uti'a'ar. Yan uti'a'ar yete(r) chäk xok.

The ancestor goes over the middle of the lagoon. He sees his sister. He plunges deep into the lagoon with his wings. He entered to see his sister. She is there. He arrived. He goes over to where his sister is. He sees her. His sister is there grinding corn. She is pregnant. The ancestor wants to take her out, he wants to take his sister out, to take her out and teach her the secret of the wings. But she is pregnant. She has a child. She is pregnant with the merman's child.

"Eh mäna'." Tan uyirik, 'otsir unuki(r) winik, *"Ma' het la'eh ti' inkik. Ma' het la'eh inharik. Ma' utsk'in ti'. Yan uti'a'ar yete(r) chäk xok, inmam."*

"Eh, it's impossible," (the ancestor says to himself). He is looking at her, the poor ancestor, *"It's impossible for my sister. I can't get her out. She's pregnant. She has a child with the merman, my brother-in-law."*

Eh tuk'atah ti' ukik, "Inmam, kik, tu' bini(h)?"

He asked his sister, "My brother-in-law, sister, where did he go?"

"Amam ma' kura'(a)n. Ti' bini(h) uyireh uchiich. Tabar uyu'(r). Ma' ne xanta(r) (u)yu'(r) tint'än."

"Your brother-in-law is not here. He went to visit his grandmother. He will come back later. He'll be back soon, I think."

"Ne poch inwichkir yeter inmam."

"I really want to swim with my brother-in-law."

"Bay. Hunch'ukteh amam. He' uyu'r. Ma' ne xanta(r)."

"Fine. Wait a while for your brother-in-law. He'll be back. It won't be long."

Lati' nukuch winik ukik tan utukrik ubah. *"Bik tarech tech wits'in,"* kih.

The ancestor's sister is thinking. *"How did you come here little brother?"*

"Ma' awohe(r) wa bine(n) intar inch'een(e')tech. Ne poch intar inch'eene't inmam. Poch intsikbar yeter inmam, ne poch."

"(Didn't) you know I was going to come visit you? I really want to come visit my brother-in-law. I want to talk with my brother-in-law, I really want to."

"Eh bay. Ma' ne sanih."

"Okay. It won't be long."

"Wayeh bäkan awatoch kik."

"So this here is your home, sister."

"Way inwatoch," kih. "Ne 'oy inwor. Ma' baay. Ma' hach tsoy tu' taren way. Ne ma' baay aktet. Tuk'ubaho'on ti' chäk xok. Tuk'ubaho'on."

"Here is my home," she says. "I am very bored. It's not the same. It's not very good here where I have come. Our father is a fraud. He gave us away to the sirens. He gave us away."

"Eh tuha(h)i(r)tuha(h)i(r), kik. Aktet, woro(r) käy (k)uhanan, woro(r) käy."

"That's true, sister. Our father just eats fish, just fish."

"Eh bay."

"Yes, that's true."

Chen bikir lati' chäk xok ti' yan uyir uchiich; lati' uchiich la' bix a' 'ayim, ahk'än 'aak. Lehih uchiich.

Meanwhile, the merman is visiting his grandmother; this grandmother of his is like a crocodile, (or) a yellow turtle. This is his grandmother.

Bay.

Okay.

Ma' ne sa(n)ih nukuch winik maan(ih) (ti' u)pach nah tuyirah yan iik. Yan ne täk'an. Yan uwich.

A while later the ancestor went around to the back of the house and saw there were chili peppers. The fruit was very ripe. There were a lot of fruits.

"Bay. Bähe', yan inbin inwichkir yeter inmam. Ne poch inwichkir yeter inmam."

"Okay. Now, I must go swim with my brother-in-law. I really want to go swim with my brother-in-law."

Eh ukik tunuukah, "Bay. Wa poch (a)wichkir yet(er) amam, ch'ukteh. Ne tabar uyu'r. Ma' ne xantar, tint'än. Ne taki(r) uyu'r."

His sister replied, "Fine. If you want to swim with your brother-in-law, wait. He'll be back soon. It won't be long, I think. He'll be back soon."

"Ne pochen; ne poch inwichkir yeter inmam."

"I really want to; I really want to swim with my brother-in-law."

Nukuch winik tan uman ukäxtik bik yirah wa yan uk'um yitha'. Le' nukuch winik tan uki'lahcha'antik uyatoch umam bik yirah uyatoch umam, bik yirah, wa yan ha' yan. Eh kuch'een(e'e)tik uyireh ahnukuch winik ti' yan äkan ti' tuts'a'(an) a' ha'.

The ancestor is going around, searching for a river at the bottom of the lagoon. The ancestor is looking around all sides of his brother-in-law's homestead, to see what it looks like, to see whether there is water. The ancestor notices a river winding there.

"Kik, tsoy wa inwichkir yeter inmam a' la'eh tuts'a'an uk'um?"

"Sister, is it all right to swim with my brother-in-law there where the river stretches?"

"Ne tsoy; lahi(h) tu' kuyichkir amam."

"It's very nice there; it's where your brother-in-law always swims."

"Bay."

"Fine."

Nukuch winik kubin ut'akik yah iik. Hunok tan uk'äb. Tutohmächa(h). Ma' ne san kutichir umam. Uk'uchur umam.

The ancestor goes and snaps off the large chilies. He seized one handful. Soon after his brother-in-law approaches. His brother-in-law arrives.

Utubur ut'an ukik, "K'uchi(h) inwits'in!"

His sister calls out, "My little brother (has) arrived!"

"K'uch(ih) awits'in. To'an awits'in? Ne poch inwirik awits'in. Ne poch in-tsikbar. Eh k'uch(ih) awits'in. Ne tsoy! K'uchech tech mam."

"Your little brother (has) arrived. Where is your little brother? I really want to see your little brother. I really want to talk (to him). Your little brother arrived. Very good! You (have) come brother-in-law."

"K'uchen, mam."

"I (have) come, brother-in-law."

"Ti' yanech mam."

"There you are brother-in-law."

"Ti' yanen mam."

"Here I am brother-in-law."

"Bay."

"Good."

Ti' kumaan. Ne tsoy uyor chäk xok, "K'uchech tech mam. Way tarech. Tawuk'usah awits'in?"

He passes through. The merman is very happy, "You arrived, brother-in-law. You came here. Did you give your little brother something to drink?" (the merman asks his wife).

"Tinwuk'usah."

"I gave him a drink."

"Eh bay. Ne tsoy." Ne tsoy uyol chäk xok k'uch(ih) umam. "Bähe', k'uchech mam. Ne tsoy inwor."

"Okay. Very good." The merman is very happy (that) his brother-in-law (has) arrived. "Now, you (have) arrived, brother-in-law. I'm very happy."

Nukuch winik ti' kura'(a)n toh tan utukrik ubah, "Bähe', ma' tsoy inwor ti' mam. Ma' tsoy inwor bähe'. Ne ts'iken. Ma' tsoy inwor yan ti' inbin t(i') inwichkir yeter inmam. Poch inbin t(i') inwichkir yete(r) yok'o(r) la' uk'um ch'ara'(a)n la' la'eh."

The ancestor is seated there, already deep in thought, "*Now I'm very unhappy with my brother-in-law. I'm very unhappy right now. I'm very angry. I'm unhappy (so) I have to go to swimming with my brother-in-law. I really want to go swimming with him in that river lying over there.*"

Bay.

Okay.

Nukuch winik uyokman iik. Ti' uta(a)n uk'äb, umächman hunok.

The ancestor holds the chili peppers in his hand. There is one handful clutched in the palm of his hand.

"Bay! Ko'ox takichkir mam."

"Okay! Let's go swimming, brother-in-law."

Chäk xok ne tsoy uyor, "Ko'ox mam! Ko'ox t(i') akichkir. Seebseeb! Le' ko'ox! Ne poch(en). Yan akichkir yok'or uk'um."

The merman is very happy, "Let's go, brother-in-law! Let's go for a swim. Hurry up! Come on! I really want to go. We must go swimming in the river."

Nukuch winik toh yan utukur bähe'. *"Ne ko'or usi'ipir inmam ten. La' ubo'ori(r) ten tuch'a'ah inkik. Ma' het inharik inkik ma' utsk'in ti' bähe'. Bähe' yan iik ten. He' inwe'esik ti' inmam wa."* Tutohtukrah ubah nukuch winik, *"Bähe' yan inharik. Yan inbin t(i') inwichkir yete(r) mam. Yan iik yan. He' inwe'esik ti'."*

The ancestor has a plan now. *"My brother-in-law's evil doing is very costly for me. This is my payback. He took my sister. I cannot take my sister out now (because) she is pregnant now. Now I have chili peppers. I will show them to my brother-in-law."* He thought to himself, *"Now I have to pull them out. I have to go swimming with my brother-in-law. There are chili peppers. I will show them to him."*

"Bay. Ko'ox mam. Ko'ox!"

"Okay. Let's go, brother-in-law. Let's go!"

Uk'uchur to'an a' uk'um tu' tuts'a'(a)n. (U)purik ubah—*bihin*—kih nukuch winik. Eh chäk xok upurik ubäh ti'—*bihin*.

They get to the stretch in the river. The ancestor dives in—*sploosh*. Then the merman dives in—*sploosh*.

"Ehhh ne tsoy mam. Ne ki' ha', ne tsoy." Tan uyichkir. K'ä(b)bihin, k'ä(b)bi-
hin.

"Ehhh this is very good, brother-in-law. The water is great," (says the
merman). He is bathing. He is splashing about.

Chen nukuch winik tan ukäxtik uyaran che' ti' utakik uho'or umam. Tan
ukäxtik.

But, the ancestor is looking for (someplace) underneath a tree to stick his
brother-in-law's head. He's looking for it.

"Mam! Way atar, mam."

"Brother-in-law! Come here, brother-in-law," (the ancestor calls out).

"Bik awa'arik mam?"

"What are you saying brother-in-law?"

"Way, atar way ka(k)ichkir näko'on(?)."

"Here, come over here so that we swim together."

"Bay!"

"Okay!"

Chäk xok ma' uyohe(r) wa yan ba'ikin kume(n)tah ti'. Mix uyohe(r); ne tsoy
uyor.

The merman doesn't know what is about to happen to him. He doesn't
know anything; he is in high spirits.

"Tubah, mam?"

"Where, brother-in-law?"

"Way! Atar way."

"Here! You come over here."

Kuk'uchur lati' xok'or tu' chara'(a)n che' ahchäk xok. Eh, nukuch winik upaayhitik uyok umam—eeeREECH. K'äk'o'a', k'äk'o'a'. Seeb k'äk'o'a'. Nukuch winik ne chich umuuk' uho'or umam (ti' u)yara(m) che' t(i') uyitha'. Tan up'isbah umam. K'äk'o'a'. K'äk'o'a'. Ka'(ah) tutekch'atah a' iikeh tuki'ki'babahk'ä'tah t(i') uyit umam.

The merman gets near to where the log is lying. Then, the ancestor yanks his brother-in-law's feet—eeeREECH. (The merman) is drowning, he is drowning. He is quickly drowning. The ancestor is very strong. He sticks his brother-in-law's head under the log in the water. His brother-in-law is struggling. He is drowning. He is drowning. Then he grabbed the chili and pounded it up his brother-in-law's anus.

—POCH, POCH—

—BAM, BAM—

Ba'axta(r) mäna' tuyirah umam. Seeb bini(h) t(i') uyit ha'. Tusipit(ah) uk'ä' t(i') umam. Hook'(ih) uyaaka' nukuch winik. Uman yaaka' to'an ukik.

Then he didn't see his brother-in-law. He went quickly under water. He let go of his brother-in-law's hand. The ancestor got out running. He went running to where his sister was.

"He' ts'o'ok awichkir, wits'in?" tuya'arah ukik.

"(Have) you finished bathing, little brother?" his older sister said.

"Ts'o'okih, kik. Bay. Bin inkah kik. 'Otsirech. Inmam ti' p'ati(h). He' usut pachir wa."

"Finished, sister. Okay. I'm going now, sister. Poor you. My brother-in-law stayed there. Perhaps he'll return later."

La'eh nukuch winik uyohe(r) ba' tume(n)tah t(i') umam. Maani(h) ut'aneh ukik. Tuya'arah ti' ukik,

The ancestor knows very well what he did to his brother-in-law. He went through to talk to his sister. He said to his sister,

"'Otsirech kik. Ma' bik inharikech. Ma' utsk'in tech. Wa ne utsk'in tech kachik, inharik tech kachik akbin. Ket ka(h)bin ne naach."

"I feel sorry for you, sister. I cannot take you out. You are pregnant. If you weren't pregnant, sister, I would have taken you. We would (have gone) together far away."

"Bay." Tan uyok'or ukik, "Bay. Xen tech, wits'in. Käräntabäh."

"Okay." His sister is crying, "Okay. Go, little brother. Take care of yourself."

Le hook'(ih). Bin(ih) nukuch winik. Hook'(ih) yet(er) uxik'. Bini(h) ch'ik naach, ch'i-i-i-k pach k'ak'na'.

Then, he went out. The ancestor left. He went out on his wings. He went very far away, fa-a-a-r away to the other side of the sea.

PART 5. THE BOY MARRIES THE KING'S DAUGHTER

Lati' ka'(ah) bini(h) ti'. Ch'ik bini(h) pach k'ak'na' ahnukuch winik. Ti' bini(h) to'an uk'aba' a' ton Rey.

Then the ancestor went there. He went way over to the other side of the sea. He went to where there is a King, as he is called.

Ti' eemi(h) nukuch winik. Lati' nukuch winik tu(?) la'eh ok(ih) usäk ch'iich'i(r). Ti' bini(h) ch'ik pach k'ak'na' ton(tu' yan?) Rey. Ti' tuyirah ulaak'. Ti' tuyirah ti'.

There the ancestor descended. The ancestor came in like the white falcon. He went there, far away to the other side of the sea where the King was. There he saw his (future) wife. There he saw her.

Rey yan u'ooxtuur uch'uprar uti'a'ar. Mäna' ulaak'. Tuworo(r) ne chichan toh. Mix k'äs xira(r) ti' mäna'. Mäna' xira(r).

The King has three daughters. They have no husbands. All of them are still young. There are hardly any men there. There aren't any men.

Rey ne tsoy uyor. Ka'(ah) k'uchi(h) nukuch winik ne tsoy uyor. Tuya'arah ti',

The King was elated. When the ancestor arrived, he was elated. He said to him,

"Seebar man. Tubah atar tech?"

"Come in quickly. Where do you come from?"

Lati' nukuch winik tuya'arah,

The ancestor said,

"Ne naach intar a' ten ch'ik pach k'ak'na'. Puts'ur inkah (ti') intet. Tuk'ub-ahen ti' chäk xok. Ne ma' tsoy intet. Inkik, tutohk'ubahen ti' chäk xok. Toh ti' yan (ti'?) chäk xok."

"I come from very far away, from the other side of the sea. I'm running away from my father. He handed me over to the mermaid. My father is wicked. He already handed over my older sister to the merman. She already belongs to the merman."

"Ehhh, ne ma' tsoy," tunuukah ahRey. "Ne ma' tsoy atet. Bek ume(n)tik, ma' tsoy. Bik yani(r) ume(n)tik atet bek? Ahhh, chen tsoy way tarech."

"Ehhh, that's not good," replied the King. "Your father is evil. It's not good that he does it this way. Why does your father do it this way? Ahhh, but it's good that you came here."

Bay.

Okay.

Rey ne tsoy uyor. Tuya'arah,

The King is very happy. He said,

"Way atar. Way yan wah, yan nah, yan o'ochi(r), yan inti'a'ar män(a') ulaak'. Inharik haräkniki(r). Wa 'uts tawich ateetik awireh inhaantikech. He' ints'ahik inti'a'ar tech."

"You (have) come here. Here there are tortillas, there are houses, there is food, there are my daughters who don't have husbands. I (will) bring my daughters out. You choose the one that you like (and) I'll make you my son-in-law. I will give you my daughter."

"Bay." Nukuch winik 'as sahak. Tantar uk'uchur. Sahak ti'.

"Okay." The ancestor is a little bit nervous. He had just arrived. He is nervous.

Seeb uhaansah. Seeb uyuk'ursa(h).

Quickly they feed him. Quickly they give him something to drink.

Lati' Rey uya'arik,

The King says,

"Seeb! Awuk'ur. Seeb! Awuk'ursik. Lati' ne 'otsir. Ne wi'h. Seeb! Seeb!"

"Quick! You drink up. Quick! Give him a drink. He is pitiable. He's very hungry. Quickly! Quickly!"

Ts'o'ok uhanan nukuch winik, Rey tuya'arah ti' uch'upra(r) uti'a'ar,

(When) the ancestor finished eating, the King said to his daughters,

"Bähe' ahook'or te' haräkniki(r) wa poch awirik."

"Now you go outside (and) see if you like him."

"Tech akäxtik inti'a'ar to'an tsoy awirik. Wa 'uts t(i') awich, ints'ahik tech. Inhaantikech."

"You look for the one you like. If she is to your liking, I will give her to you. I will make you my son-in-law."

"Bay."

"Okay," (says the ancestor).

Rey tuya'arah ti' uch'upra(r) uti'a'ar,

The King said to his daughters,

"Yan ahook'or ach'iktar te', lah 'ooxt(uu)re'ex te'."

"You have to go out and stand there, all three of you."

Uya'arik ti' nukuch winik,

He says to the ancestor,

"Bähe' ahook'or awirik to'an 'uts t(i') awich inch'upra(r) inti'a'al."

"Now you go out and see which of my daughters you like."

Nukuch winik tuya'arah, "Lati' ne 'uts ti' inwich."

The ancestor said, "I like this one."

"Ah bay. Lati' tech yani(r). Inhaanech bähe'."

"Very good. She is yours. You are my son-in-law now."

Ne tsoy uyor nukuch winik. Yan ulaak'. Ti' tuyirah ulaak' to'an Rey.

The ancestor is very happy. He has a wife. He found his wife there with the King.

Lati' Rey tume(n)tah uchemi(r) uyichkir (ti') uhaan. Tume(n)tah chemi(r) uyichkir uhaan. Ne 'otsir uyirik uhaan. Tulahme(n)tah tema' uch'a'bar ti' chäk xok, porke chäk xok yan uch'ikin bin ch'ik naach. Tu' kubin, tur ukäxtik. Chen Rey ne yan utukur. Tume(n)tah uchemi(r) uyichkir uhaan.

The King made a bathtub (for) his son-in-law. He made his son-in-law a bathtub. He cares for his son-in-law very much. He did it so that he wouldn't be grabbed by the mermaid, because the mermaid (will) follow him far (and wide). She looks for him wherever he goes. But the King is smart. He made a bathtub for his son-in-law.

Bay.

Okay.

Ne 'otsir. Ma' ucha'ik uyichkir yok'or ha', yok'or uk'umo'. Ma' ucha'ik uyok'or. (U)ki'känämah uhaan.

He cares for him. He doesn't let him swim in the water, in the rivers. He doesn't let him enter. He has taken good care of his son-in-law.

Uya'arah ti' uch'upra(r) uti'a'ar,

He said to his daughter,

"Yan ti' aki'känäntik inhaan. Ma' acha'ik uyichkir yok'or uk'um o yok'or petha'. Wa ma', aputs(s)'ik inhaan ten."

"You must take good care of my son-in-law. Don't let him swim in the river or the lagoon. If not, then you (will) lose my son-in-law."

"Bay."

"All right."

Ch'upra(r) ti'a'ar tukänäntah ulaak'. Tukänäntah nukuch winik. Tukänäntah. Ket kuhana(r) yete(r) ahRey. Ket kuhana(r) ket. Ne 'otsir uyirik uhaan.
Ne 'otsir.

The daughter looked after her husband. She looked after the ancestor. She
looked after him. They eat together with the King. They eat together. He
cares for his son-in-law very much. He cares for him.

Bay.

Okay.

Ele, chen biki(r) lati' nukuch winik tubi(h) ti'. Bini(h) yet(er) ulaak' yete(r)
t(i') uyichkir ich wa'an uk'um. Tuyirah uk'um ma' ne tam. Tuyirah tan uti-
hi(r).

And so, the ancestor forgot about (the mermaid). He went with his wife to
swim in the river. He saw that the river was not very deep. He saw that it
was drying up.

"Maanen! Ma' ne tam. Tan (u) tihir a' uk'um.

"Come in! It's not that deep. The river is drying up.

Ahhh," tuyirah. Tuts'i'o(r)tah.

Ahhh," he looked at it. He yearned (to go in).

"Ne poch inwichkir. Tint'än bähe' mäna' ahchäk xok. Ne naach, tint'an.
Tubi(h) ti' ten. Bähe' inwichkir."

"I want to swim. I think now there isn't a mermaid. She is far away, I think.
She forgot about me. Now I'm going for a swim."

Uch'upra(r) uti'a'ar Reyi(r) tuya'arah ti',

The King's daughter said to him,

"Ma', ma' awichkir," kih. "He' uch'a'ikech. Ahchäk xok. Tan ukäxtikech. Tan uch'uktikech."

"Don't, don't you swim," she said. "The mermaid is going to nab you. She's looking for you. She's waiting for you."

Ahnukuch winik, "Mäna'. Tubi(h) ti' ten, tint'an. Bähe' inwichkir. Poch inwichkir."

The ancestor (said), "She isn't there. She forgot about me, I think. Now I'm going for a swim. I want to swim."

Ok(ih) t(i') uyichkir nukuch winik. Toh ti' yan ahchäk xok. Seeb tuchukah. Ti' yan nukuch winik ti' ich uk'äb ahchäk xok.

The ancestor went in to swim. The mermaid is already there. She snatched him. The ancestor is in the mermaid's hands.

"Awirik! Bähe' ma' tech yani(r). Lati' ten yani(r)."

"You see! He's not yours, now. He's mine."

Uch'upra(r) uti'a'ar Rey hak'ar uyor, "Bix tacha'ah?" kih.

The King's daughter is astonished, "How could you take him?" she said.

Lati' uch'upra(r) ahchäk xok uyarik, "Awirik bähe' ten yani(r). Ten yani(r) lati', ma' tech yani(r)."

The mermaid says to her, "You see he's mine now. He's mine, not yours."

Tan uts'iiki(r) yete(r) uyanch'upir. Lati' yet(er) uch'upra(r) uti'a'ar Rey yete(r) uch'upra(r) ahchäk xok tan uts'iiko'.

She is getting angry with his wife. The King's daughter and the mermaid are fighting.

"Lati' bik yani(r), bik yani(r) tach'a'ah tech?"

"Why, why did you grab him?"

"Ma', ma' tech yani(r). Lati' ten yani(r) bähe'."

"No, he's not yours. He's mine now."

Chen biki(r) lati' uch'upra(r) uti'a'ar Rey yan utukur. Yan utuup. Tut'akah. Tupurah t(i') utaan uk'äb ahchäk xok. Tupurah utuup. HUUUM.

But then the King's daughter has an idea. She has earrings. She snapped (one) off. She threw it to the hands of the mermaid. She threw her earring. HUUUM.

Uya'arik ti', "Mas na'as(eh) ka'ana(n)!"

She says to her, "Raise (your hands) higher!"

Umasna'asi(k) ka'ana(n), lati' nukuch winik uhook'or uxik' ubin t(i') a' ka'an. Chäk xok ulik'i'(r) utim ti' ne ka'ana(n). Kuch'ikinbin ka'ana(n), ne ka'ana(n) uk'ä'täkche' nukuch che'; ba(y) xu(r) uch'uyu(r) chäk xok. Uka'lubul yok'or ha'.

She raises them higher. (As she does) the ancestor spreads his wings (and) goes into the sky. The mermaid jumps up (after him). She goes very high, very high up in the branches of a large tree, (where) the mermaid gets hung up. (Then) she drops back into the water.

"Ehhh, ne ma' tsoy tech. Taputs'ah inlaak'. Taputs'ah ten."

"Ehhh, you are wicked. You helped my husband escape. You helped him escape from me," (says the mermaid).

"Mäna'. Ma' tech yani(r). Tawirah, toh ten yani(r), beyin bini(h) tawirah. Ma' inputs'ba(r) tech. Toh techi(r) toh ti' yan t(i') utaan ak'äb. Aputs'ba(r)."

"No. He's not yours. You see, he is still mine, that's why he left, you see. I didn't let him escape from you. You already had him in the palm of your hand. You let him escape."

Le bini(h) nukuch winik, bini(h) tu' ya'axi(r) ka'an.

Now the ancestor went, he went to bluest part of the sky.

U'ri(h) lati' uch'upra(r) uti'a'ar Rey. Ne ts'iik utet. Tuya'arah, "Bähe' in-kins(i)kech. Ne ma' tsoyech. Taputs'ah inhaan. Bähe' bin inkah inkinsi-kech."

The King's daughter returned (home). Her father was very angry. He said, "Now I'm going to kill you. You are no good. You let my son-in-law escape. Now I'm going to kill you."

Ume(n)tik umaska lati' Rey ti' uxatik uche'(ir) ukaar uch'upra(r) uti'a'ar.

The King prepares his machete to cut his daughter's throat.

"Eeeh," uch'upra(r) uti'a'ar tuya'arah, "ma' yan (a)ki(n)siken. Ahaan he' usut. Saama(n) kuyu'r. Ma' (a)ki(n)siken ma' axatik inche'(ir). Ma'. Saaman, kuyu'r len k'ak' ch'uk'in. He' uyu'r."

"Oh," his daughter said, "you don't have to kill me. Your son-in-law will come back. Tomorrow he'll come back. Don't kill me. Don't cut my throat. Don't. Tomorrow, he'll come back at midday. He will come back."

"Bay."

"All right," (says the King).

Rey kura'(an) uch'ukteh uhaan. Tuch'ahah uk'ä'che' ts'o'ok uki' limatik umaska' ti' uxatik ukaar uch'upra(r) uti'a'ar.

The King is sitting there waiting for his son-in-law. He took his chair (and) finished sharpening his machete to cut his daughter's throat.

K'uchi(h) k'ak' chunk'in. Uyirik utichir. Uhook'or ku(r)ta(r) Rey. "Tawa'arah bähe' kuyu'r inhaan!"

He came at midday. He sees him approach. The King goes out and sits down. "You said my son-in-law (would) come back today!"

Ne 'otsir uyirik uhaan. Uch'uktik uyireh. Tan utichir. Kuyirik utichir; ne chan säk.

He likes his son-in-law very much. He waits for him. He is approaching. He sees him approach; he is a little white (speck).

"La' wa kutichir inhaan?"
"Is that my son-in-law approaching?"

"Le' lati' tet."
"That's him, father."

Utubur ut'änik uch'upra(r) uti'a'ar Rey, "Tawa'arah ma' uyu'r ahaan!"
The King's daughter blurts out, "You said that your son-in-law was not coming back!"

"Hach tuhahir. He' yu'reh haan. Ne tsoy inwor. Seeb, seeb, ame(n)tike'ex uyo'och. Seeb ame(n)tike'ex uyuk'ur inhaan."
"Yes, it's true. My son-in-law is coming back. I'm very happy. Quick, quick, all of you make his food. Quick, all of you make my son-in-law his drink."

Mas eemi(h). Mas eemi(h) säk ch'iich'. Mas eemi(h). Mas eemi(h). La'eh uyirik mas xok'o(r) lati' säk ch'iich'.

He came down lower. The white falcon came down lower. He came down lower. He came down lower. The white falcon appears closer.

"Lati' inhaan!"

"It's my son-in-law!"

Rey ne tsoy uyor, "Bähe' yan u'ri(h) inhaan. Tuhahi(r). Bähe' u'ri(h) inhaan. Ne tsoy inwor."

The King is elated, "Now my son-in-law (has) returned. It's true. Now my son-in-law (has) returned. I'm very happy."

Uyeeme(r) bin. T(i) uxur uk'aax eemi(h). Eh, uch'upra(r) uti'a'ar seeb ubin upurik unook'. Seeb ubukäntik unook', seeb utaasik (uy)uuh.

He comes down. He came down near the edge of the forest. His daughter goes quickly to (change) her clothes. Quickly she gets dressed; quickly she brings her necklace.

"Eh u'rech!" uya'arik ti' uhaan Rey. "Eh wa ma' aya(n?)u'u(k?) kachik tinkin-s(ah) inti'a'ar. Ne ts'ik inpixan tuputs'ahech inti'a'ar."

"You've come back!" the King says to his son-in-law. "If you hadn't have returned I would have killed my daughter. I (was) very angry (that) my daughter let you escape."

"Ma'," tuya'arah nukuch winik. "He' inwu'(r). He' inwu'(r). Tawu'yah uya'arik ach'upra(r) ti'a'ar: he' inwu'(r)."

"No," said the ancestor. "I (would have) return(ed). I (would have) return(ed). You heard what your daughter said: I will return."

"Eh bay. Ne tsoy inwor."

"Okay. I'm very happy," (says the King).

Reciprocity is the key theme running throughout the story. For the Lacandones, reciprocity is not only desirable but also essential to their survival in that it guarantees marriageable partners and food by binding households together under the rule of mutual exchange. A son-in-law's obligation to his father-in-law is one of those rules. The chäk xok represent marriageable partners who can demonstrate that they will be good providers not only for the spouse but also for the father-in-law. In anthropological terms this is called "bride service." The merman fulfills his bride service by giving food to his father-in-law in exchange for his daughter. Reciprocity is again revealed in the scene in which the jaguar-god gives the boy his old hat in exchange for the cooked meat.

The motifs in the story are both universal and particular to Mesoamerican cultures:

Cooked versus raw meat. This reflects two opposing principles: wild versus cultured and animal versus human. That the jaguar-gods appreciated cooked meat implies their divine aspect, thus they are not "really" jaguars.

Daughter loses son-in-law. A daughter's inability to take care of her husband not only brings humiliation to the father but also robs him of bride service.

"The other side of the sea." This signifies a mythical place and the place of origin in the mythology of the Mexican and the K'iche' (Quiche') Maya. The former call it Tollan, and the latter, Tulan. Both portray it as "a paradise of abundance where power and legitimacy are bestowed" (Sachse and Christenson 2005, 9). It is also a metaphor for rebirth.

In our story, the ancestor flies far across the water to a mythical place where he encounters a mythical king, obtains a wife, and starts a new life in a land of abundance. The story is reminiscent of the journey taken by the progenitors' sons in the *Popol Vuh* who return to Tulan, on "the other side of the sea," where they receive the insignia of the mythical lord, Nacxit (Sachse and Christenson 2005, 4).

Transformation into a bird. Birds are symbols of power, freedom, and the supernatural. They are a link between the mundane and the supernatural realms. When the ancestor learns the song of the white falcon (whom the narrator of the story thought might be a god), he is freed from his mortal limitations and enters mystical space, "the other side of the sea."

Nukuch Winik yeter Uti'a'ar yeter Ahya'axche'
'The Ancestor, His Son, and the Ceiba Tree'

Bor Ma'ax

In this story, the *chemberk'uho'* teach the errant son of an ancestor a painful lesson in respect. The chemberk'uho' are little malevolent deities who live in the rocks and caverns. They can transform themselves into jaguars by reversing their tunics. In this story one chemberk'uh approaches the boy in the guise of the boy's father. Naturally the boy is insolent toward him. So the god leads the boy to a ceiba tree where the other chemberk'uho' are gathered, and they all punish him.

Bay.
Okay.

Bin intsikbartik utsikbar uchik unuki(r) winik yete(r) uti'a'a(r) nukuch winik.
I'm going to tell the story about the ancestor and his son.

Nukuch winik yan(ih) uti'a'ar, uyanchun uti'a'ar. Ma' inwohe(r) bik yani(r) creo que mänä' utuukur. Ch'ihih, ne ch'ihih ne xuurih, ne nukuch winik. Una' utet tan ut'änik uxikin, "Ma' amentik ak'eyik ana', ma' amentik ak'eyik atet."
The ancestor had a son, his first son. I don't know why, but he didn't think. He grew up. He is mature; he is a grownup. His mother and his father advise him, "Don't yell at your mother, don't yell at your father."

Lati' uti'a'ar äknukire'ex, mix tutukrah ubäh, uya'arik, "Ten chich inmuuk', chich inwor. Mix inwu'yik ut'an inna'; mix inwu'yik ut'an intet. Ten wah ink'a't inhäts'ik intet, inhäts'ik inna'."

That son of our ancestors, he never thought much about the possible risks of doing or saying something. He says, "I am strong, I am powerful. I don't listen to my mother; I don't listen to my father. I hit my father, I hit mother whenever I want."

Äknukire'ex uya'arik, "Eh ma' inwohe(r) bik yani(r) ma' uk'uchur inmuuk' ti' akti'a'ar. Ma' ut'änik, ma' utukrik ubäh. Wa ka('ah) akt'änik, up'isik ubäh. Uhäts'ik una', uhäts'ik(en), uhätsik uyits'ino'. Mix kakt'änik. Ne sa(h)aken ti'. Yah inwu'yik uha'ats'. Ne chich umuuk'."

Our ancestor (the father) says, "Oh, I don't know why I can't stand up to our son. He doesn't speak, he doesn't think. If we say (anything) he throws his weight around. He beats his mother, he beats me, he beats his little brothers and sisters. We never say (anything). I'm afraid of him. His beatings hurt me. He's very strong."

Bay.

Okay.

Äknukire'ex kut'anik, "U'y ut'an ana'. Ma' anuuk(ik) ut'an ana'."

Our ancestor would say, "Listen to your mother. You don't (ever) respond to your mother."

"Ten ma' inwu'yik ut'an inna'. Wa ink'a't inhäts'ik inna', he' inhäts'ik."

"I don't have to listen to my mother. If I want to hit my mother, I will hit her."

Una' ut'an, "U'y ut'an atet. Kuki'a'arik tech; ukansikech. Awohe(r) yan a'eere(r). Yan k'ak'i(r) ka('ah) häts'ik atet, ma' (a)bin (a)hook'or. Yan k'ak' uto(o)kech Kisin."

His mother says, "Listen to your father. He says good things to you; he teaches you (things). You know you will have to burn. There is fire (for) hitting your father, (and) you're not going to leave. There is fire Kisin burns you with."[1]

"Ten ma' intukrik. Yan ma' inweereh k'ak'. Mix inweere(r) k'ak'. Yu'sik ti'. *Tsk*. Tus ukah."

"I don't believe it. I'm not going to burn in the fire. I'm never going to burn in the fire. He can bring it on! *Tsk*. They're lying."

"Bay," una' uya'arik. "Ma' tawu'yeh int'an. 'Otsirech. Inti'a'arech, k'äs awu'yik (in)t'an. Ma' (a)me(n)tik be'ik: ma' anuk ut'an atet; ma' anuk ut'an ana'. Wa ma [ak]t'änikech, u'y ut'an, ch'a'(eh?) [ak]t'an."

"Okay," says his mother. "You won't listen to me. Poor you. You are my son, please listen to me. Don't behave like this: you don't answer your father; you don't answer your mother. When we speak to you, you listen, take in our words."

"Ten mäna'. Ba'wih?[2] Tus ukah a' la'eh. Kuya'arik woror tus."

"No, I won't. What for? They're lying. They're telling lies."

Bay.

Okay.

Äknukire'ex utet, woro(r) (tu)bäräxhäts'tah. Wa kut'änik uti'a'ar, uyan uchuru(r) uhäts'ik utet. Wa kuya'arik ba'a(r) ti', "Xen taasik che'; xen taasik när ich kor; xen t(i') ameyah ich koor," uya'arik uti'a'ar, "Ten mäna'. Ma'. Mak'ooren. Ma' (a)tuchi'tiken—yan inchuru(r)—inhäts'ikech."

He hit his father all the time. If he talks to his son, he has a bow he beats his father with. If he says something like, "Go fetch firewood—go get the maize in the cornfield—go to work in the cornfield," the son says, "Not me. No. I don't feel like it. Don't send me—I have my bow—I'll hit you."

Kuhäts'(ik) utet. Eh ma' (u)p'is(i)k ubäh. Mix utet, kura'an mix up'isik ubäh. Yah yu'yik uha'ats'.

He hits his father. He can't fight back, his father can't do anything. He sits there, helpless. The beating is painful.

Wa una' uya'arik, "Bik yanir ahiixtik atet?" uya'arik uti'a'ar, "Xureh at'an na'! Ten, yan inchuru(r). He inhiixtikech; inhäts'ikech yet(er) inchuru(r)."

Or, if his mother says, "Why are you beating your father?" the son says, "Shut up, mother. I have my bow. I will thrash you; I will beat you with my bow."

Mix mak (k)ut'änik, mix una' mix utet. Ma' uk'uchur umuuk'. Ne chich uyor uxira(r) uti'a'ar nukuch winik.

No one says anything, neither his mother nor his father. They don't have the strength. Their son is very headstrong.

Bay.

Okay.

K'uchih tuk'in lahih uk'ini(r) yan kuxur näri(r), kuxur när. Tuya'arah ti' (ah)tet, "Xen awireh uku(')uki(r)tar när."

The time came when the corn was ripe and sweet. His father said to him, "Go and see if it is being ravaged by squirrels."

Bay.

Okay.

Lik'ih ahnukuch winik uti'a'ar, binih ich kor. Tuch'a'ah uharar, bineh yete(r). Binih t(i') ukäxtik ahku(')u)k t(i') uxuur koor, ti' kumaan ukäxtik ahku(')u)k. Yan uhana(n).

The ancestor's son got up. He took his bow and arrows and went. He went to look for squirrels around the border of the cornfield. He walks around looking for squirrels. Their food is there.

Bay.

Okay.

Ti' kuxmaan uti'a'ar ahnukuch winik, tan ukäxtik ahku(')uk. La' ka'ah tuyirah tan (u)na'akar ahku(')uk, *t-e-r-r-r*, na(k)che' na'akih, tuhi(r)t(ah) uhärär ti' uhurik. Y uhi(r)tik uhurik, TWANG. Umaan, *k'orrrech*. Ma' ts'a'apah³ uhurik. Uka'k'äpik uher uhärär. Uka'hurik. Bexir. Ka'ah maanih, *kä-r-r-r-on*, sut uman uhärär. Mix lati' uhurik.

The ancestor's son continues to look for squirrels. Then, when he saw a squirrel scurrying, *t-e-r-r-r*, up a tree, he pulled out his arrow to shoot it. And he pulls it out and he shoots. TWANG. It goes through (the air), *k'orrrech*.⁴ He shoots but (the arrow) doesn't penetrate it. He inserts another arrow (into his bowstring). He shoots again. The same thing (happens). When it passes, *kä-r-r-r-on*, the arrow veers off. It never hits (the squirrel).

(Ah)k'uh tari(h). Tumentah ubäh p'iis uwichi(r) (u)tet. P'isir unook', ubäk'er utet.

A god arrived. He made his face look like (the ancestor's) father. His clothes are the same, his body is his father's.

"Hah tawirah (ah)ku'uk, Chan K'in?"

"Well, did you see (the) squirrel, Chan K'in?"

"Mäna' tet!"

"No, father!"

"Bik? Tinwirah (a)hurik."

"What? I saw you shoot it."

"Mäna', ma' tinhurah."
"No, I didn't shoot anything."

"Maaa, ma' tus. Tinwirah ahurik."
"Nooo, it's no lie. I saw you shoot it."

"Mäna', mäna' ten. Ma' tawirah. Tus akah. Ap'a(k)tiken. Ma' tinhurah."
"No, not me. You didn't see (anything). You're lying. You're making me angry. I didn't shoot it."

"Mäna', ma' intus. Tinwirah, tinwirah ahurik. Ma' tuch'ukah (a)hurik."
"No, I'm not lying. I saw it, I saw you shoot it. Your arrow didn't come loose."[5]

"Mäna'."
"No."

Tan ute(k)ko'oxtik uchuru(r) ti' uhäts'ik utet, k'uh tumentah ubäh p'is utet. Kutar a' churu(r), ti' uhäts'ik utet, kutekchuktik a' churu(r) uti'a'ar nukuch winik. Seeb lub umuk'. Mäna' muk' uk'äb.

He is curling up his bow to beat his father, the god who made himself like his father. When the bow comes to his father, he grabs the ancestor's son's bow. His strength drops instantly. His arms don't have any strength.

"Ehhh," kutubur ut'an ahk'uh. "Len t'ärä'än, bäkan tech, paareh," kih. "Ne t'ärä'än tech, bäkan, ahäts'ik atet. Len t'ärä'än tech ahäts'ik ana'. Kut'änikech, ma' awu'yik (u)t'an. Bähe' ten h(e') awu'yik int'an. H(e') awu'yik bik inwe'esik tech, bik int'änikech."

"Ehhh," the god exclaims. "So, you're accustomed to (doing this), son," he says. "So, you're accustomed to hitting your father. You're accustomed to hitting your mother. They talk to you, but you don't answer them. Now I am the one who you will listen to. You will pay attention to what I show you (and) what I say to you."

"Mäna'!" tan uche('e)ht'an äknukire'ex uti'a'ar nukuch winik. "Mäna' ten! Yo (in)bin inhäts'ikech."

"No!" our ancestor's son snaps back. "Not me! I'm going to hit you."

Mäna'. Poch uhaats', mäna' umuuk'. Poch uhaats'. Mix. Lahlub(ih) umuuk'. T'ayal.[6] Mäna'.

(But) he can't. He wants to strike (but) he doesn't have any strength. He wants to strike. He can't. All his strength (has) vanished. (His arms) are limp. They don't have any (strength).

"Ele bähe', ne t'ärä'än bäkän ahäts'ik ana', ahäts'ik atet, kahäts'ik awits'ino'. Ten bähe' kinbin int'anikech ti' akänik usa'ah ti': Ma' (a)bin ahäts'ik ana'. Ma' (a)bin ahäts'ik atet. Ma' (a)bin ahäts'ik awits'ino'e'ex—mix mak. Ten he' int'anik axikin. Awu'yik bik int'anikech."

"So now, you're accustomed to hitting your mother and hitting your father, you hit your little brothers and sisters. Now I am the one who is going to tell you, so you learn to be afraid: Don't go hitting your mother. Don't go hitting your father. Don't go hitting your little brothers and sisters—not anyone. I am the one who will warn you. You listen to what I tell you."

Toh ahya'axche' ti' kura'an le hach ch'ik yum. Ya'axche'. Ne nuk. Yan uk'ak'a'su' uk'äb. Yan way uk'ak'a'su' uk'äb uyanchunir. Yanta(r) uhump'er uk'ak'a'su' uk'äb. Yanta(r) hu(n)p'er uk'ak'a'su' uk'äb. 'Oxk'aas uk'ak'a'su' uk'äb ahya'axche'.

A great big ceiba tree is standing there. A ceiba tree. It is very big. It has dense, closely spaced branches. There are dense stories of branches at the bottom. There is another story of dense branches. There is (still) another story of dense branches (above). There are three stories of branches.

Ba'aleh, ahk'uho', chem(b)e(r)k'u(h)o', tuworo(r) chem(b)e(r)k'u(h)o' ti' nika'an ucha'anteh. Ti' ucha'antik bik uyäräktar aknukire'ex ti' uch'iini(n) yok'o(r) (u)k'äb ahya'axche'.

So now, the little gods, the little gods that walk around, all the walking gods are sitting there to watch.⁷ They see our ancestor like a play thing: for throwing up the branches of the ceiba.

Ne pim k'uh. Chem(b)e(r)k'u(h)o' tuworo(r) ximbar k'u(h)o' tuworo(r), tu-woro(r) ahk'u(h)o' ti' yan (u)cha'anteh bik uyäräkta(r) nukuch winik.

There are a lot of gods. The little gods, all the walking gods, all of them, all the gods are there to watch how the ancestor (has) become a plaything.

Bay.

Okay.

K'uh tutohtukrah tema' cha'ah ulubu(r) way yok'o(r) lu'um, ch'ika'an way k'uh. Y ti' uk'äb yok'o(r) ya'axche' huntuu(r) ti' ch'ika'an. Huntuu(r) k'uh t(i') uher uk'ä' ya'axche' yanta(r) huntuu(r), y t(i') uyoori(r) ti' uk'äb ch'ika'an huntuu(r).

The gods (had) already decided not to let him fall to the ground. So a god is standing there (at the bottom), and on the branches in the ceiba another god is standing. On another branch of the ceiba there is another god, and on the branches at the top of the tree there stands another.

Bay.

Okay.

Nukuch winik tuyu'yah läh lub(ur) umuk'. Mäna' muuk' ubaake(r), t(i') uk'ä', tuworo(r) mix mäna' muk'. Tuyu'yah uyäräk'ta(r). Uch'iini(n). Yah-puurih, ch'iini(h), ʜᴜᴍᴍᴍ, uyahchun uk'äb. Kutar kuchukah, läp'. Pach(ir) uch'iini(n) mas ka'ana(n), HUMMM, Kutar kuchukah, läp'. Kuka'masch'iini(n) mas ka'ana(n), HUMMM, tuyoori(r).

The ancestor felt all his strength drain away. He didn't have any strength in his body, in his arms, he didn't have any strength anywhere. He felt like he had become a toy. He is hurled, he is tossed, HUMMM, (to) the first branches. When he comes, he is caught. Then he is thrown higher, HUMMM. When he gets there, he is caught. Then he is thrown still higher, HUMMM, to the top.

Ele, kuchukah tuka'ten.
And then he is caught again.

Ele, kuka'ch'iini(n) t(i') ukabar.
And then he is thrown to the bottom again.

WHOOOSH — kuka'bin.
WHOOOSH — he goes again.

Kuka'chukik.
They catch him again.

Kuka'chukah tuka'ten, kuka'ch'iini(n) mas kabar. Ele, kuka'chukah.
He is caught again, (and) again he is thrown lower still. Then, he is caught again.

(Ku)ka'ch'iini(n).
His is thrown again.

Kuka'purur mas kabar. Ma' ulubu(r) yok'o(r) lu'um. Ma' ulubur.
He is sent further down again. He doesn't fall on the ground. He doesn't fall.

Oxwäts' uch'iini(n).

Three times he is thrown.

Tuyu'yah uts'aap ubäk'er yok'or k'äb ya'axche', *puuuxxxwww, puuuxxxwww,* yok'o(r) (u)k'äb ya'axche'. Poch ut'an. Poch uyawat. Utuyu'yik ubah, *"Ma' het la'eh. Ne'aar inchi'; ma' het int'an, mäna'. Poch inwawat, pero mäna'."*

He felt his body hit the tiers of branches of the ceiba, *puuuxxxwww, puuuxxxwww,* on the branches of the ceiba. He wants to speak. He wants to yell. He feels, *"It's impossible. My mouth is heavy; I can't talk. I want to shout, but I can't."*

Ne tsoy uyirik k'uh. Uyäräk'ta(r) unukuch winik. Neee tsoy uyirik k'uh. Tan uyäräk'ta(r), p'is k'ik' uyäräk'ta(r) yok'o(r) (u)k'äb ya'axche'.

The gods really enjoy (this). The ancestor becomes their toy. The gods reeeally enjoy it. He (has) become a toy, like a rubber ball, a toy in the branches of the ceiba.

'Oxwäts' uyäräk'ta(r) unukuch winik. Tuyu'yah, *chichiiin.* Tan usaata(r) uyor. Ne mäna'. *Ch'ich'iin* ... Tan uyu'yik uyäräk'ta(r). Poch uyawat. Poch ut'an. Mäna'.

Three times the ancestor becomes a toy. He feels (himself being thrown), *chichiiin.* He is feeling dizzy. There is nothing (he can do). *Chichiiin* ... He feels he has become like a toy. He wants to yell. He wants to speak. But he can't.

A' la' uyoxwäts' kuch'iini(n). Kuxna'a(k)sa(r). Kuxch'iini(n). Kuxna'a(k)sa(r). Kuxpuru(r) kaba(r). Kuch'iini(n). Kuka'na'a(k)sa(r). Kuyeensa(h).

Three times he is thrown. He is picked up. He is thrown. He is picked up. He is flung down. He is thrown. He is picked up again. He is brought down.

Ts'o'ok.

It's over.

Wene(n) tuyu'yah.

He felt tired.

Bay.

Okay.

Uteto' ahnukuch winik t(an) utukrik, "*Tu' binih inti'a'ar? Bik yanir ma' u'rih? Ne hats'ka' binih. Bähe' mäna' k'in.*"

[Meanwhile] the ancestor's father is thinking, "*Where did my son go? Why (hasn't) he returned? He left early in the morning. Now the sun (has gone down).*"

Eh, una' nukuch winik, tan uya'arik, "Ba'i(nkin) tume(n)tah akti'a'ar? Tint'an yan ba'inki(n) tume(n)tah, bik yani(r) ma' u'rih?"

The ancestor's mother is saying, "What did our son do? I think he must have done something or why wouldn't he have returned?"

Una' äknukire'ex tuya'arah, "Bik yani(r) ma' abin awireh ati'a'ar ich koor ireh yan ba'inki(n) tumentah, wa lubih tuwa(tah) (u)yok o yan ba'i(inkin) chi'bi(r) ten kan. Tint'an xen akäxtik."

Our ancestor's mother said, "Why don't you go see your son in the cornfield to see if there is something he did, whether he fell and broke his leg or (has been) bitten by a snake. I think you should go look for him."

Uteto' ahnukuch winik, lik'ih binih ich ukor uyir(eh) uti'a'ar. Man uyirik xur koor. Eh kuyirik ne yaab uya'axkech. Ki'p'oomih(?) ya'axkech t(i') uk'ä' che'. Woror uya'axkech.

The ancestor's father got up and went to the cornfield to (look for) his son. He walked around (searching) the edge of the cornfield. And then he sees a lot of flies. The flies swarmed the branches. Flies are all around.

"Ehhh, bik yani(r) yan ne pim? Ne yan ya'axkech," utet utukrik ubäh. *"Eh, 'utsereh. Ba'i(inkin) tume(n)tah inta'a'ar?"* Umasxim(b)a(r), umasxim(b)a(r) he' uyirik naak'a'an uti'a'ar, naak'a'an. *"Ehhh mäna', inti'a'ar,"* tutukrah nukuch winik. *"Eh mäna, inti'a'al. Ma' inw(oh)e(l) ba'(inkin) tume(n)tah."*

"Ehhh, why are there so many flies?" thinks the ancestor's father. "There are so many flies. Uh-oh. What did my son do?" He walks on, he walks on and here he sees his son lying to one side. "Oooh no, my son," the ancestor thought. "Oh no my son. I don't know what he did."

Nukuch winik hook' ukuchik uti'a'ar. Tukuchah tubisah (ti') (u)ya(to)ch k'uh. (T)uk'usah (ti') uya(to)ch k'uh, seeb seeb upokik ti' k'uh.

The ancestor went (over) to carry his son. He hoisted him onto his shoulders and took him to the god house. He brought him to the god house and hastily burns offerings to the gods.

"Ba'i(nkin) tume(n)tah inti'a'ar?" ut'an uk'uh. *"Ba'(inkin) tume(n)tah inti'a'ar, yumeh? Ba'(inkin) tume(n)tah? Ch'a'eh!* 'Otsir inti'a'ar, ma' inw(oh) e(r) ba'(inkin) tume(n)tah. 'Aanten t(i') ulik'i(r), ti' uchichta(r) muuk', ti' ulik'i(r) ku(r)ta(r), ti' uxim(b)a(r)."

"What did my son do?" he prays. "What did my son do, Lord? What did he do? Take (my offering)! My poor son, I don't know what he did. Help him to get up, to become strong, to sit up, to walk."

Ne yan uk'uh ne chich umuuk'. T(an) upokik, t(an) upokik, t(an) upokik.

There are many gods with great power. He is praying and praying and praying.

(U)ch'a'ik uyiik' nukuch winik. Tan uch'a'ik uyiik'.

The ancestor (boy) takes a breath. He is breathing.

"Ehhh," nukuch winik. 'As tsoy uyor. *"Tint'an tan uyaanten k'uh. Bähe' uyaan-ten. Poch inwu'yik ba'(inkin) tumentah inti'a'ar. Ba'(inkin) usi'ipi(r)?"*

"Ehhh," (says) the ancestor. He is relieved, *"I think the gods are helping me. Now they are helping me. I want to hear what my son did. What was his crime?"* (he says to himself).

Tanux pokik. T(an) ukäxtik k'inyah ba'(inkin) usi'ipir uti'a'ar ka' cheeri(h) ich koor. Nukuch winik, seeb ukäxtik mak ukäxtik uk'inyah, t(i') uyoh(er) tik ba'(inkin) usi'ipi(r).

He is praying and praying. He is trying to determine what his son's crime was that he fell in the cornfield. The ancestor hurriedly divines which god to petition to know what the crime was.

Ts'o'ok uk'intik (ah)nukuch winik, tuya'arah ti' utet, "Ti' k'ik' ati'a'ar. Inch'eenkintah. Intsikbartik tech ink'inyah."(?)[8]

(When) the ancestor finished divining, (a god) said to the father, "It will be rubber for your son. I (will) cure your son (for offerings of rubber). I (will) tell you about it through (your?) divination."

"He' awa'arik ten ba'inki(n) usi'ipi(r) inti'a'ar?"

"Will you tell me what my son's crime was?"

"'A'arah lati' usi'ipi(r) ati'a'ar hiixpah(ih?) ati'a'ar ten k'uh. Awi(r)ik, tech tat'änah, una', tut'anah ma' k'uch umuk'. Ne seeb up'is(i)k ubah. Ne chich uyor. Up'is(i)k ubah. Lahih usi'ipi(r) ati'a'ar. Bähe', t(an) ukän(i)k usaah-ki(r) ati'a'ar."

"They[9] say that (for) your son's crime he was thrashed by the gods. You see, you told him, his mother told him (that his father) wasn't strong. (Your son) is quick to push his weight around. He is brash; he pushes his weight around. This is your son's crime. Now, your son is learning (to) fear."

Ele, ulik'i(r). Tanux pokik. Uya'arik ti' uk'uh. "Lik'ik inti'a'ar. Chich(chah)ak umuuk', ka' k'uchu(k) t(i') up'iis ubaake(r), ka' k'uchuk chich(chah)ak uximbar. Ma' inw(oh)e(r) ba'inki(n) usi'ipi(r). Wa lahih usi'ipi(r) ti' tuhiixtah utet tuhiixtah una'. He' ubo'otik tech. He' uts'ahik hu'un. He' uts'ahik chäk hu'un, k'ik', k'uxu'. He' (u)ts'ahik tech tuworo(r)—ma'ats', ba(')che'—tuworo(r). He' ubo'otik tech, ka'ah (u)lik'(ir) inti'a'ar."

And so, (the father) gets up. He keeps burning offerings. He says to the god, "May my son get up. May he become strong, may his bones regain strength, may he walk strong. I don't know what his crime was. Perhaps this crime was because he beat his father, beat his mother. He will pay you. He will give bark cloth. He will give red bark cloth, rubber, annatto—posol, balche'—everything. My son will pay you, when he gets up."

Tupokah ne yaab, ne yaab.

He prayed and he prayed.

K'uchih 'oxp'e(r) k'in tan uhook'or ut'an uti'a'ar, "Bähe' tet, he' inwuk'u(r). Ha'ri' muuk' t(i') inximba(r), mäna'. Bähe' ma' su'en ten. Sa'aseh ten. Lahih insi'ipi(r).

Three days later his son speaks, "Today, father, I will drink. Only, I don't have any strength to walk. Now I am sorry. Forgive me. This is my crime.

Bähe', insutik int'an tech, tet. Ma' su'en ti' (kin)hiixt(ik)ech. Tinhiixt(ah) inna'. Tinhiixt(ah) inbäho', inwits'(i)no'. Ma' su'en tet. Sa'aseh ten.

Now, I take back my words to you, father. I won't beat you anymore. I beat my mother. I beat my companions and my little brothers and sisters. I am sorry, father. Forgive me.

Bähe', tapokahen. Tawaantahen. Bähe', inbin inwoko(r) (in)ch'eene'et(ik); inbin intsikbartik t(i') inbäho'."

Today, you burned offerings on my behalf. You helped me (recover). Now, I'm going to go visit them; I'm going to talk to my companions."

"Eh bay," tuya'arah utet. "Ne tsoy. Ne tsoy abin atsikbartik."

"All right," said his father. "Very good. It's very good that you go talk to them."

Bay. T(an) upokik, t(an) upokik. Uti'a'ar nukuch winik bin upokik ubäh ti' k'uh. Tume(n)tah ba(')che', tulahme(n)tah tuworo(r)—hu'un, k'ik', tuworo(r)—ma'ats'. Tulahts'aah ti' kyum.

Okay. He is praying and praying. The ancestor's son went to burn offerings to the gods. He made balche', he made everything—bark cloth, rubber, everything—posol. He gave it all to the gods.

Ele, ne tsoy uxim(b)a(r). Ya, k'uch(ih) t(i') up'iis tsoy uximba(r), tsoy upeek tuworo(r), uximba(r) ubin utsikba(r) tuworo(r) winik tu' kahenkah t(an) usiih ut'an.

So then, in time he could walk well. He moves well as before. And he goes around talking to all the people living here and spreads the word.

Le' lahih ti' up'ätik utsikbar aknukire'ex, ti' (a)kbäho'.

He does this to leave the story with our ancestors, with our companions.

Tuya'arah, "Bähe', ma' (a)bin akäräxme(n)tik ana', atet, y ma' (a)bin anuukik ut'an. Yan k'uh; kut'än(a)ho'on he' kwu'yik t'an. Bähe', yan ti' ktukrik ut'an aktet, akna'. Yan ti' kch'a'ik, yan ti' kkänik kuts'ahik to('o)n. Bähe', kän(eh) usaahki(r). Ma' (a)me(n)tik ten: Ma' tinwu'yah ut'an inna'. Ma' tinwu'yah ut'an intet. Tinnukah ut'an intet. Tinhäts'(ah) intet. Teche'ex ma' (a)me(n) tike'ex. Käne'ex usaahki(r)."

He said, "Now don't go abusing your mother or your father, and don't talk back. There are gods; when they speak to us we will listen. Now, (we) must heed the words of our father (and) our mother. (We) must follow them, must learn (what) they give us. Now, you (must) learn to fear them. Don't do (as) I (did): I didn't listen to my mother. I didn't listen to my father. I didn't answer my father; I hit my father. You are not to do this. You learn to fear."

Haayok'

Bor Ma'ax

The *haayok'* are mythical birds, like ravens, that lure hungry travelers on the road with plates of steaming food. After eating the food, the travelers become drowsy. When they fall asleep, the haayok' swoop down and pluck out their eyes.

Lati' utsikbar nukuch winik yet(er) haayok' uhantik o'ochi(r).
This is a story about the ancestor who ate the food of the haayok'.

Bay.
Okay.

Uchik, nukuch winik uxim(b)a(r) ich (k'aax) (ti') ubähik pom. Ubin ubähik pom yet(er) ubäho'. Bini(h) ka't(uur)o'.
Long ago, an ancestor is walking in (the forest) (to) tap copal resin. He is going to tap copal with his brother. The two of them went.

Tup'ih ti' . . . ma' tukuchah (u)yo'och; ma' hanih ich uyatoch. Bin(ih) ich utähte', ne hats'ka'.
They forgot . . . to carry food; they didn't eat in their house. They went into the pine (forest) at dawn.

Eh, usut. Uk'uchur bix k'ak' chun k'in—ne naach ubähik upom, ne naach.
Then, they return (home). They arrive around midday—it's very far (where) they tap copal, very far.

Eh, tan usut yet(er) ubäho' wa('a)n be(r).

So, he is coming back with his brother on the road.

Eh utukrik, "Ehhh ne wi(')ihen. Ne poch inhantik o'ochir."

And he says, "Ehhh, I'm very hungry. I really want to eat some food."

Eh unuukik huntuur äknukire'ex, "P'isi(r) ten. Ne wi'ihen."

And the other ancestor replies, "Me too. I'm really hungry."

"Ehhh hah? Bik yani(r) tat'aan mix ten? Ne wi'ihen."

"Really? Why didn't you tell me? I'm so hungry."

Maa, ma' ne naachtar uximba(r) kupurik uwich äka('a)n nahwah. Äka('a)n ma'ats'. Ne chäkar. Ne k'iina(r). Nahwah, ne k'iina(r), ne chäkar, ne ts'um.

W-e-ll, they don't walk much farther when they notice tamales laid out. Posol is laid out. It's very hot. It's very warm. The tamales are very warm, piping hot (and) very soft.

"O-o-o-H. He' o-o-o'ochi(r)! Kahan(i)ko'on," kuya'arik ti' ubäho'.

"O-o-o-H. Here is f-o-o-o-d! Let's go eat it," he says to his brother.

A' huntuur yan utuku(r). "M-a-a-a'. Ma' ahantik. Ma' wa tawu'yah (u)tsik-bar yan ahhaayok'?"

The other one is worried. "N-o-o-o. You'd better not eat it. Didn't you hear the story about the haayok'?"

"Mäna'. Ma' tinwu'yah. Ele, tuus ukah. Mäna', mäna' haayok'. Haayok'? Tsk! Mäna' haayok'."

"No. I didn't hear anything. Anyway, they're lying. There aren't any, there aren't any haayok'. Haayok'? Tsk! There aren't any haayok'."

Uhuntuur uya'arik bäho', "Ma' ahant-i-i-i-k. He' uk'oyik awich. Tawu'yah yan haayok' wa'an be(r). Ma' ahantik."

The other brother says, "Don't e-e-eat it. They scoop out your eyes. You heard that there is haayok' on the road. Don't eat it."

A' huntuur nukuch winik ma' yu'yah ut'an. "Tsk! Ten ne wi'ihen. Ne p'enk'äch wi'ihen. Bin inkah hanan."

The other ancestor didn't listen. "Tsk! I'm very hungry. I am sooo hungry. I'm going to eat."

Kuk'at(ik) ubäh, purk'ä't(ik) nahwah, "xaap, xaap." Tuhantah. Tekch'a't(ik) ma'ats', "haap." Kuyuk'ik.

He turns around, reaches for the tamales, "slurp, slurp." He ate them. He snatches up the posol, "gulp." He drinks it.

"Ehhh," uhook'or ut'an. "Ele ne tak inwenen. Ne tak inwenen."

"Ehhh," he says. "Now I'm very sleepy. I'm very sleepy."

A' huntuur unukuch winik bäho', "Tintoh'a'arah tech ma' (a)hantik. Yan haayok'. Uk'oyik awich."

The other ancestor, his brother, (says), "I just told you not to eat it. There are the haayok'. They scoop out your eyes."

"Eh hah," unuukik ubäho'. "Eh hah, tuha(h)i(r), tawa'arah. Eh ten ne wi'ihen. Tinhantah. Ele, tak inwene(n)."

"Yes," his brother replies. "Yes, that's true, you said that. But I was very hungry. I ate it. And now, I'm sleepy."

Tuch'ek'ätah ubäh bin. Ma' hach tuch'ek'ätah ubah—p'än!

He laid down. It wasn't long after he laid down and—boom! (he fell asleep).

"ᴀʜ-h-o-o-o-o-o," kih, cha(a)k' uni'.
"ᴀʜ-h-o-o-o-o-o," his nose deflates [he's snoring].

A' s-a-a-sa(n) bin kutichir ahhaayok'.
A l-i-t-t-l-e later the haayok' approach.

ᴀᴘᴏᴘғғ, ᴋᴜʀʀʀᴜᴍᴘ!
ᴀᴘᴏᴘғғ, ᴋᴜʀʀʀᴜᴍᴘ! (they land).

Aaah, toh ka't(uu)ro' k'uch(ih) bin. Kuki'päktik bin tu' kura'an tu' chara'(a)n nukuch winik.
Two of them instantly arrive. They peer at the ancestor lying there.

Eh, "ʜᴀᴀʏᴏᴏ! ʜᴀᴀʏᴏᴏ! ʜᴀᴀʏᴏᴏ! ʜᴀᴀʏᴏᴏ! ʜᴀᴀʏᴏᴏ!"
"ʜᴀᴀʏᴏᴏ! ʜᴀᴀʏᴏᴏ! ʜᴀᴀʏᴏᴏ! ʜᴀᴀʏᴏᴏ! ʜᴀᴀʏᴏᴏ!"

ᴘᴜᴘғғ—bi(n).
ᴘᴜᴘғғ—(Then) they left.

Hach ma' san ubin a' la'eh ahhaayok' bin, sansa(n)[1] ulik'(ir) uku(r)t(ar) ubäh nukuch winik.
Soon after the haayok' leave the ancestor sits up.

"Oooy," kih. "Mäna' inwich," kih. "Mäna' inwich. Mäna' inwich. 'Utse(re)h. Mäna' inwich. Ma' het la'eh ma' chäk incha'(a)n!"
"Oooy," he says. "I don't have any eyes," he says. "I don't have any eyes. I don't have any eyes. Oh no! I don't have any eyes. I can't see!"

Lik'i(h) ahnukuch winik. Mana' uwich. La(h)haar uwich. Lahhiita'.

The ancestor got up. He doesn't have any eyes. His eyes had been completely scooped out. They were pulled out completely.

Ba'ale'² a' la'eh haayok' bini(h).

By now the haayok' had long gone.

"Eh 'u-u-u-utse(re)h," nukuch winik a' huntu(u)r p'aatih, a' ma' tuhantah nahwah.

"Oh m-y-y-y," (says) the other ancestor that remained, the one who didn't eat the tamales.

"'U-u-u-utsereh," kih. "Bik inbin inme(n)tik? Inbähobi(r) ma' het la'eh."

"Oh-oh," (the other one) says. "What am I going to do? My brother can't (see)."

Eh, kuyu'yik utar hum uyaakan ubarum. Uyu'yik naach utar. "I-i-i-nh, I-i-i-nh,"³ kutar ubarum.

Then he hears a jaguar's grunts coming. He hears him coming in the distance. "I-i-i-nh, I-i-i-nh," comes the jaguar.⁴

Bay.

Okay.

Äknukire'ex bin, "Mäna'. 'Utse(re)h, kubin uchi'en ahbarum. Ma' chäk inbin. Mäna' inwich. Ma' het la'eh."

The ancestor says, "(I can't see) anything. Dear me, the jaguar is going to eat me. I can't see where I'm going. I don't have any eyes. I can't (see to get away)."

A' huntu(u)r bäho' tuya'arah, "Tintoha'arah tech ma' (a)hantik kachik. Toh 'a'arah ma' (a)hantik la'eh haayok', uyo'och haayok', ti' uhaarik awich."

The other brother said, "I told you before not to eat it. I already told you not to eat it because that is the food of the haayok', (which they put there so) they (can) scoop out your eyes."

"Hah," kih. "Toh hahi(r), tanet'an(a)hen. Tanet'an(a)hen, ehhh ma'. Bähe' 'utse(re)h. Paa(y)t(eh) ink'äb. Paa(y)t(eh) ink'äb."

"Yes," he says. "It's true, you really told me. You told me and told me, but (I didn't listen). Now (I'm paying for it). Pull my hand. Pull my hand."

Tuche'paayt(ah) uk'äb ubäho' nukuch winik. Pero tuyu'yah ne xok'or utar ahbarum t(i') upach; t(i') upach tan utar uyaakan. Ele, sipitk'ä'tik t(i') ubäho'. Ele tusip(i)t(ah) ubäho' nukuch winik.

He quickly pulled his brother's hand. But he heard the jaguar com(ing) very close behind (them); behind (them) his grunting is coming. So, he drops his brother's hand. He let go of his brother.

Bay. Uxur ubin boon unaachir ubin. Eh, kuyu'yik uyawat ti' ubäho', "o-a-a-a-AGH!"

Okay. He goes as far as (he can). Then, hears his brother's screams, "o-a-a-a-AGH!"

Ya chi'b ten barum. Le 'mäna'. Chi'b.

He's just been eaten by the jaguar. He's done for. He's been eaten.

Bay.

Okay.

Nukuch winik tan utukrik ubäh. Tan uyak'tik ubäh, ka'(a)h u'ri(h) ti' uya-toch, "Bähe' mäna'. Hunt(uuri') inbäh(o') chi'b, chi'b te(n) barum. Tuhan-tah (u)yo'och haayok'."

The ancestor is brooding. He is sobbing, when he returned to his house, "Now he is no more. One of my brothers (has been) eaten, eaten by the jaguar. He ate the food of the haayok'."

Ele, nukuch winik bin utsikbarteh ti' ubäho' a' la'eh, "Bähe' wa tawirah 'äk-rik o'ochir wa'an be(r)wa tayu'yah mäna' atukur ne wi'ihech tawirah 'äkrik nahwah wa k'oor wa ba' tawirah 'äkrik, ma'ats', ma' awuk'ik. Hach tuha-hi(r). Ma' tus: hach uk'oyik awich haayok'."

And so, the ancestor goes to tell his friends, "Now, if you see plates of food laid out on the road, if you feel hungry, (and) you see tamales or stew laid out, or whatever (else) you see laid out, like posol, don't drink it. It's true. It's no lie: the haayok' really do scoop out your eyes."

"Bay," kih a' huntuur nukuch winik. Ma' tutukr(ah) ubäh wa hach tuhahi(r) (u?)tsikbar. "Ma' utus?"

"Okay," say the other ancestors. They didn't think it was a true story. "It's not a lie?" (they ask).

Bini(h) ich k'aax. Bin(ih) ubähik tähte'. Eh umaan utukur. Uya'arik, "'Uts-e(re)h, ne wi'ihen," kih. "Ne wi'ihen."

They went in the forest. They went to tap resin. And the thought crosses (one boy's) mind. He says, "Oh am I ever hungry," he says. "I'm very hungry."[5]

"Hach tuha(h)i(r)?" kih. "P'isi(r) ten. Ne wi'ihen."

"Really?" says the other one. "Me too. I'm really hungry."

Tan uxim(b)a(r) tan uxim(b)a(r). Eh kupäktik 'äka'an k'oor. K'oor 'äka'an, uk'oori(r) k'ambur. 'Äka'an wah ne chäkä(r)ta(r). 'Äka'an uma'ats'ir.

They are walking and walking. And then they spot stew laid out. Stew is laid out, stew with pheasant meat.[6] The tortillas that are laid out are still piping hot. The posol is laid out.

"Tsk! E-h-h-h h-a-h, bäkan," uya'arik ahnukuch winik ti ubäho'. "Hah bäkan tutsikbartah takuyah. Hach tuha(h)i(r). Ma' utus.

"Tsk! S-o-o-o, it's true," says the ancestor to his brother. "What he said, what we heard (him say) is true after all. It's the truth. It's no lie.

Ch'eene'eteh awireh—'äka'an k'oor, wah, ma'ats'. Lahi(h) uyo'och haayok'.'"

Look and see the the stew, laid out, and the tortillas and posol. This is the food of the haayok'.'"

Nukuch winik ne yan utukur. Tuch'a'ah la' k'oor. Tulahch'a'ah la' wah, ma'ats'. Tumeek'ah. Ma' tuhantah, tumeek'ah.

The ancestors have an idea. They took the stew. They took everything, the tortillas and posol, they held it in their arms. They didn't eat it, they held it in their arms.

U'ri(h). Tah bini(h)(h) ti' uyatoch k'uh to('a)n a' k'ur. K'uchi(r) to'an k'uh. Tuch'a'ah la' k'oor (tu)lahts'aah ti' uk'uh.

They returned (home). They went straight to the god house, where the gods are.[7] They arrived where the gods were. They took the stew (and) offered it to the gods.

"He'ra', yumeh," kih.

"Here it is, Lord," they say.

"Tsoy inhantik uyo'och haayok'.

"It would be good if I could eat the food of the haayok'.

Ma' bik uhaarik inwich.

Don't let them scoop out my eyes.

Ma' inyanhantik.
I don't eat it first.

Tech kinyants'ahik uho'(or), yumeh."
I offer it to you first, oh Lord."

Ubin ulahts'ahik t(i') uk'uh tuworor. Ulahxe'epik uwah, ma'ats'. Tuworor ahk'uh tulahts'ah ti' ahk'uh päytan.
They go and offer it to all the gods. They pinch off pieces from the tortillas, (and give some) posol. They offer all of it to all the gods first.

Ele, tutoha'arah ti' ahk'ur.
And then they addressed the gods.

"He' uyo'och haayok', yumeh.
"Here is the food of the haayok', oh Lord.

Tarak inhantik, ma' bik uhaarik inwich haayok'.
Although I eat it, don't let the haayok' scoop out my eyes.

Tu hahi(r), tinwa'arah ka'suten ne wi'hen.
It is true, I said I was very hungry when I returned.

Nen p'enkäch wi'ihen.
I was so hungry.

Toh inwoher yan haayok'.
I knew that there were the haayok'.

Ma' tinhantah.
I did not eat (their food).

He'ra' yumeh. He'ra' tech, uyanchun uho'(or) kints'ahik tech.
Here it is, oh Lord. Here it is for you, the first offering I give to you.

Ma' bik uhaarik inwich haayok'.
Don't let the haayok' scoop out my eyes.

Ka'(ah) ts'o'okor haayok' yok'or wa('a)n be(r).
May the haayok' on the road be finished.

Tarak inboho' kuya'arik, 'Wi'ih,' utukurik ubäh,
Although my brothers say, 'I'm hungry,' they think to themselves,

wi'ih wa('a)n be(r) usut,
they are hungry on the road on their return,

ke umäk'eh haayok' uyo'och."
may they eat the food of the haayok'."

Lahi(h) äknukire'ex, lahi(h) tulahts'aah ti' uk'uh. Tulahts'ahah uho'(or), hook'(ih) uhantik. Tulahhantah k'oor. Tulahhantah wah. Mix wenen. Mix haayok'. Ts'o'ok.
These ancestors of ours, they offered it all to all the gods. (After) they offered the first fruits of everything, they came out to eat it.[8] They ate up all the stew. They ate up all the tortillas. Neither did they sleep nor did the haayok' (appear). It was over.

Le' lati' ka('ah) xupi(h) haayok'. Ts'o'ok haayok'.
That was when the (time of the) haayok' ended. The haayok' were finished.

Ko'otir Ka'an 'The Celestial Eagle'

Bor Ma'ax

Hachäkyum kept large, ferocious animals as pets. One of these was the *ko'otir ka'an*, a celestial eagle. From time to time it would break loose, swoop down to earth, and haul unsuspecting people up to its aerie in the sky and then devour them. This story recounts the time when Ak'inchob 'Lord of Maize' put an end to it.[1]

Bay. Uko'oti(r) ka'an tumentah Hachäkyum. Lahih tume(n)tah ti' uyäräk' hunk'uk'.

Okay. Hachäkyum created the ko'otir ka'an. He created them as his pet eagles.

Uchik, unukuch winik bex tutsikbartah, y intet, tuya'arah, yan uko'oti(r) ka'an ich ka'an.

Long ago, so our ancestors recounted, and my father said, there were ko'otir ka'an in the sky.

Hachäkyum, lahih yani(r) uyäräk' ko'oti(r) ka'an. Ne nuk, nukuch hunk'uk'. Yan uyähkäna(h)ir Ak'inchob. Lahih kukänäntik yäräk' yäkan.

They were Hachäkyum's pets. They were enormous eagles. The person who took care of them was Ak'inchob. He took care of his father-in-law's pets.

Yan nukuch hunk'uk'. Ne nuk. Uchik kutsikbartah tuchi'ah nukuch winik. Tuchi'ah.

There were these enormous eagles. They say they ate the ancestors in the past. They ate them.

Woro(r) kuhook'or ahnukuch winik kuhook'o(r) ti' haräkniki(r) kuch'a'ik uyo'och ha' kubin t(i') uber, kutar ahhunk'uk' kutekch'uytah kubisik ch'ik t(i') uka'ani(r), (ti') uka'ani(r) ahnukuch hunk'uk'. Ti' kubisik ti' uchi'ik ahnukuch winik, ti' kuchi'k ubäk'e(r).

Every time the ancestors would go outside to fetch their water (or) would go to the toilet, an eagle would come, snatch them up, and take them hanging (from its talons) to the sky, to the sky of the enormous eagles. It took the ancestors there to eat them, to eat their flesh.

'Otsir nukuch winik. (U)bin upokik ubäh ti' k'uh. Ubin ti' uk'intik nukuch winik ba'inkin t(an)uchi'eh inboho'.

The poor ancestors. They go and burn offerings to the gods. The ancestors (try to) discover what is eating their companions.

"Ba'inkin t(an) uchi'eh? Ba'inkin (tan u)chi'eh inchan ti'a'ar, ba'inkin (tan u)chi'eh? Ba'inkin tuch'uyah, hunk'uk'?"

"What is eating them? What is eating my children, what is eating them? What snatched them up swinging, an eagle?"

Mix uyoher tu' binih. Seeb binih ich ka'an.

Nobody knows where it went. It took off into the sky.

Bay.

Okay.

Nukuch winik ts'o'okih uk'intik. Tuyohertah ba'ar k'uhir ut'aanah. Tuk'intah hunk'uk', tuk'intah hunk'uk' chi'bnah.

The ancestors finished their divination. (Now) they knew which god to address. They (also) determined it was an eagle. They determined it was an eagle that ate (their people).

Bay.

Okay.

Nukuch winik ubin utukrik bik ubin umentik yeter uhunk'uk' ti' uts'o'okor uchi'bar. Wa kuhook'or t(i') uch'ur—HAYIII—kutekch'uytik kubisik ti' uka'ani(r).

The ancestors go and think about what they are going to do about the eagle so that it stops eating them. If someone goes out to urinate—HAYIII—it snatches them up and carries them hanging (from its talons) to its sky.

Bay.

Okay.

Woror 'otsi(r) nukuch winik, tan upokik ubäh, upokik, upokik, "Ma' bik utar. Ma' bik uchi'bar. Way yok'o(r) lu'um a' uchi'ko'on. Makeh uyumeni(r)ka'an. T'aneh uyumeni(r) ka'ah uch'ukeh uyäräk' hunk'uk', ma' tsoy. Uchi'bar."

All the poor ancestors are burning offerings, burning offerings, burning offerings, "Don't let it come. Don't let it eat (us). It eats us here on the earth. Shut it up in its master's sky. It belongs in its master's sky. Tell its master when he catches his pet eagle (that) it is evil. It eats (people)."

Bay.

Okay.

Ak'inchob, uhaan ahHachäkyum, lahih tuyu'yah ut'an. Ma, k'uchih ubo'ori(r). Nukuch winik tan uts'o'oksik, tan uts'o'oksik. Yan nahwah, yan ch'ur(h)a', yan ba(')che'.

Ak'inchob, the son-in-law of Hachäkyum, heard their pleas. And their offerings arrived. The ancestors finish (giving) offerings, they finish (giving) them. There are tamales, there is posol, there is balche'.

Tan uchichk'atik ti' k'uh, "'Utsereh, ma' het la'eh, ma' het ti' akhook'or haräkniki(r), ma' het la'eh. Mix mak, mix inchanti'a'ar, mix mak uhook'o(r) ti' uber. Lati', ne sahak ti'.'"

They are imploring the Lord (Ak'inchob), "Oh dear, we can't go outside, we can't. No one, not even our children, no one goes out on the road. They are terrified of (the ko'otir ka'an)."

(Ka'ah) tuyu'yah ti', ahAk'inchob lahih bin uya'areh ti' Hachäkyum, "Eh, tan uchi'bir a(k)paare'ex. Tan uchi'bi(r) ten awäräk' hunk'uk'.'"

(When) Ak'inchob heard them, he went to tell Hachäkyum, "Eh, our children are being eaten. They are being eaten by your pet eagle."

"Eh hah," kih Hachäkyum. "Eh ma' tsoy. Ma' inw(oh)e(r) inwäräk' hunk'uk' wa tan uchi'bar."

"Oh, is that so," says Hachäkyum. "That's very bad. I was unaware of my pet eagle eating (them)."

"Tan uchi'ik a' lu'umo' bin, tun. He' kuk'uchu(r) ba(')che'; he' kuk'uchu(r) nahwah; he' kuk'uchu(r) hu'un; he' kuk'uchu(r) ma'ats'.'"

"Well, it's eating the mortals. Here, their balche' arrives; here, their tamales arrive; here, their bark cloth arrives; here, their posol arrives," (says Ak'inchob).

"Eh bay," kih Hachäkyum. "Eh ma' tsoy. Ma' inwoher wa tan uyeemer inwäräk' hunk'uk'. Tan uchi'ik inwaaro'. Eh bay, yan abin awirik."

"All right," says Hachäkyum. "This is very bad. I was unaware of my pet eagle going down and eating my children. All right, you have to go and have a look."

Ele, eemih uhaan Ak'inchob. Eemih way, yok'or a' lu'um, utunteh uyireh wa hach tuha(h)i(r), ti' uyirik ti' uwich ba'(ar) hunk'uk'ir kuchi'bar.

And so, his son-in-law, Ak'inchob, came down, he came down here to the earth, to try and see with his own eyes if it were true that this thing was the eagle and what it was eating.

Hook'ih ku(r)tar ti' uxur chi' nah, kutich'i(r). Kuyirik kutich'i(r)— WHOOOOOSH—chinchinpor kuta(r). Ma' boon uk'uchur bix uni' yor a' nu-kuch che'. Ma, (ka'ah?) tuyirah uwinki(r), ka'ah tuka'sutk'ätah ubah. Binih t(i') uka'ani(r).

He went out and sat down at the edge of the ceremonial kitchen.[2] He sees it approaching—WHOOOOOSH—it dives with its wings straight back. In no time it gets to the top of the tall trees. But when it saw its master, then it swiftly changed direction and went into the sky.

UYE-E-E-T binih t(i') uka'ani(r) ahAk'inchob. UYET binih t(i') uka'ani(r). Ma' tunahxurah turaka(r)[3] k'uchih t(i') uka'anir ahHachäkyum. Kuk'uchurkurur tuyirah ahAk'inchob.

Ak'inchob TOOK OFF AFTER it into the sky. He TOOK OFF AFTER it into the sky. They didn't stop until they got all the way to the sky of Hachäkyum. Ak'inchob saw it land on a branch.

"A' la'eh la' hunk'uk', la' la'eh kuchi'ik ahnukuch winik. Eh hah! Tinwirah lati' bä-kan, uyäräk' hunk'uk' Ekyum bäkan, kuchi'ik lu'umo'. 'Otsi(r) lu'umo'."

(He says to himself,) "That is the eagle that is eating the ancestors. Aha! Just as I suspected, it is our Lord's pet eagle that is eating the mortals. The poor mortals."

Eh ma, tukinsah. Tukinsah tupur(ah) uxik' yok'or a' lu'um. Eh tupur(ah) uxik' xok'or uxur uchi'ir (u)yatoch (ti') (u)nukuch winik. Tuyirah uche-re(r)—P'IIN.

And so, he killed it. He killed it (and) threw down (one of) its wings to the earth. He threw down the wing near the edge of the god house of the ancestors. They saw it fall—WUMPF.

Ne nuk uxik'. Batak ule' ahchäk boox[4] uxik'. Ele tuye'esah uxik'. La' ubo'ori(r) t(i') tubo'otah ti' nukuch winik. Tuyee(n)sah uxik' t(i'), uyeesik ne boon winik tuchi'ah.

It was an enormous wing. It was the size of a banana leaf. He showed (them) the wing. This is (the) compensation he offered to the ancestors. He brought down the wing, to show (them) (what had been eating all the people).[5]

Uyitber 'He at the End of the Road'

Bor Ma'ax

Among the ogres in the forest, the *yitber* is one of the most horrific. He is a jaguar that takes the form of a relative of his victims and fools them into following him down the road. When he reaches his cavern, he devours them.[1]

Transformers, such as the yitber, are usually jaguars, the symbol of warriors from the Mayan Postclassic period. The warriors would don jaguar skins and masks before going into battle, killing and cannibalizing their captives. Possibly the yitber is based on these warriors.

Bay.
Okay.

Uyitbe(r), uchik, bek tutsikbartah yan ich k'aax.
Long ago, they said the yitbe(r) was in the forest.

Nukuch winik tuyu'yah utsikbartah, tuyu'yah utsikbartah uher winik äknukire'ex.
An ancestor heard him talking, he heard another ancestor talking.

Tuya'arah,
He said,

"Käränt(eh) abäh.
"Watch out.

Wa tech kabin ich akoor,
If you go into your milpa,

wa tu' kabin abähik apom,
or where you go to tap your copal,

awa'arik t(i') alaak' ke ma' uch'uktikech, ma' upäktik wanber, upäktik uyirik
uch'uktikech, wa yan asut seeb."
tell your wife not to watch for you, not to keep checking the road watching
for your quick return."

"Bik yani(r)?" kuk'ateh äknukire'ex.
"Why?" our ancestor asks.

"Es que uyitbe(r) yan ich k'aax.
"It's that the yitber is in the forest.

Kisin.
He is the devil.[2]

Kuchi'bar; ku chi'ikone'ex. P'is barum.
He eats (people); he eats us. He is like a jaguar.

Ach'uktik—
You peer out (looking for your husband)—

wa aka'ch'uktik,
if you peer out again,

kutar, kutar wa('a)nber."
he will come, he will come down the road."

"Ah bay," kih.
"Ah, all right," (the ancestor) says.

Entonces tuya'arah tulaak',
Then (the ancestor) said to his wife,

"Bay, bin ink(ah) inbähik inpom.
"Okay, I'm going to tap my copal now.

Tint'an ma' ach'uktiken.
I think you better not watch for me.

Yan uyitbe(r). Utar, utar uchi'ikech."
There is the yitber. He (will) come eat you, he (will) come and eat you."

Ulaak' ahch'uprar mix tuyu'yah t'an.
His wife didn't listen.

Bini(h) unukuch winik ubähik upom.
The ancestor went to tap his copal.

Ne tsoy uyor ti'.
He is in high spirits.

Mix uyoher ulaak' tan uch'uktik.
He doesn't know his wife is waiting (and watching) for him.

Se(e)b usut ich uyatoch.
He hurries back (to) his house.

Ne tsoy uyor.
He is in high spirits.

Nukuch winik ma' uyohe(r) wa yan uyitbe(r).
The ancestor doesn't know that the yitber is there.

Bay.
Okay.

Ahch'upra(r) ti' yan ich nah.
The woman is in the house.

Tan uhuuch'.
She is grinding corn.

Ma' ne xanta(r), tan upurik uwich yok'or ber uyirik (wa?) yan utichir ulaak'
uxira(r).
In a little while, she looks at the road to see if her husband is coming.

Mix.
(She sees) nothing.

Ma' ne santar, kuka'purik uwich uyirik (wa) yan utichir.
A little while later, she looks again at the road to see if he is coming.

A' yooxwäts' upurik uwich bin, kutichi(r).
The third time she looks, he approaches.

Toh ubähi(r) ahxirah la'eh ulaak'i(r).
He looks like her husband.

Bähi(r) uwich,
He has the same face,

bähi(r) uho'(or),
the same hair,

bähi(r) upooxa(r), harar.
the same leather shoulder bag (and) bow and arrows.

CHIK, CHIK,[3] kutichir. Tah kuta(r) to'an kunacha(r)ta(r) ich k'an ahnukuch winik.
CHIK, CHIK, he approaches. He heads straight to the hammock where the ancestor (the woman's husband) usually lies.

Uchek'ätik ubäh.
He stretches out in it.

Uk'ochtik uk'äb.
He cradles his head in his hands.

Chara'(a)n.
He is lying down.

Mix ut'an—mix utsikba(r).
He doesn't say anything—not a word.

Mix.
Nothing.

Ulaak' ahnukuch winik ahch'uprar ma' tutukrah ubah wa hach tuha(h)i(r) yan barum wa yitbe(r).

The ancestor's wife, she didn't think if it were really true about the jaguar or the yitber.

Mix tutukrah ubäh.
She didn't think anything of it.

Na'ak(ih).
She climbed up.

Tuku(r)k'ahtah ubah tu' xaax.
She dropped down beside (him).

Chara'(a)n.
They lay there.

"'U'reh!"
"You're back!" (she says to him).

Ma' tak unuukik.
He doesn't feel like responding.

"'U'ren."
"I'm back."

Mix uyohe(r) wa barum wa yitbe(r).
She doesn't know that he is a jaguar or the yitber.

Tan uyirik ahch'upra(r) nukuch winik.
The ancestor's wife is looking at him.

Mäna' ut'an.
He doesn't speak.

Ma' tak utsikba-a-a-r.
He doesn't want to ta-a-a-lk.

Ma' uk'a't t'an.
He doesn't want to speak.

Ma' ne sanhi[4] ucha(r)tar, tak p'is hump'e(r) orah, ele kulik'ir uyitbe(r).
Not long after he lies down, about an hour, the yitbe(r) gets up.

Ele kuya'arik ti' ulaak' ahnukuch winik ahch'upra(r), "Ko'ox."
Then he says to the ancestor's wife, "Let's go."

"Bay, ko'ox!" kih ahch'uprar. "Ko'ox." Yet bin(ih) ti'.
"Okay, let's go!" the woman says. "Let's go." She went with him.

Ma, bini(h) a' la'eh ahch'uprar tupach a' yitbe(r). Bini(h).
Well, that woman followed the yitber. She went.

Ma, k'uchur to'an a' 'aktun.
And well, they arrive at a cave.

Tukinsah. Tuchi'ah ahch'upra(r).
He killed her. He ate the woman.

Bay.
Okay.

Nukuch winik tan usut.

(Meanwhile) the ancestor is on his way back.

Kuyu'ur ich uyatoch. Saah nah.

He goes into his house. The house is empty.

Tarak umaan ukäxtik ulaak, "Tu' binech? Tu' binech? Tawu'yah?," mäna'.

Although he passes through looking for his wife (and calling), "Where did you go? Where did you go? Do you hear?," there is no (answer).

Bin(ih) ya(a)ka' ukäxteh to'an uk'um tu' kunahp'o'ik uyo'och wah.

He ran off to look for his wife at the river, where she always washes maize.

Mix. Mäna'.

She isn't there either.

Man ukäxtik (t)upach uyatoch.

He goes behind the house to look for her.

Bin(ih) uyaaka' ukäxtik to'an uyäkan.

He ran to his father-in-law to see if she's there.

"Yan wa k'uchi(h) a ti'a'are'ex way?"

"By any chance did your daughter come here?" (he asks).

"Mäna'."

"She's not here," (says his father-in-law).

"He' awirik wa uyitbe(r) tuchi'ah (in)ti'a'ar."

"You will find out if the yitber ate my daughter."

"Ele hah," kih. "Ma' inw(oh)e(r) tu' bini(h)," kih, tunuukah (ah)nukuch winik.

"That could be," he says. "I don't know where she went," replied the ancestor.

"Eh 'utse(re)h," kih. "Ba'a(r) ok'⁵ tech ka'ah tap'ät(ah) ti' tuhuna(n)."

"Uh-oh," says (the father-in-law). "It's because of you when you left her there by herself."

"Hah," kih nukuch winik.

"True," says the ancestor.

"Bähe' mäna'."

"Now she's gone," (says the father-in-law).

Bin(ih) ukäxteh ti'.

(The ancestor) went to look for her.

Ti' kumaan nukuch winik tan uyak'tik ubah. Tan umaan, "'Utse(re)h, ma' inw(oh)e(r) tu' bini(h)."

As the ancestor walks along he is crying. He is going along, "Oh no, I don't know where she went."

Bay.

Okay.

Ne chich uyor nukuch winik.

The ancestor is brave.

Maan ukäxtik ulaak'. Maan ukäxtik.
He went around looking for his wife. He went around looking for her.

Saasi(r), saasi(r) tuka'ten
In the morning, the next morning

cha(ra'an) uch'ukteh nukuch winik.
the ancestor is lying down waiting.

Hach la' t(i') up'isir k'inir ka'(ah) k'uch(ih). Taki(r) k'ak' chun k'in.
Sure enough, he arrived at the same time. It's almost midday.

(Tan u)ch'uktik uyirik. (U)päktik utich(ir).
He is waiting and watching. He spots him approaching.

Tah kutar bin.
He comes right (toward him).

"Le' hah. Uyitbe(r)."
(The ancestor says to himself,) *"It's true. It is the yitber."*

Tan utukurik ubah nukuch winik, *"Lati' tuchi'(ah) inlaak'."*
The ancestor is still thinking, *"He's the one who ate my wife."*

Hach tah kutar bin —*chiik, chiik, chiik.*
He comes walking right (toward him) —*chiik, chiik, chiik.*

K'uchi(h) to'an k'an bin(ih) uchek'at(ik) ubäh.
He got to the hammock and went to stretch out in it.

Te(k)k'oocht(ik) uho'or uk'äb, eh cha(r)a'(a)n.
He puts his hands behind his head and lies there.

Mix ut'an.
He doesn't speak.

Nukuch winik, *"Leee lati',"* tutukr(ah) ubah. *"Leee lati' tuchi'(ah) inlaak'.*
The ancestor says to himself, *"Thaaat's him. Thaaat's the one who ate my wife.*

Bähe',
Now,

mäna' inpek.
I'm not going to move.

Voy inch'ukteh inwireh."
I'm going to wait and see (what he does)."

Bay.
Okay.

K'uch ma p'is hump'e(r) orah.
About an hour goes by.

Chara('a)n ich k'an.
He's (still) lying in the hammock.

Ele, kulik'ir uyitbe(r), kupurik ut'an ti' ahxirar ulaak' ahch'uprar ahnukuch winik, "Ko'ox."
And then, the yitber gets up, he announces to the woman's husband, "Let's go."

"Ko'ox," kih a(h)nukuch winik.
"Let's go," the ancestor says.

Poch uyirik to'an ulaak' ti' uyirik ti' tupurah ahyitbe(r).
He wants to see where his wife is, to see where the yitber put her.

Bay.
Okay.

Lik'i(h) uyitbe(r) bini(h). Binih
The yitber got up and went. They left.

K'uchu(r) boon ubin kuya'arik bin, "Maanen."
They get so far and (the yitber) says, "Go ahead."

Nukuch winik unuukik, "Ten ma'. Tech pä(y)tan."
The ancestor replies, "Not me. You first."

Ele, ubin.
And so, they go.

Tan ubin,
They are going,

tan ubin,
and going,

tan ubin.
and going.

K'uchur boon bin(ih) kuyirik—yaha(h) kura'(a)n 'aktun, nen ch'ikyum.

They went so far and then (the ancestor) sees it—a great, enormous cave sitting there.

Hach säkhupe'(en) kurik 'aktun.

A glowing white cave sat there.

Le' ahnukuch winik uya'arik, "Le' tuha(h)i(r). Ti' tupurah inlaak'. Ti' tuchi'ah."

The ancestor says to himself, "So it is true. This is where he put my wife. This is where he ate her."

Uk'uchu(r) to'an a' 'aktun, ma' boon tu' (u)k'uchu(r) chun a' ('a)ktun bin uyirik.

He comes to the cave (and) goes just as far as the entrance of the cave and looks in.

Purik uwich a(h)nukuch winik bin.

The ancestor peers in.

Kura'(a)n uho'or ulaak', puka'(a)n unook'.

His wife's head is sitting there, her dress is thrown down.

"*Tsk. Le' hah.*"

"*Tsk. It's true.*"

Toh ukuchba(r) umaska' nukuch winik. Ka'(a)h tupur-r-r-ah, bin(ih) t(i') uche'ir ukaar. KACHAH!

The ancestor is still carrying his machete. When he threw it, it went into (the yitber's) neck. KACHAH!

Ma' tunahcha(')ah.

(But) he didn't let go of it.

Kuka'purik. CHAAH!

He throws it again. CHAAH!

PEYIIH.

THUD (the yitber hits the ground).

Bini(h) uyaaka' uyireh. Ubin tu' puka'(a)n unook' ulaak'. Kura'(a)n uho'(or) ulaak'.

(The ancestor) went running (into the cave) to see. He goes to where his wife's dress is thrown down. His wife's head is lying there.

"Tsk. 'Utse(re)h." Ti' kunookor bin nukuch winik uyak'tik ubahi(r).

"Tsk. Oooh no." The ancestor bends over (with his face in hands) and weeps.

"'Utsereh. Ba'a(r) ok' ten ka'(ah) tinp'ätah inlaak'.

"Oooh no. It's all because I left my wife behind.

Ten insi'ipir. Tinp'ätah.

It is my fault. I left her.

Wa ma' inp'ätik kachik kuxa'(a)n inlaak' kach(ik).

If I hadn't left my wife, she would be alive.

Ten insi'ipir.

It is my fault.

Tinwu'yah tsikbar. Tinwu'yah pero ma' tinch'a'ah a' tsikbar.

I heard the story (about the yitber). I heard it (but) I didn't take it (seriously).

Ma' tinwu'yah t'an."

I didn't listen."

Ele,

And so,

nukuch winik hook'or uch'a'ik uho'or ulaak' tumukah.

the ancestor goes out and takes his wife's head and burie(s) it.

Ba'eh uyitbe(r), tukinsah.

Now as for the yitber, he killed him.

Tukinsah. Tuch'äkah.

He killed him. He chopped him.

Eh, uts'o'ok umuk(ik) uho'or ulaak', bini(h) uyireh uyäkan.

And so, (when) he finished burying his wife's head he went to visit his father-in-law.

Bin uk'ateh uher ulaak'. Yan uboho' ulaak' ch'upra(r) ma' ch'a'aha'(a)n.

He went to ask for another wife. His wife (had) unmarried sisters.

"He' wa ats'ahik ten uch'upra(r) ati'a'ar?"

"Will you give me your daughter?"

"Mäna'," uya'arah uyäkan. "Mäna' ints'ahik tech inti'a'ar.

"No," his father-in-law says. "I won't give you any of my daughters.

Ma' taki'karantah. Ma' takarantah.

You didn't look after (the first one). You didn't look after her.

Chi'bi(h) ti' uyitbe(r).

She was eaten by the yitber.

'Otsi(r) uch'upra(r) inti'a'ar. Ma' tatukrah."
My poor daughter. You didn't think about her."

"Tuha(h)i(r). Ten insi'ipir," (tu)ya'arah nukuch winik.
"That's true. It's my fault," said the ancestor.

"Tuha(h)i(r). Ten insi'ipir.
"That's true. It's my fault.

Tinp'ätah ati'a'ar tuhuna(n) ich nah.
I left your daughter alone in the house.

Inwohe(r). Tinwu'yah utsikbartah yan uyitbe(r), ma' tsoy. Kuchi'bar."
I know. I heard them say that there was the yitber, who was very bad. He (ate) (people)."

Bay.
Okay.

Ele bex utsikbar uchik unuki(r) winik yete(r) yitbe(r).
Well, that's how the story about the ancestor and the yitber goes.

Kak'och yeter Uyitber 'Kak'och and the Yitber'

Bor Ma'ax

In this story, Kak'och, the first Creator, destroys the yitber.[1]

Uchik ti' Mensäbäk Kak'och. Ti' yan uyatoch ich Mensäbäk xok'or to'an Mensäbäk, yan xok'or to'an Ts'ibanah. Ti' yan uyatoch uchik. Kak'och way yok'o(r) lu'um.

Initially, Kak'och lived in Mensäbäk. He had his house in Mensäbäk near (Lake) Mensäbäk and Ts'ibanah. Kak'och had his house here on earth before (he went to the sky).[2]

Bay

Okay.

Kak'och kubin uyirik uk'ani(r). [Ti' yan uk'anir ti' ulu'um ti' yan ne ka'ana(n).] Yan uk'ani(r) Kak'och. Yan uk'anir, uyähkänanir yatoch. Ti' yan ti' uhoor nah; mak kukänäntik, como p'iis ts'ulo'. Yan uyähkänanir yatoch. Mix mak kucha'ik uyokor—wa ma' uk'oor, ma' ucha'ik uyokor.

Kak'och goes to see his assistants. [There are exceptional (humans) who are the gods' assistants in the sky.] Kak'och has an assistant. He has an assistant, a guardian of his house. He is at the door of the house; he is the person who guards it, like the mythical jaguars. He has a guardian of the house; he does not allow anyone to enter—if they do not knock, he does not let them enter.

Bay.

Okay.

Kak'och bini(h), bini(h) ich uyatoch. Mix uyohe(r) wa bin ukah okor yitber ich uyatoch. Mix uyohe(r) Kak'och; ti' yan ich uka'an, ma' toy(ir) sutuk.

Kak'och went, he went into his house. (The assistant) doesn't know that the yitber is about to enter his house. Kak'och doesn't know (because) he is in the sky and hasn't returned yet.

Bay.

Okay.

Ti' yan mak ukänäntik uhoor nah. (U)päktik uyirik utichir. Ubähi(r) wich Kak'och, hach ubähi(r). Mix k'äs k'axa'an ubähi(r); hach uwichi(r) Kak'och. Mak uyähkänani(r) miiix, tarak uyirik, wa uyitbe(r). Mix tuyirah.

The person who guards the door is there. He sees him approaching. He's got the same face as Kak'och, just like his, nothing much is changed about him; he has the same face as Kak'och. The housekeeper doesn't (know) he is the yitbe(r), even though he looks at him, he doesn't recognize him (as the yitber).

Oki(h) yok'or (u)yatoch Kak'och. To'an uk'aan t(i') unahcha(r)tar ahKak'och, ti' ok(ih) (u)cha(r)tar uyitbe(r). Uyähkänani(r) mix uyohe(r) wa uyitbe(r) ok(ih) ich uyatoch Kak'och. Mix uyoher.

He entered Kak'och's house. The yitber came in (and went to) Kak'och's hammock, where Kak'och always lies down, and lay down there. The caretaker doesn't even know that it is the yitber who entered Kak'och's house. He doesn't even know it.

Ma' ne sanhih como ma p'iis hu(n)p'er 'ora, kupäktik utichir ubähi(r) a(h)Kak'och, hach ubähi(r), kutichi(r)—kichik, CHIK.[3] Eh, (u)yähkänanir nah, eh t(i') umaan tukur que irah ok(ih) (u)cha(r)tar ubähir Kak'och. Maxi' la', "TSK."[4]

A little while later, perhaps an hour, he observes Kak'och approaching—kichik, CHIK. The thought crosses the housekeeper's mind that he saw Kak'och come in and lie down. It wasn't him. "TSK."

Eh, kuxok'o(r) kupurik ut'an, "Ma' awohe(r) tech yumeh," kih, "okech cha(r)ta(r) way? Oksa('a)n. Okech."

When he comes closer he calls out, "Don't you know, my Lord," he says, "you came in and lay down here? You were let in. You came in."

"Ma' sutiken ten," kih. "Ten ma' sutiken."

"I didn't come back," he says. "It wasn't me who came back."

"Eh!" Ok(ih) (u)yaaka' (u)yirah bin.

"Eh!" (Kak'och) ran in to see.

(U)bähir ahKak'och ti' yan ich uyatoch. Chara'an yitbe(r) ich uk'an.

Kak'och's imposter is in his house. The yitber is lying in his hammock.

"Eh!" kuhook'o(r) (u)t'an ahKak'och. "Eh, le ma' tsoy uyitbe(r) oki(h) ich inwatoch. Ma' wa tawirah?"

"Eh!" Kak'och says. "Eh, it is not good (that) the yitber entered my house. Didn't you notice it was him?"

"Miiix," unuukik uyähkänani(r) nah. "Mix tinwirah."

"Not at all," replies his caretaker. "I never noticed him."

"Eh! Le uyitbe(r) oki(h). Ne ma' tsoy yitbe(r)."

"Eh! This is the yitber that entered. The yitber is evil."

Bay.

Okay.

Kak'och tupurah ut'an ti' Mensäbäk. Tupurah ut'an ti' Ts'ibanah, "Eh Ts'ibanah, he' wa ats'ahik inmahan tawatoch ti' (in)maa(n)s(i)k uba'(a)r inbäh?"

Kak'och called out to Mensäbäk. He called out to Ts'ibanah, "Hey Ts'ibanah, would you lend me your house to move my things into?"

"He're'," kih Ts'ibanah tunuukah. "He're'," kih.

"Of course," said Ts'ibanah. "Of course," he said.

"Tech, Mensäbäk, he' wa mahant(i)k awatoch ti' (in)but'ik uba'(a)r inbäh?"

"You, Mensäbäk, would you lend your house to put my things in?"

"He're'," tunuukah Mensäbäk. "He're', intasa(h?) uba('a)r abäh.[5] He're'."

"Of course," Mensäbäk replied. "Of course, I will bring your things. Of course."

'Oreh[6] lahaantah seebseeb ulahharik uba('a)r ubäh ahKak'och. Ulahmaa(n)sik uba('a)r ubäh to'an uyatoch Mensä(bäk), to'an Ts'ibanah. Ulahmaa(n)sik uba('a)r ubäh seeb.

They all helped to rapidly remove all Kak'och's things. They move all his things to the house(s) of Mensäbäk (and) Ts'ibanah. They move all his things quickly.

Bay.

Okay.

"Bähe'," tuya'arah Kak'och, "bähe' way kubin ts'o'okor tun. Uyitbe(r) way kubin cha(r)ta(r) ich inwatoch, way kubin 'eerer way."

"Now," said Kak'och, "now it is going to stop here. The yitber is going to be lying here in my house (and) here he is going to burn."

Bay.

Okay.

Ts'o'ok ulahharik uba('a)r ubäh. Lahmaa(n)sa('?) uba('a)r ubäh t(i') uyatoch Ts'ibanah uyatoch Mensäbäk. Ele tumakah uhoor a' nah; ulahmaka' tun. Mäna'. Pe'pe'ek.

They finished removing all his things. All his things are moved over to the house of Ts'ibanah (and) the house of Mensäbäk. Then he shut all the doors and windows of the house; they are all shut then. There is no way (to get out). (The yitber) is closed in.

Ele, ka'(ah) tut'äbah ubähi(r) Kak'och tut'äbah uyatoch. [Umak ahKak'och uyirik ti' uyatoch xa'an, xa'an, ma' tunich, xa'an.][7] Tulaht'äbah a' la'eh uyatoch ahKak'och. Lah chan ka'(ah) hoopeh, *x-i-i-i-x*, kuyee(r)er. *Bär-a-a-ax*, kih. K-A-A-A-A-AK, kuyee(r)eh. Eh, uyitbe(r) ku(r)tar (u)yawat, "uuuh! uuuh! Ne yah inweerer. uuuh!" kuyawat uyitbe(r). Tami(r)[8] ich uyatoch ahKak'och tan uyeere(r). "uuuh!" kuyawat ahyitbe(r). "uuuh!"

And then, when the Kak'och himself set fire to his house. [The roof of Kak'och's house looks like palm thatch, not stone.] Kak'och set the house on fire. When it catches fire, *sh-i-i-i-sh*, it burns. *W-o-o-osh*, it goes. *W-o-o-sh*, CR-A-A-A-A-ACK, it burns. The yitber's screams come, "uuuh! uuuh! It hurts, I'm burning. uuuh!" the yitber cries out. Deep inside Kak'och's house he is burning. "uuuh!" cries the yitber. "uuuh!"

Ba'lah ka'ah (u)lahtohhachts'ahik, uyeere(r), *b-r-r-raaahsh*, kih tun. Tan uhook'or ubuuts'i(r) t(i') upach uyatoch ahKak'och. T(a)n ulahee(r)e(r). Ele chäkan ka'(ah) tuyu'yah bin, *par-r-r-a-a-sh*, kih, hook'i(h) uyeere(r) pach t(i') uyatoch. Chen ka'(ah) lahhook'(ih) uk'ak'i(r) t(i') upach uyatoch, *b-r-r-raaahsh*, kih, tuyee(r)ah che', mehen che', lah(h)aan t(i') upach uyatoch.

But when he really gives it to him, it burns, *b-r-r-raaahsh*, then. The smoke is coming out the back of Kak'och's house. It is burning up. Then, when he heard it go *par-r-r-a-a-sh*, it bursts into flames behind his house. And when the fire ignited behind the house, *b-r-r-raaahsh*, it burned the small trees (leaving) the back of his house entirely bare.

Ele, ka'(ah) tar(ih) uyu'yeh ahbuh — PIT — kubuh(ik) ucho(o)cher uyitbe(r). Buhnah. Ele, kiim.

And then, when an owl came to smell around — PIT — he splits open the guts of the yitber. They split open. And so, (the yitber) is dead.

"Ele bähe'," tuya'arah Kak'och, "bääähe' uyitbeheh tuneh, ma' tsoy tun. Tint'an bähe' bin ukah ts'o'okor uyitbe(r), bin ukah xu(r)bur. Bähe' bin ukah ts'o'okor uyitbe(r), bin ukah ts'o'oko(r) tuworo(r) ba'(ar). Kisin way ma' tsoy."

"Now," said Kak'och, "nooow the yitber is evil. I believe this puts an end to the yitber; now he is finished. Now it is the end of the yitber, it is the end of all (his evil doings). The devil[9] here is evil."

Ele bek tutsikbartah uchik Kak'och.

So that's how (the ancestors) told the story of Kak'och.

Want'ut'k'in

Säk Ho'or

Want'ut'k'in[1] is one of several ogres that prey on unsuspecting travelers in the forest. He lures them up trees that contain beehives on the pretense that there is plenty of honey waiting to be collected. Once up in the tree, the victims are unable to get down. After a few days, Want'ut'k'in returns, retrieves his half-dead victims, and then devours them.

In this story Want'ut'k'in has lured an ancestor up a tree. Want'ut'k'in leaves the ancestor there, presumably waiting for him to ripen. While he is gone, coatimundis and a woodpecker coordinate their efforts to rescue the ancestor and defeat Want'ut'k'in.[2]

Bay.

Okay.

Uchik, ahWant'ut'k'in ne ma' paatih.

Long ago, Want'ut'k'in was very bad.

(Tu)tsikbartah uchik ahWant'ut'k'in tutusah nukuch winik. Tutusah nukuch winik. Tuya'arah, nukuch winik ne tsoy uyirik ubin uch'äk(ik) uyo'och kab, ti' ume(n)tik ba(')che', tuworor. AhWant'ut'k'in tuna'asah yok'or ya'axche' ti' uchi'ik. Tuya'arah ke Want'ut'k'in yan upek', barum.

They said long ago that Want'ut'k'in lied to the ancestor. He lied to the ancestor. They said (that) the ancestor(s) liked to go cut down honey to make balche' and other things.[3] Want'ut'k'in lures them up the ceiba tree to eat them. They said that Want'ut'k'in has dogs that are jaguars.[4]

Bay.

Okay.

Ahnukuch winik ma' uyoher wa yan Want'ut'k'in y tuyirah ne yan kab. 'A'arah ti', "A' he' ch'ika'(a)n kab. Awirik he' ch'ika('a)n a' nukuch che' kawirik ne yan kab yok'or che' a' la'eh."

The ancestor doesn't know about Want'ut'k'in and he saw a lot of honey. He is told (by Want'ut'k'in), "Right here there is honey. You see the large tree standing here, you will see that there is a lot of honey in that tree there."

Bay.

Okay.

Tuna'asah (ah)Want'ut'k'in nukuch winik. Tuya'arah Want'ut'k'in,

Want'ut'k'in lured the ancestor up. Want'ut'k'in said,

"Na'aken. Ch'äkeh a' he'! Ne yan kab ti'. Awirik ne yan kab. Ne yan kab kabin ahaareh."

"Climb up! Chop it off right here! There is a lot of honey there. You see there's a lot of honey. There's a lot of honey that you are going to scoop out."

Bay.

Okay.

Nukuch winik ne tsoy uyor. Na'aki(h) yok'or nukuch che', yok'or yahche'⁵ na'aki(h) nukuch winik. Kuna'akar yok'or nukuch k'ä'che', tuyirah mäna' kab. Tusnah Want'ut'k'in.

The ancestor is jubilant. The ancestor climb(s) up the large tree, climb(s) up the ceiba tree. When he climbs up on a large branch, he sees that there isn't any honey. Want'ut'k'in (had) lied.

Want'ut'k'in tuya'arah, "Bähe' ti(n)na'a(k)s(ah)ech," kih. "Bähe' ma' tun xikech. Tech, kinbin inchi'ech."

Want'ut'k'in said, "Now I (have) made you climb up," he said. "Now, you can't get away. I'm going to eat you."

Bay.

Okay.

Nukuch winik tutukrah ubäh,

The ancestor thought,

"Bähe' tint'an ten bin inkah kimi(n). Ten kubin uchi'en ahWant'ut'k'in."

"Now I think I'm going to die. Want'ut'k'in is going to eat me."

Bay.

Okay.

Pachir, bini(h) Want'ut'k'in. Tuch'uktah boon k'in. Boon k'in tuch'uktah. Bini(h) Want'ut'k'in; ha'ri' hach winik tuna'a(k)sah yok'or nukuch k'ä'che'. Bini(h).

Then, Want'ut'k'in left. And he waited for so many days. For so many days he waited. Want'ut'k'in left; only the ancestor (had) climbed up on the big branches. He (Want'ut'k'in) left.[6]

Pachir, tutukrah ubäh nukuch winik, "*Bik kinbin inme(n)teh ti'? Bik kinbin 'eemer? Mäna' ts'oy. Mäna' che'. Mäna' ba'(ar) ti' (in)weemer.*"

Then, the ancestor thought, "*How am I going to do it? How am I going to get down? There aren't any lianas. There aren't any trees. There isn't anything that I can get down on.*"

Ahche' ne hurehmäk, ma' bik uyeemer.

The tree is very straight, there is no way for him to get down.

Bay.

Okay.

Pachir, tuch'uktah. Tuyärtah ubäho', "oooy! Ti' yanech? Wa yan mak kuyu'yik int'an? Kawirik poch uchi'(i)ken ahWant'ut'k'in. Poch ukinsiken ahWant'ut'k'in. Wa yan mak kuyu'yik int'an? Wa yan akbohore'ex kutar uyaantiken, kutar uyaantiken ti' weemer; upahchetik uche'il ti' inweemer?"

Then, he waited. He called out to his companions, "oooy! Are you there? Can anybody hear me? You see, Want'ut'k'in wants to eat me. Want'ut'k'in wants to kill me. Can anybody hear me? Is there anyone of our friends who will come and help me, come help me get down; (anyone who will) lean a log (against the tree) so I can get down?"

Mix muk (tu)nuukah uyawat, mix muki. Ma' ne pim uchik nukir winik, mix muk uyoher.

Nobody answered his call, nobody. There weren't many people back then, nobody knows (he's struck up a tree).

Bay.

Okay.

Want'ut'k'in ne tsoy uyor. Tuna'a(k)sah. Bini(h) ukäxtik upek', ubarum. Bin(ih) ukäxteh ubarum. [Upek' awirik barum.]

Want'ut'k'in is elated. He lured him up. He went to look for his dogs, the jaguars. He went to look for his jaguars. [His dogs look like jaguars.⁷]

Bay.

Okay.

Pachir, maani(h) bäk'. Ti' yan ahnukuch winik. K'ata(r) ti', "Ba'i(n)k(in) kawak'tik?" Tuk'aatah ahhare'. (Päytan, uyanmaanih ahhare'.) Tuk'aatah (ah)hare', "Ba'i(n)ki(n) kawak'tik?"

Then, an animal passed by. The ancestor is there. He asks him, "Why are you crying?" the paca asked him. (First, a paca passed by.) The paca asked, "Why are you crying?"

"Awirik, mäna' ba'(ar). Kinwak'tik porque ma' bik inweemer. Tutusahen ahWant'ut'k'in. Tinna'akah ti' ch'äkeh kab. Tinwirah ne yan kab. Tuye'esah ten ne yan uche' kab. Pero mäna' ukab. Tutusahen."

"You see, there isn't any (honey). I'm crying because I don't know how to get down. Want'ut'k'in lied to me. I climbed up to cut down the honey-(comb). I (thought) I (had seen) a lot of honey. He showed me (where there was) a lot of honey in the branches. But there wasn't any honey. He lied to me.

Bay.

Okay.

Pachir, tuya'arah, "Ma' inwoher bik inbin (inw)eemer."

Then, he said, "I don't know how I'm going to get down."

Tuya'arah hare', "Ma' bik inweensikech, 'otsirech. Ten ma' inna'aka(r) che'. Ten yok'or lu'um kinmaan yok'or k'aax."

The paca said, "I don't know how to bring you down, you poor thing. I don't climb trees. I go along the ground through the forest."

"Bay. Ne tsoy."

"Okay. That's okay," (says the ancestor).

Pachir maani(h) yuk. Tuya'arah yuk, "Ba'inki(n) kawak'tik?"

Then a deer passed by. The deer said, "Why are you crying?"

"Mäna' awirik, Want'ut'k'in tuna'a(k)sahen yok'or che', yok'or che'ir kab ... Pero mäna'. Want'ut'k'in tutusahen. Eh, mäna' kab."

"Can't you see, Want'ut'k'in lured me up into a tree, into the branches that had honey ... But there wasn't any. Want'ut'k'in lied to me. There isn't any honey."

Tuya'arah yuk, "Eh 'otsirech. Awirik ten, ma' bik inwaantikech. Ten ha'ri' lo'obir kinhantik."

The deer said, "Oh, you poor thing. You see me, I don't know how to help you. I only (stay on the ground and) eat plants."

Bay.

Okay.

Pachir maanih ahwech'. Tuya'arah ahwech', "Ba'inkin ame(n)tik ti' ukä'che'? Ba'inkin awak'tik?"

Then an armadillo passed by. The armadillo said, "What are you doing in the branches? Why are you crying?"

"Awirik tan intukrah inbäh ma' ba'(ar). Ne wi'hen. Uk'ahen. Mix k'äs ba'(ar) inwuk'eh. Ma' bik inweemer yok'or lu'um. Ne ma' tsoy. Ma' bik inweemer. Mäna' ti' chukik inbäh."

"You see, I'm thinking that there isn't anything. I'm very hungry. I'm thirsty. I have nothing at all to drink. I don't know how to get down to the ground. It's not very good. I don't know how to get down. There isn't anything to grab hold of."

Pachir tuya'arah, "'Otsirech. Awirik ten. Wech'en ten. Ma' bik inwaantikech. Ma' bik inweensikech."

Then (the armadillo) said, "You poor thing. You see me. I'm an armadillo. I don't know how to help you. I don't know how to bring you down."

Bay.

Okay.

Pachir tari(h) ts'u'ts'u'. Tari(h) ts'u'ts'u', tuya'arah, "Ten he' inweensikech! Ten inweensikech."

Then a coatimundi came. The coatimundi came and said, "I will bring you down! I (will) bring you down."

Nukuch winik tuya'arah, "Hach tuhahir? He' aweensiken?"

The ancestor said, "Really? You will bring me down?"

"He' inweensikech." Tuya'arah, "He' inweensikech."

"I will bring you down." He said, "I will bring you down."

Bay.

Okay.

Pachir tari(h) tunse(r). Tari(h) tunse(r). "Ba'inkin awak'tik?"

Then a pileated woodpecker came. The woodpecker came. "Why are you crying?"

"Awirik, tutusahen Want'ut'k'in. Tutusahen. Tuya'arah yan kab. Mäna' kab. Bähe' tuna'asahen, ma' bik inweeme(r). Mäna' bik inchukik inbäh bik ti' inweeme(r). Ne ma' tsoy che' ti' (in)weeme(r). Ne ka'ana(n) che'. Ma' bik inweeme(r)."

"You see, Want'ut'k'in lied to me. He lied to me. He said there was honey. There wasn't any honey. He lured me up, and now I can't get down. There isn't anything for me to grab on to so I can get down. This is a bad tree to get down from. It's a very tall tree. I don't know how to get down."

"Bay," tuya'arah ahtunse(r). "He' inweensikech. He inweensikech. Pero yan incho(k')k'aatik chichin ubo'orir ti' inweensikech."

"Okay," said the woodpecker. "I will get you down. I will get you down. But I have to ask for a little compensation for getting you down."

Tuya'arah nukuch winik, "Wa he' aweensiken?"

The ancestor said, "Is it true that you can get me down?"

"'Uts yan be'."

"It'll be all right," (says the woodpecker).

"Awoher ba'i(n)k(in) kak'a'tik he' ints'ahik tech."

"(If) you know what you want, I will give it to you," (says the ancestor).

Ts'uts'u' tuya'arah ti', "Bexir ten! Ba'i(n)ki(n) achäkbo'otiken, wa achäk-ts'ahik ba'(ar) ten, ats'ahik ten när. Achäkts'(ah)ik ba'(ar) ten, he' inwee(n) sikech."

The coatimundi said, "The same goes for me! What(ever) you give me in return, if you give me anything, you give me maize. You give me a little something (and) I will bring you down."

Ne tsoy uyor nukuch winik. Ka'(ah) tuyu'yah tuya'arah ti', ne tsoy uyor.

The ancestor is heartened. When he heard what he said to him, he is heartened.

Bay.

Okay.

Tuya'arah ts'uts'u', "He' inweensikech."

The coatimundi said, "I will get you down."

Tukat(ah?) uyor yete(r) tunser. Tu(ya'arah) ti' tunser, "Tech hach'ik uhoo(r). Tech kabähik uhoor y ten kinbin inna'ak(ar) inweenseh. Kintaasik upimen inboho'. Kinna'ak(ar) inweenseh nukuch winik; tech kabähik."

He and the woodpecker agreed. He said to the woodpecker, "You peck holes. You're going to punch in holes and I'm going to climb up to bring him down. I will bring along my many brothers.[8] I'm going to bring the ancestor down; you're going to punch in (the holes).

Bay.

Okay.

Pachir k'uchi(h) t(i') up'isir k'inir, bix ka'(ah) tuna'asah a' nukuch winik ahWant'ut'k'in, (ku)k'uchur t(i') up'iis ne to'an k'in. Ka'(ah) k'uchih ahWant'ut'k'in tan utar upax. Ya(n) 'oxkur uwitsi(r), oxp'er wits ti' utar upax. [Ne k'a'am upax utar uhum upax k'a'am. K'a'am kupax, tak ahWant'ut'k'in.]

Then Want'ut'k'in arrived at precisely the same time when he (had lured) the ancestor (up the tree). When Want'ut'k'in arrived he was playing his guitar. (The sound) of his guitar came from three mountain ranges away. [The sound of his guitar is very loud. Want'ut'k'in plays loudly when he comes.]

Nukuch winik ne sahak. Ne haak' uyor, "'Utse(reh). Bähe' tint'an bin uchi'eh(e)n ahWant'ut'k'in wa ma' tuyees(ah)en seeb." "Eesen, seeb!" tuya'arah ti'. Ahnukuch winik tuya'arah ti' ahts'uts'u', "Eesen, seeb!"

The ancestor is very afraid. He is terrified, *"Oh no. Now Want'ut'k'in is going to eat me, if they don't lower me down quickly."* "Bring me down, quick!" he said to them. The ancestor said to the coatimundi, "Bring me down, quick!"

Tuya'arah ahts'uts'u', "Ma' bik inweens(i)ke(ch) seeb. Tan uyanbähik ahtunse(r). Tan uya(n)bähik uhoor t(i'?) inchuk(ik) inbäh t(i') inweensikech."

The coatimundi said to him, "I don't know how to bring you down quickly. The woodpecker (has to) punch in holes in first. He is punching in holes for me to grab to lower you down."

Bay. Tuya'arah ahts'uts'u', "Ma' tukrik abäh. Ten kinkänäntikech. Ten kinbin inkärän tech."

Okay. The coatimundi said, "Don't worry. I'll take care of you."

Bay.

Okay.

Tan umasxok'or upax. Tan uyu'yik tan umasxok'or upax. Ma' ne samtar tan umasxok'or upax. Hach winik tan utukrik ubah, "'Utse(re)h. Ma' het la'eh. Tint'an (u)bin uchi'ehen."

The (sound of the) guitar is closer. He hears the guitar (coming) closer. Soon the guitar is even closer. The ancestor is thinking, *"Oh no. It's no use. I think he's going to eat me."*

Pachir, tan uyu'yik upek'. Upek', awirik upek'. Lati' upek', barum upek'.
Barum upek'. Tan uyu'yik utar upek; tan utar uk'ey(ah) upek'. Pero k'ey(ah)
upek' lati' uhum uyawat ahbarum, uyawat barum. Tan uxok'or, *maaas*
xok'or.

Then, he hears his dogs. He sees his dogs. Those dogs are jaguars. His dogs
are jaguars. He hears the dogs coming; the barking of the dogs is coming.
But the barking of the dogs is the sound of jaguars roaring, the roaring of
jaguars. It is getting close, *muuuch* closer.

Entonces,

And then,

tan uk'uchur ti' ta' toh k'uchi(h) tu' tuna'asah nukuch winik. K'uchi(h)
Want'ut'k'in. Tuna'akar tu' tuna'asah ahnukuch winik yok'or nukuch che',
tu' tuna'asah yok'or yahah che'. Ne yoher ahWant'ut'k'in tu' tuna'asah.

he is approaching (the base of the tree), right where he (had) lured the ancestor up. Want'ut'k'in (has) arrived and is (now) climbing up the great big
tree (to) where he (had) lured the ancestor. Want'ut'k'in knows where he
(had) lured him.

"*Eh, way k'uchen bähe', tanah. Bähe' k'uchen. Lahih kinbin inkinseh. Lahi(h)*
inwo'och, lahi(h) kinbin inhanteh. Lahi(h) kinbin (in)chi'eh unukuch winik. Tin-
tusahah."

(As he approaches, Want'ut'k'in is thinking,) "*Eh, here I have arrived, now.*
Now I (have) arrived. I'm going to kill him. He is my food, (and) I'm going to eat
him. I'm going to eat the ancestor. I deceived him."

Bay.

Okay.

Pachir k'uch(ih) upek', bey yahk'uchi(h) hohxim(b)a(r) kutar ahbarum. Lahi(h) uhohxim(b)a(r) kutar upek'. Hohxim(b)a(r) kutar ahbarum. K'uchi(h) ahbarum.

Then the dogs arrived; walking with their heads bent to the ground, the jaguars come. These dogs come walking with heads bent to the ground. The jaguars come walking with their heads bent to the ground. The jaguars arrived.[9]

Na'aki(h) ts'uts'u'. Seeb na'aki(h) ts'uts'u'. Na'aki(h) yok'or k'ä'täk che'. Na'aki(h) huntuur yok'or k'ä'che'. Huntuur bini(h) yok'or k'ä(')täk che'— nen pim lahna'aki(h) ahts'uts'u' tuworor

The coatimundis climbed up. The coatimundis scampered up. They climbed up the branches. Another one climbed up the branches. Others went (up) the branches—(there were) many coatimundis climb(ing) up everywhere.

Ne ts'ik ahts'uts'u'. Kume(n)tik, "MAMAMAMAK."

The coatimundis are defiant. They (go), "MAMAMAMAK."

Ne ts'ik ahts'uts'u'. Uyäräk pek' ne ts'ik barum. Ne poch uchi'ik ahts'uts'u'. Pero, ahts'uts'u' nen pim, ma' bik uchi'ik ahts'uts'u'. Nen pim.

The coatimundis are defiant. The pet dogs are (really) ferocious jaguars. They really want to eat the coatimundis. But the coatimundis are so many that they don't know how to eat them. There are too many coatimundis.[10]

Entonces, ts'uts'u' tan uya'arik ti' ahtunse(r), "Ts'aheh, abähik t(i') useebtar, t(i') useeb(tar) t(i') inweensik nukuch winik."

And then, the coatimundis are telling the woodpecker, "Give it, punch in (those holes), faster, faster, so I can bring down the ancestor quickly."

Uya'arik, "Hanch'ukteh ti'!" (u)ya'arik ahtunse(r). "Hanch'ukteh ten. Tan inhanbähik. Nen pim; pero ma' ukuch inmuk' ne seeb."

"Just wait!" says the woodpecker. "Wait for me! I'm hammering it as quickly as I can. (The bark) is very dense; I'm not strong enough to go that fast."

Bay.

Okay.

Bin uyäräk pek' Want'ut'k'in t(i') una'ak(ar) ukinsik ahts'uts'u'. Tupur(ah) ubäh ahbarum t(i') uchi'ik. Ne yoher ahts'uts'u': tupur(ah) ubäh ti' xatik uk'o'och. Tuxatah uk'o'och.

The pet dogs of Want'ut'k'in are climbing up to kill the coatimundis. A jaguar jump(s) up to bite them. The coatimundis know (what to do): they jump out and cut its throat. They cut its throat.[11]

Bay.

Okay.

Cheeri(h) uyäräk barum. Cheeri(h).

The pet jaguar dropped. It dropped.

Kutar huntuur barum, tuch'a'ah, utim. Ahts'uts'u' ne uyoher. Tuxatah. Uher huntuur uk'a't uhanah — HÄT.

Another jaguar comes, he seized (a coatimundi), (but) it springs (out of the way). The coatimundi knows (what to do). He cut him. (Then) another one wants to eat him — CHOP.

Cheeri(h).

It dropped (too).

Bay.

Okay.

Ahts'uts'u' tuya'arah, "Awirik, ten ma' ts'ektiken. Ten ne t'a'hen, ne pimen."

The coatimundi said, "You see, you can't reduce me.[12] I am tireless (because) I am many."

Cheeri(h) ahbarum. Ka't(uu)ro' tukinsah. Ne ts'ik ahWant'ut'k'in. Awirik, ne ts'ik. Ne ma' tsoy uyor ahWant'ut'k'in, "Bik yanir talahkinsah? Ne ma' tsoye'ex tech—tech kalaheensik nukuch winik—ten inwo'och. Ten tinya(h)'ir(ah) uya(h)chuni(n)."

The jaguars dropped. (The coatimundis) (had) killed two. Want'ut'k'in is furious. You see, he is furious. Want'ut'k'in rants, "Why did you kill them all? You are wicked—you are lowering the ancestor—he's my food. I am the one who saw him first."

Pachir, tuya'arah ahts'uts'u', "Ten inwirik, ma' awo'och. He' hach winik. Lati' nukuch winik. Awirik, ma' bäk'. Ma' bäk'.

Then, the coatimundi said, "I see he's not your food. This is a man. He is an ancestor. You see, he is not meat. He is not meat.

Wa bäk', inwoher awo'och. Pero a' he' ma' bäk'."

If he were meat, I know it would be your food. But this here is not meat."

"Mäna'! Ten tinwirah. Ten tinna'asah. Ten tintusah."

"Doesn't matter! I saw him. I lured him up. I deceived him."

"Tech tatusah? Tech ne ma' tsoy tame(n)tah. Ten awirik, yan inwaantik. 'Otsir inwirik. Ma' inkä(rä)xme(n)tik."

(The coatimundi says,) "You deceived him? You are wicked because of what you did. I (saw) him and I (had) to help him. I (felt) sorry for him. I (didn't) harm him."

Bay.

Okay.

Tunse(r) tan uts'ahik ubähik uhoor t(i) useebtar t(i') uyeensik nukuch winik.

(Meanwhile) the woodpecker is hammering holes so that (the coatimundis) can bring down the ancestor faster.

Ne ts'ik. Ne ts'iik ahWant'ut'k'in. Uya'arik, "Bähe' tech, ma' tun inchi'(i)ke'ex, tan inkinsikech."

Want'ut'k'in is furious. He says, "Now as for you, I'm not going to eat you, I'm going to kill you."

Yan umaska'. Yan tan upäxik utambor t(i') uchi'ik. Ne tsoy utambor; t(an) upäxik ti' uyu'yik ne tsoy uk'aay.[13]

He has his machete. He must play his drum, so he can eat them. His drum is rousing; he plays it because he likes the melody.

Lati' uya'arik, "Ten yanir."

He says, "He's mine."

"Ma'," tuya'arik lati' ahts'uts'u'. Uya'arik, "Tech, ma' tech yanir. Ma' tech yanir. Lati' ma', ma' bäk'."

"No," the coatimundi says. "He's not yours. He's not yours. He is not meat."

Na'aki(h) tuch'a'ah umaska'. "Ma' ak'a't inkinseh? Inkinsikech tech. Päytan tech kinya(h)kinsikech."

He climbed up and grabbed the machete. (Want'ut'k'in says,) "Don't you want me to kill him? I (will) kill you. First I will kill you."

"Bay!" uya'arik ts'uts'u'. "Kinseh ten. Ten aya(h)kinsiken. Inya(h)chuni(n) ten kakinsiken."

"Fine!" says the coatimundi. "Kill me. You kill me first. I (will be) the first you kill."

Bini(h) ts'uts'u'. Na'aki ka'ana(n), mas ka'ana(n) chichin.

The coatimundi went. He climbed high, then a little higher.

Tuyirah tan uk'uchur ahWant'ut'k'in. Tupur(ah) ubah, tuch'a'ah umaska' ti'
uch'äkik. Tupur(ah) ubah ts'uts'u', tuxat(ah) uche'(ir) ukaar uk'o'och. Tuxatah uk'o'och. Luubi(h) ahWant'ut'k'in.

He saw Want'ut'k'in coming. He jumped up, (the coatimundi) seized his
machete to chop him. The coatimundi jumped up to cut his throat. He cut
his throat. Want'ut'k'in fell.

Bay. Cheerih. Cheeri(h) ahWant'ut'k'in.

Okay. He fell. Want'ut'k'in fell.

Tuya'arah ti' nukuch winik, "Bähe', Want'ut'k'in, ne ma' paatih. 'A'arateh,
ts'ikba(r)teh abäho' ma' awa'arik ti'. Utusah ti' Want'ut'k'in. Yan awu'yik
uya'arah ti', 'Na'asen. Ne yan kab.' Utusikech. Ma', ma' acha'ik ut'u'ur. Ma',
ma' ach'a'ik ut'an. Ha'ri' ti' ukinsikech."

He (the coatimundi) said to the ancestor, "Now, Want'ut'k'in is really bad.
Tell every one of your companions not to talk to him. They are being lied to
by Want'ut'k'in. You (will) hear him say, 'Climb up. There is a lot of honey.'
He's lying to you. Don't, don't let him follow (you). Don't, don't fall for his
words. He's just going to kill you."

"Eh hah." Ne tsoy uyor nukuch winik. Tuya'arah, "Eh bay. Tuhahir."

"Ah, yes." The ancestor is glad. He said, "All right. That's how it is."

Na'aki(h). Tuya'arah tunser, "Bähe' ts'o'ok inbähik."

(The coatimundi) climbed up. The woodpecker said, "I finished hammering, now."

"Bay." Na'aki(h) ts'uts'u'. Ts'o'okih tuchuk(ah) ubäh to'an ubähban ahtunse(r). Tan uhoor tuchukah tulahbut'ah uk'ä'. Huntuur na'aki(h). Tulahsin(i)kah ubäh ts'uts'u', tulaka(h) k'uchi(h) yok'or nukuch k'ä'che'.

"Okay." The coatimundi climbed up. (When) it was finished, he inserted himself where the woodpecker had hammered. There are holes (where) he inserted his paws. Another one climbed up. All the coatimundis arrived and stretched themselves out along the large tree branch.

Bay.

Okay.

Tuya'arah ti' nukuch winik, "Tech kachuk' abäh ti', t(i') chara('an) ti' inpach. Taweeme(r) ki' ts'aab aweeme(r) y achuk'ik abah yok'or inneeh, t(i') uma' sipi(k)k'äb abah."

(The first coatimundi) said to the ancestor, "You will position yourself there, lying on my flank. You are (going to) descend nice and slow, you position yourself holding on to my tail so that you don't slip."

"Bay."

"Okay," (says the ancestor).

"Ten kinchukikech, tech kaka'chuk' abah."

"I will position you, and you will reposition yourself."

Tan uchuk(ik) ubäh nukuch winik, 'eensah. Tulaka(h) 'eemi(h).

The ancestor is getting into position, (they) lowered him down. They separated (themselves) and descended.

Ka'(ah) eemi(h), ka('ah) tuya'arah ti', "Bay. Tuhahir, tech taweensahen. 'Otsi(r)ech. Ne pim bäk'. Tuhahir, 'otsir. . . . Ma' uyeensiken, porque ma' una'akahan, ma' bik una'akar yok'or nukuch k'ä'che' ti'. Tech yok'or k'ä'che' kana'aka(r)."

When he descended then he said to them, "Okay. It's true, you lowered me down. You poor things. There (were) many animals. It's true, poor things. ...They (didn't) bring me down, because they don't climb, they don't climb up the big branches. (But) you (were already) high up in the branches."

Bay.

Okay.

"Ne tsoy," tuya'arah ts'uts'u'. "Bähe', yan awirik awähwaar. Awirik he', uyär-äk' pek'. Barum, ma' pek'. (A)wirik, wa ma' taren, wa ma' (t)inyähi(rah)ech, tuchi'ahech. 'Otsir. Bähe' kabin atsikba(r)teh abäho'; kawarik t(i') abäho'e'ex keh ukäräntik ubäh, ma' uch'e'ik(?) utus ahWant'ut'k'in. Want'ut'k'in ne ma' tsoy. Orak ne tak uchi'(i)kech. Pero ten tinweensahech.

"Very good," said the coatimundi. "Now, you have to look at your attackers. You see them here, the pet dogs? They are jaguars, not dogs. You see, if I (hadn't) come along, if I (hadn't) seen you first, (they) (would have) eaten you. You poor thing. Now, you are going to tell your companions; you will say to your companions that they better take care (and) not to fall for Want'ut'k'in's lies. Want'ut'k'in is evil. He almost (ate) you. But I brought you down."

Tuk'a'tah ti', "Tech ba'inkin ak'a't?" tuk'a'tah ti' ahts'uts'u'.

(The ancestor) asked him, "What do you want?" he asked the coatimundi.

Ts'uts'u' tuya'arah, "Ten, ats'ahik ten när. Wa päk'ik ten yok'or koor, lati' ten, lati' ubo'orir ti' ten. Ne tsoy inwor. Tech aka'sut asi(h)ik ten ba'a(r), när."

The coatimundi said, "For me, you give me maize. If you sow it for me in your milpa, that will be my compensation. I (would be) happy. What you give me in return is maize."

"Bay," tuya'arah nukuch winik. "Y bik ak'a't när? Inhakik, wa ma' si(h)ik inhakik?"

"Okay!" said the ancestor. "And how do you want the maize? Do I strip it or not?"

Tuya'arah, "Ma' si(h)ik ahak'ik. Ten inwoher bik inhantik. Inwoher bik in-xupik yok'or korir."

He said, "Don't strip it. I know how to eat it. I know how to eat it up in the milpa."

Bay.

Okay.

Ne tsoy uyor. Tuts'ah(ah) ti' ts'uts'u'. "He' tech akor."

He is very happy. He gave it to the coatimundi. "This here is your milpa."

Yet(er) tuk'aatah, "Tech tunser! Tech, ba'ikin ak'a't?"

He asked (the woodpecker), "And you, woodpecker! What do you want?"

Tuya'arah ti', "Ten, akäxtik kab. Tech akäxtik kab ten. Ma' si(h)ik ach'äkik. Ma' si(h)ik ana'ak(ar) ach'äkeh. Ten inwoher bik inch'a'ik inbähi(r). Inwo-her bik inch'äkik yet(er) inwinik. Tuworor boona xi('i)ken. Inwoher bik in-harik kab."

He said to him, "For me, you look for honey. You look for honey for me. Don't cut it down. Don't climb up and cut it down. I know how to get it myself. I know how to cut it down with my people. There are many that go with me. I know how to remove honey."

"Bay. Ne tsoy." Nukuch winik tuya'arah, "Ten inbin inkäxtik."

"Okay. Very good." The ancestor said, "I'm going to look for it."

"Mee(n)teh ba'che', mee(n)teh ma'ats', mee(n)teh tuworor ba'(ar), muk xibir wah, mee(n)teh ti' ats'o'oksik ti'. Want'ut'k'in ukäräxme(n)tikech. Ne ma' tsoy."

"Make (offerings of) balche', make posol, make everything, baked tamales, make them so you put an end to him. Want'ut'k'in harms you. He is evil."

Bay.

Okay.

[Back in his village the ancestor tells his story.]

"A ver ne ma' tsoy, yan kutusah Want'ut'k'in." Bex tuya'arah ka'ah 'u'rih. Tutsikbartah ti' ubäho'. "Awirik ten ne tak ukinsiken Want'ut'k'in. Lati' uyirik p'isir Yum K'aax ke lahi(h) kukäräntik k'aax. Ne tak tukinsahen. Mix inwoher. Tinwirah p'is inbohobir, pero ma' inbäho'. Lati' ne tak tukinsahen. Ne tak tuts'ahah ten. Bähe' wa (a)bin, ma' (a)cha'ik utusikech. Want'ut'k'in, lati' ti' yan yok'or k'aax."

"You see that Want'ut'k'in is evil, he lies." This is what he said when he came home. He said to his companions, "Look at me, Want'ut'k'in nearly killed me. He looks like Yum K'aax,[14] the one that guards the forest. He nearly killed me. I don't know who he is. I saw that he resembled my companions, but he is not (one of) my companions. He nearly killed me. He nearly gave it to me. Now when you go, don't let him lie to you. Want'ut'k'in is there in the forest."

P'ikbir Ts'on yeter Kisin 'The Rifle and Kisin'

Säk Ho'or

This story recounts a contest between the rifle and the bow and arrow to kill the devil. Reflecting the advance of technology in the history of the Lacandones, the rifle wins.

Firearms were introduced to the Lacandones late in their history. First they acquired old Spanish muzzleloaders. Later, at the beginning of the twentieth century, they adopted the .22 caliber rifle (Tozzer [1907] 1978, 54). They acquired the bow and arrow relatively late also, which was possibly introduced by Mexican mercenaries from Tabasco in AD 1283 (Coe 1993, 156). Although they preferred to use rifles, the Lacandones continued to use the bow and arrow until the middle of the twentieth century. Today Lacandones still make the bow and arrow, but only for tourists. No one in the community uses them for game, and very few are even adept at using them.

Bay. Ten kinbin intsikba(r)teh bähe' p'ikbir ts'on yeter Kisin.

Okay. I'm going to tell the story now about the rifle and Kisin 'the Devil'.

Bay.

Okay.

Tutsikba(r)tah uchik, tuya'arah uchik nukuch winik ukuch(i)k uts'on. Yan uts'on nukuch winik.

They recounted it, they said that the ancestor carries his rifle. The ancestor has a rifle.

Bay.

Okay.

Nukuch winik oki(h) t(i) uta'. Bini(h) t(i') uber. Ti' tucha(r)ki(n)t(ah) up'ik-bir ts'on.

The ancestor went to the toilet. He went down the path.[1] He laid down his rifle there.

Bay.

Okay.

Pachi(r) tari(h) Kisin. Tari(h) Kisin tuya'arah ti' ts'on, "Wa h(e') ats'ahik awi-nikir ti' ten, ints'ahik bäk' tech ne yaab. Wa he' ats'ahik awiniki(r), awirik tech, ma' ukinsik bäk', mix ba'(ar) kume(n)tik tech. Mix ukinsik."

Later, Kisin came along. Kisin came along and he said to the rifle, "If you give me your owner, I (will) give you plenty of meat. Perhaps you should surrender your owner, (because) you see, he doesn't kill game for you, he doesn't do anything for you. He doesn't kill anything."

Bay.

Okay.

Nukuch winik tan uyu'yik ut'an Kisin. Tan uyu'yik ut'an yete(r) ts'on.

The ancestor overhears what Kisin is saying. He is listening to what he is saying to the rifle.

Bay.

Okay.

Uya'arik ts'on, "Ma'. Ma' ink'ubik inwinikir."

The rifle says, "No. I won't hand over my owner."

"Ma'! Ats'ah ten awin(i)ki(r)! Ts'aah ten awin(i)ki(r). Awirik awin(i)ki(r), mäna' mix ba'(ar) kume(n)tik awin(i)ki(r) tech. Awirik tech mix kakinsik bäk'; ma' uts'ah(i)k uchi'(i)k bäk'. Ma'."

"No! You give me your owner! Give me your owner. You see that your owner can't do anything for you. You see that you don't kill any game; he doesn't give (you) any meat to eat. No."

Bay.

Okay.

Ts'on uya'arik, "Ten ma' ints'ah(i)k inwin(i)ki(r), tumen awirik inwin(i)ki(r) ne 'otsi(r) (in)wirik. Lati' ukinsik inwo'och bäk'. Ukinsik. Lati' kuts'onik yete(r) ten. Lati' kuts'onik inwo'och bäk'. Lati' kukinsik bäk'. Ne tsoy inwor ti' nukuch winik. Ten ma' ints'(ah)ik inwin(i)ki(r). Ne 'otsi(r) inwirik inwin(i)ki(r) ten."

The rifle says, "I (won't) give up my owner, because, you see, I love my owner very much. He kills my meat. He kills it. He shoots with me. He shoots my meat. He kills game. I am very content with the ancestor. I'm not giving up my owner. I care about him very much."

Bay.

Okay.

Kisin tan uya'arik, "Ma' ats'(ahi)k awiniki(r) ten? Ats'ahik awiniki(r) ten!"

Kisin says, "You won't give your owner to me? You give your owner to me!"

"Ma'. Ma' ints'(ah)ik, ma' ints'(ah)ik tech."

"No. I won't give him up, I won't give him to you."

"Bay. Ma' ats'(ah)ik awin(i)ki(r)."

"Fine. You won't give up your owner."

"Ma'. Ma' ints'(ah)ik inwin(i)ki(r)."

"No. I won't give up my owner."

"Ma' ats'(ah)ik awin(i)ki(r). Bay. Ten inhi'tikech ti' inwit. Inhi'tikech ti' inwit. Mix ba'(ar) kahari(k) tech, mix chich amuuk'."

"You will not give up your owner. Fine. I (am going to) rub you on my rear end. I (am going to) rub you on my rear end. (Then) you won't (be able to) take out anything, (because) you (won't) have any strength."

Bay.

Okay.

Ts'on uya'arik ts'on, "Ten ma' ints'(ah)ik in winiki(r). Ten ma' ints'(ah)ik in win(i)ki(r). Ne 'otsi(r) inwirik inwin(i)ki(r). Lati' ukinsik inwo'och bäk'. Lati' uts'onik inwo'och bäk'. Inhana(n) yet(er) inwin(i)kir y ne tsoy inwor ti' ten inwin(i)ki(r). Yan inkäräntik inwin(i)kir."

The rifle says, "I am not giving up my owner. I am not giving up my owner. I care very much for my owner. He kills my meat. He shoots my meat. I eat with my owner, and I'm very content with my owner. I have to protect my owner."

"Ma'," Kisin.

"No," (says) Kisin.

Ts'ik chichin Kisin ma' uk'a't uk'ubik uwin(i)kir.

Kisin is annoyed that it doesn't want to hand over its owner.

Kisin tan uya'arik ti' ts'on, "Mix tech mänä' ba'(ar) kahari(k) tech, awirik.

Kisin says to the rifle, "You don't take out anything, you see.

Mix ba'(ar) kaharik tech. Awirik tech mänä'. Inchukech, inhi'tik (ti' in)wit, mix k'äs ba'(ar) kaharik."

You don't take out anything. You (will) see, there (will be) nothing for you. I (will) seize you (and) I (will) rub (you) on my rear end, (then) you (won't) take out a thing."

Ts'on, tunuukah ts'on, "Ah! Ten awa'arik ten mänä' ba'(ar) kinharik?"

The rifle replied, "Ah! You're telling me that I won't take anything out?"

Bay.

Okay.

Nukuch winik tan uch'e'extik uyu'yik utsikbar.[2]

The ancestor is crouching down listening to them talk.

Uts'on tan utsikbar, "Bay, ten tawa'arah, 'Miiix, mix ba'(ar) k(a)harik tech wa inchukech y chahi'tik(ech) (ti') inwit. Miiix ba'(ar) kaharik tech. Mänä' käs ba'(ar) kahari(k) tech'. Yuuts' tech.' Bay!" ts'on tuya'arah. "Xen tech. Abin k'äs naach abin. Mas naach abin, aktuntik. Si ma' tints'onahech o mix ba'(ar) tinme(n)tah ti' tech, tsoy ink'ubik inwin(i)ki(r) ti' tech. Achukik inba'(ar). Si ma' tachuk(ah) uba'(ar) ints'on, ma' tataasah ten uba'(ar) tech, ma' ink'ubik inwin(i)ki(r)."

The rifle is saying, "Okay, you said to me, 'You won't take aaanything out if I seize you and rub (you) (on my) rear end. You (won't) take out anything. You (won't) take out much of anything. You (will) smell bad.' Fine!" the rifle said. "Go on. You go a little farther away. (When) you (have) (gone) a little farther away, we (will) try it. If I don't shoot you or do anything to you, (then) I (will) hand over my owner to you. You catch my bullet. If you

(don't) catch my bullet, (if) you don't bring me the bullet, (then) I (won't)
hand over my owner."

"Bay," Kisin tuya'arah. "Tsoy. Aktuntik. Ne tsoy. Aktuntik."
"Okay," Kisin said. "Good. Let's try it. Very good. Let's try it."

Bay.
Okay.

Ts'on, uya'arik ts'on ti' Kisin, "Tsoy. Xen abin man. Yan mas naach abin.
M-a-a-a-s naach. Ne xok'or. Le' k'in (in)kinsikech."
The rifle says to Kisin, "Okay. Move away. You have to go farther away. F-a-
a-a-rther. You're too close. This is the day I kill you."

Bay.
Okay.

Mas naach binih. Binih k'äs naach.
Kisin went farther away. He went a little bit farther.

Bay.
Okay.

"Eh bis(eh) abäh, Kisin," tuya'arah (ah)ts'on. "Bis(eh) abäh, Kisin."
"Eh, get ready, Kisin," said the rifle. "Get ready, Kisin."

Bay.
Okay.

Kisin tubisah ubäh. Ne tsoy uyor Kisin. Ubisik ubäh, *"Bay, bähe' tint'an ten yan(ir) uwin(i)ki(r). (Ku)k'ubik ten. Yan inchukik. Yan inki'irik uba'(ar) ts'on utar. Yan inchukik."*

Kisin readied himself. Kisin is excited. He readies himself, *"Okay, now I think his owner (will be) mine. He (will) give him to me. I have to grab it. I have to concentrate on the bullet coming. I have to grab it."*

Bay.

Okay.

"Chukeh ten. Taas(eh) uba'(ar)!"

"Catch it for me. Bring the bullet!" (says the rifle).

Bay.

Okay.

Ne tsoy uyor lati' Kisin.

Kisin is gleeful.

Bay.

Okay.

Ts'on lati' ts'on ti' cha(ra)'(an). Tuhuni(n) t'aabih ts'on. Ka'(ah) tuyu'yah t'a'ba(r) ts'on. *Puuxxxuw.* Mix ba'(ar). Kisin, lubi(h) Kisin; bich'a' Kisin.

The rifle is lying there. The rifle went off on its own. When he heard the rifle go off. *Puuxxxuw.* Nothing (he didn't see it). Kisin fell; Kisin is knocked down.

Tan uya'arik ts'on, "Taas(eh) uba'(ar) ten, tan. Taas(eh) uba'(ar). E'es(eh) in-wir(ik) uba'(ar), wa tachuk(ah) uba'(ar)."

The rifle is saying, "Now, bring me the bullet. Bring the bullet. Show me if you caught the bullet."

Kisin mix tuchuk(ah) uba'(ar). Kisin, lah'eer(ih) utso'otser Kisin. Lah'eer chichin Kisin.

Kisin didn't catch the bullet. Kisin's hair is all burned off. Kisin is singed all over.

[Ne chich umuk' uba'(ar) ts'on. Ma' tuyirah. P'iis k'ak' tari(h).]

[The bullet is strong. He didn't see it. It came like fire.]

"Taas(eh) uba'(ar) ten." Tan uya'arik lati' p'ikbir ts'on, "Taaseh ten."

"Bring me the bullet." The rifle is saying, "Bring it to me."

Mix (u)taasik Kisin. "Mäna' ten uba'(ar) ts'on. Ma' tinwirah tu' bini(h)."

Kisin doesn't bring it. "I don't have the bullet. I didn't see where it went."

"Taaseh ten!" Ts'on ts'ik. Tan uya'arik, "Taaseh ten! Taaseh ten wa ma' ints'(ah)ik inwin(i)ki(r) ten. Taaseh ten. Wa (a)taasteh ten, ints'(ah)ik inwin(i)ki(r)."

"Bring it to me!" The rifle is angry. He is saying, "Bring it to me! Bring it to me or I'm not going to hand over my owner. Bring it to me. If you bring it, I (will) hand over my owner."

"Ma'. Mäna'. Ma' tinwilah tu' bini(h) uba'(al). Ma', ma' tinchukah."

"No. There isn't any (bullet). I didn't see where it went. I didn't catch it."

"Bay. Ma' tawir(ah) uba'(ar). Ta(ra)k uher hump'er. Ta(ra)k a' wa."

"Okay. You didn't see the bullet. Another one is coming. It's coming."

Bay. Ts'on, tan uyirik lati' Kisin. Uka'ch'eti(k) uyireh Kisin tan ut'a'bar ts'on.

Okay. Kisin is looking at the rifle. Kisin twists around again to see the rifle reloading.

Yan uk'ak'i(r) ts'on, yan uk'ak'i(r) kuts'onpah uni'(?).

The rifle has fire, it flares (at the end of) the rifle when it fires.

Bay. Kisin, lati' t(an) usähta(r) Kisin.

Okay. Kisin is getting scared of it.

"Taaseh ten. Wa ma' (a)taasik, awirik kuka'ta(r) uher."

"Bring it to me. If you don't bring it, you (will) see another one come!"

Bay. Kisin lik'i(h). Bini(h) Kisin. Ma' tutaasah Kisin. Bini(h). Puts'i(h) Kisin. Tuk'ana(h) yok. Ne chichir ubin Kisin. 'Aaka(')rah. Puts'i(h).

Okay. Kisin got up. Kisin left. Kisin didn't bring it (the bullet). He left. Kisin fled. He sped away as hard he could. Kisin ran away. He fled.

Bay.

Okay.

Ts'on, mix upeek ts'on la'eh. Tuyirah lati' ts'on puts'i(h) Kisin. Ne tsoy uyor ts'on, "Awirik ten, ma' ints'(ah)ik inwin(i)ki(r)."

The rifle doesn't move. The rifle watched Kisin as he ran away. The rifle is pleased, "You see, I (won't) give (up) my owner."

Bay. Kisin bini(h). Bini(h) Kisin.

Okay. Kisin left. Kisin left.

Mix.

He had failed.

Bay. Nukuch winik tari(h), u'r(ih?) uyir(eh) uts'on. Tuyir(ah) uts'on tuworo(r) ts'on. *"Mix ba'(ar). Ne tsoy ts'on. Tuworo(r) ne uts uts'on."*

Okay. The ancestor came back to check his rifle. He looked the rifle over. (He muses) *"Nothing (is different). The rifle is fine. The rifle is all intact."*

Mix uba'(ar) uts'on uyirik tuworo(r). (U)harik uts'on uba'(ar). Ne ti' yan tuworo(r) ba'(ar).

He doesn't see anything amiss. He takes out the bullets. They are all there.

Lati' nukuch winik tuyu'yah ut'an (u)ts'on. Lati' nukuch winik ka'(ah) tuya'arah, ts'on kuxa'(a)n.

The ancestor (had) heard the rifle speak. When the ancestor heard it speak, the rifle was alive.

[Ts'on, yan aki'käräntik ats'on. Yan uwiniki(r) lati' ts'on. Uchik uya'arik kuxa'(a)n. Tuhahir. Kuxa'(a)n. Tuyu'y(ah) (u)t'an, tuyu'y(ah) (u)tsikbar. Y uts'on tuta'(a)kah uwin(i)kir.]

[You have to take good care of your rifle. It has its owner, that rifle. In the past, they (said) that it was alive. It's the truth. It was alive. (The ancestor) heard it speak, he heard the conversation. And the rifle (had) protected its owner.][3]

Kisin tan uk'aatik uwin(i)ki(r), "Ts'aah ten awin(i)ki(r). Ts'aaten! Ts'aaten! Awin(i)ki(r) ma' uts'(ah)ik tech ahanan ahbäk'. Ma' (u)ts'(ah)ik achi'(i)k bäk'. Mix ba'(ar) kuts'ahik. K'ubeh ten awin(i)ki(r)." Pero ts'on tuya'arah, "Ten ma' k'ubik inwiniki(r).

Kisin asks for its owner, "Give me your owner. Give him to me! Give him to me! Your owner doesn't give you any game to eat. He doesn't give you meat to eat. He doesn't give you anything. Hand over your owner to me." But the rifle said, "I will not hand over my owner."

Ahnukuch winik tuyu'yah; tuyirah mix, mix ts'on. Ne uts tuworor.
The ancestor heard this; he saw that nothing (had happened to his) rifle. Everything was fine.

Bay.
Okay.

Kisin ne k'aa(h) ti' uyor.
Kisin remembered.

Bay.
Okay.

Kisin tuyirah härär; tuyirah härär ti' uxana(n). Tuya'arah lati' härär, "Bay tech, ba'inki(r) ame(n)tik xanakech way?"
Kisin saw an arrow; he saw an arrow leaning (against a tree.) He said to the arrow, "Hey you, what are you doing leaning here?"

"Awirik, inkäräntik inwin(i)ki(r). Inch'uktik inwin(i)ki(r)."
"I'm guarding my owner. I'm waiting for my owner."

[P'isir ts'on, tuch'uktah win(i)ki(r).]
[Like the rifle, it waited for its owner.]

"Ten tan inkänäntik inwin(i)ki(r)."
"I am guarding my owner."

Bay. Ti' tan ukänäntah uwin(i)ki(r). Tan uch'uktik.

Okay. It's guarding its owner. It's waiting for him.

"Ten inkänäntik inwin(i)ki(r)."

"I'm guarding my owner."

"Ah hah. Tan akänäntik awin(i)ki(r). Wa (a)k'ubik ten awin(i)ki(r), ne tsoy inwor. Tech, awirik awinikir ma' uts'ahik ahanan bäk'. Ma' uts'ahik achi'(i)k bäk'. Mix ba'(ar)."

"Ah, yes. You're guarding your owner. If you hand over your owner to me, I would be very happy. You see your owner doesn't give you any meat to eat. He doesn't give you meat or anything to eat."

Bay.

Okay.

Härär uya'arik, "Ma', ma'. Ma' ints'(ah)ik inwin(i)ki(r) ten ne 'otsir (in)wirik inwin(i)ki(r). Lati' uts'(ah)ik inchi'(i)k bäk'. Ukinsik ba'intäk nukuch bäk'. Lati' ne ki' inhanan. Ne 'otsir inwirik inwin(i)ki(r). Ten ma' ints'(ah)ik ti' tech. Ma' ink'ubik inwin(i)ki(r). Ta(ra)k ak'aatik ti' ten, ma' ink'ubik."

The arrow said, "No, no. I (won't) give up my owner. I care very much for my owner. He gives me meat to eat. He kills all kinds of large game. This is what I like to eat. I care for my owner deeply. I (won't) give him to you. I (won't) hand over my owner. Although you ask me for him, I (won't) hand him over."

Bay.

Okay.

Kisin ne k'aah ti' (y)or bexi(r) tume(n)tah ti' ts'on. Ne tsoy uyor Kisin.

Kisin remembered what had happened with the rifle. Kisin is jubilant.

"Ak'ubik ten awin(i)ki(r). Wa ma' ak'ubik ten awin(i)ki(r), ele a(k)tuntik."

"You (are going to) hand over your owner. If you don't hand over your owner to me, then we (will) test who is superior."

Bay.

Okay.

Härär tuya'arah, "Aktuntik? Tsoy. Xen abin ti' ta'. Waay p'ehas ti' ta' la' xuu(r)."

The arrow said, "We are going to test it? Fine. Go over there. There is far enough."

Bay.

Okay.

Härär tuhurah. K(a'ah) tar(ih) (u)härär, tuchukah Kisin. "Awirik? Mix ba'(ar) kahari(k)."

The arrow shot (itself). When the arrow (came), Kisin caught it. "You see? You (can't) take out anything."

Pero härär tuya'arah, "Ma' ink'ub(i)k inwiniki(r). Taas(eh) ten inhuur. Uts yan! Ten ma' ink'ub(i)k inwiniki(r). Ma' ten mix ba'ar. Ta(ra)k ma' tachuk(ah) inhuur, ma' ink'ubik inwin(i)ki(r) tech."

But the arrow said, "I (won't) hand over my owner. Bring me my arrow. Forget it! I (won't) hand over my owner. (You won't get) anything from me. Even though you caught my arrow, I (won't) hand over my owner to you."

"Ma' ak'ub(i)k awin(i)ki(r)?! Ne tsoy. Ma' ak'a't ak'ubik awin(i)ki(r)? Uts yan?

"You (won't) hand over your owner?! Very well. You don't want to hand over your owner? Forget it?

Bay."

Okay."

Uhach winik nuki(r) winik ti' yan t(i) uber. Lati' tuyu'yah ut'an, "Eh!"

The ancestor is on the path. He overheard them talking, "Eh!"

Tuch'e'extah tuyu'yah utsikbar härär; tan ut'an härär, "Awirik, mäna' ma' ink'ubik inwinik(ir) tech, ta(ra)k tachukah inhärär. Tachukah. 'Uts yan! Inwin(i)ki(r) ma' ink'ubik tech; ne ki' inhana(n)."

He overheard the arrow saying, "You see, I (won't) hand over my owner, even though you caught my arrow. You caught it. Forget it! I (won't) hand over my owner; I eat well."

Bay.

Okay.

Tuchukah (ah)Kisin. Tuchukah härär Kisin, tuhi'tah t(i') uyit. Tulahhi'tah t(i') utisah uyit yete(r) härär.

Kisin caught it. Kisin caught the arrow, (and) he rubbed it on his rear end. He rubbed it all over and dried his rear end with the arrow.

'Otsi(r) härär.

The poor arrow.

Tuxonkintah härär.

He stood the arrow against (the tree).

Härär tan ut'an, "Ten ma' ink'ubik inwin(i)ki(r). Tarak ame(n)tik ti' ten, ma' ink'ubik inwin(i)ki(r)."

The arrow is saying, "I (won't) give up my owner. Even though you do (that) to me, I (won't) hand over my owner."

Bay. Kisin bini(h).

Okay. Kisin left.

"Ma' k'a't ak'ubik awiniki(r). Tsoy. 'Uts yan."

"You don't want to hand over your owner. That's fine. Forget it."

Bini(h) Kisin.

Kisin left.

Bay.

Okay.

Hach winik tarih. (T)uyir(ah) uhärär. *"Ne tsoy, tuworor ne uts. Mix ba'(ar) tu-me(n)tah. Ne tsoy."*

The man came over. He looked over his arrow. (He muses,) *"Everything is fine. He didn't do anything (to it). It's fine."*

Bin uhureh uyo'och bäk'. Bin ukinsik uyo'och bäk' ma' uchukik uhuur.

He goes to shoot his game. He went to kill his game, (but) his shot misses.

'Otsi(r) (härär). Lati' ma' tsoy. Tukäräxme(n)tah u(härär) Kisin. Tarak uhur-ik ma' ukinsik bäk'. Tarak uhurik mix tah ubin.

The poor arrow. It isn't any good. Kisin (had) defiled the arrow. Although he shoots it, it doesn't kill (any) game. Although he shoots it, it doesn't go straight.

Bay.

Okay.

Hach winik tuya'arah, "Lati' härär mäna'. Ne tsoy härär ne tsoy, pero
. . . Ha'ri' (u)härär ma' tuk'ubah uwin(i)ki(r). Lati' ne tsoy. Ma' tuk'ubah
uwin(i)ki(r). Ne 'otsir uyirik uwin(i)ki(r). Tukänäntah uwin(i)ki(r). 'Ten inkänäntik inwiniki(r),' tuya'arah. 'Lati' uts'ahik ten bäk.'"

The man said, "This arrow (shoots), but it hasn't any (power). It's a good
arrow, a very good one, but . . . Only the arrow didn't give up its owner. That
one is good. It didn't give up its owner. It really cared about his owner. It
protected its owner. 'I am going to guard my owner,' it said. 'He gives me
meat.'"

Bay.

Okay.

Kisin bini(h). Ts'o'ok.

Kisin left. It's finished.[4]

Bay.

Okay.

Hach winik lati' tuya'arah tubäho', tutsikba(r)tah, "Awirik inhärär. Kuxa'(an)
härär. Härär yan uwin(i)ki(r). Härär tukänäntik ten. Ts'on tukänäntah ten.
Pero ints'on," tuya'arah, "ints'on mas ne chich umuuk' ts'on. A' ts'on uta('a)
kikech. Hach tuhahir.

That man said to his companions, he told them, "You see my arrow? The
arrow is alive. The arrow has its owner. The arrow looked out for me. The
rifle looked out for me. But my rifle," he said, "my rifle is stronger. The rifle
protects you. It's the truth.

Bin(ih) ich k'aax ts'on. Wa uyirik Kisin, saha(k) ti' ts'on. Ne chich ut'a'bar,
p'iis uhats'k'uh. Ne chich umuk'. Ne ne seeb—mix uyirik uba'(ar) ts'on."

The rifle went into the forest. When Kisin sees it, he is afraid of the rifle.

It ignites mightily, like lightning. It's powerful. It's very quick—one can't see its bullet.

Härär tuhahir tukäräxme(n)tah. 'Otsi(r) härär. Tukäräxme(n)tah. Härär ma' chich umuuk'. Ma' ukinsik Kisin. Ne seeb tuchukah."

As for the arrow, it's true that (Kisin) ruined it. The poor arrow. He ruined it. The arrow isn't strong. It doesn't kill Kisin. He promptly caught it."

"Eh tuhahir."

"Ah that's true," (says his companions).

[Bay. Tint'an taki(r) bähe' p'aati(h) (u)tsikabar. Taki(r) bähe' uya'arik uchik taki(r) bähe' ts'on o p'ikbir ts'on kuxa'an uwin(i)ki(r). Yan uwin(i)ki(r). Wa yan kinsah, awirik upeek ts'on. Uk'usik uba'(ar).

[Okay. I think that story has remained up to now. To this day, they say that the rifle, or shotgun, lives for its owner. It has its owner. If there is war, you (will) see the rifle move. It brings the bullet.

Eh, umaska', p'isi(r) maska', kupeek maska' lehi(h) uch'äkik ubäho' o kah wa yan ukinsah, upeek maska', *puxxx, puxxx*. Lati' upeeksik ubäh. Poch ukinsa'.

Eh, the machete, the same goes for the machete; when it moves it (is going to) cut companions or villagers. If there is a war, the machete moves, *swish, swish*. It moves itself. It wants to kill.

A' ts'on, poch ukinsa'. Lati', bähe', tuya'arah bähe' ts'on kuxa'an.]

The rifle wants to kill. Today they say that the rifle is alive.]

'Ayim yeter Chem 'The Crocodile and the Canoe'

Säk Ho'or

In this story an old crocodile teaches a brand-new canoe how to glide through the water.[1]

According to the Lacandones, the crocodile-teacher must be an old, weathered canoe, because of its rough, gray exterior, alluding to the wisdom and experience that comes with old age. Säk Ho'or's story evokes the connection between crocodiles and canoes expressed in ancient Mayan cosmology, in which the crocodile is associated with the ceiba tree. Apart from their similar appearance—both have bulging protuberances—the ceiba and the crocodile are associated with the earth, water, and renewal (see Freidel et al. 1993 and Schele and Villela n.d.). In Säk Ho'or's story the theme of renewal is expressed in the transference of power, wisdom, and experience from the old canoe-crocodile teacher to his young apprentice.

Bay. Uchik unuki(r) winik bex tuyiro'; tuyirah unuki(r) winik uchik. Tuya'arah uchik aknuki(r) winik, "Chem ne tum(b)en, ne tum(b)en chem ma' uyoher, ma' uyoher bik ubin yok'o(r) petha'. Mix uyoher bik ubin." Tuya'arah, "'Ayim chem. Lati' sukunbi(r) 'ayim. Lehi(h) sukunbi(r), chem le(hih) its'i(n)bi(r). Uka'ans(ik) uba'ab, bik ubin."

Okay. The ancestors saw it like this; the ancestors saw it formerly. Our ancestors said, "A brand-new canoe doesn't know how to travel in the lagoon. It doesn't know how to travel." They said, "The crocodile is a canoe. That crocodile is the older brother. He is the older brother and the canoe is the younger brother. (The crocodile) teaches (the canoe) how to paddle, how to travel."

Bay.

Okay.

'Ayim kuka'ansik. Leh(ih) kuka'ansik chem.

The crocodile teaches it. He teaches the canoe.

'Ayim tutsikbah aak'bir. Kuya'arik ti' chem, "Awirik" kih, "int'än yan akänik tech bik abin. Awirik ten bik inba'ab? Awirik ten bik inbin yok'o(r) ha', ne tsoy inpees(i)k ink'äb, ne tsoy inpeesik inwok tuworo(r)? Bay. Tech yan t(i') akänik. Bähe', int'än yan akäni(k) tech, tech ne tumech."

The crocodile talked (to the canoe) at night. He said to the canoe, "You see," he says, "I think you have to learn how to travel. You see how I paddle? You see how I go through the water, (how) well I move my hands, (how) well I move my feet, (how well I move) everything? Okay. You have to learn (how to do) it. Now, I think you have to learn it, (because) you are brand-new."

"Bay," chem tuya'arah. "Tsoy. Inkänik."

"Okay," the canoe said. "Good. I (will) learn it."

'Aak'be(r) kuka'ansah.

(The crocodile) teaches at night.

Bay.

Okay.

[Chem, ti' yan chem ne tum(b)en, be'in tuya'arah uchik, ch'upra(r) ma' tsoy una'aka(r); ma' tsoy (u)na'aka(r) ich chem ne tum(b)en ... (Wa) (kuy)okor na'aka(r), chem kubuhur. Kubuhu(r) chem.]

[(If) there is a brand-new canoe, as they said in the past, it's bad (if) a woman climbs in. It's bad for her to climb in, because the canoe is brand-new ... (If) a woman climbs in, the canoe (will) split in two. The canoe (will) split in two.]

Tuya'arah ti' (ah)'ayim, "Si wa ka'(ah) una'aka(r) ahch'uprar, kukäräxme(n) tikech. Ma' tsoy, ne kupeeksikech. Ne ma' tsoy.

The crocodile said to (the canoe), "If a woman climbs in she will wreak havoc on you, because she (will) move you about too much. That (would be) very bad.

Yan ka'bu(h)k'ä' k'in kuch'uktik. Ka'bu(h)k'ä' kutar hu(n)buh ok, ne tsoy una'akar."

A woman must wait ten days. After ten or fifteen days, it is all right (for her) to climb in."

Bay.

Okay.

Pachi(r), tuya'arah, "Awirik ten. Yan akänik."

Then, he said, "You watch me. You have to learn it."

Chem tuya'arah, "Ten its'in, ma' inwoher bik inbin."

The canoe said, "I am the younger brother, (so) I don't know how to travel."

"Yan ats'(ah)ik t(i') awin(i)ki(r) käy. Ats'ahik siih ti' käy. Yan t(i') ats'ahik ti' tuworor. Yan akänik."

"You have to give your owner fish. You give him a gift of fish. You have to give it all to him. You have to learn how (to travel)."

Bay.

Okay.

Bin utunteh. Tupee(k)sah ubäh 'aak'bir. Kubin chem, kubin t(i') uxim(b)a(r).

He went to try it. He moved himself at night. The canoe was going along, the canoe was going for a "stroll."

Ka('ah) tuya'arah 'ayim, "Yan akänik. Awirik bik inbin ten? Ne tah inbin."

Then the crocodile said to him, "You have to learn it. See how I go? I go very straight."

Pachi(r), ne tsoy ubin chem.

After that the canoe goes along very well.

(Tu)ya'arah, "Bay. Bähe' takänah. Ts'o(')okih bähe', awoher bik ame(n)tik abah. Awoher bik abin."

(The crocodile) said, "Okay. Now, you (have) learned it. You now know how to do it yourself. You know how to go."

Ahsaay 'The Leafcutter Ants'

Bor Ma'ax

This story recounts the time when the *ahsaay* 'the leafcutter ants' were constantly demolishing a farmer's corn stalks. He was so angry and desperate that he scuffed the path that they made to his field. One day he was confronted by the lord of the leaf-cuter ants, who asked him what the matter was. The farmer explained the situation and vowed to continue to erase their path. The lord of the leafcutter ants suggested that the farmer show the ants where his field was so that they could clear it for him (after the harvest). This way, he explained, they would all benefit. The farmer agreed, and the result was an abundance of corn.

Although the ants seem only interested in the leaves, in other Mayan myths of creation ants are given credit for the discovery of corn.[1] Echoing this belief, the Lacandones used to sow their corn in the anthills of leafcutter ants.

Nukuch winik ma' uyoher wa ahsaay ulahhantik unär ich (u)kor.
The ancestor doesn't know the leafcutter ants are eating all his corn in his cornfield.

Ne tsoy uyor äknukire'ex, tan upäk'ik unär. Ne kuxa'an unär.
Our ancestor is happy, as he is sowing his corn. The corn is really growing.

Mix uyoher wa yan naat'ar.
He doesn't know they have pincers.

Päytan, ahsaay oki(h) ich nah tu' äkan uyo'och när.
At first the leafcutter ants entered the corncrib where his corn is spread out.

Tu' kura'an uyo'och wah utar saay.
Along come the leafcutter ants to where his corn is standing.

Ne pim utar.
They come in droves.

Ulahhantik uyo'och wah.
They eat up his corn.

Wa uyirik ukoh när ulahkuchik ulahhantik.
If they see corn kernels they carry them off and eat them up.

Nukuch winik uch'a'ik uk'äbche' ule' che' ulah hi'ixtik ahsaay—BUH.
The ancestor seizes branches of leaves (and) whips the leafcutter ants—
BUH.

Ulahhi'ixtik.
He whips them all away.

"Xen saay! Ma' atar tech! Ma' atar tanah way. Tan alahhantik inwo'och!"
"Go away leafcutter ants! Do not come! Do not come here. You're eating all
my food!"

Uhi'ixtik—BUH—ich uber, uber ahsaay.
He whips them—BUH—in the road, the road of the leafcutter ants.

Mix, ahsaay mäna' uyu'yik t'an.
The leafcutter ants don't listen at all.

Okor ukah k'in utar.
They come in the early evening.

Uhantik.

They eat (the corn).

Uka' häts'ik—BUH.

He beats them again—BUH.

"Xen saay! Ma' atar akäräxme(n)tik inwo'och när. Awirik, mäna' inwo'och när, mäna'. Wi'ih inkah."

"Go away, leafcutter ants! Don't come wreck my corn. You see there isn't anything left of my corn. There isn't any left. I'm going to starve."

Mix. Ne pim ahsaay utar ukäräxme(n)tik uyo'och när.

It was no use. The leafcutter ants come in droves and wreck his corn.

Bay.

Okay.

Woror uhäts'ik uber. K'uchih tuk'in bini(h) ukarik ukoor äknukire'ex.

He beats all their paths. When the time came our ancestor went to clear his cornfield.

Bini(h) upäk'ik unär.

He went to sow his corn.

Woror bin ulahhantik ule' unär, be'iki(r) uhi'ixtik—BUH—t(i') uber ahsaay.

They all go eat up the leaves of his corn, and like before—BUH—he scuffs up the leafcutters' path.

"Bay, saay, xen ich k'aax!
"Okay, leafcutter ants, go off into the forest!

Abin ahantik ule' che'."
Go off and eat the leaves of the trees."

Bin ulahp'uchik yok'or ulu'uma(').
He scuffs up the ground.

Ulahp'uchik.
He scuffs it all.

Up'uchik yok'or ulu'uma' yok'or (u)muur.
He scuffs up the earth on their ant hill.

—BUH—
—BUH—

Tan ut'änik, tan uk'eeyah ahnukuch winik, "Ne ma' tsoy ahsaay. Alahkäräx-
me(n)t(i)k inwo'och när. Ba'(inkin) inhanteh ten?"
He is warning them, the ancestor is scolding them, "Eh, you're very bad,
leafcutter ants. You're wrecking all my corn. What will I eat?"

Eh, kuyu'yik utubur ut'an uts'uri(r) yumir ahsaay, "Eh ba'i(kin) tume(n)t(ah)
inwinik tech?"
Then, he hears the lord of the leafcutter ants exclaim, "Ehhh, what did my
people do to you?"

"Mäna'! Ba'i(inkin) tume(n)tah awinik? Tan ulahhantik inwo'och när."
"There isn't anything (left)! What did your people do? They're eating all
my corn."

"Hachah!"

"Indeed!"

"Tuhahir. Ma' intusikech! Ba'i(n)ki(r)in kawirik ne ts'iiken—tulahkäräx-me(n)tah inwo'och när—tulahhantah inwo'och wah—mäna' inwo'och när. T'äka'(a)n. Tulahkucha(h) ten!"

"It's true! I'm not lying to you. You see I'm very angry—they wrecked all my corn—they ate all my corn—I don't have any corn. It's snapped off. They carried it away on me!"

"Ehhh hah. Ba'i(n)kin tume(n)tah tech?"

"Uh-huh. What (else) did they do to you?"

"Bex bähe'—tan ulahhantik inpak'arnär.

"Like what (they're doing) now—they're eating all my corn plants.

Bähe' ne ts'iiken ti', tan inhi'ixtik, tan inhäts'ik uber. Ya ma' wo(r)or utar ukäräxme(n)t(ik) inwo'och när."

Now I'm so angry with them, I'm scuffing it, I'm beating their path. This (way) they (won't) come and wreck all my corn."

Uyumin ahsaay tuya'arah, "Bay. Wa tan unaat'ar inwinik tech, tint'an he' usutik uher tech, he' uyaantikech. Ha'ri' kawe'esik to'an akor, he' upaaktik akoor ti' apäk'ik awo'och när."

The lord of the leafcutter ants said, "Okay. If my people keep coming to (your cornfield), I think they will come back again to you, they will help you. Just show them where your cornfield is, and they will clear your corn-field for you to sow your corn."

"Ehhh bay," kih nukir winik. "Hach tuhahir? Ma' atusiken?"

"Ohhh, okay," says the ancestor. "Really? You're not lying to me?"

"Mäna'! Ma' intusikech. Inwinik h(e') uyaantikech."

"Not at all! I'm not lying to you. My people will help you."

"Ehhh!" ne tsoy uyor nukuch winik. "Bähe' ts'o'ok inhi'ixtik awinik tech. 'Oy inwor ti' woror ukäräxme(n)tik ten inwo'och när."

"Ohhh!" the ancestor is elated. "Now, I (will) stop rubbing out your people. I was so tired of them always demolishing my corn on me."

Uyuminir ahsaay tuya'arah, "Bähe' tso'oki(h) ukäräxmentikech inwinik. Bin kuyaantikech; kupaaktik akoor."

The lord of the leafcutter ants said, "As of today, my people have stopped bothering you. They are going to help you clear your cornfield."

"Ehhh bay," tuya'arah nukuch winik ti' uyumin ahsaay. "Bähe' ts'o'ok. Inwe'esik tech to'an inkor ubin upaaktik ten inkoor."

"Oh, okay," the ancestor said to the lord of the leafcutter ants. "Now it's over. I (will) show you where my cornfield is. (And) they are going to clear my cornfield for me."

"He're'," tuya'arah uyumir saay. "He're', upaaktik. Uyaantikech. Bähe' ma' ayan bin apäkteh akor. Ch'ukteh oxp'er k'in abin awireh."

"Of course," said the lord of the leafcutter ants. "Yes indeed, they'll clear it. They will help you. Now, you must not go look at your cornfield. Wait three days before you go visit it."

"Bay."

"Okay," (says the ancestor).

Tuch'uktah oxp'er k'in bini(h) uyireh ukoor. Tuworor tulahki'lahmiistah. H-ä-n-n-kareh (u)koor, 'äkrik. "*N-e-e-e tsoy ti' upäk'nar.*"

He waited three days (and then) went to visit his cornfield. They (had) swept it all nice and clean. The cornfield is cl-e-e-e-a-r and level. "*This is perfect for planting corn,*" (he thinks).

Bini(h) aknukire'ex. Tucha'ah unär. Tupäk'ah tuworor ukoorir.

Our ancestor left. He took his corn. He sowed it throughout his cornfield.

Ne ch'ih(ih) unär; ne nukir tuworor. Bin(ih) uts'aheh uho'(or) ti' k'uh.

His corn really grew; all of (the ears) were large. He went to give the first of the fruits to the gods.

Tuya'arah nukuch winik, "Bähe' ne tsoy inwor. Tuyaant(ah)en ahsaay. Yan när ten. Bähe' ts'o'okih unaat'ar ahsaay."

The ancestor said, "Now I'm happy. The leafcutter ants helped me. (Now) I have corn. Now the leafcutter ants have stopped their pinching."

Tuts'a'ah uho'(or) när. Ne tsoy uyor nukuch winik.

He offered the first fruits of corn. The ancestor is very pleased.

Aht'u'ur yeter Barum 'The Rabbit and the Puma'

Säk Ho'or

This story features the rabbit as trickster and his inane dupe, the puma. In this story the rabbit outsmarts the puma repeatedly, until he is beaten by a cat. Versions of this story are told throughout Mesoamerica.[1]

Bay. Äht'u'ur ti' kura('an) tan ubuhik uche'.

Okay. The rabbit is sitting there, he is splitting his firewood.

K'uchi(h) ähchäk barum. Kuya'arik ähchäk barum, "Ba'inki(r) kame(n)tik?" kih.

A puma arrived. The puma says, "What are you doing?"

"Mix ba'(ar)," tuya'arah äht'u'ur.

"Nothing," the rabbit said.

"Awirik ten; tan inbuhik inche'."

"You can see me; I'm splitting my wood."

"Ahhh, tan abuhik ache'," tuya'arah (äh)chäk barum.

"Ahh, you're splitting your wood," said the puma.

Ts'o'oki(h) ubuhik tuya'arah, "K'aar ubaat." Tuya'arah äht'u'ur, "Bik yani(r) ma' awaantiken? Bik yani(r) ma' awaantiken, tumen tech ne nukech ne k'äb? Tech, ne nukech. Ne chich amuk'. Tech hach chich amuk'."

(When) he finished splitting, he said, "The axe is stuck." The rabbit said, "Why don't you help me? Why don't you help me, because your arms are very strong? You are very big. You are very strong."

(Chäk barum) tuya'arah, "Inwaantikech."
(The puma) said, "I (will) help you."

Bay.
Okay.

Chäk barum tubut'ah uk'äb yok'o(r) che'. Tubut'ah k'äb yok'o(r) ubuhik che'.
The the puma put his hand in the wood. He put his hand in (and) split the wood.

Tuya'arah äht'u'ur, "Ten kinhiitik ubaat, ten kinhitik ubaat."
The rabbit said, "I'll take out the axe, I'll take out the axe."

Tuhiitah ubaat. K'aar uk'äb ähchäk barum.
He took out the axe. The puma's hand got stuck.

'Otsi(r) ähchäk barum. Ok'o(r) ukah (äh)chäk barum. Kuya'arik, "Mix muk kuyaantiken."
Poor puma. The puma is crying. He says, "No one will help me."

"Awirik?" äht'u'ur tuya'arah. "Ha ha ha! Ne tsoy inwor. Tintusahech. Awirik ten, ten äht'u'uren. Ne ma' paaten. Ne ma' tsoyen," tuya'arah äht'u'ur.
"You see?" the rabbit said. "Ha ha ha! I'm very happy. I lied to you. You see me, I am the rabbit. I'm very naughty. I'm very bad," said the rabbit.

Bay.
Okay.

Ähchäk barum, ne pim ubäho' umaan. Tan umaan, tuya'arah ubäho'.

The puma (has) many companions that pass by. His companions are passing by.

"Chen ma' bik yani(r) ma' awaantiken?" tuya'arah ähchäk barum.

"But why don't you help me?" the puma said.

"Ma' bik inwaantikech." Maani(h) hare'. Maani(h) ähyuk. Maani(h) ähtsub. Maani(h) ähbo(r)ay. Maani(h) tuwo(r)o(r). "'Otsirech ma' bik inme(n)tik tech. Ma' bik inwaantikech."

"I don't know how to help you." A paca passed on by. A deer passed by. An agouti passed by. A tiger cat passed by.[2] Everything passed by (saying), "Poor (you), I don't know what to do for you. I don't know how to help you."

"Ten mäna' ink'äb. Wa yan ink'äb he' inwaantikech."

"I don't have hands. If I had hands, I would help you."

Bay.

Okay.

Pachi(r), tari(h) ubäho' chäk barum. Tuya'arah, "Ba'inki(r) kame(n)tik?"

Next, a puma friend came by. He said, "What are you doing?"

"Awirik, äht'u'ur tutusahen. Tuya'arah, ''Aanten inbuheh che',' aht'u'ur tuya'arah ten, 'Buheh (a') che' ten kinhiit(i)k ubaat.' Bay, (äh)t'u'ur, (ku)ts'o'ok(or) tutusahen, tutäkah ink'äb, ma' het la'eh inhiitik."

"You see, the rabbit lied to me. He said, 'Help me split wood,' the rabbit said to me, 'Split the wood (and) I will take out the axe.' Okay, (when) the rabbit finished lying to me he stuck my hand in, (and) I can't pull it out."

Ubäho' tuya'arah ähchäk barum, "Eh 'utse(r)eh. 'Otsirech. Ma' ba'i(nkir) inme(ntik) tech, porque ten mäna' ink'äb ten. Lah ke(et) to'one'ex. Mäna' ink'äb."

His friend the puma said, "Oh no. Poor you. I can't do anything for you, because I don't have any hands. We're just the same. I don't have hands."

Bay.
Okay.

Pachi(r) bini(h). Tuya'arah t(i') ubäho', "Kinseh inwäwaar äht'u'ur. Ne ma' paati(h). Kinseh! Äht'u'ur awirik p'is ch'upra(r). Ne tsoy uwich tinwirah. Ne tsoy uwich; ne mäna' tuxuur äht'u'ur. Mäna'ta ch'uprar uxuur. Ne p'enk'äch tsoy uwich; ne uts t(i') uwich. Tutusahen."

Then he left. He said to his companion, "Kill my attacker, the rabbit. He's very bad. Kill him! The rabbit you see looks like a woman. I saw that she was very pretty. She was very pretty; no other woman compares with the rabbit. She is the ultimate. She is incomparably beautiful; she is good-looking. She lied to me."

"Bay," tuya'arah (äh)chäk barum. "Bay. Inkinsik awäwaar."
"Okay," the puma said. "Okay. I (will) kill your attacker."

Bay.
Okay.

Pachi(r), bini(h) chäk barum. Bin(ih) ukäxteh
Then, the puma went. He went to look for him.

Tuka'irah, "Ba'inki(r) ame(n)tik? Tech tatusah inbäho'."
He saw him again (and said), "What are you doing? You lied to my companion."

"Eh. Tuhahir; ten ma' inwoher ten. Ten awirik ten way yanen. Ten äht'u'uren. Ten mix ba'(ar) kinme(n)tik ten. Ten mix ba'(ar). Ma' inwa'arik intusikech. Mix intusikech."

"Eh. That (may be) so; I don't know. You see, here I am. I'm a rabbit. I'm not doing anything. I didn't do anything. I'm not lying to you. I (would) never lie to you."

"Ma'aa. Atus," tuya'arah chäk barum. "T-u-u-u-s a-k-a-a-a-h tech. Tech tus akah. Tech takäräxme(n)tah inbäho'. Bähe' bin inchi'(i)kech. Inbin inkinsikech inchi'(i)kech."

"Nooo. You lie," said the puma. "You are l-y-y-y-i-i-i-ng. You are lying. You harmed my companion. Now I'm going to eat you. I'm going to kill you (and) eat you."

Bay, äht'u'ur tuya'arah, "Kinsen. Kinsen."

So, the rabbit said, "Kill me. Kill me."

Pachi(r), äht'u'ur tuwaays(ah) ubäh ch'uprar.

Then, the rabbit turned itself into a woman.

"Ne tsoy awich ch'uprar; mäna'ta ch'uprar uxuur. Mäna'ta ne p'enk'äch tsoy awich. Ne tsoy awich," tuya'arah (äh)chäk barum. "Ne tsoy awich. Ba'i(n)k(ir) inme(n)tik tech?" tuya'arah.

"You are a very beautiful woman; there is no better woman. There is no other. You are the lovliest of all. You are very beautiful," said the puma. "You are very beautiful. What can I do for you?" he said.

"Ne tsoy awiriken?" tuya'arah äht'u'ur.

"Do you like me?" said the rabbit.

"Ne tsoy inwirikech," tuya'arah ähchäk barum. "He' inch'a'ikech."

"I like you very much," said the puma. "I will take you."

"Ma'. Ten ma' (a)bik ach'a'iken, porque ne nuk awich. Ne nuk awich."

"No. You will not take me, because your eyes are too big. Your eyes are too big."

"Pero bik inme(n)tik ti' inwich? Ne 'otsi(r) inwich."

"But what am I going to do about my eyes? I (need) my eyes."

"Ten ink'a't kahiit(i)k awich."

"I want you to remove your eyes."

"Porque bik yani(r) inhiitik inwich?"

"Why should I remove my eyes?"

"Awiich'ak, ne nuk awiich'ak. Awiich'ak ne nuk. Akoh ne nuk. Uts wa lehi(h) k'in ameek'iken lehi(h) k'in aleep'(t)iken."

"(And) your claws, your claws are too big. Your claws are too big. Your teeth are too big. Whenever you embrace me you will scratch me."

"Bay," tuya'arah ähchäk barum. "H(e') ach'a'iken (in)hiit(eh) inwiich'ak?"

"Okay," said the puma. "Will you take me (if) I take out my claws?"

"Lahhiiteh awiich'ak."

"Take out all your claws," (says the rabbit).

"Bay," barum tuya'arah. "Inhiitik inwiich'ak."

"Okay," the puma said. "I (will) take out my claws."

Tuhiitah uyiich'ak huhunp'e(r). Tuworo(r) (u)yiich'ak tura(h)hiitah, pach-i(r) tuya'arah, "Bähe' tsoy awiriken?"

He took out his claws one by one. He took out all his claws, then he said, "Now do you like me?"

"Ma'! Ma' tsoy inwirikech. Akoh ne nuk. 'Uts wa lehi(h) k'in, ats'i'o(r)tiken h(e') achi'(i)ken."

"No! I don't like you. Your teeth are too big. Everytime you desire me you will bite me."

Tuya'arah, "Ma' bik inhiitik. Wa kinhiitik inkoh, ma' bik inhana(n). Mix kinbin inchukeh inwo'och."

He said, "How am I to take them out? If I take out my teeth, how would I eat? I would never be able to catch my food."

Äht'u'ur tuya'arah, "Ma'! Wa ma' ahiitik akoh, ma' ach'a'iken. Ma' ach'ahiken."

The rabbit said, "No! If you don't take out your teeth, you (will) not take me. You (will) not take me."

Chäk barum tuya'arah, "Bay, inhiitik inkoh."

The puma said, "Okay, I (will) take out my teeth."

Tuhiitah ukoh. Tula(h)hiitah ukoh. "Bähe' tsoy awiriken?"

He took out his teeth. He took out all his teeth. "Now do you like me?"

"Ma'! Ma' tsoy inwirikech. Awirik, ma' tsoy inwirikech porque ne nuk awich. Ne ma' tsoy awich. Ne nuk p'is ahbuh awich."

"No! I don't like you. You see, I don't like you because your eyes are too big. Your eyes are very ugly. Your eyes are very big, like an owl's."

Chäk barum tuya'arah, "Bik yani(r) inhiitik inwich? Si wa mäna' inwich, bik kinbin inwireh ba'(ar)? Bik kinbin inwireh? Bik kinbin inchukeh inwo'och? Bik kinbin (in)hanan?"

The puma said, "Why would I take out my eyes? If I don't have eyes, how am I going to see things? How am I going to see? How am I going to catch my food? How am I going to eat?"

Tuya'arah äht'u'ur, "Ma' ahiitik awich mix ach'a'iken."

The rabbit said, "(If) you don't take out your eyes you (will) never take me."

Bay.

Okay.

Tutukrah ubäh (äh)chäk barum. Tuya'arah, "Inhiitik inwich." Tuhiitah uwich. "Bähe' atukriken?"

The puma thought about it. He said, "I (will) take out my eyes." He took out his eyes. "Now (what) do you think of me?"

Pachi(r), tuya'arah äht'u'ur, "Ha ha! Ten intus. Hach ten mix ats'ahik ten. Ha'ri' ten ne chich inmuuk'. Ha'ri' ten. Chan mihinen, ten ne tahen t(i') intus. Awirik ten tinhachlahtusah abäho'; Tuworo(r) abäho' ten tintusah. Ha'ri' ten."

Then, the rabbit said, "Ha ha! I lie(d). You're never going to outdo me. I'm the only strong one. Only me. I'm very small, (but) I'm clever at lying. You see, I really lied about everything to your companion; I lied to all your companions. Only me."

Tuk'in kuyu'u(r) che'eh, "ha ha", kuhäts'ik uho(r) yok'or chunche'.

When he hears the rabbit laugh, "ha ha," he hits his head on the trunk of a tree.

Pachi(r) tuya'arah, "Turah inkinsikech," tuya'arah (äh)chäk barum. "Turah inkinsikech. Ne ma' paatech, t'u'ur. Ten tawa'arah ten ti' inhiitik inwich. Tech tawa'arah ten ti' inhiitik inwiich'ak. Tech tawa'arah ten ti' inhiitik inkoh. Tech ne ma' tsoy. Ne ma' paatech."

Then he said, "I have to kill you," said the puma. "I have to kill you. You're wicked, rabbit. You told me to take out my eyes. You told me to take out my claws. You told me to take out my teeth. You're very bad. You're very naughty."

Bay.

Okay.

Äht'u'ur ne tsoy uyor. Bini(h).

The rabbit is very happy. He left.

'Otsi(r) chäk barum

Poor puma.

Maani(h) uher barum. [Ne pim barum.] Maani(h) äh boray, ähyuk, tuwor-o(r) maani(h); hare', wech'.

Another puma passed by. [There are many pumas.] A tiger cat, a deer, everything passed by; a paca, an armadillo.

"'Otsirech. Ba'inki(r) tame(n)tah?" tuk'aatah ti'. "Ba'inki(r) tame(n)tah?"

"Poor you. What did you do?" he asked him. "What did you do?" (the puma says).

"Awirik tutusahen tutusahen äht'u'ur. Tutusahen: lati' tuya'arah ten ke ne nuk inwich, ne ma' tsoy; ne yan inwiich'ak, ne yan inkoh."

"You see, he lied to me, the rabbit lied to me. He lied to me: he told me that my eyes were too big, they were ugly; I had lots of claws, lots of teeth."

"Eh hah. 'Otsirech," tuya'arah ti' (äh)chäk barum. "'Otsirech. Ma' ba'(ar) in-me(n)t(ik) awirik? La ke(e)t to'one'ex. Lah yan inwiich'ak ten lah p'is tech, ma' bik inwaantikech mäna' ink'äb."

"Eh, uh-huh. Poor you," the puma said to him. "Poor you. How can I do anything for you, we're the same (says the other puma)? I have claws the same as you. How do I help you (when) I don't have any hands?"

"Bay." Pachi(r) tuya'arah chäk barum, "Tech sukun. Tech kabin akinseh in-wäwar. Tech kabin akinseh. 'Aanten. Tech kink'ubik tech (ka)kinseh."

"Okay," (says the puma). Then the puma said, "You're the older (brother). You are going to kill my attacker. You are going to kill him. Help me. I leave it to you to kill him."

Bay. T'u'ur bini(h).
Okay. The rabbit left.

Pachi(r), tuk'in ka'(ah) bini(h) ukäxteh, tuyirah äht'u'ur ti'yan yok'o(r) wits yok'o(r) haban 'aktun. "Ba'inki(r) ame(n)tik?" kih.[3]

Then, when the puma went to look for him again, he saw the rabbit on top of a cave on a hill. "What are you doing?" (asks the puma).

"Mix ba'(ar). Awirik ten, kink'oochik 'aktun. Ten kink'oochik lu'um. Ten kinlahkuchik tuworo(r)."

"Nothing. You see me, I'm carrying the cave on my shoulder. I'm carrying the earth on my shoulder. I'm carrying everything."

"Eh hah. Tech takins(ah) inbäho'. K'aa(h)i(h) tech tatusahen inbäho'? Ne yaab ba'(ar) takäräxme(n)tah ti' ka't(uu)ro' inbäho'. Takinsah. Tarahkinsah inbäho'."

"Uh-huh. You killed my companion. (Do) you remember (that) you lied to my companions? You did many bad things to two of my companions. You killed them. You killed all my companions."

"Ten ma' inwoher. Ten mix inwoher ba'inki(r) tume(n)tah abäho'. Ten ma' inwoher. Awirik ten, ten kinkuchik a' he' wits. Ten kinkuchik haban 'aktun. Awirik ten, ten kink'oochik. Awirik? Cha('a)nteh awireh kinsiptik."

"I don't know. I don't know what happened (to) your companions. I don't know. You see me, I'm carrying this here hill. I'm carrying the cave. You see me, I'm carrying it. You see? Watch and see me drop it."[4]

Kusiptik, kuhene(n) ts'uyu(r). Tan ula(h)hene(n) k'aax; tan (u)la(h)heen tuworo(r).

He drops it; it goes tumbling down. All the mountains are caving in; everything is caving in.

"Awirik?" Kuka'k'oochah. "Awirik, ten ma' intus. Hach tah, hach tah ba'(ar) kinwa'arik, hach tah. Hach tuhahir. Ten ma' tus inkah."

"You see?" He loads up again. "You see, I'm not lying. What I tell you is correct. It's true. I'm not lying."

"Eh hah."

"Uh-huh," (says the puma).

"Wa kakinsiken," tuya'arah äht'u'ur, "wa kakinsiken bähe' a' lu'um ts'o'oki(h) ti' tech. Tuworo(r) tech bin akah (a)lahkimi(n) tuworo(r). Ha'ri' ten kink'oochik way lu'um yok'o(r) a' way, yok'o(r) haman 'aktun."

"If you kill me," said the rabbit, "if you kill me now, the earth is finished for you. You're all going to die. It is only I who carries the earth in here, in the cave."

"Eh hah," tuya'arah (äh)chäk barum. "Bay, bik yanir ma' inkinsikech."

"Uh-huh," said the puma. "Okay, so that's why I (won't) kill you."

Bay.

Okay.

Pachi(r), tich'i'k'ä' aht'uur; tan uk'oochik.

Then, the rabbit raises it high (over his head); he is carrying it.

Pachi(r) tuya'arah äht'u'ur, "Oken, 'aan(ten) t(i') ink'oocheh, tumen tech ne nohochech, ne nukech, ne chich amuuk'. Awirik ten, ma' ak'aatik boon ya'axk'in mix kinwuk'u(r), mix kinhana(n). Mix ba'(ar). Umaanen (u)ya'axk'in woro(r) ten kink'oochik 'aktun tu(men) m(a') ula(h)heene(n) wits tuworo(r)."

Then the rabbit said, "Step in and help me carry it, because you're so big and strong. You see me, don't ask me how many years (that) I (haven't drunk) or (eaten) anything. Nothing. The years pass (and) all I do is hold up the cave so that the entire hill doesn't completely cave in."

"Eh hah."

"Uh-huh," (says the puma).

"Aanten t(i') inbin t(i') inhana(n), t(i') inbin t(i') inwuk'u(r). Ma' uxanta(r) inka'sut. Hach seeb' insut, (t)ume(n) ukuchu(r) amuk' ak'oocheh. Aanten!"

"Help me so I can go eat, so I can go drink. I'll be back soon. I'll come back quickly, because you are strong enough to carry it. Help me!"

"Bay," Chäk barum tuya'arah. "Inwaantikech."

"Okay," the puma said. "I (will) help you."

Bay, chäk barum ok(ih) uk'oocheh. Tuki'p'is(ah) ubäh uk'oocheh. Neki'ka'ni(h) chäk barum. Umaanen k'in tuk'oochah.

So, the puma stepped in to carry it. He really exerted himself carry(ing) it. The puma got very tired. All through the day he carried it. (He says to himself:)

"Tu' bini(h) äht'u'ur? Lati' tutusah inbäho' bäkan. Wa tak intuk(ur) hach tintoh-kinsah. Ma' puts'ih."

"Where did that rabbit go? After all, he lied to my companions. If I (were) thinking, I (would have) just killed him outright. He (wouldn't have) escaped."

Chäk barum tan uhanp'is(i)k ubäh uk'oocheh.

The puma is really straining to carry it.

Bay. Chäk barum (tu)tukrah, *"Int'an inbin insiptik inwireh wa uhene(n) wa hach tuhahir."*

Okay. The puma thought, *"I think I'm going to drop it and see if it really caves in."*

Bay. Chäk barum tusiptah. Mix upeek, mix k'aax, mix. Tuworo(r) ne uts. Ma' uhene(n) wits, mix ba'(ar), mix 'aktun, mix upeek.

So, the puma dropped it. Nothing moves, neither the mountains nor (anything else). Everything is fine. The hill doesn't collapse, neither does the cave, it never moves.

Bay. Chäk barum tutukrah, *"Int'an inputs'u(r). Inbin inwirik hach tuhahir."*

Okay. The puma thought, *"I think I'll run away. I'm going to see if it's really true."*

Bay. Chäk barum tuwaarah ubäh uyaaka'. Ch'ik bini(h). Ch'ik bini(h) tuch'uktah uyireh.

Okay. The puma runs hard. He went far away. He went very far, (then) waited to see.

M-i-i-i-x ba'(ar). Mix uhene(n). *"Woro(r) tus ukah lati' äht'u'ur. Lehi(h) ubäh(ir) tutusahen lati' tukäräxme(n)tah inbäho' bähe' inbin inkinsik bähe'."*

No-o-o-thing. Nothing collapses. *"That rabbit (was) lying all the time. This one who lied to me is the one who harmed my brothers. Now I have to kill him."*

Bay. Bini(h). Bini(h) tuka'ten tuyirah ti' kura'(a)n.

Okay. He went. He went again and saw him sitting there.

"Ba'inki(r) kame(n)tik t'u'ur? Tech tatusah inbäho'. Bähe' ma' tuni' xi'ikech. Tur inhantikech. Tur ints'ahik ti' tech, tur ints'ahik ti' tech. Bähe' tur inkinsikech."

"What are you doing, rabbit? You lied to my companions. Now you can't (get away). I have to eat you. I have to give it to you. Now I have to kill you."

T'u'ur tuya'arah, "Ten tinwirah way; maani(h) way äht'u'ur; tinwirah inbäho' ubin inbäho' way. Bini(h). Aaka' bini(h). Ne ka'ni(h) ka'(ah) tinwirah umaan."

The rabbit said, "I saw him here; the rabbit passed through here; I saw my brother go by here. He left. He went running off. He was very tired when I saw him pass through."

"Mäna'. Tus akah tech!" tuya'arah chäk barum. "Tech tus akah, tech. Tatusahen. Tats'aah(eh?); tarahkins(ah) inbäho'. Tats'aah(ah) ink'oochik 'aktun. Tats'aah ink'oochik 'aktun — m-i-i-i-x ba'(ar). Tawirah tinhachki'harah inmuk' tinp'isah inbäh, mix ba'(ar). Woro(r) tus."

"No. You're lying!" said the puma. "You're lying. You lied to me. You gave it (to them); you killed all my companions. You gave me (orders) to carry the cave. You gave me (orders) to carry the cave and n-o-o-o-thing. You saw (that) I mustered all my strength, I really exerted myself, and nothing (happened). They were all lies."

Bay. Tuya'arah, "Bähä' inbin inchi'(i)kech."

Okay. He said, "Now I'm going to eat you."

"Ma' achi'(i)ken," tuya'arah äht'u'ur. "Awirik ten, ten kinlahuk'(ik) a' ha'. Ten kinlahxupik a' petha'. Si wa mäna' ten turah ulahbin, porque tuworo(r) petha', k'ak'na'. Mix k'äs k'aax, tula(h)k'up(char yeter) woro(r) ha'. Mix tu' abin. Lahkimine'ex tuworo(r)."

"Don't eat me," said the rabbit. "You see that I'm drinking the water. I'm finishing up the whole lagoon. If I (don't) it's all going to overflow; the entire lagoon (will become) an ocean. There (won't be) any forest left; it (will be) submerged under water. There (would be) nowhere you (could) go. You (would) all die."

Chäk barum tuya'arah, "Atusiken."

The puma said, "You're lying to me."

"Ma'. Awirik."

"No. See this."

Äht'u'ur tan uyuk'ik ha'. Tuye'esah, tuya'arah, "Awirik: ma' usap'a(r) ha'.
Awirik: bähe' sa(p')ih ha'. Si wa ma' inwuk'ik ten ma' usap'ar ha'. Sino que
ha' tan umasnebuurur. Tan aklahkimi(n). Bay. Aant(en) inwuk'ik," tuya'arah
ti' chäk barum. "Aant(en) inwuk'ik."

The rabbit is drinking water. He showed him and said, "You see: the water
does not drain off. You see: now the water (has) drained. If I don't drink
it, the water won't drain. On the contrary, the water rises even more. We
are all (going to) die. So, help me drink it," he said to the puma. "Help me
drink it."

Tutukrah (äh)barum. Chäk barum tuya'arah, "Inwaantikech."

The puma thought about it. The puma said, "I (will) help you."

Bay.

Okay.

Tuyaant(ah) uyuk'eh—ne yaab ha'. Tuyuk'ah chäk barum, tuya'arah, "Ne
na('a)hchahen."

He helped him drink—there's a lot of water. The puma drank it, (and) he
said, "I'm getting very full."

"Ma'. Awirik ten. Ten mas ne yaab inwuk'ik' p'is tech. Awirik mas ne yaab
inwuk'ik."

"No," (says the rabbit). "Look at me. I'm drinking more than you. You see,
I am drinking a lot more."

Tuya'arah. "Hach tuhahir." Tup'is(ah) ubäh yuk'eh, tup'is(ah) ubäh yuk'eh.
Pachi(r) chäk barum tuya'arah, "Bähe' ts'o'oki(h) inwuk'ik. Ya ne tak inbu-
hur. Bin inkah buhur," tuya'arah chäk barum.

(The puma) said, "That's true." He forced himself to drink and drink. Then
the puma said, "Now I've finished drinking. I'm about to burst. I'm going
to burst," said the puma.

"Ma'. Aanten."
"No. Help me," (says the rabbit).

"Ya p'ehas inwuk'ik. Ts'o'oki(h). Ne na'ahchahen."
"I've already drunk enough. I'm finished. I've become very full," (says the
puma).

Bay.
Okay.

Bini(h) chäk barum. Ti' yan k'i'ix. Tulamah uchoocher, buhnah choocher.
The puma left. There was a thorn. It pierced his belly, (and) his belly burst.

Buhnah (u)choocher, lehi(h) a' la'eh ka'(ah) ts'o'oki(h) äht'u'ur.
(When) his belly burst, this is when the rabbit finished (him) off.

[Ts'o'oki(h) a' la'eh tsikba(r) tanah.]
[So, that's the end of (the puma's story) now.]

Bini(h) ti' ähmiis.
(The rabbit) went to the cat.

Bay. [Ähmiis its'i(n)bi(r). Ähchäk barum, sukunbi(r).] Bini(h) ti' ähmiis. Ne hats'ka', tan umarik uye'ex äht'u'ur.

Okay. [The cat is the little brother. The puma is the big brother.] He went to the cat. It's very early morning, and the rabbit is collecting his trousers.

Bay. Ähmiis tan uch'uktik uyo'och. Tari(h) äht'u'ur, tari(h) tupach, "Ba'in-ki(r) kame(n)tik?" tuk'aatah ti' ähmiis.

Okay. The cat is lying in wait for his food. The rabbit came up behind (him), "What are you doing?" he asked the cat.

"Mix b-a-a-a'(ar). Ten kurukben."

"N-o-o-o-thing. I'm sitting."

"Eh. Tuhahir. Toh mix tawir(ah) intar, tuk'in ka'(ah) taren tapach. Wa kinch'aheh kachik che(n?) tinhäts'ah a ho'(or). Mix kawirik, tumen tech chan muts' awich. Ne chan mehenech. Ne chan chichinech. Chan muts' awich kurukech."

"Ah. That's true. You didn't even see me, when I came up behind you. If I were to grab you I would've just hit you over the head. You don't see anything, because your eyes are a little shut. You're very small. You're tiny. You're seated there with your eyes a little shut."

Miis tunuukah, "Awirik ten ne mihinen, ne chan chichinen. Ten tinwi(r)ah (a)tar. Ma' poch inkinsikech. Ma' poch inchi'(i)kech. Bey ma' tinkins(ah) ech."

The cat replied, "You see, I am very small; I am tiny. (But) I saw you come. I didn't want to kill you. I didn't want to eat you. So, I didn't kill you."

"Mix awirik intar. Tus akah. Tech mix. Mix tawirah intar. Chan muts' awich kurukech."

(The rabbit said,) "You didn't see me come. You're lying. You never did. You never saw me come. You were seated there with your eyes a little shut."

"Ahh, la' ton? Ten ma' tinwirah?"

"Ahh, is that so? I didn't see you?"

Bay. Lik'i(h) ä(h)chan miis. Lik'(ih) ähmiis tuchukah kukurun. Uyawat äht'u'ur, "Hah tawa'arah. Hach t(uh)a(hir) ba'(ar) tawa'arah. Hach tuhahir ba'(ar) tawa'arah tech. Ma' kuch' inmuuk' ti' tech. Ma' tinkäräxment(ah) tech. Tech hach chich amuuk'. Bähe', kubi(n) p'aato' tuworo(r) bähe' inti'a'ar, tuworo(r) lehi(h) kubi(n) p'aato' yok'o(r) lu'um, yok'o(r) k'aax. Tuworo(r), ch'ik binih, woro(r) ma' nuk. Kubi(n) p'aato' ti' tech; kubin p'aato' bähe' mehen t'u'ur, inka'ti'a'ar kuka'lik'ir."

Okay. The cat got up. The cat got up and pounced on him. The rabbit shrieks, "What you said is true! The things you said are true. It's true the things you said. I'm not as strong as you. I didn't harm you. You are very strong. Now, all my children are going to remain. All of them are going to remain on the land, in the forest. All of them, wherever they go, they will not be large. They will remain here for you; they will remain as little rabbits. My next generation will remain (as) little rabbits when they grow up."

Ch'ämäk yeter Chäk Barum 'The Fox and the Puma'

Bor Ma'ax

The puma and fox are related: they are brothers-in-law. The little fox is mischievous and bothersome. And the puma tries to shake him off. Unable to shake him off, the puma demands that he address him as "Señor Maestro," and then teaches him how to take down game (in this case, it is a farmer's cow). After they succeed, the fox runs off to get his mother to help him carry home his portion of the meat. When he returns with his mother, the puma is gone, and so is the meat. The fox enlists his mother to help bring down another cow in the same way the puma had taught him to do. But it does not go as well as he planned.

Bay.

Okay.

Ahchäk barum tan umaan. Tan umaan ukäxtik uyo'och bäk' e kuyu'yik "I-I-I-H," kih habanche'. Ha'k'ih uyor ahchäk barum. Ha'k'ih uyor. "Ba-a-a'inkin tinwu'yah?"

The puma is going along. He is going along looking for meat and he hears, "I-I-I-H," (coming) from a rotten log. The puma was startled. He was startled. "Wha-a-at's that I heard?"

Uka'me(n)tik ah ch'ämäk,[1] "I-I-I-H."

The fox does it again, "I-I-I-H."

Ti' yan ich haban che'.

He is in a hollow log.

Eh, ne ha'k' uyor ahchäk barum. "Ba-a-a'inkin?" Uka'sut ti' uki'yirik.

The puma is really startled, "Wha-a-at?" He turns around to take a closer look.

Uhook'or uche', "HAHAHAHAHA. Mameh. Ha'k'areh awor, mameh? Ha'k'ih awor mameh?"

"HAHAHAHAHA," comes out of the tree. "Brother-in-law. Are you frightened, brother-in-law? Were you frightened, brother-in-law?"

"Ahh, chichin ha'k'(ih) inwor, äs ha'k'i(h)," unu(u)kik ahchäk barum, "äs ha'k'(ih)."

"Ahh, I was a little startled, a little startled," replies the puma, "a little startled."

"Eh, ma' mameh. Tu' kabin mameh?"

"Don't be, brother-in-law. Where are you going, brother-in-law?"

"Eh," tunuukah ahchäk barum. "Ten kinbin a' he' inkäxtik inwo'och."

"Eh," replied the puma. "I'm going there to look for food."

"Tsoy inwor. Intar t(i') apach, mameh!"

"I'm so happy. I'll follow you, brother-in-law!"

"Eh, ko'ox. Poch atar, ko'ox."

"Well, come on. You want to come, let's go."

"Bay mam! He' intar!"

"Okay, brother-in-law! I'm coming!"

Ne tsoy uyor bin ahch'ämäk. Tan ubin. "Ko'ox, mam!" kih.

The fox is overjoyed. He is going along. "Let's go, brother-in-law!" he says.

K'uchu(r) bin yok'or paakche' kor. Ne yan saak'. "TERRRIN-TERRRIN," kih.

They get to a fallow cornfield. There were many grasshoppers. "CHIRRUP-CHIRRUP," they say.

"He'ra' mam!" kut'an ahch'ämäk. "He'ra' mam! Ka(k)han(i)ko('o)n a' he'-re'; he' kakchi'eh

"Look here, brother-in-law!" the fox says. "Look here, brother-in-law! We could eat (them); let's munch on them."

"A' le' ten, mäna'," tunuukah ahchäk barum. "Ten mäna', yo'm kuchi'bi(r) yaha ahsaak'. Mihin."

"Not those," replied the puma. "Not for me, the large grasshoppers are spongy when eaten. They're too small."

"Ma', mameh. Ko'oten. Ne ki'!"

"No, brother-in-law. Come. They're really tasty!"

Tan uch'a'ik ahch'ämäk p'iis. XA-XA-XAH, kuchi'ik.

The fox is taking (one). CHOMP-CHOMP-CHOMP, he eats it.

"Ahhh mäna' ten," tunuukah ahchäk barum. "Ten mäna'. Ma' ink'a't. Ne mihin saak'; yo'm kuchi'bi(r) saak'."

"Ahhh, not for me," says the puma. "Not for me. I don't want any. Grasshoppers are too tiny; grasshoppers are spongy when eaten."

"Bay. Way kap'ata(r) tech," tuya'arah chäk barum. "Way kap'ata(r) tech, mam. Bin inkah ten."

"Okay. You're going to stay here," said the puma. "You're going to stay here, brother-in-law. I'm leaving."

"Ma', ma', mam! Ch'u(k)te(h) ten! He' intar!"

"No, no, brother-in-law! Wait for me! I'm coming!"

Bay.

Okay.

Chäk barum tan ubin, tan ubin. K'uchu(r) boon ubin tan uk'aatik, "Tu' ka-bini wa mam?"

The puma is going along and going along. He gets so far, and the fox asks, "Where are you going, brother-in-law?"

"Eh, a' la'eh, kinbin a' la'eh."

"Eh, over there, I'm going over there."

"Ahh bay."

"Ahh, okay," (says the fox).

Tan ubin, tan ubin. Tuyu'yah bin ahtsub, "tseeeh, tseeeh," uyawat.

They go along, they go along. (Then) they heard a paca cry, "tseeeh, tseeeh."

"He'ra' mam," kih. "He'ra' bäk'."

"There, brother-in-law," (the fox) says. "Meat is right there."

"Ma'," tunuukah (ah)chäk barum. "Ma'. Ne mihin. Ma' k'uch inwu'yik."

"No," replied the puma. "No. It's too small. It doesn't fill me up."

"Ah, bay, mameh."

"Ah, okay, brother-in-law," (says the fox).

"Xen a' tech," tuya'arah (ah)chäk barum. "Xen a' tech. Xen chukeh."

"You go ahead," said the puma. "You go ahead. Go and grab it."

Bin ahch'ämäk bin. "Bay mam!" kih. "Ch'uk(teh) ten—IIIIYAH!"

The fox went. "Okay, brother-in-law!" he says. "Wait for me!—IIIIYAH!" (he whoops).

Hach saanxi'ik/chik(?) ti' utar (u)yawat, "TSIIAAH!"

A short time later and there comes a "SQUAWK!"

"TSIIAAH!" kih ahtsub. "TSIIAAH!"

"SQUAWK!" cries the paca. "SQUAWK!"

"He'ra' mam! Ko(')oten mam! 'Aanten! Ko(')oten! 'Aanten!"

"Here it is brother-in-law! Come brother-in-law! Help me! Come! Help me!"

Mix chäk barum; ch'ika'an uch'eene'. Ch'e'exteh uyu'yeh.

The puma (does nothing); he is standing there peering out. He listens.

"Ko(')oten mam! He'ra'! Bin inputs'(s)eh! He'ra' mam! Ko'oten!"

"Come brother-in-law! Here! I will lose it! Here brother-in-law! Come!"

"Leee ma'."

"Not thaaat," (says the puma).

"Se(e)b atar. Bin ink(ah) inputs'(s)eh."

"Come quick. I'm going to lose it!" (says the fox).

Chäk barum ch'e'extik uyu'yik to'an ahch'ämäk.

The puma listens intently where the fox is.

"CHIIII!" kuyawat ahtsup'. Tuputs'(s)ah. Bini(h).

"CHIIII!" shrieks the paca. (The fox) let it escape. It went.

"Ehh! Kutichi(r) ne ka'ani(n). Neee ka'ani(n), mameh. Ma' tarech awaan-ten mam."

"Ehh! He appears way up high (in the tree)," (says the fox). "He's way up high, brother-in-law. You didn't come help me, brother-in-law."

"Ma', ma' taren. Tint'an h(e') akinsik."

"No, I didn't come. I thought you would kill it."

"Le' ma', mameh. Tinputs'(s)ah. Ma' k'uch inmuk' ti'. Ne ch'ik yum."

"No, brother-in-law. I let it escape. I wasn't strong enough. It was really powerful."

"Eh hah, mameh."

"Yes, that's true, brother-in-law," (says the puma).

"Tinputs'(s)ah. Beeeh. Ah bay. Ele, to'an tu' kabin, mameh?"

"I let it escape. It's gooone. Okay. So, where are you going, brother-in-law?"

"Ele, bin inkah te'."

"Well, I'm going over there."

"He' intar, mam!"

"I'm coming, brother-in-law!"

"Ko'ox."

"Let's go," (says the puma).

Bay.

Okay.

Bähe' tan ubin. Tan ubin ahchäk barum. Ho(h)xim(b)a(r) kubin ahchäk barum. Ele, kuk'uchu(r) bin tu' ya(n) to'an chaak'an ahwakäx bin. Ti' yan tu' kuyuk'u(r) ha' ahwakäx ti' puuman ahche'.

Now they are going along. The puma is going along. The puma is walking bent to the ground. They arrive at a cow pasture. They are where the cows drink by a bent-over tree.

Ele, ti' na'ak'(ih) ahchäk barum, ku(r)ta(r) t(i') upach.

Then, the puma climbed up there and (sat) down on the back (of the tree).

"Tu' kabin, mameh?"

"Where are you going, brother-in-law?"

"Le te' kinbin a' he' ku(r)ta(r)."

"I'm going to sit down here."

"Eh bay, mameh."

"Okay, brother-in-law."

Ele, kura'(a)n bin ahchäk barum (ti' u)pach ahche'; tu' yahah puum(an) ahche' ti' nahku(r)ta(r).

So, the puma is sitting there (on the) back of the tree; he leans against the great bended tree.

Bay.

Okay.

Xok'or tu' uk'uchur ahwakäx tub uyuk'ur ha'—toh (u)yoher to('a)n k'in ahchäk barum, to('a)n k'in tunahuk'ur ha' ahwakäx—t(i') up'iis k'ini(r) k'uchi(h). Kura'(a)n.

Near to where the cows arrive to drink water—the puma already knows what time the cows go to drink water—he came at the same time. He is sitting there.

"Mameh," kih. "Lah kutichir, mameh!" kih.
"Brother-in-law," (the fox) says. "They are all approaching!"

"Tuhahi(r). Tinwirah," (u)nuukik ahchäk barum. "Tuhahi(r). Tinwirah. Bähe' ma' at'äniken amamehtiken," tuya'arah ahchäk barum.
"That's right. I (see) them," the puma replied. "That's right. I (see) them. Now quit calling me your brother-in-law," said the puma.

[Ti' kuya'arik ti' ahch'ämäk, "Bähe' ma' (a)t'äniken amamehtiken."]
[This is what he says to the fox, "Now don't call me your brother-in-law."]

"Bik kint'änikech?"
"What do I call you?"

"At'äniken, Señor Maestro."
"You call me Lord Master."

"Ahhh bay!" tuya'arah (ah)ch'ämäk. "Ah bay. Bähe' int'änikech, Señor Maestro."
"All right!" said the fox. "All right. Now I call you, Lord Master."

Eh kura'(a)n bin ahch'ämäk.
The little fox is sitting there.

Bay.
Okay.

Ahwakäx tan utichir. Ne pim tan utar ti' yuk'ur ha'. Ne uk'ah. (U)k'uchu(r) lähta(r).

The cows are getting closer. There are many of them coming to drink water. They're very thirsty. They come in procession.

Tan uteetik ahchäk barum; lehi(h) kuteetik ne nuk ahwakäx.

The puma is sizing them up; he picks out this really big cow.

"La' kutichir mam," kih.

"They're approaching, brother-in-law," says (the fox).

"Ma' t'äniken amameh ti' tinwa'arah tech. Ma' t'äniken amameh. At'äniken Señor Maestro. Wa ma', inlisik inwiich'ak; kalubur kuhäptikech 'ayim."

"Don't call me your brother-in-law, I told you. Don't call me brother-in-law. You call me Lord Master. If not, I (will) raise my claws; when you fall the crocodiles will slurp you up."

"Aaah ma'. Señor Maestro!"

"Ohhh no. Lord Master!"

"Eh, ne tsoy inwirik at'äniken. Be'ik at'äniken."

"I would like you to call me (that). This is how you address me."

Kura'(a)n ch'ämäk.

The fox is sitting there.

Ele, tuyirah ahchäk barum ne nuk ne bäk'er uka'anan.

And then, the puma saw a really big and tall one.

Ele tuya'arah chäk barum, "Lech ten kinyanbin wa. Pä'h teneh wa. Pachir, tech kahiit(i)k uneeh."

And then, the puma said, "Now I'll go first. Wait for me. Then, you'll pull its tail."

"Ehhh, BAY mameh!"

"OKAY, brother-in-law!"

"Xureh awa'arik amamehtiken," tuya'arah (ah)chäk barum. "Ma' awa'arik amamehtiken. Wa ma', kinpurik inwiich'ak, hun iich'ak; kalubur kuhapti-kech 'ayim."

"Now stop saying you are my brother-in-law," said the puma. "Don't say you are my brother-in-law. If not, I will let fly one of my claws; when you fall the crocodiles will slurp you up."

"Ma', Señor Maestro!"

"No, Lord Master!"

Leti' kura'(a)n chäk barum; le' bin ukah lik'ir usiit', ti' uchukik uyo'och waa-käx. Hach hook'or ut'an ahchäk barum, "Le' ko'ox tun, mameh! Hiit(eh) uneeh wa!"

The puma is sitting there; he is about to jump up to grab his cow. The puma (yells) out, "Come on then, brother-in-law! Pull its tail!"

"Bay!" kih.

"Okay!" says (the fox).

Na(k)'lik'(ih) usiit' ahchäk barum. TIMMM![2] Ti' bin t(i') uche'i(r) ukaar ahwaakäx, ti' uch'uy. Kuhook'or ut'an ahchäk barum, "Hiit(eh) uneeh mam!"

The puma sprang up. TIMMM! He went for the cow's neck, where he hung on. The puma (yells) out, "Pull his tail, brother-in-law!"

Eh, ch'ämäk ulik'il ti'. "KWAANG," ti' ch'uuy ti' (u)neeh. Ti' ch'uya'(a)n t(i') uneeh tun. Chich uchukik uneeh.

The fox gets up from there. "KWAANG" (he shrieks), and he hangs on to its tail. He is hanging on to its tail now. He holds on tight to its tail.

Ahbaram ne chich umuk' ka'wäts' uhook'or (u)t'an, "Hiit(eh) uneeh ma-meh!"

The puma is very strong. He (yells) out a second time, "Pull his tail, brother-in-law!"

"BAY!" ti' tunuukah (ah)chan ch'ämäk. "BAY, mam!"

"OKAY!" replied the little fox. "OKAY, brother-in-law!"

Ma' ne naacheh, (ku)k'uchur bin a' "BEEEH." Cheer(ih) ahwakäx. LUB.

Not very far away, there comes a "BEEEH." The cow fell down with a THUD.

Bay.
Okay.

Ch'ämäk ne tsoy uyor.
The fox is jubilant.

"Le' takinsah, mam."
"You killed it, brother-in-law."

"Tinkinsah bähe'."
"I killed it, now."

Ne tsoy uyor chäk barum. Ts'o'ok. Tuyu'yah kimi(n) tun. Tute(k)kuch-tah. Bin upureh to'an tuworo(r) ... Be' k'i'ix, be' chäk k'i'ix ti' bin t(i') usu' ahchäk k'i'ix ti' tupurah (u)yo'och waakäx, ti' bin uts'oor (u)yoot'er.[3]

The puma is very pleased. It's finished. He sensed it was dead, now. He immediately loads it on his back ... He put his food in a thicket of brambles, the red cat's claw thicket, to peel off its skin.

Ele, kura'(a)n ahch'ämäk bin. Ne tsoy uyor.

And so, the fox is sitting there. He is jubilant.

"Leeh, he' (a)khanan mam."

"Sooo, let's eat, brother-in-law."

"Le' he're'," (tu)nuuk(ah) ahchäk barum.

"Yes, of course," replied the puma.

"Ehhh, bay."

"Great," (says the fox).

Ts'o'ok ulahts'i(r)ik ahchäk barum uyo'och. Tulahts'irah uyo'oter. Tulahts'irah, ele, chan p'uyah ti' chichin ubäk'er t(i') utunteh.

The puma finished skinning his food. He skinned it all. He skinned it all and then he chopped it into little bits of meat to try.

"Atunt(eh) awu'yeh."

"Try it to see how it tastes," (he says to the fox).

"Aaahhh mameh," kih. "Ne p'enk'äch ki'."

"Aaahhh, brother-in-law," says (the fox). "This is sooo tasty."

Eh baarah, chäk barum tan uts'o'okor ulahk'upah. Tulahhaarah uyoot'er. (Tu)chants'irk'uptah ti' t'ä(r)k(u)nta(h) ti' t(i') upach.

So now, the puma finishes slicing it all up. He removed all the skin. He shredded into pieces and laid (the meat) on (the fox's) back.

"Eeeeh! Eeeeh, mameh, ma' kuch' inmuk'! Ne 'aar, mameh. Eenseh ten."

"Eeeeh! Eeeeh, brother-in-law, I'm not that strong! It's very heavy, brother-in-law. Take them off of me."

Eh tupayeenstah chäk ba(rum), tuchaki(n)tah t(i') (u)lu'um.

He pulled them off and laid them on the ground.

"Eh bay, ma' kuch' amuk' ti' akuch."

"Okay you're not strong enough to carry it," (says the puma).

"Le' ma' mameh," tuya'arah ahch'ämäk, "Mameh," kih. "Bin ink(ah) inpääy inna'. Inna' yan upach ba'ay. Yan upach ba'ay inna'. He'r utar uyaantiken inkucheh. Wa h(e') ach'ukt(i)ken ma(meh)? (A)chanxet'k'upt(ik) ubäk'er, ten kinch'a'eh inwe'esik inna'."

"No, brother-in-law," said the fox. "Brother-in-law," he says. "I'm going to go call my mother. My mother has a backpack. My mother has a backpack. She will come and help me carry it. Will you wait for me, brother-in-law? You cut up small pieces of meat, and I will take them to show to my mother."

"Eh bay," kih ahchäk barum. Tuxatah hunxet' ubäk'er tuts'aah ti'.

"Okay," says the puma. He cut a piece of meat and gave it to him.

"Bay."

"Okay," (says the puma).

"Bin inkah, mam," kih ch'ämäk. K'ana(n) uyok chan ch'ämäk bin upäy una'.

"I'm going now, brother-in-law," says the fox. The little fox runs off to call his mother.

Eh, p'aata(r) yahah chäk barum, p'aat tuchi'i(r?) yo'och waa(kä)x.

So, the great puma stays behind, he stayed behind with his cow.

Ele bin ahchan ch'ämäk. Bin upäy una'. Hook' (ti') (u)kuuch(ir) t(i') una'.

And so the little fox left. He went to call his mother. He went out to his mother's place.

"Na'eh!" kih. "Tintaasah. Tintaasah bäk', na'!" kih. "Ma' uk'uch(ur) inmuuk' ink'uch(eh); ne 'aar. Atech he' atar awaanten."

"Mother!" he (calls out). "I brought it. I brought meat, mother," he says. "I'm not strong enough to carry it; it's very heavy. You have to come help me."

Lik'i(h) una' ahch'ämäk. "Bay, ko'ox!"

The fox's mother gets up. "Okay, let's go!"

Hook'(ih). Bin(ih) ket.

They went out. They left together.

"Ko'ox, na'! Seeb!"

"Let's go, mother! Quickly!"

Kuk'uch(ur) ubin tu' tuts'oorah bin, tu' tuchi'ah ahwaakäx yet(er) ahchäk barum. Mix ba'(ar), chen uk'ik'er puka'(an).

They arrive at (the place) where (the puma) (had) skinned it, where he ate the cow with the puma. There isn't anything, just congealed blood.

"Eh to'an awa'arah tun?" kuya'arik a' na' ahch'ämäk. "To'an tawa'arah tun?"

"So where is it, you say?" the fox's mother says. "So where is it, did you say?"

"Le' hah. Mäna'."

"So it's true. There isn't any."

Ne ts'iik bin (ah)chanch'ämäk. Ti' kumaan. Tuk'eyah. Ne ts'iik.

The little fox is furious. He walks around. He yelled. He is fuming.

"Mäna'. Ma' inwoher tu' bin xi'ik inmam. Ma' la' tuch'ukah inmam. Chen ten tinch'ukah. Wa mäna'en kachik mäna' ba'(ar) ukinsik mam."

"There isn't any. I don't know where my brother-in-law went. My brother-in-law didn't wait. But I waited (for him). If it weren't for me, my brother-in-law wouldn't have killed anything."

Una' ti' kumaan ulahleets'(eh) uk'ik'er. "Leets'eleets'," kih. Ta(ra)k man ukäxtik mix k'äs ba', mix ubäk'er, mix k'äs p'aatih. Man ahchäk barum, tulahk'uchah ubiseh, tukuchah.

His mother goes around lapping up all the blood. "Slurp, slurp." Although she goes around searching for (some meat), there isn't much of anything (left); there isn't any meat; hardly anything at all is left. The puma (had) gone around, loaded it all up, and carried it off.

Ele, ti' kuka'maan uleets'e(r) uk'ik'er. Mix k'äs ba'; mix ubäk'er, mäna' p'ata(r) ti'.

And then, she goes around again, lapping up the blood. There is hardly any; there is nothing left of the meat.

Ele, ka'(ah) bini(h) chan ch'ämäk bin, la' bixi(r) tuyirah chäk barum be-ki(r) tume(n)tah. Hook' uka'na'akar pach ahche' t(i') upuuma'an ahche'. Ele, tuya'arah ti' una',

Well, then the little fox went and did it the same way that he saw the puma do it. He went out and climbed up the back of the bent tree again. And then, he said to his mother,

"Ko'ox na'. Way ana'akar." Ele, la' bixi(r) tume(n)tah chäk barum, beki(r) ti' (ah)chan ch'ämäk yeter una' na'ak ku(r)tar.

"Let's go, mother. You climb up here." And in the same way the puma did it, the fox and his mother climbed up and sat down.

Bay.
Okay.

Ahwakäx, ne tak k'ak'chun k'in, uk'uchur xäktar uyuk'eh uyo'och ha'.
It's almost midday (and) the cows arrive and stoop to drink their water.

Uya'arik ti' una', "Le bähe', awoher ma' at'äniken awaarehtiken'. Ma' awa'arik awaarehtiken'. At'äniken, Señor Maestro."
He says to his mother, "Okay, now you know you are not to call me your child. Don't call me your child. You call me, Lord Master."

"Ehhh bay," unuukik una' ahchan ch'ämäk. "Ehhh bay. Eh, ma' int'änikech inwaareh."
"Oookay," replies the little fox's mother [she whispers]. "Ooookay. I won't call you my child."

"Eh ma' at'äniken awaarehtiken. At'äniken, Señor Maestro."
"Don't call me your little child. You call me, Lord Master."

Leti' tukanah bekir tukanah chan ch'ämäk (ti') chäk barum.
She learned it just like the little fox learned it from the puma.

Tan uteetik lahi(h); kuteetik. Kutichir ahwaakäx, (ku)tichir ahwaakäx p'uruknäk' ... Ma' la' kuteet(eh) kuk'uchu(r) t(i) uyuk'ur ha'—ma' ne nuk. Lehi(h) kuteet(ik) le' ne nuk, ne nuk, nukuch ubäk'er.

He is selecting them; he selects (one). A cow approaches with a swollen belly ... (But) he doesn't choose the one that comes to drink water—it's not very big. He selects the much bigger (one), it's a very big (one), a really tall (one).

Ele, kuhook'or ut'an bin una', "La' wa he' kutichir inwaareh?" kih.

And then, his mother calls out, "How about that one approaching, son?"

"Ma' at'äniken awaarehtiken!" kih. "Ten kinlisik ink'äb; kuhäp(ti)kech 'ayim wa."

"Don't call me your son!" he says. "I will raise my hand; when you fall the crocodiles will slurp you up."

"Eh! Ma'!" Ha'k' uyor una' ahch'ämäk.

"Oh! No!" The fox's mother is startled.

Chan kura'(a)n una'. Mix upeek. Lati' kura'(a)n kuyirik tan uk'uchur ahwaakäx; t(an) uk'uchur ti' uyuk'ur ha'.

His mother is seated. She doesn't move. She is sitting there watching the cow arriving; it is arriving to drink water.

K'uch(ih) ahwaakäx—ne 'uk'ah bin. K'uch(ih) uyuk'ur ha', *suuu*. Xäkih.

The cow arrived—it was very thirsty. It arrived to drink water, *slurrrp*. It stood on all fours.

"Lech, HIITEH uneeh ten wa na'!"

"Now PULL its tail for me mother!"

"Bay!" nuuk una' ahch'ämäk bin. "Bay!" kih.

"Okay!" his mother replied. "Okay!"

Hach tuna'ak(ar) che' ahch'ämäk bin. HUAAAH. Ti' ch'uy t(i') uche'i(r) ukaar ahwaakäx bin. Ta(ra)k uts'ahik, "norrrot-norrrot," kih, mix k'äs okih ukoh. Ma' nuk ukoh, ma' okih. Ne tsuy uyoot'er ahwaakäx.

The fox goes scrambling up the tree. HUAAAH. He hangs on to the neck of the cow. Although he is giving it to it, "chomp-chomp," his teeth hardly enter (its hide). His teeth aren't large, they didn't go in. The cow's hide is very tough.

Tuya'arah ti' una', "Hiiteh uneeh na'. Hii(r)teh uneeh na'!"

He said to his mother, "Pull its tail, mother! Pull its tail, mother!"

"Bay!" kih.

"Okay!" she says.

"Ts'aah! Ma' axurik! Hiiteh uneeh!"

"Give it! Don't stop! Pull its tail!"

Tarak uts'ahik ahch'ämäk, "norrrot-norrrot," mix mäna' okih. Mäna' k'äs cheeri(h) waakäx.

Although the fox is giving it, "chomp-chomp," (his teeth) didn't go in. The cow hardly wavered.

Täk'än (u)wich; (tuyirah) tun(?) tan uk'uchur to'an uwiniki(r), xok'or to'an uyatoch uwiniki(r).

Then he noticed he was moving toward its master's house.

Ele tak ut'änik, "Na'eh, hiiteh uneeh. Hiiteh uneeh, na'."

He wants to call out, "Mother, pull its tail. Pull its tail, mother."

"CHIIIN," kih.

"CHIIIN," (a sound of something snapping).

Mix unuukik una'.

His mother doesn't answer.

Ele, ne tuyirah ne xok'or nah. Tupur(ah) ubah ahchan ch'ämäk. *Pih.*

Then, he saw that the cow is very close to the house. The little fox jumped down. *Flumppf.*

Tarak ut'änik, "NA'EH. TU' BINECH NA'EH?"

Although he says, "MOTHER! WHERE DID YOU GO, MOTHER?"

mäna' una'.

his mother isn't there.

"TU' BINECH NA'?"

"WHERE DID YOU GO, MOTHER?"

Hook'(ih) uka'sut ukäxtik una'. He' uyirik tu' bin(ih) una'. Tarak ut'änik, "Na'! Tu' binech, na'?" Mänaaa'.

He went back to look for his mother. He will see where his mother went to stand. Although he calls out, "Mother! Where did you go, mother?" She doesn't answer.

Eh, kuyirik una' käpa'(a)n t(i') uxaay che'. Kimen.

Then, he sees his mother in the fork of a tree branch. She's dead.

" EHhhh mäna' inna'. Ki(m)ih inna'."

"EHhhh my mother is no more. My mother died."

Ta(r)ak una'ak'ar ahch'ämäk, upoch kuhiitik una', mäna'. Ne chich tak'i(h) yok'or uxaay che'.

Although the fox climbs up, he wants to release his mother, it's impossible. She is really stuck in the fork of the tree.

"EHhhh 'utsereh. Bähe' mäna' inna'. Tinkinsah inna'. Ten insi'ipi(r)." Ok'or ukah ahch'ämäk.

"OHhhh dear. Now my mother is no more. I killed my mother. It's all my fault." The fox is crying.

"Bähe' mäna' inna'," ki(h). Ahch'ämäk tan uyok'or, "Mäna' inna'. Kimen."

"Now my mother is gone." The fox is crying, "My mother is gone. She's dead."

Hachäkyum yeter Ahbäb 'Hachäkyum and the Toad'

Säk Ho'or

This story explains how the toad got his warty skin.[1] One day Hachäkyum gathered all the mosquitoes and gnats and stuffed them in a bag. He asked the toad to take the bag and pitch it at the end of the world. He warned him not to look inside. Curiosity overcame the toad, and he opened the bag. He was immediately enveloped in mosquitoes and gnats, which bit him all over.

Bay.
Okay.

Hachäkyum uchik tulahchukah tuworor ah'us, tuworor ahchibar. Mix ba' hump'eri' tulahchukah.
Hachäkyum caught all the gnats (and) all the mosquitoes. There wasn't one he didn't catch.

Bay.
Okay.

Ahbäb, tuya'arah ti', tuya'arah ti' bäb,
He said to the toad,

"He' wa (a)bin apureh bähe' pach k'ak'na'," tuya'arah Hachäkyum.
"Will you go now and throw them on the other side of the sea," said Hachäkyum.

"Bay," ahbäb tunuukah. "He' inbin pureh. He', he' inbin pureh."

"Okay," the toad replied. "I'll go and throw them away. Yes, I'll go and throw them away."

"Ch'iktar tahan t(i') upach k'ak'na'."

"Stop way over on the other side of the sea," (Hachäkyum says).

"Bay!"

"Okay!"

"Ka'ah wu'(r), kak'aatik ten awoher ba'i(n)ki(r) pochech tech. Kabin ak'aat-eh ten, insihik tech."

"When you come back, you will ask me for anything you think you want. You're going to ask me for it, I (will) give it to you."

"Bay." Ahbäb tucha'ah.

"Okay." The toad took it.

"Pureh ch'ik bähe' pach k'ak'na'. Ma' ahe'ik! Ta(ra)k uba'i(n)k(ir) awu'yik 'ᴋ'-ᴏ-ᴏ-ɴ' kih, ma' ahe'ik."

"Throw it way over on the other side of the sea. Don't open it! Although you hear something like 'ᴋ'-ᴏ-ᴏ-ɴ,' don't open it."

Bay.

Okay.

Ahbäb bin upureh. Bin upureh. K'uchih chumuk ber ahbäb, tuyu'yah, "ᴋ'-ᴏ-ᴏ-ɴ" kih.

The toad set off to the throw it away. He set off to throw it away. The toad got half way up the road (and) he heard, "ᴋ'-ᴏ-ᴏ-ɴ."

"Ba'inkin a' la'eh?" kih.
"What's that?" he says.

Tutukrah ahbäb, *"Tint'an inhe'ik inwireh."*
The toad thought, *"I think I'll open it and see."*

'Otsir bäb. Tuhe'ah. Ka'(a)h lahxibk'ah — ahchibar, tuworor ah'us — ka'(a)h lahxibk'ah (tu)lahbäräxtah ahbäb.
Poor toad. He opened it. When they broke free — the mosquitoes, all the gnats — when they all broke free they bit the toad all over.

(Tu)lahbäräxtah.
They bit him all over.

(Tu)lahbäräxtah.
They bit him all over.

'Otsi(r) bäb. Kuputs'ur. Kubin haban che'. Kubin bähe' yok'o(r) petha'.
Poor toad. He runs away. He goes to a log. Now he goes into the lagoon.

Tupur(ah) ubäh yok'o(r) petha', yok'or ha'. Tupur(ah) ubah.
He threw himself into the lagoon, into the water. He threw himself in.

'Otsi(r) ahbäb.
The poor toad.

Bay.
Okay.

Kuka'hook'or, kubäräxtah. (Ku)tich'ik uho'or, kubäräxtah.

When he gets out again, they bite him all over. When he sticks his head out, they bite him all over.

'Otsi(r) bäb.

Poor toad.

Bay.

Okay.

Pachi(r) ahbäb tuya'arah, "Bay. Ma' k'uch(en) inpureh."

Then the toad said, "Okay. I didn't get there to throw it away."

Tichih. Kutichir, uyir(ik) Hachäkyum.

He got out. When he gets out, he sees Hachäkyum.

"Ehhh, ba'i(nkin) tume(n)tah, ahbäb? Ba'i(nkin) tume(n)tah ahbäb? 'Otsi(r) bäb, ba'i(nkin) tume(n)tah?"

"Ehhh, what happened, toad? What happened, toad? Poor toad, what happened?"

"Awirik, Hachäkyum, ma' k'uch(en) inpureh. Tulahbäräxten ahchibar. Ah'us tulahbäräxten."

"You see, Hachäkyum, I didn't get there to throw it away. The mosquitoes bit me all over. The gnats bit me all over."

Bay.

Okay.

Hachäkyum tunuukah, "Bähe', teche'ex ti' kubin p'aata(r) binet k'in. Bähe' tech, kubin p'aata(r) tech. Yan awoot'e(r), kisinkisin awoot'e(r), t(i') kubin p'aata(r)."

Hachäkyum replied, "Now all of you (toads) are going to stay (like this) forever. Now it's going to stay this way for you. You have hideous skin, (which) is going to remain."

'Otsi(r) bäb, tutukrah ubah, "*Bik yani(r)?*"

Poor toad, he thought to himself, "*Why?*"

"Bex kubin p'aata(r) teche'ex, tuworor ati'a'ar woro(r) bex kubin p'aata(r). Wah he' axi'ikech apureh (tu)pach k'ak'na', bähe' mäna' ahchibar. Mäna' ich k'aax. Mäna' 'us. Mäna' tuworo(r) ba' bähe'. Ne tsoy."

"It will stay like this for all of you, all of your children everywhere will remain this way. If you had gone and thrown it to the other side of the sea, there wouldn't be any mosquitoes now. There wouldn't be any in the forest. There wouldn't be any gnats. There wouldn't be any of them now. It would have been fine."

Hachäkyum tuya'arah ti', "Bähe' ti' kubin p'aata(r binet k'in ti' teche'ex. Tuworo(r) ka('a)h chan ti'a'ar kuka'lik'i(r), tuworo(r) amehen ti'a'ar kulik'i(r), binet k'in² woro(r) bex kup'aata(r) ahbäb."

Hachäkyum said to him, "Now it's going to stay like this forever for all of you. When all your children grow up, when all your little ones grow up, the toad will stay like this forever."

Pek' yeter 'Ayim 'The Dog and the Crocodile'

Säk Ho'or

This story explains why the dog has a long tongue while the crocodile hasn't any.

Uchik, pek' ma' ch'ukuch uyaak'.
A long time ago, the dog didn't have a very long tongue.

Bay.
Okay.

'Ayim tuyirah pek'. Tuya'arah, "Ba'i(in)k(ir) ame(n)tik?"
The crocodile saw the dog. He said, "What are you doing?"

"Mix ba'." Pek' tan uyuk'u(r) ha'.
"Nothing." The dog is drinking water.

'Ayim tuya'arah, "Tech, bik yani(r) ma' ak'axik awaak'? Ten kints'ahik inwaak' tech, tech kats'ahik awaak' ten. Chen, ints'ahik a' ma(h)a(n) t(i') inwaak', h(e') aka'sutik ten."
The crocodile said, "Why don't you change your tongue? I give you my tongue and you give me your tongue. But (if) I loan you my tongue, you will return it to me."

Pek' tuya'arah, "Inka'sut(i)k awaak'."
The dog said, "I'll return your tongue."

"Hach tuhahil(r)? He' aka'sutik ten? Ma' awaak'ir ten ma'."
"Honestly? You will return it to me? My tongue is not yours."

Pek' tuya'arah, "Ma', ma', ma' inch'a'ik tech awaak' porque tech yani(r) awaak'. Tech yani(r). Ma' ten yani(r)."
The dog said, "No, no I won't take your tongue from you, because it's your tongue. It's yours. It's not mine."

Pach(ir) tuya'arah, "Ints'ahik tech. Ama(h)a(n)tik, he' aka'sutik ten."
Then (the crocodile) said, "I (will) give it to you. You borrow it, (then) you will return it to me."

Bay.
Okay.

Pek' tuch'a'ah uyaak'; tuk'ax(ah) uyaak' yete(r). "Ch'a'(eh) inwaak'."
The dog took his tongue; he exchanged tongues with him. "Take my tongue," (says the dog).

Tuch'a'ah tutäkah uyaak'. Tuch'a'ah.
(The crocodile) took it and stuck in his tongue. He took it.

Pach(ir) tuya'arah 'ayim, "Bay, he' inwaak'."
Then the crocodile said, "Okay, here's my tongue."

Bay.
Okay.

Pachi(r) pek' tutunt(ah) uyuk'ur ha'.

Later, the dog tried to drink water.

Tuya'arah pek', "Ahhh ne tsoy uyaak' 'ayim. Ne tsoy. Int'an bähe' poch inch'a'ik."

The dog said, "Ahhh, the crocodile's tongue is excellent. It's very good indeed. Now I think I want to (keep) it."

Pek' ma' poch uka'sutik. Pek' poch unahch'a'ik uyaak'. Poch uyaakrik uyaak' 'ayim.

The dog doesn't want to give it back. The dog wants to keep his tongue. He wants to steal the crocodile's tongue.

Bay.

Okay.

'Ayim tuya'arah, "Bähe' bin aka'sut(ik) inwaak'."

The crocodile said, "Now you're going to give me back my tongue."

"Y bik yani(r) (in)sutik awaak'? Tech tawa'arah ten, 'Ch'a'(eh) inwaak'. Insihi(k) tech.'"

"And why (should) I return your tongue? You told me, 'Take my tongue. I am giving it to you.'"

'Otsi(r) 'ayim tuya'arah, "Ne ma' paatech, pek'. Ha'ri' tech ne ma' paatech. Talah'akrah inwaak'. Talahtak(ah) inwaak'. Ten yani(r) inwaak' lahi(h). Ten ma' tinsiyah. Tints'ahah mahanteh."

The poor crocodile said, "You're wicked, dog. You're just plain wicked. You just stole my tongue. You took my tongue in. That's my tongue. I didn't give it away. I loaned it."

Pek' tuya'arah, "Bähe' ma' insutik tech. Ten yani(r). Ne tsoy inwirik. Ne tsoy inwuk'u(r) ha' ne tsoy."

The dog said, "I'm not going to give it back to you, now. It's mine. I really like it. I can drink water perfectly. It's very good."

'Ayim tuya'arah, "Tur inkinsikech. He' uk'uchu(r) k'in tur inhantikecheh, tur inchi'ik abäk'er."

The crocodile said, "I have to kill you. The day will come when I (will) have to eat you, eat your flesh."[1]

'Otsi(r) 'ayim. Binet k'in, tuya'arah taki(r) bähe' uyaak' pek' lehi(h) uyaak' 'ayim. Uyaak' 'ayim lati' uyaak' pek'.

The poor crocodile. They said it stayed this way forever. Up to now, the dog's tongue is the crocodile's tongue (and) the crocodile's tongue is the dog's tongue.

How the Toucan Got His Red Beak

Antonio Martinez

Hachäkyum told the keel-billed toucan to eat the fruits of the *k'o'och* tree. But the toucan got confused and went for an ancestor's throat, which is also called *k'o'och*. This is an example of word-play, which is ubiquitous in Mayan literature. The story explains how the toucan got his red beak.[1]

La' pän, ahHachäkyum umentik.

Hachäkyum (made) the toucan.[2]

Ku(r)a'an. Ts'o'ok uch'urha' bin aknukire'ex yet(er) ti' kura'(a)n. Ts'o'ok a' ch'urha', 'u'ri(h).

(Hachäkyum) is seated there. He finished the ritual offering of posol. Our ancestors are sitting there with him. (When) the posol is finished, he came.

Eh, bin(ih) utunteh ti' uwich ahk'o'och, la' k'o'och uwich ahk'o'och. Toh hach winik tubah uk'o'och bin(ih) ahpän.

Eh, (the toucan) went to taste the fruit of the pumpwood tree, the fruit of the pumpwood tree. (But) it was really a person's throat that the toucan went to.[3]

A-a-a-h kimi(h) hach winik.

A-a-a-nd the person died.

"Eh, ma' tinwa'arah ti', 'Ma' la' ahk'o'och?'"

"Eh, didn't I tell him, 'It's not that k'o'och?'" (says Hachäkyum).

Ahk'o'och (ti' yan) yok'or k'aax. Kuya'arik ahk'o'och. Uwich kuhantik la' pichik'. Bin ti' (u)wich ahk'o'och tuhahir ti' bin yok'or k'aaxeh wich che' tuhantah.

The pumpwood tree (is) in the forest. They call it k'o'och. The collared araçari eats its fruit. He went to the fruits of the real k'o'och. He went into the forest and ate the fruit of the tree.[4]

Ahpän, la' kura'an uk'ik'er t(i') ukoh. Te' nu' ukoh tu' leh uk'ik'er winik.

As for the toucan, the blood is sitting on his beak. There, on his beak was a lump of the blood of the person.

Ch'iksa(n)[5] kimi(h). Tukinsah.

A while later (the person) died. He killed him.

"Ehhh ma' bikih. Ma' tsoy ahpän."

"Ehhh, he can't (go around doing that). The toucan is bad," (says Hachäk-yum).

Ehhh, nahku(r)a'(an) ti' uk'ik'er.

Ehhh, (the person's) blood was sitting there (on the toucan's beak).

"Eh, ne ma' tsoy ahpän."

"Eh, the keel-billed toucan is very bad."

Ch'iksa(n) bähe' ahpichik eh, bin ti' uwich ahk'o'och, tuhahir k'o'och.

A while later, the collared araçari goes to the fruit of the real k'o'och, the pumpwood tree.

Toh ka'(ah) lik' ahpän, toh t(i') uk'o'och winik ...

(But) when the toucan ascends, he (goes) straight for the man's throat ...

"KIIS, KIIS!" t(an) uyawat. Ch'uuy tu' himpah[6] way.

"KIIS, KIIS!" he screeches. (The blood) hangs off of where (his beak) got flattened. [Antonio points to his nose showing where the red spot sits on the toucan's beak.]

Eh, ka'(ah) tutäkche't(ah) täkäch, bini(h).

Eh, (after) he stabbed him, he left.

Bähe' nahkura'(a)n uk'ik'er meen yok'or koh.

Today the blood is sitting there on his beak.

4

Songs

Uk'aay Barum 'The Jaguar Song'

Antonio Martinez

Lacandones sing this song to protect themselves from jaguar attacks when on their way to the milpa or walking through the forest. The song was given to them by K'ak' 'the God of Courage and War'. K'ak' was the model of a Maya warrior, dressed in jaguar skins. K'ak' was the first one to slay a jaguar. It was a premeditated plan of Hachäkyum to test K'ak''s courage and skill. K'ak' proved his prowess after slaying the fearsome, two-headed jaguar, *Ka'wäts'äk uho'or* (see "Ka'wäts'äk uho'or Barum yeter K'ak'" 'The Two-Headed Jaguar and the Lord of Fire', this volume). Hachäkyum declared that K'ak''s courage would be his legacy to the mortals.

This song is meant to lull the jaguars to sleep. It is the only text I know of that mentions Lacandon musical instruments, of which there were four: guitar, flute, drum, and rattle. In pre-Columbian times, drums, flutes, and conch shells were played as the warriors went into battle. The Lacandon guitar resembles an African-style zither, undoubtedly introduced by African slaves during the Colonial period. The rattle and the drum were played only in ceremonial contexts, inside the god house.

This song is one of at least ten versions, according to Antonio.[1] In this version and some others (Bruce 1968, 1976) the singer and the jaguar are having a conversation.

Eh, ka' tawu'y(ik) utar ink'aay,
Eh, when you hear my song come,

tan aw(u'y)iken wits'ineh hunkur uwits.
you are hearing me, oh little brother, one mountain (away).

Tan atarer wits'ineh; huhunts'it t(an) ahiitik ak'äb.

You are coming, oh little brother; one by one you are drawing out your paws.

Tan upeek aneeh.

Your tail is moving.

Tan upeek.

It is moving.

Tan atar t(i') inpach;

You are coming behind me;

tsay way ki' ubok.

a delicious scent follows here.

Huhunts'it tan upeek aneeh,

One by one your tail is moving,

tan uwawar aneeh.

your tail is swaying.

T(i) uwe're('e)n aneeh, t(i') uwe're('e)n axikin,

From your painted tail to your painted ears,

tan utar huhunts'it te' wits'ineh, ka' taw(u'y)ah.

your (paws) are coming here, one by one, oh little brother, when you heard it.

Ka' tawu'yah, he' wits'in.

When you heard it, here little brother.

Tinchukah tan inpax.

I took my guitar (and) I am playing it.

Ka' tawu'y(ah) utar inpax,

When you heard my guitar coming,

ka' tawu'y(ah) utar inpax,

when you heard my guitar coming,

utar inchur, t(an) utar

(and) my flute coming, they are coming

ne ch'ik naach yok'or nah wits.(?) T(an) awu'yik utar.

very far off in the hills. You are hearing (the sound) come.

Ma' xok'o(r) uyareh wits'(in)eh. Ma'.

The (mountain) range is not near, oh little brother. It is not.

Ka' tinnuukah ak'aay, tinnuukah ten, ket aknuukik. Ket akoreh, wits'(in)eh.

When I answered your song, I answered it, we answer each other. We are in harmony, oh little brother.

...

...

Le' mäna' tak inwene(n), tak'a(')t ten tak inwene(n). (In)käxtik ich hene(n) che'

I am not sleepy, you want me to be sleepy. I look for a log

k'ataki(h) nahkor, xantarkih lo'obi(r).
lying across the milpa, leaning against the brush.

Ts'o'ok upeek inneeh. Ts'o'ok upeek ink'äb. Ts'o'ok upeek inxikin.
My tail stopped moving. My hands stopped moving. My ears stopped moving.

Tan inwirik.
I am looking (at you).

He' inchi'ikecheh.
I am going to eat you.

Mäna' achi'iko'(on).
You are not going to eat us.

T(an) awu'y(ik) (in)nuuk te', wits'in. Tan utar inpax.
You are listening to my reply there, my little brother. My guitar is coming.

Ka' tar(er) uk'aay,
When the song came,

ka' tare(r) ch'ik naach boon utan k'aax,
when it came from far off in the forest,

ka' tichi(h) ink'aay, tawu'yah,
when my song approached, you heard it,

he' wits'ineh.
here, oh little brother.

Huhunts'it ak'äb
One by one your paws (come)

ka' binech ich hene(n)che';
when you went into the log;

tak awenen.
you are sleepy.

Tarak inmaanen, wits'ineh,
Although I walk past, oh little brother,

ki' awenen.
you are sleeping soundly.

Cha(ra)kech.
You are lying down.

Mäna' ma' hanech, wits'ineh.
You didn't eat anything, oh little brother.

Ka' tawu'yah (u)tar inpax,
When you heard my guitar come,

ka' tawu'yah upak'ar inpax,
when you heard (the sound of) my guitar spread,

upak'ar inchureh, wits'ineh,
(the sound of) my flute spread, oh little brother,

ts'o'ok ahiit(i)k ak'äb.
you stopped dragging your paws.[2]

Huhunts'it ts'o'okih.
One by one they stopped.

Ma' aw(oh)e(r) wa ta min(?) t(an) intar awa'a(n)ber, wits'ineh?
Don't you know I am coming (along) your path, oh little brother?

Ma' aw(oh)e(r) wa(h) tan intar?
Don't you know I am coming?

Tan intar ten.
I am coming.

Kaka'tare(r) wits'ineh, ka'(ah) tawu'yah,
When you come again, oh little brother, when you heard it,

ts'o'ok ulahmakar axikin.
your ears all folded down.

Talahwäts'a(h).
You folded them up completely.

Talahmeek'ah axikineh, wits'ineh.
You tucked in your ears, oh little brother.

Mäna' ma' het la'eh.
There is nothing (you can do to me now).

Bin akah ti' wenen ich hene(n) che'.
You are going to sleep in the log.

Okech yaram lo'obir
You went into the underbrush

tawenen.
and went to sleep.

Mäna'.
There is nothing (you can do to me now).

Ne tak awenen, wits'ineh.
You are very sleepy, oh little brother.

Ka' tawu'yah inchur,
When you heard my flute,

ka' tawu'yah inpax,
when you heard my guitar,

ts'o'oki(h) tasähtahen.
you stopped frightening me.

Tak awenen. Ma' up'iir awicheh, wits'ineh.
You are sleepy. Your eyes do not open, oh little brother.

Eh, ka'ah tawu'yah utar inso'ot, inchur.
Oh, when you heard my rattle (and) my flute come.

Uk'aay Box 'The Gourd Song'

Antonio Martinez

This is a drinking song[1] an accused liar sings to prevent himself from vomiting *balche'*, the Lacandon ceremonial liquor.[2] It is a song that is sung in a ritual context, conducted by members of the community to bring a suspected liar to account, by forcing him to drink copious amounts of balche' to the point of vomiting. As such, the event is a ritualized form of punishment (Davis 1978, 267). But the aim is to cleanse the liar of his crime, to obviate punishment in the afterlife. On the social level his confession restores harmony to the group.[3]

The accused liar tries to prove his innocence and remain in a state of inebriation by singing the song to the balche' cup (Bruce 1976, 108). But his song is addressed to a woman, imploring her not to "cast him away," but to keep him in her embrace. "Cast away" implies elimination, expressed in this song as rejection and purging. Her embrace implies ecstasy and intoxicated delirium.[4]

The associations between balche' and a young woman, and between inebriation and sexual ecstasy, are made by a play on the near homophonous words *lek* 'balche cup' and *laak'* 'female consort'.[5] The filled cup is likened to the swell of a young woman's breasts; the bark cloth ribbon tied around the balche' urn is her braided hair. The correspondence between balche' and femininity is also inferred via honey (McGee's (1987, 112–14). An extended metaphor in the *Chilam Balam of Chumayel* (Roys [1933] 1973) associates the beehive and the balche' tree with parts of a woman's body:

> The entrails of his daughter are an empty beehive. Her bone, the flexible bark of the balche'. Her thigh, its trunk. Her arm, its branch. (Roys [1933] 1973, 95)

The song takes the form of a conversation between the singer and the woman. Only the woman's speech is enclosed in quotations.

Kära'anen. Ne kära'anen. Eh, t'anen k'aseh inwik'.
I am drunk. I am very drunk. Oh, call me, set me straight.

Mix inwu'yik tu'bah way yanen. Tan inwok'ot . . .
I can't feel anything where I am here. I am dancing . . .

Ne wu'yik inwok(')ot.[6] K'äs t'anen.
I really feel like I'm dancing. Please call me.

Tawu'yah t'anen. Tan ink'äyik ti' box.[7] Tan ink'äyik.
You heard me call. I am singing (the song) to the (balche') cup. I am singing it.

Laak' chaneh, laak' chaneh,
Oh little wife, oh little wife,

tan uturankär laak' chan,
you are filling up little wife,

t(i') ap'iis;[8] mäna' tsoy kurenmäk awiim.[9]
in your measuring cup; there is nothing lovelier than your growing breasts.

Chichanech tsitsi(k)näk aho'or. Tints'i(b)o(r)tikech.
You are youthful and your hair is nicely combed. I am longing for you.

Bähe' ma' saamänen laak' chan; ma' apuriken; ma' atench'intiken.
I haven't vomited yet(?) little wife; don't throw me down; don't push me away.

Tarak awirik tinnets'i'o(r)t(ik)ech, he' inmeek'ikech, ma' ameek'(ik)en.

Although you see that I am longing for you, I will embrace you, you don't embrace me.

Tinpurahech; tintench'intahech. Ma' 'uts t(i') inwich. Tinpurahech. Ma' tsoy.

I threw you down; I pushed you away. You don't appeal to me. I threw you down. You are wicked.

Pachi(r) tinwirahecheh, ne chichanech.

Then, I looked at you there, you are so youthful.

Tsitsi(k)näk aho'or, ch'ikrikech. Tinwirah turemäk ap'iis, tan uturankär.

With your hair so nicely combed, you stood. I saw your measuring cup brimming full; it is filling up.

Tinnets'i(b)o(r)tahech laak' chaneh. Mäna' tech; ne tsoyech kurenmäk awiim.

I was longing for you, oh little wife. There is no one like you; you are beautiful with your growing breasts.

Mäna'; pichik' awiimeh. Ch'uprareh tinwirahech.

There is nothing (finer); like guavas are your breasts. I saw you as a woman.

Eh laak' chan tinwirah tsitsiknäk uho'or, p'is ch'uprar ch'ikrik ti' inwich. Mäna'tar uxur inwirik.

Oh little wife, I saw your nicely combed hair, like a woman standing in my view. I see nothing that comes close (to you).

Ha'ri' ten ma' apuriken.
Just don't throw me down.

"Ma' he' ink'asik awik'."
"I will not bring you to your senses."

K'aseh inwik'.[10] T'anen.
Bring me to my senses.[11] Call me.

"Ma' int'änikech."
"I won't talk to you."

Tarak ma' ukuchur inmuuk', int'änikech. Kära'an awiriken.
Although I have no strength, I call you. You can see that I am drunk.

Tatench'intahen, ya bähe' ma' int'änikech. Mäna'aneh.
You pushed me away, so now I don't call you. It's too late.

Ma', laak' chan, k'aseh inwik'eh, laak' chan.
Don't, little wife, bring me to my senses, little wife.

Tinwirah ... pichik' awiim.
I saw them ... your breasts are like guavas.

Talak awiriken, tapulahen.
Although you see me, you threw me down.

Bähe' mäna' int'änikech. Ts'o'okih.
Now I don't call you (anymore). It's over.

Uk'aay Käkah 'The Cacao Song'

Juana Koh

This is a women's work song that is sung while preparing the ceremonial cocoa beverage. The singer invokes the *tsukil* sarsaparilla vine to release its juice to help her froth the cacao. Like other Lacandon women's work songs, it is sung to help relieve the workload and hasten the process.[1]

This song also serves a pedagogical purpose, by listing and describing each step in the preparation of the beverage. First the tender tips of the vine are crushed and the juice squeezed out. Then the juice and vine pulp are added to the cacao beans, which have been roasted, ground, and mixed with water. After this the beverage is beaten with a wooden beater to raise a froth. Finally, the beverage and the chocolate foam are added to corn gruel.

Most of the preparation takes place in the ceremonial kitchen, located beside the god house. One of the rare occasions when women are allowed into the god house is to froth the cacao, which they do in front of the god pots that will receive the offering.

The structure of the text reflects Juana Koh's delivery. Line spaces indicate long pauses, punctuation marks off prosodic features and syntactic constituents, semicolons and commas signal a hiatus in the stream of speech, and periods mark off sentences.

Eh, ink'eerik inkäkah eh,
I toast my cacao,

innuts'ik uk'ak'ir inkäkah.
I push the fire together for my cacao.

Inch'a'ik uk'ak'ir inkäkah, inch'a'ik.
I fetch the fire for my cacao, I fetch it.

Inmaan inmarik uche'ir inkäkah.
I walk around collecting firewood for my cacao.

Innuts'ik uk'ak'i(r).
I push the firebrands together.

Inch'a'ik uxet'er ukumir inkäkah.
I fetch the pieces of my cacao for my pot.

Inch'a'ik uche'i(r); inpeeksik inkäkah; ink'ee(r)ik.
I fetch the wood; I stir my cacao; I toast it.

Inwät(i)k; inwät(i)k inkäkah.
I break it up; I break up my cacao.

Inpeeksik inkäkah.
I move my cacao around.

Inp'o'ik upohche' inkäkah.
I wash the table for my cacao.

Inmaan inch'a'ik uya'ri(r) inkäkah.
I go fetch the water for my cacao.

Inmaan inch'uyik uya'ri(r).
I go carry the water.

Inch'a'ik uluuchi(r).
I fetch the cup.

Inp'o'ik uluuchi(r) inkäkah.
I wash the cup for my cacao.

Inp'o'ik upohche'i(r).
I wash the table.

Inch'a'ik umorinuhi(r).
I fetch the beater.

Inpuk'ik inkäkah.
I beat my cacao.

Inmaa(n)s(i)k inkäkah.
I pass my cacao through.

Inhuch'ik inkäkah.
I grind my cacao.

La' morinuh,
The beater,

es inkäkah,
it is (for) my cacao,

la' morinuh.
the beater.

Inpeeksik inkäkah eh.
I move my cacao around.

Inch'a'ik uchan suuri(r) inkäkah ti' uyo'och äkyum.
I fetch the small cup of my cacao for the food of our Lord.

H(e') atar awirik inbo'or ti' kyum.
You will come see my offering to our Lord.

Inpeeksik; ink'eerik inkäkah.
I move it around; I toast my cacao.

La' morinuh,
The beater,

inpeeksik ya; inch'a'ik utsukiri(r) inkäkah.
I move it around; I take the sarsaparilla vine for my cacao.

Inp'ikiko'
I snap off (the tips of)

utsukiri(r) inkäkah.
the sarsaparilla for my cacao.

Inmaa(n)sik utsuki(r).
I pass the sarsaparilla (through the beater).

Inhuch'ik inkäkah.
I grind my cacao.

Inmaa(n)sik inkäkah.
I regrind my cacao.

Inch'a'ik umorinuhi(r).
I fetch its beater.

Inch'a'ik uluuchi(r) inkäkah.
I fetch the cup for my cacao.

Inmaa(n)sik.
I regrind it.

Inpuk'ik.
I dissolve it.

Inpuk'(ik) inkäkah.
I dissolve my cacao.

Inpeeks(i)k inkäkah.
I move my cacao around.

Inhäx(i)k^2 inkäkah.
I beat my cacao.

Inmaxik inkäkah.
I mash my cacao.

Inmuxi(k).
I crush it.

Inch'a'ik uchan suuri(r) ti' kyum.
I fetch the small cup of our Lord.

Inbo'otik ti' kyum.
I offer it to our Lord.

Inch'a'ik umorinuhi(r) inkäkah.
I fetch the beater (for) my cacao.

Inbin inch'a'ik umorinuhi(r).[3]
I am going to fetch the beater.

Inp'e'ik.
I chip (the cacao).

Wa 'uts (ti') awich, yanech ahkoke' ak'eh.
If it pleases you, you are the sarsaparilla.[4]

Ko'oten awirik ti' inbo'or ti' kyum.
Come, see my offering to our Lord.

Yan apurik awits, k'uyuch ak'eh, koke' ak'eh,
You must throw down your juice, oh twisted vine, oh sarsaparilla,

a' he', abut'(i)k awits ti' . . .
right here, you put in your juice . . .

Inp'ikik intsuki(r).
I snap my sarsaparilla.

Awirik?
Do you see it?

Inmaa(n)s(i)k intsukiri(r).
I regrind my sarsaparilla.

Inpurik ti' ka'(ah) atar awirik.
I put it there when you come see it.

Inmuxik.
I crush it.

Inmaa(n)sik.
I regrind it.

Inmaa(n)sik inkäkah.
I regrind my cacao.

Inmaa(n)sik; inpuk'ik inkäkah.
I regrind it; I dissolve my cacao.

In(k)'eerik inkäkah.
I toast my cacao.

Inbo'otik ti' kyum.
I offer it to our Lord.

Yan atar awirik.
You must come see it.

Kinbin inhäxik (ti') uyatoch k'uh.
I am going to beat it (in) the god house.

(K)inbin inhäxik
I am going to beat it

t(i') uchi' uleki(r) kyum.
at the edge/mouth of our Lord's plate.[5]

(K)inbin ink'eerik inkäkah.
I am going to toast my cacao.

Tan inmaan.
I am walking through.

Kinpuk'ik.
I dissolve it.

Inlaar(ik) ulek.
I empty the bowl.

Inbin yeter uchan suuri(r).
I go with the small cup.

Inbin inwahkuntik,
I go set it up,

t(i') uchi' uleki(r) kyum,
at the edge/mouth of our Lord's plate,

uchan suuri(r).
the small cup.

Inhäxik inkäkah.
I beat my cacao.

H(e') atar apurik awits ten,
You will come throw down your juice for me,

koke' ak'eh.
oh sarsaparilla.

Tu' yanech ahkoke' ak'eh?
Where are you, oh sarsaparilla?

Ko'ten apureh awits ten.
Come put in your juice for me.

Tan awirik inp'ikik.
You are watching me snap (your vine).

…

…

Tan inp'i(k)ikech.
I am snapping you off.

Inmaa(n)sik inkäkah.
I regrind my cacao.

Tan inbut'ikech yok'or inkäkah.
I am putting you in my cacao.

Tan inmaa(n)sik yeter.
I am regrinding it with it.

Inyu(r)maa(n)sik yok'o(r) ka'.
I grind it smooth on the millstone.

Inmaa(n)sik yok'or inpohche'.
I regrind it on my table.

Tan inmuxik.
I am crushing it.

Tan inyaach'tik utsukir(ir) inkäkah.
I am smashing the sarsaparilla for my cacao.

Tan inmaa(n)s(i)k inkäkah.
I am regrinding my cacao.

Atar awi(ri)k inbo'o(r) ti' kyum.
You come see my offering to our Lord.

Tech ka'(ah) tar awirik te('),
When you come to see it here,

tsuk'i(r) ak'eh, koke' ak'eh,
oh sarsaparilla vine, oh sarsaparilla,

tech way amuuch'ik abäh.
you gather together here.

Uk'aay Käy 'Fish Song'

Antonio Martinez

This song is like a charm, sung to catch a large quantity of fish and ensure that the hook does not break free.[1] The song calls upon various creatures to help the fisherman. He calls upon the orb spider to throw out its "line" and its "claw" (the fishhook).[2] He calls to the otters to drive the fish away from the shore and into the lagoon. He calls to the turtles to propel the fish toward the edge of the canoe. He mentions a kite, which flies in circles above the lagoon and assists in the roundup.

Chäk sahareh,[3] eh chäk sohoneh,[4]
Oh red *sahar*, oh red *sohon*,

ko'oten muruteh[5] t(i') uchi' inchem. Ku(ru)ken t(i) uyit inchem.
come, shoal at the side of my canoe. I am seated at the stern of my canoe.

Maraach'[6] ts'ibanar, kawirik una'akar burur kuna'akar tan uturankar burur.
Ducks, anhingas, you see (the water) rise, when it rises, the (lagoon) is rising.

Hook'en muruteh, chäk sahar, chäk sahareh.[7]
Go out and shoal, red sahar, oh red sahar.

Hook'en ireh chäk sohon,[8] ya'ax sahar.[9]
Go out and see it, red sohon, green sahar.

Kumurutik uk'anir le'on, uyiich'akir inle'on.

They swarm the fishing line, the fishhook of my line.

Kumurutik uk'anir le'on, uyiich'akirir a' le'on, (u)yiichak'irir a' le'on.

They swarm the fishing line, the hook (at the end of) the line, the hook (at the end of) the line.

Ka'ah tinch'uktah utar ha', ka'ah hook'ech amurut(eh) ya'ax sahar.

When I waited for the rain to come,[10] then you went out to shoal, green sahar.

Chäk sohoneh, tan awirik uya(a)rar utar.[11]

Oh red sohon, you are looking at the line (of fish) come.

Kurukbahe'ex maraach', ts'ibanar. Käyunkäy[12] le'ekbar. Tan awirik käyunkäy xit'a'an utan ha'.[13] Tan awirik.

You are seated, ducks, anhingas. The *käyunkäy* is hovering. You are looking at the käyunkäy gliding over the surface of the water. You are looking at it.

Tan upäxha'tik paato' maraach', ts'ibanar, käyunkäy kumaan.

The ducks and the anhingas are flapping their wings on the water, (while) the käyunkäy passes over head.

Tan ulubu(r) uk'anir le'on. Uyiich'akir le'on, la' uyiich'akiri(r) ahtäkay.[14]

The fishing line is falling (in). The hook is the claw of the *täkay*.

Uyiich'ak'iri(r) uchichiri(r) inpäräm ba' inluts.[15]

Its claw is the hardness of my sinker.

La' uwich ahchäk sahareh, la' ahchäk sohon la' awich.
It is the eye of the red sahar, the eye of the red sohon.

Upäräm ba' inluts la' uwicher chäk sahareh, ya'ax sahar.
The sinker of my fishing line is the eye of the red sahareh, the green sahar.

Chäk sohoneh, ka'ah ahook'ech awireh le' bakxaache' apach uchi'bir apa-che(r) bakxaache'.
Red sohon when you go out to see, the dorsal fin is (on) your spine, it is the dorsal fin.

Tenen chäk sohoneh. Ka'ah tawirah, ka'ah tinpurah uk'anir luts,
I am the red sohon. When you saw (it), when I cast out the fishing line,

ka'ah tinhiitah, tan awirik uyiich'akir le'on.
when I pulled it out, you are looking at the hook of my fishing line.

Tan uweher chintok'.[16] Kopo'[17] kuwehe(r).
The fruit of the ironwood tree is scattering. The fruit of the fig tree scat-ters.[18]

Le ule' che' kuwehe(r).
The leaves of the trees scatter.

La' kawirik una'akar awo'och su'uk. K'än 'aak, xen ak'aasteh (wich) ten. Xen ak'aasteh uwich.[19]
This you see as your food of grass rising. Yellow turtles, go round up the fruit for me. Go round it up.

Xen ach'a'eh uwich ten, ch'ik tupach ti' chi' petha'.

Go and fetch the fruit for me, on the far shore of the lagoon.

Xen alahtaaseh, tsura'ir ha' beh.

Go bring it all to me, otters.

Utsura'i(r)ha', xen ala(h)k'aasteh uwich.

Otters, go round up (the fish).

Na'(k)taki(r)ha', chi'taki(r?) uk'um, xen alahkäxteh ten. Kalahtaaseh t(i) uchi' inchem, t(i) una'akar buru(r).

(At) the edge of the water, the shore of river, go find it for me. You will bring them all to the edge of my canoe, where (water) rises.

Unaachban su'uk. La' (a)wirik (k)utarer chäk sahareh, chäk sohoneh, ya'ax sahar.

The grass is clenched (in the mouths of the fish). You see the red sahar come, oh red sohon, green sahar.

Yäräknäk utar kawirik burureh.

You see them come en masse (like) a flood.

Uk'aay ti' Huuch' 'Song for Grinding'

Juana Koh

This is one of the few women's work songs, which are sung to help speed up and enhance the result of distaff tasks. Juana Koh is singing while she makes ceremonial tamales and the *ch'ulha'*, atole[1] that her husband will then offer to the gods. She calls upon a variety of birds to help her wash the maize, grind it several times, pat out the dough, and fold the tamales. They must work steadily throughout the morning to have it ready by midday, when her husband's ritual is to commence.[2] The amount and variety of foods required for ceremonies, especially if they involve many participants, are huge. Women must get up well before dawn to start preparing the offerings. This explains why, at certain junctures in the song, Juana pleads to the birds (or the gods) to stop the sun from rising.

Anthropologist Jacques Soustelle noted that although Lacandon women were prohibited from taking part in the religion (except on the rare occasion), they nevertheless were indispensable because they prepare the food offerings (Soustelle 1935a, 177–78).

Inhuuch'. Yan atar awaantiken,
I (am) grind(ing). You must come help me,

awaantiken ti' inmeyah....
help me with my work....

Inhuch'ik inhu';[3] yan atare'ex way.
I grind my corn; you must come here.

Boona 'ibi la boona, chiro' la boona.
How many *'ibi*,[4] how many there are, how many quail there are.

Lah way atare'ex amuuch'ik abähe'ex ten ti' inmeyah way, ti' äkyum way, Hesu,
You all come together for me, for my work here, for our Lord Jesus,

way, ti' äkyum way ti' inmeyah way, inhuuch' way.
here, for our Lord, here for my work here, my dough here.

Yan atar ahuch'ik ten way, tinhuch'ik way.
You have to come grind it for me here. I am grinding it here.

Yan atar awirik inmeyah way ti',
You have to come see my work there,

inbo'or ti' kyum.
my offering to our Lord.

[long pause]
[long pause]

A' boona chiro'e'ex la' boona.
How many quail you are, how many there are.

Ähwaan, la boona; ähnookor la' boona;
How many partridges and tinamous there are;[5]

way atare'ex (ich?) way awaantiken
you come (in?) here and help me

t(i') äkmeyah way, ko'oten awaantiken ti' inhuuch' way; yan atar awaantiken way,

for our work here, come help me with my grinding here; you have to come help me here,

ti' inmeyah way.

with my work here.

Yan atar awaantiken ahuch'ik ten way.

You have to come help grind it for me here.

Yan ahuuch' way.

You have to grind here.

Yan atar awaantiken, nukuch t'ut', kacho'.

You have to come help me, large parrot, blue-crowned mealy parrot.

La' boona mo' la' boona.

How many macaws there are. How many there are.

Nukuch t'ut' yan atare'ex

Large parrots you all have to come

awaantiken ti' inmeyah way,

you have to help me with my work here,

inbo'or ti' kyum way.

my offering for our Lord here.

Yan atar awaantiken ti' inmeyah way ti' äkyum.
You have to come help me with my work here for our Lord.

Yan atar awahik ten.
You have to come crush it for me.

Yan atar ap'e'ik. Yan atar
You have to come chip it. You have to come

alahwahik way.
crush it all up here.

Kacho', chiro', tuworor humpuur atare'ex way.
Blue-crowned mealy parrot, quail, you all come here at once.

Tsiir,
Ani,

la' way atar way ti' inmeyah ti' kyum way.
you come here to my work for our Lord here.

[pause]
[pause]

(A)tar awaantiken way
(You) come help me here

ti' inbo'or ti' kyum way.
at my offering for our Lord here.

Yan atar awaantiken way ti' inbo'or.
You have to come help me (with) my offering.

Ti' usee(b)tar,
So that it goes faster,

amuu(ch'i)k abähe'ex way ti' ameyah way, ti' äkmeyah t(i' ä)khuuch' way,
you gather together here to work here, to our work, for us to grind (it) here,

ti' awahik ten.
to crush it for me.

Yan alah p'e'ik ten way.
You have to (peck) it all up for me here.

[pause]
[pause]

Yan awahik ten way.
You have to crush it all up for me here.

La' boona
How many are the

ts'ak'ak',
chestnut-capped brush-finches,

tsiir, 'itsana(r),
the ani, the *itsanar*,[6]

la' way amuuch'ik abähe'ex way,
you all gather together here,

ti' äkmeyah way ti' kyum way.
to our work for our Lord here.

Ti' yan ach'eeh ti' useebtar uts'o'okor,
So that you must break (it) up so it finishes faster,

ti' useebtar.
so that it goes faster.

Seeba(') kut'arar,
It piles up quickly,

akmeyah ti' äkyum way.
(this) our work for the Lord here.

Ti' useebtar ti' uts'o'okor way,
So that it finishes faster here,

awaantiken way.
you help me here.

[*pause*]
[*pause*]

Yan awaantike'ex i(n)maa(n)sik.
You all have to help me regrind it.

Inmaa(n)sik inmeyah.
I regrind my work.

Yan awaantiken (yeter?).
You have to help me (with it?).

Seeb (atar?), ti' useebtar uts'o'okor;
You (come?) quickly, so it finishes faster;

la boona nukuch t'ut' la' boona; kacho' la' boona;
how many large parrots there are; how many blue-crowned mealy parrots;

ba'axtäk;
(so many) kinds;

'itsana(r)täk. Tuworor way (a)lahmuuch'(i)k abähe('e)x way.
every kind of itsanar. All of you gather together here.

Tech way ameyah ti' äkyum way,
You are here to work for our Lord here,

ti' useebtar äkmaa(n)sik, ti' useebtar, ti' useebtar ti' ut'arar,
so our regrinding goes faster, so it goes faster, so it piles up faster,

ti' useebtar.
so it goes faster.

Boona atar; boona. Apimene'ex k'äbche' tu' nika'ane'ex (ti'?) k'ä'che'. Lah boona.
How many of you come; how many (you are). You are many where you are (perched) in the branches. So many.

Pukchiro' la' woror; la boona xure'ex.
Quails all around; how many of you stopped.

Lah way amuuch'ik abähe'ex way.
All of you gather together here.

Tech(e'ex) awirik(e'ex) inmeyah ti' äkyum way.
You all see my work for our Lord here.

Woror boona xure'ex. Teche'ex way,
So many of you stopped here. You are here,

lah way awaantiken way.
you are all here to help me here.

Awirik useebtar uts'o'okor maa(n)sik,
You see that the regrinding finishes faster,

ti' äkpätik nahwah,
so we can fold the tamales,

ti' äkmentik ti',
so we can make them,

ti' useebtar ut'arar.
so that they pile up faster.

Ma' asiptik una'akar k'in.
Don't let the sun rise.

Ma' asiptik una'akar k'in.
Don't let the sun rise.

Xureh hats'kab.
Stop the dawn.

Ma' asiptik una'akar k'in ti' äkmeyah way.
Don't let the sun come up on our work here.

[*pause*]
[*pause*]

Ma' asiptik una'akar k'in, ti' äkmeyah way,
Don't let the sun come up, for our work here,

ti' useebtar ti' äkpätik.
may we fold them faster.

Ach'a'ik ulekir ti' (ä)kbut'ik, ti' useebtar ut'arar (ä)kpätik,
You bring the plate for us to fill, so that our folding them piles up faster,

ti' useebtar ut'arar äkmentik way.
so that our making them here piles up faster.

. . .
. . .

Uturur ulekir way, ti' useebtar.
The plate overflows here, so that it goes faster.

[pause]
[pause]

Boona apimene'ex way, la' way amuuch'ik abäh way. Boona.
How many you are here, you all gather together here. How many there are.

K'ambur, lah boona.
Curassow, how many there are.

Koox, lah boona; way amuuch'ik abähe'ex way, ti' kwahike'ex way.
Crested guan, how many there are; here you all gather together here, so we
can crush it here.

Ba'axtäk ch'iich'ir tuworor,
All kinds of birds everywhere,

lah way amuuch'ik abähe'ex way,
you all gather together here,

ti' kmeyah ti' kyum way;
for our work for our Lord here;

ti' useebtar ti' äkpätik, ti' useebtar.
so it goes faster, so our folding them goes faster.

Ma' asiptik una'akar k'in,
Don' t let the sun rise,

ma' asiptik una'akar,
don't let it rise,

ti' useebtar.
so it goes faster.

[pause]
[pause]

Ti' useebtar ti' ut'arar,
So it piles up faster,

ti' useebtar,
so it goes faster,

way alahmuuch'ik abähe'ex way,
here you all gather together here,

[pause]
[pause]

ti' kmeyah, äkmaa(n)seh, (Ku)ts'o'okor, kwarik ti'. Kuts'o'okor ti' kwarik
yok'o(r) (u)pohche'ir,
for our work, our regrinding it. When it finishes, we will roll it into a ball.
When it finishes we will roll it into a ball on the table,

ti' useebtal äkpäteh.
so that our folding will become quick.

(A)ch'a'ik ulekir, kapätik.
You fetch the plate, (and) fold them.

Amiistik ulekir.
You sweep its plate.

Aki'miistik ulekir, äkbut'ik.
You sweep its plate well, (then) we fill it.

[pause]
[pause]

Way alahmuuch'ik abähe'ex way. Boona apimene'ex way. Alahmuuch'ik
abähe'ex.
You all gather together here. How many you are here. You all gather
together.

[pause]
[pause]

La' äkhuch'ik yok'or ka'.
This we grind on the millstone.

Ti' äkwahike'ex. Ko'o(t)en, käkwaheh,
There we crush it. Come, let's crush it,

[pause]
[pause]

ti' useebtar.
so it goes faster.

[pause]
[pause]

Tech chich amuk'e'ex; awahik way; chich amuk'.
You are very strong; you crush it here; you are very strong.

Alahwahik ukoho' närir.
You crush the corn kernels completely.

[pause]
[pause]

Ach'a'ik ya'rir awarik,
You fetch the water to roll it into a ball.

(Ku)ts'o'okor ti' umaa(n)sa'.
(When) you finish rolling it, it is reground.

Tinmaa(n)sik.
I am regrinding it.

Inmaa(n)s(i)k inhuuch'. Inmaa(n)sik.
I regrind my ground dough. I regrind it.

Inwarik inhuuch'. Inwarik
I roll my dough into a ball. I roll

inbo'or ti' kyum.
my offering to our Lord.

[pause]
[pause]

Ta(n) (a)tar awaantikene'ex. Tuworor boon apimene'ex.
All of you are coming to help me. How many of you there are everywhere.

Tu' yane'ex ch'ik naache'ex. Yan(e'ex) lah way; alahmuuch'ik abähe'ex.
You come from far away. Here you all are. You are all here; you all gather
together.

Way atar way t(i') ameyah.
Here you come to work.

Boona ba'axtäk uch'iich'ir.
How many kinds of birds there are.

[pause]
[pause]

Mehen ch'iich'o' tuworor, huhump'er lah way amuuch'ik abähe'ex—
Small birds everywhere, one by one, you all gather together here—

tsir,
ani,

ts'ah k'ak',
chestnut-capped brush-finches,

tuworor.
all of them.

Lah way amuuch'ik abähe'ex awaantiken inmeyah,
You all gather together here to help me with my work,

ti' useebtar uts'o'okor.
so that it finishes faster.

Yan atar awahik ten inhuuch', ti' useebtar uts'o'okor.
You come to mill my dough for me, so that it finishes faster.

T'arar inhuuch'.
My dough piles up.

Seeba(r) kut'arah.
It piles up quickly.

Seeba(r) kut'arar; inhuch'ik,
It piles up quickly; I grind it,

ti' useebtar ti' ut'arar.
so that it piles up faster.

A' boon, tuk'in (in)pät(i)k t'arar,
Oh so many when (I) fold them (they) increase,

tuk'in (in)pät(ik), ti' usee(b)t(ar) uturur ulekir.
when (I) I fold (them), the plate fills up quickly.

[pause]
[pause]

Uher, uher ulekir kach'a'ik wa tinbut'ik,
Another and another plate you fetch, when I am putting them on,

ti' ut'arar.
the plates fill up.[7]

[pause]
[pause]

Ne tsoy upatar,
The folding goes very well,

ti' usee(b)ta(r).
it goes faster.

Lah boona pukchiro'.
How many quail there are.

Lah boona 'iirih.
How many speckled hawks there are.

Lah boona ba'axtäk ch'iich'ir.
How many kinds of birds there are.

K'än ch'iich', tuworor, huhump'er a' way, kamuuch'ik abäh way ti' äkwahik,
ti' äkpätike'ex, ti' useebtar uts'o'okor ti' äkyum, ti' inbo'or ti' kyum,

Yellow birds, everywhere, one by one you gather together here so we can crush it, so we can fold (the tamales), so that it finishes faster for our Lord, for my offering to our Lord,

ti' inbo'otik ti' kyum, ti' useebtar.
so that I can offer it to our Lord, so it goes faster.

Axeep'ik uchi' aka'täk'ik uchi',[8]
You pinch (a piece) off the edge (of the tamale wrapper) and stick it on the edge,

ti' inbo'or ti' kyum.
for my offering to our Lord.

Ats'ahik uchi'ir yok'or uxibir unahwahir.
You give the "bite" of leaf of the tamale.[9]

Kuts'o'ok(or) inmaa(n)sikeh, katar awaantiken pätik.
When my regrinding finishes, you come to help me fold (the tamales).

Atal awaantikene'ex, k(a')ah la' way amuuch'ik abäh way.
You come to help me, when you all gather together here.

La' way amuuch'ik abäh, ti' äkpätik yok'or (u)pohche' way.
You all gather together here, so we can fold them on the table here.

Inp'o'ik ukumir unahwahir. Inp'o'ik ukumir. Inchäkik.
I wash the pot for the tamales. I wash the pot. I cook them.

Inchäkik wah. Kuts'o'okor upatar, kuchakar.
I cook the tamales. When the folding finishes, they will cook.

Seeb käkmuuch'ik äkbähe'ex äkpätik, ti' useebtar, ti' äkchäkik.

Quickly we gather together to fold them, so it goes faster, so we (can) cook them.

Ya ts'o'ok inmaa(n)sik nahwah. Äkpäteh toh.

I've just finished regrinding the tamale (dough). Let's fold them now.

Yan äkpätäk yok'or lekir, but'ik yok'or lekir. Bin inwareh.

We have to fold them on the plate, put them on the plate. I'm going to roll (the dough).

...

...

Seeb, ko'otene'ex ti' äkmeyah way. Xen ach'a'ik uya'rir ten.

Quickly, all of you come to our work here. Go fetch the water for me.

Ko'oxe'ex äkch'uyeh ya'rir ti' uwarar.

Let's go carry the water for rolling (the dough).

Yan ap'o'ik ukumir. Yan ti' chakar a' nahwah.

You have to wash the pot. The tamales need to cook.

Yan uch'am.

There is the grill rack.

Yan mahaas uch'am, mahaas uch'am.

There is the *canela*[10] grill rack, the canela grill rack.

Yan atar awaantiken ti' inmeyah. Yan atar awaantiken.

You have to come help me with my work. You have to come help me.

Toh ts'o'okih. Tan inp'o'ik upohche'.
It's ready. I am washing the table.

Lah p'o'ah upohche'.
The table is all washed.

Yan atar awaantiken ti' khuuch' yok'or ka'.
You have to come help me with our grinding on the millstone.

Yan awaantikene'ex ti' inmeyah, meyah way yok'or ka' way.
You have to come help me with my work here on the millstone here.

Yan awaantikene'ex.
You have to help me.

La' boona ch'iich'o' lah way amuuch'ik abäh ten way ti' inmeyah way.
How many birds there are. Here you all gather together for me here, for my work here,

Tsir, ts'ah k'ak', tuworor.
Ani, chestnut-capped brush-finches, everyone.

Kacho', mehen t'ut', näkrehkum, tuworor, way (a)muuch'ik abähe'ex.
Blue-crowned mealy parrots, little parrots, brown-hooded parrots, every-one, here you all gather together.

Äh k'iri',
Parakeets,

alähmuuch'ik abähe'ex ten.
you all gather together for me.

Lah way amuuch'ik abähe'ex ti' ameyah way, ti' äkmeyah ti' äkyum,
You all gather together to work here, for our work for our Lord,

ti' äkbo'or ti' äkyum way,
for our offering to our Lord here,

ti' useebtar ut'arar, ti' useebtar.
so that it piles up faster, so that it goes faster.

Tuworor nukuch t'ut', tuworor; lah kacho', lah boona.
All the large parrots, all of them; all the blue-crowned mealy parrots, how many there are.

Ähnäkrehkum tuworor, lah way amuuch'ik abäh(e'ex?) way ti' äkmeyah way.
Brown-hooded parrots, you all gather together here for our work here.

La' awaantiken ti' inmeyah way.
You help me with my work here.

Yan atar awaantiken ti' inmeyah, ti' useebtar uts'o'okor.
You have to come help me with my work, so that it finishes faster.

Ma' asiptik una'akar k'in.
Don't let the sun rise.

Ma' asiptik uts'o'okor ti' una'akar.
Don't let the sun finish rising.

Ma' asiptik uk'uchur k'ak' chun k'in.
Don't let the midday arrive.

Ma' asiptik hats'kab.
Don't let it dawn.

Chukeh k'in, k'äs. Xur(eh), ti' äkpätik,
Grab the sun, please. Stop it, so we can fold (the tamales),

ti' äkpätik ti' äkyum, ti' äkmeyah ti' äkyum.
so we can fold them for our Lord, so we can work for our Lord.

Awaantiken ti' inmeyah way.
You help me work here.

Ach'a'ik ulekir. Kabut'ik, ... Akpätik, abut'ik yok'or ulekir,
You fetch the plate. You fill it, ... We fold (the tamales) (and) you put them
on the plate,

but'ik yok'or lekir inmeyah ti' äkyum.
put my work for our Lord on the plate.

Lah woror nukuch t'ut', tuworor,
All the large parrots, everywhere,

kacho', tuworor,
blue-crowned mealy parrots everywhere,

boona mo', tuworor,
how many macaws there are, everywhere,

lah way amuuch'ik abähe'ex ten.
you all gather together for me.

Lah boona 'itsanar;
How many finches there are;

lah way amuuch'ik abähe'ex ti' inmeyah ti' äkyum way,
you all gather together here for my work for our Lord here,

ti' äkwaheh ti' äkyum way,
so we can crush it for our Lord here,

ti' useebtar kut'arar, ti' useebtar kut'arar usäkänir.
so that it will pile up faster, so that the dough will pile up faster.

Tinmeyah ti' äkyum.
I am working for our Lord.

Seebar, kut'arar inpätik, seebar kut'arar ti' inmeyah ti' äkyum.
Quickly, my folding piles up, quickly it piles up for my work for our Lord.

T'arak yok'or lekir, awaantikene'ex äkmentik yok'or lekir.
May they fill up on the plate, you help us make them on the plate.

Yan ti' aki'lahmiistik ulekir.
You have to sweep the entire plate well.

Aki'puustik ulekir.
You dust off the plate well.

Aki'but'ik.
You fill it well.

Yan awirik; ap'o'ik upohche'ir. Yan alahp'o'ik upohche' ti' äkhuuch' ...
You must look at (the table); you (must) wash the table.[11] You must wash the
table completely, (before) we grind ...

Xen ach'a'ik uya'rir.
Go fetch the water.

Ch'a'ik uya'rir, ti' kmeyahe'ex, ti' akhuch'ik.
Fetch the water, for our work, for us to grind it.

Yan ap'o'ik uk'u'umir.
You have to wash the cooked corn.

Yan ap'o'ik.
You have to wash it.

Ach'a'ik uxaakir.
You fetch the basket.

Kap'o'ik uk'u'umir,
When you wash the cooked corn,

ach'a'ik uxaakir ap'o'ik ink'u'um.
you fetch the basket to wash my boiled corn.

Ko'ox äkp'o'eh.
Let's go wash it.

Yan awaantikene'ex inch'uyik uya'rir.
You have to help me carry the water.

Yan atar awaantikene'ex ti' äkmeyah way, ti' huuch' yok'or ka' way,
You have to come help me with our work here, to grind on the millstone here,

äkmeyahe'ex way yok'or pohche',
we work here on the table,

ti' useebtar ut'arar. T'arak usäkänir . . .
so that it piles up faster. May the dough pile up . . .

Seeba(r) kut'arar inpätik.
Quickly, my folding tamales pile up.

Seeba(r) kut'arar.
It piles up quickly.

Seeba(r) kuts'o'okor inhuch'ik.
My grinding it finishes quickly.

Seeba(r) kuts'o'okor.
It finishes quickly.

Tech chich amuk'e'ex tech.
You are very strong. How many there are.

Lah boona k'ambur, la boona.
How many curassows there are.

Koox, lah boona.
How many crested guans there are.

Ut'arar inhuch'ik. Seeba(r) kut'arar.
My grinding piles up. It piles up quickly.

Seeb utar ähwaan, kachok', tuworor,
Quickly the partridges, the blue-crowned mealy parrots, all of them come,

k'iri', tuworor,
all the parakeets,

way amuuch'ik abäh(e'ex?) way, ti' inmeyah ti' äkyum way.
you all gather together here, for my work for the Lord here.

Inch'o'ik uk'u'umir.
I scrub the cooked corn.

Inch'o'ik uk'u'umir.
I scrub the cooked corn.

Inp'o'ik ti' useebtar.
I wash it so that it goes faster,

ti' inbut'ik,
so I can fill (the pot),

ti' inchäkik ti' äkyum.
so I can cook it for our Lord.

Inbin inchäkeh (ti' u)yatoch k'uh,
I am going to cook it in the god house,

uyatoch k'uh,
the god house,

ti' ints'o'oksik kut'anir inlaak' (ku)ts'o'okor.
to finish it when my husband's prayers finish.

Seebar, uts'o'okor ti' inchäkik. (Ku?)ts'o'okor uch'urha'ir inchäkik uch'urha'ir.
Quickly, it finishes so I can cook it. (When) the (corn for) the atole (is ready)
I cook the atole.

Inmentik uch'urha'ir useebtar,
I make the atole go faster,

ti' inbo'otik ti' äkyum.
so I can offer it to our Lord.

(In)chäk(ik) uch'urha'ir.
I cook the atole.

Int'achkuntik uch'urha'ir.
I place the atole on the fire.

Inchäkik.
I cook it.

Kuts'o'okor, kinhuch'ik uch'urha'ir.
When it finishes, I will grind the atole.

Inhuch'ik uch'urha'ir ti' inbo'otik ti' äkyum ...
I grind the atole to offer it to our Lord ...

Ap'o'ik uhama'ir.
You wash the cups.

Ti' useebar ... ap'o'ik uhama'ir,
So it goes faster ... you wash the cups,

ti' int'ahik ...
so I can fill them ...

(Ku?)ts'o'okor inpuk'ik, kint'ahik.
(When) I finish dissolving (the atole), I will fill them.

Apimenee'ex, kalahmuuch'ik abähe'ex ti' inwahik ti' äkyum.
You are many, when you gather together so I can crush it for our Lord.

Alahwahik, tech kawahik ukoh kawaantik inwahik.
You completely crush it, you crush the kernels, you help me crush them.

Yan awaantiken inhuch'ik.
You have to help me grind it.

Yan awaantikene'ex ti' inmeyah way,
You have to help me with my work here,

ti' inbo'otik ti' äkyum.
so that I can offer it to our Lord.

Uk'aay ti' K'uuch 'Song for Spinning Thread'

Juana Koh

This is a woman's work song[1] that invokes the spiders and the bees to enhance the volume of thread on her spindle and her weaving shuttle.[2] Throughout the song the singer alludes to the act of spinning with a drop spindle. She appeals to the creatures to produce the great volume of thread needed to weave a single *xikul*, the traditional two-piece tunic. Hand-spun and woven tunics are for ceremonial use only. Worn by men, they are large and long, taking a month or more to complete. The song also mentions the process of weaving on a backstrap loom.

The art of weaving was abandoned after the introduction of commercial fabric in the mid-1800s. Thread is still spun from homegrown cotton, but in small quantities and only for curing strings, primarily given to new mothers and their newborns as protection against contracting fatal illnesses. In Lacandon myth, the curing strings were introduced by the Haawo', revered ancestors who had knowledge of medicine. But the curative power of the strings traces further back to the aged Moon Goddess in Mesoamerican mythology, who represents, among other feminine matters, weaving and medicine. Mayan iconography portrays the aged Moon Goddess with a ball of unspun cotton wound round a spindle on her head and carrying weaving swords.

Juana Koh was the only woman willing to sing this song. While most women know how to spin cotton, only some older Lacandon women know how to weave. This would explain why younger women claimed not to know the song. The other elderly women whom I approached all claimed not to know it well.[3]

Eh, tu' yanech ähtakay?
Oh, where are you, orb spiders?

Eh boona mehen takay,
How many you are, little orb spiders,

k'äbche' takay,
orb spiders of the branches,

lah way amuuch'ik abäh apits'ik ten.
you all gather together here to spin it for me.

Atar awaantiken,
You come to help me,

abut'ik ak'uuch ten ti' ink'uuch ti' ut'ahar ink'uuch way.
you put your silk into my thread for me, so that my thread will expand
here.

Atar awirik yok'or inpecheech way.
You come to see it on my spindle here.

Awaantiken ti' inpiits'.
You help me spin.

Lah boona mehen takay, lah boona nukuch takay, lah mak lah boona,
How many are all the little orb spiders, how many are all the large orb spiders, how many are all the trapdoor spiders,

tuworor,
all of them,

chinkoh, tuworor, lah way amuuch'ik abähe'ex way,
tarantulas, all of them, you all gather together here,

ti' ink'uuch way,
for my spinning here,

ti' innook'.
for my cloth.

Yan atar at'a(h)sik ten
You have to pile it up for me

ti' ut'aa(ha)r inpits'
so that my cotton piles up

ti' ut'a(ah)ar.
so that it piles up (on my spindle).[4]

Yan (a)tar ti' awaantiken inpits'eh,
You have to come help me spin,

tu' way yane'ex a' kabar lah boona.
where you are here below, how many (you) all are.

Kab(ar) awaant(iken).
Below you help (me).

Ku(r)e(n) but'(eh) awaar te(n) way.
Sit down and put your brood in for me here.

Yan atar abut'ik.
You have to come fill it.

Yan atar ats'äpik ten inpits' a' way.
You have to come and stack it on my thread here.

Yan atar ats'äpik ten a' way.
You have to come stack it on for me here.

Lah boona ähchi',
How many chi' there are,

lah boona,
how many,

k'än säk k'oho', lah boona[5]
yellow *säk k'oho'*, how many

'aktun kab,[6] lah boon.
cave bees, how many.

Lah way la' boon yuus lah way,[7]
All the many *yuus* are all here,

amuuch'ik abahe'ex ten
you gather together for me

ti' ats'äpik inpits' ten,
to stack up my cotton for me,

ti' atar abut'ik awaar way.
to come and put in your brood here.

Te' atar ats'äpik ten way,
There you come to stack it on for me here,

ti' ut'arar,
so that it piles up,

ti' ut'arar ink'uuch,
so that my thread piles up,

ti' ut'arar,
so that it piles up,

ti' useebtar ut'arar.
so that it piles up faster.

Tu' way yanech mehen takayeh.
You are here, oh little orb spiders.

Lah boona takay ti' ut'arar ink'uuch,
How many orb spiders there are (that come) to pile up my thread,

ti' u'ra('n), atar awirik yok'or inpecheech way.
to have arrived here, you come to see (the thread) on my spindle here.

Yan atar abut'ik ak'uuch ten yok'or ink'uuch,
You have to come and put your silk on my thread

tu' kinwarik, tu' kinpirixtik.
where I roll it into a ball,[8] where I wind it up.

Inpirixtik ink'uuch ti' ka'(a)h atar abut'ik way ak'uuch tech.
I wind up my thread, so that when you come you stuff your silk in here.

Yan awaantiken ink'uchik.
You have to help me spin it.

Yan awaantiken ink'uchik.
You have to help me spin it.

Awu'yik ink'uuch.
You hear me spin.

Ink'uchik.
I spin it.

Kuts'o'okor ink'uchik, kinpirixtik.
When I finish spinning it, I will wind it up.

Ka'(a)h atar awaantiken,
When you come help me,

kinwäkik ink'uuch.
I will enlarge my (ball of) thread.

Atar awaantiken
You come to help me

insäktik innook' way. He' inch'a'ik uhärärte'.⁹
weave my cloth here. I will fetch the weaving rods.

He' inch'a'ik uxuunche'ir,
I will fetch the end rods,

katar awaantiken xuunche'tik way.
then you will come help me stretch the warp on the end rods here.

Atal awaantiken.
You come help me.

Tu' way yane'ex.
You are here.

Lah boona takay lah boon.
How many you are, orb spiders, how many you are.

Boon apimene'ex lah way.
How many you all are here.

Ka'(a)h atar amuuch'ik abäh kat'asik ak'uuch ten ti' ut'arar ti' ink'uuch
When you come gather together you will pile your silk on my thread for
me, so that my thread expands

ti' innook', ti' ut'arar.
for my cloth, so that it piles up.

Atar awaantiken insäktik way tu' uxuunche' to'an uhärärte'.
You have to come to help me weave it here on the end rods, where the weaving sword is.

Tan awaantiken.
You are helping me.

Lah boona takay, mehen takay tuworor.
How many are all the orb spiders, the little orb spiders everywhere.

Tu' yanech ch'ik yok'or ka'an,
You are far up in the sky,

tu' yanech yok'or k'äbtak nukuch che'.
you are on the branches of the big trees.

Lah 'eemseh abäh way,
All of you, come down here,

awirik ti' ink'uuch.
you see that I am spinning here.

Lah awaantiken ink'uuch way.
You help me with all my spinning here.

Awaantiken ti' ink'uuch, atar awaantiken ti' ink'uchik innook',
You help me spin, you come help me spin my cloth,

ti' useebtar ut'arar tuk'in insäktik
so that it may pile up faster when I weave it

yok'or inbut'u'o'och,
on my shuttle,

tuk'in inbut'ik unookir t(i') uchara' . . .
when I put the cloth where it lies . . .

tu' chawak uakpachir,
where it hangs along the length of the back,[10]

ti' atar awaantiken.
you come help me there.

Yan atar awaantiken ti' ink'uuch way.
You have to come help me with my spinning here.

Yan atar awaantiken ink'uchik ti' useebtar ut'arar
You have to come help me spin it so that it expands faster

yok'or inpecheech.
on my spindle.

Ti' useebtar ut'arar,
So that it expands faster,

yan atar awaantiken ti' innook'.
you have to come help me with my cloth.

Yan atar abärik ten way, tu' kinbärik,
You have to roll it for me here, where I am rolling it,

ti' useebtar ut'arar ink'uuch.
so that my thread piles up faster.

Awaantiken.
You help me.

Ko'oten. He' ak'ucheh ink'uuch.
Come. You will spin my thread.

Yan atar awaantiken way ti' ink'uuch ti' innook' wa.
You have to come help me here spin thread for my cloth.

Yan atar awaantiken ti' ink'uchik way yok'or pecheech,
You have to come help me spin it here on the spindle,

ti' useebtar ut'arar ti' innook'.
so that it may expand faster for my cloth.

Tan ink'uchik innook'.
I am spinning my cloth.

Atar awirik yok'or uxuunche'.
You come see it on the end rods.

Tech katar abut'eh ten ak'uuch.
You will come stuff in your silk for me.

Takay mehen, takay,
Little orb spiders, orb spiders,

tuworor yok'or ulek ink'uuch,
everywhere on the bowl of my thread there,[11]

ti' katar awirik.
when you come you see it there.

Yan atar awirik ti' ka'(a)h atar.
You must come see it when you come.

Abut'ik ten.
You put in (your silk) for me.

Tan insäktik innook'.
I am weaving my cloth.

Tan ink'uchik innook'.
I am spinning my cloth.

Tinmentik inook'.
I am making my cloth.

Katar awirik yok'or uxuunche'. Katar awirik te' yok'or 'akpach
You come see it on the end rods. You come see it there on the warp(?)

tu' kinsäktik.
where I weave it.

Ka('ah) atar awirik,
When you come see it,

ka'(a)h atar awirik innook', abut'ik ak'uuch ten,
when you come see my cloth, you stuff in your silk for me,

ti' useebtar, ti' inpits'ik, ti' inwakik,
so that it goes faster, so that I spin it, so that I make it swell,

ti' inwakik innook'.
so that I can swell my cloth.

He' innook' ti' inxuunche'.
This here is my cloth on my end rods.

Inch'a'ik uhärärte'ir.
I take the beater.

Inka'hi'ik.
I smooth down (the weft) again.

Kinka'hi'ik ti' uheets'e(r).
I smooth it down again so it is snug.

Ko'oten, but'eh ak'uuch yok'or.
Come, stuff your silk on.

'Aak'ä'chär.
Night is falling.

Ko'ten but'eh ak'uuch yok'or.
Come, put on your silk.

'Aak'ä'chär tuk'in inwakik,
It is nightfall when I swell it,

tuk'in intap'ik cha(r)tar.
when I cover it and lay it down.

Yan awaantiken insäktik.
You have to help me weave it.

Atasik yaab ak'uuch kabut'ike'ex.
You bring a lot of your silk, which you put in.

Awaantikene'ex ink'uuch ten, ti' insäktik innook',
You all help me spin thread, so that I can weave my cloth,

uxikul inlak' insäktik,
my husband's tunic is what I weave, so that it expands,

ti' ut'arar ti' useebtar.
so that it piles up faster.

Tarak chukuch uwaan, ti' useebtar umootsor.
Although it is very long, may it shrink faster.

Yaab ak'uuch ka'(a)h abut'ik 'ichir.
You have a lot of silk that you put inside.

Awaantiken ti' useebtar inmeyah.
You help me so that my work goes faster.

Tarak inlik'ir ti',
Although I get up from there,

inlik'ir inbin ti' inber,
I get up and I go on my way,

awaantiken tech;
you help me;

ten inp'ätikech, atar awaantiken ti' abut'ik ak'uuch ti' ink'uuch,
I leave you, (and) you come help me by stuffing your silk in my thread,

ti' useebtar ut'arar.
so that it may pile up quickly.

Tech awaantiken ti' unook' inlak',
You are the ones that help me with my husband's cloth,

ti' useebtar uts'o'okor.
so that it finishes faster.

K'uchur 'oxp'er k'in, ts'o'okih,
In three days, it is finished,

'uher, 'uher kinsäktik.
and I will weave another one.

Tech chich amuk'.
You are very strong.

Awaantiken.
You help me.

Tech ähtoy,
You are the spider,

mehen takayeh.
the dear little orb spider.

Lah boona takay.
How many you are, orb spiders.

Yan awaantiken ti' inmeyah.
You have to help me with my work.

Yan awaantiken ti' ink'uuch.
You have to help me spin.

Ka'(a)h atar abut'ik ak'uuch yok'or inpecheech,
When you come put your silk on my spindle,

tan awirik inpecheech.
you are watching my spindle.

Tan atar abut'ik tu' kinlik'sik ka'anan utaan nah.
You are coming to stuff in (your silk) where I raise it up high in the rafters.

Inwahkuntik yok'or ka'anan, ti' katar abut'ik ak'uuch
I set it up above, so that you will come stuff your silk

yok'or inpecheech.
on my spindle.

Tech chich amuk'e'ex ti', ka'(a)h atar abut'ik.
You are very strong, when you come and stuff it in.

Awaantiken ink'uchik.
You help me spin it.

Awaantiken.
You help me.

Tech t'asik ak'uuch abut'ik ten.
You are the ones that pile up your silk (and) stuff it in for me.

Atar abutw'ik uyo'och insäkär,[12]
You come fill the woof of my woven cloth,

tu' chara'an,
where it is laying,

tu' kinwakik,
where I expand it,

abut'ik uyo'och insäkär.
you put in the woof of my woven cloth.

Atar awaantiken.
You come help me.

Uk'aay Torok 'The Iguana Song'

Antonio Martinez

This song is sung during the creation of the new god pots, the Lacandon means of communicating with the gods.[1] Made from clay, these bowls are embellished with anthropomorphic faces of the deities who will receive offerings of food, copal, and rubber. The pots are whitewashed with calcium lime and painted in red and black designs appropriate to their gender: male pots have vertical stripes, while female pots have a cross-hatched pattern. These stripes correspond to the stripes on the iguana, which the singer draws to the pots, conceivably to be offered to the gods. Thus, mention of the stripes on the god pots evokes the stripes on the iguana, and vice versa.

Bay. Bähe' kinbin ink'äyik uk'aay torok ti' uts'iiba(r) tum(b)en läk.
Okay. Now, I'm going to sing the song of the iguana for the stripes (on) the new god pots.

Torok ka'(ah) at'ä(r)ta(r) nikte', eh torok,
Iguana, when you sit upon the frangipani vine, oh iguana,

päpäknäk,[2] torok, uts'iibar.
the stripes (on your head) are bobbing, iguana.

Kapa'an (ti'u) pach utsimi(n),
Seated astride the back of a horse,

kaprik torok xok'or up'iis k'ax ho'or.
the iguana is mounted near the measure of bark headband.[3]

Way yan, torok, uts'iibarar.
Here they are, iguana, his stripes.

Ka'ah na'aki(h)[4] ti' tum(b)en läk torok,
When the iguana leaned against the new god pot,

uts'iibar t'äräkbar t(i') uts'iibar torok.
the stripes are put in place on the stripes of the iguana.

Ek' uts'ibar torok.
Black are the iguana's stripes.

T'ä(r)ta(r) nikte' torok,[5]
The iguana remains in place on the frangipani vine,

päpäknäk.
bobbing (his head).

Torok t'är(r)ik t(i') upach che'.[6]
The iguana is placed on the back of a tree.

T'ära'an t(i') upach che', torok.
Seated on the (bark) of a tree, is the iguana.

Kapa'an t(i') upach utsimin, torok,
Mounted on the back of his horse, is the iguana,

kapa'an,
mounted,

kapa'an ti' upach uche'.
mounted on the (bark) of a tree.

Yan uts'iibar, torok.
There are his stripes, iguana.

Uts'iibar uho'or torok,
The stripes of the iguana's head,

uts'iibar uho'or
the stripes of his head

tupach uts'iibar, upach uche', uyeek'er uyok,[7]
the stripes on his back, the back of his neck(?), the colors of his feet,

uyeek'er uk'äb, torok,
the colors of his hands, iguana,

uyeek'er uho'or, torok,
the colors of his head, iguana,

tu' xok'or t(i') uts'iibar torok, ka'ah na'akt'ärt'ar, torok.
(the stripes on the god pot are) near the stripes of the iguana, when he stretched out on top.

Umaan k'ineh, torok.
The days pass, iguana.

Umaan äkna', torokeh.
The months pass, oh iguana.

Päpäknäk, torok. T'är(r)ik t(i') ulekir.

The iguana is bobbing (his head). He sits on top the god pot.

Ka'ah na'akt'ät'är t(i') upach utsimin, t'ärik.

When he stretched out on the back of his horse, he is placed on top (of the god pot).

Tan inwirik uts'iibar.

I am looking at his stripes.

Ya'ax uts'iibar.

Green are his stripes.

Chäk uts'iibar, torok.

Red are his stripes, iguana.

Chäk uts'iibar, torokeh.

Red are his stripes, oh iguana.

La'eh ka'ah na'ak usukun kyum[8] torok; t'är(r)ik uts'iibar ya'ax kabar, ya'ax kabar uts'iibar, ka'ah na'ak(ih) t'ärtar uts'iibar.

These (are the stripes) of your older brother iguana when he climbed up; his green stripes are placed below, green are his stripes below, when he climbed up his stripes remain in place.

Ya'ax kabar, ka'ah na'ak(ih) t'ärtar uts'iibar, torok.

(They are) green below, when he climbed up the stripes of the iguana remain in place.[9]

T'ära'an t(i') upach ulekir innohwah. T'ära'an t(i') ulekir, t'äräkbar, torok.

He is stretched out on the back of my plate of tamales. Stretched out on the plate, the iguana is stretched out.

Päpäknäk, torok,

The iguana is bobbing his head,

t'är(r)i(k) t(i') upach utsimin, torok.

the iguana lies stretched out on the back of his horse.

T'äräkbar t(i') ulekir. Le' ka'ah na'ak(ih), t'ärtar, torok.

The iguana is stretched out on top of the plate. When he climbed up, the iguana remains in place.

Ya'ax uts'iibar.

Green are the stripes.

Chäk uts'iibar torok.

Red are the stripes (of the) iguana.

Ch'ik naach ka'ah na'ak t'ärtar torok

(It is) far away when the iguana climbed up and remain(ed) in place

t(i') utaan ulekir,

on the front of the god pot,

ti' utaan nah,

on the front of the house,[10]

ka'ah na'akt'ärtar, torokeh.

when he stretched out on top, oh iguana.

Ka'ah eemih torok, eemih t'ärtar t(i') uts'iibar uyeek'er torok.

When the iguana descended, he descended and the stripes of the iguana remained in place (there).

Uk'aayir Ma'ax 'Song of the Monkeys'

Antonio Martinez

This song is sung to attract monkeys to offer to the gods.[1] The gods relish monkey meat more than any other food offering. Monkey meat was also the Lacandones' favorite game.

As is the case in Mayan ritual language, Lacandon chants and charms are rife with allusion. Words and offerings undergo a transformation that typically entails a reversal of the meaning of the words or qualities of offerings when they reach the gods. In this song the three-layered mountain ridges allude to the three stacks of tamales, each tamale composed of alternating layers of meat (or beans[2]) and corn dough. These are called *nahwah* 'great bread' in ceremonial contexts. Like the mountain ridges, the stacks of tamales are lined up.

The song of the monkeys alludes to the meat; the spreading of the song across the mountain ranges alludes to the fatty meat (inside the tamales).[3]

Ma'axo', ma'axo', ka'ah paak'(ih) uk'aay, ma'axo',
Spider monkey, spider monkey, when the song spread, spider monkey,

ma'axo', ka'ah lik'ih.
spider monkey, when it rose.

Ne ch'ik naach utar uk'aay, ka'ah paak'(ih) uk'aay
From far away the song comes, when the song spread

(ti') hunyära' wits, ka'ah k'uch(ih) uk'aay.
(from) one mountain ridge, when the song arrived.

Tan awu'yik upaak'ar, ma'axo', ma'axo', kuk'aay
You are listening to it spread, spider monkey, spider monkey, he sings

ch'ik t(i') uyooxyära' wits, ka'yära' wits kuk'aay.
far off from the third mountain ridge (then) the second mountain ridge,
he sings.

Ka'ah paak'(ih) uk'aay ti' äkyum,
When the song spread to our Lord,

ka'ah k'uchih ku(r)tar t(i') ulekir wah,
when it arrived and sat down in the tortilla plate,

ti' uyum(bir)ir ka'an,
of the Lord of Heaven,

ka'ah paak'(ih) uk'aay,
when the song spread,

ka'ah tinbut'ah ts'u'ts'u' wah,
then I put it in the soft center of the tortilla,

ten tinbut'ah ti' tum(b)en lekir ti' wah.
I put it in the new tortilla plate.

Ka'ah paak'(ih) uk'aay
When the song spread

'ooxyära' wits, yäri(k)wits, ka'ah paak'(ih) uk'aay,
three stacked mountain (ridges), when the song spread,

ka'ah k'uch(ih) uk'aay, tum(b)en (lek?) yan,
when the song arrived, there is a new (plate?),

tu' kura'an uyumi(r) ka'an.
where the Lord of Heaven is seated.

Ka'ah k'uch(ih) uk'aay, ma'axo', ma'axo',
When the song arrived, spider monkey, spider monkey,

ka'ah paak'(ih) uk'aay.
when the song spread.

'Ooxyära' wits, ka'ah k'uch(ih) uk'aay, tan aw(u'y)ik uk'aay.
Three mountain ridges away, when the song arrived, you are listening to
the song.

Tinbut'ah 'ooxyära' yärik t(i') uleki(r) wah, t(i') uleki(r) mukxib(bir) bäk',
ka'ah yärak uk'aay.
I put three stacks of layered (tamales) on the tortilla plate, on the plate of
baked meat tamales, when the song lines up.

Ka'ah na('a)kku(r)tar (te'?) ti' kyum,
When it climbed up and sat down for our Lord,

ka'ah tinku(r)kintah uk'aay.
then I set the song down (inside the tamales).

Tinkurkintah t(i') uleki(r) wah, t(i') uleki(r) innohwah ti' kyum,
I set (the song) down on the tortilla plate, on my tamale plate for our Lord,

ka'ah k'aaynah (ah)ba'ats'.
when the howler monkey sang.

'Ooxyära' wits, ka'ah paak'(ih) uk'aay ba'ats',
Three mountain ridges away, when the song of the howler monkey spread,

ka'ah paak' uk'aay
when the song spread

humpat heeba(n),
through the canyon,

ka'ah k'uchi(h) uk'aay,
when the song arrived,

ten uyumir ka'an,
for(?) the Lord of Heaven,

ka'ah paak'(ih) uk'aay ba'ats',
when the song of the howler monkey spread,

ka'ah paak'i(h).
when it spread.

Ka'ah paak'(ih) uk'aay, ka'ah tinbut'ah
When the song spread, then I put in

'ooxyära' yärik wah,
three stacks of layered tortillas,

ka'ah k'uchih ti' tum(b)en lek ti' kyum.
when it arrived at the new god pots for our Lord.

…

…

'Ooxyära' yäriko' yaari(r) wah,
Three stacks of layered tortillas,

ka'ah tinbut'ah ti' tum(b)en ulek,
when I put them in the new (god) pot,

ten uyumir ka'an.
I am(?) the Lord of the sky.

La' ka'ah paak'(ih) uk'aay tu' bin t(i') akna' yete(r) Hachäkyum.
When the song spread, it goes to our Mother and Hachäkyum.

Lati' bu'urir,
They are beans,

mäna' bu'urir wah,
(but) they are not (really) bean tamales,

mukxi(b)bi(r) bäk',
(but) baked meat tamales,

ka'(a)h k'aaynah,
when they sang,

'ooxyära' wits,
three mountain ridges (yonder),

ba'ats'o',
the howler monkey,

ma'axo',
the spider monkey,

ka'ah paak'(ih) uk'aay,
when their song spread,

ka'(ah) tawu'yah upaak'ar uk'aay.
when you heard their song spread.

Ka'(ah) binen inwireh ba'ats',
When I went to (look for) the howler monkeys,

ka'(ah) binen inwireh ma'ax,
when I went to (look for) the spider monkeys,

ch'ik naach,
(they are) very far away,

ka'(ah) tintaasah.
when I made them come.

Ka'ah k'uchi(h) ku(r)ta(r) t(i') uleki(r) bu'ur,
When they arrived and sat down on the plate of beans,

mukxib(b)i(r) bäk',
the (plate of) baked meat tamales,

'ooxyära' yaari(r) wah ti' tum(b)en lek ti' kyum.
there are three stacks of layered tortillas on the new god pot of our Lord.[4]

La' ti' uyorir ka'an ti' utukur yaari(r) t(i') uleki(r),
These are for the Lord of Heaven (who) thinks about the layered (tortillas) in his plate,

'ooxyära' ya(a)ri(r) upaak'ar uk'aay t'ärik,[5]
three stacked layers of their song are piled up,

ka'ah tawu'yah upaak'ar.
when you heard it spread.

Boon lah wits ch'ik naach, ma' xok'or yan,
So many mountain (ridges) away, they are not close,

ka'ah k'aaynah ba'ats'o', ma'axo',
when the howler monkeys, the spider monkeys, sang,

ka'ah paak'(ih) uk'aay.
when their song spread out.

Siinte(h?) ti' (ku)k'uch(ur) uk'aay chäksiineh,
Stretch out for when the song arrives red mucus (bark headbands?),

ka'ah paak'i(h) uk'aay.
when their song spread out.

Parok uchooche(r) ma'axo',
(It is) the greasy gut of the spider monkey,

parok uchooche(r) ma'axo',
the greasy gut of the spider monkey,

ka'ah paak'i(h) uk'aay.
when the song spread out.

Ka'ah tinbut'ah ts'u'ts'u' wah,
When I put it in the soft center of the tortilla,

ka'ah okih ti' innohwah,
when it entered my great tamale,

ka'ah tinpurah ten ti' ti' kyum,
when I put it there for our Lord,

la' uyumir ka'an ti' utukur ti' inmukxib(bir) bäk'.
the Lord of Heaven thinks it is my baked meat tamale.

Uk'aayir Tok' 'Song of the Flint'

Antonio Martinez

This chant is like a charm, recited to give strength to the antler punch and the stone hammer and to ensure that these tools slice straight, hard flakes.[1] In this chant the flint knapper invokes plant and bird species that possess qualities of durability, strength, and straight lines to help him with his task: *Pahok* and *'akte'* both have the strongest stems of the Arecaceae family; the spines of the *'akte'* palm are long, straight, and hard; *hach bo'oy, säk bo'oy, ch'ibix, k'eben,* and *säk wawal* all possess straight midribs; *ko'otma'ax* and *balum hunk'uk'* have large, powerful talons and strong bones, particularly the upper wing; the *säktan kos* 'white-breasted sparrow hawk' is invoked because of its hard head and soft breast, the latter being a valued feature of the striking platform; and *chäk p'ookin* is a small but vociferous bird that makes a "chit-chit-chit-THWAK" sound, like that of someone knapping flint.

He' ka'ah kuren ti' intok'
Here when I sat down (at) my flint

la' uho'(or) säktan kos,
it is the head of the white-breasted hawk,

la' uho'(or) ahkos, ka'ah kuren.
it is the head of the hawk, when I sat down.[2]

Ka'ah kuren inp'ep'eh, intaskunteh uch'ibi(r),[3]
When I sat down to chip, I make the ridges,[4]

(u)hook'sik yaaka' (in)nahbaatay (u)naachk'a't(ik) ho'(or).

my antler swiftly removes (the flakes) (when) it strikes the head.

Ka'ah kuren inp'ep'eh usäbkir, kuren inp'ep'eh, la' innak'a' säktan kos.[5]

When I sat down I chip the cortex, sat down to chip, my hammer is the white-breasted hawk.

La' inch'ini' ko'otma'ax la' unahchaakber ubaaker, . . .

The quartz is the thigh bone of the harpy eagle, . . .

ta' 'utsaan la' uba(a)ker inbaak, la' uchichir inbaak, la' uchichir intok'.

the calf bone is the bone of my antler, it is the hardness of my antler, the hardness of my flint.

Ka'ah kuren inp'ep'eh usäbkir, hook'sik yaaka' (in)nahbaatay (in)naachk'a't(ik) uho'(or).

When I sat down to chip the cortex, my antler swiftly removes (the flakes).

Ka'ah kuren inp'ep'(eh) usäbkir,

When I sat down to chip the cortex,

k'ak'na'[6] tintäsah, säk wawar tintäsah uch'ibi(r).

I laid out the ridges of the sea, I laid out the midribs of the calathea.[7]

La' tintäsah la' uch'ibi(r).

The lines that I laid out are the (bevel) ridges.

La' ch'ibix lahtäsa'an, säk bo'oy, la' (t)in täsah uch'ibi(r), ka'ah (u)hook'sik yaaka' innahbaatay.

The parlor palm[8] is all laid out, the white chamaedorea I laid out its midribs, when my antler swiftly removes the flakes.

Tintäsah ti' usäkbir, ka'ah kuren inp'ep'eh.
I laid them out on the cortex, when I sat down to chip.

Chäk p'ookin—
Red-capped woodpecker—

la' umuk' uxik' chäk p'ookin—
the strength of the red-capped woodpecker's wings—

la'ten ka'ah' kuren intsasteh intok', la' uyiich'ak barum hunk'uk',
that is why when I sat down to flake my flint, they are the talons of the black hawk-eagle,

la' yiich'ak barum hunk'uk'; ko'otma'ax la' yiich'ak.
they are the talons of the black hawk-eagle; they are the talons of the harpy eagle.

Ka'ah kuren inp'ep'eh, tintäsah uch'ibi(r), ka'ah kuren (tin)ki'täs(ah) intok'.
When I sat down to chip, I lined up the ridges; when I sat down, I laid out the ridges well.

(U)hook'sik uyaaka'; lahtäsa'an uch'ibi(r).
(My antler) swiftly removes them; the veins are all lined up.

Ka'ah kuren inp'ep'eh, la' intok'.
When I sat down to chip, they are my flint.

Säktan kos la' innak'a';
The white-breasted hawk is my hammer;

uho'(or) (in)k'äxank'ä'teh.
the head is tied to my hand.

La' uho'(or) la' inch'ini' säktan kos.
The head of the white-breasted hawk is my quartz.

La' innak'a'.
It is my hammer.

La' ka'ah hook'sik yaaka' innahbaatay.
It is when my antler swiftly removes the flakes.

Nika'an ka'ah kuren ti' (in)nahbaatay.
They are piled up when I sat down at my antler.

Tinnaachk'a'(tah) uho'(or).
I hit the head.

La' uchichir intok'.
It is the hardness of my flint.

La' ka'ah kuren inp'ep'eh, chäk p'ookin.
When I sat down to chip, it is the red-capped woodpecker.

Ule' pätan tintäsah uch'ibi(r).
I laid out the vein of the plantain leaf.

Säk wawar, säk muxan, la' täsa'an uch'ibi(r).
The veins of the white calathea, the *heliconia librata*, their veins are laid out.

La' tintäsah k'eben la' uch'ibi(r),
I laid out (the veins of) the fishtail palm,[9]

ahk'eben, ahch'ibix, 'akte' uk'i'ixer, la' täsrik ule' ch'ibix, 'akte' uk'i'ixer.

the veins of the fishtail palm, the spines of the chocho palm, the leaf of the parlor palm, the spines of the chocho palm are laid down.

Axonk'a'teh kuxu(r)när, la' ukoh när la' intok', ka'ah' kuren inp'ep'eh.[10]

The kernels of shelled young maize are my flint chips, when I sat down to chip.

Ka'ah kuren intsaasteh uyiich'ak barum hunk'uk', (u)yiich'ak ko'otma'ax,

When I sat down to flake the talons of the black hawk-eagle, the talons of the harpy eagle,

la' innak'a' (ah)säktan kos, la' inch'ini', ka'ah tinkäxtah uho'(or).

my hammer is the white-breasted hawk, it is my quartz, when I searched for the head.[11]

Ka'ah' tinki'täs(ah) uch'ibi(r) intok' beh,

When I laid out the ridges of my flint well,

(in)nahbaatay naachk'a'teh t(i') uho'or, (u)hook'sik yaaka'.

my antler abutting the head removes the flakes rapidly.

La' uchichir inbaaker 'akte', la' uchuur intok'. Le' inbaak. La' uchichir pahok la' uchichir inbaak.

The hardness of my antler is the 'akte', it is the hardness of the core of my flint. This is my antler. The hardness of the pahok is the hardness of my antler.

La' uchichiri(r) ubaaker 'utsaan ko'otma'ax.

It is the hardness of the calf bone of the harpy eagle.

Unahkuuk xik', la' uho'or ukuuk xik'.

It is the elbow of his great wing, the head of his great wing.

La' uchichir intok' ka'ah kuren inp'ep'eh innaxk'a't(eh) uho'(or).

It is the hardness of my flint when I sat down to chip, I strike the head.

(U)hook'sik yaaka' (in)nahbaatay.

My antler removes the flakes rapidly.

La' ka'ah'h kuren inp'ep'eh intok' usäbki(r),

When I sat down to chip away the cortex of my flint,

la' ka'ah tinlahharah usäbki(r),

when I removed all the cortex,

(u)hook'sik uyaaka' (in)nahbaatay.

my antler removes the flakes rapidly.

Ka'ah kuren inp'ep'eh intok' chäk p'ookin la' umuuk' uxik' la' uchichir intok'.

When I sat down to chip my flint, the strength of the wing of the red-capped woodpecker is the hardness of my flint.

Ka'ah' tinhuhuuxtah, la' chäk p'ookin intok'.

When I grind down (the edges), it is the red-capped woodpecker on my flint.

Uk'aayir Xux 'Song of the Yellow Jacket Wasps'

Säk Ho'or

This is a charm sung to the yellow jacket wasps,[1] to prevent them from stinging. A similar charm can be found in the *Ritual of the Bacabs*, a book of Maya incantations written in the latter part of the eighteenth century but likely copied from an earlier manuscript, circa the seventeenth century (Roys 1965, vii). It is called "The words for kanpetkin-wasp poisoning" (*u thanil kanpetkin yah lae*) (48). The speaker, like Säk Ho'or in the present charm, assumes the role of the birds who drill for and eat the larvae of the wasps. Another wasp-poisoning charm, "Kanpedzkin on the head of a man" (*kanpedzkin tu pol uinic*) (46–47), contains Säk Ho'or's phrase verbatim, "I am your mother; I am your father" (48); yet, these two charms are dissimilar in content and purpose.

Xuxeh ka'(ah) tinwi(r)ah ch'uyike'ex bin,
Oh wasps, when I saw you were hung up there,

ti' ch'uuye'ex yok'o(r) ule' insahar
you hung on my dry (leaves)

ti' ch'uuye'ex bin,[2]
there you hung,

yok'(or) le' xibi(r).
on the *xibil* leaves.[3]

Ti' ch'uuye'ex bin
There you hung

yok'o(r) ule' inchukuch xibi(r),
on the leaves of my long leaves,

ka'(ah)tawi(r)ah inta(r) bin.
when you saw me come.

Ka'(ah) tawi(r)ah inta(r),
When you saw me come,

yok'o(r) ule' ink'eben bin,
(you were hanging) on the leaves of my fishtail palm,

k'än xuxeh.
oh yellow wasps.

Ka'(ah) tawi(r)ah inta(r),
When you saw me come,

ti' ch'uuye'ex bin tu ya(r)am che'.
there you were hanging below the tree(s).

Ti' ch'uuye'ex bin tu' yaram lo'obir,
There you hung beneath the brush,

tu yaram sahar.
beneath the dead leaves.

Ti' ch'uuye'ex tu yaram k'ä'che'.
There you hung beneath the branches.

Ti' ch'uuye'ex bin.
There you hung.

K'an xuxeh,
Oh yellow wasps,

ka'(ah) tawirahen bin
when you saw me

ka'(ah) ta(r)en bin
when I came

tu' kura'(an) anahpaak' bin,
to where your nest was sitting there,

ka'(ah) k'uchen ku(r)ta(r).
when I arrived and sat down.

Ka'(ah) k'uchen ku(r)ta(r) inwir(eh) apaak',
When I arrived and sat down to (visit) your nest,

ka'(ah) ta(r)en inwireh bin,
when I came to (visit) it,

eh ka'(ah) ta(r)en inwi(r)eh bin,
oh when I came to (visit) it,

ka'ah lik'en bin.
then you rose.

Ka'(ah) tink'ätmachtik ink'uuts bin.
Then I grasp my cigar.

Ka'(ah) tink'ätmachtah ink'uuts,
When I grasped my cigar,

ka'(ah) tinp'u(r)ustah tech,
when I blew it at you,

ka'(ah) tinp'u(r)ustah uyiik' ink'uuts,
when I blew the puff of my cigar,

ka'(ah) tarih bin,
when it came,

(in)nahik k'ak',
(I) collect(ed) the (smoke?),

ka'(ah) tar unukuch iik' ink'uuts,
when the large puff (of) my cigar came,

ka'(ah) tarih bin.
when it came.

Ka'(ah) tarih bin,
When they came,

k'än xuxeh bin,
oh yellow wasps,

ka'(ah) tarih,
when they came,

ka'(ah) tarih sinik,
when the ants came,

ka'(ah) tarih,
when they came,

ka'(ah) tarih saka(r),
when the army ants came,

ka'(ah) tarih,
when they came,

ka'(ah) na'akih, (tu)lahpa'ah awaar.
when they climbed up, they completely broke apart your brood.

Na'ak'ih (tu)lahhantah awaar bin,
They climbed up (and) ate up your brood,

ka'(ah) tarih.
when they came.

Ka'(ah) tari(h) hooch',
When the fire ants came,

ka'(ah) tarih saakar,
when the army ants came,

ka'(ah) tari(h) chäk waayah,
when the *chak waayah*[4] came,

ka' tari(h) na'aki(h),
when they came they climbed up,

lahtari(h) bin.
they all came.

Ka'(ah) na'aki(h) bin (tu)lahpa'ah awaa(r).
When they climbed up, they completely broke apart your brood.

Ka'(ah)na'aki(h) (tu)lahhantah awaa(r).
When they climbed up, they ate up your brood.

Ka'(ah)na'aki(h) (tu)lahp'e'ah awaa(r).
When they climbed up, they completely pecked apart your brood,

ka'(ah) na'akih.
when they climbed up.

K'än xuxeh bin,
Oh yellow wasps,

ka'(ah) tink'ätmachtah,
when I grasped it,

ka'(ah) tink'ätmachtah bin, ink'uuts bin,
when I grasped my cigar,

ka'(ah) tinp'urustah tech.
then I blew (the smoke) at you.

Ya ma' het la'eh alisik ak'i'ixe(r).
Already you cannot raise your stingers.

Ma' het la'eh bin.
It is impossible.

'Aarak' ak'i'ixe(r).
Your stingers are tame.

'Aarak' bin.
They are tame.

'Aarak' aho'(ol).
Your heads are tame.

'Aarak' bin.
They are tame.[5]

Ma' het la'eh alisik ak'i'ixe(r),
You cannot raise your stingers,

ka'(ah) tinwa(ar)kuntah ak'i'ixe(r),
when I made your stingers heavy,

ka'(ah) tinti(r)iskuntah,
when I made them flutter,

ka'(ah) tinti(r)istah ak'i'ixe(r),
when I flicked your stingers,

ka'(ah)tinti(r)istah.
when I flicked them.

K'än xuxeh,
Oh yellow wasps,

ka'(ah) tinwi(r)ah ch'uyike'ex bin,
when I saw you hung up,

ka'(ah)k'uchen, (t)inpepee(k)s(ah)e'ex bin.
when I arrived, I shook you.

Ma' het la'eh (a)lisik abäh,
You cannot rise.

Ma' het la'eh alik'i(r) bin.
You cannot rise.

Ka'(ah) tink'ätmachtah uyor ink'uuts,
When I grasped the tip of my cigar,

ka'(ah)tink'ätmachtah bin,
when I grasped it,

ka'(ah)tinbärähe'ex yok'o(r) yor ink'uuts,
when I rolled you up on the tip of my cigar,

ka'(ah)tinbah(ah)e'ex bin,
when I tapped you,

eh, ka'(ah) tinp'urustah bin.
oh, then I blew (the smoke).

Ka'(ah) tinp'urusah yok'o(l) uyiits ink'uuts,
When I blew on the resin of my cigar,

ma' het la'eh ak'äslisik abäh,
you can barely rise,

k'än xuxeh.
oh yellow wasps.

Ma' het la'eh bin.
It is impossible.

Ma' het la'eh alisik ak'i'ixe(r),
You cannot lift your stingers,

ma' het la'eh.
it is impossible.

Tinwa(a)lkunt(ah) (a)ho'(or).
I made your heads heavy.

Tinwärak'tah bin.
I tamed them.

Tinwa(a)rkunt(ah) (a)xik'.
I made your wings heavy.

Tinwa(a)rkuntah bin.
I made them heavy.

Tinwa(a)rkuntah ayaach.
I made your stingers heavy.

Tinwa(a)rkuntah bin.
I made them heavy.

Tinwa(a)rkuntah tech bin, k'än xuxeh,
I made you heavy, oh yellow wasps,

ma' het la'eh alisik ak'i'ixe(r).
you cannot lift your stingers.

Ka'(ah) tawi(r)ah uta(r) achiich,
When you saw your grandmother come,

ka'(ah) tawir(ah) utar ana',
when you saw your mother come,

ka'(ah) tawi(r)ah uta(r) asukun,
when you saw your elder brother come,

ka'(ah) tawirah bin,
when you saw him come,

ten ayumen bin.
I am your lord.

Ma' het la'eh (a)lisik ak'i'ixe(r).
You cannot raise your stingers.

Ma' het la'eh bin.
It is impossible.

Ma' het la'eh,
It is impossible,

ten ateten,
(for) I am your father,

ten asukun,
I am your older brother,

ten bin.
I am.

Ten ana',
I am your mother,

ten bin.
I am.

Eh ma' het la'eh, ten
It is impossible, (for) I am,

tuworo(r) bin, ten.
all of them, I am.

Eh, ma' het la'eh alisik ak'i'ixer,
So, you cannot lift your stingers,

ka'(ah) tinwa(a)rkunteh tech ak'i'ixer.
when I made your stingers heavy.

Ka'(ah) k'uchen ku(r)ta(r) bin,
When I arrived and sat down,

ka'(ah) tink'ätmachtah ink'uuts,
when I grasped my cigar,

ka'(ah) tink'ätmachtah ink'uuts bin,
when I grasped my cigar,

ka'(ah) tinp'urustah ti' anahwaaro' bin,
when I blew (the smoke) at your brood,

tan atar ka'(ah) tawi(r)ah bin.
you come when you (see) it.

Eh purusin che'
Oh *purusin che'*[6]

ka'(ah) tinpurah bin,
when I knocked it down,[7]

ka'(ah) na'aken bin,
when I climbed up,

(tin)lahhantah bin.
I ate up (the brood).

Tinlahpa'ah awaa(r) bin.
I broke your brood all apart.

Eh, ma' het la'eh bin.
So, it is impossible.

Ma' het la'eh alisik ak'i'ixe(r),
You cannot lift your stingers,

ka'(ah) tinpurah tech bin,
when I sent it to you,

ka'(ah) tinpur(ah) uyiits ink'uuts,
when I sent the resin of my cigar,

ka'(ah) tinpur(ah).
when I sent it.

Ka' tinbärahe'ex bin ti' uneek' ink'uuts,
When I rolled you on the seeds of my tobacco,

ka'ah tinbärahe'ex ti' uyiits in k'uuts bin,
when I rolled you in the resin of my cigar,

ma' het la'eh (a)k'äslisik ak'i'ixer,
you can barely raise your stingers,

ma' het la'eh' bin.
it is impossible.

Ma' het la'eh ak'äslisik ak'i'ixe(r),
You can barely lift your stingers,

ka'(ah) tinpepee(k)sah aho'(or).
when I shook your heads.

Ka'(ah) tintiri(r)stah ayatoch,
When I quickly flicked your house,

ka'(ah) tintiri(r)stah ayaach,
when I flicked your stingers,

ka'(ah) tintiri(r)stah axik',
when I flicked your wings,

ka'(ah) tintiri(r)stah bin,
when I flicked them,

ka'(ah) tintiri(r)stah aho'(or),
when I flicked your heads,

ka'(ah) tintiri(r)stah, k'än xuxeh,
when I flicked them, oh yellow wasps,

ma' het la'eh ak'äslisik abäh.
you can barely get up.

Eh, ma' het la'eh,
So, it is impossible,

ka'(ah) tar(ih) asukun,
when your older brother came,

ka'(ah) tar(ih) ana',
when your mother came,

ka'(ah) tar(ih) atet,
when your father came,

ka'(ah) tarih,
when they came,

ma' het la'eh.
it is impossible.

Ka'(ah) tarih inpitskan 'ox,
When my red-crowned ant-tanager came,

ka'(ah) tarih.
when it came,

ka'(ah) tarih ink'än kux,[8]
when my yellow trogon came,

ka'(ah) tarih bin,
when it came,

na'akih ch'uch'uuy t(i') awaa(r),
they climbed up and hung all over your brood,

na'akih (tu)lahhantah awaa(r) bin.
they climbed up and ate up your brood.

Eh, ma' het la'eh alisik abäh.
Eh, you cannot get up.

Ma' het la'eh
It is impossible

ka'(ah) tintiri(r)stah bin,
when I flicked them,

ka'(ah) tintiri(r)stah.
when I flicked them.

Eh, ka'(ah) tari(h) bin nah iik',
So, when a great (puff of) breath came,

ka'(ah) bin(ih) nukuch iik',
when a large puff went,

ink'uuts bin uyiik' ink'uuts,
(of) my cigar, the puff of my cigar,

ka'(ah) tari(h) bin ti' tech,
when it came to you,

ma' het la'eh alisik bin.
you cannot rise.

Eh, ka'(ah) tinsarah ta'an tech bin,
So, when I blew the ashes at you,

ka'(ah) na'aki(h) ka'ana(n) bi,
when they rose high,

k'än xuxeh,
oh yellow wasps,

ma' het la'eh bin.
it is impossible.

Ti' ch'uya('a)n yok'o(r) yaram le' che'eh, ti' ch'uya(a'n)e'ex bin.
There hanging on the underside of the leaves of the tree(s), there you are hanging.

Ti' ch'uya('a)n(e'ex) yok'or ule'(t)äk luuch,
There you are hanging on the leaves of the calabasa tree,

yok'o(l) yaramtäk hama',
on the underside of the gourd bowls,

yok'o(l) ule'täk saha(r),
on the dry leaves,

ti' ch'uy(a'an)e'ex bin.
there you are hanging.

Ma' het la'eh ak'äslisik ak'i'ixe(r),
You can barely lift your stingers,

ka'(ah)tinwa(a)rkunteh tech bin.
when I made you heavy.

Ma' het la'eh.
It is impossible.

Ma' het la'eh, k'än xuxeh,
It is impossible, oh yellow wasps,

ka'(ah)tintiri(r)stah axiik',
when I flicked your wings,

ka'(ah)tintiri(r)stah aho'(or),
when I flicked your heads,

tintiri(r)stah.
I flicked them.

Eh, ka'(ah) na'aki(h) siinik,
So, when the ants climbed up,

ka'(ah) ta(r)i(h) siinik,
when the ants came,

ka'(ah) ta(r)i(h) chäk waayah,
when the chäk waayah came,

ka'(ah) ta(r)i(h) chäk siinik,
when the red ants came,

ek' siinik,
the black ants,

ka'(ah) na'aki(h) (tu)lahpa'ah bin.
when they climbed up they broke apart (the nest).

Eh, ka'(ah)ta(r)i(h) hooch',
Eh, when the fire ants came,

ka'(ah) na'akih lahchi'eh awaa(r),
when they climbed up to eat up your brood,

na'akih (tu)lahhantah awaa(r),
they climbed up and ate up your brood,

na'akih (tu)lahpa'ah.
they climbed up and broke them apart.

Eh, ma' het la'eh alisik abäh,
Eh, you cannot get up,

ka'(ah)tintiri(r)stah ak'i'ixe(r),
when I flicked your stingers,

ka'(ah)tintiri(r)stah,
when I flicked them,

ka'(ah) tintiri(r)stah ak'i'ixer, ma' het la'eh ak'äslisik abah.
when I flicked your stingers, you can barely rise.

Eh,
So,

ten asukunen bin.
I am your elder brother.

Ten ana'en.
I am your mother.

Ten ateten bin.
I am your father.

Uteten bin.
I am the father.

Ma' het la'eh ak'äschi'iken,
You can barely bite me,

ma' het la'eh ak'äslisik abah.
you can barely get up.

Ka'(ah) k'uchen ku(r)tal bin t(i') anahpak',
When I arrived and sat down at your nest,

ka'(ah) k'uchen bin,
when I arrived,

ka'(ah) k'uchen ku(r)ta(r) t(i') anahpak',
when I arrived and sat down at your nest,

ma' het la'eh (a)k'äslisik abäh.
you can barely get up.

Ma' het la'eh.
It is impossible.

Ka'(ah) k'uchen ku(r)ta(r) t(i') anahpak', ka'(ah) tink'ätmacht(ah) uyor ink'uuts,
When I arrived and sat down at your nest, when I grasped the tip of my cigar,

Ka'(ah) tinbärahe'ex yok'or t(i') uyor ink'uuts,
When I rolled you on the tip my cigar,

ma' het la'eh;
it is impossible;

ma' het la'eh alik'ir.
you cannot rise.

Bähe' ma' het la'eh alik'ir, k'än xuxeh,
Now, you cannot get up, oh yellow wasps,

ma' het la'eh bin.
it is impossible.

Ka'(ah) na'akih (tu)lahhanteh awaa(r) bin,
When (they) climbed up they ate up your brood,

ka'(ah) na'akih.
when (they) climbed up.

Eh, ka'(ah) tari(h) bin inpitskan 'ox,
When my red-crowned ant-tanager came,

ka'(ah) tari(h) inpitskan 'ox,
when my red-crowned ant-tanager came,

ka'(ah) ta(r)i(h) inchukuch neeh,
when my quetzal came,[9]

ka'(ah) tari(h) ink'än kuux,
when my yellow tanager,

ka'(ah) tari(h) inchäk mo' bin,
when my scarlet macaw came,

ti' ch'uuye'ex bin yok'o(r) le'täk k'eben, t(i') ule'täk chukuch xibi(r),
there you hung on the leaves of the fishtail palm, on the leaves of the heliconia,

ma' het la'eh ak'äslisik.
you can barely rise.

Ka'(ah) tinp'urustah nukuch iik' ink'uuts tech,
When I blew a great puff from my cigar at you,

ka'(ah) ta(r)i(h), tinp'urustah tech uyiik' ink'uuts,
when it came, I blew a puff from my cigar at you,

ma' het la'eh ak'äslik'i(l) bin.
you can barely rise.

Ka'ah tintiri(r)stah ak'i'ixe(r),
When I flicked your stingers,

tintiri(r)stah ayaach,
I flicked your stingers,

tintiri(r)stah aho'(or),
I flicked your heads,

ma' het la'eh.
it is impossible.

Ka'ah tintiri(r)stah a cría,
When I flicked your brood,

ma' het la'eh ak'äslisik abah bin.
you can barely get up.

Asukunen.
I am your elder brother.

Ateten.
I am your father.

Ma' het la'eh bin.
It is impossible.

Ma' het la'eh alik'ir bin.
You cannot rise.

Ma' het la'eh achi'ah.
You cannot bite.

Ma' het la'eh bin.
It is impossible.

'Aalak' aho'(or).
Your heads are tame.

'Aarak' ayaach.
Your stingers are tame.

'Aarak' bin.
They are tame.

Eh, ka'(ah) tink'ätmachtah[10] uyor ink'uuts,
So, when I grasped the end of my cigar,

ka'(ah) tinp'urustah tech,
when I blew (the smoke) at you,

ma' het la'eh.
it is impossible.

Eh,
Eh,

ka'(ah) tinp'urustah ti',
when I blew it at (your nest),

ka'(ah) tari(h) bin,
when it came,

ka'(ah) tar(ih) iik' innukuch k'uuts,
when the puff of my large cigar came,

ka'(ah) tinsarah ta('a)n tech,
when I blew ashes at you,

ka'(ah) na'ak'e'ex ka'anan bin,
then you rose high,

a' ka'an bine'ex.
to the sky you went.

Tu' yalam ka'an
Under the sky[11]

kabin t(i') uya'axeh ka'an
you go to the blue sky.

A' ka'[12] bine'ex bin,
When you went,

ti' yan tu' yaramtäk hama',
it is to the undersides of the gourd bowls,

t(i') uyaramtäk ule' xibi(r),
to the undersides of the heliconia leaves,

t(i') uyaramtäk ule' saha(r),
to the undersides of the dry leaves,

ti' yane'ex bin,
is where you are,

yaramtäk che' bin.
the undersides of the trees.

Ma' het la'eh bin.
It is impossible.

Ka'ah tar (u)nukuch iik' ink'uuts,
When the big puff (of smoke) of my cigar came,

bähe' ma' het la'eh bin.
now it is impossible.

5

Ritual Speech

Invocations, Chants, and Charms

Ahhooch' 'The Hooch''

Juana Koh

The following *sekreto* 'secret' is recited to prevent the *hooch'*, a kind of 'panther ant' (*Pachycondyla purpurascens*), from biting.[1] Lacandones describe it as large and black with a powerful stinger on its abdomen.[2]

Tu' way yanech ahhooch'eh,
Where you are here, oh hooch',

ka'(ah) tawir(ik) intar ahhooch'eh,
when you see me come, oh hooch',

ka'(ah) tinluk'sik umuuk' awaach,
then I remove the strength of your stinger,

ka'(ah) tinluk'sik umuuk' uk'ak'(ir) ak'i'ix.
then I remove the strength of the fire from your stinger.

Ahsiinikeh,
Oh ants,

tuk'in kawirik intare(r),
when you see me coming,

h(e') awi(rik) utare(r) inwoke(r) uk'ara'n tsub inwok.
you will see my feet come enclosed in agouti (pelts).

Ti' ti(n)tak'ah t(i') uk'are(n) tsub t(i') utaan inwok.
There I fastened the agouti slippers on the soles of my feet.

Ti' tinhantap't(ah) utaan inwok yet(er) uk'aren tsub.
There I quickly wrapped my soles with the agouti slippers.

Tu' way yane'ex ahsiinkeh, hooch'eh,
Where you are here, oh ants, oh hooch',

ka'(ah) tawir(ah) atiristik inwok.
when you (see) them, you tap my feet.

Tan atiristik inwok.
You are tapping my feet.

Tan apeeksik ak'i'ix.
You are moving your stingers.

Tan apeeksik awaacher.
You are moving your stingers.

Ten kinlubs(ik) umuk' awaach.[3]
I reduce the strength of your stingers.

Ten kinlubs(ik) umuk' ak'i'ixer.
I reduce the strength of your stingers.

Ahsiinikeh, tu' yane'exeh,
Oh ants, where you are,

'äx p'utun mu(ur) siinikeh, 'äx p'utun,
lumpy mounds of ants' nests, lumpy mounds,

tu' yane'ex to'an awaal tanah.
you are where your brood is now.

Inpeeksik awaar.
I move your brood.

Tan inwätik awaar.
I am scrambling up your brood.

Tan inpeeksik amuur.
I am moving your nest.

Tan inhu(r)che'(e)tik amuur ten.
I am poking your nest with a stick now.

Ma' achi'iken ten.
You don't bite me.

Awi(ri)k utar inwok.
You see my feet come.

Chäkhare'(en) inpik, utar inwok yet(er), inwok yet(er) uk'aren tsub,
Bright red is my skirt, my feet come with (them), my feet with the agouti slippers,

hooch'eh,
oh hooch',

kala(h)wir(ik) intare(r), hooch'eh.
when you see me come, oh hooch'.

Ahts'in 'The Manioc'

Juana Koh

This is a charm to protect the manioc. It calls upon the animals of the milpa, especially those with grasping paws, to help harvest the manioc before the other animals can get at it.

Manioc is one of the Lacandones' primary crops, after maize. They plant the slips when the moon is half full (K'ayum Paniagua, pers. comm.). The flesh of one variety is used to make tortillas. Two other varieties are baked or boiled and sweetened with honey or sugar.

Tu' yanech ahaak'ä'bäk'?

Where are you, raccoon?

Tu' yanecheh? Ahamp(i)tik inwo'och ts'in.

Where are you? You pull out my manioc.

Yan atar hamp(i)tik inwo'och ts'in ten 'ooch, hori(r)ch'o'.

You must come pull out my manioc for me, opossum rat.

Yan ahamp(i)tik ten.

You must pull it out for me.

Yan ahamp(i)tik inwo'och ts'in. Ne yan atar ahamp(i)tik inwo'och ts'ineh, aak'ma'ax.

You must pull out my manioc. You really must come and pull out my manioc, night monkey.[1]

Haayok',[2]

Haayok',

yan atar ahamp(i)tik inwo'och ts'in.

you must come pull out my manioc.

Ma' (bik) upu(k')ta(r) inwo'och ts'in ten. Yan ahamp(i)tik inwo'och ts'in.

Don't let my manioc rot on me. You must pull out my manioc.

—HOM HOM HOM —[3]

—HOM HOM HOM —

Tub(ah) yan(ech) hori(r)'ooch, hori(r)ch'o'?[4]

Where are you opossum rat?

To'an t(an) umaan t'eche(r)xikin ch'o', way alahmuuch'(i)k abäh ten.

Where the long-eared rats are passing through, you all come together here for me.

A' boona hare' lah boona way. Amuuch'(i)k abäh ten ahamp(i)tik inwo'och ts'in.

How many spotted cavies[5] there are here. You gather together for me to pull out my manioc.

—HOM HOM HOM —

—HOM HOM HOM —

Lah boona amuuch'(i)k abäh ten ti' inwo'och ts'in ti' ala(h)hamp(i)tik inwo'och ts'in.

How many there are of you who gather together at my manioc to pull out all my manioc.

Tu' kinmukik inwo'och ts'in, ma' utu'utar ten.
Where I bury my manioc, it doesn't rot on me.

Tech ahhaayok';
You are the haayok';

tech ah'aak'ma'ax;
you are the night monkey;

lah way amuuch'(i)k abäh ten t(i') inwo'och ts'in ti' inhantik.
you all gather together here for me at my manioc so that I can eat it.

Alahhamp(i)tik inwo'och ts'in ten
You pull out all my manioc for me

—HOM HOM HOM.
—HOM HOM HOM.

An Offering Chant during the Preparation of Balche'

Antonio Martinez

This chant was performed during the preparation of a balche' ceremony hosted by Antonio. I had requested that he prepare the ceremony for documentary purposes. Antonio determined the occasion and the kinds of offering required to be made. The occasion was a supplication to the gods to remove an illness that had taken hold of the community. The offering included *ch'urha'kih* 'sacred water', a kind of cooked corn gruel.[1]

The following text has been extracted from the first of the three rituals in the ceremony. In this ritual Antonio sits in front of the god pots offering them balche' from a rolled leaf spoon while he chants.[2] He interrupts this ritual, walking outside the god house to offer balche' to the gods not in attendance. This action is also accompanied by chanting.

The monotonic chanting is punctuated by bursts of rapid, intonationally oscillating speech. In the transcription the chanting is presented in plain text, whereas the spoken words are given in italics.

La'he' Chobeh, uho'(or) ch'ur(h)a'kih. 'Eeseh uyori(r) ka'an.

Here it is, Chob,[3] the first offering of ch'urha'kih. Show the Heart of Heaven.[4]

Ok' awichi(r), Chobeh.[5] Sahkunteh la' siim. Tarak ne hets'a yeheh yahi(r),[6]

You cry, oh Chob. Dry up the mucus. Although there is much pain relief (?),[7]

pureh ta beh.

send it away.

K'äs 'aak'(ä')kunteh uwich uchäkwirir se'em.
Please, darken the eyes of the fever of the flu.[8]

Mäna' uts'aakeh, Chobeh.
There is no medicine, oh Chob.

T'än(eh) awäkan, kyum
Tell your father-in-law, our Lord

kurik yok'o(r) ka'(a)n beh.
who is seated in the sky.

Ma' pimo'(on).
We are not many.

'Otsi(r), ku(ru)ko'on beh.
We are pitiful, seated here.

K'äs sahku(n)teh chäkwi(rir), uyahi(r) se'emi(r).
Please reduce the fever, the pain of the flu.

Ma' ucha'ik utar ha'.
Don't let it rain.

Kura'(an) he' beh se'em.
The flu is here.

Itsanar, ma' ucha'ik utar ha' beh.
Itsanar, don't let it rain.[9]

Seebar kuyaak'ä'chah uwich ye'h yahi(r) beh.
Quickly the eyes of the illness darken.

Pur(eh) ak'ä' beh.
Throw out your hand.

Tarak tubah ti' k'aax,
Although where it is in the forest,

ch'ik naach utar yahi(r).
the illness comes from far away.

Pureh ak'ä' beh.
Throw out your hand.

Pureh naach, ka'(ah) xi(')ik beh.
Hurl it far away, that it might go.

'Otsi(r) kur(u)k aleki(r).
Your god pots set (here) are pitiable.

Ma' het la'eh beh.
They are inadequate.

Itsanah ne tech t(an) awirik uho'(or) la'
Itsanar, you are seeing the first offering (of)

ya'ahk'in.
the ya'ahk'in ceremony.

T(an) awirik ya'ahk'in.
You are seeing the ya'ahk'in.[10]

T(an) awirik beh.
You are seeing it.

Way, kabin awireh uyo'och chäk hu'uni(n) ya'ahk'in.

Here, you are going to see the red bark cloth offering of the ya'ahk'in.

Ka'(ah) (a)wireh te' (Ak)na',[11] kuren.

When you see Our Mother there, sit down.

Yant'o', he' beh.

Akyant'o', here it is.

Kyant'o', boon pimin tu' kura'(a)n beh.

How many there are where Akyant'o' is.[12]

Tu xaax ahAkyant'o' kints'a(k)ik uhu'un. Ma' acha'ik uluubur ye'eh yahi(r) way beh, yok'or a' k'aax. Ma' pimeno'(on).

Next to Akyant'o' I give the bark cloth. Don't let the illness fall here, in the forest. We are not many.

Kaho' bähe' yan ts'aak. Ti' yan uts'aaki(r) kuluk'ur beh.

The villagers[13] now have medicine. There is their medicine they swallow where (they are).

To'on way tu' kura'an aleki(r).

We are here where your god pots are seated.

Mäna' ts'aak beh. Na'aken t'äneh Akyant'o' ne tech beh.

There is no medicine. Akyant'o' go up and summon (Hachäkyum) on your behalf.

Ne buun upimin ume(en)kahi(r) Akyant'o'. Tukupah k'aax to'on.

How very many are the creations of Akyant'o'. They (have) filled up our forest.

Tarak ne chich utar se'em,

Although the flu comes on strong,

sahkunteh.

reduce it.

Ti' yan awirik beh.

You see them there.[14]

T(an) inme(n)t(ik) (ti') (u)ho'or. T(an) awirik hu'un, ti' wah, ti' k'uxub beh.

I am making (the offerings to the) head. You are seeing the bark cloth, the tortillas, the annatto.

Bin(ih) insuku'uno'.

My elder brothers are gone.

Lahkimi(n).

They are all dead.

Ma' kuxt(ar)kih.

They are not alive.

Lah ma' suut a' hu('u)n; ma' suut lah chäk hu'un; tumen lah wah tuts'ah ma' suut a' hu'un,

The bark cloth didn't return; the red bark cloth headbands didn't return; because they gave all the tortillas the bark cloth headbands didn't return.[15]

'Otsi(r) beh.

It's pitiable.

Bähe' mäna' beh.
Now there isn't any.

He' ch'urha'kih.
Here is the ch'urha'kih offering.

He' inwuk'ur ba'che'.
This is my balche' drink.

Uki'aa(n)t(i)ko'(on) beh.
It really helps us (get well).[16]

Bin(ih) insuku'uno'.
My brothers are gone.

Lahkim(in).
They are all dead.

Ma' kuxt(ar)kih.
They are not alive.

Na'ak'e(n) t'äneh uyori(r) ka'an, ne intech beh.
Go up and tell the Heart of Heaven, it is your duty.

Le' tarak ye'eh yahi(r) chäkwirir,
Although the threat of the illness of fever is very strong,

uchäkwirir se'em utar yeter beh uxeeh yet(er) uhubnäk'ir,
the fever of the flu comes with vomiting and diarrhea,

chi'ba(r) hämneneh beh.
stomach ache.

Lahman(ih) uxeeheh; boona lah yah hämneneh,
A great deal of vomiting goes on; how much stomach pain there is,

xeeheh beh.
and vomiting.

Tarak tub(ah) utar,
Although where it comes,

ch'ik naach utar,
(from) far away, it comes,

ma' (a)cha'ik uheets'e(r) way beh.
don't let it take hold here.

Sahkunteh to'on.
Reduce it for us.

Offering under a Tree

Antonio Martinez

Antonio performed this ritual under a tree by a stream in 1990. He placed a shard of *tähte'* 'pitch pine' in a small boat made from a leaf, lit it, and floated the burning offering down a small stream while chanting the following text. In this chant he asks Ak'inchob to deliver his petition to Hachäkyum asking him to prevent branches from falling on the people while they walk through the forest. Many people get injured, and some are killed, by falling branches, especially during the rainy season.

Bay yumeh. Le' bähe' umuxur matan che', yumeh.
All right, oh Lord. This now is the offering, oh Lord.

Tech tawir(ik) umuxur matan che'. Ma' bik ulubur uk'ä'che'.
You see the offering. Don't let the branches fall.

Ma' bikir lubur tuk'in maano'(on). Ma' bik upeets' che', ma' bik upeets', yumeh.
Don't let them fall when we pass. Don't let the tree branches crush (us), don't let them crush (us), oh Lord.

'Otsi(r) ku(ru)ken yumeh. Na'aken t'äneh kyumeh ma' bik upeets'tikeno'(on) che'.
Pity me, sitting (here), oh Lord. Go up and tell our Lord not to let the trees crush us.

Ma' lubu(r) uk'ä'che' tuk'in (in)man. Ma' bik uchi'ikeno' ukani(r) uk'ä(')täk-
che' tuk'in (in)maana(n),

Don't let the branches fall when I pass. Don't let the branch snakes bite me
when I pass,

tuk'in inkoorok, yumeh. 'Ostir. Ma' pimeno'(on).

when I pull trees down (in the milpa). Pity us. We are few.

Ma' bik upeets' che' yumeh.

Don't let the tree crush (us), oh Lord.

Eh tech uyori(r)ka'an. Tech la' ya'rir k'in. Tawirah. He', yumeh.

You are the soul of the sky, oh Lord. You are the one (who makes the rainy
season). You see (the offering). Here it is, oh Lord.

T'äneh uyori(r)ka'an, yumeh, tawirah umuxur matan che', yumeh.

Tell the soul of the sky, oh Lord, you saw all the offerings (by the) tree, oh
Lord.

Way tintook(ah) pom. Way 'eerer way.

Here I burned the incense. Here, it burns here.

(T)'a(b)bi(r) pom tech yumeh.

The copal is lit for you, oh Lord.

Tawirah umuxur matan che', yumeh.

You saw the copal offering (by the) tree, oh Lord.

Ut'anir Ba'che' 'The Secret of the Balche''

Antonio Martinez

Balche''[1] is a sacred, ceremonial beverage that is offered to the gods in every ritual large or small, because the gods like to get drunk and enjoy seeing their mortals drunk too.[2] Hachäkyum created the balche' tree for its properties and taught the mortals how to make it and then offer it to him. He erred the first time by making a poisonous tree (*ya'ax ba'che'*), which killed his assistants.[3]

"Ut'anir Ba'che''" is a charm that is recited to promote the fermentation of this ceremonial beverage. In this charm the singer invokes venomous creatures, entities with piquant properties, and others who can move the solution. Antonio explains that one needs to repeat the chant many times, up to four times, to ensure that the balche' ferments properly. Clearly this is an example of sympathetic magic, the idea that like produces like: venom, stingers, hot chilies, for example, will make the drink piquant. And the number of times the chant is repeated will imbue the balche' with greater strength. At the same time, the venomous objects invoked in the song are meant to prevent a hangover (Davis 1978, 88). Why a strong liquor should be prevented from causing a hangover may be based on the principle of reversal: what is strong will be weak and vice versa. Principles of parallelism and reversal are predominant in Lacandon mythology and ritual (23).

Säkhure'(n)hure'(n) t(i') ink'äb,[4]

White light in my hand,

te' inwahboren.[5]

here is my true Bor.[6]

Te' inwahetsere(n).[7]

Here is my true *etsel* cup.

Sä(k)hure'(n)hure'(n) t(i') ink'äb.

White light in my hand.

Te' inwahbor(en).

Here is my true Bor.

Te' inwahetsareh(n).

Here is my true etsel cup.

Te' inwahbore(n).

Here is my true Bor.

Ka'ah (u)lik'(ir) (u)yoom inchaaka(r),[8]

When the foam of my pot of food rises,

tech te(k)cha'anteh teno' ukuumir inpuk'o',

you immediately watch the pot of our solution for us,

ukuumir inchaaka(r),

the pot of my food,

ti' (u)lik'(ir) (u)yoom beh. Ka'ah (u)lik'(ir) ko'oten, peekseh te(n), chäk xok beh.[9]

so that the foam rises. When it rises, come, move it for me, chäk xok.

Chäk xok ch'ika('a)n t(i') unoh. Bu(r)k'äranka(r)[10]

The chäk xok is standing on the right side. It moves from side to side[11]

t(i') unoh inchemo',
on the right side of our canoe,

t(i') uts'iik inchemo'.
on the left side of our canoe.

Ka'ah (u)lik'(ir) (u)yoom inchakaa(r),
When the foam of my pot of food rises,

ko'oten, peekseh ten upuk'ur inba'che'.
come, move it for me (so) my balche' dissolves.

Lah ko'oten, pureh ten.
All come throw it in for me.

Bu(r)k'ära(n)ka(r) t'int'a 'aak beh, k'än 'aako'.
The *t'int'a*[12] turtles, the yellow turtles move from side to side.

Lah ko'oteno'.
All come.

La' maayok[13] kän 'aako' beh. Chakraw beh, chäkar beh, sohom beh, ko'oten peekseh teno' ti' ukuumir inpuko'.
The yellow turtles paddle. Striped mojarras, red mojarras, *sohom*,[14] come move our solution.

Ko'oteno'.
Come.

Hach 'aak bu(r)k'äranka(r).

The *hach 'aak*[15] moves from side to side.

Ha(ch) t'int'a 'aak beh, ha(ch) let' beh,

T'int'a turtles, snapping turtles,

ko'oten, peekseh ten ukuumir inchaaka(r),

come, move my pot of food,

la' ukuumir inpuko'.

the pot of our solution.

La' kuhum bu(r)k'äranka(r).

This makes a noise when it moves from side to side.

K'än 'aako' kuhum waan inchemo'.

The yellow turtles make a sound (along) the length of our canoe.

Chäk xok ch'ika'an t(i') unoh inchemo'. Ch'ika'an t(i') uts'iik inchemo',

The chäk xok is standing on the right side of our canoe. She is standing on the left side of our canoe,

ka'ah (u)lik'(ir) (u)yoom inchaaka(r).

when the foam of my pot of food rises.

Te(n) (in)hoops(ik) uk'ak'eh t(i') uneeh ahch'eero'.

I am the one who kindles the fire (with) the tail of the penelopina.[16]

La' ubi(n) upikitik k'ak'.

It is going to fan the fire.

Tinpikitik (ti') unohinohi(r) inchemo'.
I am fanning it on the (far?) right side of our canoe.

Ka'ah (u)lik'(ir) (u)yoom inchaaka(r),
When the foam of the pot of my food rises,

ko'oteno', chikix kano',
come, rattle snakes,

ko'oten chi'(eh) uk'ab luucho'.
come bite the hand cups.

Chi'(eh) insuuro'.
Bite our small cups.

Chi'(eh) ink'a'luuch beh.
Bite my hand cup.

Chi'(eh) inmehen suuro'.
Bite our small cups.

Chi'(eh) inpako'.[17]
Bite our balche' urn.

Chi'(eh) ink'a'luuch beh.
Bite my hand cup.

Chi'(eh) innukuch luucho'.
Bite our large cups.[18]

Chi'eh teno'.
Bite them for us.

Ko'oten, pureh (u)ya'r(ir) akoh,
Come, throw down the venom of your fangs,

chikix kano',
rattle snakes,

k'uk'ur kano',
feathered serpents,

ek'ren kano',
black snakes,

säbä(k) kano'.
soot snakes.

Chi'(eh) unoh inba'che'.
Bite the right of my balche'.

Chi' uchun(in) inba'che'.
Bite the base of my balche'.[19]

Ka'ah (u)lik'(ir) (u)yoom inchaaka(r), hoops(eh) uk'ak'i(r).
When the foam of my pot of food rises, kindle its fire.

Ka'ah (u)lik'(ir) (u)yoom beh,
When the foam rises, (the balche')

bu(r)k'äranka(r).
it moves from side to side.

La' kuhum t(i') unoh inchemo'.
This makes a sound on the right side of our canoe.

Te' (in)wahbore(n).
Here is my true Bor.

Ka'ah (u)lik'(ir) (u)yoom beh,
When the foam rises,

chikix kano' la' uk'ax inchemo'.
the rattle snakes are the ties of our canoe.

La' upix inchemo'. Upix inchemo' laa(r) tsah beh, hach tsah beh.
The cover of our canoe.[20] The cover of our canoe (are) nettles, the devil nettles.

Ak'i(r) tsaho', le' ink'äxma(n) uk'ax inchemo'.
The vines of the nettles, these are my ties that tie our canoe.

K'ä'che' kano' la' uk'ax unoh inchemo', uk'ax inchemo'.
The branch snakes are the ties (on) the right side of our canoe, the ties of our canoe.

K'ä'che' kano',
Branch snakes,

säbä(k) kano',
soot snakes,

k'uk'ur kano',
feathered serpents,

ek'ren kano',
black snakes,

säbä(k) kano',
soot snakes,

ko'oten pur(eh) (u)ya'r(ir) akoh t(i') inchemo'.
come throw the venom from your fangs into our canoe.

Chi'(eh) uts'ik inchemo'.
Bite the left side of our canoe.

Chi'(eh) uchuni(n) inchemo'.
Bite the base of our canoe.

Ko'oteno'.
Come.

Ko'oten puk's(eh) inba'che'.
Come make my balche' dissolve.

Ko'oten chi'(eh) uchuni(n) inba'che',
Come bite the base of my balche',

ek'ren kano',
black snakes,

säbä(k) kano',
soot snakes,

k'uk'ur kano.'
feathered serpents.

Ek'ren kano',
Black snakes,

ch'ikix kano',
rattle snakes,

ko'oteno'.
come.

Chi'(eh) unoh inchemo'.
Bite the right side of our canoe.

Chi'(eh) inba'che'.
Bite my balche'.

Chi'(eh) uts'iik inba'che'.
Bite the left side of my balche'.

Chi'(eh) uchuni(n) inba'che'.
Bite the base of my balche'.

Ka'ah (u)lik'(ir) (u)yoom inchaka(r),
When the foam of my pot of food rises,

hoops(eh) uk'ak'eh.
kindle the fire.

Bu(r)k'äranka(r)chäk xok beh.
The chäk xok is moving from side to side.

'Ayinkäyo' beh, bu(r)k'äranka(r).
The garfish are moving from side to side.

Säbä(k) kano', ko'oten.
Soot snakes, come.

Pur(eh) uya'r(ir) akoh t(i') ink'ä' luucho',
Throw down the venom from your fangs in my hand cups,

t(i') innukuch luucho',
in my large cups,

nukuch k'ä' luucho'.
the large hand cups.

Chi'(eh) inpako'.
Bite our balche' urn.

Peekse(h) ten ukuumir inpuko'.
Move the pot of our solution for me.

Ko'oteno', chikix kano', ek'ren kano', uk'ax inchemo' laar tsah beh.
Come, rattlesnakes, black snakes, the nettle ties of our canoe.

Säk yo(r)te' iko',
The white walking stick chili peppers,

ka'ah tinki'mäxah, ka'ah tinmuuch'ah beh,
when I mashed them thoroughly, when I gathered them up,

ka'ah ti(n)wäch'k(')a(b)na(h) t(i') unoh inchemo',
when I released them at the right end of our canoe,

ka'ah (u)lik'(ir) (u)yoom beh,
then the foam rises,

bu(r)k'äranka(r).
(the balche') roils.

La' kuhum beh t(i') unoh inchemo'.
This makes a sound on the right side of our canoe.

Kekech'[21] beh, la' kuhum beh.
It is the frog that makes the sound.

Chäk 'aako',
Red turtles,

k'än 'aako',
yellow turtles,

säbä(k) kano',
soot snakes,

ek'ren kano',
black snakes,

te' imwahbore(n).
here is my true Bor.

6

Descriptions of Meteorological and Astral Phenomena

’Äxp’äri’ ‘The Solstice’

Antonio Martinez

In this text Antonio describes the winter solstice. As he describes the movement of the sun he draws lines in the dirt to show the direction of the sun's path.

Like other Mayas, the Lacandones believe that the sun is a sentient being, but unlike other Mayan groups, including the southern Lacandones, they do not consider him a god. A summary of Antonio's descriptions follows.

At the beginning of the December solstice (’*äxp’ari’*)[1] he is young and weak. He leaves the earth rising slowly above the horizon and stays there a little longer each day. He is fed sardines and pumpkin seeds. On these foods he gains a little more strength each day: his heat and light gradually become stronger and last longer as he journeys north. When he reaches the north, he is fed beans to help preserve his energy during the long days. Then he turns south and begins his journey south, to the base of the sky.[2]

This cycle described by Antonio is represented in Classic Mayan images on the lids of royal sarcophaguses, depicting an immature ruler both in death and as the newborn sun (ruler) rising in the east (see Stuart 2015).

Kubin ahkahtich’k’ä’e’ex[3] tutseer ka’an; kubin tutseer. Kuk’uchur uyah-chun tu’ kura(’a)n tunah ya’axk’in.[4] Kuts’a’bar uhana(n) ten äkyum. Woro(r) säktaan, uneek’ k’um kuts’a’bar ti’. Lehi(h) kuts’a’bar. Lehi(h) kura’(an) up’äreh. Tan up’ärik tan ubin . . . Ha’ri’ uneek’ k’um, woro(r) lehi(h) tan up’ärik. Tan ubin tan uhana(n).

Our sun goes to the side of the sky; it goes to the side (of the sky). When it arrives at first, where it is sitting, (it is) in the spring. It is given food by Hachäkyum. Purely sardines (and) calabash seeds are given to it.[5] This it is given. It sits there shelling (the seeds). It is shelling them. It is shelling them as it goes ... Only calabash seeds, these are all (the sun) is shelling. It is eating (them) (as) it goes.

... Way tan ulik'ir uyaaka'. Eh tan umasna'akar k'in. Tan umashook'or. Kuka'lik'ir uyaaka'. Tan uchichtar ubin. Tan uximba(r), tan uhana(n) tan ubin.

... Here it is rising rapidly. The sun is climbing higher. It is coming out more. (When) it rises again, (everyday) it is more quickly. It is becoming stronger (as) it goes. It is traveling across, eating as it goes.

Kuka'k'uchur ku(r)ta(r), utar uher uyo'och, tuworo(r) käy. Mäna' uts'a'bar ti' bix a' bu'ur ... Toh ha'ri' uyo'och kuts'a'bar ti' ka'p'ero' neek' k'um.

When it arrives again and sits (in the middle of the sky), another (kind) of food comes, just fish. Nothing else is given to it, like beans ... The only (other?) food it is given is two calabash seeds.

...

...

Ki'ts'abi(r) up'ärik. Ele, kulik'ir uyaaka'. Ne 'omo' uyoko(r) k'in ti' to'one'ex way.

Very slowly it shells them. And then, it rises rapidly. The sun sets slowly on us here.

Ele, nah 'äxp'äri', le' kubin tutseer. Le' kusut ti' mayo'eh tumen uyok ha'.

So then, (during) the (main?) solstice, it will go to the side (of the sky). It returns in May because the rains begin.

Le' seebseeb uhana(n). Uts'a'bar ti' bu'ur. Woro(r) bu'ur kuhantik. Seeb ubin tutseer ka'an. Be'in a'ara' 'äxp'äri' uk'aba'. Be'in a'ara' äxp'äri'. Ne seeb

ubin uximba(r). Ma' uxanta(r) hora uku(r)ta(r). Mäna', ma' chukuch ube(r)
tu' kubin. Tutseer ka'an kubin.

It eats quickly. It is given beans. It eats only beans. Quickly it goes to the
side of the sky. That's why it's called *'äxp'äri'*. That's why they say it is called
'äxp'äri'. It travels swiftly. It doesn't take much time. The path it follows isn't
very long. It goes to the side of the sky.

Ele, tuyirah äknukire'ex, tuyirah Haawo'. Bek kuku(r)ta(r) umeyah uber a'
k'in winik.

And then, the ancestors saw it, the Haawo' saw it. Like (this?) they set to
work on the path of the sun. (They sweep the path clean).

T(an) uhans(ik) tu' kubin.

They are feeding it where it goes.

Kuk'uchur hach tutseer ka'an, kuka'sut tupach. P'isi(r) tan uhana(n). Seebseeb uhana(n).

When it reaches the (far) side of the sky it comes back again. It is eating the
same as before. Rapidly it eats.

Ele, kuk'uchur a' nah ya'axk'in, abrir, kusut k'uchur.

And so, when spring arrives, in April, it returns.[6]

Ele, tan ubin. Tan uhana(n). Tu' ne hats'ka', ne xantar uhook'or ne hats'ka'.
Tan uhachhanan. Tan una'akar, uneek' k'um tan uts'a'bar ti' . . . Sikir, ku-
taas(ik?) uneek'. Lahp'ärik tan ubin. Ele, tan ubin. Ne xantar ubin. 'Omo'
uyaak'ä'chär.

And so, it is going. It is eating. At daybreak, it comes out very slowly. It is
eating a lot. As it is climbing, the calabash seeds are being given to it . . .
They bring the seeds of the large calabash.[7] (The sun) shells them all as it is
going. And so, it is going very slowly. Nightfall comes slowly.

Le' 'äxp'äri', nah ya'axk'in uk'aba', 'äxp'äri' nah ya'axk'in. Eh tan chumu-ki(r) ya'axk'in.

This is the solstice, the summer solstice, the summer solstice it's called. It happens in the middle of the year.

Lu'um Kab 'The Rainbow Gods'

Bor Ma'ax

Lu'um kab is the name for a class of terrestrial deities who travel across the sky along the rainbow. The rainbow is called *uber lu'um kab* 'the road of the lu'um kab'.[1]

La' lu'um kab t(an) uto(o)k(ik) ube(r).
The lu'um kab burn their road.

Tup'ätah bin 'uchik ahk'uh ka'(ah) lahkimih.
They left them behind, they say, before the gods all died.[2]

Lahi(h) p'ati(h) uk'anir, a' way uyaram k'aax.
They stayed behind as their assistants, here in the forest.[3]

Kutook(ik) ube(r), kuna'akar yok'o(r) ka'an.
They burn their road, when they rise into the sky.

Eh kut'äbik chäkhare'n (u)be(r) tu' kubin.
They set it alight, their road is ablaze, when they go.

Ti' yan way kahaneh, ti' na'ak(ih) ka'an.
They live here, (but) they climbed to the sky (to talk to Hachäkyum).

Wa ne toh tekts'o'ok tutsah yok'or ka'an, uts'o'ok yaram ka'an ti' na'aki(h).

When (the rainbow) follows directly (behind) the sky, it ends below the sky, (this is) where they went up.

Le' took bin uber; kutook ube(r) kuximba(r).
This is the road they burn; they burn their road as they walk.[4]

Bähe', mäna', 'otsir. 'Uchik kuna'akar.
Today, there is no (road for them), poor things. A long time ago they used to climb to the sky.

La' la'eh be'ik kuya'arah ahlu'um kab.
That is what they say about the lu'um kab.

Wa kir utsitsi(ts) bähe', kuya'arik äknukire'ex huntuu(r), "Eh tan utookik uber. Bin ukah tsitsi(ts) ha'."
If it is about to sprinkle, one of elders will say, "They are burning their road. It is just about to sprinkle."

Ma ha'ri' utookik uber ti' ubineh. Tan utosor ha' utookik uber ti' ubin ka'ana(n).
So they just burn their road to go. (When) it drizzles, they burn their road to go high.

Bek tutsikbartah intet, inna'. Uka'tsikbar unuki(r) winik.
That's how my father and mother explained it. The ancestors might have (had) another explanation.

Eh, ha'ri' kawirik utookik ube(r) ti' ubin.
Eh, you only see them burn their road (when) they go.

Säkber Akyum 'Our Lord's White Road'

Antonio Martinez

Antonio describes the Milky Way as the footprints Hachäkyum left behind after he strode across the sky, as phenomena in the sky mirror phenomena on earth.[1]

La' tichir. Ka'(ah) tuyirah ti' bini(h) Chichen 'Itsah bino'.
It arrives. When they saw it, it went to Chichen Itza.[2]

Ti' maanih Hachäkyum ti' bini(h) uyireh, lehi(h) yani(r) ha'ha'nahk'uh.
It was what Hachäkyum went along to visit the ha'ha'nahk'uh.[3]

Lahi(h) kir utar xämän, xämän tarih.
It came from the north, from the north it came.

Lehi(h) ka'(ah) luk'ih bi(n) ka'(ah) tuyeensah uyoker.
It appeared when he put down his feet (in the sky).

Maanih ti' akaasike'ex, ti' atsikbartik ti' abäh(o')e'ex, mak uyoher usäkber akyum.
He passed through so that you would remember him, for you to tell your companions to realize that it is his white road.

Ka'(ah) maani(h) tan chumuk ka'an, tu' maan(ih), bura'an-tar(?) usasta(r).
When he passed through the center of the sky, where he passed through became filled with radiance.

Bini(h) nohor. Ka'(ah) binih, ma' yähsutbäh Hachäkyum, . . . tume(n)tah uyok. Tuxit'kintah uyok.

He went south. When he went, Hachäkyum didn't return at first, . . . he made his footprints. He stretched his footprints across (the sky).

Eh, lehih uber tu' bini(h). Tawirah säktäre('en) tuts'tik.

So, this is the path he went along. You (have seen) the glowing white (band) stretched out.

Bex utsikbartar. Eh ma' yaab.

That's how the story goes. It's not very long.

APPENDIX 1

Lacandon Onen, Ceremonial Names, and Distribution

The following table of onen and corresponding "ceremonial" names combines information from previous scholars and travelers in the Lacandon forest who described Lacandon settlements they encountered between the nineteenth and mid-twentieth centuries. The locations and composition of the settlements provided in the table is mainly based on the descriptions of Blom and Blom (1969), Sapper (1897), J. Soustelle (1935a), and Tozzer ([1907] 1978).

The table omits the dates when the settlements were discovered and the names of the scholars who discovered them. That information is provided in figure 5 (map of four Lacandon areas) in the gallery. On the maps the location and composition of the settlements display the distinct affiliation of onen with patrilineages and make clear that these patrilineages were in distinct areas of the forest. This suggests the Lacandones were part of a larger sociopolitical structure, more than a mere collection of disparate ethnic groups. The maps also show that the onen allied through patrilineal descent or political affiliation are widely dispersed, suggesting periodic or constant shifting of alliances. Finally, the maps show that the settlement patterns occurred within two distinct territories located on either side of an invisible horizontal line that originates at Yaxchilan. Despite the two groups' social, cultural, and religious dissimilarities, the central and most important common ground the southerners and the northerners share is Yaxchilan.

Table 2 presents this information in columns starting from the left with Lacandon animal onen names, followed by ceremonial names, and then the location of their settlements.

To recap, "ceremonial" name corresponds to a patronym, which, as discussed previously, is the name of a Maya group that settled in the Lacandon forest in the seventeenth and eighteenth centuries. An onen is the name of a Lacandon group that shares the same patronym. The patronym is named after an animal. The Lacandon onen system groups these onen into pairs following a folk-classification system, which categorizes and names species of plants and animals on the basis of their attributes (e.g., wings, fur) or concepts (e.g., predatory feline). Those sharing the same attributes are grouped together to form a large category. For example, *ma'ax* 'spider monkey' and *ba'ats'* 'howler monkey' form a pair; *k'ek'en* 'white-lipped peccary' and *kitam* 'collared peccary' form another pair. These pairs of onen form a larger group called Garcia (or Karsiyaho') and Koho', respectively. The -o' is the general plural suffix, thus indicating groups of people with the same name. In this case one is called Karsiyah and the other Koh.

The double naming system suggests that the Lacandones were once part of a larger social organization that traces back to the Postclassic and early Colonial periods. A description of the Mayan lineages and probable associations with Lacandon onen follows table 2.

Table 2. Lacandon onen, ceremonial names, and distribution (listed in alphabetical order by ceremonial name)

ONEN	CEREMONIAL NAMES	LOCATION
k'ambur	Chan	Chankahla
aak'ä'bäk', ts'u'ts'u' [see *koton*]	Haawo'/Jague(?)	Yaxchilan
-?-	Itsa'o'	Petén, southeastern Chiapas,
ma'ax 'spider monkey'	Karsiyaho'~Garcia	Naha', Monte Líbano, Arena, Petha' (El Guineo), Piedras Bolas, Piedras Negras
ma'ax	Karsiyaho'	Petha' (El Guineo)
ba'ats 'howler monkey'	Karsiyaho'	Chancala (El Cambio), upstream of the Rio Seco
chilu' 'quail'	Kobaho'	Lacantún River (east)
wan 'partridge' -?-	Kobaho' Chan Kah (Cline 1944)	Chancalá (El Cambio)
keh 'mule deer' yuk 'white-tailed deer'	Keho'	San Quintín, (east) R. Lacantún
k'ek'en 'white-lipped peccary'	Koho'	(share territories with *ma'ax*)
k'ek'en	Koho'	Lacanha', (upper?) Lacantún River
kitam 'collared peccary'	Koho'	Lacanha', (upper?) Lacantún River

ONEN	CEREMONIAL NAMES	LOCATION
-?-	Kowoh	-?-
mo' 'macaw'	Miso'	Tenosique
kacho' 'mealy (blue-crowned) parrot'	Miso'	-?-
t'ut' 'small parrot'	Miso'	Chancala River (near El Cambio)
k'ambur 'great curassow, pheasant'	Nawäto'/Naguate [nawate]	Tenosique, Santa Clara River
koox 'crested guan'	Nawäto'	San Hipolito
hare' 'spotted cavy'	Nistisyaho'	San Hipolito
tsup 'agouti'	Nistisyaho'	Lacantún River
-?-	Peten	between R. Azul and R. Perlas
barum 'jaguar'	Puko'	Tenosique
chäk balam 'red jaguar'	Puko'	-?-
kotom [sic] (Tozzer 1907) 'male coatimundi and male raccoon'	Taxo'	Anaite (1)
sanhor (tsahon) 'tayra'	Taxo'	Tzendales, Anaite
uuk 'pigeon'	Uuko'	Rio de la Pasión
ts'ur 'dove'	Uuko'	
hunk'uk' 'eagle'	Witso'	hills
yaxum 'lovely cotinga'	Yaxuno'~Yaxumo'	-?-
aak'ma'ax 'night monkey, kinkajou'	-?-	Petén

DISCUSSION

The following describes only those onen that have a plausible correlation with a specific Mayan patronym.

At least three personal names of rulers survived in the Lacandon naming system. Puc, Coboh (Covoh, Cobov, Coboj), and Hau (Haw) were leaders of their respective lineages that lived in the Petén in AD 1697 (Hellmuth 1971). These names correspond to the Lacandon "ceremonial" names, Puko', Kowoh, and Haawo'.

Peten, Itza, and **Kowoh** are names mentioned in Lacandon myths, but they lack Lacandon onen affiliation. This suggests that these lineages were external to the Lacandon onen system.

Peten is mentioned in one southern Lacandon myth (Boremanse 1986) and refers to one character who is described as a ladino (Hispanicized person).

Itzas are portrayed in Lacandon narratives as enemies of the Lacandon ancestors. One story from the northern Lacandones recounts an episode in which the Itzas attacked Yaxchilan and tried to destroy the city's *hach biraam*, a statue of the Hachäkyum, to prevent it or him from destroying the world (see Boremanse 1986, 134–39).

The Itza were a dominant power in the Petén up to AD 1697 and had subjugated several other Mayan groups in the area. Before they were called the Ah Itzá, they are believed to have been a group of Putún, "Mexicanized" Chontal Maya merchant-warriors from Tabasco (Coe 1993, 129, 155). They are also believed to have originated in Motul de San José near Lake Petén Itzá during the Classic period (Drew 1999, 373). They migrated to the Yucatan at the end of the Classic period (circa AD 900) and again in the eleventh century (AD 1224–1244) (Coe 1993, 155), conveying Mexican ideology and the political structure of the Toltec (Mexican) regime. During AD 1441–1461 they were driven out of the Yucatan by the Xiu. They returned to the Petén, where they established the city of Tayasal on Lake Petén Itzá.

Kowoh was a powerful group linked with the Xiu. They occupied a region northeast of Petén Itzá near Lake Yaxha' (De Vos [1980] 2015, 9315). They were mortal enemies of the Itza. Kowoh is spelled Couoh, Cobog, Coboje, and Covoje in colonial manuscripts. The seventeenth-century church records register the surname Cobog for a group of Maya who settled briefly at San José de Gracia Real, near Palenque (see De Vos [1980] 2015; McGee 2002). The name Couoh is also remembered as a powerful lineage and polity in the Yucatan. Fray Diego de Landa, bishop of the Roman Catholic Archdiocese of the Yucatán, mentions a group called the Covohes ([1937] 1978, 20, 42). A Lacandon subgroup called the Cobojes [kobohes] was settled on the upper Santa Cruz River at the end of the nineteenth century (Sapper 1897, 259). The variant spellings of the name obfuscate the lineage name, the spelling discrepancies reflecting the Spanish chroniclers' orthographic conventions and their inability to hear and transcribe the sounds of the indigenous languages. Lacandon /b,ɓ/ and Spanish /b/ are often pronounced as [ß], a bilabial approximant that sounds like a [w]. Spanish *v* and *b* are pronounced the same, only the *v* is pronounced "softer" than a /b/. Spanish /j/ usually sounds like an English /h/. Finally, the letter *c* is the written form of the sound /k/. Given these phonetic details, the Coboj/ Covoh/Couoh/Kowoh were the same people. The -es is the Spanish plural, which corresponds to the Lacandon plural -o'.

Aak'ä'bäk' 'night animal, raccoon' is the animal onen of the Haawo'. Aak'ä'bäk' is associated with *chunk'inbäk'* 'day animal, coatimundi' under the rubric of *koton*. Koton refers to the male of both of these species. Koton is also used to refer to the Haawo'. According to Tozzer ([1907] 1978), the koton associates with the Taxo' people. The southern Lacandones refer to the coatimundi as the *lo'k'in*, the cannibals of Lacandon lore (see Boremanse 1986, 346–49).

Aak'ma'ax is the animal onen 'kinkajou' (*Potos flavus* Schreber, 1774). There is no information on these people, and thus their ceremonial name is uncertain. I believe they might have been affiliated with the Taxo', given their resemblance to coatis and raccoons.

Chan is only mentioned in Cline (1944). The Lacandones called them Chan Ka(h), literally 'little villager'. They say that they lived in or near a place called Chankalá, situated northwest of the northern Lacandon communities. Their onen was the *k'ambul* 'great curassow'. During the Colonial period, Yucatec-speaking Mayas with the Chan surname were living in various settlements, including Yucum (1697), Petenacte (1709), Batcab (1696), Pakeken (1696), and Maní (1697); Pakeken was predominantly Chan, with 126 registered Chan names (De Vos [1980] 2015, 4948–49). Chan was also a prominent lineage in Cozumel and northeastern Yucatan during the Postclassic period (De Vos [1980] 2015, n45). The Chan were not native Yucatecans, but "Mexicanized" Mayas, likely the Chontal Maya of Tabasco. As members of the Lacandon k'ambul, they were allied with the Nawäto'.

Cobox is listed as another semiautonomous Itza group that lived northeast of Lake Petén Itzá (Schwartz 1990, 34). Kob'ox appears as an alternate pronunciation of Kowoh, in Jones (1998, Table I.I).

Haawo' are the revered Lacandones ancestors who lived at Yaxchilan.

They guarded the sacred hach biraam, a statue that Lacandones believe represents their principal god, Hachäkyum. They belonged to the koton onen.

Jague/Haawo' are different groups. Following Spanish orthographic conventions, Jague would be pronounced [hagwe], which does not come close to haawo'. More likely, Haawo' derives from Hau, another Yucatec-Maya patronym.

Koho' is the patronym of the Lacandon onen *k'ek'en* 'white-lipped peccary' onen and *kitam* 'collared peccary'. Most researchers claim that Koho' is synonymous with Kowoh. I believe that these are two separate names. As discussed above, Kowoh derives from Couoh; a sound change from /w/ to /h/ is uncommon. Rather, Koho' could be *koh* 'puma' or 'tooth, tusk'.

Kobaho' may come from Cobá, the name of the impressive Classic Maya ruins in Quintana Roo, Mexico (see J. Thompson, Pollock, and Charlot 1932, 6, in Roys [1933] 2008, 198n197). There is also a lake east of Tenosique, Tabasco, called El Cobá. Coba survives as a common surname in the Yucatan. Typically, lineage names derive from place names. Hence, *kobaho'* 'people of Cobá' designates a lineage or a community from Cobá.[1] In addition to lineages the community of smaller lineages often adopted the name of the ruler or that of the group with the largest population (see Restall 1999, 28). Given this, kobaho' may have designated the polity under the leader or house called Cobah. The *Chilam Balam of Chumayel* (Roys [1933] 2008, 98) describes a leader and a place by the name of Ah Kinchil Coba.

Nawäto' <nawat-o', obviously derives from Nawat, a language spoken by the Nahuas. The language is also called Pipil. Nawat also refers to Nahuatl language varieties spoken in southern Veracruz, Tabasco, and Chiapas. Additionally, Nahua was the family name of some Mayan governors (De Vos 2015, 9315). Despite belonging to a separate linguistic and ethnic group, the Lacandones describe the Nawäto' as relatives, in the sense that they refer to them as hach winik (see Boremanse 1986, 356). The Nawäto' are said to have inhabited a large region stretching from San Quintín to Tani Perlas (Pasión River) (Boremanse 1986, 356n8). In one southern Lacandon story (354–57), the Nawäto' had access to machetes before the southern Lacandones did, but they lacked the Lacandon bow and arrow, using instead a weapon that is described as an *atlatl* (spear thrower) (354). The

Nawäto' venerated a deity called Me'ex K'uk' Chan, who lived on a hill at the entrance to Lake Miramar (354). Me'ex K'uk' Chan may refer to the deified ruler Ah Mex Cuc of Chichén Itzá (c. thirteenth century) (see J. Thompson 1970, 14). The book of the *Chilam Balam of Chumayel* reports that he was "one of the four greatest men of the Maya" (Roys [1933] 2008, 188n76).[2] These four great men were Itza who (re)entered the Yucatan in the thirteenth century and went on to reign over the eastern half of the peninsula.

In the same Lacandon story an ancestor of a southern Lacandon group married into a community of Nawäto'.

Nistisyaho' is unclear. I am unable to analyze it as a Yucatec word or phrase and have not found anything similar to it in Ch'ol, Chontal, Chorti', Kek'chi, or Quiche' languages. The closest approximation I have found is *nitzitzih*, which means 'to come or move towards slowly' in the Chuj language (Hopkins 2012). The Nistisyaho' occupied the lower Lacantún River, northeast of the Chuj in San Mateo Ixtatán, Guatemala. The southern Lacandones are said to have traded with the Chuj for salt.

Sanhor 'tayra' were affiliated with the Taxo' living at Anaite and the Tzendales. They may have been allied with *koton* Taxo', who lived in Anaite (see Tozzer [1907] 1978).

Wech 'armadillo' and **Saay** 'leaf-cutter ant' are additional onen identified by the southern Lacandones (see Boremanse 1986).

Yaxum may designate the people from *Yaxumcabil* 'land of the lovely cotingas',[3] which was an historic Cehach settlement in the northern Petén (see J. Thompson 1977, 34–35).[4] The name derives from *ya'ax* 'green' and the archaic suffix *-um* 'bird' (Roys [1933] 2008, 182n34). The location of the *yaxum* onen has never been determined. Interestingly, the eighth century ruler of Yaxchilan was called Yaxun B'alam IV (a.k.a. Bird Jaguar IV).

Gods and Men in Lacandon Mythology

Ak'inchob 'Lord of Maize' is the guardian of the milpa and the Lacandones' emissary to Hachäkyum. He was the only solar deity to have been born naturally, rather than emerging from the sacred tuberose. Hachäkyum threw dirt over the spot where Ak'inchob was born to hide the "indecency," whereupon the blood-soaked dirt transformed into ants. Ak'inchob married Akna' (Äkna'), who corresponds to the youthful Moon Goddess (God I) in the Classic Mayan pantheon, and who was the daughter of the Lacandones' Creator couple, Hachäkyum and Xk'ale'oox.¹ Ak'inchob is a dutiful son-in-law: after the second destruction of the world he built Yaxchilan for Hachäkyum and the other solar deities; he resowed the land after the world destructions; he protected Hachäkyum's mortals, curing the sick and reviving the dead. He also rescinded their right to immortality, after a husband and wife disobeyed him. Up until that time he was living on earth among the Lacandones. After that point he ascended to the sky, leaving the mortals with incensories and instructions for petitioning the lords for protection. He also gave men their curing chants and songs.² Ak'inchob also delivered their offerings to Hachäkyum. And, finally, according to Boremanse (1986, 113), he introduced polygyny.

   Another one of Ak'inchob's names is *ki'chäkchob* (Bruce 1968, 131). The first morpheme could be *kih* or *kit*, rather than *ki* 'good, tasty'. *Kih* means 'sun or sun god' in the Quiché, Cakchiquel, Zutuhil, and Pokoman Mayan languages (J. Thompson 1970, 235). *Kit* is an honorific meaning "father"³ and is the first element in the title *kit kan* bestowed on petty monarchs or co-rulers in a junior position to the principal rulers (Jones 1998, 91). See also Jones (1998, 89, 95, 451n88). The last element, *chäkchob*, could be the compound *chäk=chob* 'red maize' (Bricker 1998, 59). Although Bruce translates *chob* as 'squinting, blinded', the word for blind is *ch'oop* in the Yucatecan languages.⁴

   Ak'inchob corresponds to the southern Lacandon deity K'äbilam 'branches of the ceiba tree' (Boremanse 1986, 272).⁵ *See also* Hach Biraam.

Akna'i(r) Ak'inchob 'Our Lady of Ak'inchob' is the wife of Ak'inchob and daughter of Hachäkyum and Xk'are'ox. She corresponds to the youthful aspect of the Moon Goddess (a.k.a. God I). She shares the role with her mother as the Goddess of Childbirth and the Loom and represents fertility and sensuality. She lives on a small island in the Usumacinta River across from Yaxchilan.

Akna'i(r) Akyant'o' 'Our Lady of Akyant'o'' is the *xunan* 'foreign' wife of Akyant'o' 'Lord of Foreigners'. She and Akyant'o' introduced Western medicine to the Lacandones (Boremanse 1986). Women petition her to mediate on their behalf to Xk'ale'ox (Bruce 1968).

Akna'i(r) Sukunkyum 'Our Lady of Sukunkyum' is the wife of the Lord of the Underworld in northern Lacandon mythology. Along with her husband she scrutinizes the souls of the dead and protects those that are "good" from Kisin 'the Devil'.

Akyant'o' (Äkyant'o') is the Creator God of the foreigners, or the Christian God and the father of Hesuskristos (Jesus Christ). He was the second of the main gods to emerge from the sacred tuberose. He is responsible for introducing foreign goods, domestic animals, currency, Western diseases, and medicine to cure them.

His name has caused some confusion among both Lacandones and researchers. It is spelled as Akyantho by Bruce (1968).[6] The name would be more intelligible if it were analyzed as *Ak-ya(a)m-t'o'* < (*t'o'oh* 'esteemed one') and glossed as 'Our Middle Lord'. At least this form would define not only his birth position in the hierarchy of the divine triumvirate but also his position in a three-level universe. Under this view I have taken the liberty of rewriting his name.[7]

Akyant'o' corresponds to Hoylob in the pantheon of the southern Lacandones (Boremanse 1986, 272n3). *See also* Hoilob.

Bol Menche (Menche Bol) was the leader of the last of the three thousand Mayan infidels to yield to the Spanish. They occupied an extensive zone between Ocosingo and the forest to the east, in the ranges running between Tabasco and Yucatan, and in the Usumacinta basin fed by the rivers of the Passion, the Chixoy, the Xocoljá, the San Pedro, and the Lacantún. Menche was a constant threat to the Christianized residents, raiding the towns, murdering inhabitants, and setting fire to their communities. Despite continuous expeditions to the area, the Spanish were never able to conquer him. In 1837, however, a Petenero by the name of Julian Segura won him over with flattery (Soza 1957).

Edwin Rockstroh encountered Menche in Yaxchilan while surveying the ruins. Impressed by this affable leader, he named the site Menche Tinamit.

Later another nineteenth-century explorer, Teobert Maler, renamed the site Yaxchilan (Morley 1920 [1883–1948], 23).

The name Menche may be a mispronunciation of Manche, the name of a Ch'ol group who were never completely subdued (Palka 2014, 28). The Manche Ch'ol occupied an area extending from the southern boundary of the Guatemalan Petén to southeastern Belize. Whether Menche and his people were the illustrious Haawo' in Lacandon mythology is uncertain. Stories of the Haawo' recount attacks made on them and Yaxchilan by the Itzas and Spanish. The name Haawo' appears to derive from Hau (Jaw), a patronym among the Itza and the Tipu (Itza) living in the Petén between the sixteenth and eighteenth centuries (Jones 1998, 24–27).[8] *See also* Coati mundi.

Bor 'Lord of Balche' is a solar deity who prepares Hachäkyum's balche', ceremonial liquor made from fermented balche' bark (*Lonchocarpus* sp.). He is represented on earth as a large clay urn with a face modeled on the front. This urn functions as a serving bowl from which balche' is dipped out by the gourd and poured into individual drinking cups.

Chäk xib 'red men' are two of Hachäkyum's sons. One is called *k'ak'bak'akyum chak xib* and the other, *uparakyum chak xib*. They lost favor with their father for having tried to murder their little brother T'uup 'Lord of the Sun'. In a Lacandon myth they killed T'uup's "proxy." Because of this Hachäkyum cut off the route to his sky realm, stranding them on earth. These elder brothers parallel Hun Chouen and Hunbatz in the *Popol Vuh*. Marion (1999) claims that the chäk xib correspond to the Mayan rain gods, chaacs.

Chembe(r)k'uho' 'pedestrian gods' are minor deities who live in the rocks and trees of the forest and milpas. They are transformers that take the form of jaguars on earth and humans when in the sky realm. Mischievous and malicious, they steal the harvest and unleash the mythical jaguars on unsuspecting humans. They compare with the *wayantekob* in southern Lacandon mythology.

Cher (ah) is the name for the female rubber figurines offered during certain Lacandon ceremonies. The name likely corresponds to Ixchel, God O (the aged Moon Goddess) or to both the aged Moon Goddesses (God O) and her youthful counterpart. See Taube (1992).

Coati mundi (chunk'in bäk, ts'u'ts'u', [male] koton) was the animal onen of the *lo'k'in* people, according to southern Lacandon mythology (Boremanse 1986, 346–49). The lo'k'in were adversaries of both the northern and southern Lacandones. In a southern Lacandon myth the lo'k'in were killed off by a certain military captain under orders from the Lacandones' principal deity, Ik Yum,[9] because they tried to avert the end of the world by preventing the fragments of Ik Yum's statue at Yaxchilan from reassembling (*see also* Hach Biraam). A similar northern Lacandon myth recounts an assault on Yaxchilan by the Itza (in the company of Spanish soldiers). The lord, Hachäkyum, and the Haawo' thwarted the attack by roiling the waters of the Usumacinta, capsizing the canoes, and drowning the warriors. These two myths suggest that the lo'k'in and the Itza were the people.

Haawo' were Lacandon ancestors who belonged to the *aak'ä'bäk* 'raccoon' onen. They were decimated by an epidemic (yellow fever?) after eating food that was purposefully contaminated by a Nawäto' man. Hachäkyum revived them, and thereupon they were transformed into demigods. They live in the ruins of Yaxchilan where they take care of the hach biraam, a large, headless stone statue of Hachäkyum. They present themselves only to the most devout Lacandones, relaying messages and warnings from the gods.

Hach Biraam is the name of the headless stone sculpture of Hachäkyum. It is actually the statue of Bird Jaguar IV, Yaxchilan's most famous ruler, who ruled from AD 752 until 768. The Lacandones believe that when the world comes to an end, his head will affix to his shoulders, and his eyes will light up and scan the earth for miscreants. Then he will end the world.

Hachäkyum 'Our True Lord' is the principal god of the northern Lacandones. He goes by other names as well—Yumbirir Ka'an 'holy lord of the sky',[10] Akchanyum 'Our Little Lord', and Äkyum (Akyum) 'Our Lord'. As the Creator, he corresponds to Itzam Na of the Classic Yucatec Mayas. He was the third of the divine triumvirate to emerge from the tuberose.

Hachir Hachäkyum 'in-law of Hachäkyum' is the father of Ak'inchob. Otherwise an ill-defined deity. The Lacandones in Petha' believed he controlled the population of venomous snakes and, in general, guarded the forest (Bruce 1968, 128). He lives in Bonampak. According to the southern Lacandones in Lacanha' Chan Sayab, the Jaguar God depicted in the murals represents Hachir Hachäkyum, but they say little else about him. He was the eighth god to be born from the tuberose.

Ha'ha'nahk'uho', ha'nahwiniko' literally 'rain house gods' are the water deities who fulfill the orders of Mensäbäk 'Maker of Soot'. They are associated with the four cardinal directions and two intercardinal directions: Xäman '(Spirit of the) north'; Tsetser xäman '(Spirit of the) northeast'; Burha' kirutark'in '(Spirit of the) flood of the east'; Tsetser nohor '(Spirit of the) southeast'; Nohor '(Spirit of the) south'; and Chik'ink'uh 'deity of the west'. Three of them carry a macaw's tail with which they sprinkle *säbäk* 'soot' on the clouds. They receive this soot from Mensäbäk. Instead of soot, the 'Spirit of the south' receives a dry wind with which it "fans" clouds back to the 'Spirit of the north' (Bruce 1968, 127). The north is the direction from which come flooding rains during the winter months. These are aptly called xämän. They carry very big fans to oscillate the winds and carry axes, which they strike together to make lightning. When lightning strikes the land, the Lacandones say that Kisin has shown the ha'ha'nahk'uh his bare buttocks, provoking the ha'ha'nahk'uh to fire at him.

Hoilob (Hoylob) is the southern Lacandon name for the God of Foreigners (Boremanse 1986, 314). His name may be analyzed as *hoil-ob* (*-ob* is a plural suffix). Hoil (or Joil) is not only a common surname in the Yucatan but also the surname of the Mayan missionary Juan de la Cruz Hoil, who accompanied the governor of the district of Petén, Modesto Méndez, to "explore a peace settlement" with the Mayan rebels of Chichanha in 1851. It is possible that the southern Lacandones applied the blanket term Hoilob to all missionaries and their converts. *See also* Akyant'o'.

Itsanah is the first assistant of Hachäkyum and Kak'och, although his functions are vague. His name is evocative of Itzam Na (Itzam Nah, Itzamna, Itzamnaaj), who was the Creator God of the Classic Maya. His origin is reptilian, although he assumed various aspects and functions. He lived in the sky and sent rain to the earth (J. Thompson 1970, 210). He was exclusively venerated by the Mayan elite; the peasants, most of them farmers, worshipped the terrestrial rain gods called chacs (/chak/). According to Thompson, when the Maya elite lost their prominence in the affairs of the people, so too did Itzam Na, as he is "completely absent from present-day peasant rites in the Yucatan" (211). This may also account for why Itsanah is a subordinate god in the Lacandon pantheon.

Itsanohk'uh (< its-an noh-k'uh) is the maker of the hail, the guardian of the lakes, and the regulator of the alligator population (Bruce 1968, 128). He lives on a lake by the same name, close to his brother Mensäbäk 'Maker of Soot', the Lacandon god of rain. He was the seventh god to emerge from the tuberose. He may correspond to the Classic Mayan god Itzam Na, who is associated with reptiles and water. The name could also be a derivation of *Itza noh k'uh*, roughly glossed as the 'great god of the Itza'. Nohk'uh is also a Lacandon god living in Yaxchilan. I suspect that this is his former home before the gods vacated it after the second destruction of the world. Nohk'uh is said to be residing in some ruins in the northern Lacandon community of

Mensäbäk (Palka 2014, 182), but I think this is Itsanohk'uh and not a sepa-rate deity called Nohk'uh.[11] Finally, the Mayas of the Yucatan say the *nohk'uh* are spirits of the milpas (Tozzer [1907] 1978, 97).

K'ak' 'Lord of Fire, the Hunt, and Courage' is renowned for his bravery in hunting and his custom of removing hearts and painting himself with the blood. In ceremonial contexts, he is referred to as *ah bo'oray*, which corre-sponds to Ah Bolay, the name of the Yucatec Mayas' God of the Hunt. *See also* Nuxib K'ak'.

K'akoch (derivation is unclear) is the original Creator of the world, the sea, the first sun and moon, and the sacred tuberose, the birthplace of the gods. As the Lord of the Gods, he corresponds to Ixpiyacoc, the remote god in the creation story of Quiché Maya, and to Ometecuhtli of the Toltec/Aztec people (Bruce 1968).

Kanank'aax 'Guardian of the Forest' is not a single deity, but a class of for-est guardians who live in old ruins and rock shelters throughout the forest (Bruce 1968, 129). They frequently appear to humans in the form of a jaguar.

K'ayum 'Lord of Song' is a solar deity and one of Hachäkyum's assistants. He provides the music at ceremonies, for the gods as well as for mortals (Bruce 1968, 130). He is represented by a clay drum with a human face modeled on one side. This ceremonial drum was played in ritual contexts.

K'in (Ah) '(The) Sun' is the god of incense, the flute, and ceremonies in the northern Lacandon pantheon (Bruce 1968, 130). The northern Lacandones regard him as an assistant of their principal god, Hachäkyum (Bruce 1968, 130). K'in is the name of the principal god Ik Yum of the southern Lacan-dones (Boremanse 1986).

k'in (ah) 'squirrel cuckoo' is a bird in southern Lacandon legend that would sound the alarm—*KIPCHO! KIPCHO!*—at the approach of enemies, espe-cially the *Lo'k'in* (Boremanse 1986, 346; Nations and Valenzuela 2017, 108). This avian sentinel is evocative of the avian sentinel *kinchil coba* 'chachalaca bird of the sun' of the Itza Maya at Tayasal (see J. Thompson 1970, 324).

Kinchil Coba is the name of a statue of a man, AhKinchil Coba, which was placed on a hillock overlooking the Itza capital, Tayasal, to stand guard over the city (Roys [1933] 1973, 239n632). The connection between him and the avian sentinel called *kinchil coba* is unclear. Kinchil Coba was also a name of a place that the man founded. This place was likely Cobá, a Classic Maya site in Quintana Roo, Mexico (J. Thompson, Pollock, and Charlot 1932, 6, in Roys [1933] 1973, 198n197).

K'inich Ahau 'Sun-Faced Lord' is the younger brother of Sukunkyum and the older brother of Ik Chan Yum in the southern Lacandon pantheon. The ancient Mayan Creator, Itzam Na, is sometimes associated with the sun god Kinich Ahau.

Kisin 'Lord of Death, demon' was created by Hachäkyum to be the messenger of death, to punish the souls and perform all the disagreeable functions unworthy of the other gods (Bruce 1968, 134). Envious of Hachäkyum for having mortals who adored him, Kisin tried to create his own people. But Hachäkyum foiled the attempt by turning them into animals. Many of the animals became onen (lineages) of the Lacandones. After enduring Kisin's constant harassment, Hachäkyum finally interred him and his family in the underworld. In bursts of rage, Kisin kicks the pillars supporting the earth to break free and destroy Hachäkyum's world. The rumbling of earthquakes is called *kisin upeek*. *Kisin* is also used to refer to his two sons, who took over all evil deeds when Kisin became old and decrepit (Bor Ma'ax, pers. comm.). Kisin has a daughter who protected the Mole Trapper while he was in the underworld. He became her husband and the son-in-law of Kisin. Kisin is also the general term for 'demon'.

Kisni(n) is a dead person's spirit or ghost.

Kohoh (k'ohoh?) is the name of the male figurine burned as an offering to the Lacandon gods during specific ceremonies. The etymology of the name is unclear. Koho' is the ceremonial name for the people of Lacandon k'ek'en lineage. K'oh is the Yucatec word meaning 'mask or image' (Freidel, Schele, and Parker 1993, 65, 416n9).

Kowoh (Couoh) were a lineage of the Xiu Maya that entered the Petén from Mayapan (Yucatan) in the late Postclassic period. They were enemies of the Itza. The northern Lacandones regard the Kowoh as their ancestors.

K'uk'urkan 'feathered serpent' is a kind of malevolent being described variously as a two-headed snake that lives near Lake Miramar and eats people, a species of saurian approximately three meters long and one meter wide, and a kind of enormous snake with narrow scales protruding from the back of its head like feathers (Bruce 1968, 135; Tozzer [1907] 1978, 96). His association with the cultural hero K'uk'ulkan is lost among the Lacandones.

K'urer[12] were inspectors of the milpa in the service of Hachäkyum, conceivably corresponding to civic and religious offices of the Postclassic Maya (Bruce 1968, 130). The k'urer is regarded as a single entity with multiple aspects, such as a whirlwind, a female spider monkey, and one of the assistant deities at the service of Hachäkyum (Perera and Bruce 1982, 31). According to Bor Ma'ax, the k'urer splits in two, and each half is assigned the job of inspecting the cultivated fields for Hachäkyum. Antonio Martinez says that there were three k'urer; two of them were dishonest, and the third was honest. The two dishonest k'urer lied to Hachäkyum when they told him that the fields were ready for rain when they were not and that the fields were not ready for rain when they were. They were resentful for not getting their fair share of the produce, so they decided to ruin the harvest for Hachäkyum.

kuxtey k'uh (< kuxtalel?) is a nebulous class of minor gods. The Lacandones say they are the souls of the dead or demigods in the service of the major gods. They inhabit the Classic Mayan ruins and were responsible for carving the stelae and lintels (Bruce 1968, 137). Kuxtey seems to be cognate with *kuxtälel*, the Ch'ol word meaning 'life force'.[13] Ah Kushtal is the god of birth in the Yucatec Maya pantheon (Tozzer [1907] 1978, 157).

Luumkab (lu'umkab) 'spirits of the land and the stones' are of relatively little importance, except when they are offended, whereupon they render the milpa sterile. Lacandones believe that the rainbow is their road, associating the colors with dye running from their tunics.

Me'ex K'uk' Chan was the principal deity of the Haawo' and *k'ambul*, the great curassow onen of the Nawäto people (Boremanse 1986, 354). His "home" is situated on a hill at the entrance of Lake Miramar (Boremanse 1986, 121) in the territory formerly occupied by the Ch'ol-Lacandon in the seventeenth century. He may be a deified Ah Mex Cuc (Chan), who was the lord of Chichén Itzá in the thirteenth century (see Roys [1933] 1973, 28; J. Thompson 1970, 14).

Mensäbäk 'Lord of Rain', literally 'soot maker', is also called *yum kanansäbäk* 'Lord Guardian of the Soot', which signifies his control over the rain clouds. He provides soot to his assistant rain gods, the *ha'nahwininko'*,[14] to seed the clouds. As such, he is also the Lord of Lightning and Thunder. Mensäbäk' corresponds to the Mexican (Toltec) rain god, Tlaloc. He lives around Lake Mensäbäk in the northern Lacandon forest. A rock painting above his abode has been identified as Tlaloc, drawn by an ancient Mayan hand. The Lacandones believe that Mensäbäk created the Tzeltal Mayas, whom they call *kah* 'villager'. He was the fifth god born from the tuberose (Bruce 1968, 127).

Murikna' <muur-ikna' 'mound-moon' is the general name of goddesses who

occupy small islands in bodies of water. Specifically, Murikna' refers to the daughter of Mensäbäk 'Lord of Rain'. She lives on a small mound in Lake Mensäbäk.

Nuxib K'ak' 'Venerable Lord of Fire' is another name for the 'Lord of Fire' (*see* K'ak'). He differs from AhK'ak' Mensäbäk, who is a helping god, or perhaps the assistant of the rain god, Mensäbäk (see Bruce 1968, 126). According to Boremanse (1986, 72n5), Nuxib K'ak' is the assistant of Sukunkyum 'Lord of the Underworld'.[15]

Säkäpuk is an assistant god with ill-defined functions (Bruce 1968, 130; Tozzer [1907] 1978). He may correspond to Zacal Puc [sakal puk], a leader of one of the four Itza lineages that invaded the Yucatan (Roys 1939, 5). After his death, he was deified and honored in the residences of the Cocom (Itza) aristocracy (J. Thompson 1970, 12, 317). If Säkäpuk is Zacal Puc, then his god pot in Lacandon temples implies that the Lacandones continued the practice of ancestor worship.

Sukunkyum 'Our lord's elder brother' was the first god to emerge from the tuberose. He descended into the underworld where he took up his duties as "judge of souls" and the warden of Kisin 'the Devil'. His most important duty, however, was retrieving the sun after it sank in the west and transporting it through the underworld to the East. This task is reflected in another one of his names, Chan Yum K'in 'Little Sun Lord'. In ceremonial contexts, he is called Itsanachaak (<Itsam-nah-chak). This name is evocative of the divine pillars that support the four corners of the universe in Classic Maya cosmology.[16] Chak refers to the Cha(a)c rain gods, the patrons of agriculture. Situated at the four cardinal directions, each personifies a phase in the life cycle of a plant, and the main steps for agricultural practices include sowing (burial), gestation (entombment), germination (birth), and harvesting (maturation and decline).

Associated with the place of the rising sun, Itzam-na-chak embodied fertility and rebirth.[17] Sukunkyum's association with the east, in addition to the underworld, is implied in northern Lacandon beliefs about death, judgment, and the final destiny of the soul: Sukunkyum assesses the souls' conduct on earth and then releases them to Kisin for the appropriate punishment. He then retrieves those whom he deems sufficiently cleansed from Kisin's fires, brushes them off, and then sends them to live with Mensäbäk or one of his brothers (Itsanohk'uh 'Lord of Lakes, Hail, and the controller of the population of crocodiles' and Ts'ibanah 'Painter of Houses/Lord of the Graphic Arts'). Relatives of the deceased give Sukunkyum offerings in return for treating their loved ones with leniency.

Sukunkyum is also associated with fertility of the land. Before cultivating their milpas, Lacandones conduct ceremonies dedicated to him for a bountiful harvest. By his association with death, resurrection, and fertility, Sukunkyum corresponds to the Yucatec gods (Itzam Na) Kauil '(Itzam Na) (of the) Bountiful Harvest' and Bolan Dz'acab 'God of Lightning, Fertility, and Dynastic Descent'. According to J. Thompson (1970, 216), these two gods represent two of the many aspects of the omnipresent god, Itzam Na. He also corresponds to the Classic Mayan god Moan Chan, who possesses both mortuary and life-giving attributes (Taube 1992, 81).

Ts'ibanah[18] is the lord who painted the houses of the gods with the blood of the mortals during the second destruction of the world. Many buildings at Yaxchilan, the gods' second terrestrial residence, show traces of red paint, which signified blood to the Lacandones.

T'uup 'Lord of the Sun' is the youngest son of Hachäkyum. He was made Lord of the Sun while his malevolent elder brothers, the *chäk xib* 'red men' were relegated to the periphery of the earth for denigrating their father and conspiring to murder T'uup. As the guardian of the sun while it is in the sky, and in his position as the third son of the principal god, T'uup resembles Piltzintecuhtli 'God of the Rising Sun' and is associated with Tonatiuh 'Youthful Sun' in Nahuatl (Mexican) mythology (Fernandez 1992, 154). In his role as guardian of the sun he is also responsible for the eclipse. When Hachäkyum decides to end the world, T'uup covers the sun with his tunic. The northern Lacandones assert that T'uup's tomb is under the Temple of the Inscriptions in Palenque. The tomb belongs to the renowned Classic Mayan ruler K'inich Janaab Pakal.

Want'ut'k'in is an ogre who lures hapless victims up trees to collect honey and strands them there to "age" before he returns to eat them. His name translates as 'partridge-parrot-cuckoo', but I can find no mythological significance for each of these three names. Conceivably it refers to a person called Juan T'ut' K'in. T'ut' is a Lacandon onen that may correspond to Tut, the name of a Xiu lineage in the Yucatan. Their leader was Tutul Xiu.

Xäkeh is a vague deity. According to Bruce (1968, 136), Nawäto' members of the *k'ambul* 'curassow' onen made human sacrifices to xäkeh until relatively recently. The name could be a mispronunciation (or misspelling) of *sakeh*. If so, this god likely corresponds to *sac ke* 'bright, white sun', the Kekchi

(Q'eqchi') name for the sun god (see J. Thompson 1970, 236). *Saq'e* is the modern Kekchi word for sun (Kahn 2006). The largest population of Kekchi speakers is concentrated in northern Alta Verapaz and southern Petén, on the periphery of the southern Lacandon territory. Contact between the Kekchi people and the Lacandones located in the southern Lacandon forest may have occurred, given that the Nawäto' venerated the sun.

Xk'are'ox (xk'änre'ox), the aged Moon Goddess, is the consort of Hachäkyum, the northern Lacandones' creator. Her name translates as 'she of the yellow breadnut leaf/leaves' or 'she of the branches of the breadnut tree'. Likened to the Mayan breadnut (*Brosimum alicastrum*), a tree that produces abundant yields of nutritious nuts several times a year and provides a reliable supply of food, the Moon Goddess is a symbol of fertility, productivity, and support. As the main creator of the fourth generation of mortals in Mayan mythology, she has a strong connection to nourishment. The material she used was maize, the main sustenance of the Mesoamerican peoples. In Lacandon mythology she created women, while her husband created men. As the symbol of birth and procreation, she is petitioned to help women conceive and to protect their unborn children. In Mayan society, she is regarded as a diviner and curer, and among the Yucatec Maya she is the Goddess of Medicine. Her connection to life and sustenance is but one side of her character. In the pantheon of the Classic Mayas, she is God O, the aged Moon Goddess of medicine, weaving, and midwifery and is associated with disease, death, and the underworld. She is the embodiment of the moon as it wanes, gradually disappearing into the underworld. In her New Moon phase, she rests in the dark, primordial waters. Her youthful counterpart, God I, emerges from the underworld. Likened to the waxing moon, the youthful Moon Goddess swells more each evening until she develops into the full, round symbol of fertility and abundance. *See also* Akna'i(r) Ak'inchob.

Xtabay 'She of the Rope' are a class of minor goddesses created by Hachäkyum to be the lovers of the *chemberk'uh* 'pedestrian gods' (who had no wives). They live in houses with their consorts, bearing them lots of little girls. But they also seduce Lacandon men, especially those who are observing abstinence during important, protracted ceremonial periods, such as the god pot renewal ceremony. Similarly, in Yucatec Mayan folklore the Xtabay are incomparably beautiful seductresses who lure men to their deaths. The name Xtab is the feminine counterpart of Ahtab 'hangman', evoking her association with hanging or the snares, particularly the spring snare, which

hoist the game into the air. Mayas in the sixteenth century hanged themselves instead of being taken by the Spanish. They are said to have been accompanied by the Xtab to the otherworld (see Tozzer 1941, 132).

yiihman are seeds that have been saved for next year's sowing. This is also the
term used for descendants.[19] *See also* yixmehen Kisin.

yitbeh (yitber) 'he at the bottom of the road' is a kind of ogre that transforms
into a human being who is familiar to his victim, such as a woman's husband. By doing so he can easily lure victims into his cave and then eat them.

yixmehen Kisin 'the seeds of Kisin' refers to Kisin's children (Bruce 1968, 136).

Yum K'aax 'Lord of the Forest' is a supernatural who is an ape-like being that
lives alone in a cave in the forest. In a northern Lacandon myth (Boremanse
1986, 169–75), he abducts two brothers who are hunting in the forest. He
takes them back to his cave where he befriends them because he wants their
company. They escape, and the enraged Yum K'aax sets off after them, vow-
ing to eat every human being in sight. The Lord Hachäkyum captures him
and locks him up in a cave. See J. Thompson (1930) for a similar version
from Belize.

NOTES

Preface

1. Baer and Baer (1948, 1952); M. Baer (n.d.); Boremanse (1986); Bruce (1968, 1974, 1976); Bruce et al. (1971); Cline (1944); G. Soustelle (1959); Tozzer ([1907] 1978).

Introduction

1. See especially Baer and Baer (1952); Baer and Merrifield (1971); Boremanse (1986, 1998a); Bruce (1968, 1974, 1975); Bruce, Robles, and Ramos Chao (1971); Cook (2016); De Vos ([1980] 2015); Marion (1999); McGee (1990); G. Soustelle (1959, 1961); J. Soustelle (1933, 1935a, 1935b); Tozzer ([1907] 1978).
2. Barbara Godard, "Oral Literature in English," *Canadian Encyclopedia*, 2006, Historica Canada, revised June 23, 2015, https://www.thecanadianencyclopedia .com/en/article/oral-literature-in-english/.

The Lacandones

1. Figures vary.
2. Arguments complete the meaning of the predicate (or verb).
3. It is assumed that the northern Lacandon dialect spoken in Mensäbäk is the same as that spoken in Naha'; I have not conducted research in Mensäbäk to determine if this is true or not.
4. A hypothetical ancestral language reconstructed from attested languages sharing similar linguistic features.
5. Tone is a distinctive pitch level carried by the syllable of a word that provides the meaning of that word, e.g., *míis* 'broom' vs. *mìis* 'cat', where acute accent indicates high tone and the grave accent, low tone.
6. J. Soustelle (1935a, 172) comments on the similarity between the dialect of the *k'ek'en* onen in the southern Lacandon community and the dialect spoken in the Yucatan. He contrasts the k'ek'en speakers' dialect with the dialect of the northern Lacandon speakers who belong to the *ma'ax* onen. The contrast he identifies is in vocabulary, citing the word for corn as *nol* in the northern dialect but *isim* in the southern dialect. Speakers from San Quintín and Cedro-Lacanha' can still be differentiated based on their distinctive dialects as well. Tone, or the lack thereof, is the main feature that differentiates these dialects. See Hofling (2014, 2).
7. The term *lowlands* is a misnomer, as the area encompasses various land formations and vegetation, from low dry scrub forest plains in the northern area to high plateaus and densely forested mountain ranges in the central area.

8. K'uk'ulkan to the Mayas.

9. Also spelled Kowoj, Kowoh.

10. See Jones (1998, 19–28) and Rice and Rice (2005).

11. Variously spelled as Kejach, Kejache, Quejache.

12. A Nahuatl phrase meaning 'hedge of cane', alluding to the stockades surrounding the settlements. These people were also referred to as Tulumkih, meaning 'agave surround', in Yucatec Maya. Chinamitla refers to any settlement of a lineage. The word derives from *chinamit*, the Nahuatl term for a territorial and residential unit (Sharer 1994, 507).

13. See Cogolludo ([1688] 1868, bk. 12, chap. 3–7).

14. The word may derive from the Mayan phrase *akan-tun* meaning 'stone pillar' (Perera and Bruce 1982) or 'roaring stone' (Tozzer [1907] 1978), or even *lakam tun* 'big, great, wide stone'.

15. Also spelled Cobog and Cobogués.

16. Also spelled Haw and Jaw.

17. Also spelled Karsiya and Kasyho.

18. See Bruce (1975); De Vos ([1980] 2015, 5103); McGee (2002, 10). See also Feldman (2000) and Lee and Markman (1977) for details and descriptions of the ethnic groups.

19. Spelled *yucum* in the extant publications, the word is analyzed as *y-uk'um*, where *y-* occurs on third-person possessive prefixes before vowels, i.e., *uy-uk'um*.

20. Logging operations in the Lacandon forest were run by La Constancia, a Spanish company owned by the Romano Brothers.

21. "Mexico," *Encyclopaedia Britannica*, https://www.britannica.com/topic/land-reform/Mexico, accessed June 2018.

22. This group may have been from south of the Mexican Guatemalan border, possibly Ixcan. The word Tzendales may be Tzeltales. The Tzeltales are a Mayan ethnic group that speak a Tzeltalan (Maya) language. Over most of the Colonial period until the Mexican Revolution, they and other indigenous groups were forced to work in the mines, mills, and haciendas.

23. *Petha'* means 'lake', and the name was ascribed to these people because they lived in the lacustrine area.

24. One Lacandon myth, "Les Nawat-o" (Boremanse 1986), mentions that the Nawäto', Lacandon ancestors, did not use the bow and arrow, but a weapon that, from its description, resembles an atlatl. Boremanse, however, supposes it is a blowgun (1986, 356n7).

25. See Cook (2016) for a comprehensive description of the plants and their uses in Lacandon culture.

26. K'ek'en is also represented in the north, where they are allied with the ma'ax

through marriage. However, Bor Ma'ax explains that these k'ek'en are different people from the k'ek'en group in the south (pers. comm.).

27. Each group disparages the other's speech.

28. A ruthless fanatic who led a violent campaign to stamp out Mayan idolatry, destroying almost all the Mayan hieroglyphic texts, which contained invaluable information on Mayan religion, civilization, and history.

29. Conceivably thirteen represented the number of astral bodies that moved in procession across the night sky, reminiscent of characters in a zodiac who follow the sun across the celestial sphere. Twenty represents the "bundles of time" they carried in endless relay.

30. God A (Kisin 'Lord of Death'), patron deity of number ten, God G (K'inich Ahau 'Sun Lord'), patron deity of the number four, and God B (Chac 'Lord of the Rain'), patron of number thirteen (Sharer 1994, 539).

31. A composite god, or a collection of gods that included gods of the Oxlahun ti' K'uh when they passed through the underworld after disappearing below the horizon. See Sharer (1994, 536).

32. His name is spelled variously as Äkyantho'/Akyantho'/Kyantho in the Lacandon literature. I have changed the spelling to reflect what I believe is the meaning of his name.

33. The town of one of the Spanish reducciónes 'mission settlements' where the "indios de la montaña" were corralled.

34. Ak'inchob's birth is the shortest and most obscure event in the creation story. It mentions Ak'inchob was born on earth, and his parents were Hachäkyum's future in-laws. Hachäkyum throws sand on the blood, to "cover the indecency," and the blood-soaked sand turns into ants (Bruce 1974, 43–44). In many Meso-american myths, ants are associated with maize, and by extension, Ak'inchob symbolizes the "birth of maize." This Lacandon passage evokes the Classic Mayan myth of the reincarnation of the Baby Jaguar as the Maize God. One of three divine brothers, Baby Jaguar was the illegitimate child of God N (Itzam Na) and Lady Wayaab' ("the Old Goddess"). Because of this, he was killed and buried. After this he emerged from the earth as the Maize God (see Valencia and Capistrán 2013). K'awiil is associated with lightning, serpents, fertility, and maize. He corresponds to Bolon Dzacab, who plays an important role as "seed bearer" in the cosmogonic myth in the Book of Chilam Balam of Chumayel. Baby Jaguar is also referred to as Chak K'awiil (Valencia and Capistrán 2013, 43), which can be glossed as 'Red K'awiil'. Ak'inchob's other name is Chäk Chob, which can be glossed as 'Red Corn'.

35. "When Hachäkyum, our true lord, becomes angry, there may be a solar eclipse. If he wishes to, he grabs the sun and holds it tight. Then he lowers the sky of the vulture. They say when the sky of the vulture hangs there, the sun cannot go on

its way anymore because the vulture's round sky hangs in its way" (Rätsch and Ma'ax 1984, 183; author's translation).

36. "Mayan Symbols," Ancient-Symbols.com, https://www.ancient-symbols.com/mayan_symbols.html, accessed February 2019.

37. Often spelled Itsanal in the Lacandon literature.

38. Spelling varies from one source to another: k'ulel (Bruce 1968), kurel (Davis 1978), and Ah-kulel (Roys [1933] 2008).

39. Roys describes the Ah-kulel as a "mediator or deputy and . . . the title of a certain class of town-officials. They were inferior to the *ah-cuch-cab*, or councillors, and superior to the *tupil*, whom the Spaniards considered a sort of constable" (Roys, 235n588).

40. Lacandones believe that without wives they would die of starvation. Moreover, without women, who prepare the food, men would be unable to satisfy the gods with offerings and thereby provoke the gods to end the world.

41. *K'än* 'yellow' is the direction of nadir, south, and the direction of death. Yellow is maturity, the color of ripe maize. *Ox* 'ramon tree' produces an abundance of nutritious nuts that were eaten during times of famine, which plagued the Mayas throughout their history.

42. Marion (1999) notes two flowers, *chaknikte'* (*Plumeria rubra*) and *saknikte'* (*Plumeria alba*), as does Tozzer ([1907] 1978). In my version and that of Bruce (1974) it is a single tuberose (*Polianthes tuberosa*).

43. A Classic period city where three rulers and gods, called the Triad, resided.

44. Following Bruce (1968), I refer to them both as Chäk Xib.

45. These three sons evoke the elder and younger sets of twins, Hunbatz and Hunchouen, and Xbalanque and Hunahpu in the *Popol Vuh*.

46. Ak'inchob may also correspond to the sun god, owing to the *k'in* 'sun' element in his name. If associated with maize and the sun, he corresponds to K'awiil 'sustenance and lightning', who partners with the sun god to form the celestial god Oxlahun ti' K'uh mentioned in the books of the *Chilam Balam*. That Ak'inchob is the son-in-law of the preeminent creator, Hachäkyum, strengthens this hypothesis.

47. This animosity evokes the ongoing struggle between the lords of the underworld and the lords of the heavens in other Mesoamerican cosmogonic myths, e.g., *Chilam Balam* of Chumayel.

48. The Lacandones refer to the Tzeltales as *kah* 'village dweller'. The Tzeltales constitute the largest group of settlers in the Lacandon forest.

49. According to the version in Rätsch and Ma'ax (1984, 42–46), it never became dark, because when the sun "went out of" (set?) Kak'och's sky, Hachäkyum's sun rose. Additionally Rätsch and Ma'ax say that Hachäkyum clothed the sun and painted an eagle on his chest (42), and when he made the moon, he painted a rabbit on her chest (43).

50. In Marion (1999). My consultants were vague on this point.
51. Incidentally, human sacrifices donned headbands. At the peak of the temple their hearts were removed, and their bodies were thrown down the step. Priests at the bottom removed the skin and wore it as a mantel (Durán 1964, 121–22, cited in Léon-Portilla 1988, 142–43). This might be the origin of the chak hu'un headbands and the reason why both celebrants and the god pots wear them.
52. *Chel* is the word for "rainbow" and the name of the Mayan Moon Goddess, called Ixchel. *Kohoh* may allude to mask. *Koh* also is the patronym of the k'ek'en and kitam people.
53. The etymology of the phrase is uncertain. *K'an* (or *k'aan*) means 'cord', and by extension 'support', as in hammock (*k'a[a]n*) and stool (*k'anche'*), but also 'high', as in corncrib (*ka'anche' när*). *K'an* also means 'to use'.
54. A version of the chant to awaken the copal and rubber figurines is provided in Davis (1978, 137–38) and is replicated in McGee (1983, 132–33).
55. The large tamales are called *yariyar* (Davis 1978, 205) < *yal* 'layer'.
56. In the extant Lacandon literature the phrase is translated as 'give it to the head'. Lacandones reject this translation, although when asked, my consultant, Bor Ma'ax, was unable to provide a precise meaning. I suspect it means 'give the head', which puts the focus on the offering, which is the head or top of the crop, rather than on the head of the god pot.
57. McGee's spelling. I have a feeling the word is *baaker* 'bone, corn cob', not *bäk'el* 'meat, flesh; body'.
58. Bruce notes the strong cultural relations between Palenque and Yaxchilan, on the one hand, and the association of the northern Lacandones with Palenque and southern Lacandones with Yaxchilan, on the other (Bruce 1968, 12). The affinity the northern Lacandones have with Palenque was likely established when the Yucum people were taken to Palenque by Father Calderon in the early eighteenth century. Conceivably, some of the Lacandones' ancestors were living in the area before then.
59. Tozzer ([1907] 1978, 89, 171n8) states the stone inside is the life force of the servant to the god represented by the god pot. Other researchers say that the god pot is a living replica of the god that it represents (e.g., McGee 2002, 139). There is some confusion over whether the stone is one "idol" and the god pot another. See Tozzer (138–39) for more.
60. I imagine the cacao pod signifies the most prestigious offering, apart from blood, that can be offered to the gods. Cacao was a precious commodity in ancient times; it was the food of the elite and gods alike, in addition to serving as currency.
61. This evokes the ancient Maya faith in the apotheosis of dead kings rising as the sun god, their ascent into the sky coinciding with the start of a new era.

Northern Lacandon Oral Literature

1. Boremanse (1986, 8) found that the Lacandones do not expand their classification of their literary genres beyond *tsikbal* 'story', *k'aay* 'song', and *t'an* 'charms'. He also asserts that they do not distinguish between recent and old stories. I think what Boremanse means is that they do not have words for these kinds of stories.
2. See the Moyers interview with Joseph Campbell (Moyers 1988).
3. See Bratcher (1973, 61).
4. In the story, Christ punishes a disrespectful farmer by turning his crop to stone.
5. There is a third kind, called *käräsh k'aay* 'vulgar songs' (Davis 1978, 263).
6. See also Hofling (2017, 37).
7. Spelled *k'asäl*, in Bruce (1975, 177).
8. Cf. *k'a'ahs* < k'a'ah [Yuc.] 'remember' (Bricker, Yah, and Dzul de Po'ot 1998); *k'a'jsik* [S. Lac.] 'remember' (Hofling 2014); *k'ajsik* [Mop.] 'remember' (Hofling 2011); *k'ajsik, k'asik* [Itz.] 'remember' (Hofling and Tesucún 1997).
9. Tozzer ([1907] 1978) makes the same observation.
10. Divination is also performed to determine which of the gods are willing to be represented in the supplicant's god house. For details see Tozzer ([1907] 1978, 100–101) and Davis (1978, 261).
11. Cf. *póokb'aar*, afv. 'pray, cure' [S. Lac.] (Hofling 2014); *pokol, pokik* 'pray, worship, sacrifice' (Bruce 1975).
12. Säk Ho'or and Bor Ma'ax had gained the extensive experience working with linguists and anthologists.

Birth of the Gods

1. There is more than one version of the creation story. In M. Baer's "Lacandon Creation Stories" (n.d.), there were four creator gods, each responsible for the creation of a particular human population: Hachäkyum created the Lacandones; Mensäbäk 'The Powder Makers [a.k.a. Lord of Rain]' created the other Mayan groups and Mestizos (Mexican indigenous people); Äkyant'o' created all foreigners; and Kisin 'the Devil' created beings that Hachäkyum subsequently turned into animals and deemed as the onen (lineages) of his Lacandones. Additionally, Baer mentions that Hachäkyum's youngest son, T'uup, attempted to make mortals, but his jealous brothers cut off their heads. From the severed heads ceiba trees sprouted. See also Baer and Baer (1957).
2. Spelled several ways and with several possible meanings (Bruce, Robles, and Ramos Chao 1971, 76), this god corresponds to the remote creator Xpiyacoc in the *Popol Vuh*. I have spelled his name according to the pronunciation of my Lacandon consultants. In addition to the tuberose, Kak'och created the water, the first sun, the moon, the sand, and maize (Bruce 1974; Bruce, Robles, and

Ramos Chao 1971). The creation of maize is undeveloped in northern Lacandon myths recounted in Naha'.

3. J. Thompson (1970, 202–3) states that the gods' birth flower was the plumeria, since this flower is also considered the gods' birthplace in creation myths from the Yucatan. Baer and Baer (1952) add that the Lacandon gods were born from white and red varieties of the plumeria. Bruce claims that the Lacandon deities emerged from a water lily and the tuberose (Bruce 1967, 1974, 1975). Cook's (2016) ethnobotany identifies the birth flower as *Polianthes tuberosa*, as does Petryshyn (1976, 486n2). Although Petryshyn was unable to find a Yucatecan origin for the name, I believe it is a Lacandon translation for the Nahuatl word *omixochitl* 'bone flower' (*Polianthus tuberosa*) (Trueblood 1973, 158), as *baknikte'* can be analyzed as *ba(a)k* 'bone'-*nik* 'blossom'-*te'* 'tree'. Incidentally, there is a red variety of omixochitl, the Nahuatl name for which is *tlapal-omixochitl*. The wild species are found in central Mexico and north of the Volcanic Belt. Omixochitl and its cultural associations are very old. The connection between flowers and the solar deities is portrayed by the four-petal logogram *k'in* meaning 'sun, day, prophesy, and priest'. This logogram occurs in the glyph names of various Mayan gods. Flowers are often associated with the fetus or umbilicus in Mesoamerican mythology (Sasson and Law 2008), underscoring the link between the flower and the birth of the gods. In a painting depicting the birth of the gods by Lacandon artist K'ayum Ma'ax the three primary solar deities emerge from three separate blossoms of a single white flower. In Mayan iconography, one of the symbols for the sacred umbilicus is a rope ending in a *sak nik* 'white flower' (Schele and Mathews 1998, 114). The umbilicus is also portrayed as a two-headed snake, called the *kuxum-sum* 'living cord' that connects important gods to the source of their cosmic power (Schele and Villela n.d., 3, 7, fig. 5; Schele and Mathews 1998, 143). On an astronomical level the umbilicus is associated with the ecliptic, the circular path on the celestial sphere that the sun appears to follow over the course of a year. According to Schele and Villela, in Mayan iconography, deities representing the "Mayan zodiac" are depicted hanging from the ecliptic.

4. Northern Lacandones also refer to Sukunkyum as Itsanachaak (Bruce 1968, 124). This name seems to correspond to Itzam Na Chak, the Yucatec deity who was conceived of as four *chacs* 'rain gods' positioned at each of the cardinal directions (J. Thompson 1970, 212). As the supreme Mayan god, Itzam Na assumed numerous aspects and functions, including perhaps Bolon Dz'acab (a.k.a. GII), an underworld deity associated with lightning, fertility, and dynastic descent (Taube 1992; J. Thompson 1970, 226). Both aspects of Itzam Na are evoked in Sukunkyum, the Lacandon lord of the underworld. Before the cultivation cycle commenced, Lacandones held agricultural ceremonies giving

Sukunkyum offerings in return for his assurance of fertile soils and good harvests.

5. Antonio Martinez, father-in-law of Bor Ma'ax, added this comment.

6. Tozzer ([1907] 1978, 93) remarks that Nohochakyum 'Our Great Lord', another name for Hachäkyum, was created by the union of his father, the red frangipani (*Plumeria rubra*), and his mother, the white frangipani (*P. rubra*). See note 2.

7. McGee (1993, 5) includes a version of the Lacandon creation story. In his version stone hills emerge after Hachäkyum disperses the sand. He notes a parallel between this event and the placement of the three-stone hearth, the future birthplace of the God of Maize, in the creation story inscribed on tablets in the Classic Maya period city of Palenque (Chiapas, Mexico) and on Stela C at Quirigua (Izabal, Guatemala).

8. Sound effect of someone's foot suddenly sinking.

9. The term *nahb* usually refers to a small body of freshwater, but essentially it can designate any body of water. *K'ahk'-nahb* refers to sea, ocean, or large bodies of salt water, and appears to derive from the Proto-Ch'olan *k'äk'-nahb* (Kaufman 2003): in Ch'olti', the form is *cahnab* (Ara [1548] 1986); in Q'eqchi', it is *k'ak'naab* 'laguna, laguneta' (ALMG 2004); in Itza', it is *k'a'naab* (Hofling and Tesucún 1997); and, in Yucatec, it is both *k'ak'nab* and *k'anaab*. While the gloss of the first element of the compound, *k'a(h)k'/k'a'*, is uncertain, the second element, *na*, means 'water' or related to water. The original meaning of the sign *na* is water, attested in the early Mesoamerican Isthmian script; in Mayan imagery the logograms for water include water lily flowers, lily pads, dotted lines, water stacks, and scrolls (Kettunen and Helmke 2013, 20–22).

10. According to Chan K'in and Antonio, Uhachil Hachäkyum resides in the ruins of Bonampak.

Hachäkyum and Akyant'o' Create People

1. Other versions of this story can be found in M. Baer (n.d.), Baer and Baer (1957), Boremanse (1986), Bruce (1974), and Cline (1944). McGee (1983, 188–89) provides an abridged English translation of Bruce's narrative.

2. In Chan K'in Viejo's version collected by Bruce (1974, 112) and Cline (1944), Hachäkyum made the males and his wife made the females. In Cline's version white clay was used (1944, 110), whereas in Bruce's version clay and sand were used.

3. Sukunkyum went to live in the underworld. Akyant'o' went to "the other side of the sea." Hachäkyum remained in the forest.

4. Cf. *ma' tooyi'* [S. Lac] 'not yet' (Hofling 2014), *ma' toj* [S. Lac] (Canger 1970), *toj* [Itz.] 'still' (Hofling 1997), *toj* [Mop.] (Hofling 2011).

5. Hach winik is the name the Lacandones call themselves.

6. Square brackets enclose narrator's asides.

7. These are small clay braziers in which offerings are burned. Among the offer-

ings are little rubber figurines which transform into child assistants to the gods (Bor Ma'ax, pers. comm.).

8. In another version of this story the hair was to be fair, and the skin was to be red and green (Cline 1944).

9. Bor Ma'ax points to his armpits and crotch, to show where the paint remained. Cline's Lacandon narrator says that Hachäkyum's mortals were originally white skinned and had fair, curly hair (Cline 1944, 111).

10. They do this by wafting smoke from burning copal with a chamaedorea leaf over the bodies.

11. This is the narrator's exclamation, not the sound of the animals.

Hachäkyum Makes the Ants and Snakes

1. In Bruce's version narrated by Chan K'in Viejo (1974, 43–44), the ants were created when Hachäkyum threw sand on the blood left behind from the birth of Ak'inchob 'Lord of Maize'. In another, similar version (P. Baer n.d.), the blood belonged to "a child" born to Hachäkyum and his wife.

2. Cf. *wäk* 'make thread' [S. Lac.] (Hofling 2014, 425).

3. Sound effect. Also used to describe someone grinding corn on stone metate, which involves a downward motion and a flick of the wrists.

4. Cf. *p'a'ta'ch* [S. Lac.] (onom.) 'sound of falling rain on leaves' (Hofling 2014, 272).

5. <*tutz*' P. 'stretch out'. Cf. *tutz'tal* pv. 'lie, be stretched out lengthwise' < *tutz'* 'push'; *tutz'al* part. 3. 'left (long thing)'; *tutz'a'an* part. 1. 'pushed' (Hofling and Tesucún 1997, 611).

6. 'They push out'. See note 5.

7. Cf. *jáartik* 'rub with hand' [S. Lac.] (Hofling 2014, 152).

8. Cf. *yära* 'last one left' [S. Lac.] (Hofling 2014, 403).

9. Refers to the ants.

Hachäkyum Makes the Sky

1. Baer and Baer (1957, 3) mention an additional sky, just above Hachäkyum's, in which his son, T'uup, lived. The authors refer to the son as *u par Äkyum* 'the son of our Father'. According to these authors, T'uup remained behind in the underworld to guard Kisin while Sukunkyum ascended to help Hachäkyum make his celestial realm.

2. In contrast to most of the creation myths in the region, the Lacandon creation myth recounted in Naha' fails to elaborate on the sun and the moon in any significant way. In almost all Mesoamerican myths the sun and the moon were mortals and culture heroes before they rose to the sky. In many versions the sun and moon were children; in others the sun and moon were brothers, and in still others they were husband and wife or lovers. See J. Thompson's (1970) chapter on Maya creation myths, especially pp. 330–60.

3. In another version (Rätsch and Ma'ax 1984, 44–46) the two suns produced too much light, so Hachäkyum created another sky layer (closer to earth) and stuck the new sun there.

4. As the sun travels across the sky, the Haawo' take over, feeding it specific foods throughout its annual journey. See "'Äxp'äli'" 'The Solstice' (this volume).

5. Tozzer's northern Lacandon consultants (from Lake Petha') claimed that the sun and the moon are servants of the Hachäkyum (Tozzer [1907] 1978, 158). Whereas the northern Lacandones believe that the sun is a man, the southern Lacandones believe he is a god. They refer to him as *ikyum* 'our father' and his consort, the moon, *ikna'* 'our mother' (Canger 1970). The northern Lacandones of Naha' (at least) believe the moon is only the sun's companion, who follows behind it along his path. (See also Tozzer [1907] 1978, 98.) They too refer to her as *äkna'* 'our mother'. *Na'* is also the word for month. Lacandones whom Baer and Baer (1957) interviewed said that Hachäkyum made the sun and the moon, and that they are husband and wife. They also said that initially Mensäbäk had made the sun, but it shone all the time, which displeased Hachäkyum because his mortals were unable to sleep. He rectified this by setting the sun on its present course. According to the Baers' consultants, the sun is cared for by certain gods. Sukunkyum 'Lord of the Underworld' retrieves it in the west and carries it through the underworld at night, setting it up on the eastern horizon in the morning. When the sun reaches zenith, "another god" feeds it tortillas and posol (Baer and Baer 1957, 6). Other Lacandones have said that Sukunkyum feeds the sun in the underworld.

6. Chan K'in Viejo described the mortals' sky as a cloud of smoke in McGee (2002, 127). P. Baer's (n.d) consultant said that Hachäkyum divided the earth and sky by stretching clouds over the earth. The clouds were also part of the upper world.

7. Hachäkyum had two houses on earth, one in Palenque and the other in Yaxchilan. The latter was built by Ak'inchob following one of the world destructions.

A Star Falls and Creates the Lagoon

1. Tozzer ([1907] 1978, 157) notes that some Mayas (from the Yucatan) believe that when a meteor falls it creates a lake full of alligators.

2. May correspond to the feathered serpent, K'uk'ulkan, portrayed in Mayan iconography as a serpent encrusted with diamonds of light that represent its body. On the spring and fall equinoxes the shadow of the serpent descends the stairs of the pyramid of K'uk'ulkan at the Maya ruins of Chichén Itzá (Anthony Aventi, "The End of Time," lecture given at Marlboro College, September 13, 2010, https://www.youtube.com/watch?v=exQGTvZ5aKw). The illusion of the snake slithering down the northern staircase manifests the sacred, by symboli-

cally joining the heavens, the earth, and the underworld, and the day and the night.

3. Velásquez (2006) provides a detailed account of the Flood Myth and the Decapitation of the Cosmic Caiman. Decapitation mythology appears to be associated with the death of a ruler, and hence the end of his term of rulership.

Hachäkyum, T'uup, and the Devil

1. Similar versions are published in Boremanse (1986), Bruce (1974), and McGee (2002). Baer and Baer (1957) provide an English synopsis of the same story. According to the version in Baer and Baer, Ak'inchob also played a role in creating the underworld by erecting the pillars.
2. Kisin is the name of the Devil and his family. It is his two sons that cause all the trouble in the stories.
3. This is reminiscent of the scene in the *Popol Vuh* in which the Hero Twins decapitate the Lords of the Underworld (see Tedlock 1985, 153–54).
4. The "real Hachäkyum" as opposed to his body double.
5. This is a large, high-walled gourd vessel.
6. In another version of this story the ancestor discovered that after Hachäkyum had drunk the posol, the gourd was still full (see Boremanse 1982a). In effect, Hachäkyum had only imbibed the essence of the posol, as the gods do with copal smoke. In Lacandon rituals in which offerings of copal are burned, the gods ingest the fragrance. This parallels the belief held by the Quiche' Mayas, who say that the gods only ingest [the aroma] of maize, "because they have been created without an anus" (Christenson 2005, 9). In Boremanse's (1982a, 74, 95) translation, it is the *pixan* 'soul' of the posol that the gods drink.
7. Bor Ma'ax explains that the ancestor is traipsing all over the milpa to mask Hachäkyum's scent with his own.
8. It is only Hachäkyum's body double that dies.
9. They know Hachäkyum's soul will emerge, and they are ready to beat it back.

Hachäkyum, T'uup, and Chäk Xib

1. Southern and northern Lacandon versions of a similar story are published in a work by Didier Boremanse (1982a, 71–98). These are accompanied by a detailed structural analysis based on the two groups' cultural practices and cosmological beliefs. In the southern version, the elder brothers are banished to fringes of humanity. No location is mentioned. The northern Lacandon version identifies both Palenque (Boremanse 1982a) and Yaxchilan (Bruce 1968). According to Marion (1999, 41), there were three Muchachos Rojos 'Red Boys' who remained on earth and eventually served as intermediaries between the Hachäkyum and his mortals. The Muchachos Rojos correspond to the *wayantekob* in the mythology of the southern Lacandones living in Lacanha' (Marion 1999, 41n39).

The wayantekob are forest spirits or deities in charge of preparing the soul for its passage to the underworld (Marion 1999, 317). See note 3 in this chapter.

2. Although only one is mentioned in this story, there are two elder sons. Both are portrayed as antagonists.

3. Chäk Xib is reminiscent of Chac Xib Chac 'the Red Rain-god' and the name of the ruler of Chichén Itzá who was overthrown by Hunac Ceel in the tenth century (see Roys [1933] 1973, 216n397). The chacs were the Classic Mayan rain deities (Coe 1993, 182), and official positions within the Postclassic political structure were occupied by the *xib chac*, literally 'man chac'. There were five *chac* gods, four of which were stationed at each of the cardinal directions and the fifth one in the center of the world. Each direction was associated with a color — red with east, yellow with south, black with west, white with north, and green with center. Chak Xib Chac was stationed in the east. An indirect association can be made between the Chäk Xib brothers and the xib chac if one considers that, like the rain gods situated at the corners of the world, the Chäk Xib brothers were relegated to the periphery of the earth (Bor Ma'ax, pers. comm.). Marion (1999, 41) notes that they became intermediaries between the celestial gods and the mortals, but that they also terrorized the mortals with hurricane-force winds and torrential rains, especially when the mortals neglected Hachäkyum (Marion 1999, 42). For more information on the Chäk Xib, see appendix 2.

4. T'uup is aware that Hachäkyum's body is only his proxy. T'uup is only weeping to fool Kisin into believing that the real Hachäkyum is dead.

5. When a woman shares a meal with a man, she is his wife. By refusing to accept his niece's food, T'uup not only rejects her as a wife but shames his brother, Chäk Xib.

6. Leaves of the fan palm, guano, or sabal palm.

7. It is the pileated woodpecker (*Hylatomus pileatus*).

8. I am not sure how to gloss this particle.

9. Sound effect.

Hachäkyum Cuts the Mortals' Throats

1. McGee (2002, 149) remarks that this event was the first destruction.

2. According to Bruce, Robles, and Ramos Chao (1971, 17), this occurred at Palenque.

3. Boremanse (1998b, 203) says that the blood of virgins was collected.

4. Ak'inchob is the protector of the mortals. He is the one they petition for help most often. As their emissary, he delivers the mortals' messages and offerings to Hachäkyum.

5. Yaxchilan is the second home of Hachäkyum. It is also an important Classic Maya ceremonial center, situated on the west bank of the Usumacinta River. In

Lacandon cosmology it is the center of the world. Until recently Lacandones made pilgrimages to the site to collect stone relics from the temples of the gods for their god pots. The word *yax* means 'first', but in this context it may be a truncated form of *ya'ax* 'green'. Or it may mean both 'first' and 'green'. In Mayan cosmology, green is the color of the fifth cardinal point on the Mayan compass and the center of the universe from which emerged the sacred *ya'axche'* (*yaxche'*) 'ceiba tree', the Mayan Tree of Life.

6. Literally 'upper Usumacinta River'. The upper Usumacinta is south of the northern Lacandon territory. *Xokla'* may be derived as *xok-ol ha'* 'water (or river) of the *xok'* (Bruce 1975, 246). The *chäk xok* are sirens that live in the lagoons and rivers, cruising around to snatch unsuspecting bathers and haul them down to their watery abode. See the story "Chäk Xok" 'The Sirens' in this volume.

7. Yahanah is a deity who lives in the lake of the same name. Ts'ibanah 'painter of houses' is the Lord of Graphic Arts, and Mensäbäk 'soot maker' is the Lord of Rain. They live close together on lakes that carry their names.

8. McGee's Lacandon consultant, Chan K'in Viejo, said that the ancestor who escaped was Haawo', who implored Hachäkyum to spare his family. Hachäkyum agreed on the condition that Haawo' make offerings of balche' and nahwah to him. Haawo' obeyed, and his family went on to repopulate the earth. In another story, all the Haawo', save one man, were wiped out by an epidemic introduced by the Nawäto' people (Boremanse 1986).

9. Bor Ma'ax described the pot as a large, gold caldron.

10. Cf. *t'is* 'line up' (Hofling 2014).

11. *Yiiman* (*yi'ihman*) refers to the seeds saved from the last harvest for resowing the following year. Root is likely *yi'ih* 'corn tassel or silk, staminate flower of corn plant'. Cf. *yi'j* (Hofling 2014). Cf. *yix-mehen* 'begotten' (Bruce, Robles, and Ramos Chao 1971, 99). Bruce states that *yix < ix* 'urinate'; however, the word for urinate is *wi(i)x* in Lacandon, Yucatec, Itzaj, and Mopan. *Yix < y-ixim* 'maize kernels'?

Äkiche'ex 'Our Eyes'

1. Reference to this event appears in Boremanse (1986, 33).

2. In the *Popol Vuh* Huracan 'Heart of Sky, Heart of Earth' is the Quiché Maya god who created humanity (Tedlock 1985, 343). The fourth attempt at making beings to venerate the gods was finally successful; the humans were everything the gods had hoped for. But there was one problem yet to be resolved: they could see far and, therefore, had divine knowledge. The gods were alarmed that beings who were merely manufactured by them should be like themselves, to know all and see all. So Huracan clouded their eyes to shorten their sight.

3. Bor Ma'ax says that rest stops are located approximately one kilometer apart.

4. Sound effect.

5. The town of Palenque is a four-hour drive from Naha'. It is named after the major Classic Maya ceremonial center in the southern Lowlands.
6. Square brackets enclose narrator's asides.

Nacimiento 'Birth'

1. In more ancient times the ancestors retrieved their babies from under a ceiba tree. This changed when the gods realized that having the women journey into the forest to find the ceiba was too inconvenient. So they gave the ancestors papaya seeds to plant in their milpas. That the ceiba's substitute is a papaya tree is fitting, as the fruit of the papaya resembles a womb.
2. Reminiscent of the tribute rural Mayan farmers were compelled to pay to the state ruler. See Davis (1978, 245–48) for an interesting discussion on the correspondence between historical Maya politico-social structure and the Lacandon "first fruits" ritual.
3. Cf. Genesis 3:4–5.
4. Compare the same pronouncement in the Bible: "To the woman [God] said, 'I will surely multiply your pain in childbearing; in pain you shall bring forth children.'" Genesis 3:16. The Fall explains why sin and misery exist in the world.
5. Another title for the story is *utoop'il chun put* 'birth at the base of a papaya tree'.

Uyählehir Bah 'The Mole Trapper'

1. Versions of this story, or parts of it, are published in Boremanse (1986) and Bruce (1974).
2. It is unclear whether the Mole Trapper looked like a monkey to Kisin, but Kisin relishes monkey meat as much as he does human flesh.
3. Gods do not have body odor. Conceivably Sukunkyum's old tunic neutralizes the Mole Trapper's mortal odor. In Boremanse's (1986) version Sukunkyum gives the Mole Trapper his loincloth, which doubles as a snake. A discussion about the significance of snakes and loincloths in Lacandon mythology can be found in Marion (1999, 349).
4. The word derives from Mictlan, the Nahuatl word for the underworld. Rather than a place of torture, Mictlan is the final destination of the souls of the dead. Like the underworld described in the *Popol Vuh*, Mictlan consists of nine distinct levels, which take four years to descend. The souls are aided on their journey by Xolotl, the god associated with lightning, death, and the sunset. Like the Lacandon Lord of the Underworld, Sukunkyum, Xolotl protects the sun as it travels through the underworld each night.
5. The act of sneezing is also associated with coming back to life, or waking up. The *äsäb*, the "awakening instrument" the Mole Trapper uses to resurrect the dead, is stuck up the corpse's nose, causing it to sneeze. The force of sneezing jolts the dead person back to life (see also McGee 1983, 148). Chili and gagging

are associated in many Mayan myths that incorporate the chili-blowgun motif (see J. Thompson 1970, 359, 364–66). Most of these stories are about the hero twins who become the sun and the moon. The sun/boy incapacitates his lover's father by filling his blowgun with chili.

6. This scene is recounted in many stories throughout the Maya region. The hummingbird as lover is a ubiquitous motif in Mesoamerican mythology, in which it becomes a boy (or man) and later ascends to the sky and becomes the sun. See J. Thompson (1970, 358–66, 370–71) for cultural variants of the story. Another similar story is told in the Nahua town of Mecayapan, Veracruz (H. Law 1957).

7. The version in Bruce, Robles, and Ramos Chao (1971, 26) describes the escape a little differently: "*Nuxi' (Nuxib)* [the Mole Trapper] is instructed by Sukunkyum to brew *balche'* and get Kisin drunk on it. Before the Mole Trapper can escape, he must ensure that his own house is swept clean, so as not to leave anything of himself in [the] underworld. But Kisin finds a little dirt that has been over-looked, gathers it up and with that, forces his daughter to remain in the under-world" (translated by the author).

8. Bruce, Robles, and Ramos Chao (1971) provide a slightly different account.

9. In the Nahua version (H. Law 1957), the bird lover is up in the nance tree, spies the grandmother's bald head below, and throws a fruit at it to punish her for cooking him and then grinding him up (348–49).

10. The sun is sinking and has reached the tree tops.

11. Unclear form. Cf. *soli(l)man (u bäh)* 'pudriéndose' (to rot) [Lac.] (Bruce 1974, 78); *ku-sòl* 'molt' [S. Lac.] (Canger 1970); *soolmaj* prfv. 'has peeled', *sooltik ub'aj* rv. 'to shed skin' [Itz.] (Hofling and Tesucún 1997, 567). Bor Ma'ax explains that the soul is housed within a shell. When a person dies, his soul leaves the shell and travels to the underworld.

12. The small opening is made so that the ancestor can breathe.

13. Chaxnuk is the name of Sukunkyum's wife. It is a common woman's name in the northern Lacandon area. The underlying form is likely /*chan x-nuk*/ 'little esteemed woman'.

14. Eastern horizon.

15. Sometimes Kisin is referred to in the singular and at other times in the plural. According to Bor Ma'ax, Kisin's two boys took over the work of Kisin when he became old and decrepit.

16. Identified by Antonio Martinez as *Campylopterus hemileucurus*.

17. Or, "she is looking for flowers to give it to drink."

18. More precisely, they are Kisin's sons.

19. After the sun sets in the west, Sukunkyum retrieves it and carries it through the underworld to the east.

20. Bor Ma'ax explains that the monkeys represent one of two souls that a person

has: the one referred to in this story is the *pixan* 'real soul', or the eternal soul, which can leave the body as it sleeps. It appears like a monkey to Kisin, who tries to kill it. If he succeeds, the body dies three days later. See also McGee (1983, 151), whose Lacandon consultant, Chan K'in Viejo, gives a similar explanation.

21. The idea that monkeys are the remnants of the ruined generation of mortals is advanced by Marion, who says, "the pathetic singing of the monkeys responds to the murmurs of men, remembering the day already far away in which Kisin, for wanting to match the creator, caused his [down]fall" (Marion 1999, 366). Although my Lacandon consultant, Antonio Martinez, denies that monkeys were once mortals in a previous era, there does seem to be a connection between Kisin's "murder" of Hachäkyum, whose onen is the spider monkey, and the belief that Kisin kills the mortals' monkey-souls.

22. An example of binary opposition. Phenomena on earth are reversed in the underworld. Therefore, whatever is perceived as low on earth is perceived as high in the underworld and vice versa.

23. This is the traditional leather shoulder bag men carry.

24. Itsanal, Mensäbäk, and Ts'ibanah.

25. Or, "Why doesn't he burn it severely?"

26. The text in square brackets is the narrator's aside.

27. According to Bor Ma'ax, Itsanal guards the gate to a place on a lake by the same name. Itsanal is a kind of way station through which the souls pass on their way to Mensäbäk. I believe Bor Ma'ax intended to say Itsanohk'uh, whose home is on the lake by the same name that adjoins Lake Mensäbäk.

28. Literally 'he made them his wives/partners'. When a couple sleeps together they are considered married.

29. Kisin only has one arrow, so he can only kill one monkey at a time (Bor Ma'ax).

30. Pronounced [santar].

31. Kisin decides which kind of animal the soul will become. If they have committed incest, the souls become Kisin's horses with worms in their genitals. If the soul was a murderer, it may become a chicken or a rooster (depending on the gender of the person). Souls that have committed lesser transgressions are not transformed into animals (Bor Ma'ax).

32. This might also be translated as "that soul works for Kisin all year round."

33. Kisin is angry that Hachäkyum imprisoned him in the underworld, and so he kicks the pillars to collapse the earth and release the underworld jaguars to devour Hachäkyum's mortals.

34. *Laak'* means 'companion of the opposite sex'. A couple need not be married to be considered laak', according to Bor Ma'ax and his wife (pers. comm.).

35. In another version (Bruce, Robles, and Ramos Chao 1971), Kisin's daughter gave

birth to four pairs of moles. Hachäkyum instructs the Mole Trapper to replace the moles that he had killed by taking them back to earth and placing two at each of the four cardinal directions, where they would repopulate the world. Evidently, those moles he had trapped and eaten were the children of Kisin's daughter (which she evidently had before she met the Mole Trapper) (Boremanse 1998a, 90). According to Bruce, Robles, and Ramos Chao (1971, 116), these moles correspond to the ancestors of the first "men of mud" in the *Popol Vuh* that had escaped the cataclysmic flood and went underground to become the Xibalbans 'Lords of the Underworld'. The hero twins, Hunahpu and Xbalanque, later vanquish the Xibalbans to avenge the murder of their father and uncle in the underworld (Bruce, Robles, and Ramos Chao 1971, 102; Tedlock 1985). According to Bruce, Robles, and Ramos Chao (1971), the Mole Trapper's elimination of the moles parallels the twins' defeat of the Xibalbans. The Lacandon story differs from the *Popol Vuh* in that Xquic, the daughter of one of the lords of the underworld, did ascend to the earth and gave birth to the hero twins, Hunahpu and Xbalanque. After they had vanquished the lords of the underworld, they ascended to the sky where they became the sun and the moon (or Venus), respectively. In the Lacandon story Kisin's daughter remained in the underworld; had she escaped with the Mole Trapper, she would have given birth to Kisin's descendants, and humankind would have transcended mortality, since Kisin is loath to kill his kin (Bruce, Robles, and Ramos Chao 1971, 26, 116). See also Boremanse (1998a, 90–91).

36. The narrator was vague about why the Mole Trapper died, but in another version of the story (McGee 1983, 148–49), he died after his (human) wife had discovered his äsäb, the instrument that he used to resurrect the dead. Having uncovered it, the Mole Trapper's wife had defiled it. Thus, the Mole Trapper and all the people that he had resuscitated died. Immortality had come to an end. See also Boremanse (1998a, 90–91).

The World Ends with the Flood

1. For a survey of Mesoamerican flood myths, see Horcasitas (1988).
2. For an astronomical analysis of the creation story and the associated symbolism, see Freidel, Schele, and Parker (1993).
3. The Haawo' were once mortals living in Yaxchilan. Then an epidemic hit and decimated all but one man. He appealed to Hachäkyum to revive his family. After he did so, Hachäkyum put the Haawo' in charge of guarding Hach Bilam, a headless stone statue that sits in Structure 33 at Yaxchilan. The Lacandones claim it portrays Hachäkyum. They say that when Hachäkyum decides to end the world again, the head of the statue will affix itself to the shoulders, the eyes will light up, and the head will turn as the Hach Bilam scans the earth with

his penetrating eyes. The Haawo' were also permitted to visit the gods in their celestial realm and hence were privy to the gods' activities and intentions. They relayed this information to the mortals.

4. *Uch'upi(r)* is a term used for female creatures. Women are called *ch'uprar*.
5. *Terminalia amazonia* (J. F. Gmel.) Exell.

Äkyant'o' Prevents the End of the World

1. Similar versions of this story are found in Boremanse (1986, 105–11) and Bruce (1974, 183–95).
2. An episode in a myth from the southern Lacandones, "Notre Mère et Notre Père" (Boremanse 1986, 277–82), mentions that K'inich Ahau, the southern Lacandon equivalent of Akyant'o', is the one who threatens to end the world.
3. In the beginning the Haawo' were human beings, but at some point they were deified by Hachäkyum for being exceptional people. They deliver critical information about the gods' discussions and activities to only the most devout Lacandones. Antonio says that it has been a very long time since anybody has seen or been visited by the Haawo'. According to Davis's Lacandon consultant, the Haawo' were not gods but a group of Lacandones who knew how to cure illness and were able to speak directly to Hachäkyum for assistance (Davis 1978, 38). They apparently possessed an apothecary and introduced the cotton curing strings that Lacandon women still spin and give to pregnant women and newborns to protect them from illness and death.
4. Hachäkyum had already destroyed the world three times before, and he continued to threaten to end the world.
5. Cause an eclipse.
6. As the Lacandones' emissary, Ak'inchob passes on their offerings to Hachäkyum.
7. These are incensories in which offerings are burned.
8. Square brackets enclose narrator's asides.
9. In other words, "They're all you have."
10. In other words, "The world will start over, will be renewed."
11. Indicating the sun has come up.
12. They stop because the sun has been restored in the sky, thus the ending of the world has been halted.
13. Possibly *ch'erir < ch'eh* [Yuc.] 'extinguish'. Cf. *ch'eehel* 'extinct' (Bricker, Yah, and Dzul de Po'ot 1998).
14. Literally 'cast/fling the head' refers to the offering of the first fruits. Head refers to both the god pot, which resembles a head with a face modeled on the front, and the "top" or first portion of every new crop or product made from it. Before drinking balche', all participants in the ceremony flick drops of the beverage to the gods who are not present while the host flings small amounts of balche' to

the four cardinal directions. The gods are also required to offer the first fruits to their creator, Kak'och.

15. Cf. *ma' tooyi'* [S. Lac.] (Hofling 2014), *ma' to* [Mop.] (Hofling 2011), *ma' toj* [Itz.] (Hofling and Tesucún 1997).

16. Refers to the bark paper strips, painted red with annatto paste; formerly included the blood from the supplicants. These were burned in the braziers. There were other bark paper strips with designs cut or painted on them that were worn by ceremonial participants and then relinquished to the gods present in the ceremony. They were tied around the rims of the anthropomorphic pots simulating, perhaps, the conferral of the royal headdress to the incoming Mayan ruler at the beginning of new era, every fifty-two years.

17. Alternate pronunciation of Akyant'o'.

'Ähah

1. The name 'Ähah resembles the Maya word *ahau*, which was the title of Mayan rulers. It is unclear if there is some latent connection between the two.

2. A version of this story is published in Boremanse (1986, 159–62).

3. Loincloths were a common piece of attire of Maya, Aztec, and Inca men.

4. This alludes to the symbolic association between serpents and fertility (and serpents and rain); in Mesoamerican ceremonial art, the rain gods are portrayed wearing a serpent for a loin cloth (Bruce 1975, 327). The serpent also symbolizes the connection between the physical and spiritual world. The shadows of serpents descending the stairs of Mayan pyramids portray the union of earth and sky, and the mundane and the spiritual realms (Markman and Markman 1989, 31). The shedding of a serpent's skin also symbolizes death and rebirth. This is expressed in the Lacandon belief that the souls of the dead shed their skin before embarking on their journey to the afterlife. Marion (1999, 95) provides a Spanish translation of a similar story she collected from the southern Lacandon community of Lacanha' Chan Sayab. The character is called Oja and collects honey like the 'Ähah. Marion interprets the honey that Oja collects as semen, thus concluding that the story is about fertility.

5. The ha'ha'nahk'uh 'water deities' are assistants of Mensäbäk 'Lord of Rain'. There are six ha'ha'nahk'uh, each one associated with a cardinal direction: *xämän* 'north', *tsetsel xämän* 'northeast', *nohol* 'south', *tsetsel nohol* 'southeast', *(bulha') kil utalk'in* '(inundation from) east', *chik'in* 'west' (Bruce 1968, 127). According to Antonio, they live in a cave near Chichén Itzá. Their main duty is to seed the clouds with soot using the tail feathers of a macaw. The feathers also serve as their fans, which they use to whip up the winds to blow in the clouds.

6. Akna', literally 'our mother', is the name given to all the wives of the gods. It also means 'moon', but it may be a mistake to believe that all goddesses are the moon. This point has never been clarified.

7. *Bucida buceras* and/or *Ulmus mexicana.*

8. Literally, 'he put his hand on the flesh of bodies where we urinate from'.

9. Square brackets enclose narrator's asides.

10. The hanging flesh is the dewlap.

11. *Basiliscus basiliscus* L.

12. This is the narrator's reaction, not that of the character.

13. The consultant glossed *chiiin* as 'silence'. Cf. *chin* ONOM. 'rattle' (Hofling and Tesucún 1997, 206).

14. This fan is also described as the tail feathers of the macaw. According to the Lacandones (Cline 1944), "inside the guacamaya (macaw) tail are dead caribes [a.k.a. Lacandones] who help the Santo ['Saint']. They have rocks which they strike together, and that is the noise of thunder. When the rocks strike together, there are sparks. That is lightning" (Cline 1944, 113).

15. Bor Ma'ax explains that the ha'ha'nahk'uh must fly at edge of the wind because it is too strong to fly through it.

16. There are several different ways this word is represented in the Yucatec Mayan literature: *y-alkab'* [Itz.] (Hofling and Tesucún 1997), *'aalka'* [Yuc.] (Bricker, Yah, and Dzul de Po'ot 1998), *y-akab* [S. Lac.] (Canger 1970), *y-akab/w-akab* [S. Lac.] (Baer and Baer 2018), *'aakab'* [S. Lac.] (Hofling 2014). Therefore, I have written it as it is pronounced.

The Two-Headed Jaguar and the Lord of Fire

1. A similar story by Chan K'in Viejo is published in *El Libro de Chan K'in* (Bruce 1974). In that version Hachäkyum tests K'ak''s courage by releasing the two-headed jaguar. In southern Lacandon mythology this jaguar has a master called Känän Beh K'in 'Guardian of the Sun's Path', who is responsible for not only guarding the sun's path but also feeding the sun when it reaches its zenith (Boremanse 1986, 188).

2. The chemberk'uho' release the two-headed jaguar on unsuspecting travelers in the forest, presumably under the orders of Känän Beh K'in. He can prevent them from doing so if he receives offerings (Boremanse 1986, 188). In this story, however, the chemberk'uho' appear to have lost control over the two-headed jaguar.

3. Bruce (1968, 126) is inferior to the one described here. In Bruce's view K'ak' and his counterpart K'ak' ti' Mensäbäk, Mensäbäk's assistant, parallel the ancient Mayan Nacom warriors whose job was to remove the hearts of captives for sacrifice (see also Coe 1993, 182). On a cosmological level, Bruce equates them with the survivors of the "wooden men" in the *Popol Vuh*, the Quiche' Maya book of council (1975, 236).

4. See Saunders (1998, 26).

5. The *nah ts'ulu'* are mythical jaguars residing in the subterranean and celestial

realms (Bruce 1975, 236). The name is analyzed as either 'great foreigners' or 'house of the foreigners'. *Dzul (/ts'ul/)* is a surname of Mayan origin that goes back to the Dzul royal lineage. The semantic change to 'foreigner' was motivated by ethnic conflicts throughout subsequent epochs of Mayan history (Bricker and Orie 2014, 388). Jaguars are depicted as invaders during crises and world cataclysms in Mesoamerican myths. Mayan warriors conned their captives and often ate their hearts. Lacandones conceive the jaguar as capable of transforming into a human form, who then lures his unsuspecting victims into the forest and eats them. In Lacandon myths of world destruction, the nah ts'ulu' are unleashed and devour the mortals, thereby preserving the association between jaguars and invaders. Today dzul refers to the white descendants of Spanish conquerors and (male) Caucasian foreigners.

6. Several Lacandones provided this translation for *ak'ätik abah*. Cf. *k'at* (2) 'lie athwart, block, cross' [Yuc.] (Bricker, Yah, and Dzul de Po'ot 1998, 149). This translation makes sense if the jaguar has a head on either end of his body. Bruce (1974) translates *ak'ätik abah* as 'stay (there)'.

7. Cf. *b'a'axban* 'stiff with grime' [Yuc.] (Bricker, Yah, and Dzul de Po'ot 1998, 27), *b'aax* [S.Lac] 'stain' (Hofling 2014).

8. Cf. *chak-ya'p'é'en* [Yuc.] 'red (many fruits on tree; many tomatoes)' (Bricker, Yah, and Dzul de Po'ot 1998, 61).

Mensäbäk and the Ancestor He Killed

1. Similar versions of this story are published in Bruce (1974, 68–98) and Boremanse (1986, 64–70). In Bruce's version it is Ak'inchob whom Mensäbäk envies.

2. The cave of Mensäbäk is where the souls of the dead go after they exit the underworld.

3. Mensäbäk has no role to play in the death of mortals. His responsibility is to protect the souls once they reach his realm. Moreover, in this story he seems to have forgotten that the soul must be reunited with the body within four days of death, which would account for his inability to revive the Hachäkyum's assistant.

4. Chan K'in Viejo recounts a true story about a meteor that crashed into the cliff above Lake Mensäbäk (Davis and Standard 1997). Whether this event became melded with the existing myth or inspired it is unclear.

5. See "Uk'aay Box" 'The Gourd Song' (this volume).

6. Honey is the food of the gods. Mortals cannot survive on the gods' food (Bor Ma'ax, pers. comm.).

7. These are Mensäbäk's helpers who seed the clouds with soot to bring on the rain.

8. He is talking to the gods that helped him push the star away. Gods call each other "lord."

9. Hachäkyum had just received offerings from his mortals.

10. A kind of cicada with an exceptionally loud song (Bor Ma'ax). Bruce (1975) lists two kinds: *ähch'anex* 'cicada', which sings during the day, and *ähmaas* 'cricket', which sings at night. *Umaasi ka'an* may be glossed as 'crickets of heaven' and 'its passing (-on) of heaven', exemplifying the Mayan literary style of exploiting similar sounding words for multiple meanings.

Kak'och and His Human Assistant

1. Kak'och, The First Creator, and Hachäkyum, the Lacandones Creator, each have a set of assistants with the same names and perform the same duties (Bruce 1968, 130). The Lacandones have a similar set of helpers and ritual functionaries. The reiteration of structure and function pervades Lacandon religious cosmology.

2. Akin to *psychoducts*, a hollow tube that runs up from the tomb to the floor of the temple above. They were installed as conduits for the souls of Mayan rulers to travel between the underworld, the earth, and the sky. They are also believed to be portals for communication between the rulers and their living descendants during rituals, as is thought to be the case for Pakal the Great in the Temple of Inscriptions (Schele and Mathews 1998, 109, 119, 130).

3. Neither *k'an-* nor *kan-* appears in any Yucatecan language dictionary that I've consulted meaning helper, assistant, aid, subordinate, or other synonyms for the meaning provided by my Lacandon consultant.

4. All the important solar deities have assistants. My Lacandon consultant, Bor Ma'ax, says these assistants are human. While Bruce (1968) equates the gods' assistants with people of rank that existed in the Mayan religio-political hierarchy, it is unclear whether the two assistants in this text belong to this ilk or are yet another class of beings with superhuman strength and abilities who had earned the privilege to serve the gods.

5. *Guatteria anomala* R. E. Fries.

6. Root may be *ti'*. Cf. *ti'ri'* [S. Lac.] 'apart, separated' (Hofling 2014); *ti'ri'ri'* [S. Lac.] 'distinct' (Canger 1970).

Ak'inchob Takes a Human Wife

1. It is unclear what this god's name means. A(k)k'in 'our lord, our sun/priest', is clear. Chob is not so clear. Most scholars follow Bruce (1968) in glossing it as 'squint, squinting'. However, "squint" is *muts'-ich*, in northern and southern Lacandon. The word may mean 'blind'; if so, the spelling is *ch'oop*, cf. *ch'oop* noun 'blind person' (Bricker, Yah, and Dzul dePo'ot 1998, 86), in Yucatec; *ch'oop* 'blind' (Hofling 2014, 474). Yet my Lacandon consultants pronounce the word as [*chob*] or [*chop'*] (final b often sounds like p'). This being the case, then the word means 'corncob'. Cf. *chòob'* noun 'cob', *chak chòob'* 'red corn' (Bricker, Yah, and Dzul de

Po'ot 1998, 71). Given this translation, Ak'inchob can be translated as 'Our Corn-cob Sun Lord'. According to Bruce (1968, 131), Ak'inchob is the God of Maize in the northern Lacandon pantheon. Another one of his names is *ki'chäkchob*, which could be translated as 'good/father red corn'. According to Bruce, *ki'chäkchob* is used exclusively as a ceremonial reference. This name is phoneti-cally similar to *chichacchob*, which Landa describes as the "demon" venerated by the Yucatec Maya.

2. The association between honey and death is unclear. Mensäbäk inadvertently kills Hachäkyum's human assistant by feeding it only honey (see "Mensäbäk yeter Hach Winik Tukinsah" 'Mensäbäk and the Ancestor He Killed', this vol-ume). It could be that as honey is the food of the gods, it is unfit for human con-sumption. Moreover, humans need more than honey to survive.

3. Boremanse (1986, 113–18) provides a similar version but includes a lengthier lead-in. From page 115 onward his version is practically identical to the story presented here.

4. Supplying firewood to a future father-in-law is one of the rituals involved in Lacandon courtship.

5. Cutting firewood is one of the main services a new son-in-law performs for his father-in-law, while cutting wood before marriage is part of the ritual required of a suitor. Bor Ma'ax said that he has yet to cut wood for his father-in-law, even though he has been living with the man's daughter for decades. Because he had not performed this duty, he and his partner are not technically married.

6. Lacandon marriages are uncomplicated events. However, requesting a wife in the northern Lacandon community is lengthy and tiring for the suitor, who must endure several nights of verbal dueling with his prospective father-in-law to demonstrate his worthiness as a husband.

7. She is Ak'inchob's first wife. Perhaps a better gloss is 'other wife', although the word for "other" is *uher*.

8. In polygamous marriages, the elder wife refers to the younger wife as 'little sis-ter', while the younger wife refers to the elder wife as 'older sister'. In many of these marriages the women are biological sisters.

Maya Kimin 'The Mayan Death'

1. Two other versions of the story are found in Bruce (1974) and Boremanse (1986). In the *Book of the Chilam Balam of Chumayel*, Maya Cimil alludes to the yellow fever epidemic that struck Merida in 1648. Molina Solis mentions that this epi-demic began in Guadeloupe, later broke out in Campeche, Mexico, in June of that year, and persisted for two years (Roys [1933] 2008, 226n490).

2. Steven Doerr, "Yellow Fever," MedicineNet.com, http://www.medicinenet.com /yellow_fever/page2.htm, accessed February 2017.

3. This comment is ambiguous: The narrator may mean either that the Lacan-

dones had never experienced sickness before then or that they had never suffered from yellow fever before.

4. < *be'-in, ba'-in* (?).

5. Future generations.

Chäk Xok 'The Sirens'

1. Chan K'in Viejo, describes the chäk xok as water spirits that look like short humans who wear pants, hats, and shoes, and eat people. He said that there is also a fish that is called chäk xok (Davis 1978, 95n22).

2. Other versions of the story are published in Bruce (1976, 141–43), Marion (1999, 365–66), and Boremanse (1986, 232–41).

3. *Eugerres plumieri* Cuvier (Schoenhals 1988, 271). Cf. *chäklau* 'a red fish' (Tozzer [1907] 1978, 54).

4. Square brackets enclose narrator's asides.

5. Men carried small shoulder bags equipped with hunting paraphernalia.

6. *Chemberk'uho'* are a class of terrestrial deities who live in the rocks and in the milpas (Bruce 1975, 143; Davis 1978, 19, 23). These little deities turn into jaguars when they reverse their tunics: the inside is spotted like the coat of a jaguar. They are vengeful little spirits who harm mortals or render their milpas sterile. They also release the dreaded two-headed jaguar under the orders of the Känän Beh K'in 'Guardian of the Sun's Path' (Boremanse 1986, 188).

7. *Puma concolor* L. mountain lion, cougar, puma, panther.

8. This assumes that the method of making fire was still unknown.

The Ancestor, His Son, and the Ceiba Tree

1. Kisin 'Lord of Death' punishes the souls for their bad deeds on earth. He metes out the form and degree of punishment accordingly. For example, for talking back to your parents Kisin burns one's mouth with firebrands.

2. Cf. *b'a'wiir* [S. Lac.] (Hofling 2014).

3. *tz'äp* 'sink in' (Hofling 1997, 635).

4. Sound effect. Cf. *k'oro'och* [S .Lac] 'make a scraping sound' (Hofling 2014).

5. In other words, the arrow stuck in the squirrel.

6. Cf. *t'àayal* [Yuc.] adj. 'dangling, hanging down (strings of mucus)' (Bricker, Yah, and Dzul de Po'ot 1998).

7. The narrator described how the gods treated the boy: bix kuba'axtik a' k'ik' ts'uro', bik uba'axtik a' k'ik'o', bek a' bix la'eh tumentah chem(b)erk'uho' 'Like foreigners playing with a rubber ball, that is how the little gods treated him'.

8. Unclear. Perhaps the god is saying, "I'll tell you about it through your divination." I don't believe the god is divining.

9. Unclear who "they" are. Perhaps they are the chemberk'uho', the walking gods.

Haayok'

1. Cf. *sáan-sáam* [S. Lac.] (Hofling 2014).
2. Cf. *b'a'ale'* [Yuc.] 'but, however' (Bricker, Yah, and Dzul de Po'ot 1998).
3. The narrator makes a low wheezing sound.
4. Jaguars have a variety of vocalizations. In addition to roaring and mewing, they grunt. This is a rough approximation of the sound the consultant provided, but it is not really what the grunt sounds like, which is more nasal and sounds something like a donkey's bray.
5. Bor Ma'ax corrected himself, saying it was *hach pom* that they were tapping. In the old days they used hach pom, which is found growing in Yaha'petha' and Mensäbäk. Today they use the resin of the *tähte'* (*Pinus pseudostrobus, P. oocarpa*), which grows in abundance in Naha'. Antonio said that was the main reason the northern Lacandones chose Naha' as their settlement.
6. To be exact, it is the curassow *Crax rubra* L.
7. Refers to the god pots through which Lacandones communicate to the gods.
8. "They" refers to all the people in the community.

Ko'otir Ka'an 'The Celestial Eagle'

1. The name *ko'otir ka'an* likely derives from Greater K'iche'an *koht* 'bicephalic eagle'. See Kaufman (2003, 608).
2. The *chi' nah* is a small, open-sided hut beside the god house where offerings are prepared by sponsors' wives. Women are prohibited from entering the god house except on special occasions that involve the preparation of certain food offerings and during rites of passage ceremonies.
3. ? Cf. *tulakal* [Itz.] 'all, every' (Hofling and Tesucún 1997).
4. A variety of banana with a red stalk and leaves.
5. The translation of the Lacandon transcription is "how many people it ate," but the narrator explained to me that Ak'inchob threw the wing down to show the people what was eating them and that it was now dead. So, I changed the translation accordingly.

Uyitber 'He at the End of the Road'

1. *Yitber* is reminiscent of the *k'ebatun* in the lore of the southern Lacandones of San Quintín. According to Boremanse (1986, 381), he is a jaguar that transformed himself into the father of two girls so that he could lure them to his cavern. Bruce (1968, 136), however, reports that the San Quintín Lacandones say the character is like "La Llorona" (The Weeping Woman) of Spanish American folklore.
2. Kisin is the name of the Devil, but the word is also used to refer to demons. I am not sure if the narrator is referring to Kisin or a demon here.

3. Sound effect of his walking. Cf. *chik* [Yuc.] 'shake, rattle' (Bricker, Yah, and Dzul de Po'ot 1998), *chik* [S. Lac.] 'shake, vibrate' (Hofling 2014).
4. Unclear form. Cf. *sáan-sáam* [S. Lac.] 'in a little while' (Hofling 2014).
5. Unclear form.

Kak'och and the Yitber

1. See "Uyitber" 'He at the End of the Road', this volume.
2. Mensäbäk 'Lord of Rain' lives in the lagoon near the northern Lacandon settlement of Mensäbäk, about one hour's drive north of Naha'. His brother, Ts'ibanah 'Lord of Graphic Arts', stands at the entrance of Lake Ts'ibanah, the first stop on the souls' journey to the underworld (Bor Ma'ax, pers. comm.). Lake Ts'ibanah is connected to Lake Mensäbäk.
3. A sound effect of him walking.
4. Sound of sucking teeth.
5. *Intasa uba('a)r* is unclear. Shouldn't it be *intaa-s-ik uba('a)r*? A transitive verb 'bring, make come' from the intransitive verb, *tal* 'come'. Cf. *taaks-ik* 'bring it', *taaks-ah* 'brought it' [S.Lac.] (Hofling 2014).
6. *'Oreh* is unclear. It might be an adverbial expression of some kind.
7. *Sabal mexicana* Mart.
8. < *tam* 'deep'.
9. Refers to a demon, not Kisin, the Lord of Death.

Want'ut'k'in

1. It has been proposed that *want'ut'k'in* is a multiword compound, each morpheme referring to a kind of bird: partridge, parrot, and squirrel cuckoo. Rätsch and Ma'ax analyze the name as *wan* 'big coot', *t'ut'* 'parrot', *k'in* 'the prophet' (Rätsch and Ma'ax 1984, 134n1). Although the origin of the name is, as yet, unknown, it may be a reanalysis of Juan Tut K'in, perhaps a historical personage. Tut (T'ut'?) was a lineage of the Xiu named after Tutul Xiu, the head of the lineage and the ruler of the province of Maní in the Yucatán (Sharer 1994, 746). *K'in* means both 'sun' and 'priest', concepts that are associated with divine rulers. As for Juan, many Mayas received Christian names during and after the Conquest.
2. Other versions of this story are published in Boremanse (1986) and Rätsch and Ma'ax (1984).
3. Lacandones collect wild honey by cutting down the hive from trees or removing hives from fallen logs and then scooping out the honey with their hands.
4. Dogs are referred to as jaguars in stories from other Mesoamerican cultures. These "jaguars" may have been the mastiffs brought by the Spanish conquistadors. See Saunders (1998, 35).
5. Unclear what the narrator means, either ceiba tree or great big tree.

6. I think Want'ut'k'in is waiting for the ancestor to ripen in the tree before eating him.

7. Square brackets enclose narrator's asides.

8. Coatimundis move in troops.

9. Recall that the Want'ut'k'in's dogs resemble jaguars. In Lacandon myths, all supernatural dogs are really jaguars.

10. I take this to mean that even though there are many coatimundis to choose from, they are jumping all around, making it impossible for the jaguars to focus on any one of them.

11. The tense/aspect of the Lacandon original is inconsistent, so I have changed it to the present tense in the English translation.

12. *Ts'ah* 'give' is used idiomatically to mean 'give it to someone' or 'clobber'.

13. Note that the instrument Want'ut'k'in plays is now a drum, whereas before it was a guitar. *Pax* usually means 'guitar' in Lacandon. But in Yucatec Maya *pax* means 'drum'. This linguistic interference may be why the instrument is now a drum. I believe this is a mistake on the part of the narrator. In another version of this story (Boremanse 1986), the instrument is a guitar.

14. Ka'anan K'aax 'Lord of the Forest', is another forest ogre.

The Rifle and Kisin

1. A euphemism for going to the toilet in the bush. In the old days there were no bathrooms (Bor Ma'ax, pers. comm.).

2. *Ch'e'extik* is unclear. It could be *ch'e(e)x ti' k-uy-u'yik* 'crouch to listen to something'.

3. Square brackets enclose narrator's asides.

4. Unclear. Either the contest is over and Kisin is the victor, or this part of the story is over.

The Crocodile and the Canoe

1. See *La Pirogue et le Crocodile*, narrated by a southern Lacandon (Boremanse (1986, 396–97). In Boremanse's story, a crocodile tries to buy the oarsman from the canoe to eat him (396).

Ahsaay 'The Leafcutter Ants'

1. See Bierhorst (1990).

The Rabbit and the Puma

1. A French translation of a similar story is available in Boremanse (1986, 254–60).

2. *Boray* is like an ocelot but much smaller (Bor Ma'ax). It may be *Leopardus tigrinus* Schreber, a close relative of the ocelot (*Leopardus pardalis* L.) and the mar-

gay (*Leopardus wiedii* Schinz). Cf. *bo'olay* "the ceremonial title of *K'ak'*, the god of hunting, courage, arrow-making and originally, of war" (Bruce 1976, 56).

3. Holding up the cave (or hill) is a common motif in stories of deception, including a story from the Warao of the Orinoco Delta of Venezuela and Guyana. See Wilbert (1970, 256–68). See also story synopsis 2.5 in Bratcher (1973, 61).

4. I believe that the rabbit is pretending to hold up rather than carry the hill/cave. The word *k'ooch* means to carry on the shoulder or head, whereas *kuch* means 'to carry something'.

The Fox and the Puma

1. *Urocyon cinereoargenteus* Schreber.
2. Sound effect.
3. Cf. *b'e'b'* [S. Lac.] 'cat's claw vine' (Hofling 2014, 83).

Hachäkyum and the Toad

1. This story appears as an episode in a longer story about Tamákasti, a culture hero of the Gulf Nahuat speakers. The story comes from Mecayapan, Veracruz, collected by Howard Law (1957). The focus of this story is the illicit affair between the daughter of a she-devil, Tsitsimilama, and a supernatural bird. See a similar Lacandon story, "Uyählehir Bah" 'The Mole Trapper' (this volume). In this episode Tamákasti entrusts a toad to take a crate containing the ashes of his grandparents (whom he had killed and burned) and throw them across the ocean. But the toad just dropped the crate on the shore. It broke open and freed the mosquitoes, flies, and gnats that were inside.

2. Possible analysis, *bin-yet-k'in* 'go with day'.

The Dog and the Crocodile

1. Lacandones lose many of their dogs to crocodiles.

How the Toucan Got His Red Beak

1. Reference to this this event appears in Boremanse (1986, 33).
2. *Ramphastos sulfuratus*.
3. *Cecropia* spp. The fruit grows in bunches of long, narrow fruit that looks like crumpled trachea. A common name for the fruit is "snake fingers."
4. *Pteroglossus torquatus* is similar to the keel-billed toucan (*Ramphastos sulfuratus*) but without the red beak.
5. *san* < *saam* 'a while ago'. Cf. *sáam* [S. Lac.] 'a while ago' (Hofling 2014).
6. Unclear word. Cf. *hi'm* adj. 'dry' [S. Lac.] (Hofling 2014, 157), *hi'* 'crush, flatten' (157), *hi'* 'rub, smooth, iron' [Yuc.] (Bricker, Yah, and Dzul de Po'ot 1998, 104).

Uk'aay Barum 'The Jaguar Song'

1. Other versions are published in Bruce (1968, 1976), Baer and Baer (1948), and Rätsch and Ma'ax (1984).
2. This movement refers to the way cats move when they are stalking.

Uk'aay Box 'The Gourd Song'

1. Versions of this song are published in Bruce (1974, 1976) and Rätsch and Ma'ax (1984).
2. See also Uk'aayir ti' Box, in Bruce (1976, 107).
3. Davis (1978, 268) mentions that women and children also undergo the forced drinking ritual. This author provides a detailed description of the ceremony and a version sung by Chan K'in Viejo (1978, 267–73). Another version by the same performer is published in Bruce (1974, 292–95; 1976, 107–11). McGee (1983) provides an excellent description of the event and discusses the metaphorical significance of the song with respect to the pan-Mayan association between beehives and honey and women. He includes his version of the song (McGee 1987, 109–10).
4. See also Bruce (1976, 108).
5. *Laak'* is frequently reduced to *läk'*, strengthening the homophony.
6. Unclear. Consultant translated the word *buy* as 'drunk'. May be from *bul* 'sink', 'submerge', *b'uul* 'drown' [Yuc.] (Bricker, Yah, and Dzul de Po'ot 1998, 38) or *buy* 'hard, decompose'.
7. A large, high-walled gourd vessel from which participants drink balche'.
8. The measuring cup refers to the cup used to ladle balche' from the serving bowl, called Bor, into the individual drinking cups.
9. Unclear form. It may be *kuruur umak* 'round caps/covers', *kur'a'an mak* 'seated covers', *kurunak* 'rounded, rounding' derived from either *ku(u)r* (1) 'round' or *kul* (2) 'seat, settle'. The sense of these alternatives is the same. "Growing breasts" is the translation provided me by a Lacandon woman.
10. Another expression. *Wiik'* is either *w-iik'* 'my/your breath' or 'my/your wind/air'.
11. This is the consultant's translation. The root is probably *k'as* 'bad', cf. *kàak'as 'iik'* 'evil wind [that makes people sick]' [Yuc.] (Bricker, Yah, and Dzul de Po'ot 1998, 148). *Kàak'as* appears in compounds to denote a bad situation, e.g., *kàak'as-nak'* lit. bad stomach 'indigestion', *kàak'as-koha'anil* 'incurable disease', *kàak'as-kan* 'poisonous snake' (148). K'as appears in compounds that express a partial situation, e.g., *k'as-k'oha'an* 'half sick', *k'as-kimen* 'half-dead' [Yuc.] (148). Therefore, *k'as-wiik'* could be glossed 'delirious, feeling no pain, three sheets to the wind'.

Uk'aay Käkah 'The Cacao Song'

1. This word is pronounced several ways, e.g., *käkah, käkaw, käkow*.
2. She is twisting the beater back and forth in her hands. The term *häxik* refers to the motion of rolling any long object between the palms, such as a fire drill or twine, or rubbing clay in one's hands, producing a long rope.
3. Also pronounced as *murinu(h)* (Bruce 1975, 195).
4. *Smilax lanceolate*.
5. The god pots have anthropomorphic faces molded onto one side of the pot. The mouth has a large, protruding bottom lip on which food offerings are placed.

Uk'aay Käy 'Fish Song'

1. Versions of this song are published in Bruce (1974, 1976).
2. Bruce (1976, 105) surmises that the fishhook is the leg of a spider.
3. *Le' che'* refers to both the leaves of a type of tree and the gills and scales of the fish (Antonio).
4. *Sohon/sohor* is a type of fish, called *tenwayaca* in the Spanish dialect of the area. Sahar may be the same fish or a pile of leaves (see Bruce 1976, 102n3).
5. *Murut* means the massing of fish (Antonio). Cf. *mùulut* N. 'swarm' [Yuc.] (Bricker, Yah, and Dzul de Po'ot 1998, 190).
6. *Maraach'* is a kind of duck.
7. Presumably a type of fish.
8. According to Säk Ho'or, this is a type of black fish, bigger than a mojarra. They call it *tehuayaca* in Spanish. *Tenguayaca* is a very tasty river mojarra of Tabasco (Schoenhals 1988, 282). Cf. *Eugerres plumieri* 'striped mojarra' (309). Cf. *sohom* (Tozzer [1907] 1978, 54); Bruce (1974, 305; 1975, 219); *tsau* 'large fresh-water mojarras' (Motul., in Roys 1931, 340).
9. A kind of sardine that has a blue back (Antonio).
10. Rains that flood the lagoon (Bor Ma'ax).
11. The narrator explains, "fish travel together in lines."
12. This is a type of eagle or hawk (Antonio).
13. They are flapping their wings on the water's surface (Antonio).
14. This is possibly a small kind of harmless, black spider that makes a web (Säk Ho'or). Koh Paniagua identifies it as an orb spider. It is also the name of a type of yellow bird with a white head that sits at the edge of the lagoon (Bor Ma'ax), undoubtedly a kind of flycatcher. According to Bor, the fish eat their poop.
15. Word not found in Bricker, Yah, and Dzul de Po'ot (1998), Bruce (1975), Canger (1970), or Hofling (1997). It may derive from *pool* N. 'head, leader'. *Ba'* is likely *ba'al* 'thing'.
16. *Krugiodendron ferreum* (Vahl) Urb.
17. *Ficus* spp.

18. Bruce (1976, 104) explains that the dropping fruit of the *kopo'* near the shore of the lagoon attract fish, which "swarm in a state of constant agitation, and will strike at practically anything thrown into the water." The Lacandones take advantage of this and throw in their lines.

19. Bor Ma'ax says this is a common expression that means 'herd, round up'. Cf. *k'aas* N. nc [Yuc.] 'divider [room, land]'; 'column, section'; ap. 'divide, obstruct, block' (Bricker, Yah, and Dzul de Po'ot 1998, 148).

Uk'aay ti' Huuch' 'Song for Grinding'

1. Literally, 'sacred water' <ch'ul=ha'. Cf. *ch'uura'* [S. Lac.] 'sacred' (Hofling 2014), *ch'ul* [Tzotzil], *ch'uhul* [Tzeltal], *ch'ujul* [Ch'ol] 'sacred'. *Atole* is a kind of sweetened corn gruel.

2. In Mayan religious cosmology, when the sun reaches zenith, it is a god. To the ancient Mayas, the sun was the most highly revered deity. They conducted elaborate ceremonies that included offerings to nourish the god and sustain the sun at the same time. Although the northern Lacandones (of Naha') do not regard the sun as a god, I suspect the midday sun still carries the same, albeit latent, significance.

3. Huuch'?

4. An unidentified bird.

5. Bor Ma'ax identified this bird as the thicket (rufescent) tinamou (*Crypturellus cinnamomeus* Lesson). Cf. *nok no:käh, ?U-no:käh-Ir 'codorniz* (quail)' [S. Lac.] (Canger 1970).

6. Antonio identified this bird as the *Sporophila minuta* 'ruddy breasted seedeater'.

7. It could also be the number of plates that increases.

8. This meaning of the text is unclear. The consultant says that it refers to evening the edges of the tamale dough and sticking dough in places where it needs to be evened out: When women pat out tortillas, they work from the center and push the dough outward, and it usually involves pinching out a lump of dough from the center to make the tortilla the same thickness from center to edge. However, Juana Koh explained that when making the tamales, you stick a piece of the leaf of the tamale wrapper on the edge of the tamale dough before wrapping up the tamale. As Davis (1978, 205) explains, this strip is called *uchi' nahwah* 'the mouth of the tamale', which indicates the cure for which the god is being paid. Ceremonial tamales are arranged in stacks of five, the fifth representing the uchi' nahwah, which, as described, will be offered to the gods. The other four will be distributed among the ceremonial participants.

9. Davis explains that the leaf tucked inside the tamale is referred to as "the mouth of the tamale" or "Hachäkyum's bite." This tamale is reserved for offering to the gods. Every fifth tamale in a stack is marked this way (Davis 1978, 205).

10. *Quararibea funebris* (La Llave) Vischer.

11. In other words, "you have to look at the table and make sure it's clean."

Song for Spinning Thread

1. The author follows Davis (1978), by calling the songs sung by women "work songs."

2. The appeal to spiders is clear enough. Far less transparent is the association between bees and spinning, until we consider that bees are embedded in a network of symbolic associations. One primary association is their link with femininity, fertility, and procreation. Fertility, procreation, and productivity are symbolized by the Moon Goddess. The Moon Goddess is both youthful and aged, depending on the phases of the moon that she personifies. The youthful, waxing Moon Goddess is associated with sensual pleasure and fertility. Her aged aspect is associated with weaving and spinning. Bees are associated with spinning and weaving via their association with Hummingbird, who visits the Moon Goddess in the underworld (conceivably the goddess represents the new moon). Hummingbird and the Moon Goddess have an illicit love affair, after which they ascend to the sky to become the sun and the moon (Chinchilla 2010). Parallel episodes are found in Mixe, Chatino, and Aztec narratives (J. Thompson 1970, 370–71). The sexual connotation of the hummingbird is also present in the Lacandon story about the Mole Trapper (this volume). In Classic Mesoamerican art Hummingbird is sometimes portrayed as an insect that resembles a mosquito (Chinchilla 2010, 1). In the Lacandon song the bee, with its stinger, evokes the mosquito, with its proboscis. The singer's appeal to bees could be construed as an invitation to procreate, but apart from their association with fertility, bees also symbolize communal and mutual support and industry in most (all?) cultures.

3. The text is easier to understand for those who know anything about spinning with a drop or supported spindle. For those who do not, see "Spinning Cotton on a Takli Support Spindle" (https://www.youtube.com/watch?v=RUHMT sfhshY) and "What Is Backstrap Loom Weaving?" (https://mayaweavings.com /pages/what-is-backstrap-weaving).

4. Juana Koh is asking the spiders to add their silk to her carded ball of raw cotton while she is spinning, perhaps while she is drafting the lengths of the cotton fiber. Evidently, silk has longer fibers than cotton.

5. *K'än säk k'oho'* may be a variety of *säk k'oho'* (*k'oho'n*) (*Apis mellifera*). This species was introduced from Europe. Bor Ma'ax says that it has a nasty sting. According to Lacandon beekeeper Atanasio, the villagers (Tzeltales) raise them in hives. Apart from Atanasio, no one in Naha' raises bees.

6. Mentioned also is a kind of short, stingless honeybee (Antonio).

7. A small species of stingless, gray honeybee. Its hive is found in fallen logs. The hives yield up to two liters of honey, according to Atanasio.

8. Refers to winding the twisted thread at the bottom of the spindle.

9. *Häräte'* refers to individual weaving sticks and, according to Antonio, the entire loom.

10. Perhaps Juana Koh is describing weaving the weft into the warp.

11. Juana Koh is referring to the small bowl in which the tip of the spindle is supported.

12. Cf. *sakal* [Yuc.] 'length of woven cloth' (Bricker, Yah, and Dzul de Po'ot 1998, 241).

Uk'aay Torok 'The Iguana Song'

1. A version of this song along with a description can be found in Bruce (1976, 71–75).

2. This is the description Antonio and Bor Ma'ax gave. But Bruce (1976, 74nn3–4) glosses it as 'flattened out, crawling, or hugging (a tree limb or the ground)'. Cf. *päk* (2) 'lean, fold' (Hofling 2014), *pak* 'brood, lean over' (Bricker, Yah, and Dzul de Po'ot 1998). Cf. *pak* (1) [S. Lac.] 'sit with head on shoulder' (Hofling 2014). I suspect that the duplication, *pa-pak-*, implies continuous up and down movement of the head from the shoulder.

3. The headbands referred to are called *chäk hu'un* 'red bark cloth', which are worn by ceremonial participants and given as offerings during such ceremonies. The serving urn, called Pak or Bor (Lord of Balche') also wears one of these. The "royal headband" was worn by Mesoamerican rulers and nobility (Stuart 2015). Bark paper headbands were a symbol of royal authority, the presentation of which was an important part of accession ceremonies among the Classic Maya (Baron 2016, 133). God pots and ceremonial participants wear these headbands during special ceremonies—notably during the ceremony dedicated to renewing the god pots, which occurred at the turn of a new year and involved the "killing" of the soot-encrusted censors with new ones. This most important ceremony among the Lacandones started to peter out; the events were delayed for extended periods until the ceremony was completely abandoned in the late twentieth century.

4. Cf. *na'ak'* [Yuc.] 'be laid aside, placed near' < *nak'* 'lean against' (Bricker, Yah, and Dzul de Po'ot 1998); cf. *näk* [S. Lac.] 'lean' (Hofling 2014).

5. Cf. *t'ot'ol nikte'* 'flattened out, hugging the nikte' vine' (Bruce 1976, 73). Cf. *t'äl* 'put in place', *t'aar* 'hang, hung' (Hofling 2014), *t'al* [Yuc.] 'stretch out', *t'ol* 'line up, align', *t'ó'ot'ó'ol* 'striated' (Bricker, Yah, and Dzul de Po'ot 1998).

6. Cf. *-ik* intransitive completive (Bricker, Yah, and Dzul de Po'ot 1998). Appears on positional verbs in Lacandon, e.g., *kurik* < *kul* 'sit', *kaprik* 'mounted' < *kap-l*.

7. *Uyeek'er* < *(e)ek'* 'black' also means 'color', according to Bor Ma'ax (pers. comm.). It is also translated as 'spots', in reference to the markings on a jaguar.

8. *Sukun* is 'elder brother', but *usukun kyum* means 'Sukunkyum, the eldest brother of the deity Hachäkyum'. It could be that the god pot in question belongs to the god Sukunkyum, as each god has its own god pot.

9. I interpret this to mean that the imprint of the iguana's stripes remain on the god pots.

10. The god pots are sometimes referred to as houses of the gods.

Uk'aayir Ma'ax 'Song of the Monkeys'

1. A version of this song, entitled "U K'ayil Ma'ax ti' Nahwah," is published in Bruce (1976, 81–85). Antonio's version (here) differs considerably from Bruce's: it omits mention of the clouds and bark cloth headbands in Bruce's version. But it contains the metaphor that the monkeys' song is the offering. Bruce notes two levels of symbolism in his version: "On the one hand the song alludes to live monkeys climbing through the trees ... on the other hand it alludes to the Song of the Monkeys coming from beyond the clouds, where they have gone as offerings to *Hachäkyum*" (82). I have made a stab at interpreting Antonio's song to the best of my ability: Lacandon songs are rife with allusions created by a play on words, and I cannot say that I have done it justice. See also Bruce (1974, 296).

2. Antonio mentioned that if there is no actual monkey meat to offer, beans will suffice, because they appear as meat to the gods. This is another example of the transformation of an object as it goes from one level of existence to another.

3. Bruce (1976) provides a different interpretation, explained in note 1.

4. Each tamale is composed of five alternating layers of meat or beans and corn dough. Cf. *yariyar* 'one five-layered tamale' (Davis 1978, 25).

5. The consultant explained that this expression meant "stretched out in a line." Cf. *t'aal* [Yuc.] 'line' (Bricker, Yah, and Dzul de Po'ot 1998). Cf. *t'är* 'put in a place', *t'aar* 'hang, hung' (Hofling 2014); *t'äräkb'aar* 'put in place', and *t'aarakb'aar* 'lying suspended in a hammock' [S. Lac.] (Hofling 2014); *t'alakb'al* [Yuc.] 'stretched out, lying unconscious' (Bricker, Yah, and Dzul de Po'ot 1998). In other versions of this song the word *sintebäh* 'stretch out yourselves' is used (Bruce 1974, 297).

Uk'aayir Tok' 'Song of the Flint'

1. Another version, entitled "Chant to the Flint/Canto al Pedernal," can be found in Bruce (1976, 61–70).

2. Half of the stone is the striking surface, called "the head." The flakes are referred to as *ch'ibix bo'oy*, a species of chamaedorea palm, or simply *bo'oy*.

3. Bruce (1976) glosses this word as 'grain in the stone'. Literally, it means 'vein'.

4. He creates beveled edges, or ridges, that he will then knap.
5. Cf. *kòos* [Yuc.] 'a nocturnal hawk?' (Bricker, Yah, and Dzul de Po'ot 1998, 134); *kòs* [S. Lac.]. 'sparrow hawk' (Canger 1970).
6. Possibly refers to the ridges of waves.
7. *Calathea lutea* (Aubl.) Schultes.
8. *Chamaedorea elegans* Mart.
9. *Chamaedorea ernesti-augusti* H. Wendl.
10. The singer mentions shelling corn in hopes of producing as many flakes (Bor Ma'ax).
11. Bor Ma'ax explains this is the sweet spot on the chert.

Song of the Yellow Jacket Wasps

1. There is almost an identical song sung to the *ek'ren xux* 'black-faced wasps'.
2. *Bin* is a euphonic element in this text. In other texts by other performers the word is variously pronounced as [*be*], [*beh*], and [*ber*]. Tozzer ([1907] 1978) also comments on the occurrence of this element in the texts that he collected.
3. *Heliconia* spp.
4. My consultants describe this as a kind of red ant with a nasty bite; like an army ant it destroys things. There is a story about a child who fell into their ant hill and died from the bites (Bor Ma'ax, Säk Ho'or).
5. Säk Ho'or said that by uttering these words he was "dominating" the wasps.
6. Unclear. Bor Ma'ax says this is a kind of tree that smells bad.
7. Unclear.
8. Antonio identified this bird as a trogon with breast bands, i.e., mountain trogon, collared trogon, elegant trogon, and citreoline trogon.
9. *Pharomachrus* spp.
10. The consultant translates this word as *agarro* 'I hold'. This word also shows up in the "Uk'ayir Tok'" 'Song of the Flint' and refers to the way the flint knapper holds the antler punch between the forefinger and the baby finger.
11. Unclear. It could mean the point where the clouds meet the sky.
12. Unclear.

Ahhooch' 'The Hooch"

1. John Longino (pers. comm.)
2. Refers to the hypopygium, a modified ninth abdominal segment on male insects designed to retain the female.
3. *Waach* and *k'i'ix* 'thorn, spine' are used interchangeably to mean 'stinger'.

Ahts'in 'The Manioc'

1. *Aotus lemurinus.*
2. According to Bor Ma'ax, *haayok'* is like *chan barum*, a little (predatory) feline

that is striped and about the size of a large house cat. It only eats fruit, especially the fruit of the *ya'* (*Manilkara, Pouteria, Chrysophyllum*). Nations and Valenzuela (2017, 88) identify haayok' as *Bassariscus sumichrasti* (a.k.a. *cacomistle* < *tlahcomiztli*, a Nahuatl word meaning "half cat" or "half mountain lion" [Merriam-Webster]). It is like the ring-tailed cat, *Bassariscus astutus*, which is smaller than a house cat. It is a solitary, nocturnal, arboreal mammal that is completely dependent on forest habitat.

3. This is the sound of the animals routing out the tubers.

4. Roys identifies "holil-och" as the *Marmosa gaumeri* 'grayish mouse opossum' (Roys 1931, 333). Cf. *joorir-'ooch* 'small weasel' [S. Lac.] (Hofling 2014, 162), *hóoli-'ooch* 'fox-like rodent' [Yuc.] (Bricker, Yah, and Dzul de Po'ot 1998, 109). *Horir ch'o* is likely a synonym, but I have translated it as 'rat'; reference to a "long-eared rat" appears earlier in the text. *Horir* < *hol-* 'to perforate, bore, or prick'.

5. Spotted cavy (*Cuniculus paca*) is a large, white-spotted burrowing rodent. A nuisance to farmers, it is hunted for its meat, adding valuable and delicious protein to the Lacandones' vegetarian diet.

An Offering Chant

1. *Ch'urha'kih* is also the name of the ceremony in which *ch'urha'* is the main offering (Davis 1978). According to Bruce (1975, 170), the suffix *-kih* refers to a balche' ceremony.

2. See Davis (1978) for detailed descriptions of many ceremonies that she attended in the community of Naha'.

3. Ak'inchob, Lord of Maize.

4. Refers to Hachäkyum.

5. Another name for Ak'inchob.

6. ? Cf. *jetz'-yajil* [Itz.] 'relieve pain' (Hofling 1997, 308).

7. Unclear. I think Antonio is referring to other villages that have medicine to relieve the pain. He is telling the gods to send the sickness back to them.

8. Säk Ho'ol explains that the fever is a little man that walks around at night shooting his victims with arrows.

9. Itsanar is the first assistant deity to Hachäkyum, but his functions are imprecise (Bruce 1968, 130).

10. *Ya'ahk'in* is a ceremony held to pay the gods for curing a seriously ill person or aiding in a successful birth of the sponsor's child. Unlike other ceremonies with the same purpose, this ceremony in more complex and involves copious offerings (Davis 1978, 274–80).

11. Äkna' may refer to Äkna'il Hachäkyum 'Our wife of Hachäkyum' and her daughter. Both are associated with protection.

12. Akyant'o' is the god who made all human races except for the Lacandones, their Mayan neighbors, and Mestizos.

13. Refers to other Mayan groups in villages surrounding Naha'.
14. Refers to the offerings Antonio is making.
15. Antonio is referring to the dearth of offerings he has. The ya'ahk'in ceremony calls for a large variety of offerings, which Antonio did not have on hand.
16. Balche' is believed to purge oneself physically and spiritually.

The Secret of the Balche'

1. The word *balche'* is pronounced several ways. In Lacandon publications is it is transcribed as *baache'*, *bache'*, *ba'che'*, although its underlying form is written *balche'* or *ba'alche'*, meaning 'thing of the tree'. I have elected to transcribe the word as *ba'che'* and the underlying form as *balche'*.
2. Other versions are provided in Tozzer ([1907] 1978, 177), Davis (1978, 90–100), and Rätsch and Ma'ax (1984, 270–82). Rätsch notes that a Maya in Campeche said that "they" also have a balche' song (*u k'àyil bà'lché*), which, like Antonio's version, invokes venomous creatures to help fermentation. Unfortunately, Rätsch does not supply the Campeche version. He refers to the Lacandon host of the balche' ceremony as *h-mèn*, the title for shaman among the Maya of the Yucatan. However, this title does not exist in Lacandon culture.
3. See Cook (2016, 112).
4. Tozzer transcribes and translates this phrase as *samea hule* 'the wood of my balche' pass over my hands' (like a sleeve) (Tozzer [1907] 1978, 177). It is unclear what *samea* is. In the chant presented here the phrase sounds like [*sa(k)-hur-e'en*]. The primary meaning of *hur* is 'thrust, plunge', but its extended meanings are 'focus', 'light', or 'focus light', as in 'flashlight', in Yucatec Maya (Bricker, Yah, and Dzul de Po'ot 1998, 115). The phrase could also be /*säk hole'en*/ 'flam(ing) white', since /o/ is frequently pronounced [u]. Cf. *ya'ax=jol-e'en* [Itz.] 'blue/green (flames of fire)' (Hofling 2000, 174). *E'en* (or -*e'*) is a suffix appended to color terms. See Cook (2004).
5. Antonio may also be assuming the role of Bor, the Lacandon deity responsible for making balche' for the gods (see note 7).
6. Bor is both the name of the balche' urn and the lord who makes the balche' for the gods. Another name for the balche' urn is *pak* 'large clay vessel'.
7. *Etser* is a small, shallow gourd cup that the supplicant uses to scoop out a small portion of balche'. He holds it in his hand while he chants. After he is finished, he pours the contents back into the canoe, mixing the power-infused solution into the rest of the balche'. The word may also be *eets'ar*, as the glottal stop is difficult to detect in this chant. *Eets'ar* means 'reflection' from the root, *ets'* 'echo'. The idea conveyed by this word in the context of the chant is to clarify the solution (Antonio pers. comm.). Both translations were provided by my Lacandon consultants. The first translation was chosen to create semantic parallelism with *inwahboren*.

8. The material in the parentheses is inserted by the author. Although grammatically correct without the added material it sounds awkward in English translation. Furthermore, the performer habitually clips the suffixes and prefixes from the words.

9. The *chäk xok* comprise male and female sirens, who snatch humans in lakes and rivers and then carry them off to the bottom where they are held captive as wives or husbands. They are also called *miim 'aak* 'grandchildren of the turtle' (Bruce 1975, 246).

10. The consultant sometimes translated this word as *revocarse* 'roll about' and sometimes as *sumergirse* 'submerge'. I have also translated it as 'roil', to refer to the churning action of the balche'. When referring to the action of specific aquatic beings performing the action, I have translated the word as 'move from side to side'. Cf. *b'urk'äráankär* [S. Lac.] 'move from side to side' (Hofling 2014, 91).

11. It is agitating the balche' in the canoe.

12. Likely this is the name of a kind of turtle, possibly based on the root *t'in* 'stretch'. The second morpheme of the word is unclear.

13. Unclear form. Could be *maay* 'hoof'-*ok* 'foot'.

14. My Lacandon consultants described this as a type of black fish that is larger than a mojarra. Cf. *sohom* (Tozzer [1907] 1978, 54) (Bruce (1975, 305). Cf. *tsau* 'large fresh-water mojarras' (Roys 1931, 340).

15. Identified as *Dermatemys mawii* by Baer and Merrifield (1971). My consultants identified three species: (1) *Dermatemys mawii* 'Central American river turtle', (2) *Kinosternon leucostomum* 'white-cheeked mud turtle', and (3) *Kinosternon scorpioides* 'red-cheeked mud turtle'.

16. Antonio identified this species as *Penelopina nigra* and *P. purpurascens*.

17. *Pak* is a large clay pot into which Lacandones transfer balche' from the canoe and from which they fill the gourd drinking cups. It is also referred to as *Bor*. Cf. *b'oor* [Itz.] 'wooden tub' (Hofling 1997, 186).

18. These are all names for the different sizes of gourd cups used for drinking and measuring the balche'.

19. The stern of the canoe. The "nose" is the bow.

20. The balche' canoe is covered with palm leaves, which are tied down with vines. These vines are what Antonio is referring to.

21. My consultants applied the name to numerous species, including a variety of tree frogs. The word is glossed as 'toad' in Hofling (1997) and Canger (1970). The significance of the frog etched on the side of the balche' urn appears to harken back to ancient times, when balche' was used as an intoxicant to transform the shamans into their alter egos (Rätsch 2005, 726). Figures 26a and 26b in the Codex Tro-Cortesianus depict God F with the hands of a tree toad or tree frog. According to Rätsch, "the [poisonous] secretions of such tree-dwelling amphibians were likely added to the balche' drink." (726).

'Äxp'äri' 'The Solstice'

1. Analyzed as *äh-x-p'äli'* (Bruce 1975, 127). Derivation unclear. Äh MASC.-X-INSTR.?-p'äl 'open, shell beans', hence 'the bean sheller'??

2. See Marion (1999, 341–44) for a detailed description of the solar year from a Lacandon perspective.

3. Pronounced [*ahkähtich'k'ä'y*]. Possible suffix is the possessive /-ir/. The translation has greater depth than 'sun'. Antonio described it as "ne saasir uk'ak" 'a very bright/clear fire'. Cf. *tich'k'ab't(ik)* [Yuc.] 'illuminate, light [with candle or flashlight]' (Bricker 1998, 275). Stem is *ti(i)ch'k'ab'-ncpd [v+n]* 'illumination, light', with the added sense of rays of sunlight.

4. "*Nah ya'axk'in* is the middle of the year, when there is no rain, and the old leaves drop and new leaves come out" (Bor Ma'ax). The literal translation of *ya'axk'in* is 'main green-time'. According to Chan K'in Viejo, ya'axk'in is a time when it just rains and rains (in Bruce 1975, 252). *K'in* 'time' also means 'sun', 'day', 'prophesy', and 'priest'.

5. Sardines and calabash seeds are associated in Lacandon dream interpretation, for to dream of sardines foretells seeing gourd seeds (Bruce 1975, 216).

6. Bor Ma'ax translated this as *llega en el medio año* 'it arrives in the middle of the year.'

7. *Cucurbita argyrosperma* is a relatively inedible squash that is mainly cultivated for its protein-rich seeds.

Lu'um Kab 'The Rainbow Gods'

1. Cline (1944) and Marion (1999) equate the lu'um kab with the *ha'ha'nah k'uh*, the rain gods of northern Lacandon mythology. The northern Lacandones in the community of Mensäbäk call the rainbow deity Ah Xuce (Baer and Baer 1952, 238). In ancient Maya cosmology the moon goddess, IxChel, is associated with the rainbow.

2. I think the narrator is saying that the gods, who once lived on earth, "died" and then ascended to their celestial realm.

3. Although the lu'um kab are relatively insignificant, they can render the milpa impotent if they are offended (Bruce (1968, 136).

4. The rainbow is the road of the lu'um kab, who create it ahead of them in a manner like spraying gasoline and lighting a match (Bor Ma'ax). Other Lacandones say that the colors of the rainbow are caused by the dye running from the colored stripes on the tunics of the lu'um kab. Cline's Lacandon consultant says, "Sometimes after the rain the tail of the macaw stays a little while in the sky" (Cline 1944, 113). See also Marion (1999, 345), who says, "Sometimes after a storm, they leave in the sky the long tail of the macaw with its beautiful plumage and thus produce a rainbow" (author's translation).

Säkber Akyum 'Our Lord's White Road'

1. The Milky Way is also conceived of as the path souls take on their way to the afterlife. But according to the northern Lacandones, the souls follow the path of the sun in the underworld, where they arrive at the threshold of the house of Sukunkyum 'Lord of the Underworld', who then directs them to a "short and narrow path" that leads to their final destination.
2. Chichén Itzá is the name of a classic Maya city in northeastern Yucatán. It means 'the mouth of the well of the Itza'. The city rose to prominence toward the end of AD 600, expanding its power between AD 900 and 1050.
3. According to Antonio and Bor Ma'ax, the ha'ha'nahk'uh live in a cave somewhere in or near Chichén Itzá. This cave may be Balancanché, inside of which are a small lake and a sanctuary consisting of the "Altar of the Jaguar" and the "Altar of Pristine Waters." The cave was commemorated to Chaac 'God of Rain' (see "Balankanche," Wikipedia, https://en.wikipedia.org/wiki/Balankanche).

Appendix 1

1. In addition to places of origin, the Maya (surnames) were based on their positions and abilities or names of flora, fauna, or astral bodies. For example: *Dzib* (*Ts'ib*) is attributed to scribes; *Chel* is the Mayan name for the chachalaca bird (*Ortalis* spp.); *Cocom* also refers to a climbing plant with yellow flowers; *Itza'* can be translated literally as 'water witch' or 'enchanted waters' (Schele and Mathews 1998, 63); and *Pech* means 'tick' (Jorge Ivan Canul Ek, "History of Mayan Last Names," http://www.yolisto.com/topic/5514-history-of-mayan-last-names/).
2. For more on Ah Me'ex Cuc, see Roys ([1933] 2008, 28).
3. Probably the lovely cotinga (*Cotinga amabilis*), a blue "perching bird" found in the tropical forests of Central and South America. Ya'ax, in Yucatec Maya.
4. *Yaxuna* (< *yaxum nah* 'house of the yaxum') is an archaeological site in the municipality of Yaxcabá 'place of green earth', located northeast of the city of Mérida. Yaxuna is also the alternate name for Cetelac, a town just south of Chichén Itzá (see map in Roys [(1933) 2008, 180, 190n111]; Chase and Rice [2014, 70]).

Appendix 2

1. Their daughter is called Ertub in Tozzer ([1907] 1978, 94).
2. The maintenance of physical and spiritual health of the community is the purview of Lacandon men.
3. *Cit* 'sire' is mentioned in the *Ritual of the Bacabs* (Roys 1965, 58), a book of medical incantations from the Yucatan peninsula. But as Roys points out, "the word has survived only in the terms *citbil* 'God the Father' and *ixcit* 'paternal aunt'" (58n123).

4. See Hofling (1997, 2011, 2014) and Bricker, Yah, and Dzul de Po'ot (1998).
5. Spelled *k'äb'iraan* 'god of ancestors' in Hofling (2014, 196).
6. Bruce (1968, 125) only glosses the last syllable, *tho*, as 'of the door', leaving the rest of the name untranslated.
7. This analysis reopens the discussion about the meaning of his name and presents an opportunity for further research on Lacandon mythology and ideology.
8. In addition to Jones (1998), De Vos ([1980] 2015) and Hellmuth (1971) provide comprehensive lists of Mayan patronyms from the registries of colonial missions and government documents.
9. The southern Lacandon pronunciation of Äkyum. Äkyum is another name for Hachäkyum in the northern Lacandon pantheon.
10. Cf. *yùum b'ìil* 'holy father' [Yuc.] (Bricker, Yah, and Dzul de Po'ot 1998, 319).
11. Itsanohk'uh is said to live at Lake Petha'. Lake Petha' (a.k.a. Pelja) is another name for Lake Mensäbäk. Mensäbäk is also referred to as *yaha petha'* 'Great Lake', as it is the largest of the lakes in this lacustrine region (Palka 2014, 20–21).
12. The Ch'ol Maya word *ch'ujlel (ch'ulel)* 'soul' is cognate with *k'urer* (Josserand and Hopkins [1996] 2001, 28).
13. Tozzer ([1907] 1978, 157) mentions Ah Kuxtal 'God of Birth' but does not specify if this is a Lacandon or a Yucatec Maya deity.
14. Also spelled *ha'ha'nahwiniko'* < *ha'-ha'* 'water-water' =*nah* 'house' =*winik-o'* 'people'.
15. See also Bruce, Robles, and Ramos Chao (1971).
16. There were four Itzam Na (or Itzam Na Chak) stationed at the four cardinal directions. Each is named after the color associated with the direction. For example, Itzam Na K'an Chac (/itsam na k'an chak/) is the rain god of the south, named after the directional color yellow. South is associated with the underworld. Yellow is associated with pallor, illness, and decay. The fruit of the nance tree (*Byrsonima crassifolia*) is a soft yellow cherry that emits a rank odor reminiscent of cheese and is associated with underworld deities in the creation stories throughout the Maya area (J. Thompson (1970, 212). West is associated with the color black, represents death, and is the direction in which the souls of the dead go to enter the underworld. East is associated with the color red and represents (re)birth. North is associated with the color white, representing the highest point of the sun in the sky (midday) 90° above the horizon, and the highest point along the zenith passage of the sun. At Chichén Itzá this event occurs on May 26 and July 20. These two zenith events have a key role in the development of the Tzolk'in calendar as it relates to the movements of the zenith sun and the growing cycle of corn, the nine cycles of the moon, and the gestational period of humans (Smithsonian 2018). The Dresden and Madrid codices (ancient Mayan screen-fold books) describe a burner ritual conducted to ensure

abundant rains. Priests are personified as the four Chaacs, each playing a different role: one takes the fire, one begins the fire, one fans the fire, and one extin-
guishes the fire. Hearts of sacrificial animals were cast into the fire, and then all
four Chaacs poured jugs of water on it (Maestri 2017). The sequence mirrors the
slash-and-burn practices of rural Mayan farmers. The Lacandones do not conduct this burner ritual. However, the sequence is alluded to in a narrative about
the *k'urer*, inspectors of the milpas who report to Hachäkyum when to send rain
and when to hold off on rain.

17. Bruce analyzes the last morpheme as *ch'ak* and interprets the full name as 'lord
of the lying downs', with reference to the dead (Bruce 1968, 124–25).

18. Spelled *Ts'ibatnah* in Bruce (1968). Lacandon consultant Bor Ma'ax said that the
word was pronounced without the /t/, hence [*ts'ibanah*]. Perhaps the /t/ registered by Bruce was simply his consultant's idiomatic pronunciation, or the consultant said *ts'iba'an ti' nah* 'painted on house' rapidly.

19. Could be < *yi'h* 'stamen, corn tassel'.

REFERENCES

Academia de Lenguas Mayas de Guatemala (ALMG). 2004. *K'iche' Choltzij, Vocabulario K'iche': K'iche'-Kaxla'n Tzij, Kaxla'n Tzij-K'iche'*. Guatemala City: Academia de Lenguas Mayas de Guatemala.

Amram, David, W. Jr. 1937. "Eastern Chiapas." *Geographical Review* 27: 19–36.

———. 1948. "Eastern Chiapas Revisited." *Geographical Review* 38: 120–26.

Andrade, Manuel J. 1955. *A Grammar of Modern Yucatec*. Microfilm Collection of Manuscripts on Middle American Cultural Anthropology Series 7, no. 41. University of Chicago Library.

Ara, Domingo de. [1548] 1986. *Vocabulario de Lengua Tzeldal según el orden de Copanabastla*. Estudio de la Cultura Maya, no. 4. Mexico DF: Instituto de Investigaciones Filológicas, Centro de Estudios Mayas, Universidad Nacional Autónoma de México.

Aveni, Anthony F. 2001. *Skywatchers*. Austin: University of Texas Press.

———. 2006. *Uncommon Sense: Understanding Nature's Truths across Time and Culture*. Boulder: University of Colorado Press.

———. 2012. "Beginnings and Endings: Prophecies and Time of the Maya and the Milky Way, Powhatans and the Giant Hare." *CW Journal*, Autumn. http://www.history.org/Foundation/journal/autumn12/beginnings.cfm. Accessed March 2018.

Baer, Mary. 1970. "The Rabbit and Mountain Lion: A Lacandon Myth." *Tlalocan* 6: 268–75.

Baer, Phillip. N.d. "Lacandon Creation Stories." Bartholomew Collection of Unpublished Materials. SIL International–Mexico Branch. http://www.sil.org/resources/language-culture-archives. Accessed October 2018.

Baer, Phillip, and Mary Baer. 1948. "The Lacandon Song of the Jaguar." *Tlalocan* 2: 376.

———. 1952. *Materials on Lacandon Culture of the Pethá (Pelhá) Region*. Microfilm Collection of Manuscripts on Middle American Cultural Anthropology, no. 34. University of Chicago Library.

———. 1957. *Legends of the Lacandones*. Bartholomew Collection of Unpublished Materials. SIL International–Mexico Branch. http://www.sil.org/resources/language-culture-archives. Accessed October 2018.

———. 2018. *Diccionario Maya Lacandón*. Serie de vocabularios y diccionarios indígenas "Mariano Silva y Aceves," no. 51. Mexico City: Instituto Lingüístico de Verano, A.C. https://www.sil.org/resources/archives/75363. Accessed November 2018.

Baer, Phillip, and William R. Merrifield. 1971. *Two Studies on the Lacandones of Mexico.* Norman: Summer Institute of Linguistics, University of Oklahoma.

Barnhart, Edwin L. 2005. *The First Twenty-Three Pages of the Dresden Codex: The Divination Pages.* https://www.mayaexploration.org/pdf/DresdenCodex1-23.pdf. Accessed March 2018.

Baron, Joanne. 2016. *Patron Gods and Patron Lords: The Semiotics of Classic Maya Community Cults.* Boulder: University Press of Colorado.

Barrera Vásquez, Alfredo, and Silvia Rendón. 1948. *El Libro de los Libros de Chilam Balam.* Mexico: Fondo de Cultura Económico.

Bassie, Karen. 2002. *Maya Creator Gods.* Mesoweb. http://www.mesoweb.com/features/bassie/CreatorGods/CreatorGods.pdf.

Bassie-Sweet, Karen. 2008. *Maya Sacred Geography and the Creator Deities.* Civilization of the American Indian Series, no. 257. Norman: University of Oklahoma Press.

Bauman, Richard. 1986. *Story, Performance and Event: Contextual Studies of Oral Narrative.* Cambridge: Cambridge University Press.

———. 1991. "A Genre in Folklore." In *Folklore, Cultural Performances, and Popular Entertainments: A Communications-Centered Handbook,* edited by Richard Bauman. Oxford: Oxford University Press.

Benson, Elizabeth P. N.d. "The Vulture: The Sky and the Earth." http://www.mesoweb.com/pari/publications/RT10/Vulture.pdf.

Bierhorst, John. 1986. *"The Monkey's Haircut" and Other Stories Told by the Maya.* New York: William Morrow.

———. 1990. *The Mythology of Mexico and Central America.* New York: William Morrow.

———. 1998. *The Deetkatoo: Native American Stories about Little People.* New York: William Morrow.

Blom, Gertrude Duby, and Franz Blom. 1969. "The Lacandon." In *Handbook of Middle American Indians,* vols. 7 and 8, edited by E. Z. Vogt, 276–97. Austin: University of Texas Press.

Boremanse, Didier. 1981a. "A Comparative Study of Two Maya Kinship Systems." *Sociologus* 31 (1):1–37.

———. 1981b. "A Southern Lacandon Maya Account of the Moon Eclipse." *Latin American Indian Literatures* 5 (1): 1–6.

———. 1982a. "A Comparative Study in Lacandon Maya Mythology." *Journal de la Société des Américanistes* 68: 71–98.

———. 1982b. "Tomorrow: *The Day of the Jaguar.*" *Latin American Indian Literatures* 6 (1): 1–8.

———. 1986. *Cuentos y Mitología de los Lacandones: Tradición Oral Maya.* Guatemala: Academia de Geografia e Historia de Guatemala.

———. 1989. "Ortogénesis en la Literature Maya Lacandon." *Mesoamérica* 17 (June): 61–104.

———. 1998a. *Hach Winik: The Lacandon Maya of Chiapas, Southern Mexico.* Institute for Mesoamerican Studies, monograph 11. Albany: State University of New York at Albany.

———. 1998b. "Representaciones Metafóricas de los Antiguos Mayas en Mitos y Ritos Religiosos Lacandones." *Journal de la Société des Américanistes* 84 (1): 201–9.

Brasseur de Bourbourg, Charles Étienne, ed. 1861. "Popol Vuh: Le Livre Sacré et les Mythes de L'antiquité Américaine, avec les Livres Héroïques et Historiques des Quichés." In *Collection de documents dans les langues indigènes, pour servir à l'étude de l'histoire et de la philologie de l'Amérique ancienne*, vol. 1, edited by A. Bertrand.

Bratcher, James T. 1973. *Analytical Index to Publications of the Texas Folklore Society, Volumes 1–36.* Publication of the Texas Folklore Society. Dallas: Southern Methodist University Press. texashistory.unt.edu/ark:/67531/metadc77207/. Accessed October 31, 2018.

Breedlove, Dennis. E. 1981. *Flora of Chiapas.* Vol. 1: *Introduction to the Flora of Chiapas.* San Francisco: California Academy of Sciences.

Bricker, Victoria. R. 1981. *The Indian Christ, the Indian King: The Historical Substrate of Maya Myth and Ritual.* Austin: University of Texas Press.

———. 2007. "Literary Continuities across the Transformation from Maya Hieroglyphic to Alphabetic Writing." *Proceedings of the American Philosophical Society* 151 (1): 27–42. https://www.jstor.org/stable/4599042.

———. 2014. *The Indian Christ, the Indian King: The Historical Substrate of Maya Myth and Ritual.* Austin: University of Texas Press. Kindle.

Bricker, Victoria R., and Olanike O. Orie. 2014. "Schwa in the Modern Yucatecan Languages and Orthographic Evidence of Its Presence in Colonial Yucatecan Maya, Colonial Chontal, and Precolumbian Maya Hieroglyphic Texts." *International Journal of American Linguistics* 80 (2): 175–207.

Bricker, Victoria R., Eleuterio Po'ot Yah, and Ofelia Dzul de Po'ot. 1998. *A Dictionary of the Maya Language as Spoken in Hocabá, Yucatán.* Salt Lake City: University of Utah Press.

Brown, Marley. 2019. "The Maya Animal Kingdom." *Archaeology*, January/February, 46–47.

Bruce S., Roberto D. 1967. "Jerarquía Maya Entre los Dioses Lacandones." *Anales del Instituto Nacional de Antropología e Historia* 20: 93–108.

———. 1968. *Gramática del Lacandón.* Departamento de Investigaciones Antropológicas, no. 21. Mexico City: Instituto Nacional de Antropología e Historia.

———. 1974. *El Libro de Chan K'in.* Colección Científica, no. 21. Mexico City: Instituto Nacional de Antropología e Historia.

———. 1975. *Lacandon Dream Symbolism.* Vol. 2: *Dictionary Index and Classifications of Dream Symbols.* Mexico City: Ediciones Euroamericanas Klaus Thiele.

————. 1976. *Textos y Dibujos Lacandones de Naja*. Colección Científica (Lingüística), no. 45. Mexico City: Instituto Nacional de Antropología e Historia.

Bruce S., Roberto D., Carlos Robles U., and Enriqueta Ramos Chao. 1971. *Los Lacandones 2—Cosmovision Maya*. Departamento de Investigaciones Antropológicas, no. 26. Mexico City: Instituto Nacional de Antropología e Historia.

Campbell, Lyle. 1985. "The Pipil Language of El Salvador." *Mouton Grammar Library*, no. 1. Berlin: Mouton.

————. 2017. "Mayan History and Comparison." In *The Mayan Languages*, edited by Judith Aissen, Nora C. England, and Roberto Zavala Maldonado, 1–20. Abingdon, UK: Routledge. https://www.researchgate.net/publication/266138323 _Mayan_history_and_comparison. Accessed April 2018.

Canger, Una. 1970. "Vocabulary of San Quintín." Unpublished MS.

————. 1988. "Subgrupos de los Dialectos Nahuas." In *Smoke and Mist: Mesoamerican Studies in Memory of Thelma D. Sullivan*, edited by J. Kathryn Josserand and Karen Dakin, 473–98. Oxford: BAR International Series 402, pt. 2.

Chase, Arlen F., and Prudence M. Rice, eds. 2014. *The Lowland Maya Postclassic*. Austin: University of Texas Press.

Chávez-Gómez, José Manuel A. 2011. "Waterways, Legal Ways, and Ethnic Interactions: The Ríos District of Tabasco during the Seventeenth and Eighteenth Centuries." In *Negotiation within Domination: New Spain's Indian Pueblos Confront the Spanish State*, edited by Ethelia Ruiz Medrano and Susan Kellog. Boulder: University Press of Colorado.

Chinchilla, Oswaldo. 2010. "Of Birds and Insects: The Hummingbird Myth in Ancient Mesoamerica." *Ancient Mesoamerica* 21: 45–61. https://doi.org/10.1017 /S0956536110000155.

Christenson, Allen J., ed. 2003. *Popol Vuh: Literal Poetic Version: Translation and Transcription*. Norman: University of Oklahoma Press.

————. 2005. "Tulan and the Other Side of the Sea: Unraveling a Metaphorical Concept from Colonial Guatemalan Highland Sources." Mesoweb. www.meso web.com/articles/tulan/Tulan.pdf.

————, ed. 2007. *Popol Vuh: The Sacred Book of the Maya*. Vol. 1. Norman: University of Oklahoma Press.

Cline, Howard. 1944. "Lore and Deities of the Lacandon Indians, Chiapas, Mexico." *Journal of American Folklore* 57 (224): 107–15.

Coe, Michael D. 1992. *Breaking the Maya Code*. London: Thames and Hudson.

————. 1993. *The Maya*. 5th ed. London: Thames and Hudson, 1993.

Coe, Sophie D. 1994. *America's First Cuisines*. Austin: University of Texas Press.

Cogolludo, Diego López. 1688. *Historia de Yucathan: Compuesta*. Madrid: J. Van Garcia Infanzon.

Cook, Suzanne. 2004. "Lacandon Colour Terms." *Santa Barbara Papers in Linguistics* 15: 3–8.

————. 2016. *The Forest of the Lacandon Maya: An Ethnobotanical Guide*. New York: Springer Science and Business Media.

Craine, Eugene R., and Reginald C. Reindorp. 1979. *The Codex Pérez and the Book of Chilam Balam of Maní*. Norman: University of Oklahoma Press.

Cucina, Andrea, Vera Tiesler, and Joel Palka. 2015. "The Identity and Worship of Human Remains in Rockshelter Shrines among the Northern Lacandons of Mensabäk." *Estudios de Cultura Maya* 45 (45): 141–69. https://doi.org/10.1016/S0185-2574(15)30005-8. Accessed March 2018.

Dähnhardt, Oskar, ed. 1907–1912. *Natursagen: Eine Sammlung naturdeutender Sagen, Marchen, Fabeln und Legenden*. 2 vols. Leipzig: B. G. Teubner.

Davis, Virginia Dale. 1978. "Ritual of the Northern Lacandon Maya." PhD. diss., Tulane University.

Davis, Virginia Dale, and Charles Standard. 1997. "Celestial Phenomena in Lacandon Maya Song and Lore." In *Latin American Indian Literatures: Messages and Meanings*, edited by Mary H. Preuss, 47–51. Lancaster CA: Labyrinthos.

Devitt, Amy J. 2004. "A Theory of Genre." In *Writing Genres*, 1–32. Carbondale: Southern Illinois University Press.

De Vos, Jan. [1980] 2015. *La Paz de Dios y del Rey: La conquista de la Selva Lacandona, 1525–1821*. Mexico City: Fondo de Cultura Económica. Kindle.

————. 1988. *Oro Verde: La Conquista de la Selva Lacandona por los Madereros Tabasqueños, 1822–1949*. Mexico City: Instituto de Cultura de Tabasco.

Doerr, Steven. N.d. "Yellow Fever." https://www.medicinenet.com/yellow_fever/article.htm. Accessed February 2017.

Dorson, Richard M., ed. 1982. *Folklore and Folklife: An Introduction*. Chicago: University of Chicago Press.

Drew, David. 1999. *The Lost Chronicles of the Maya Kings*. London: Weidenfeld & Nicolson.

Edmonson, Munro. S., ed. 1971. *The Book of Counsel: The Popol Vuh of the Quiche Maya of Guatemala*. New Orleans: Middle American Research Institute, Tulane University.

————. 1985. "Quiche Literature." In *Supplement to the Handbook of Middle American Indians*, vol. 3: *Literatures*, edited by Victoria R. Bricker, 105–32. Austin: University of Texas Press.

Farriss, Nancy M. 1987. "Remembering the Future, Anticipating the Past: History, Time, and Cosmology among the Maya of Yucatan." *Comparative Studies in Society and History* 29 (3): 566–93. http://www.jstor.org/stable/179039. Accessed September 2017.

Feldman, Lawrence H. 2000. *Lost Shores, Forgotten Peoples: Spanish Explorations of the South East Mayan Lowlands*. Durham NC: Duke University Press.

Fernández, Adela. 1992. *Dioses Prehispánicos de México*. Mexico City: Panorama Editorial.

Foster, Lynn V. 2005. *Handbook to Life in the Ancient Maya World*. Oxford: Oxford University Press.

Freidel, David, Linda Schele, and Joy Parker. 1993. *Maya Cosmos: Three Thousand Years on the Shaman's Path*. Austin: University of Texas Press.

Gillespie, Susan D. 2000. "Rethinking Ancient Maya Social Organization: Replacing 'Lineage' with 'House'." *American Anthropologist* 102 (3): 467–84.

Goetz, Delia, and Sylvanus Griswold Morley, eds. 1954. *Popol Vuh: The Book of the People*. Los Angeles: Plantin Press.

Gossen, Gary, H., trans. 1979. *Los Chamulas en el mundo del sol: Tiempo y espacio en una tradicion oral Maya*. Series: Colección INI, no. 58. Mexico City: Instituto Nacional Indigenista.

———. 1984. *Chamulas in the World of the Sun: Time and Space in a Maya Oral Tradition*. Prospect Heights IL: Waveland Press. First published in 1974 by Harvard University Press.

Grofe, Michael J. 2016. "Eternity in an Hour: The Astronomical Symbolism of the Era as the Maya Agricultural Year." In *Astrology in Time and Place: Cross-Cultural Questions in the History of Astrology*, edited by Nicholas Campion and Dorian Gieseler Greenbaum, 245–80. Newcastle, UK: Cambridge Scholars.

Gubler, Ruth. 1997. "The Importance of the Number Four as an Ordering Principle in the World View of the Ancient Maya." *Latin American Indian Literatures Journal* 13 (1): 23–57.

Guiteras-Holmes, Calixta. 1961. *The Perils of the Soul: The World View of a Tzotzil Indian*. New York: Free Press of Glencoe.

Hanks, William F. 1989. "Elements of Maya Style." In *Word and Image in Maya Culture: Explorations in Language, Writing, and Representation*, edited by William F. Hanks and Don S. Rice, 92–111. Salt Lake City: University of Utah Press, 1989.

Hellmuth, Nicholas M. 1970. *Preliminary Bibliography of the Chol Lacandon, Yucatec Lacandon Itza, Mopan, and Quejache of the Southern Maya Lowlands, 1524–1969*. Katunob, Occasional Publications in Mesoamerican Anthropology no. 4. Greeley CO: Museum of Anthropology, University of Northern Colorado.

———. 1971. "Progress Report and Notes on Research on Ethnohistory of the 16th–19th Century Southern Lowland Maya." Pt. 1: "The Cholti-Lacandon of Dolores (Sac Balam), Chiapas, 1695–1712." Pt. 2: "The Yucateco-Lacandon of San Jose de Gracia Real." Rev. ed. Guatemala. Mimeograph (originally produced in 1970).

Hill, Robert, and John Monaghan. 1987. *Continuities in Highland Maya Social Organization: Ethnohistory in Sacapulas, Guatemala*. Ethnohistory series. Philadelphia: University of Pennsylvania Press.

Hofling, Charles Andrew. 2001. "La Historia Lingüística y Cultural del Maya Yucateco Durante el Último Milenio." Paper presented at the Congreso Internacional de Cultural Maya, Mérida, Yucatan.

————. 2004. "Language and Cultural Contacts among Yukatekan Mayans." *Collegium Antropologicum* 28, Suppl. 1: 241–48.

————. 2009. "The Linguistic Context of the Kowoj." In Rice and Rice, *Kowoj*, 71–79.

————. 2011. *Mopan Maya-Spanish-English Dictionary.* Salt Lake City: University of Utah Press.

————. 2014. *Lacandon Maya-Spanish-English Dictionary.* Salt Lake City: University of Utah Press.

————. 2017. "Itzaj and Mopan Identities in Petén, Guatemala." In *The Only True People: Linking Maya Identities Past and Present,* edited by Bethany J. Beyyette and Lisa J. LeCount, 73–90. Boulder: University of Colorado Press, 2017.

Hofling, Charles Andrew, and Felix Tesucún. 1997. *Itza Maya-Spanish-English Dictionary.* Salt Lake City: University of Utah Press.

Hopkins, Nicholas A. 2012. *A Dictionary of the Chuj (Mayan) Language as Spoken in San Mateo Ixtatán, Huehuetenango, Guatemala, ca. 1964–65.* Tallahassee FL: Jaguar Tours. http://www.famsi.org/mayawriting/dictionary/hopkins/ChujEnglish Dictionary2012.pdf. Accessed March 2018.

Hopkins, Nicholas A., and J. Kathryn Josserand. 2012. "The Narrative Structure of Chol Folktales: One Thousand Years of Literary Tradition." In *Parallel Worlds: Genre, Discourse, and Poetics in Contemporary, Colonial, and Classic Maya Literature,* edited by Kerry M. Hull and Michael D. Carrasco, 21–44. Boulder: University Press of Colorado, 2012. http://www.jstor.org/stable/j.ctt4cgkrh.5. Accessed July 2017.

Horcasitas, Fernando. 1988. "An Analysis of the Deluge Myth in Mesoamerica." In *The Flood Myth,* edited by Alan Dundes, 183–219. Berkeley: University of California Press.

Houston, Stephen D. 1999. "Classic Maya Religion: Beliefs and Practices of an Ancient American People." *Brigham Young University Studies* 38 (4): 43–72. http://www.jstor.org/stable/43042817. Accessed March 2018.

Houston, Stephen D., John S. Robertson, and David S. Stuart. 2000. "The Language of the Classic Maya Inscriptions." *Current Anthropology* 41 (3): 321–38.

Houston, Stephen D., and David Stuart. 1996. "Of Gods, Glyphs and Kings: Divinity and Rulership among the Classic Maya." *Antiquity* 70: 289–312.

Hull, Kerry M. 2000. *Cosmological and Ritual Language in Ch'orti'.* FAMSI. http://www .famsi.org/reports/99036/99036Hull01.pdf.

————. 2016. "Ch'orti' Maya Myths of Creation." *Oral Tradition* 30 (1): 3–26.

Jones, Grant D. 1998. *The Conquest of the Last Maya Kingdom.* Stanford CA: Stanford University Press, 1998.

————. 2000. "The Lowland Maya, from the Conquest to the Present." In *The Cambridge History of the Native Peoples of the Americas,* vol. 2, pt. 2, edited by

Richard E. W. Adams and Murdo J. Macleod, 346–91. Cambridge: Cambridge University Press, 2000.

Joralemon, Peter D. 1971. "A Study of Olmec Iconography." *Studies in Pre-Colombian Art and Archaeology*, no. 7: 1–95. http://www.jstor.org/stable/41263412. Accessed January 2019.

Josserand, J. Kathryn. 1991. "The Narrative Structure of Hieroglyphic Texts at Palenque." In *Sixth Palenque Roundtable, 1986*, edited by Merle Greene Robertson, 12–31. Norman: University of Oklahoma Press.

———. 2003. "Story Cycles in Chol (Mayan) Mythology: Contextualizing Classic Iconography." FAMSI. http://www.famsi.org/reports/01085/01085Josserand01 .pdf. Accessed March 2017.

Josserand, J. Kathryn, and Nicholas A. Hopkins. [1996] 2001. *Chol Ritual Language.* FAMSI. http://www.famsi.org/reports/94017/index.html. Accessed November 2018.

———. 2011. *Maya Hieroglyphic Writing Workbook for a Short Course on Maya Hieroglyphic Writing.* 2nd ed. Tallahassee FL: Jaguar Tours. http://www.famsi.org /mayawriting/hopkins/MayaGlyphWritingWrkBk_part1.pdf.

Kahn, Hillary E. 2006. *Seeing and Being Seen: The Q'eqchi' Maya of Livingston, Guatemala, and Beyond.* Austin: University of Texas Press.

Kaufman, Terrence. 2003. "A Preliminary Mayan Etymological Dictionary." FAMSI. http://www.famsi.org/reports/01051/pmed.pdf. Accessed May 2017.

Kettunen, Harri, and Christophe Helmke. 2013. "Water in Maya Imagery and Writing." *Contributions in New World Archaeology* 5: 17–38.

Knowlton, Timothy. 2010. *Maya Creation Myths: Words and Worlds of the Chilam Balam.* Boulder: University of Colorado Press.

Landa, Diego de. 1864. *Relación de las cosas de Yucatáan.* Translated by Brasseur de Bourbourg. Paris: Trübner.

———. [1937] 1978. *Yucatan before and after the Conquest.* Translated by William Gates. New York: Dover. Originally published as publication no. 20 by the Maya Society, Baltimore, 1937. The work is a translation of *Relación de las cosas de Yucatán*, a manuscript of 1566.

———. 1941. "Relacion de las cosas de Yucatán. In *Papers of the Peabody Museum*, vol. 18, translated and edited by Alfred M. Tozzer. Cambridge MA: Harvard University.

Lastra de Suarez, Yolanda. 1986. *Las Áreas Dialectales del Náhuatl Modern.* Mexico: Instituto de Investigaciones Antropológicas, Universidad Nacional Autónoma de México.

Laughlin, Robert. M. 1977. *Of Cabbages and Kings: Tales from Zinacantan.* Smithsonian Contributions to Anthropology, no. 23. Washington DC: Smithsonian Institution.

Law, Danny. 2014. *Language Contact, Inherited Similarity and Social Difference: The*

Story of Linguistic Interaction in the Maya Lowlands. Current Issues in Linguistic Theory, vol. 328. Amsterdam: John Benjamins.

Law, Howard W. 1957. "Tamakasti: A Gulf Nahuat Text." *Tlalocan* 3 (4): 344–60.

Lee, Thomas A., and Sidney D. Markman. 1977. "The Coxoh Colonial Project and Coneta, Chiapas Mexico: A Provincial Maya Village under the Spanish Conquest." *Historical Archaeology* 11: 56–66. http://www.jstor.org/stable/25615317.

Lewis, Paul M., Gary F. Simons, and Charles D. Fennig, eds. 2015. *Ethnologue: Languages of the World*. 18th ed. Dallas: SIL International, 2015.

López Austin, Alfredo. 1997. *Tamoanchan, Tlalocan: Places of Mist*. Boulder: University Press of Colorado.

Maestri, Nicoletta. 2017. "Chaac, the Ancient Maya God of Rain, Lightning, and Storms." *ThoughtCo*, March 28. http://thoughtco.com/chaac-ancient-maya-god -of-rain-lightning-and-storms-171593. Accessed June 2018.

Maler, Teobert. 1901 and 1903. *Researches in the Central Portion of the Usumatsintla Valley: Reports of Explorations for the Museum*. Memoirs of the Peabody Museum, nos. 1 and 2. Cambridge MA: Peabody Museum.

Malmström, Vincent H. 2014. "The Maya Inheritance." http://www.dartmouth.edu /~izapa/The_Maya_Inheritance.pdf. Accessed January, 2018.

Marcus, Joyce. 1978. "Archeology and Religion: A Comparison of the Zapotec and Maya." *World Archaeology Journals* 10 (2): 172–91.

Marion, Marie-Odile. 1999. *El Poder de las Hijas de Luna: Sistema Simbólico y Organización Social de los Lacandones*. Mexico City: Conaculta-INAH/Plaza y Valdes.

Markman, Peter T., and Roberta H. Markman. 1989. *Masks of the Spirit: Image and Metaphor in Mesoamerica*. Berkeley: University of California Press.

Martin, Simon, and Nikolai Grube. 2000. *Chronicle of the Maya Kings and Queens: Deciphering the Dynasties of the Ancient Maya*. London: Thames and Hudson.

Maxwell, Judith, and Robert M. Hill, trans. 2006. *Kaqchikel Chronicles: The Definitive Edition*. Austin: University of Texas Press.

McGee, R. Jon. 1983. "Sacrifice and Ritual Cannibalism: An Analysis of Myth and Ritual among the Lacandon Maya of Chiapas, Mexico." PhD. diss., Rice University.

———.1987. "Metaphorical Substitution in a Lacandon Maya Ritual Song." *Anthropological Linguistics* 29 (1): 105–18.

———. 1989. "The Flood Myth from a Lacandon Maya Perspective." *Latin American Indian Literatures Journal* 5 (1): 68–80.

———. 1990. *Life, Ritual, and Religion among the Lacandon Maya*. Belmont CA: Wadsworth.

———. 1993. "Palenque and Lacandon Maya Cosmology." *Texas Notes on Precolumbian Art, Writing, and Culture*, no. 52: 1–8.

———. 1997a. "Narrative Structure of Lacandon Creation Myths." *Latin American Indian Literature Journal* 13 (1): 1–20.

————. 1997b. "Natural Modelling in Lacandon Maya Mythology." In *Explorations in Anthropology and Theology*, edited by Frank A. Salamone and Walter Randolph Adams, 175–90. Lanham MD: University Press of America.

————. 2002. *Watching Lacandon Maya Lives*. Boston: Allyn & Bacon.

McQowan, Norman A. 1967. "Classical Yucatec (Maya)." In *Handbook of Middle American Indians*, vol. 5, edited by Robert Wauchope, 201–48. Austin: University of Texas Press.

Mendez, Alonso, and Carol Karasik. N.d. "Centering the World: Zenith and Nadir at Palenque." https://www.academia.edu/2368146/Centering_the_World. Accessed January 2019.

Milbrath, Susan. 1999. *Star Gods of the Maya: Astronomy in Art, Folklore, and Calendars*. Austin: University of Texas Press.

Monaghan, John D. 2000. "Theology and History in the Study of Mesoamerican Religions." In *Handbook of Middle American Indians*, supplement to vol. 6, edited by John D. Monaghan and Barbara W. Edmonson, 24–49. Austin: University of Texas Press.

Morley, Sylvanus Griswold. 1920. *The Inscriptions at Copan*. Carnegie Institution of Washington no. 219. Washington DC: Carnegie Institution of Washington.

Murfin, Ross C., and Supryia M. Ray. 2003. "Myth." In *The Bedford Glossary of Critical and Literary Terms*, edited by Ross C. Murfin and Supryia M. Ray, 2nd ed. Boston: Bedford-St. Martin's.

Nations, James D. 2006. *The Maya Tropical Forest: People, Places, and Ancient Cities*. Austin: University of Texas Press.

Nations, James D., and Chan K'in José Valenzuela. 2017. *Maya Lacandón: El Idioma y el Medio Ambiente*. James D. Nations.

Neuenswander, Helen. 1987. "Reflections of the Concept of Dualism in Maya Hieroglyphic Pairing, Halving, and Inversion." In *Memorias del Primer Coloquio Internacional de Mayistas: 5–10 de Agosto de 1985*, 715–34. Mexico City: Universidad Nacional Autónoma de México, Centro de Estudios Mayas.

Palka, Joel W. 2005. "Residence in Colonial and Independence Periods." In *The Postclassic to Spanish-Era Transition in Mesoamerica: Archaeological Perspectives*, edited by Susan Kepecs and Rani T. Alexander, 183–202. Albuquerque: University of New Mexico Press.

————. 2014. *Maya Pilgrimage to Ritual Landscapes: Insights from Archaeology, History, and Ethnography*. Albuquerque: University of New Mexico Press.

Perera, Victor, and Robert D. Bruce. 1982. *The Last Lords of Palenque: The Lacandon Mayas of the Mexican Rain Forest*. Berkeley: University of California Press.

Petryshyn, Jaroslaw Theodore. 1976. "Some Findings Concerning the Nomenclature and Functions of Certain Lacandon Deities." In *The Realm of the Extra-Human*, vol. 1, *Agents and Audiences*, edited by Agrhananda Bharati, 485–500. Berlin: Walter de Gruyter.

Pugh, Timothy. 2009. "The Kowoj and the Lacandon: Migrations and Identities." In Rice and Rice, *Kowoj*, 368–84.

Rangel-Villalobos, Héctor, Viviana M. Sánchez-Gutiérrez, Miriam Botello-Ruiz, Joel Salazar-Flores, Gabriela Martínez-Cortés, José F. Muñoz-Valle, and Christopher Phillips. 2012. "Evaluation of Forensic and Anthropological Potential of D9S1120 in Mestizos and Amerindian Populations from Mexico." *Croatian Medical Journal* 53 (5): 423–31.

Rätsch, Christian. 2005. *The Encyclopedia of Psychoactive Plants.* Rochester VT: Inner Traditions International.

Rätsch, Christian, and K'ayum Ma'ax. 1984. *Ein Kosmos im Regenwald.* Cologne: Eugen Diederichs Verlag.

Recinos, Adrián, ed. 1947. *Popol Vuh: Las Antiguas Historias del Quiché.* Mexico: Fondo de Cultura Económica, 1947.

Redfield, Robert. 1941. *The Folk Culture of Yucatán.* Chicago: University of Chicago Press.

Restall, Matthew. 1999. *The Maya World: Yucatec Culture and Society, 1550–1850.* Stanford CA: Stanford University Press.

Rice, Prudence M. 2009. "The Kowoj in Geopolitical-Ritual Perspective." In Rice and Rice, *Kowoj*, 21–54.

Rice, Prudence M., and Don S. Rice. 2005. "Sixteenth- and Seventeenth-Century Maya Political Geography." In *The Postclassic to Spanish-Era Transition in Mesoamerica: Archaeological Perspectives*, edited by Susan Kepecs and Rani T. Alexander. Albuquerque: University of New Mexico Press.

———, eds. 2009. *The Kowoj: Identity, Migration, and Geopolitics in Late Postclassic Petén, Guatemala.* Boulder: University Press of Colorado.

———. 2018. "The Itzas of the Northern Lowlands and Their Allies." In *Historical and Archaeological Perspectives on the Itzas of Petén, Guatemala*, edited by Prudence M. Rice and Don S. Rice. Boulder: University Press of Colorado.

Roys, Ralph L. 1931. *The Ethno-Botany of the Maya.* New Orleans: Department of Middle American Research, Tulane University.

———. [1933] 1973. *The Book of Chilam Balam of Chumayel.* Washington DC: Carnegie Institution; reprint, Norman: University of Oklahoma Press, 1973.

———. [1933] 2008. *The Book of Chilam Balam of Chumayel.* Washington DC: Carnegie Institution; reprint, London: Forgotten Books.

———. 1939. *The Titles of Ebtun.* Washington DC: Carnegie Institution.

———. 1965. *Ritual of the Bacabs.* Norman: University of Oklahoma Press.

Sachse, Frauke, and Allen J. Christenson. 2005. "Tulan and the Other Side of the Sea: Unraveling a Metaphorical Concept from Colonial Guatemalan Highland Sources." Mesoweb. www.mesoweb.com/articles/tulan/Tulan.pdf.

Sapper, Karl. 1897. *Das Nördliche Mittel-Amerika nebst einem Ausflug nach dem Hochland von Anachuac.* Braunschweig: Friedrich Vieweg und Sohn.

Sasson, Vanessa R., and Jane Marie Law, eds. 2008. *Imagining the Fetus: The Unborn in Myth, Religion, and Culture.* New York: Oxford University Press.

Saunders, Nicholas J., ed. 1998. *Icons of Power: Feline Symbolism in the Americas.* London: Routledge.

Schele, Linda, and David Freidel. 1990. *A Forest of Kings: The Untold Story of the Ancient Maya.* New York: William Morrow.

Schele, Linda, and Peter Mathews. 1998. *The Code of Kings: The Language of Seven Sacred Maya Temples and Tombs.* New York: Simon and Schuster.

Schele, Linda, and Mary Ellen Miller. 1986. *The Blood of Kings: Dynasty and Ritual in Maya Art.* Fort Worth: Kimbell Art Museum.

Schele, Linda, and Khristaan D. Villela. N.d. *Creation, Cosmos, and the Imagery of Palenque and Copan.* http://www.mesoweb.com/pari/publications/RT10/Creation .pdf. Accessed September 2017.

Scholes, France, and Ralph L. Roys. 1948. *The Maya Chontal Indians of Acalan-Tixchel.* No. 560. Washington DC: Carnegie Institution.

Schoenhals, Louise C. 1988. *A Spanish-English Glossary of Mexican Flora and Fauna.* Mexico City: Summer Institute of Linguistics.

Schwartz, Norman B. 1990. *Forest Society: A Social History of Petén, Guatemala.* Philadelphia: University of Pennsylvania Press.

Sharer, Robert J. 1994. *The Ancient Maya.* 5th ed. Stanford CA: Stanford University Press.

Sharer, Robert J., and Loa P. Traxler. 2006. *The Ancient Maya.* Stanford CA: Stanford University Press.

Smithsonian National Museum of the American Indian. 2018. *Living Maya Time: Sun, Corn, and Calendar.* Smithsonian Institution. https://maya.nmai.si.edu /calendar/calendar-system. Accessed May 2018.

Soustelle, Georgette. 1959. "Observaciones sur la Religion des Lacandons du Mexique Méridional." *Journal de la Société des Américanistes* 48 (1959): 141–96.

———. 1961. "Observaciones sobre la Religión de los Lacandones del Sur de México." Translated by J. L. Arriola. *Guatemala Indígena* 1 (1): 31–105.

Soustelle, Jacques. 1933. "Notes sur les Lacandon du Lac Peljá et du Río Jetjá (Chiapas). *Journal de la Société des Américanistes* 25 (1): 153–80. https://www.jstor .org/stable/pdf/24601583. Accessed December 2018.

———. 1935a. "Les Idées Religieuses des Lacandons." *La Terre et la Vie,* no. 4: 170–78.

———. 1935b. "Le Totemisme des Lacandones," *Maya Research* 2: 325–44.

Soza, José María. 1957. *Pequeña monografía del Departamento del Petén.* Guatemala: Editorial del Ministerio de Educación Pública.

Spero, Joanne M. 1991. "Beyond Rainstorms: The Kawak as an Ancestor, Warrior, and Patron of Witchcraft." Originally published in *Sixth Palenque Round Table,* 1986, edited by Virginia M. Fields. Norman: University of Oklahoma Press.

http://www.mesoweb.com/pari/publications/RT08/BeyondRainstorms.pdf. Accessed January 2019.

Stacy, Anna. 2014. "Of the Same Stuff as Gods: Musical Instruments among the Classic Maya." *Collegiate Journal of Anthropology* 2. http://anthrojournal.com /issue/may/article/of-the-same-stuff-as-gods-musical-instruments-among-the -classic-maya. Accessed January 2019.

Stuart, David. 2005. "The Inscriptions from Temple XIX at Palenque: A Commentary." San Francisco: Pre-Columbian Art Research Institute.

———. 2011. *The Order of Days: The Maya World and the Truth about 2012.* New York: Harmony Books.

———. 2015. "Birth of the Sun: Notes on the Ancient Maya Winter Solstice." *Mayan Decipherment: Ideas on Ancient Maya Writing and Iconography.* https://decipher ment.wordpress.com/2015/12/29/birth-of-the-sun-notes-on-the-ancient-maya -winter-solstice/#comments. Accessed February 2017.

Tate, Carolyn. 1980. "The Maya Cauac Monster: Formal Development and Dynastic Implications." Master's thesis, University of Texas at Austin.

Taube, Karl Andreas. 1992. "The Major Gods of Ancient Yucatan." *Studies in Pre-Columbian Art and Archaeology,* no. 32: i–v, vii–viii, 1–160. Dumbarton Oaks, Trustees for Harvard University. http://www.jstor.org/stable/41263477. Accessed May 2017.

Tedlock, Dennis, ed. 1985. *Popol Vuh: The Mayan Book of the Dawn of Life.* New York: Simon and Schuster.

Thompson, J. Eric S. 1930. *Ethnology of the Mayas of Southern and Central British Honduras.* Edited by Berthold Laufer. Field Museum Natural History, Anthropological series 17 (1).

———. 1950. *Maya Hieroglyphic Writing: Introduction.* Washington DC: Carnegie Institution.

———. 1970. *Maya History and Religion.* Norman: University of Oklahoma Press.

———. 1971. "Estimates of Maya Population: Deranging Factors." *American Antiquity* 36 (2): 214–16.

———. 1977. "A Proposal for Constituting a Maya Subgroup, Cultural and Linguistic, in the Petén and Adjacent Regions." In *Anthropology and History in Yucatán,* edited by Grant D. Jones, 3–42. Austin: University of Texas Press.

Thompson, J. Eric, Harry E. D. Pollock, and Jean Charlot. 1932. *A Preliminary Study of the Ruins of Cobá, Quintana Roo, Mexico.* Washington DC: Carnegie Institution.

Thompson, Stilth. 1955. *Motif-Index of Folk Literature: A Classification of Narrative Elements in Folktales, Ballads, Myths, Fables, Mediaeval Romances, Exempla, Fabliaux, Jest-books and Local Legends.* Vol. 4. Bloomington: Indiana University Press.

Tiesler, Vera, and Andrea Cucina. 2006. "Procedures in Human Heart Extraction and Ritual Meaning: A Taphonomic Assessment of Anthropogenic Marks in Classic Maya Skeletons." *Latin American Antiquity* 17 (4): 493–510.

Tozzer, Alfred M. [1907] 1978. *A Comparative Study of the Mayas and the Lacandones.* London: Macmillan.

————, ed. 1941. "Landa's Relacion de las Cosas de Yucatán. A Translation." *Peabody Museum Papers,* vol. 18. Cambridge MA: Harvard University.

Trueblood, Emily W. Emmart. 1973. "'Omixochitl' the Tuberose (*Polianthes tuberosa*)." *Economic Botany* 27 (2): 157–73.

Vail, Gabrielle, and Christine Hernández. 2013. *Recreating Primordial Time: Foundation Rituals and Mythology in the Postclassic Maya Codices.* Boulder: University of Colorado Press.

Valencia Rivera, Rogelio, and Hugo García Capistrán. 2013. "In the Place of the Mist: Analysing a Maya Myth from a Mesoamerican Perspective." ACTA *Mesoamericana* 29. *The Maya in a Mesoamerican Context: Comparative Approaches to Maya Studies: Proceedings of the 16th European Maya Conference, Copenhagen, December 5–10, 2011,* edited by Jesper Nielsen and Christophe Helmke, 35–50. Markt Schwaben, Germany: Verlag Anton Saurwein, http://www.academia.edu/6991991/. Accessed February 2019.

Vanderwarker, Amber. 2010. "Archeology and Anthropology: Western Hemisphere." In *Britannica Book of the Year 2010,* edited by Encyclopaedia Britannica, 204–5. Chicago: Encyclopedia Britannica.

Velásquez, Erik García. 2006. "The Maya Flood Myth and the Decapitation of the Cosmic Caiman." PARI *Journal* 7 (1): 1–10. www.mesoweb.com/pari/publications/journal/701/Flood_e.pdf.

Villa Rojas, Alfonso. 1988. "Appendix A: The Concepts of Space and Time among the Contemporary Maya." In *Time and Reality in the Thought of the Maya,* by Miguel León-Portilla, 113–59. Norman: University of Oklahoma Press.

Wilbert, Johannes. 1970. *Folk Literature of the Warao Indians: Narrative Material and Motif Content.* Los Angeles: Latin American Center, University of California at Los Angeles.

Zralka, Jarosław, Wiesław Koszkul, Katarzyna Radnicka, Laura Elena Sotelo Santos, and Bernard Hermes. 2014. "Excavations in Nakum Structure 99: New Data on Proclassic Rituals and Precolumbian Maya Beekeeping." *Estudios de Cultura Maya* 64: 85–117.

In the Native Literatures of the Americas and Indigenous World Literatures Series

To order or obtain more information on these or other University of Nebraska Press titles, visit nebraskapress.unl.edu.